MW01038588

Diplomatic Tradecraft

As universities and governments seek to prepare the next generation of diplomats to manage international affairs, they finally have a teaching tool focusing on the practical knowledge and skills that in the past could be learned only on the job. Edited by Nicholas Kralev, founder of the Washington International Diplomatic Academy, *Diplomatic Tradecraft* brings together 18 career diplomats with decades of experience to lift the curtain on a mysterious but vital profession, and to pass on the insights and abilities they gained to those who will succeed them. Beginning with an overview of diplomatic institutions and protocols, the text considers the key attributes of diplomatic communication and negotiation, as well as core specializations, including economic, consular and public diplomacy. With compelling narratives, case studies and exercise scenarios, the chapters on various aspects of diplomatic practice form a cohesive and comprehensive volume, written in an accessible and engaging style.

Nicholas Kralev is the founding executive director of the Washington International Diplomatic Academy, an independent organization that provides practical professional training in diplomacy. A former *Financial Times* and *Washington Times* correspondent specializing in diplomacy and foreign affairs, he covered and accompanied U.S. Secretaries of State Hillary Clinton, Condoleezza Rice, Colin Powell and Madeleine Albright on their travels around the world. He is the author of *America's Other Army: The U.S. Foreign Service and 21st-Century Diplomacy* and holds a master's degree in public policy from Harvard's Kennedy School.

"Editor Nicholas Kralev has assembled a group of superbly qualified former practitioners to relate from personal experience manifold perspectives of diplomatic conduct and practice. They offer us the kind of ground truth about diplomacy that cannot be found in Ivory Towers. A very practical guide for those interested in better understanding the workings of our profession."

John Negroponte, former U.S. Permanent Representative to the United Nations and former Deputy Secretary of State

"Nicholas Kralev has devoted much of his career to improving and developing the practice of diplomacy, and to understanding the strengths and weaknesses of the U.S. Foreign Service and our national security agencies. As founder of the Washington International Diplomatic Academy, he brings aspiring and practicing diplomats from our country and around the world to Washington and introduces them to some of the most accomplished and inspiring members of the diplomatic profession. In this superb book, Kralev brings together perspectives and recommendations from some of the greatest diplomatic leaders and thinkers that our country has produced. Read this book to understand how our country got to where it currently stands in the world, and what it needs to do to restore and revive its influence and leadership in a rapidly changing global environment."

Eric S. Rubin, former U.S. Ambassador to Bulgaria

"Kralev has done more than anyone else to understand what diplomats, and American diplomats in particular, actually do. It is a world quite apart from the abstract removes of international relations theorists. In this volume he draws on a team of outstanding veteran diplomats. Topic by topic they not only review the character of the work; they share lifetimes of insights about how to do it. There is no better introduction currently in print. It deserves to become a standard text for would-be professionals, starting with America's own trainees."

Philip Zelikow, Senior Fellow, Hoover Institution, Stanford University

"It's not simply that we have more armed conflict in today's world. It's also that these fights involve so many governments, each with its idiosyncratic political culture and its unique set of interests. This is why the world so badly needs more thoughtful and expertly trained diplomats, and why Nicholas Kralev's *Diplomatic Tradecraft* is such a valuable addition to their education and ongoing work."

Ian Bremmer, President and Founder, Eurasia Group

"I wish that I'd had *Diplomatic Tradecraft* to assign in my course on modern diplomacy. Nicholas Kralev's comprehensive and lively textbook by leading American diplomats is a much needed addition to the literature on the making of US foreign policy. The book should be required reading for all aspiring US Foreign Service Officers, as well as required reading in university courses on international relations and American foreign policy. It is the best reality-based study of diplomacy that I've read."

Derek Shearer, former U.S. Ambassador to Finland and Director, McKinnon Center for Global Affairs, Occidental College

"*Diplomatic Tradecraft* by Nicholas Kralev presents an illuminating inside look at all aspects of diplomatic service through a student-centric approach. The knowledge and wisdom of 18 career ambassadors embedded in this volume, provide a comprehensive and engaging experiential learning environment for readers to develop skills necessary for future diplomatic service and for the Fourth Industrial Revolution."

Baktybek Abdrisaev, former Ambassador of the Kyrgyz Republic to the U.S. and Canada and Lecturer of Political Science, Utah Valley University

"*Diplomatic Tradecraft* is an elegantly-written, thorough introduction to diplomacy in practice. Timely and lucid, free of jargon, and salted with memorable and revealing anecdotes, it is a pleasure to read. The authors have taken a complex and tangled profession and made its essentials clear, digestible, and memorable. They have also taken the trouble to give budding diplomats concrete and actionable career advice. This book will be invaluable to academics trying to help our students begin careers in a profession almost as confusing to us as to them. Every graduate and undergraduate student intending to pursue a diplomatic career should be pointed to these pages."

Richard Jordan, Assistant Professor of Political Science, Baylor University

Diplomatic Tradecraft

Edited by

Nicholas Kralev
Washington International Diplomatic Academy

CAMBRIDGE
UNIVERSITY PRESS

CAMBRIDGE
UNIVERSITY PRESS

Shaftesbury Road, Cambridge CB2 8EA, United Kingdom

One Liberty Plaza, 20th Floor, New York, NY 10006, USA

477 Williamstown Road, Port Melbourne, VIC 3207, Australia

314–321, 3rd Floor, Plot 3, Splendor Forum, Jasola District Centre, New Delhi – 110025, India

103 Penang Road, #05-06/07, Visioncrest Commercial, Singapore 238467

Cambridge University Press is part of Cambridge University Press & Assessment, a department of the University of Cambridge.

We share the University's mission to contribute to society through the pursuit of education, learning and research at the highest international levels of excellence.

www.cambridge.org
Information on this title: www.cambridge.org/highereducation/isbn/9781009100410

DOI: 10.1017/9781009118668

First published 2024

A catalogue record for this publication is available from the British Library

Library of Congress Cataloging-in-Publication Data
Names: Kralev, Nicholas, editor.
Title: Diplomatic tradecraft / Edited by Nicholas Kralev, Washington International Diplomatic Academy.
Description: First edition. | New York, NY : Cambridge University Press, 2024. | Includes bibliographical references and index.
Identifiers: LCCN 2023048659 (print) | LCCN 2023048660 (ebook) | ISBN 9781009100410 (hardback) | ISBN 9781009114936 (paperback) | ISBN 9781009118668 (epub)
Subjects: LCSH: Diplomats–Vocational guidance. | Diplomatic and consular service. | International relations–Vocational guidance. | Career development.
Classification: LCC JZ1405 .D559 2024 (print) | LCC JZ1405 (ebook) | DDC 327.2023–dc23/eng/20240116
LC record available at https://lccn.loc.gov/2023048659
LC ebook record available at https://lccn.loc.gov/2023048660

ISBN 978-1-009-10041-0 Hardback
ISBN 978-1-009-11493-6 Paperback

Additional resources for this publication at www.cambridge.org/kralev.

....

Contents

List of Contributors   ix

Foreword: **What Is Diplomatic Tradecraft?**   1
Nicholas Kralev

1 **The Diplomatic Landscape**   5
Nicholas Kralev

2 **Diplomacy as an Instrument of Statecraft**   31
Chas W. Freeman

3 **Key Diplomacy Skills**   51
David Lindwall and Chas W. Freeman

4 **The Interagency Foreign Policy Process**   78
Daniel Fried and John Tefft

5 **How Does an Embassy Work?**   100
Charles Ray and Janice Jacobs

6 **Political Tradecraft**   125
Eunice Reddick and Gina Abercrombie-Winstanley

7 **Economic Tradecraft and Commercial Diplomacy**   150
Lisa Kubiske

8 **Diplomatic Reporting and Communication**   174
Douglas Silliman and Eunice Reddick

9 **Public Diplomacy**   197
Bruce Wharton and Nicole Finnemann

10 **Consular Affairs and Crisis Management**   221
Janice Jacobs and James Zumwalt

11 **Diplomatic Protocol, Privileges and Immunities**   245
Eunice Reddick

12 **Multilateral Diplomacy**   264
    Jeffrey DeLaurentis and Tressa Rae Finerty

13 **Health and Science Diplomacy**   286
    Jimmy Kolker

14 **Cyber Diplomacy**   305
    Heli Tiirmaa-Klaar

15 **Diplomatic Negotiation**   320
    Thomas R. Pickering and Nicholas Kralev

    Afterword: **Diplomacy Is the World's Best Hope**   350
    Nicholas Kralev

    Glossary   353
    Acronyms   355
    Notes   358
    Index   385

Contributors

Gina Abercrombie-Winstanley is a former U.S. ambassador to Malta and consul general in Jeddah, Saudi Arabia. During more than three decades as a career diplomat, she also served in Iraq, Egypt, Israel and Indonesia. She was the State Department's first chief diversity officer.

Jeffrey DeLaurentis is a former U.S. alternate representative at the United Nations with the rank of ambassador and chargé d'affaires at the U.S. Embassy in Cuba. During his 27-year Foreign Service career, he was posted to Geneva and Colombia, and also served as deputy assistant secretary of state for Western Hemisphere affairs and director for inter-American affairs on the National Security Council staff.

Tressa Rae Finerty has been a U.S. Foreign Service officer in the political career track since 2002, with postings to Malaysia, Iraq, Armenia and Thailand, as well as to the United Nations in New York and Geneva. Most recently, she served as the State Department's deputy executive secretary.

Nicole Finnemann has been a U.S. Foreign Service officer in the public diplomacy career track since 2011, with postings in Nicaragua, Zimbabwe, Afghanistan, Mexico and Spain. She also served as head of strategic communications for the Bureau of Western Hemisphere Affairs at the State Department.

Chas W. Freeman is a former U.S. ambassador to Saudi Arabia and deputy chief of mission in China and Thailand. During nearly three decades in the Foreign Service, he was also principal deputy assistant secretary of state for African affairs and assistant secretary of defense for international security affairs.

Daniel Fried is a former U.S. assistant secretary of state for European and Eurasian affairs. During his four decades in the Foreign Service, he was ambassador to Poland and also served in Russia and Serbia, as well as serving as senior director for European affairs on the National Security Council staff.

Janice Jacobs is a former U.S. assistant secretary of state for consular affairs, ambassador to Senegal and Guinea-Bissau, and deputy chief of mission in the Dominican Republic. During her 34-year Foreign Service career, she was also posted to Ecuador, Egypt, Ethiopia, France, Mexico, Nigeria and Thailand.

Jimmy Kolker is a former U.S. assistant secretary for global affairs at the U.S. Department of Health and Human Services. During his 30-year Foreign Service career, he was ambassador to Uganda and Burkina Faso and deputy chief of mission in Denmark and Botswana.

Lisa Kubiske is a former U.S. ambassador to Honduras and deputy chief of mission in Brazil and the Dominican Republic. During 35 years in the Foreign Service, she also served in Mexico, China and Hong Kong, and was deputy assistant secretary of state for economic and business affairs.

David Lindwall is a former U.S. deputy chief of mission in Sweden, Afghanistan, Haiti and Guatemala, and consul-general in Guayaquil, Ecuador. During his 34-year Foreign Service career, he was also posted to Iraq, Paraguay, Nicaragua, Honduras, Spain and Colombia.

Thomas R. Pickering is a former U.S. undersecretary of state for political affairs and assistant secretary of state for oceans and environmental affairs. During more than four decades in the Foreign Service, he was also ambassador to the United Nations, Russia, India, Israel, Jordan, Nigeria and El Salvador.

Charles Ray is a former U.S. ambassador to Zimbabwe and Cambodia, deputy chief of mission in Sierra Leone, and consul-general in Ho Chi Minh City, Vietnam. He is a retired U.S. Army officer, who also served as deputy assistant secretary of defense for prisoners of war and missing personnel affairs.

Eunice Reddick is a former U.S. ambassador to Niger, Gabon and São Tomé and Príncipe. She spent 37 years in the Foreign Service and also served in Zimbabwe, China and Taiwan. Most recently, she was chargé d'affaires in Burundi.

Douglas Silliman is a former U.S. ambassador to Iraq and Kuwait and deputy chief of mission in Turkey. During his 35-year Foreign Service career, he also served in Jordan, Pakistan, Tunisia and Haiti, as well as in several senior positions in Washington.

John Tefft is a former U.S. ambassador to Russia, Ukraine, Georgia and Lithuania. During his 45 years in the Foreign Service, he also served in Italy, Hungary and Israel, and as a deputy assistant secretary of state for European and Eurasian affairs.

Heli Tiirmaa-Klaar is a former ambassador-at-large for cyber diplomacy at the Estonian Ministry of Foreign Affairs, as well as a former chief cyber policy coordinator for the European External Action Service and cybersecurity policy adviser at NATO.

Bruce Wharton is a former U.S. ambassador to Zimbabwe, former acting undersecretary of state for public diplomacy and public affairs, and deputy chief of mission in Guatemala. During his 35 years in the Foreign Service, he also served in Argentina, Chile, Bolivia and South Africa.

James Zumwalt is a former U.S. ambassador to Senegal and Guinea-Bissau and deputy chief of mission in Japan. He was also deputy assistant secretary of state for East Asian and Pacific affairs, and served in China and the Democratic Republic of Congo.

Foreword
What Is Diplomatic Tradecraft?

NICHOLAS KRALEV

The first time I remember being aware of diplomats was a television news report I saw at age 10 in 1984, about a meeting between U.S. Secretary of State George Shultz and Soviet Foreign Minister Andrei Gromyko. In the next five years, as I watched more television footage of Shultz and his successor, James Baker, coming down the stairs of a white-and-blue plane with "United States of America" emblazoned on it, I wondered why these men's frequent travels commanded seemingly endless media attention.

As a child in Bulgaria, I had a hazy notion that, when American and Soviet leaders met, they discussed matters of war and peace. But I was far removed from any global centers of power and could not relate to what I saw on television. I certainly had no reason to think that I would ever meet the likes of Shultz and Baker. Then the Berlin Wall fell in 1989, and the United States, along with other Western countries, set out to help former communist states behind the Iron Curtain, including Bulgaria, to transition to democracy and market economy. I realized that international diplomacy was not so distant after all – in fact, it affected my own life. The end of the Cold War opened up opportunities I would have never had otherwise, and it brought me closer to the highest levels of diplomacy than I ever thought possible.

The first time I flew on that white-and-blue plane I had seen so many times on television was in 2000. Now living in the United States and working as a journalist, I was part of the traveling press corps covering another secretary of state, Madeleine Albright. On that whirlwind trip to Iceland, France, Germany and Egypt, I began to understand the critical role of career diplomats, or Foreign Service officers, in carrying out U.S. foreign policy and managing international relations. At every stop during the trip, they made my work easier. As soon as we deplaned and jumped in the motorcade, the officers assigned to the traveling press made sure we had everything we needed to report, write and file our stories. It was in the motorcade where I first learned about the Foreign Service and its unique way of life.

Over the next few years, as I traveled with Albright's successor, Colin Powell, I became more and more interested in the lives and careers of the officers I met. It was a turbulent and consequential time in U.S. foreign policy – right after the terrorist attacks on September 11, 2001 – and the policy stories my colleagues and I wrote from Washington made front-page news. But I often found the personal stories of the career diplomats I met even more intriguing and compelling.

1

I also realized that the general idea I had about what diplomats did was superficial and outdated. And if that was the case with me, what of the public's perceptions? As I continued to travel with two more secretaries of state, Condoleezza Rice and Hillary Clinton, I decided to write a book about the Foreign Service at the beginning of the twenty-first century titled *America's Other Army*, which was published in 2012. During my research, I interviewed about 600 Foreign Service officers at 77 embassies, consulates and other diplomatic missions on five continents. I found that their work directly affected the everyday lives of Americans, including their safety and security, their ability to travel and communicate with people in other countries, and their employment and overall prosperity.[1]

I made two astonishing discoveries. First, almost all officers I met told me that they did not know what they were getting themselves into when they joined the service. They had only a vague notion of what diplomacy was about, based on what they knew from academia, the media and movies. They had no knowledge about what they would be required to do in a diplomatic career, let alone how to do it. As I traveled from country to country, I also met diplomats of dozens of other nationalities and asked whether they had the same experience. They did. A sobering realization sank in. Governments around the world expected their diplomats to represent their countries abroad and advance their national interests, move around every few years and commit to a long career, because recruiting and onboarding new officers was a costly investment. Yet there was no way for aspiring diplomats and even new recruits to gain true understanding of what the diplomatic profession entailed and how to prepare for it.

The lack of proper training and professional development was my second big surprise. New officers were thrown into the deep end with few skills, and it took them years to reach the necessary level of competence. As I presented my book at several countries' ministries of foreign affairs, it became clear that they did no better at training than the United States – in fact, many did worse. They recruited entry-level officers with master's degrees in International Relations, expecting them to know how to practice diplomacy. What they apparently did not appreciate was that International Relations is an academic discipline, not diplomatic practice, and the difference is crucial.

This is largely still the case today. In this context, professional diplomacy training becomes essential to learning how to navigate a foreign country in order to get specific things done that advance one's national interest. Given the state of global diplomacy in recent years, I was so convinced of the urgent need for such training that I literally put my money where my mouth was, creating the Washington International Diplomatic Academy (WIDA) in 2017. From the beginning, I was determined to focus exclusively on teaching **diplomatic tradecraft**, defined as **the set of skills, duties and responsibilities required in the daily work of modern diplomacy** – and to have career ambassadors and other senior diplomats with decades of experience teach it. As far as I could tell, no such organization had ever existed.

Many of our alumni, who come from dozens of countries, wish they had learned what we taught them when they were in college or graduate school. Some of them must have spoken highly of our training to their universities, because we have noticed rising interest in academia in offering diplomacy courses that go beyond theory and history, aiming to teach practical skills. However, universities are running into a serious problem: there are no adequate textbooks they can use. It was a natural step for me to try filling that void, and I decided to adapt the material we at WIDA have been teaching and produce this volume, with contributions from some of our instructors and other experienced diplomats. Unlike other published works on this subject, whose focus is on the "what" and "why" of diplomacy, we go deeper and explore the "how." Many of our case studies come from their authors' experiences. They either managed the processes they write about or were active participants in them. You will notice the similar writing style across chapters – evidence that I was a very active editor. I saw part of my job as making sure the text reads like one coherent book, rather than a collection of disparate chapters.

As the book makes clear, there are different definitions of diplomacy, which is a testament to its complexities and intricacies. I define it as **the profession or activity of managing international relations with measures short of war**. Diplomacy is also a tool for implementing a country's foreign policy by engaging and influencing nation-states, multilateral organizations and other actors on the world stage; I believe it should be the tool of first resort. It is not this book's intention to analyze, debate or assess policy, or to deal with diplomatic theory and history. Rather, in the case studies and other examples from the authors' experiences or the historical record, we have included discussion of policy processes and decisions to illustrate diplomats' role in them. Although we recognize the need for modernizing the current system, it is not our goal to criticize it and offer recommendations for its improvement.

It will not be a surprise that we focus on U.S. diplomacy and use examples from its practice; all but one of the contributors to the book are Americans. We recognize that U.S. diplomatic ambitions and resources may be bigger than those of other countries. However, the skill sets we aim to teach are fundamental to the profession and universally applicable. National, cultural and bureaucratic differences by no means negate the importance of superb interpersonal, communication, analytical and negotiating skills, among others. For example, different governments may deploy distinct communication tactics, but every diplomat should be able to write clearly, succinctly and persuasively, even about complex and confusing matters.

Political leaders around the world have long failed to appreciate professional diplomacy and to understand how much it can help them achieve their policy objectives. As a result, they have starved their diplomatic institutions of resources and ignored the need for training. Few realize that transactional diplomacy rarely works, especially in the long term. Embassies and other permanent diplomatic missions exist to give diplomats the time and opportunities to learn a country's language, history and culture, and to understand how its government and society function. Great diplomats use the relationships they build and cultivate to understand how their foreign interlocutors think and where they are coming from when making decisions. Those accumulated insights, experience and – ideally – a reservoir of goodwill in the host-country come into play in times of crises or strained official relations.

No one is born with the skills to practice international diplomacy. They have to be acquired. But as one of our contributors, Chas Freeman, writes, "Professional diplomatic doctrine – a body of interrelated operational concepts describing how to influence the behavior of other states and people by mostly nonviolent means – does not exist. So there is no diplomatic equivalent of military doctrine. This is a very big gap in statecraft. The absence of diplomatic doctrine to complement military science eliminates most options short of the raw pressure of sanctions or the use of force. It increases the probability of armed conflict, with all its unpredictable human and financial consequences. Working out a diplomatic doctrine with which to train professional diplomats could have major advantages."

In other words, as I wrote in the *New York Times* in 2018, "with more professional diplomacy, the world might just become less of a mess."[2] I hope this volume is a modest contribution to making sure that day dawns soon.

1 The Diplomatic Landscape

NICHOLAS KRALEV

Janice Jacobs was almost as petrified as the woman she was trying to help escape from an abusive marriage. It was 1981, and the women, both in their mid-30s, stood in front of an immigration officer at the airport in Lagos, Nigeria, their hearts racing. The woman next to Jacobs, a fellow American, had sought assistance from the U.S. Embassy after her Nigerian husband, who had repeatedly beaten and tormented her, took away her passport to prevent her from leaving the country. The embassy issued her a new passport and tasked Jacobs, a consular officer on her first tour in the U.S. Foreign Service, with ensuring that the woman flew out of Nigeria, as she wished.

The abusive husband, however, was a high-ranking official in the Nigerian Immigration Service and had instructed the officer at the airport not to let his wife through. It took Jacobs all the persuasive power, stamina and persistence she could muster, but they finally made it to the gate. Their relief turned out to be short-lived. The husband was standing menacingly in the gate area, and airport security officers, several times bigger than the petite Jacobs, blocked the woman's way as she tried to board her plane. Jacobs, despite her delicate frame, outmaneuvered the burly men and hurried her charge onto the aircraft. The woman was soon on her way to the United States, and Jacobs happily reported to the embassy that the job was done.

In 1996, in another West African country, Sierra Leone, another American diplomat worked to resolve an even bigger problem. It was election day, which the officer, Charles Ray, viewed as a personal victory of sorts. For years, along with other Western diplomats, he had pressured the country's ruling military junta to allow multiparty elections. When it finally did, Ray and his embassy colleagues helped to bring in American observers as part of an international monitoring mission. Some of them were sent to parts of the country on the front lines of a civil war between the junta and rebels from the Revolutionary United Front. In the run-up to the election, there were reports that the rebels had cut off several villagers' hands to prevent them from voting.

On the day before the election, in a provincial capital surrounded by rebel-held territory, a pro-government militia known as the Hunters captured a rebel and dragged him in front of the hotel where U.S. observers were staying. Then the Hunters beheaded him in public view. Not surprisingly, the Americans were shocked and terrified. It fell on Ray to calm them down and ensure their safety, so he put his wide network of local contacts to work. The defense minister explained that the decapitation was proof that the Hunters were protecting the Americans, and they had nothing to worry about. The election proceeded without incident, and the observers left the following day. But the civil war, marked by rape, mutilation and murder on both sides, would rage on for more than five years.[1]

In 2003, on another continent, another U.S. diplomat coped with a very different crisis. When Lisa Kubiske arrived in the Dominican Republic, she found an economy in freefall. A popular Caribbean tourist destination, the country had been a bright spot in an unstable region until recently, in spite of poverty, corruption and weak institutions.

However, months before Kubiske began her tour at the U.S. Embassy, the third-largest Dominican bank, Banco Intercontinental, collapsed. Investigators discovered that it had kept two sets of books for more than a decade, covering up massive bad loans and lavish spending. The crisis widened to include other banks and led to the first economic contraction since 1990, and to soaring inflation and unemployment. The number of Dominicans fleeing to the United States and intercepted by the U.S. Coast Guard jumped more than 20 times compared to two years earlier.[2] The economic crisis significantly complicated Washington's plans to include the Dominican Republic in a Central America free trade agreement it hoped to negotiate. It believed such a pact would benefit both U.S. businesses and consumers. Kubiske and her embassy colleagues helped clear the way for a negotiation by helping the Dominican government claw its way back from the abyss. We will see what they did in Chapter 7.

In 2014, another U.S. diplomat crisscrossed Europe to conduct another kind of negotiation. Not long after Russia annexed Ukraine's Crimean Peninsula and invaded the country's eastern Donbas region, Washington started working on the first-ever broad set of sanctions against Moscow. It preferred to enact such penalties in concert with the European Union (EU). So the White House dispatched Daniel Fried, along with officials from the Department of the Treasury and other agencies, to EU member-states to negotiate an agreement. We will discuss further details of that process in Chapter 4.

These stories from the experiences of four of the contributors to this volume provide a rare glimpse into some of what diplomats do, though they represent a very small part of the duties and responsibilities of the career Foreign Service. Each of the chapters ahead adds to the diverse elements of modern diplomatic practice and lifts the curtain on various aspects of a unique type of tradecraft and profession. Diplomacy seldom produces quick results, and its victories are rarely celebrated. A diplomatic win is much more often "the patient accumulation of partial successes," in Henry Kissinger's words.[3]

A country's diplomatic service is – or at least should be – the steward of its national interests abroad. International civil servants, who work on the staff of multilateral organizations like the United Nations and the EU, are supposed to serve global or regional interests. Both bilateral and multilateral diplomats manage and participate in the daily conduct of international relations. In carrying out their duties, they work within a diplomacy architecture – systems that have been established at the national and global levels. Before we discuss these systems, we need to understand how diplomacy relates to other key terms and concepts, such as national interest, national security and foreign policy.

National interest and international relations

Why does diplomacy exist? How does it contribute to a country's national interest? How critical is it to national security? The answers to these questions are important as much for people inside the system as for those on the outside. Professional diplomats are truly effective and successful only if they understand where and how they fit in large bureaucracies, and how their work can benefit their country and compatriots. Politicians and the public can better appreciate how diplomacy can improve their lives, provided they have a grasp of what diplomats do, and why it is important for the success of both domestic and foreign policies.

Scholars of international relations tend to date the beginning of their field of study to around 500 years ago,[4] but interactions across borders have existed for much longer. Centuries before globalization, statesmen realized that no country could survive in isolation. The Mesopotamian city-states of Lagash and Umma concluded treaties as far back as the 25th century B.C.[5] The ancient Greek city-states dispatched envoys to negotiate on specific matters, such as war and peace or commercial relations, though they did not have representatives permanently posted in each other's territory.[6]

The terms "diplomacy" and "diplomat" were first used in the 18th century, when the French word *diplomate* came to refer to a person authorized to negotiate on behalf of a state. The word is derived from the ancient Greek *diplōma*, composed of *diplo*, meaning "folded in two," and the suffix *ma*, meaning "an object." The folded document conferred a privilege on the bearer, and the term came to denote documents through which princes granted such favors. It later applied to all solemn documents, especially those containing agreements between sovereigns. But eventually, diplomacy's direct tie to documents lapsed, and its meaning became much broader.[7]

Today, "diplomacy" and "international relations" are often used interchangeably, which is not quite right. Diplomacy is the machinery of international relations. It is governed by the 1961 Vienna Convention on Diplomatic Relations, a treaty under the auspices of the United Nations. It is supplemented by another treaty, the 1963 Vienna Convention on Consular Relations, as we will see later. Diplomacy also represents the peaceful conduct of international relations, as opposed to the use of force.

If a country's diplomacy is meant to serve the national interest, who and how defines that interest? Every government has the right to determine it, and some profess more interests than others. In the same country, one administration may proclaim that combating climate change or ending a conflict on another continent is a national interest, and the next may not. Politics and ideology sometimes play a role, which makes it difficult for public servants, who are supposed to be nonpartisan. Diplomats may disagree with their own government on whether something is in the national interest, but they are expected to set their own views aside and carry out the administration's policies.

For the purposes of diplomacy, what matters most is a country's core national interest, defined pragmatically and fairly broadly. Harry S. Truman, U.S. president from 1945 to 1953, is said to have been asked once, "What are our vital interests?" He replied: "Survival and prosperity."[8] In recent years, government documents, such as the National Security Strategy of the United States, have identified security and prosperity as the core national interests.[9] Some administrations have also included American values and their defense. That has been controversial, because interests and values are often considered rivals, and conflicts between the two have kept many policymakers up at night. A classic example of such a clash is U.S. policy in the Middle East. American values dictate that Washington shun oil-rich autocratic regimes there, but it has argued for decades that U.S. strategic interests require maintaining close relationships in the region. The bottom line for American diplomats is that their government wants both interests and values to guide its foreign policy, and they need to manage a balancing act.

Diplomats represent and work for their compatriots as much as for their government. So years ago, I decided to conduct an experiment and find out what most mattered to some of the citizens of the countries I would visit during my frequent travels. As I researched my book *America's Other Army*, I asked participants in informal focus groups in dozens of countries what they most cared about in their everyday lives. The answers, in their overwhelming majority, revolved around two main themes. The first had to do with safety or security – people wanted to make it through the day unharmed. Their other major concern was their economic well-being. Not everyone wanted to be rich – for most, a decent job that made it possible to have a home and a car, and to be able to pay for their children's education and go on vacation once a year, was enough.

Not every country's foreign policy is guided by values or includes their promotion, which is mainly a Western tradition. But security and prosperity can reasonably be applied to the national interest of most nation-states. The way I see it, everything diplomats do should contribute in some way to their country's security or prosperity. We will illustrate and elaborate on that link in the chapters that follow.

National security and foreign policy

Although there can be more than one definition of national security, for the purposes of this volume, we define it as **the provision, protection and defense of the security of a country and its people**. The national security toolbox contains both domestic and foreign policy instruments. Without discounting the former, which include law-enforcement, political, economic and social matters, this book naturally focuses on the latter.

A country's foreign policy is a set of policies aimed at countering external threats, furthering interests and taking advantage of opportunities. Traditionally, the main tools in the foreign policy toolbox have been diplomacy, intelligence and the use of force. More modern tools include development, science and technology, among others. This is partly a result of the definition of national security having expanded to include economic security, because many governments view the lack of economic opportunity as a potential cause of instability and conflict.

The above definition of national security includes the security of a country and its people. By "country" I obviously mean its sovereignty and territorial integrity. But what counts as providing, protecting and defending the security of its citizens? Is guarding against external and internal physical threats enough? Or should a government protect its people's lives from all kinds of threats? What about health, the water supply and the environment, food and energy security? Does failure to provide a reliable, equitable and affordable healthcare system mean a dereliction of duty in national security terms? Very few governments would say yes, even if many have acknowledged how inadequately they responded to the Covid-19 pandemic, beginning in 2020.

In the aftermath of the terrorist attacks on September 11, 2001, senior U.S. policymakers suggested that other countries' economic well-being is in the American national security interest. Condoleezza Rice, who served as national security adviser and later secretary of state in the George W. Bush administration, told me in a 2012 interview that helping other countries improve their economies and governance is "not a matter of largesse and compassion – it's a matter of security." Poorly governed countries "that can't act as responsible sovereigns end up giving their territory over to terrorists, drug traffickers and human traffickers. And those are then dangerous places from which a lot of transnational threats emerge," Rice said.

Hillary Clinton, Rice's successor as secretary of state during President Barack Obama's first term, agreed that Washington had an interest in improving people's lives around the world. "More peaceful, prosperous and democratic countries are not only good for the people living in them, but also good for the United States and our global goals," she told me, also in 2012. "There is no doubt that, where people feel that their aspirations can be addressed through their political and economic systems, and where they have accountable governments, they are more likely to be partners in helping us solve problems."[10]

When it comes to attention and funding, not all components of national security are created equal. For example, the U.S. defense budget is consistently more than 12 times bigger than spending on diplomacy and international affairs. In its 2023 budget proposal, the Joe Biden administration requested from Congress $773 billion for the Pentagon and $60 billion for the State Department and the U.S. Agency for International Development (USAID).[11] As of this writing, the Foreign Service has about 13,507 members, 7,996 of whom are considered diplomats.[12] In the military, there are about 1.2 million active-duty members and about 800,000 reservists.[13]

Figure 1.1 Nicholas Kralev, the founding executive director of the Washington International Diplomatic Academy (WIDA), speaks at a WIDA event in Washington, D.C., in 2018. Photo courtesy of WIDA.

In 2013, I conducted a survey of congressional staff attitudes toward diplomacy and the State Department for the American Foreign Service Association (AFSA). The respondents were evenly divided between Democrats and Republicans, and between the House of Representatives and the Senate. When asked whether they believed that most members of Congress associated diplomacy with national security, only 43 percent said yes. "They see it as not necessarily vital," a Senate Democratic aide said, while a House Democratic aide added that members thought that "defense trumps diplomacy." Asked whether they thought the American public associates diplomacy with national security, only 4 percent of those interviewed said yes. In theory, they probably "know that diplomatic attempts are made to avoid wars," a senior Senate Republican aide said.[14]

Much broader and more scientific polling than my modest effort conducted more recently has provided better news for diplomats. According to a 2019 survey among Americans by the Pew Research Center, 73 percent of respondents said that "good diplomacy is the best way to ensure peace." In addition, 68 percent said that the United States "should take the interests of allies into account, even if it means making compromises."[15] A 2022 survey by the RAND Corporation showed that more than 65 percent of respondents thought that "diplomacy contributes to national security."[16]

There is no doubt that a country's armed forces are the pillar of its security. But a problem or crisis will be resolved long before they need to worry about it if diplomats do their job well. In a way, by serving on the front lines of world affairs, diplomats are a country's first line of defense.

Defining diplomacy

The terms "foreign policy" and "diplomacy" are another pair often used inter-changeably, which is inaccurate. Diplomacy is just one tool in the foreign policy toolbox, as noted above – preferably, the tool of first resort. In the foreword, I defined it as the profession or activity of managing international relations with measures short of war. When it comes to implementing a country's foreign policy, diplomats do so by engaging and influencing nation-states, multilateral organizations and other actors on the world stage.

Diplomacy has often been described as an art – from "the art of the possible" to "the art of letting someone else have your way." One of the more unusual and memorable definitions is "the art of telling people to go to hell in such a way that they" – depending on the version of the quote – either "look forward to the trip" or "ask for directions." It is often attributed to Winston Churchill, even though there is no evidence he actually said it. The definitions of various dictionaries are quite different, with most focusing on only one aspect of diplomacy. The Merriam-Webster Dictionary describes it as "the art and practice of conducting negotiations between nations."[17] The Cambridge Dictionary defines it as "the management of relationships between countries."[18]

The stories at the beginning of the chapter showed that the practice of modern diplomacy includes a much wider variety of duties and responsibilities. The impetus and motivation for using diplomacy can be very different as well. It is usually associated with trying to achieve or maintain peace, or to resolve differences. Even when relations between two countries are good, there is daily state business to be carried out, which is done through diplomacy – George Shultz used to call it "tending the diplomatic garden."[19]

Historically, diplomacy has also been used to produce an impasse or insult meant to trigger a war. In those cases, leaders thought that a war was necessary to accomplish an adjustment in relations with other states. Chas W. Freeman, a veteran diplomat and contributor to this volume, cites such an example in his writing. In the mid-1800s, there were 39 German states. One of them, Prussia, was led by Otto von Bismarck. In 1870, he concluded that his effort to unite Germany under his leadership required a war. But he needed France to appear to be the aggressor, because an apparently defensive war would activate treaties that placed the Prussian king, Wilhelm I, in command of all German armies, including those in the Prussia-suspicious south. By altering a telegram and releasing it to the public, Bismarck made it sound as if Wilhelm had demeaned a ranking French envoy. Provoked by this apparent insult, as Bismarck had supposed it would be, France declared war on Prussia. In response, all German states united. As Bismarck had calculated, the victory of a Prussian-led German army over the French paved the way for the creation of a German empire under Wilhelm.[20]

Freeman points out that sometimes diplomacy can be a means of deception that conceals the intention to use force to effect change. During 1990 negotiations with Kuwait, Iraqi President Saddam Hussein convinced the Kuwaitis and other Gulf

Arabs that there was no imminent danger of his forces attacking them. An hour after abruptly breaking off the talks, Iraq invaded Kuwait.[21]

As one of the dictionary definitions above makes clear, negotiating is the activity most often associated with diplomacy. Although high-level and high-stakes negotiations are what makes the news, most diplomatic negotiations are done quietly by career professionals and have much more to do with run-of-the-mill and even mundane matters, such as embassy operations and visits by senior officials from headquarters, than with peace treaties or trade agreements. That does not mean that diplomats are absent from peace talks and trade negotiations, but that such high-profile activities take up a small part of the average diplomatic career.

Diplomacy has its limits. As soon as an armed conflict breaks out somewhere in the world, many foreign leaders tend to issue calls for negotiations. Those who start wars, however, rarely heed such calls quickly. In 2022, Russia had no interest in diplomacy either before or after it invaded Ukraine. The Kremlin was apparently certain that force was the only means of achieving its objective. Given what that goal was – subjugating Ukraine – it is reasonable to assume that no country would agree to such terms at the negotiating table. When the invasion began, Ukraine broke off diplomatic relations with Russia and closed its embassy in Moscow.[22] Still, it was more interested in talks than Russia was, and its president, Volodymyr Zelenskyy, offered to meet with his Russian counterpart, Vladimir Putin. But when Ukraine started scoring major military successes, Zelenskyy changed his mind.[23]

Not all diplomacy stopped as the fighting continued. With help from mediators, Russian and Ukrainian officials worked out a way to export Ukrainian grains, on which many countries relied to feed their people. No other foreign embassy in Moscow was closed, even if many were downsized. Despite punishing Russia with the most draconian economic sanctions in history, the United States and the European Union decided that they needed lines of communication with Moscow to remain open. The negotiation to move Ukrainian shipments through the Black Sea was a rare example of diplomacy that produced tangible results in the short term. For the most part, diplomacy is a long game that requires patience, persistence, flexibility and multiple adjustments. Results may not be achieved for years or even decades, as was the case with the Cold War – or they may be impossible to measure. It is difficult to make the case to anyone but insiders that the absence of conflict is a reason to give someone credit.

Who is a diplomat?

Career diplomats often say that diplomacy is a "people business," regardless of whether one works at home or abroad. At headquarters, many feel more like bureaucrats and do not enjoy the same privileges they have abroad, such as exemption from sales tax, immunity from prosecution, and free housing and schooling for their children. What makes someone a diplomat? This can be a loaded question. The

1961 Vienna Convention does not once use the term "diplomat." It says only that "the members of the diplomatic staff are the members of the staff of the mission having diplomatic rank."[24] So, is holding a diplomatic passport enough? Not quite: such passports are issued to family members of diplomats as well.[25] Not everyone working in a diplomatic mission is a diplomat, either. This is obvious in the case of a nurse or security guard, but what about a representative of the Federal Bureau of Investigation (FBI) or the National Aeronautics and Space Administration (NASA)?

In practice, there are two main categories of diplomats: permanent and transitory. The first category belongs to a country's career diplomatic service, usually known as its Foreign Service. These diplomats believe that diplomacy requires know-how acquired through training, on-the-job experience and mentoring. The transitory category includes three subcategories: domestically based civil servants on occasional "excursion tours" abroad, usually when a position cannot be filled by a Foreign Service member; representatives of various agencies at headquarters, other than the Ministry of Foreign Affairs, posted abroad; and noncareer appointees in senior roles, such as ministers and their deputies, as well as some ambassadors. All these categories of diplomats are full-time employees of their government at the time of their service. That is usually not the case with so-called honorary consuls, most of whom are private citizens with another occupation, appointed in an unpaid, part-time capacity. We will discuss details in Chapter 5.

The sending government is supposed to declare intelligence operatives to the receiving country. That usually works in allied states whose intelligence agencies cooperate routinely. But many countries have spies posted under diplomatic cover somewhere in the world. When those operatives are found out, they may be expelled for "engaging in activities not consistent with their duties," as declared to the host-country. In fact, "the receiving state may at any time and without having to explain its decision notify the sending state that the head of the mission or any member of the diplomatic staff of the mission is *persona non grata*," or an undesirable person, the 1961 Vienna Convention says. "In any such case, the sending state shall, as appropriate, either recall the person concerned or terminate his functions with the mission."

The term "recall," as used today, may be misleading in some circumstances. From time to time, you may read or hear in the news that an ambassador has been "recalled." That usually happens when the sending government is displeased with the receiving state. The media has the habit of omitting what comes after "recall" in an official statement, which is "for consultations," meaning that the ambassador has been ordered home for a few days to make a point and will return to post. That was what happened in 2021, when the United States and Australia announced a deal for U.S. nuclear-powered submarines to replace older Australian diesel-electric vessels, as part of a trilateral security partnership with Britain. This meant that Australia would break an earlier agreement with France to provide submarines. Paris was outraged as much over the deal as for being kept in the dark, and it recalled its ambassador in Washington for consultations.[26]

Diplomacy is not just a career but a way of life, with frequent moves and uprooting of families. Governments usually impose a time limit on diplomatic assignments, also known as tours. The average tour lasts three to four years. That may seem counterintuitive, because it makes it difficult to develop deep expertise, but it is done to prevent diplomats from becoming too close to their host-countries, which some in the business call "clientitis." Tours in high-risk places may last only one or two years. Some countries are less strict than others in their limits, allowing diplomats to remain at the same post for more than five years, sometimes to save on significant moving expenses.

The bilateral diplomacy system

Every nation-state has its own structures and mechanisms for making and implementing foreign policy. They include a system that enables the government to conduct diplomacy with other countries, both at headquarters and abroad. Those systems share many similarities, because they are based on the Vienna Conventions, but there are some differences, influenced by culture, history, and political and bureaucratic traditions, among other factors. We have already used the terms "home-country" and "host-country" to indicate the state diplomats represent and the one to which they are accredited. The terms "sending country" and "receiving country" are frequently used as well. There are also both similarities and differences between bilateral and multilateral diplomacy. We will first focus on the former, which is defined as **the management of relations between two nation-states**.

The diplomatic headquarters

In most countries, the executive branch makes and executes foreign policy. The legislative branch also plays a role in foreign affairs, particularly in democracies. On occasion, so does the judiciary. Every government has an executive agency charged with conducting diplomacy – usually, that is the Ministry of Foreign Affairs, with some name variations, such as the U.S. Department of State, the German Foreign Office and Britain's Foreign, Commonwealth and Development Office.

There are other government agencies with a stake in foreign affairs, such as those responsible for defense, finance, trade, justice, health, etc. Many countries – democracies in particular – have policymaking structures meant to bring together different agencies involved in a certain matter. The U.S. government uses the term "interagency" to describe both a structure and a mechanism through which policies are supposed to be developed, debated and presented to the National Security Council (NSC), which is headed by the president and includes the Cabinet secretaries who lead the relevant executive departments.[27] We will discuss details in Chapter 4.

The minister of foreign affairs – sometimes called minister of external affairs, secretary of state or foreign secretary – is usually considered a country's chief diplomat, though heads of state and government often engage in diplomacy as well. It is important to keep in mind that, although in a presidential republic such as the United States, the president is both the head of state and government, that is not the

Figure 1.2 A U.S. flag flies at half-staff outside the State Department in Washington, D.C., on September 12, 2012, to honor U.S. Ambassador J. Christopher Stevens and three other Americans killed in an attack on the U.S. Consulate in Benghazi, Libya.
Photo by Alex Wong/Getty Images.

case in much of the world. The British prime minister and the German chancellor are heads of government. In Britain, the monarch is the head of state, and so is Germany's president, even if the post is largely ceremonial. We will discuss how political leaders use diplomacy as a tool of statecraft in the next chapter.

A Ministry of Foreign Affairs, often referred to as Foreign Ministry or by the acronym MFA, is usually staffed by civil servants working at its headquarters, as well as diplomats who alternate between service at home and postings abroad. A country's career diplomatic service may include officers not just from the Foreign Ministry, but from other parts of the government. Although the vast majority of the U.S. Foreign Service members work for the State Department, there are also officers from USAID and the Departments of Commerce and Agriculture.

Foreign ministries are typically organized by geographic regions, such as Europe and Asia, and so-called functional issues like economic affairs and consular services. At the State Department in Washington, the top official is the secretary of state, followed by two deputy secretaries, six undersecretaries with responsibilities in broad areas, including political affairs and management, and assistant secretaries heading bureaus for different regions and functional issues (see Figure 1.3). In each bureau, the assistant secretary has several deputies who manage narrower parts of the respective portfolio. For example, in the Bureau of African Affairs, there are deputy assistant secretaries for West Africa, East Africa, Southern Africa, etc., who oversee offices with responsibilities for the countries in that subregion. Every office

Figure 1.3 U.S. Department of State leadership posts that require Senate confirmation. Ambassadors must also be approved by the Senate.

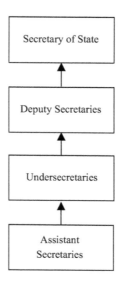

has country desks dedicated to one or more countries. The staff working there are known as desk officers – along with the deputy assistant secretaries, they are the workhorses of the management of diplomatic relationships.

Although the U.S. Congress does not play a direct role in diplomacy, it has constitutional responsibilities that affect the conduct of diplomacy. The first is its budget and appropriations authority – there is no diplomacy without money, and the budget must be approved by both the House of Representatives and the Senate. The second responsibility is oversight of the State Department, which is exercised through committees on foreign relations in both chambers. They hold hearings, conduct investigations, and their members regularly travel abroad. Third, laws affect relations with other countries. The Senate in particular must ratify every international treaty signed by the United States. These legislative functions are common in most democracies. The U.S. Senate has an additional responsibility assigned by the Constitution: senior diplomatic appointments are made by the president, with the "advice and consent" of the Senate. The nominees who must be approved by the chamber include ambassadors and State Department officials with the rank of assistant secretary and higher.

There is another U.S. practice that is unique, especially among advanced democracies: for decades, about one-third of ambassadors have been noncareer appointees from the private sector, academia, politics and other fields, often with no qualifications to practice diplomacy. They are usually selected because of political connections or as a reward for helping to get the president elected, often through fundraising.[28] The Senate approves almost all of them. Very few political ambassadors, as they are known, have done an excellent job. Most have been below average, making little or no impact, but managing to avoid scandal, though some have caused embarrassment, and a few have been fired. This spoils system brings amateurism to diplomacy and significantly affects the work of professional diplomats. In comparison, other advanced democracies may have one or two political ambassadors at any given time.

In addition to the legislative branch, a country's judiciary sometimes plays a role in foreign relations and diplomacy. In 2014, Devyani Khobragade, Indian deputy consul general in New York, was indicted by a grand jury for lying on a U.S. visa application for a domestic worker she had brought with her to the United States.[29] Khobragade had been arrested and released by a judge after posting bail. Diplomats serving at a consulate do not receive full immunity, as we will see in Chapter 11. The incident sparked a diplomatic crisis, and the State Department struck a deal with the Indian government: Khobragade was transferred to the Indian Mission to the United Nations, which allowed the department to grant her full immunity, though it also made her leave the country.[30] It does not happen very often, but the judiciary does get involved in diplomacy.

Diplomatic missions

A country's outposts beyond its borders are officially designated as "diplomatic missions" – they can be embassies, consulates general, consulates, representative offices, presence posts or permanent missions to international organizations, including the United Nations and the EU. Both member-states and nonmembers can have such missions. The United States is a U.N. member but does not belong to the EU; still, it has missions to both. The embassy of a country that is part of the British Commonwealth, which includes some of Britain's former colonies, in another Commonwealth state is called "high commission." Whatever the name, the 1961 Vienna Convention mandates that "the receiving state is under a special duty to take all appropriate steps to protect the premises of the mission against any intrusion or damage, and to prevent any disturbance of the peace of the mission or impairment of its dignity."[31]

An **embassy** is traditionally located in the host-country's capital, and its main building is known as the chancery. Two countries may have diplomatic relations without necessarily having an embassy on each other's territory, or only one of the two may have an embassy in the other. For example, as of this writing, Bulgaria has an embassy in Australia, but Australia does not have one in Bulgaria. The United States has several "embassy units" housed in third countries. After it closed its embassy in Venezuela because of strained relations in 2019, it opened a unit at its embassy in neighboring Colombia. In Iran and North Korea, with which Washington has no diplomatic relations, Switzerland and Sweden act as its "protective powers," respectively.

An embassy is led by a head or chief of mission, who is usually given the title "ambassador extraordinary and plenipotentiary." The 1961 Vienna Convention allows for a head of mission to be accredited to more than one state. Having secured the host-country's *agrément*, "the head of the mission is considered as having taken up his functions in the receiving state, either when he has presented his credentials or when he has notified his arrival and a true copy of his credentials has been presented to the Ministry for Foreign Affairs of the receiving state," the convention says. Can one be a chief of mission without being an ambassador? Yes. In the years before the U.S. Embassy in Venezuela was closed, its chief of mission did not have the title of ambassador to signify the downgrading of relations. Can one be an ambassador without being a chief of mission? Yes again. The title can be given to an official who is not even posted abroad.

The second-in-command of an embassy is the deputy head or deputy chief of mission (DCM). If the ambassador is the chief executive officer and the face of the sending state in the host-country, the DCM is the chief operating officer who oversees the overall management and functioning of the mission. The latter is arguably the more difficult job, as we will see in Chapter 5. "If the post of head of the mission is vacant, or if the head of the mission is unable to perform his functions, a *chargé d'affaires ad interim* shall act provisionally" in that capacity, the 1961 Vienna Convention says. Usually, the DCM becomes *chargé* in the absence of an ambassador, but sometimes the home-government may send another official. Because of the revolving door of U.S. political ambassadors and the significant time it takes the Senate to confirm them, many of the posts they occupy are often vacant, especially when a new administration takes office. In some cases, Washington dispatches active-duty or even retired senior Foreign Service officers from the United States to serve as *chargés*.

An embassy is typically divided into sections, such as political, economic, commercial, consular and public diplomacy, among others. Its size determines whether it has both economic and commercial sections, or if the economic section also has commercial responsibilities. Even though the front office and the political section serve as the liaison to the Foreign Ministry on a daily basis, the other sections manage various aspects of the bilateral relationship. We will discuss in detail how an embassy works in Chapter 5.

What is the difference between a consulate general and a consulate? It depends largely on the services they offer. A **consulate general** provides the full range of consular services, such as those for home-country citizens visiting or residing in the host-country, as well as entry visas for travelers to the home-country. A consulate general is headed by a consul general and is normally located in a big city outside the capital and may have several other sections, including those listed as parts of an embassy above. Some consulates general, especially in places like Hong Kong and Dubai, may be bigger than embassies. A **consulate** provides limited or no consular services. A consulate without a consular section may seem odd, but the home-government may decide that a certain city or province in the host-country is important enough to justify local diplomatic presence. There are five U.S. consulates general and consulates in Germany, but only two of them, in Frankfurt and Munich, offer consular services.

Representative offices and **presence posts** are smaller than consulates and may have only one assigned diplomat, or even just local staff. For all practical purposes, **multilateral missions** function as embassies, with two major differences: they do not have a consular section and do not manage bilateral relationships. Instead, they manage the relationships with the international organizations to which they are accredited.

Table 1.1 shows the number of diplomatic missions of 10 countries, based on the most recent data published by each government as of this writing. China recently

Table 1.1 Diplomatic missions and Foreign Service personnel abroad by country

Country	Diplomatic missions	Foreign Service personnel abroad
Australia	120	2,363
Brazil	208	1,552
Canada	193	2,517
China	279	Est. 4,500
Germany	225	3,048
India	193	850
Russia	247	Est. 4,500
Turkey	251	1,796
United Kingdom	235	Est. 5,000
United States	275	8,843

surpassed the United States, with 279 to 275 posts. Digging up the numbers of Foreign Service personnel working at those missions was no easy task. Few countries publish accurate and updated information. We could find no official data from China and Russia, so we used expert estimates. Even the British government publishes just a rough number. It is clear, however, that the U.S. Foreign Service has by far more official personnel abroad than any other diplomatic service.

According to the 1961 Vienna Convention, a mission's premises "shall be inviolable. The agents of the receiving state may not enter them, except with the consent of the head of the mission. The premises of the mission, their furnishings and other property thereon, and the means of transport of the mission shall be immune from search, requisition, attachment or execution." In addition, "the person of a diplomatic agent shall be inviolable. He shall not be liable to any form of arrest or detention. The receiving state shall treat him with due respect and shall take all appropriate steps to prevent any attack on his person, freedom or dignity. The private residence of a diplomatic agent shall enjoy the same inviolability and protection as the premises of the mission."

The importance of the local staff of any diplomatic mission cannot be overstated, and a mission cannot run properly without them. There are usually many more of them than the diplomats, and their knowledge, insight, experience and connections are invaluable – not something diplomats can gain during a tour. They are not just support staff but legal advisers, economists, engineers, political analysts and financial specialists as well. In 2022, there were more than 50,000 local employees in U.S. missions around the world, compared with 8,843 official Americans.[32]

The multilateral diplomacy system

Most of today's challenges do not recognize national borders and cannot be resolved by any one country alone. To have any influence in the 21st-century international system of multiple centers of power, a country must engage in skillful multilateral diplomacy, defined as **the management of relations among three or more nation-states**, both within and outside international organizations. The United Nations is the largest global organization. Although the public tends to think of it in terms of its two principal organs, the U.N. Security Council (UNSC) and the U.N. General Assembly (UNGA), it is a sprawling system involved in all the main aspects of international life. That system includes dozens of specialized agencies and programs, such as the Food and Agriculture Organization (FAO), the World Bank, the U.N. Educational, Scientific and Cultural Organization (UNESCO), the World Health Organization (WHO) and the International Atomic Energy Agency (IAEA).

In addition to its headquarters in New York, the United Nations has permanent seats in Geneva and Vienna, as well as other offices around the world. As of this writing, it has 193 member-states, which are all represented in the UNGA, with one vote each. The assembly is "the main deliberative, policymaking and representative organ," where "decisions on important questions, such as those on peace and security, admission of new members and budgetary matters, require a two-thirds majority." The UNSC has responsibility "for the maintenance of international peace and security." Five of its 15 members – the United States, Britain, France, China and Russia – are permanent and have veto power, while the rest are elected for two-year terms. The U.N. Secretariat is the organization's executive arm, headed by the secretary-general, who is elected by the assembly on the recommendation of the UNSC for a five-year renewable term.[33]

Both member-states and permanent observers, such as the Holy See and Palestine, can have diplomatic missions to the United Nations in New York, Geneva, Vienna and elsewhere. The diplomats serving in those missions usually come from the same Foreign Service pools that staff bilateral missions. The main value of multilateral diplomacy is its ability to reduce the complexity of international relations in everyday life, including traveling, sending mail and solving crimes across borders. It produces agreements that are much more practical and less costly than a web of bilateral arrangements between individual countries, and it sets common standards that enable collaboration among scientists, engineers and businesses around the world. Multilateral diplomacy has added complexity compared with managing bilateral relations and requires particular abilities, as we will see in Chapter 12. But it is still diplomacy, and the main skill sets discussed below still apply.

Outside the U.N. system, there are regional international governmental organizations that contribute to the multilateral diplomacy architecture, such as the EU, the North Atlantic Treaty Organization (NATO), the African Union (AU), the Organization of American States (OAS), the Association of Southeast Asian Nations (ASEAN), as well as global groups like the Organization for Economic Cooperation and Development (OECD). Many countries have permanent diplomatic missions to all these bodies. As mentioned earlier, not all multilateral diplomats represent a country. Many serve on the international staff of the various organizations. The United Nations alone has tens of thousands of international civil servants.

Multilateral diplomacy is also practiced every day at bilateral missions around the world – as mentioned above, global threats such as climate change, transnational crime and pandemic diseases are too complex and interconnected to bear an artificial division into bilateral and multilateral. U.S. embassies in certain countries even have positions dedicated to multilateral matters, on which they work with the host-governments.

Diplomatic duties and responsibilities

William J. Burns was a U.S. Foreign Service officer for 32 years, beginning in 1982, and rose to become deputy secretary of state, only the fourth career diplomat in that position. Before he became director of the Central Intelligence Agency (CIA) in 2021, he used to tell our students at the Washington International Diplomatic Academy that "a diplomat serves many roles: a translator of the world to Washington and Washington to the world; an early warning radar for troubles and opportunities; a builder and fixer of relations; a maker, driver and executor of policy; a protector of citizens abroad and promoter of their economic interests; an integrator of military, intelligence and economic tools of statecraft; an organizer, convener, negotiator, communicator and strategist."[34]

Vienna Convention on Diplomatic Relations

Article 3

1. The functions of a diplomatic mission consist, inter alia, in:
    (a) Representing the sending state in the receiving state;
    (b) Protecting in the receiving state the interests of the sending State and of its nationals, within the limits permitted by international law;
    (c) Negotiating with the government of the receiving state;
    (d) Ascertaining by all lawful means conditions and developments in the receiving state, and reporting thereon to the government of the sending state;
    (e) Promoting friendly relations between the sending state and the receiving state, and developing their economic, cultural and scientific relations.
    2. Nothing in the present convention shall be construed as preventing the performance of consular functions by a diplomatic mission.[35]

The 1961 Vienna Convention identified five functions performed by diplomatic missions, as shown above. Today, those duties and responsibilities can be divided into six broad areas, very similar to those in the convention. The first and oldest is **representation**. A diplomatic mission is considered part of the country it represents.

The building and the flag in front of it are the most visible expressions of that state's presence. An ambassador is the face of the sending country and, in most cases, the personal representative of the head of state. All diplomats represent their country 24 hours a day, not just during business hours. This means that they are always on the job.

The second set of duties falls under **consular affairs**. The most important role of embassies and consulates is assisting their fellow citizens residing in or visiting the host-country. They provide consular services, including everything from issuing reports of birth abroad to visiting detained or imprisoned compatriots to issuing death certificates. Diplomats help victims of crime and abuse, as Janice Jacobs's experience with the American woman in Nigeria showed at the beginning of the chapter. They also facilitate child adoptions, as well as evacuations from zones of natural disasters and violent conflict.

The other major consular function is screening for and issuing entry visas to host-country and third-country citizens who wish to travel to the home-country. Consular officers have the dual responsibility of helping to facilitate and boost legitimate travel while keeping away those who may pose a threat. In that sense, they are the first line of defense when it comes to border security. After the 9/11 terrorist attacks, the U.S. visa system became the most complex and cumbersome in the world. While many countries have embassies with just one or two consular officers, U.S. consular sections are often the largest at post, issuing millions of visas globally every year. As noted earlier, consular relations between states are governed by the Vienna Convention on Consular Relations of 1963.[36] We will discuss further details in Chapter 10.

The third set of duties at a diplomatic mission abroad is **relationship management**. Even though an embassy's front office is responsible for dealing with the host-country's political leadership, all sections are involved in some aspect of the relationship, including economics and trade, science and health, and education and culture, among others. This set of duties complements representation, but they are not the same. A country may have an embassy in a foreign capital, but not much of a relationship with the receiving state. If it does have one, there may be dozens of contacts between embassy officials and people from various ministries or departments in the host-government every day.

When the use of email, instant messaging and video conferencing became widespread, the consensus in many circles was that they would render diplomats unnecessary. The logic was that host-country officials would communicate directly with their counterparts in the home-country, bypassing the embassy. Officials in different capitals certainly talk frequently, but great leaders understand the value of diplomats abroad. Modern technology can only take you so far. By living in other countries and engaging with their hosts, diplomats gain invaluable insight into the local society, culture, thinking and decision-making. That makes them more influential in the host-country and better policy advisers to their own government.

This takes us to the fourth set of diplomatic duties: **reporting and analysis**. If relationship management is a way to explain your country to your hosts, diplomatic reporting is a means of explaining the host-country to your headquarters. Policymakers back home need to know what is happening in other countries from reliable sources, because the best decisions are not made in a vacuum but take into account the situation and players on the ground. Diplomatic reporting has much more in common with journalism than with spycraft. Diplomats gather information overtly, rather than covertly. A diplomatic cable – this term is still used, even though reports are no longer sent by cable – is similar to a story in a serious newspaper. However, a good cable should provide insights that cannot be found in the media. Diplomats often have access to sources that may not be comfortable talking to reporters. On occasion, diplomats may also offer policy recommendations to their headquarters. We will discuss details in Chapter 8.

Diplomats are generally not policymakers, though some of the more senior among them participate in and even drive the policy process. Most are implementers of policy, and when a decision is made in their home-capital, they have to carry it out in the host-country. This brings us to the fifth set of diplomatic duties: **advocacy, influence and negotiation**. Diplomats spend much of their time not just explaining, but also advocating for home-country policies and actions. That is reflected in some of the stories in the beginning of the chapter. Daniel Fried advocated for European sanctions against Russia after its annexation of Crimea, and Lisa Kubiske advocated for cleaning up corruption after the banking scandal in the Dominican Republic. American diplomats also regularly seek host-country support for U.S. positions in the UNSC.

Sometimes diplomats are tasked with preventing their host-country from doing something that is deemed harmful to home-country interests. For example, they routinely monitor draft bills considered by the local legislature, and if they detect any language that might disadvantage or hurt their country, they try to find a way to have it changed or removed before the bill in question becomes a law. Governments that are about to be sanctioned by Washington instruct their diplomats to lobby both Congress and the executive branch against such a move.

Influence is the most essential marker of diplomatic success. Countries with big international ambitions view their embassies and other missions not just as representational posts that look after relationships, but as opportunities to influence host-country policies and actions. The most masterful way to do so is to persuade the other side that the decision or step you want it to take is in its own interest. In addition to what we already discussed about negotiation, we will focus on it in more detail in the last chapter.

Compared to the intricate and dexterous diplomatic art of suasion, the sixth set of duties – **mission operations** – may seem trivial, but it is vital. If an embassy does not have a proper building that is run well, if its communications equipment does not function properly, or if its staff and their families lack decent living conditions, effective diplomacy is very difficult to pull off. Big countries like the United States have embassies with substantial management or administrative sections, whose job is to make sure the mission runs smoothly. While many on the staff are engineers, accountants and other specialists, the sections' leadership and some employees are

Foreign Service officers. Because diplomacy is not just a profession but a way of life, embassies need to take care of their people and keep them safe, both inside and outside the office. To do that, they need constant cooperation with the host-country, which cannot always be taken for granted. We will discuss details in Chapter 5.

Expeditionary diplomacy

Matthew Ference shared an office trailer with five colleagues, and a living trailer with two others – his room was about 8 feet by 8 feet. "The bathroom trailer, with showers, was about a 50-foot walk," he told me in 2012 in reference to his tour in the Iraqi city of Karbala the previous year. "We had a gym, cafeteria, basketball court with a broken rim and a volleyball court. The ground was gravel and dirt, and became very muddy when it rained." James Miller lived in similar conditions in the capital Baghdad when rocket fire destroyed the trailer next to his. "People I worked closely with died – one was an Iraqi-American interpreter and the other was an Army major," Miller told me. "We used to stay late at the office, and one of the reasons was, the less time you spent in your trailer, the less chance you had of being hit."[37]

These experiences bear no resemblance to the glitz and glamor many people associate with diplomacy, but they are part of Foreign Service life. Not all diplomats live and work in comfort and enjoy modern-day luxuries. Some serve in war zones and places where electricity is scarce and clean drinking water is difficult to find. Others contend with heavy pollution and diseases that have been eradicated in most of the world. For years, thousands of diplomats served in Afghanistan and Iraq in a time of war, many of them on provincial reconstruction teams (PRTs) in various provinces, like Ference. These civilian-military units were created to help rebuild Iraq and Afghanistan, and their leadership came from more than a dozen countries.

Diplomatic service in conflict zones and other high-risk locations is known as expeditionary diplomacy. Cameron Munter had spent his entire 20-year career in Europe before heading up the first PRT in Iraq – in the city of Mosul, capital of the Nineveh Province – in 2006. His team's offices were in a building with no running water, on a military base with about 3,000 troops. "We worked from 8 a.m. straight until about 10 p.m., because there was nothing else to do," Munter told me. "Every time I left the base, I had nine gunners and three armored vehicles. The bad guys would either shoot at us or try to hit us with roadside bombs. What was much more frequent than that was the so-called indirect fire – the shelling of the base with either mortars or rockets."[38]

In spite of the risk, Munter directed his team, which he had divided into govern- ance, economic, rule-of-law and reconstruction groups, "to leave the base and take care of their projects" around the province. "If it's our job to be at the cutting edge, it's no good to be sitting at our desks like bureaucrats," he said. "We sent people every day to inspect projects, talk to local mayors, take a trip around the province and find out what was going on." One of the main jobs of all PRTs was to "put the provincial government in touch with its constituents," Munter said. "Provincial officials had never left Mosul to visit people outside the city. We actually flew them to meet with their constituents in small towns." Representatives of the U.S. Department of Justice conducted seminars for judges "to teach them the rules of conduct in court," and "an officer from the U.S. Army Corps of Engineers managed the tender process by which reconstruction was done in the province," he added. Around Iraq, the PRTs built hundreds of schools, hospitals and parks.

Diplomats at the U.S. Embassy in Baghdad faced much tougher restrictions on their movements outside the heavily fortified compound. Unless accompanied by a security detail, they were not allowed at all in the so-called Red Zone, which was beyond the protected international area known as the Green Zone. When I visited the embassy in 2012, Douglas Silliman, one of the contributors to this book, was the political section chief. "You can't go anywhere without a lot of armed men," he said. "The security people are very good and try to be unobtrusive, but there are a lot of them. The ambassador and I are going to the Foreign Ministry today, and we'll have a large security detail and several cars to take us to the Red Zone." The embassy had a sophisticated threat-warning system, and announcements about possible incoming fire were made on average several times a day during my stay. "This technology has saved lives," said Mark Hunter, the chief security officer. "You get a warning, and it gives people the time they need to seek shelter."[39]

Governments rarely give their diplomats specific training before expeditionary assignments. Even before heading to a war zone, Miller "had a week of basic familiarization," including "medical-response training, how to recognize explosives and how to shoot," even though diplomats are not armed. Once in Iraq, Ference said, "we had to improvise, and hope that the Foreign Service selection process brings in people who have versatility and adaptability."[40]

Diplomatic skill sets

So what type of people make good diplomats? Naturally, they have to be globally aware, but they also must be deeply connected to the country they represent. They must have empathy for the views of others in order to understand their thinking. They have to be able to operate in foreign societies and flourish in different cultures, so they should enjoy living abroad and moving around every few years. They must possess a high level of curiosity and revel in learning new things. They must be good at listening and talking to people, and they must be able to set aside their own politics and personal policy views and serve whatever government is in power.

Diplomats are expected to perform most, if not all, of the sets of duties and responsibilities listed above during their careers – and often at the same time. One may have to engage in representation, relationship management, reporting and analysis, and advocacy and influence in the same week. What about expertise? In much of the world, a career diplomat is a jack-of-all-trades or, officially, a generalist, doing jobs as different as repatriating a deceased compatriot's remains, reporting on anti-government protests in the host-country and trying to increase trade and investment. Even if a Foreign Service officer has formally chosen the economic career track, they may end up in a public diplomacy or operational management job – either because they were encouraged to be versatile to get promoted faster, or because an economic job was not available in the country or region where the officer wanted to serve during that particular tour.

Diplomats from some countries, such as China and Russia, are regional experts and work in the same geographic region during their entire careers. Foreign Service officers from the United States and other Western countries do not have a formal specialization and move between regions. Many officers naturally develop expertise in a certain area, but they nonetheless take assignments outside of it. The average U.S. diplomat spends most of their career on two continents, in addition to serving in Washington.

The key diplomatic skills sets, on which we will focus in detail in Chapter 3, include some we have already mentioned, such as communication (writing, editing, speaking and listening), networking, advocacy and persuasion, understanding and analysis of policy. Being a quick study, as well as having leadership and management skills, are also essential, as is the ability to navigate a complex and sometimes opaque government bureaucracy. The term "diplomatic" is often used as a synonym for "polite" or "tactful," but in reality, diplomats have to be direct, forceful and even threatening at times. When that is necessary, calm and composure usually prove to be effective.

It is not easy to come up with a recipe for a successful Foreign Service career. No two officers' careers are the same. Some are talented and possess the necessary skills but have trouble working in a large bureaucracy. Others are just average but happen to be in the right place at the right time. William Burns is considered one of the best U.S. diplomats in recent decades. At 32, after six years in the Foreign Service, he was charged with running the Middle East office of the NSC staff at the White House in 1988 by Colin Powell, who was President Ronald Reagan's national security adviser. Burns became an ambassador – to Jordan – at 42. When Powell became secretary of state in 2001, he chose Burns to be assistant secretary for Near East affairs. After a tour as ambassador to Russia, Condoleezza Rice made him undersecretary for political affairs, and Hillary Clinton promoted him to deputy secretary in 2011.

Several former secretaries of state have tried to describe what made Burns stand out. He is "not ideological, calls it like he sees it, and everybody has confidence in him," James Baker told me in 2009. He "speaks truth to power in an understated way." That same year, Rice said that Burns did "the most difficult of tasks with a sense of optimism and equanimity" and "a great sense of humor,"[41] and Clinton told me that he was a "model of dedication to our country." In 2013, John Kerry told me that Burns understood "not just where policy should move, but how to navigate the distance between Washington and capitals around the world."

For his part, Burns said that there was no Foreign Service officer he admired more than Thomas Pickering, another contributor to this book. Having joined the State Department in 1959, Pickering went on to become ambassador seven times, as

Figure 1.4 William J. Burns, a former deputy U.S. secretary of state and ambassador to Russia and Jordan, speaks to students at the Washington International Diplomatic Academy in 2019. Photo courtesy of WIDA.

well as undersecretary of state for political affairs, before retiring in 2001. "Tom is as principled, big-hearted and modest as he is skillful and professionally accomplished," Burns told me. "Encyclopedic in his grasp of issues, whether nuclear throw-weights or the widgets in the embassy boiler room, a superb advocate of American interests and values, an unsurpassed problem-solver and negotiator, and a tireless champion of his colleagues and embassy communities."

How does one become a diplomat?

Diplomats have long been considered part of a country's elite. More consequential for certain parts of society was the reality that one had to belong to the elite to be considered eligible for diplomatic service. In much of the world, that is no longer the case, which does not mean that it is easy to become a diplomat. Today, the main barriers to entry are difficult entrance exams, a large number of applicants, and a very limited number of slots for new Foreign Service officers because of small budgets for diplomacy.

There are two ways to become a professional diplomat. The first is to join your country's diplomatic service, typically as an employee of the Ministry of Foreign Affairs or its equivalent. The second is as an international civil servant at the United Nations or another multilateral organization. In both cases, you will endure a lengthy application process, though the selection criteria may vary – for example, some governments and organizations prize academic achievements, while others prefer practical experience and real-life knowledge. Diplomacy is not a science or a profession like the law, and there is no uniform approach to evaluating candidates.

There are two paths to a career at the United Nations. The first is its Young Professionals Programme, which accepts university graduates no older than 32 years of age from countries that are underrepresented in the U.N. system. The eligible countries can be different every year.[42] Successful candidates serve in various positions at the U.N. Secretariat. The other option is to enter the system through a specific job opening advertised on the U.N. career website.[43]

As for joining a Foreign Service, in some countries like Brazil, candidates must be graduates of a specific institute run by the Ministry of Foreign Affairs. In others like India and Turkey, applicants must pass a standard exam required to work in any part of the Civil Service, with an additional, more specialized exam or interview round. The German entrance process is one of the most elaborate. It includes an extensive written and oral exam, an interview with a panel of diplomats and one with a psychologist. The French requirements include a master's degree or an equivalent, as well as exams. In China, a graduate degree is not mandatory, but there is a heavy emphasis on academic achievement nonetheless. Most countries require that applicants speak fluent English, and often at least one other language.[44]

Americans, however, do not need fluency in a foreign language to become career diplomats. Officially, a bachelor's degree is not mandatory, either. The only requirement, other than being at least 21 years of age, is to pass a written exam and an oral assessment. Even before filling out an application, you must select one of five career tracks: political, economic, management (formerly administration), consular or public diplomacy. If you are not sure, this book will help you decide. As part of the application, you have to write six short essays, which the State Department calls "personal narratives." They "describe the knowledge, skills and abilities the candidate would bring," based on six "core precepts" believed to be "predictors of success in the Foreign Service: leadership, interpersonal, communication, management, intellectual skills and substantive knowledge."[45]

Then all applicants must take the written Foreign Service Officer Test (FSOT), which is offered three times a year, both in person and online. In the meantime, computer software assesses their educational and professional qualifications, as well as the six personal narratives, in a process called the Qualification Evaluations Panel (QEP). Candidates are ranked based on the combined score from the "computer-QEP" and the FSOT, and the top tier in each career track advances to an "assessor-QEP." The human assessors manually score those files, and the top candidates are invited to the Foreign Service Oral Assessment (FSOA). That number may vary by career track and selection cycle, based on the State Department's budget and hiring needs.[46]

The selection process has changed slightly in recent years to include artificial intelligence and to increase diversity in the service. For decades, most changes to any part of the diplomacy system have been cosmetic, which frustrates many career diplomats. They lament the apparent difficulty of the system to modernize and keep pace with a rapidly changing international landscape. In my book *America's Other Army*, I outlined some insider critiques and suggestions for updating the way the Foreign Service recruits, selects, trains and promotes its officers. Diplomats around the world agree that the system's risk-averse culture and lack of creativity and innovation are impediments to more effective diplomacy. Perhaps future generations will change both the culture and the system.

The key ingredients of a good diplomat, however, will likely endure. "We need people who are as good at getting things done on the ground overseas as they are in the Situation Room at the White House, driving the policy debate," William Burns told me. "That is not a common combination, but it is what we need to aim for. You have to find wherever the ball is rolling on the field, and with a sense of vision and strategy, move it down the field." At the same time, the reality of the system is that "how well you do depends a lot on who you work for and what you work on," Burns added. "I was really lucky, but I know people who were not so lucky."[47]

Track II diplomacy

In 2016, nearly a dozen former U.S. diplomats, academics and former military officers spent two days at a guest house in the northeastern Chinese city of Jilin, not far from the border with North Korea, discussing concerns about the regime in Pyongyang. The host was a Chinese government-funded think tank, and the American group was under the auspices of the EastWest Institute in New York, a nonprofit dedicated to what is known as Track II diplomacy, which is an informal process outside official government channels used by countries in disagreement to find common ground. Cameron Munter, having retired from the Foreign Service, was president of the institute, which closed down in 2021.

Often called a back channel, Track II helps to create a climate in which foreign policy has a chance of being implemented. "Because we were Americans, foreigners correctly assumed that we would communicate with U.S. policymakers at a high level, in a discreet way," Munter, who participated in several such efforts, including the visit to China, told me in 2023. "Because we were not government officials, foreigners assumed, also correctly, that we could approach problems and potential solutions with more flexibility than those in office."[48] At times, Track II can include current officials, as was the case in the Jilin talks, which were part of a series of engagements Munter's institute had with senior Chinese officials and experts, known as the Sanya Initiative Dialogue.

The first phase of Track II diplomacy usually involves breaking down barriers and building trust. At this stage, "the cultural differences of Chinese and American participants were acknowledged and accepted, or even joked about," Munter recalled. "We shared our experiences with one another, and there was inevitably a key role for *maotai*, the very potent liquor that appears – or at least used to appear – at high-level gatherings in China. Then the conversation moved on to the issues at play – defining those issues took a great deal of time and was more difficult than actually addressing them. Then the discussion devolved into specifics, with everyone looking at the clock and realizing that both sides wanted to have something to take home for the next phase, which is assessing whether there is, in fact, a way forward that can be useful to the two governments. That was the subject of the final dinner, again replete with *maotai*, during which various participants summed up the discussions and suggested where to go next."

After all that, the process had only begun. Both sides had to collect and systematize their thoughts and share them with their respective constituencies in their capitals to see if any creative suggestions for solutions to serious problems made sense – and if they did, how realistic putting them into practice was. Once agreed by the two governments, the ideas had to be shopped around to other interested parties, which in turn would trigger an official negotiating process, as we will see in Chapter 15. "Track II allows freer exchange of ideas than formal diplomacy," Munter said. "Without it, it is much harder to find out what the other side is thinking, and to reflect in a self-critical way on whether what our side wants is possible."

ADDITIONAL RESOURCES

G. R. Berridge, *Diplomacy: Theory and Practice*, 6th ed. (Palgrave Macmillan, 2022).

Andrew F. Cooper, Jorge Heine and Ramesh Thakur, eds., *The Oxford Handbook of Modern Diplomacy* (Oxford University Press, 2013).

Robert Hutchings and Jeremi Suri, eds., *Modern Diplomacy in Practice* (Palgrave Macmillan, 2019).

Pauline Kerr and Geoffrey Wiseman, eds., *Diplomacy in a Globalizing World: Theories and Practice*, 2nd ed. (Oxford University Press, 2017).

Nicholas Kralev, *America's Other Army: The U.S. Foreign Service and 21st-Century Diplomacy*, 2nd ed. (Amazon, 2015).

2　Diplomacy as an Instrument of Statecraft

CHAS W. FREEMAN

Most Americans imagine that they achieved independence either on the day it was declared, July 4, 1776, or on October 19, 1781, when the United States, with France's help, defeated the British at Yorktown, Virginia. In fact, U.S. separation from the British Empire was only secured when the British conceded it. It took John Adams, Benjamin Franklin, John Jay and Thomas Jefferson nearly two years to persuade Britain to accept that the necessary consequence of its military defeat was American independence. This became a legal reality on September 3, 1783, when Britain and the United States signed the Treaty of Paris.[1]

Two centuries later, the United States was one of two superpowers in the bipolar world of the Cold War. One of its major geopolitical challenges was in Southern Africa. In addition to trying to end military interventions on the continent by the Soviet Union, the other superpower, Washington wanted to help free South West Africa (today's Namibia) from South African occupation. Chester A. Crocker, assistant secretary of state for African affairs, proposed a policy called "linkage": it linked the demands of different parties and conditioned them on each other. If Soviet-backed Cuban forces, whose intervention in Angola the South African government viewed as a threat, were to withdraw, and if elections replaced civil war in Angola, and if South Africa withdrew from Namibia, all sides would be able to claim victory. Crocker succeeded by rearranging the strategic geometry of the region. It was a classic exercise in balance-of-power diplomacy and offshore balancing in support of U.S. objectives.[2] It was also politically friendless, which may be why it remains essentially unstudied. At the time, I served as Crocker's principal deputy assistant secretary.

Crocker's diplomacy was under constant attack in Washington from both the political Left and Right. The Left saw dealing with South Africa under the apartheid system of racial segregation and discrimination as immoral. Dealing with adversaries like the Soviet Union and Cuba, which had intervened in the region militarily, contradicted the Right's determination to punish them. As American politicians saw it, diplomacy offered an unrighteous and unrealistic distraction from their ideological agenda and preference for the use of force to counter Soviet intervention in what was called the Third World. However, George Shultz, President Reagan's secretary of state, resolutely backed Crocker's diplomacy. Reagan backed Shultz. And Crocker had the courage of his convictions. That made all the difference.

Although rarely understood, the centrality of diplomacy as an instrument of statecraft is essential to war termination, gaining sovereignty and shifting the balance of power. It is not about "making nice," nor is it just a delaying tactic before we send in the Marines. Diplomacy is a political performing art that informs and determines the decisions of other states and peoples. It shapes their perceptions and calculations, so that they do what we want them to do, because they come to see that doing so is in their own best interest. Sometimes diplomacy rearranges their appraisal of their strategic circumstances – and when needed, the circumstances themselves. Ultimately, it aims to influence their policies and behavior through measures short of war, though it does not shrink from war as a diversion or last resort. It is normally, though not always, overtly noncoercive.

Diplomacy succeeds best when it embraces humility, and respects and preserves the dignity of those to whom it is applied. Most of what diplomats do is unseen, and it is relatively inexpensive. Its greatest triumphs tend to be preventing bad things from happening, but it is hard to get credit for something that was avoided. So diplomats are more often blamed for what did happen than credited for what did not. Diplomacy stages no parades in which ambassadors and their political masters can strut among baton-twirling majorettes or wave to adoring crowds.

How does diplomacy benefit statecraft?

Statecraft is generally defined as the **skillful management of state affairs**.[3] The term "statesman" implies a higher level of skill – even mastery – compared to the abilities of an average ruler. No political leaders can manage their country's affairs in isolation from the rest of the world, which is why they have foreign policies. To be successful, they need to understand and deal with other governments and societies. We will detail the key skills a professional diplomat should have in the next chapter. In this one, we will focus on the big picture from a statecraft perspective. How can diplomacy benefit the conduct of state affairs? What do statesmen need to know, so they can utilize diplomacy in the most effective way to achieve their objectives? If there is a skill set to be mastered in this case – in addition to a solid grasp of how the world works – it has to do with the ability to recognize when to listen to diplomats and be secure enough as a leader to trust them.

That is much harder than it sounds. Politicians tend to distrust diplomats. In the United States, both Republican and Democratic presidents and other top leaders have harbored suspicion of the Foreign Service for decades. They have often sidelined or ignored it. "There is always a bias in Washington against the State Department, and when you have a conservative Republican administration, it's worse," Colin Powell told Nicholas Kralev in 2005, shortly after leaving office as secretary of state in the George W. Bush administration. "The perception is that diplomats are bad – they want to talk people into things, while soldiers fight or get ready to fight."[4]

Successive U.S. administrations have institutionalized this lack of trust by drastically increasing the number of political appointees in key diplomatic and foreign policy positions. They have argued that such appointees are necessary to make sure that career officials implement the president's policies, because he was elected by the American people. The apparent implication is that otherwise the Foreign Service may carry out some other policies. They mistake the explanation of foreign positions by diplomats for advocacy of them, especially when those positions contradict their own views as wrong, irrational or malicious. Such an attitude is not limited to the United States. In 2022, French President Emmanuel Macron was so displeased with his Foreign Service that he issued a decree aimed at dismantling it.[5] His plan was to fold it into the much larger Civil Service and have its members work in various ministries in Paris, with occasional stints abroad. In the meantime, employees from across the government would be sent abroad to staff embassies and consulates.[6] French diplomats went on strike to protest the plan weeks later. One of their concerns was that Marcon's reforms could open the door to a U.S.-style practice of handing out ambassadorships as political favors. The decree took effect in January 2023.[7]

Many politicians' distrust of diplomats comes from a misunderstanding of what diplomats actually do, as well as from failure to appreciate how useful they can be in statecraft. Political leaders have the power to instruct their diplomats, and as the main managers of state-to-state communication, diplomats need instructions from their capital every day. If they receive poor or no instructions, they cannot respond effectively to unexpected developments. This was the case with the U.S. ambassador to Iraq, April Glaspie, when she met President Saddam Hussein on the eve of his annexation of Kuwait in 1990. Glaspie could not take a position on his complaints against Kuwait without authorization from Washington, and she had none. Diplomats make easy scapegoats. Like many before her, Glaspie ended up taking the fall for officials in Washington who had ignored her warnings and failed to respond to her repeated requests for instructions. Having told Hussein that the United States had "no opinion" on Arab–Arab conflicts, she was accused of failing to warn him against invading Kuwait, which some interpreted as effectively giving him a green light.[8] At the time, I was the U.S. ambassador to neighboring Saudi Arabia.

Great statesmen understand how to consume intelligence, which is processed information that is useful to statecraft, and know that they are dependent on diplomats and spies to receive it. The main difference between the two is that diplomats gather information overtly. There is no substitute for direct conversations with decision-makers in foreign governments. Effective political leaders also know that what works in one political culture may very well be ineffectual or off-putting in another. Without the expertise of diplomats, political leaders risk engaging in "mirror-imaging," the supposition that foreigners see their interests and make decisions the same way as one's own political culture and government. In reality, each country has its own ways.

For example, to get things done in Japan, it helps to understand that government ministers or corporate chief executives seldom make decisions on their own. They

Figure 2.1 Chas Freeman, a former U.S. ambassador to Saudi Arabia and deputy chief of mission in China, meets with Chinese President Hu Jintao in Washington in 2006.
Photo by Jonathan Ernst/AFP via Getty Images.

see their role as ratifying recommendations that have percolated upward from mid-level experts in the institutions they head. In the case of Japanese government ministries, almost no decision is made without final vetting by an administrative vice minister – the senior career official in the ministry. Raising an idea at the ministerial level in Tokyo without ensuring that it has first gained support at lower levels is almost invariably a waste of time. In China, decisions have historically been made by the Communist Party apparatus. Even during the increasingly authoritarian rule of Xi Jinping, it is a culturally parochial mistake to assume that the country's president and party chief has personal executive authority equivalent to that of the U.S. president and can engage in similarly freewheeling discussion. Chinese officials, however senior, have no authority to commit their country to actions that its state and party apparatuses have not reviewed and approved.

Diplomatic engagement must not be seen as a favor to the other side, but as a convenience to one's own. It is a means by which to convey one's position directly to an adversary, to listen to its reasoning about its position on the issues in contention, to argue for changes in that reasoning, and to warn, cajole and probe for evidence of willingness to concede specific points. It may be good domestic politics to pound the policy table in support of popular narratives and nationalist postures, and to reject foreign positions as irrational, disingenuous or even malevolent. In a policy process driven more by how things will look to potential domestic critics than by a determination to change the behavior of foreigners, diplomats are easily marginalized.

But when they are backed by strong-minded leaders who want results abroad, they can accomplish a great deal. Chester Crocker certainly had such backing when he set out to implement the Southern Africa "linkage" policy he had proposed in the 1980s. His strategy proved that patient diplomacy, based on accurate assessments of the perceived needs of the parties to apparently intractable conflicts, can maneuver them toward peace when reflected in hard-nosed policies.

Diplomacy as strategy

Diplomacy is an essential part of any international strategy. It involves molding the decisions and actions of others to one's advantage, as well as making one's own moves. It is a protracted game that is almost rule-free, far more complex than chess and has real-world consequences. To formulate sound diplomatic strategy, one must assure that the words applied to foreign relations both correspond to reality and are relevant to analysis, deliberation and planning.

A strategy is **a plan of action designed to achieve a desired objective through the lowest possible investment of effort, resources and time, and the fewest adverse consequences for oneself**. In chess, a strategy that consists only of an opening move consistently yields failure. Myopic moves in foreign policy – moves that do not anticipate the probable perceptions and countermoves of others – also guarantee defeat. The American invasions of Afghanistan and Iraq in the 2000s were such exuberant military operations with no planned follow-up, definition of victory or concept for war termination. Calling a statement or a collection of military campaign plans a strategy does not make it one. Strategies cannot be wishful thinking. They must match resources to objectives and focus on specific and attainable goals.

No one can play chess without understanding the capabilities and potential uses of the various pieces on the board, both on one's own side and on that of one's opponent. Knights move differently and do things that bishops and pawns cannot, and vice versa. Each piece must be deployed or countered differently. The same is true in foreign affairs, with the added complications that the contest has actions other than attack and defense, that one sort of piece can at any moment change into another, that there are often multiple players maneuvering independently but simultaneously in the same space, and that, even when the king is cornered, the game does not end. It just enters a new phase.

During the Cold War, diplomacy for the most part resembled trench warfare, with confrontations along well-established fronts that seldom moved. Its purpose was to hold the line and prevent intrusions by each superpower into the other's sphere of influence. Such spheres are assertions of an exclusive right to supervise or participate in deciding the alignments and affairs of another country or countries in relation to others, either in general or in specific domains. They are manifestations of international contention between peers and can be formal or informal, defensive or domineering. In the rivalry between the United States and the Soviet Union, each side sought to exploit local strife – in Vietnam, Laos, Angola, Mozambique and other countries – to its advantage. But neither was willing to provoke war with the other that might escalate to the nuclear level. Struggles between them took the form of proxy wars. Within their respective spheres of influence, diplomacy was a form of imperial administration, holding subordinate states and their politicians in line.

Despite its overall strategic immobility, the Cold War was not entirely without dramatic paradigm shifts and examples of exceptional statecraft. Two of them were President Richard Nixon's 1972 outreach to China and Egyptian President Anwar Sadat's 1977 opening to Israel. They exemplified diplomatic breakthroughs through grand gestures aimed at building new strategic relationships. Such grand diplomacy seeks to bypass fruitless bargaining over insuperable but arguably petty differences with an adversary. Its purpose is to enable the two sides to make a fresh start at seeking common ground, to begin a process of expanded strategic cooperation to mutual advantage, and to defer apparently intractable problems until more favorable conditions for resolving them can emerge.

By traveling to their enemy's capital while making no specific demands of it, Nixon and Sadat, each in his own way, followed Churchill's advice: "Appease the weak, defy the strong."[9] Each gave his longtime adversary the crucial psychological satisfaction of being treated with respect. Each implicitly acknowledged the legitimacy of his opponent's national security concerns and the need to address them eventually. Grand diplomatic gestures are gifts that call for grand responses, not haggling. Nixon's gesture enabled the United States and China to end two decades of hostility in Sino-American relations. China famously takes the long view, and it opened to the strategic relationship Nixon sought. Though the immediate results of their maneuvers were different, Nixon's and Sadat's breakthrough diplomacy illustrates an important canon of statecraft: when there appears to be no effective answer to a question, one should consider whether the question one has been asking is the wrong one.

In the case of China, if the issue was how to contain and retard its development, it made sense to pursue a policy of strategic distraction through support for separatists in Taiwan and Tibet, diplomatic embargo, economic and financial sanctions, as well as military deterrence. But if the question was how to use China to offset Soviet power, or how to limit the impact of Mao Zedong's revolution on the world order, then acceptance of its government's legitimacy and diplomatic engagement, as well as promotion of trade and investment, were more appropriate. In the Middle East, if the issue was how to prevent the consolidation of a Western-backed Jewish state on Arab land, Egyptian ostracism and confrontation with Israel were logical policies. But if the question was how to develop the Egyptian economy in partnership with the United States and under conditions of peace, engaging and establishing a *modus vivendi* with Israel was essential.

Today, the impasse between the United States and North Korea invites a change in the questions on which U.S. policies have been based. The primary purpose of the North's nuclear weapons program has been to develop a deterrent to possible American, rather than Chinese, attack, and U.S. attempts to outsource the problem with North Korea to China have always represented wishful thinking, rather than a coherent strategy. The so-called six-party talks, which started during the George W. Bush administration, represented one such attempt. They included the United States, North Korea, China, Japan, South Korea and Russia. Perhaps the right question is not how to force Pyongyang to abandon its nuclear program, but how to convince it that it is secure enough from the possibility of U.S.-instigated regime change to have no need for nuclear weapons. If the questions are changed, the policy answers to them change as well.

Diplomacy as tactics

If the key to sound strategy is whether one is asking the right question, the key to sound tactics is to ask "And then what?" before taking action. Strategy must be set at the top, but tactics are best driven from the bottom up and from the field in. Those on the front lines are best positioned to judge the most effective tactics for pursuing strategic objectives in the circumstances they face. Diplomacy is the verbal tactics of foreign relations. It is the alternative to the use of force, as well as its prelude, facilitator and finale. It is both the implementer of policy by measures short of war and the translator of the results of war into durable outcomes. It uses words to portray capabilities and convey intentions in order to shape the calculus of foreign partners and opponents, and cause them to make desired changes in their policies and behavior.

The end of hostilities does not mean winning a war. To achieve peace, there must be a leader among the defeated populace with the authority to commit them to it. This is why the United States left the Japanese emperor on his throne after World War II. During the run-up to the 2003 U.S. invasion of Iraq, the failure to consider the question of who might be able to commit Iraqis to cooperation with the Americans – and what would be required to persuade them to do so – accounted in no small measure for the anarchy that followed the removal of Saddam Hussein's regime. Diplomatic tactics for war termination are an essential element of any successful war strategy. They translate military triumph into political victory. Failure to allow diplomats to negotiate postwar adjustments in relations is a major reason why so many wars spin on without end or abate, only to resume in altered form.

Diplomacy and war are often viewed as a discontinuous dichotomy. But diplomacy does not halt when war begins. Nor does the role of military power end when peace replaces war. Effective diplomatic communication is essential to escalation control. It is also necessary to persuade enemies to make concessions that justify ending wars with them on agreed terms. War is the pursuit of policy through violent coercion, up to and including mass murder. It does not supplant the need to pursue policy by other means. Enemies must be made to see that it is in their interest to agree to terms, rather than to suffer devastation or annihilation.

This makes diplomatic communication more important than ever in times of war. Even when the objective of war is unconditional surrender – generally, a counter-productive posture that incentivizes maximum resistance by the enemy – diplomacy is important to lay the basis for the postwar order. It is not the military end state that vindicates strategy; it is the political end state. For wars with limited objectives to end, the combatants must be able to end their combat through a negotiated resolution of differences on terms they consider acceptable. The fact that they are fighting makes it all the more important that they talk. This consideration is why China – contrary to Western practice – left its embassies in place during its conflicts with India and Vietnam in 1962 and 1979, respectively. The need to preserve the negotiability of differences is also why Otto von Bismarck counseled that one should be polite even when conveying a declaration of war.[10]

Diplomacy in the run-up to war and during it serves to prevent still other adversaries from becoming enemies, to preclude the formation of hostile coalitions, to deny alliances to adversaries, and to divide enemies from their allies and partners. Wartime diplomacy works to bolster one's own alliances and partnerships, to extract concessions from actual and potential belligerents, and to lay the groundwork for order and stability to succeed mayhem. Far from ending during warfare, diplomacy complements military operations and enables them to fulfill their political purposes. It is how the warring parties translate the results of their combat into adjustments in relations between them.

As important as diplomacy is to the fruitful conduct of war, it is also the principal and most effective alternative to it. In some respects, diplomacy can be likened to jujitsu (柔术), the Japanese system of unarmed combat and physical training – the use of an opponent's energy, strength, desires, preconceptions and mode of coercive action to match, misdirect, disarm and counter him. Success depends on knowing what one wants, understanding one's opponents' preoccupations, being prepared, seeing one's objective through one's opponents' eyes as well as one's own, exemplifying stamina and resilience, and knowing when to exploit openings as they appear.

In addition to translating military success into territorial adjustments and other concessions, diplomacy can play a role in expanding a country's borders in peacetime, in which case it often involves financial transactions. In 1803, President Thomas Jefferson purchased France's Louisiana Territory for $15 million, doubling the size of the United States. Jefferson's negotiators, James Monroe and Robert Livingston, took advantage of Napoleon's recent defeat in Haiti and need for money, and sensed that he was ready to write off French colonial ambitions in the Western Hemisphere. It took them just two weeks to complete the agreement.[11] When Secretary of State William Seward negotiated the acquisition of Alaska from Russia in 1867 for $7.2 million, that ended Russia's presence in North America and ensured U.S. access to both the Pacific's northern rim and the Arctic.[12]

In normal times, diplomacy is not concerned with redefining frontiers, but with arranging and policing the terms of trade and investment across borders. Military power persuades by menacing the life, liberty and happiness of those to whom it is applied. Economic ties, on the other hand, draw their power from the gains that countries, companies and individuals make from exchanging what they have for what they do not. Like a string, economic power connects people and businesses, and enables them to pull each other together. This makes economic measures ideal tools of any strategy aimed at building communities or other cooperative international relationships, as the political effects of removing trade barriers in the EU illustrate.

But the fact that economic power links and encourages exchanges of goods and services – instead of sundering or discouraging them – also makes it a poor tool of coercion. This is why economic sanctions, a frequently used tool by the United States in recent years, rarely work. You can pull on a string, but you cannot push on it. Sanctions can be essential bargaining chips to be traded for concessions by their target, but this requires that they be part of a negotiating strategy, not a punitive end in themselves. They are useful as threats. The fear of sanctions, the precise effects of which can seldom be modeled with accuracy, is generally more compelling than their actual impact. If sanctions are imposed, their only utility becomes their removal in exchange for concessions that are part of a deal.

Hard and soft power

"Do economic sanctions represent hard or soft power?" This was the first question students at the Washington International Diplomatic Academy asked Joseph Nye during a 2022 session. "Hard power," quickly responded Nye, a Harvard political scientist widely known for coining the term "soft power" in 1990. Back then, he had written that, while "hard power – the ability to coerce – grows out of a country's military or economic might, soft power arises from the attractiveness of a country's culture, political ideals and policies."[13] In the class, he described **"soft power"** as **"the ability to attract and persuade," not to threaten and intimidate**.

Because diplomacy involves talking, rather than fighting, it is often viewed as an equivalent to soft power. Understanding why that is incorrect is key to statecraft. Although the appeal of a country's political system or culture can help statesmen and their diplomats, it is almost never enough to get another country to do something. Ideally, they would use the power of persuasion to influence foreign counterparts, but in reality, they might have to resort to coercion or threats. These are still part of diplomacy, as is the case with economic sanctions. Such penalties sever relationships and unravel ties that bind parties together. The immediate damage they cause is almost always reciprocal. Groups and activities on both sides suffer, and the pain usually falls on parts of the private sector and indirectly on the public at large – not on the government or the elite.

The purpose of economic sanctions is to compel changes in behavior by their target. That rarely happens, even if the penalties cause significant economic damage. When the United States and the EU imposed unprecedented sanctions on Russia soon after it invaded Ukraine in 2022, the impact on the Russian economy was noticeable within months. But that did not stop the war. Some have argued that U.S. sanctions on Iran pushed the regime in Tehran to negotiations that produced a deal aimed at preventing it from building a nuclear weapon in 2015. Iran has denied that, and it is difficult to make a definitive conclusion. Usually, ostracism does not persuade, it enrages. Unacceptable demands are not made acceptable by maximum pressure and attempted public humiliation, unless they are accompanied by a credible negotiating process. Countries are at their most dangerous when they perceive an existential threat or an injustice from which there is no potential relief through diplomatic dialogue. We will explore the topic further in Chapter 7.

More than two millennia before Nye first wrote about soft power, Confucian moralism held that the key to influence outside one's own state was not military power projection but domestic virtue that would cause others to see one's nation as a society they should emulate.[14] In the 17th century, John Winthrop, one of the founders of the Massachusetts Bay Colony, wrote about the power of American rectitude to inspire other societies. Americans' traditional idealism, their oft-stated aspiration to apply higher-than-usual standards to themselves, and the demonstrated capacity of American society to embrace change, for decades gave Washington a uniquely persuasive voice in world affairs. Worldwide admiration for the wisdom of the U.S. statesmen who created the post-World War II order legitimized the United States' international stature as the natural leader of global governance. The appearance of virtue can add to a country's power by associating it with justice, compassion, probity and wisdom.

It is no secret that foreign perceptions of the United States have deteriorated in recent years. People in other countries see a deeply divided society, gridlocked government, endemic racism, rife homelessness, frequent gun massacres and inequality of opportunity. That has made the work of American diplomats much more challenging. They need to recognize their country's deficiencies and address them. Their political bosses need to up their performance and return to managing risks to freedom and prosperity by investing in more effective and creative diplomacy.

Diplomacy as risk management

At its most basic level, diplomacy is the management of foreign relations to reduce risk to the country while promoting its interests abroad. In this task, diplomacy's success is measured more by what it precludes than by what it achieves, as noted earlier. It is the means by which a state builds political capital, sustains a reputation for reliability and responsiveness to foreign partners and events, and interacts with them from day to day. The management of alliances, relations with dependencies, neutrals, adversaries and enemies is a never-ending task that diplomats necessarily carry out around the clock.

The ideal outcome of diplomacy is the assurance of a life for the country that is as tranquil and boring as residence in the suburbs. The previous chapter noted George Shultz's "gardening" analogy. Like suburban life, in its day-to-day manifestation, diplomacy involves harvesting flowers when they bloom, and fruits and berries when they ripen, while laboring to keep the house presentable, the weeds down, the vermin under control, and the predators and vagrants off the property. If one neglects these tasks, one is criticized by those closest, regarded as fair prey by those at greater remove, and not taken seriously by much of anyone.

Viewed this way, the fundamental purpose of U.S. foreign policy is the mainten-ance of a peaceful international environment that leaves Americans free to enjoy the prosperity, justice and civil liberties that enable our pursuit of happiness. This agenda motivated the multilateral systems of governance the United States created and relied upon after World War II – the Pax Americana. Institutions like the United Nations and its specialized agencies, as well as related organizations, such as the International Monetary Fund (IMF) and the World Bank, sought to regulate specific aspects of international behavior, manage the global commons, provide frameworks for the resolution of international disputes, and organize collective responses to problems.

In the aggregate, these offspring of U.S. diplomacy established and sustained widely accepted norms of behavior for decades. International law drew on consen-sus to express these norms as rules. To the extent they were accepted internationally, the rules constrained state actions that could damage the common interests of the society of nations the rules had brought into being. Despite its uneven performance, the Pax Americana assured a relatively high degree of predictability in world affairs that facilitated peaceful international interactions. It did so on the same philosoph-ical basis as the rule of law in domestic affairs – a belief that rules matter, and that process legitimizes outcomes, rather than the other way around. Today, that phil-osophy and its ethical foundations are under attack both at home and abroad. With the fading of previously agreed codes of conduct, what could once be taken for granted in managing relations with other states must now be repetitiously renegoti-ated and affirmed bilaterally. Escalating uncertainties are driving some countries toward unrestrained unilateralism and disregard for international law.

Historically, there have been four relationship categories that include or imply obligations: alliances, ententes, protectorates and client states. Today, thanks in large part to the atrophy of diplomatic vocabulary during the Cold War, almost the only words used to describe any sort of remotely cooperative international ties – however ephemeral – are "ally" and "alliance." These words have been so stretched and blurred in meaning that they have become semantic nulls.

An ally is a partner that has accepted an obligation to offer broad support or assistance to one's country, because it wishes to receive reciprocal support for its own interests and objectives. The usual purpose of alliances is to add the power of others to one's own. However, the spheres-of-influence landscape of the Cold War did not conform to this model. The United States and the Soviet Union embarked on a protective mission directed at denying their respective spheres to the adversary. Security guarantees to others became part of a strategy of containment and deter-rence, not one focused on power aggregation. There was little, if any, expectation that the Europeans in NATO and its rival Warsaw Pact would add much, if anything, to the military or economic capabilities of the two superpowers. They were made "allies" to bring them under protection for purposes of strategic denial.

The Cold War ended in 1989, and the Soviet Union collapsed in 1991. But this history continues to shape American thinking about "alliances" and "allies." The U.S. government considers it its duty to safeguard its "allies" from their enemies, who are – by extension and adoption – also ours. Any country not overtly hostile to the United States that is in some way cooperative with it can be a so-called "ally," worthy of American protection. But the impulse to defend "allies" coexists with the suspicion that they may be playing America for a sucker. Hence the inherent appeal of the populist demand that "allies" reimburse the United States for protecting them.

During World War II, Britain, France, the United States and the Soviet Union were known as the "allies," but that was an instance of limited partnership in entente – a commitment to cooperate under particular circumstances, for specific purposes, for as long as this served common interests. Entente confines both commitments and risks to agreed contingencies, rather than leaving them open-ended. Unlike alliances, limited partnerships pursuant to entente rely on policy coordination and parallel actions, not joint operations or unified commands. Like alliances, when they are public, ententes deter challenges to the interests of their participants. When they are aggressive rather than defensive, however, they are often kept secret to maximize strategic ambiguity, prospects for entrapment of foes or surprise.

A symbiotic relationship based on exchanges of concrete benefits, such as military bases or transit rights, is a protectorate. The protected power seldom feels a sense of obligation to its protector but recognizes the need to provide it with recompense for its support. Protection may be soundly grounded in the interests of the parties to it, but it does not involve reciprocal undertakings. The U.S. commitment to Saudi Arabia, Japan and South Korea is an example of protectorates. It is significant that relations with Japan now seem to be evolving away from dependency and toward entente.

Client-state relationships – in contrast to alliances, ententes and protectorates – are based on a one-way flow of support from the patron to the client. Client states owe no allegiance and benefits to their patrons. The misuse of the word "ally" to describe them implies honor-bound mutual obligations that do not exist. Client states add no significant political, economic, cultural or military power of their own to that of their patrons, though they may add base and transit rights or other facilities that improve the patrons' geopolitical circumstances. Sometimes they are clients only because their independence frustrates a strategic rival, and it is therefore desirable to guarantee it. Client states in the Middle East like Egypt, Israel and Jordan have received enormous strategic support from the United States. But none feels obliged to do anything in return.

In the current world disorder, relationships are more fluid than they were in the 20th century. Transactionalism seems set to replace fixed friendships and animosities. Relationships that embody obligations are diminishing, freeing states to maneuver in accordance with their interests, as they see them. Alliances are eroding, and with them, the predictability they provide. The limited and temporary partnerships characteristic of entente are multiplying. Protectorates are losing credibility. Client states are increasingly unconstrained and dismissive of their patrons. There are likely to be many ententes, but fewer alliances and protectorates. The rivalries in a multipolar state system are unlikely to support many client states – free riders on the ambitions of a single great-power patron. Smaller states are likely to consider strategic promiscuity a safer course than bonding with a particular patron.

Diplomatic capability and readiness

What does all this mean for diplomacy as an instrument of statecraft? It means that the current environment rewards diplomatic agility, flexibility, versatility and responsiveness to change, which underwrite adaptation, resilience and innovative approaches to deal with new problems and opportunities. And it penalizes diplomatic immobility and incompetence. Diplomatic preparedness requires constant attention to other countries and their views. Showing that one's government is interested in and understands what others think encourages them to be more receptive to one's own ideas. Attentiveness to their needs, views and doubts signals willingness to work together and cultivates readiness to cooperate in defending common interests.

The regular nurturing and reaffirmation of relationships is what makes it possible to call on a network of friends in times of need. Responding politely and considerately – in the least offensive way one can – to others' messages conveys respect as well as substance. It invites their sympathetic study of the logic, intent and interests behind one's own messages. Constant diplomatic engagement promotes stability and predictability. It inhibits inimical change, reducing the risk that amicable states will become adversaries or that adversaries will become enemies. And it provides situational awareness that reduces surprise and enables governments to respond intelligently and tactfully to trends and events. All this may seem obvious, but it takes a sustained commitment by national leaders, public servants and well-trained diplomats, as well as reliable funding, to carry it off.

During the Cold War, the United States learned to rely more on deterrence than diplomacy to address potentially explosive situations. This made sense in a world order with essentially fixed frontiers between two great blocs of states, in which Washington enjoyed unmatched coercive power. But in the context of disorder and fluid relations between states, deterrence should not be the first resort of statecraft. It leaves the causes of potential conflict to evolve for the worse, stimulates arms races, invites countermeasures and often precludes cooperation on unrelated matters. Its effect is to prevent problems from exploding now, but to leave them to explode later. Sometimes the passage of time erases or alleviates the danger that disputes might erupt in armed conflict. But it can also permit them to fester and enlarge their potential to produce catastrophe.

The dangers of substituting protracted deterrence for diplomacy are well illustrated in the confrontation between the United States and North Korea. For decades, U.S. policy toward the regime in Pyongyang has consisted of containment through ostracism, embargo, confrontation and military shows of force. U.S. officials have repeatedly said that Washington does not seek regime change. At the same time, at no point has the United States, which is unquestionably the stronger party, developed a strategy for coexistence with North Korea. There has been no American initiative to negotiate a replacement of the 1953 armistice that ended the Korean War with a peace treaty, despite the commitment of its signatories to do so. Instead, Americans have consistently projected the collapse of the North's regime. In the meantime, Pyongyang has mounted a desperate drive to develop nuclear weapons.

Some international relationships are bound to be adversarial. Diplomacy must seek to forestall the transformation of adversaries into active enemies. That is, unless – as is rarely the case – overt hostility by one foreign party can stimulate rapprochement by a larger, more capable country whose support would facilitate the pursuit of other, more important interests. It is usually in the national interest to inhibit the evolution of relations from skepticism to passive resistance to active opposition on issues. Such evolution can lead to broadly adversarial relations, which can easily become broad hostility or outright enmity.

Talking with adversaries is usually better than not talking, provided you know what you are going to say and are confident you know what your counterpart can and cannot accept. Direct communication with North Korea's leader on terms that convey respect for his power, but not his policies, may prove to be the key to a breakthrough. But it could also produce a catastrophe if Washington does not address the fears that underlie North Korea's policy. From Pyongyang's perspective, the United States essentially has been saying, "If you do not disarm yourself, we reserve the right to kill you, so give up your deterrent now, and we will see what we can work out" – though not in so many words. It will be very difficult to persuade Kim Jong-un, the North's leader, to place his trust in the United States.

Meeting with adversaries is the theater in which diplomacy best struts its stuff. Its purpose should not be just to reach agreement with the other side, but to achieve the end state that one's strategy requires. The object of a negotiation is to persuade one's opponent to embrace the need to accommodate one's demands, absent a better alternative. The participants in a diplomatic negotiation have the option of resorting at any time to the use of force against each other. They can choose to accept or ignore the prevalent norms and rules of international law. Implicit agreement on rules by one side cannot assure that the other side will adhere to them.

Very occasionally, not talking can be a form of negotiation. It can allow time to ripen circumstances conducive to concessions by one's adversary – for example, by inciting quarrels between it and third parties, encouraging insurrection against it, or demonstrating one's coercive capabilities against a third party. Or it can mean using talks to shelve issues, stall for time to strengthen one's position, allow the situation to evolve in one's favor, create a crisis that forces the other side to make decisions it would otherwise evade, or make the other side appear to have been so unreasonable as to leave no alternative to the use of force against it. Stalling for time can also mean entering talks but conceding only minor points, insisting that the major issues or principles be reserved until they can be resolved to one's advantage.

Direct dialogue can lend gravitas and the credibility of body language to threats or carefully articulated offers to compromise in ways that written messages or communication through intermediaries cannot. It can help develop constructive ambiguity; repair bruised egos; facilitate cooperation on issues of common concern, notwithstanding confrontation on other matters; develop personal relationships that ease the resolution of disputes or enable collusion once opportunities ripen for it; and provide a distraction for the media. If negotiations fail, the result is protracted impasse, escalating tensions or armed conflict, not a lawsuit leading to a court decision and penalties. The stakes in international negotiation are higher than those in domestic transactions; all the more reason to demand excellence from those charged with conducting it.

Less tangibly and less visibly to the public, diplomatic interactions are a major element in government awareness of foreign thinking, planning and actions that affect the national interest. Reporting by U.S. diplomats overseas often provides a substantial part of the material that intelligence agency personnel charged with all-source analysis rely upon to brief policymakers in Washington. There is no substitute for ground truth, artfully captured and examined in light of U.S. interests, in making sufficient sense of events in foreign countries and cultures to enable officials to respond intelligently. The cultivation of contacts in the host-country is the key to collecting information relevant to statecraft. It is also the most effective means of accurately and persuasively conveying one's government's views to the host-government.

The physical security of diplomats is important, but information security is truly vital to their work. Honest discourse on sensitive matters requires reliable assurances of confidentiality, whether it is to lawyers' clients, physicians' patients or diplomats' interlocutors. In democracies, the people have a right to know what policies their government is following and why. They have no legitimate interest in the sources and methods by which their government gains information from foreigners or influences their decisions. Analysis should be disclosed, but the details of diplomatic conversations and reporting on the views of foreign governments and individuals should be privileged. Breaches of professional privilege degrade the candor and reduce the effectiveness of exchanges of information. That was the consequence of the 2010 indiscriminate release by WikiLeaks of about 250,000 State Department cables,[15] which we will discuss in Chapter 8.

The need for diplomatic doctrine

Diplomacy is a universal skill, not the preserve of any particular country or its history. There is a great deal to be learned from the ways in which the statesmen of other countries manage or fail to manage the issues that confront them. We should use this period of diplomatic fecklessness to recruit, train and deploy a new generation of diplomats, who will face greater challenges than those of us no longer in government, and they must be more competent and professional. Most of today's problems are not amenable to military solutions. Excellence in diplomacy is at least as essential as excellence in the conduct of war. In the case of the United States, neither war nor the threat of war can restore its lost global leadership. Only an upgrade in competence at formulating and implementing domestic and foreign policies, coupled with effective diplomacy, can do that.

The U.S. military has the healthy habit of conducting after-action reviews to learn from what went right, what went wrong, and what might have been done better in an engagement. Sometimes what is learned is sufficiently important to be incorporated into doctrine. More commonly, it provides insights into how training can be improved. However, professional diplomatic doctrine – a body of inter-related operational concepts describing how to influence the behavior of other states and people by mostly nonviolent means – does not exist. So there is no diplomatic equivalent of military doctrine. This is a very big gap in statecraft.

The absence of diplomatic doctrine to complement military science eliminates most options short of the raw pressure of sanctions or the use of force. It increases the probability of armed conflict, with all its unpredictable human and financial consequences. Working out a diplomatic doctrine with which to train professional diplomats could have major advantages. This effort must begin with restoring precision to our diplomatic terminology and reasoning processes, sharpening our analysis of international realities and rediscovering diplomacy as strategy.

The constant review of experience is essential to extract and test the hypotheses that constitute the doctrine of any profession – its institutional memory and essential skill sets. The substance of diplomacy involves maneuvers between states and people. These are both intellectually fascinating and emotionally engaging. Much ink is spilled describing and analyzing them. Both policymakers and diplomats easily become fixated on the policy issues with which diplomacy must grapple and fail to focus on the process and methodologies by which such grappling must be done. But such a focus is indispensable in mastering the diplomatic arts.

Some diplomatic chores yield immediate gains. Others are long-term investments in garnering goodwill and building rapport – laying down strata of fossil friendship that can be mined in the future, or keeping warm memories of past cooperation suggestively alive. When these chores are not done, the country loses in both the short and the long term.

Case Study 1: "Linkage Diplomacy" in Southern Africa

When Chester Crocker became U.S. assistant secretary of state for African affairs in 1981, he inherited a failed policy focused on shaming and sanctioning South Africa into implementing a U.N. Security Council (UNSC)-mandated independence process for its Namibian colony. He replaced this with diplomacy that enlisted American power to ensure that none of the key actors in the region could get its way on the issues it most cared about unless all others did, and Namibia gained independence. This kind of "linkage" diplomacy required dealing forthrightly with several of America's and the world's most prominent bêtes noires: apartheid-era South Africa, Cuba and the Soviet Union. The Cubans and the Soviets had earlier humiliated both

Case Study 1: (cont.)

South Africa and the United States by intervening militarily in Angola to forestall elections and install a Soviet-backed government.

The decolonization of Namibia was the focus of U.N. diplomacy in Southern Africa, but it was not a top priority for any of the main players in the region. South Africa, which viewed the Cuban troops in Angola as a threat, wanted them removed. The priority of the Angolan government and its Cuban sponsors was consolidating control of Angola by defeating insurgents from the National Union for Total Independence of Angola (UNITA),[16] as well as the South African expeditionary forces that supplied and fought alongside it. The Cubans wanted to demonstrate their power to help end colonialism in Africa. For the overextended Soviets, the goal was cutting the costs of their policies, while showing that they were still a great power whose interests could not be ignored by the United States or regional powers. All concerned wanted better relations with the United States.

The main U.S. objective in Southern Africa at the time, derived from the Cold War grand strategy of containment, was the reduction and prevention of further advances in Soviet influence in the region. Linking Cuban troop withdrawal to the UNSC's demand that South Africa grant Namibia its independence gave U.S. policy a claim to

Figure 2.2 Chester Crocker, U.S. assistant secretary of state for African affairs (third from right, with glasses), meets with senior officials from South Africa, Angola and Cuba in 1988, as part of his negotiations on Angola's civil war and Namibia's independence.
Photo by Mike Nelson/AFP via Getty Images.

Case Study 1: (cont.)

international legitimacy that enabled very useful backstage support from senior U.N. diplomats. A time-honored tool of diplomacy is shameless repetition of an unwelcome proposition, so that it becomes so familiar that it is no longer ruled out. With persistence on the part of the United States and other countries that quietly cooperated with American diplomacy, the initially recalcitrant parties came to see that there could be something for everyone in a deal based on "linkage." Otherwise, the fighting in Angola would continue, with American favor withheld, the Namibian issue unresolved and South Africa ostracized.

The Cubans could take pride in having stabilized Angola and helped to end colonialism in Africa; the South Africans could rid themselves of the Cuban-Soviet threat and take pleasure in American and Soviet recognition that they were the greatest power in their region; the ailing Soviet Union would no longer have to subsidize Cuban intervention in a region that was of only marginal strategic importance to it; the Angolans could pursue an end to the civil war; the United Nations could finally oversee the independence of Namibia; and the United States would show its diplomatic mettle while removing significant Soviet influence from Southern Africa.

Much to the surprise of its many detractors, "linkage" diplomacy eventually led to the deal it had set out to produce. Crocker ended up accepting semi-clandestine aid to UNITA as a way to pressure the Angolan regime and its Cuban and Soviet patrons to agree to negotiate a regional agreement. South Africa withdrew from Namibia, which declared independence in 1989.

Case Study 2: U.S. Arms Sales to Taiwan

The "Taiwan question" is the issue of what political relationship Taiwan should have with the rest of China. It arose from the confluence of two wars. After the defeat of Chiang Kai-shek's Republic of China on the China mainland in 1949, he retreated to the Chinese province of Taiwan. In 1950, as Mao Zedong's People's Liberation Army prepared to pursue Chiang to his island redoubt, North Korea invaded South Korea. The United States interpreted this as part of a broader Soviet-bloc move to break out of "containment." It interposed the U.S. Seventh Fleet between the Chinese combatants in the Taiwan Strait to prevent the Korean War from spilling over to Taiwan and adjacent areas of the Chinese mainland.

With U.S. support, Taipei then continued to represent China internationally and to affirm its intention to reconquer the Chinese mainland. Meanwhile, Beijing stressed its determination to complete its victory in the Chinese civil war by "liberating" Taiwan. As part of "containment," the United States undertook to ensure Taiwan's defense against assault from the mainland. Each party to the unfinished civil war constantly proclaimed its intention to use force to reunite China under its rule. Washington took

Case Study 2: (cont.)

the measure of the military balance in the Taiwan Strait, including U.S. forces, and then offered or added what seemed necessary to maintain that balance.

But in the 1970s, the United States stopped using Taiwan to contain China and turned to using China to contain the Soviet Union. In 1978, Washington recognized Beijing, rather than Taipei, as the seat of the Chinese government. Beijing pledged to do its best to resolve the Taiwan question by peaceful means. The withdrawal of all U.S. forces and military installations from Taiwan and the undertaking to exercise restraint in future sales of "carefully selected defensive weapons" to Taiwan had facilitated this Chinese policy change. The United States appeared to have consolidated China's alignment with it against the Soviet Union, while successfully extricating itself from all but indirect military involvement in the residuum of the Chinese civil war. By disengaging militarily, Washington seemed to have laid the basis for realizing its stated policy interest "in a peaceful settlement of the Taiwan question by the Chinese themselves."[17]

However, during the 1980 U.S. presidential campaign, Ronald Reagan, the Republican nominee, pledged to return to a policy of unrestricted arms sales to Taiwan.[18] This led to a Sino-American crisis over the issue after he took office. But both China and the United States had a stake in at least the appearance of solidarity in their opposition to the Soviet Union. Toward the end of 1981, Beijing and Washington began exploring the possibility of a renewed *modus vivendi*. Beijing saw an American commitment to temper and eventually end arms sales to Taiwan as essential to justify its normalization of relations and overt cooperation with the United States. Washington wanted Chinese public commitments both to stand with the "free world" against the Soviet Union and not to use force against Taiwan.

On August 17, 1982, the last of three U.S.–China joint communiqués was issued. Neither side got all it wanted, though each got enough to reaffirm cooperation against Moscow. More important, the agreement put in place an understanding on how U.S. arms sales to Taiwan should be handled. In return for a U.S. pledge to cap the quality and gradually reduce the quantity of arms sales to Taiwan, China affirmed and implemented a "fundamental policy" of striving for reunification by peaceful means. As intended, these parallel policy shifts caused both Taipei and Beijing to rethink how best to pursue their respective strategic interests.

China's policy of peaceful reunification and its rapid modernization made worst-case analyses of the military balance in the Taiwan area increasingly problematic. It was becoming ever more evident that the indefinite maintenance of military parity between an island of 23 million people and the emerging great power across the strait was not feasible. Beijing's acceptance of a political, rather than military, approach to reunification enabled the United States to incorporate an appraisal of Chinese intentions into the analysis of what arms sales might be necessary to "maintain a sufficient self-defense capability" for Taiwan, as U.S. policy required.[19] As the threat diminished, so might the need for U.S. arms transfers to Taiwan. This made it very much in Beijing's interest to emphasize its peaceful intent.

The prospect of steadily diminishing American military assistance had the predictable effect of focusing Taipei on realistic alternatives to military confrontation as a

Case Study 2: (cont.)

response to the threat Taiwan faced from the mainland. Within a decade, it had stopped challenging Beijing as the government of China and decided that it was in its interest to respond to Beijing's offers of political dialogue. In meetings in Hong Kong in 1992 and in Singapore in 1993, Taipei and Beijing found a framework to justify ongoing dialogue and negotiations between them. Without prescribing any particular course of action on the Taiwan dispute to either party, U.S. policy had created circumstances that induced the parties to set aside military confrontation in favor of a "peaceful settlement of the Taiwan question" between themselves.

The realization by both Beijing and Taipei that dialogue offered a better prospect than military approaches to the management of cross-strait differences took time to take root. But it did take root. To the surprise of many, it survived the abrupt abandonment by the United States of the agreed limits on its arms sales to Taiwan. In the 1990s, the collapse of the common Soviet enemy, the deterioration in U.S.–China relations after the Tiananmen Square massacre, and a long-running campaign by proponents of military approaches to securing Taiwan came together to produce a massive sale of advanced fighter aircraft to Taiwan, the largest such package to any single purchaser to date. The U.S. turnabout predictably encouraged defiance of Beijing by Taiwan independence advocates and provoked the remilitarization of cross-strait relations.

Subsequent twists and turns in cross-strait relations included attempts by some in Taipei to repudiate previous understandings with Beijing, and Chinese and U.S. shows of force in the Taiwan area. But in 2005, Taiwan and the mainland extended their rapprochement in a detailed program of cooperation based on their earlier understandings. Many Americans still advocate a purely military approach. In response, Beijing has reciprocated with its own military buildup. Few in the United States noticed until 2022, when Beijing reacted to a visit by U.S. House Speaker Nancy Pelosi to Taipei with a show of its new military might.[20]

Neither the Taiwan story nor the risks it presents to Sino-American relations is over. The danger remains that, if Sino-American disagreement about Taiwan is not addressed creatively, it will lead eventually to a bloody rendezvous between American honor and Chinese nationalism.

ADDITIONAL RESOURCES

Hal Brands and Jeremi Suri, *The Power of the Past: History and Statecraft* (Brookings Institution Press, 2015).

Henry Kissinger, *Diplomacy* (Simon & Schuster, 1994).

J. Robert Moskin, *American Statecraft: The Story of the U.S. Foreign Service* (St. Martin's Press, 2013).

Margaret Thatcher, *Statecraft: Strategies for a Changing World* (HarperCollins, 2002).

3   Key Diplomacy Skills

DAVID LINDWALL AND CHAS W. FREEMAN

It did not take long for American diplomats around the world to be proven right. It was 2002, and the State Department in Washington had sent a cable to more than 100 U.S. embassies abroad with the same instructions. The Rome Statute establishing the International Criminal Court (ICC) was about to enter into force. The court would have jurisdiction over war crimes, aggression, genocide and crimes against humanity, perpetrated "on the territory of any state-party" to the statute.[1] Although the United States was not an ICC member, the administration of President George W. Bush worried that Americans serving in the military and stationed overseas may face prosecution.

A loophole in the statute's Article 98 allowed ICC member-states to exempt the citizens of nonmember countries from the court's jurisdiction. So the Bush administration rushed to secure bilateral agreements with as many governments as possible. The cable the State Department sent out instructed every embassy to deliver a diplomatic démarche – a request or demand to another government – aimed at beginning negotiations. It was clear to any Foreign Service officer that the cable was not written by a professional diplomat. It insisted on identical demands to all ICC member-states and did not give posts leeway in how to present the request. The reaction from most ministries of foreign affairs was negative. Still, the department dispatched lawyers and senior officials to capitals around the world to negotiate Article 98 agreements,[2] as they would become known, meant to protect American troops from ICC prosecution. Some of those officials were experienced negotiators, but they spent only a day or so in each country, often going to meetings straight from the airport, and did not take the time to learn the particular concerns and circumstances of the host-governments.

David Lindwall, one of this chapter's authors, served as the political counselor, or head of the political section, at the U.S. Embassy in Guatemala when the push for Article 98 accords started. A few years later, when he was back in Guatemala as deputy chief of mission, officials from the State Department came for a day to negotiate an agreement. Lindwall was in the meeting where Guatemalan officials showed no interest in the U.S. proposal, even after the visiting Americans mentioned that the Bush administration was considering suspension of military assistance for countries that refused to cooperate – they did not seem to know that Guatemala had not received such aid since 1990. The two countries never reached a deal.

Even though dozens of ICC member-states eventually signed Article 98 agreements, they did not include the countries where most of American forces were stationed, such as Germany, Italy, Japan and South Korea. In fact, no member of the EU or NATO went along with the U.S. initiative. The administration's inability to persuade its closest allies to agree was no surprise to career diplomats. The 2002 cable's one-size-fits-all approach was the first clue. They knew it would not work and asked Washington for flexibility and creativity in their attempts to bring the countries that really mattered onboard, but the administration would not budge.

What might have made a difference? The short answer is: key diplomacy skills on the part of the officials in charge of the negotiations. They failed to understand the importance of designing a specific approach to address each country's particular circumstances and concerns. They did not take the time to learn much about their counterparts, let alone their history, culture and way of thinking. They insisted on an all-or-nothing proposition, giving other countries no opportunities to save face with measures somewhat short of the U.S. demand but much better than nothing. They also lacked interpersonal skills that would have been conducive to building trust, a vital ingredient in any diplomatic effort.

There is no guarantee that possessing the above skills would have yielded agreements with all countries that host large numbers of American forces abroad. Some of them harbored such negative feelings toward what they perceived as the Bush administration's unilateralism and disregard for allies that perhaps even master diplomats would have failed. Others were opposed in principle to blanket immunity for American troops. Still, the chances of reaching at least some understanding would have been higher. What about career diplomats? Could they have worked harder to secure Article 98 accords? Should they get some of the blame? Well, many of them tried but were told that the negotiations were being handled by a special team. Their advice and ideas were rarely heeded. Could they have been more persistent and creative, without being accused of insubordination and undermining the administration's agenda? More collaborative relationships with political appointees and navigating the bureaucracy more skillfully might have helped, indeed.

Diplomacy skills matter, and the widespread perception – including among politicians – that anyone with common sense can be trusted with a diplomatic position, even without proper qualifications, is misguided and dangerous. Diplomacy is a serious business, and as Nicholas Kralev noted in Chapter 1, diplomats are the guardians of a country's national interests abroad. The matters they deal with are too important to be left to amateurs. There are careers that do not require a new hire to possess any special skills on day one. Diplomacy is not such a profession.

Diplomats must have most basic skills before they hit the ground running. In fact, they are expected to have them before joining the Foreign Service, because most governments do not provide much substantive training to new officers. As such an officer in 1985, Lindwall was sent to the U.S. Embassy in Colombia to head the immigrant visa unit in the consular section. He was 26, fresh out of graduate school and had not managed people before. But in Bogotá, he had to supervise four local employees, interview dozens of visa applicants in Spanish every day and make judgment calls on whether they fulfilled all the requirements of U.S. immigration law. Outside the consular section, he was expected to help the ambassador entertain official guests at events, and to establish a relationship with the American missionary community in Colombia, so the embassy could respond more effectively to its growing security concerns.

Other than a brief course in applying U.S. immigration law, Lindwall had not received much substantive training before leaving the United States. Along with his peers, he was thrown into the deep end of the pool, where the only options were to swim or sink. He was lucky enough to find informal mentors who helped him navigate the system and refine his skills. But not every new officer is so lucky – and relying on luck is hardly a responsible way to build a diplomatic career. Throughout his 34 years in the Foreign Service, Lindwall watched many new diplomats flourish, but he also witnessed many get stuck in a rut and fall behind, because they lacked key skills. Although the different career tracks, which are oddly known as "cones" in the U.S. Foreign Service – political, economic, consular, management and public diplomacy – require some specialized knowledge and abilities, most diplomatic skill sets are universal. This chapter does not represent an exhaustive list of everything a good diplomat needs to know. But it covers the key aspects of diplomatic tradecraft, on which the rest of the book will elaborate and expound.

Empathy

What distinguishes diplomats from courtiers, securocrats and other bureaucrats is a reliance on empathy. The basis of diplomacy is empathy for the views of others – the ability to see the world through the eyes of your interlocutors, and to use this insight to induce them to see their interests the way you want. A diplomat schooled in strategy can determine what circumstances are required to persuade foreign leaders that doing what the diplomat wants them to do is not yielding to superior power, but deciding on their own to do what is in their country's best interest.

Empathy does not imply alignment or agreement with the views of others, just understanding of them. It is not the same as sympathy, which identifies with the others' perspectives. At times, the objective of diplomacy is to persuade others to continue to adhere to established policies, because they are beneficial. But more commonly, it is to change the policies, behavior and practices of other countries or individuals, not to affirm or endorse them. To succeed, diplomats must cleave to their own side's interests, convictions and policy positions, even as they grasp the motivations and reasoning of those whose positions they seek to change. But they must also be able to see their country and its actions as others see them, and to accept these views as an operational reality to be acknowledged and dealt with, rather than denounced as irrational or duplicitous. To be able to advocate for their governments' policies effectively, diplomats must rely on developing expertise that enables them to nudge the decision-making processes of the governments whose decisions they seek to guide in the desired direction.

Diplomats must be concerned not only about how foreigners interpret what they say; they must be careful not to foster distrust among officials back home. Their effectiveness as envoys depends on the host-country's confidence that they have the support of their own government. Sustaining such support is more difficult than it might appear at first. Most capitals are prone to groupthink and averse to dissenting views. Officials with no experience on the ground abroad are likely to have false images of its topography and to mistake descriptions of it for "clientitis" – identifying with the host-country's interests.

Helping policymakers at headquarters to formulate policies and actions that have a chance of influencing a foreign country's decisions is central to diplomatic work. Diplomats habitually find themselves called upon to explain how and why that country's history and circumstances make it see things in a particular light and act the way it does. In the U.S. government, most officials in senior foreign policy positions did not work their way up the ranks. They are much more familiar with domestic interest groups and their views than with foreign societies and how they work. For a career diplomat, retaining credibility requires avoiding frontal assaults on the often unrealistic narratives that dominate the discourse in your own capital. You must keep your focus on your country's national interest, even as you interpret the incompatible views foreigners may have of theirs, explain them to your government and suggest ways to reshape the foreign perceptions and policy positions you are analyzing.

The lack of empathy in politics and international relations is at least partially responsible for the current ineffective state of global diplomacy. Sino-U.S. ties are one of the most prominent examples. Neither side shows much empathy in its approach to the other. As it looks at its rival, each sees itself, attributing its own motivations and reasoning processes to the other. American contempt for the legitimacy of the ruling Chinese Communist Party is more than matched by hubristic Chinese disdain for the incompetence of governance in the United States. Americans see China as uppity and exploitative. Chinese view the United States as insensitive and overbearing. Neither side has shown much empathy or responded to the frustrations of the other. These differences are a problem that is likely to persist until the United States gets its groove back or China suffers a sobering setback, or both. Neither development seems imminent.

The case study in the previous chapter about Chester Crocker's "linkage" diplomacy in Southern Africa in the 1980s is an example of empathy making a difference in achieving a diplomatic objective. Crocker was able to recognize and appreciate the interests, limits and aspirations of the South Africans, Namibians and Angolans, even if he did not identify with them. At the same time, he did not compromise U.S. interests and had the backing of his president and secretary of state, even if he endured the slings and arrows of both left-wing and right-wing politicians in Washington.

The wisest diplomats cultivate a reputation for integrity, fairness and determination to follow through on commitments. Demonstrating that their government will back them in delivering on the promises they make is as important as reaching agreement on the business at hand. Doing so raises the probability of productive future interactions with foreign counterparts, which can help prevent ongoing disputes from solidifying into impasse and irremediable hostility. So can the maintenance of good personal relations with adversaries at the negotiating table. Keeping issues in a state of negotiability, rather than accepting deadlock, is a key precept of sound diplomacy. Optimism is to diplomats what courage is to soldiers.

Empathy is not a character trait we expect or desire from soldiers. They are experts in the application of force, not in peaceable statecraft. But empathy is essential for diplomats. In addition to the above benefits, it inhibits killing.

Language ability

Empathy is most effective when grounded in a sophisticated understanding of the host-country's language, culture, history and intellectual habits. Language and area training enable diplomats to imagine the viewpoints of foreign leaders, to see the world as they do, to analyze trends and events as they would, and to evaluate the pros and cons of actions as they might. Language is the principal weaponry of diplomacy. Interpreters are its foot soldiers. But language is more than words and syntax. The body often speaks before the mouth, and it does so even when the mouth is silent. Body language, too, differs across cultures.

Mastery of a language in all its dimensions is a path to avoiding misunderstandings and miscalculations that give rise to conflict. It is essential to understand how the native speakers of the language think. That is the key to transnational communication and cooperation. Ability to think in the language of one's foreign counterparts is also the antidote to a mistake made by home-based analysts and their political masters: the earlier-mentioned tendency to view one's foreign partners and competitors as mirror images of oneself. It is a grave error to project your own values and thought processes onto foreigners.

The widespread use of English as a *lingua franca* has not obviated the need for diplomats who are native English speakers to learn foreign languages and communicate effectively. Nor will machine translation and its perfection do so. Nothing conveys understanding of a foreign culture better than the effective use of its language. Diplomatic language relies on subtlety to convey a message in the least confrontational way possible. While some cultures are forgiving of foreigners who make a good-faith effort to speak their language even if they are not fluent, other cultures are less indulgent.

In the experience of Francis Ricciardone, a former U.S. career ambassador to Egypt, people there are of the first kind. "The first time you go there and speak in Arabic – not just classroom Arabic, but taxicab Arabic – it's like a dog riding a bicycle," he told Nicholas Kralev. "No one notices that the dog rides in a wobbly way. They don't notice the errors and the circumlocutions. Even if you are at the 2,000-words-of-vocabulary level and some basic grammar, they think you are a genius, because nobody can master their language. They also see that you made an effort to get to know them. That tends to demonstrate modesty and respect, which can help to disarm or disabuse foreigners predisposed to think that we are arrogant and bossy."[3]

The lack of fluency, however, can cause embarrassment or even scandal. During David Lindwall's first week as head of the political section at the U.S. Embassy in Paraguay, he went to the Ministry of Foreign Affairs to deliver a démarche. After the meeting, the North America desk officer, with whom he hoped to establish a good relationship, walked him out. She was surprised there was no embassy car waiting for Lindwall, but he said he would catch a taxi (*coger un taxi* in Spanish). Having grown up in Central America, he was fairly confident in his Spanish and had used that phrase many times before. The ministry official, however, was shocked to hear a diplomat using what she took as offensive language. Her reaction mystified Lindwall, and when he returned to the embassy, he asked one of the local employees what was wrong with the word *coger*. It turned out that in Paraguay, as well as in Argentina and Chile, it had an extremely vulgar meaning. Lindwall never used it again.

Many of those attracted to diplomatic service already speak one or more languages before they are hired. As noted earlier, most governments require such proficiency. A rare exception is the United States. The State Department provides rigorous language instruction before postings abroad: six months for Western languages like Spanish, French and German; almost a year for those considered moderately difficult, such as Russian, Turkish and Hungarian, and two years for Chinese, Japanese, Korean and Arabic. Most American diplomats develop expertise in two main foreign languages and build their careers around them. It is no secret that mastering a foreign language is much easier at a young age. So if you want to speak on television abroad when you become an ambassador, start learning early.

In addition to taking classes, there are some practical habits you can adopt to improve your language skills. Start reading local newspapers as soon as you arrive at a new post. They use a limited, technical vocabulary that is very similar to that of diplomatic work, avoiding idiomatic expressions not familiar to a non-native speaker. Following media stories as they develop from day to day provides context and makes it easier to guess the meaning of unknown words. In addition, watching television news enhances your proficiency, as the images on the screen reinforce the understanding of the spoken script, and the audio helps to pick up the correct pronunciation of words you read in the newspapers. If you already have a good command of a language but want to take it to the next level, there are few resources better than the original literature of your host-country. It will give you invaluable insight into the national psychology, mentality and way of thinking of your audience.

Even though you will have plenty of opportunities to speak the host-country language, it is very easy not to take advantage of them. It is a mistake to limit your socializing to your embassy community and other foreign diplomats in the capital. With English being so prevalent, many diplomats from the United States, Britain and other English-speaking countries make that error. Even if your hosts prefer to practice their English, try to talk to local embassy staff, any domestic workers you may have, local officials and anyone you meet in their language. Encouraging them to correct your mistakes would be even better. If you speak with foreign counterparts in your own language, they will appreciate it if you do not talk too quickly and avoid using idiomatic phrases. If you are American, idioms like "break a leg," "taking stock" and "kicking the can down the road" may baffle your interlocutors. If you are British speaking to Americans, they may not be familiar with "fortnight" and "peckish."

Intellectual curiosity

A diplomat's principal job is to navigate the distance between headquarters and another capital, and to influence the latter's policies and actions, as explained earlier. Understanding the cultural and historical underpinnings of foreign countries is the basic building block of a diplomatic career. It is very hard to advance your own national interests and influence others if you fail to grasp what makes people and nations tick. Succeeding, on the other hand, will make you more empathetic, unlocking the benefits discussed above.

Diplomats with a high level of intellectual curiosity and a persistent appetite for learning are much more effective than those who prefer to spend most of their time in the office and treat their work as a 9-to-5 job. When Chas Freeman, this chapter's co-author, was deputy chief of mission at the U.S. Embassy in China in the 1980s, he often commended the head of the political section. Every afternoon, the officer would tell anyone he saw sitting at a desk in his section that they did not need to be in Beijing to do that. The value they added to the embassy's understanding of the country was their ability to get out and about. He would suggest that they either make an appointment to see a Chinese official or go sit in the park and talk to ordinary Chinese.

When David Lindwall served as deputy chief of mission in Afghanistan in the mid-2010s, he worked with another political section head insatiable for constant learning. Having recognized that the complexity of Afghanistan's interweaving of tribal, ethnic, linguistic and religious factions had a decisive impact on how political decisions were made, the officer took advantage of every opportunity to learn nuances that escaped foreigners. Afghan officials delighted in talking to her, and even though several officers at the embassy outranked her, she was always the one the ambassador sought out for counsel. When she completed her assignment, Ashraf Ghani, the Afghan president at the time, awarded her a medal, which even ambassadors rarely received.

Developing expertise on the host-country should start before a diplomat arrives there. One must not rely on formal training. With a wealth of information on just about anything so readily available nowadays, there can be no excuse for failing to acquire at least basic knowledge. As with language, one of the most revealing ways to learn about a country's culture is to explore its literature. For example, it is hard

Figure 3.1 David Lindwall (left), U.S. deputy chief of mission, meets with Afghan Foreign Minister Salahuddin Rabbani at the presidential palace in Kabul in 2016.
Photo by Shah Marai/AFP via Getty Images.

to truly understand Colombia without reading the works of Gabriel García Márquez. Once in the host-country, closely following the local media, building a network of contacts who can add to a diplomat's understanding of the society, and following prominent opinion leaders on social media should become a daily routine.

Lindwall did not understand why diplomats went to so many cocktail parties until he himself was thrust into the circuit. He realized that it was a very efficient way to exchange information with a large number of people and learn about developments and perspectives that otherwise could only have been gleaned by holding many time-consuming meetings.

For more than two decades, U.S. Foreign Service officers have been required to work in a consular section for at least a year at the beginning of their careers, even if they have a different career track. The main reason for that is the huge demand for consular services abroad, especially the issuing of U.S. entry visas. But consular work brings significant benefits to new diplomats, providing unique insights into the functioning of key host-country institutions like prisons, courts, hospitals, police stations and ports. Having that knowledge and a network of local contacts is indispensable in times of natural disasters, civil unrest or other crises, as we will see in Chapter 10.

It is important to remember that a country is much more than its capital. Citizens frequently identify not only with their country, but with their home-region. A diplomat who travels widely and is familiar with regional dynamics will find more common ground and respect from host-country interlocutors. In Afghanistan, Lindwall was once invited to dinner by a parliamentary delegation from Herat Province, which wanted to confront him about the upcoming closure of the U.S. Consulate there. Having been to Herat, Lindwall described the "magical beauty" of the Musalla minarets, remnants of a 15th-century complex now in ruins, and the tension in the room lifted. The legislators were still unhappy with the decision to close the consulate, but they appreciated that their American interlocutor knew and valued their province.

History and culture are by no means the only areas in which diplomats must have a solid knowledge foundation. They need a broad understanding of government, politics, economics, science and technology, and the ability to apply it in everyday judgments and decisions. As generalists, they are not expected to know everything, but they should know where and how to find experts when needed. A good diplomat is also a quick study, capable of learning enough about a subject in a very short period to be able to discuss it in a meeting or even publicly. Marc Wall, another retired Foreign Service officer, knew almost nothing about biotechnology, and even less about conflict minerals. But in the 2000s, he had to fill those gaps quickly when he ended up in a job in the State Department's Bureau of African Affairs that required him to deal with matters related to biotechnology and conflict minerals. One never knows exactly what might come up in relations with other countries, "so we constantly have to take on new issues and learn about new areas as priorities change," Wall told Nicholas Kralev.[4]

Career diplomats sometimes say that diplomacy is a great profession for people who get bored quickly and want to move on to something else. Traci Goins is one of them. A registered nurse from South Carolina, she worked for a health insurance company and later became a lawyer. But she kept getting tired of each career, and none of them felt right. Then a friend told her about the Foreign Service. "I thought it was perfect," she told Kralev in 2011 in Singapore, her first posting. "Every couple of years, you get to reinvent yourself and have new bosses and co-workers. How exciting is that!"[5]

Analytical skills

Until the late 20th century, news from the other side of the world took a long time to reach Washington or any other capital. Newspapers, including those with foreign correspondents, had a limit to what they could publish, because of both cost of reporting and print space. Government officials at headquarters could not rely on the media to learn what was happening in most other countries. So they counted on their diplomats abroad to report on developments that would inform policy decisions. Those dispatches became known as diplomatic cables, because they were sent by cable – and as noted earlier, the name has survived the technological revolution.

Today, however, diplomatic reporting cannot compete with the news media. Policymakers have television sets in their offices and get breaking news on their phones. What they need from diplomats in the field is to distill and analyze information, explaining not just what happened, but why it happened, what it means for the interests of the home-country, what the media is not reporting, and what officials at headquarters should do, if anything. Analytical thinking is the heart of diplomatic reporting. Living in other countries allows diplomats to know insights, details and nuances about institutions and players that policymakers back home can never gain. The value added of having diplomatic missions abroad is the combination of that knowledge and a solid analytical skill set, which helps to put into perspective political, economic, social and cultural developments.

Even in the era of 24-hour news and instant communication, original diplomatic reporting is still needed – mostly on closed-door meetings of embassy representatives with host-country officials, to which journalists do not have access, as well as on conversations with sources of information outside the government. Good reporting officers also dig up their own stories that do not make it in the media but can add value to headquarters' understanding of the situation on the ground.

It is essential that diplomats remove any personal bias from their reporting and analysis. As long as they have a firm grasp of their national interests and nuanced knowledge of the varying perspectives on an issue in the host-country, they should be able to provide an objective and accurate picture on any given subject. In the political section at the U.S. Embassy in Nicaragua in the early 1990s, David Lindwall supervised an officer who had strong ideological views and built a wide network of like-minded contacts. But he did not even try to understand opposing views, which made it difficult to analyze developments from any other perspective but his own. Lindwall and the ambassador consistently felt the need to edit the officer's cables to add some balance and objectivity.

A frequent mistake diplomats make is to become too engrossed in minute details about local politics and economics but ignore or lose sight of the priorities at headquarters. Keeping in mind what your audience finds useful is a good rule of thumb in reporting and analysis. Policy is not constant and priorities change all the time. As a manager, Lindwall encouraged his subordinates in the field to make at least one trip to Washington during their tours to ensure that they remained in tune with the agenda back home. That, however, does not mean that one should spare facts, analyses and recommendations that policymakers may not want to hear. Speaking truth to power often carries a career risk in a risk-averse culture, but great leaders are grateful for it, because they understand its value. The State Department has a "dissent channel" where diplomats can criticize policies or procedures and propose improvements, without fear of retribution. We will discuss details in Chapter 6.

Communication skills

It seems obvious to aspiring diplomats that diplomacy requires strong communication skills, and most think they possess them. But when they take a written exam, it turns out that conveying information and making a point precisely and succinctly, in an engaging and impactful way, is a much bigger challenge than they thought. Communication is diplomats' bread and butter. They do not brandish weapons or blow things up. They communicate both verbally and nonverbally, orally and in writing with other governments and societies, as well as within their own government. Whether they brief their boss in the hallway on the way to a meeting, advocate for a certain action in a cable or memo, or deliver a démarche, they need to express their thoughts clearly and briefly to busy policymakers. Listening is at least as important as talking, as we will see shortly.

Writing

The most efficient way diplomats can communicate their ideas, especially when they are posted abroad, is in writing. Effective diplomats are those whose writing is impactful. They have an extensive vocabulary and correct grammar, know how to formulate arguments and are confident in their personal writing style. Diplomatic writing has some unique characteristics, which are influenced mainly by its intended audience of senior officials with little time to spare, and it requires particular skills. It is important to understand what your readers expect from your memos, cables and other documents. They will not look at them to admire your beautiful prose or enjoy suspenseful narration, but to learn something they need to know to do their job or to make a decision.

When you write for busy people, there is nothing they appreciate more than brevity and getting to the point as soon as possible. A document that is a page long will get a much larger readership than one of three pages. Short and clear sentences with active verbs and precise words and phrases go a long way. If removing a word will not change the meaning, there is no reason for it to be there. Most of us say variations of "many different countries." What would change if we took out "different"? Absolutely nothing – the countries would still be many. Avoid too much detail about an issue. Displaying the extent of your knowledge is unlikely to win you any points, but it is almost certain to distract the reader from your main argument. Phrases like "as you know" have no place in a good document. If your readers already know whatever you are prefacing, why are you wasting their time? You would do well to delete that whole sentence.

If you are used to academic writing and taught to begin your documents with an introduction, you would have to unlearn that approach. The diplomatic style is much closer to journalism – in fact, some refer to diplomatic cables as official journalism. You need to make your point quickly and give your audience a reason to keep reading. The U.S. military uses the acronym BLUF, which means "bottom line up front." The most essential information and conclusions should be in the first two or three sentences. Just like objective news reporting, diplomatic reporting should be impersonal and dispassionate. Its purpose is to convey accurate information and provide unbiased analysis. Good writers avoid language that hints at their personal views and feelings. Even when writing a memo at headquarters meant to advocate a certain course of action to your boss, you have to keep your personal biases in check. Your country's interests are what matters, not your own agenda. Before making a recommendation, you have to present all sides of an issue and analyze the pros and cons of each side. We will discuss writing various types of documents in detail in Chapter 8.

Listening

In Western culture, we typically listen with the intent to respond. A good diplomat, however, listens first and foremost with the intent to understand. That has also been described as "active listening." It applies not only to conversations meant to help a diplomat collect information, but to persuade an interlocutor to support or adopt a certain policy position, including démarches. An active listener can decipher what the other person is really saying, which may not be the same as the words coming out of their mouth, as well as what they are not saying, and even what their motivation might be. Are they really saying "yes" to a request, or are they just being polite and sparing you a "no"? Was it their decision to renege on a promise, or were they influenced by another government?

During David Lindwall's first Foreign Service tour in Colombia, he once asked an association of flower exporters to share profit statistics with him. When they said that they would see what they could do in an amiable tone, it sounded like a "yes" to him. He soon learned that he had been mistaken. During Lindwall's next tour in Spain, he requested production figures from a group of automotive suppliers. They had no problem telling him directly that would not happen. Even though both countries spoke the same language, the Spaniards' "no" was very different from that in Colombia. Americans tend to be frank and direct, which has its advantages. But when U.S. diplomats exhibit such characteristics, some foreign officials interpret them as showing a lack of interest in the host-country's point of view or any constraints its government may be facing. Even if you end up disagreeing with your interlocutors, it is important to ensure they know that you have thoroughly considered their position and understand the context of their statements. One way to make that clear is by summarizing or paraphrasing their remarks, and even reflecting on them.

A confluence of previously mentioned skills can be very helpful in active listening. Empathy, language ability and intellectual curiosity are essential in understanding nuances. Skill sets we will discuss shortly, such as judgment and interpersonal skills, are useful in detecting body language and picking up other nonverbal cues. Although exercising judgment is important, it may be advantageous to refrain from judging the other side's position during your meeting and part amicably, except in the very unlikely event that your instructions call for confrontation.

Public speaking

Career diplomats are known as people who work quietly behind the scenes and, apart from ambassadors, rarely receive public attention. That perception has become less accurate in recent years. Foreign Service officers are often called upon to engage with foreign publics, and even with their fellow citizens. That engagement usually involves public speaking. While only ambassadors and designated embassy spokespersons may appear on the record in the media, all officers can find public-speaking opportunities, no matter how junior they are or in what section they work. Those opportunities include giving speeches and talks before various youth organizations, business groups, professional associations, universities and other schools, as well as participating in conferences and seminars.

Public Speaking Tips

- Know your topic well. You do not need to be an expert, but you should be comfortable talking about it without a script.
- Accept as many invitations as you can, provided your boss does not object, particularly in the beginning of your career. Adding to your experience will lower your anxiety level and polish your style.
- Practice, then practice again, and then practice some more, ideally in front of a mirror.
- Speak clearly and project, so that the audience seated in the last row can hear you well. If your voice does not carry and there is no microphone, ask for one.
- Have water next to you. A dry mouth is no friend to a public speaker.
- Make sure you are familiar with the venue and comfortable with the setting. Work out with your host details such as whether you would be speaking while standing or sitting, at a podium or a table. Avoid surprises.
- Know your audience. Ask for a list of attendees, and if one is not provided, try to get a sense of the type of people you will be speaking to.

When you are posted abroad, your speaking engagements are always done in your official capacity as a representative of your country and government. For all intents and purposes, your personal views are irrelevant. You may have to defend a policy you find abhorrent or an action you deem a grave mistake. Even if you work in a consular section and the topic of your talk is how to apply for a student visa, you must be prepared for all kinds of audience questions. It is useful to remember that you have to respond to them, but not necessarily answer them.

There is no secret recipe or winning formula for building self-confidence as a public speaker. The sooner you accept that it is part of your job and get over any anxiety, the better for you and your audiences. If you performed in school plays when you were younger, those skills will likely prove very helpful. While you may not be able to control your nerves and prevent butterflies in your stomach, especially as a novice speaker, there are things you can do to improve your performance.

Inexperienced speakers often wonder if they should read a speech or give a talk. Generally, your presentation would be much more effective if you establish a connection with the audience. That is difficult to pull off if your eyes are buried in pieces of paper the entire time – you are not likely to have a teleprompter at your disposal. It might help to write out your full remarks, but not necessarily as a way of memorizing them, which can be counterproductive if you forget a part somewhere and get stuck. Rather, it would make your ideas flow better and keep the speech within the allotted time. You can have the printed text – or an outline – with you for assurance, in case your mind freezes during the event. You can also use cards with the main points you plan to make, and even walk around with them onstage. Today's audiences often expect slides to add a visual element to what they hear. Slides can be even more useful to a speaker, serving as a prompter to what should come next.

There are instances in which these tips do not apply. The first is when your embassy directs you at the last minute to give a speech that the ambassador or another senior official is not able to deliver. In that case, reading the prepared text is the only realistic option. Make sure to go over it as many times as you can, even if you do so in the car on the way to the event. Second, if you are making an official policy statement, it is in your best interest to read what the embassy has given you verbatim, especially if the matter is sensitive or controversial, or if you have to do it in a foreign language. Third, if you have to acknowledge certain members of the audience in your opening remarks, it is best to read their names and titles, unless you know them well. Speaking in the local language will win you points with the audience, but it may also get you into trouble. Madeleine Albright spoke French fluently and enjoyed engaging with audiences in France in their native tongue. However, when she was secretary of state in the Bill Clinton administration in the late 1990s, almost every time she was asked a tricky or controversial question, she responded in English, at least partially, to avoid any chance of misunderstanding or misinterpretation.

Cross-cultural communication

"Culture" is another term with multiple definitions. The Merriam-Webster Dictionary defines it as "the customary beliefs, social forms and material traits of a racial, religious or social group," as well as "the integrated pattern of human knowledge, belief and behavior that depends upon the capacity for learning and transmitting knowledge to succeeding generations," among several other defin-itions.[6] The first of many meanings in the Cambridge Dictionary is "the way of life, especially the general customs and beliefs, of a particular group of people at a particular time."[7]

Most of us associate culture with countries and nations. Diplomats preparing to move to new countries need to learn as much as possible about local cultures. Although the terms "country" and "nation" are often used interchangeably, they are not the same. There can be more than one nation in a particular country, each with its own culture, such as England, Scotland and Wales. One nation can be divided across two countries, as is the case with the Irish and Korean nations. Understanding those differences is critical to a diplomat's effective communication across cultures. The study field of cross-cultural communication has grown significantly in recent decades, with widely accepted concepts, such as "enculturation" (the process of acquiring one's primary culture), "acculturation" (acquiring a secondary culture) and "third-culture kids" (children raised in more than two cultures, like those of diplomats). Edward T. Hall, one of the most influential scholars in the field, divides culture into "high context" (also known as traditional, with an emphasis on nonverbal communication) and "low context" (or modern, with reliance on verbal communication).[8]

For diplomats, effective cross-cultural communication abilities are invariably tied to a high degree of empathy and excellent listening and language skills. Mastering a country's language unlocks rare insights into its culture, as noted earlier. Empathy enables nuanced understanding and deep appreciation of that culture, as well as history, values and national psychology. It is almost impossible to earn the trust of key host-country interlocutors without showing respect for their culture. Examples of diplomats described as arrogant, imperious or disdainful abound in literature and popular culture. Some people interpret indifference or insensitivity toward their cultural identity as disrespect for them personally, and if they sense such an attitude, they will most likely filter your communication through a negative and even hostile lens.

The ways to show respect differ from one country to another. When David Lindwall served as deputy chief of mission in Sweden, he quickly learned that what was considered respectful was to arrive for meetings exactly on time – not 10 minutes early and not 10 minutes late. In Latin America, where he had spent most of his career, showing up exactly on time was often viewed as a sign of disrespect, even as imposing American notions of punctuality. Lindwall's every meeting in Latin America began with small talk, which lasted until his hosts switched to substance – it was not his place to do so. Following that pattern was meant to build trust. In Sweden, however, small talk was kept to a minimum. The Swedes saw it as a waste of time and much preferred cutting to the chase.

In line with Lindwall's earlier example of Colombians' reluctance to say "no" directly, the Spanish word *fijese* is a key element of communication in Latin America – a cultural construct more than a linguistic one. Literally, it means "notice" but can also be translated as "look." What people in Guatemala and other countries in the region really want to convey is, "No offense, but what you expect will not happen." If a diplomat goes to a meeting at the Ministry of Foreign Affairs expecting to receive a document, and the conversation starts with *fijese*, it should be clear that the document's arrival is not imminent.

No diplomatic communication can be truly effective unless the diplomat has unquestionable integrity. The two main elements of integrity are honesty and morality. Diplomats are expected to possess a strong moral compass, but can they always be honest? What if their instructions call for misleading another government or hiding something important? Thomas Pickering, the former ambassador and a contributor to this book, advises students at the Washington International Diplomatic Academy (WIDA) the following: "While diplomats are not compelled to tell the whole truth all of the time, they are compelled to speak the truth, even if they choose at times to leave certain things out – as long as they do not mislead. Misleading becomes evident much more rapidly than you think. It is not just an embarrassment, but it undermines your credibility and character."[9]

Cameron Munter, the former Foreign Service officer, could not agree more. He was the U.S. ambassador to Pakistan when his phone rang at 3 a.m. on May 2, 2011. "We hear there has been a helicopter crash," Foreign Secretary Salman Bashir said. "Do you know anything about it?" The only response Munter could give Bashir was, "I have to get back to you," he told Nicholas Kralev.[10] The reason was not that he did not know the answer to Bashir's question. In fact, he had watched on a video screen as one of two helicopters, which U.S. Navy SEALs used to raid a compound not far from the capital Islamabad, malfunctioned and was destroyed. In a house on the compound, the Americans had found Osama bin Laden, the leader of the al-Qaeda terrorist network, and killed him.[11] President Barack Obama had decided to keep the Pakistani government in the dark, fearing leaks that could have compromised the operation. Munter was not allowed to say anything until Obama made an official announcement.

"People think that diplomats lie," Munter said. "But we cannot lie. We have no weapons and barely any money. We have only our word and our relationships. Once you lie, you will not be effective as a diplomat. But you have to be able to keep a secret." Is an omission a lie? One could debate that for a long time, but diplomats often have to make decisions in a split second and have no time for debates. Foreign government officials understand that you cannot divulge everything you know. Still, unless they come away from a conversation convinced that you were clear and straight with them, they will not trust you.

Judgment and creativity

Days after the bin Laden raid, the White House instructed Munter to meet with the powerful Pakistani army chief of staff, General Ashfaq Parvez Kayani, and deliver a démarche with a list of demands. The Obama administration had angered Islamabad further by accusing it of either complicity, for sheltering the world's most-wanted terrorist, or incompetence, if it had no idea that bin Laden had lived undetected under its nose for years, as it claimed. The administration felt that now it had more leverage to secure better cooperation from the Pakistanis in the fight against extremists in the country. It was the lowest point in bilateral ties in decades. Three months earlier, in the city of Lahore, a CIA contractor, Raymond Davis, had shot and killed two Pakistanis.[12]

Against that backdrop, Munter walked in to find Kayani seething. When the ambassador handed the list from Washington to the general, he exploded. He knew that accepting the U.S. demands would be seen as capitulating. He "tossed the piece of paper" at Munter. "I have rarely been insulted to my face as a diplomat, but he just threw me out of his office," Munter said. "Is this the way you treat people when they are down?" he recalled the general asking. What should have Munter done? Leave without saying another word? Apologize to Kayani? Try to calm him down and reason with him? Call him out on his rudeness? Defend the Obama administration's position? Say that he was just doing his job and following orders? He had no instructions on how to respond to such a reaction, and there was no time to consult anyone. All he could rely on was his judgment. He told the general that he always preferred to look ahead despite current difficulties and left.

Judgment is almost as difficult to teach as integrity. Both authors of this chapter have worked with brand-new officers whose life experiences had given them rock-solid judgment, as well as with senior officers who had unfailingly bad judgment. Exercising your best judgment is a key part of being a good diplomat. Unlike integrity, which is a quality, judgment is a skill. On any given day during your career, you may have to do something you have never done before, even when you rise to the senior ranks. This book tries to prepare you as best as possible, and any training in diplomatic tradecraft you take would be helpful, but diplomacy is a very unpredictable profession. The only certainty is that you will face uncertainty at some point. There will be no books to consult and probably no colleagues who can give you the advice you need. Your boss or mentor will most likely say, "Use your judgment."

One diplomatic duty that will test your judgment on a daily basis is carrying out instructions from headquarters. Many instructions for démarches from the political hothouse of one's capital are written as much for the domestic policy community as for the diplomats who must execute them in the field. But the delivery of démarches is a personal and oral art, not an institutional and written one. Instructions may be composed by diplomatically inexperienced officials, who are not aware of locally prevalent prejudices and sensitivities, or are inclined to be dismissive of them, as was the case with the Article 98 negotiations in the Bush administration. Good diplomats learn to focus on the results the instructions aim to produce, rather than on the suggestions for how to present the arguments that accompany them.

During his three decades in the Foreign Service, Chas Freeman was asked to arrange many things overseas that the local context made obviously counterproductive. Fortunately, he had been born with a sense of the absurd and the gift of laughter. He very seldom questioned an instruction, no matter how bizarre. Occasionally, he even succeeded in bringing off some maneuver conceived in Washington, as preposterous as it might have been. But there was one instance when he refused to do what he was told, which illustrates the gap between Washington and foreign realities.

As noted earlier, during the 1991 Gulf War, Freeman served as U.S. ambassador to Saudi Arabia, an austere Islamist state whose ferocious anti-communism had precluded diplomatic relations with the Soviet Union. As the war progressed, a constantly expanding circle of U.S. bureaucrats discovered that the Saudis had a lot of money, and requests from Washington for their largesse multiplied, becoming more and more outlandish. Having lost the Cold War and struggling to survive, the Soviet Union was in dire straits, with serious food shortages. Next door in Poland, there was

Figure 3.2 Chas Freeman (left), U.S. ambassador to Saudi Arabia, briefs General Colin Powell, chairman of the Joint Chiefs of Staff, and General Norman Schwarzkopf, commander of U.S. Central Command, in 1991.
Photo by HUM Images/Universal Images Group via Getty Images.

a surplus of ham. Someone in Washington noticed this and brought it to the attention of the deputy secretary of state, Lawrence Eagleburger, a career diplomat for whom Freeman had great personal regard. Freeman was astonished when Eagleburger told him to ask the Saudi king, a Muslim who abhorred pork in any form, to buy up the Polish ham surplus and give it to the starving Soviet communists.

Having pondered the proposal overnight, the next morning Freeman told Eagleburger that asking the king to purchase ham for Soviet communists would be like asking the pope to buy condoms for Bangladeshi Muslims. Freeman said that he would not do it and still believes that Eagleburger never forgave him. But diplomats cannot be doormats. They are meant to exercise judgment in the interest of their country.

So how do you build the judgment ability needed to make the right decisions most of the time? First, even though Foreign Service officers are generalists, you should become as much of an expert on the main issues of your assignment as possible, as quickly as possible. Read everything you can find on a subject, consult with real experts and ask them as many questions as you can to fill any gaps in your knowledge. Being comfortable with the substance of your subject matter will make it much easier to exercise judgment when facing a decision or a difficult situation. Whether you are working on cyber diplomacy, terrorism financing or arms control, understanding how things work in practice will minimize the need to take guesses and lower any risks you cannot avoid.

Second, carefully choose a few senior officers early in your career to be your mentors and learn from them as much as possible. Shadow them, read their writing and ask questions about it, attend their meetings and serve as their notetaker. Ask them to critique drafts of your own writing. Use every opportunity to learn about their previous experiences, and how they handled tricky and challenging situations. Learn from their mistakes as much as from their successes. If a recent development sparks questions in your mind about how your government might deal with it, ask your mentors what they would do and go over a list of alternatives. Do not just listen; write everything down.

Third, study every policy document even remotely related to your current subject matter that comes out of your capital and the country where you are posted. Read every word publicly uttered by your ambassador, assistant secretary, secretary of state or minister, and president or prime minister. Doing so will keep you up to date on any change in policy direction, give you a sense of the thinking in your government and provide you with talking points and arguments you can use in your engagement with foreign interlocutors. In most countries, people want to know how the United States views a certain issue and what it might do about it. So if you are a U.S. diplomat, you will face questions often, both in private and in public. You should not be caught unprepared to respond to them, even if you do not answer them directly.

Fourth, master the intricacies of your government bureaucracy and learn to use it to your advantage. You may be a brilliant policy expert with exceptional ideas, but unless you know how to navigate the system to make those ideas work, and how to secure the support of influential colleagues, your chance of success will not be high. Your mentors can be a great resource in this effort, as can the management section at your post. Making friends in the human resources department at headquarters early in your career can pay dividends throughout your time in government.

Fifth, test your judgment in low-stakes or even hypothetical situations, and with help from mentors and other colleagues, analyze your performance to understand why there might be a better alternative to the solution you came up with. Think through the likely consequences of the various options and explore how they might influence your decision-making.

Diplomacy is usually viewed as hierarchical, risk-averse and resistant to change. Conformity and following rules are highly prized and career-enhancing, while creativity and innovation are rarely encouraged, as noted earlier. However, finding creative solutions to problems, and even breaking down bureaucratic barriers, is sometimes necessary. When Chester Crocker was responsible for U.S. policy in Africa in the 1980s, he had three competing problems to resolve – in Angola, South Africa and Namibia. It was his creative thinking and sense of strategy that produced his "linkage" diplomacy, as discussed earlier. In the story that opened Chapter 1, Janice Jacobs had to secure the escape of an American woman abused by her husband from Nigeria. No one told Jacobs how to overcome the hurdles she faced at the airport. She had to get creative to make sure the woman got on that plane. Generally, there are more opportunities for creativity abroad, where diplomats are implementers. Jobs at headquarters are focused mainly on policy and tend to be more structured, though great officers find ways to be creative anywhere.

Interpersonal skills

In 2010, a devastating earthquake struck Haiti, killing more than 300,000 people, including nine American and Haitian members of the U.S. Embassy staff. Most American employees who survived were evacuated to the United States the next day, along with their families. The small crew that remained had to keep the mission running, provide support to the massive recovery Haiti needed and carry out the largest evacuation of U.S. citizens since the fall of Saigon in 1975. Everyone worked double shifts and no one got more than four hours of sleep a night for two weeks. David Lindwall was the deputy chief of mission. He and most of his colleagues slept at the embassy, because their houses had collapsed from the seismic shock.

It took the full range of diplomatic skills discussed in this chapter to mount the recovery effort and maintain the necessary morale among the embassy staff. But in a crisis of that magnitude, nothing was more important than interpersonal skills. Not getting along and not being able to work together would have made the entire operation impossible to pull off. Although some officers buckled under the pressure and had to be medically evacuated, the embassy never stopped providing services to stranded Americans and relief to the Haitian people.

The ability to work with others is the most cross-cutting skill set needed in a Foreign Service career. One officer can accomplish little alone. Whether in their dealings with host-country officials and other contacts, or in their relationships with co-workers, interpersonal skills affect all aspects of a diplomat's profession and way of life. They determine their ability to collect information and influence their interlocutors. Those who come across as empathetic are much more likely to succeed than someone who appears detached or imperious. An embassy team is a community whose members' lives are intertwined both inside and outside the office. They often live near each other, shop at the same commissaries, work out in the same gyms and send their children to the same schools. As noted earlier, there are representatives of many home-country government agencies in a diplomatic mission, each with its own bureaucratic culture and agenda. Failure to get along can result in deadlock and hurt embassy objectives, and even harm the national interest.

When Foreign Service officers bid on their next assignments, their prospective bosses are more likely to be interested in their interpersonal skills than almost anything else. Managers are painfully aware that even one problematic officer can poison the entire atmosphere in both the embassy and the larger community. Still, some members of the U.S. Foreign Service manage to get promoted in spite of their poor interpersonal skills, including one of Lindwall's ambassadors at a stressful overseas post. He would bully his staff, scold them in public and even throw things at them. In the end, however, his reputation caught up with him. He had done a good job from a policy standpoint, but he was forced to retire as soon as he was eligible, although he wanted to stay in the service longer.

Managing people

Clearly, that ambassador's poor interpersonal skills were only part of the problem, because they naturally affected his management style as well. Few new diplomats realize how significant a component of their work managing people will be throughout their careers. As noted earlier, Lindwall had to supervise four Colombian employees during his first overseas tour at age 26. As deputy chief of mission in Afghanistan, he had supervisory responsibility for over 650 official Americans, more than 900 local employees and about 7,000 contractors, even if most of them reported to other direct managers.

In many countries' diplomatic services, new officers have to manage one or more locally engaged staff members even if they have no management experience, simply because they are officials of the sending state. In most cases, they have received no training in personnel management, which is one of the biggest failures of the diplomacy system globally. No matter how brilliant a policy expert or linguist an officer may be, nonexistent or poor management skills will hurt both colleagues and mission objectives. In his book *America's Other Army*, Nicholas Kralev tells the story of a U.S. officer who had a "horrible boss" during his second tour in the Foreign Service. "He made that experience the most horrible time of my life," said the officer, whose wife and children were also affected by his problems at work. "I was literally sick," he recalled. "I didn't want to go to work every day. I even thought about quitting." The boss in question was not promoted to the senior Foreign Service.[13]

Absent formal management training, diplomats can use informal resources to improve their skills. Among the best such resources are the local employees they supervise. In most cases, these are talented and hardworking staff members who have been in their jobs for years, if not decades, and know how the embassy functions much better than a junior diplomat. There is nothing demeaning about learning from your subordinates. In time, you may find more efficient ways for them to perform their duties, or to do your job better than your predecessor, but they will help you begin your tour productively. Your own boss is another great resource, as are your other colleagues. They have more experience and can coach and mentor you. Just ask them.

If you want to be a good manager, in addition to learning from your subordinates, show that you respect them and value their expertise and opinions. Trust them to do their work well, but have an audit mechanism. Recognize and reward good performance and share responsibility for your team's failures. Avoid making changes for the sake of change and keep an open mind when something does not work as it should. Make sure your employees know that you are there to help them with anything they need.

Sometimes a staff member's performance may just be beyond repair. Kristie Kenney, a former U.S. career ambassador to Thailand, the Philippines and Ecuador, had a first-tour officer at one of her posts who actually recognized her own deficiencies. "She needed more coaching and mentoring, and we provided that," Kenney told Kralev. "Her immediate boss brought it to me very quickly, and we gave her every opportunity to learn and get extra help. But in the end, it was not enough. We all recognized it was not a great fit. It was entry level, so the system took care of it" – the officer did not get the required tenure and had to leave the service.[14]

Managing programs

During his assignments in Afghanistan and Iraq, David Lindwall supervised State Department weapons-abatement programs for buying back sophisticated weapons, such as shoulder-fired anti-aircraft missiles, from individuals and militia members who had acquired them amid the conflicts in the two countries. The embassies contracted local organizations to run the programs and Lindwall oversaw the contracts and reported to Washington on their implementation. In Iraq, he also managed a program aimed at closing a refugee camp and finding a new home for its residents – Camp Ashraf was the headquarters of an Iranian resistance group designated by the State Department as a foreign terrorist organization.

If classic diplomacy is about collecting information and reporting back to head-quarters, a big part of modern diplomacy has to do with managing programs. Over the last four decades, the State Department has gone from administering very few programs with negligible economic implications to running hundreds of them worth billions of dollars a year and ranging from counternarcotics and rule of law to human rights and climate change. Many are mandated by Congress, which keeps adding new ones, so at some point in their careers most U.S. diplomats either manage a program directly or supervise someone who does.

All sections of an embassy are involved in program management. The political section may provide training to host-country law-enforcement officials or election observers. The economic section may run a program promoting the home-country's textile industry. The consular section may contract a local company to collect biometric data from visa applicants. Most programs, however, are run by the public diplomacy section, including educational and cultural exchanges, scholarships and fellowships, academic and civil society outreach, media campaigns and social media engagement.

The key to successful program management is designing a mechanism to measure success and ensure the integrity of projects, which are funded by taxpayer resources. During Lindwall's service in Guatemala, he worked with an officer from the political career track serving in a public diplomacy position, with little experience managing programs. He was authorized to sign grants up to a certain amount without approval from the ambassador or the deputy chief of mission. At the end of his first year in the job, an audit found that many of the programs he had initiated were economic development projects in the indigenous villages of the highlands that had little or no connection to public diplomacy. They supported a key embassy priority but were not a proper use of public diplomacy funds. The officer should have recognized his lack of experience in both managing programs and public diplomacy and sought advice from his superiors early on.

Advocacy and negotiation skills

In the early days of formal diplomatic relations between states, the representational function discussed in Chapter 1 was the focus of diplomats' work. The 20th century saw a sharp rise in diplomatic reporting, and in its final quarter, advocacy became more prevalent than ever before. In addition to démarching host-governments on various issues behind closed doors, U.S. and other Western embassies started advocating publicly for or against certain host-country policies and practices.

The beginning of that trend is often associated with Jimmy Carter's presidency in the late 1970s. Following revelations about serious human rights abuses by communist rulers in Eastern Europe and military regimes in Latin America, some of which Washington had backed, Carter decided to make human rights a key tenet of U.S. foreign policy, and their advocacy became a major part of American diplomacy. Diplomats were instructed to meet openly with dissidents and human rights activists in autocracies and dictatorships, to show public support for their causes and to criticize governments that violated what the West viewed as their citizens' basic rights. Congress started including requirements for human rights promotion abroad in legislation and created a new bureau at the State Department to oversee those activities.

Over the following decades, diplomatic advocacy spread to democracy promotion, freedom of speech and of the press, labor rights, environmental protection, women's and LGBTQ rights, among other areas. During Lindwall's career, political officers attended trials of human rights activists in Guatemala to show solidarity, the U.S. Embassy in Paraguay bought a printing press for the Ministry of Education to produce materials for a drug-prevention program in the local schools, and diplomats in Ecuador ran a marathon to raise money for environmental protection. American diplomats, including ambassadors, now march in LGBTQ pride parades around the world and fly rainbow flags on embassy buildings, sometimes to host-governments' annoyance.

As advocates, diplomats seek to persuade foreign leaders, counterparts and elites of the merits of the home-government's views and policies. In a way, like lawyers, they represent a client, but the client is always the same, and there is no court from which they can seek a ruling. Lawyers need not believe in their clients' innocence to defend them. Diplomats need not agree with their governments' positions, but they have a professional obligation to make the best case they can to win support for

Figure 3.3 Victoria Nuland, U.S. undersecretary of state for political affairs, talks to the press at the 29th Summit of the Organization for Security and Cooperation in Europe in Poland in 2022. Photo by Artur Widak/Anadolu Agency via Getty Images.

those positions. They may dissent and argue for different policies in classified internal channels, provided their government tolerates that, but not in public or where they might be overheard by someone not in their chain of command. If they are responsible for the direct implementation of policies with which they fundamentally disagree, they must make a choice between continuing to serve or resigning in protest.

Victoria Nuland is a prominent example of Foreign Service officers who have been entrusted with high-level positions in administrations with opposing worldviews and very different approaches to diplomacy. During the Republican administration of George W. Bush, Nuland was an adviser to Vice President Dick Cheney, who was known for having little patience for diplomacy and championing unilateral policies. In the Democratic administration of Barack Obama, Secretary of State Hillary Clinton named Nuland the State Department spokesperson. In the Biden administration, she was appointed undersecretary of state for political affairs. "My fundamental starting point is that everybody in these top jobs, whether Dick Cheney or Hillary Clinton, has a single common thread, which is that they love their country and want to do what's best for America," Nuland told Kralev. "Then you have to be willing to politely challenge assumptions that you think are wrong. However, once you have made your case, and if they choose to move forward in a different direction, your job is to implement what they chose to do, or to say that you cannot, and you'd like to be somewhere else."[15]

Regardless of how diplomats feel personally about positions they are tasked with promoting and defending, they must have a solid grasp of the subject matter and good understanding of advocacy campaigns. They also need excellent command of most other skill sets included in this chapter: empathy, language ability, communication and interpersonal skills, creativity and rock-solid judgment. Advocacy work is often very sensitive and requires constant adjustment. It is critical not to stray beyond the instructions from headquarters, but at the same time to adapt them to the local environment to increase their chances of success. As we pointed out earlier, good diplomats in the field know best how to tailor instructions to host-country realities. Because advocacy involves taking a public stand, it also requires no small reservoir of personal courage and risk-taking, especially when criticizing the receiving state.

Persuading another government to change a position or policy usually involves some type of negotiation. It may be bilateral or part of a multilateral effort. It may be conducted by embassy staff or higher-ranking officials from headquarters. It may take several days, several months or longer. Diplomatic negotiation, which is the topic of the last chapter, is a teachable art. It differs from negotiation in other contexts in that it takes place between nation-states, not citizens subject to coercion by their government's sovereign authority. It is how diplomats and statesmen conciliate and mediate between states. Mediation is a skill that involves the simultaneous exercise of empathy with multiple conflicting parties. Handling such complexity demands professional awareness and competence well beyond what is required for resolving simpler human equations.

Like advocacy, negotiation brings together the other skill sets discussed above. Not everything can be taught in a book, of course. Practice and interaction with experienced and skillful diplomats is essential in acquiring and honing the skills of diplomatic tradecraft. This is why about half of the training at WIDA is spent in exercises, assignments and simulations, most of which are taken from the instructors' long diplomatic careers. All responsible countries should aim to train and field diplomats who are as skilled in the profession of persuasion as their military services are in the profession of arms. In the process, they should also finally develop diplomatic doctrine.

Case Study: Repealing a Belgian Law

Hans Wechsel joined the U.S. Foreign Service in 1999. His second tour took him to Brussels, where he was responsible for the embassy's counterterrorism portfolio. In that capacity, he had frequent interactions with various parts of the Belgian judicial system, and in 2003, he learned about an obscure law. "Belgium came up with the idea that, for certain crimes against humanity, regardless of where they took place and who committed them, Belgium had the obligation and competence to pursue a case," Wechsel told Nicholas Kralev. "It was commonly referred to as 'universal jurisdiction.' That concept was mixed with the idea that any citizen could bring a criminal complaint, and force at least a cursory investigation."[16]

Case Study: (cont.)

The law, which had no connection to the ICC, had been passed in 1993, five years before the court's Rome Statute was adopted. For a decade, the United States paid no attention to the Belgian legislation. However, shortly before the 2003 Iraq War started, victims of a Baghdad bombing during the first Gulf War in 1991 filed a complaint against top U.S. officials from that time, including President George H. W. Bush, Defense Secretary Dick Cheney and Colin Powell, who was then chairman of the Joint Chiefs of Staff. Cheney was now vice president, and Powell was secretary of state, which made him Wechsel's boss. Although arrests could not be made just on the basis of a complaint, Wechsel explained, "at a certain point during an investigation, a judge could decide that there was enough evidence to make an arrest. While arrests were hugely remote possibilities, there was no absolute guarantee that they wouldn't happen" if the named officials went to Belgium, which hosts the headquarters of both the EU and NATO.

Wechsel brought the matter to his superiors, and they all decided to work toward dismissing the complaint and repealing the law. In Washington, the George W. Bush administration waged a very public pressure campaign and threatened to move the NATO headquarters. But it was the embassy's effort, including Wechsel's, that made the most difference. Career diplomats had the contacts and relationships in Brussels needed to navigate the Belgian system. They were able to see the issue from their host-country's perspective, make persuasive arguments and propose solutions that would not harm Belgium's interests. They used all forms of written and oral communication effectively and applied good judgment and creativity. Within months, the Belgian parliament repealed the law.[17]

"Both my government and the Belgian government recognized me as an expert on the issue, and I was in meetings with the Belgian prime minister," Wechsel said. "I had contacts with different perspectives and agendas. I knew the lawyer for the NGO [nongovernmental organization] that was helping file those complaints, as well as the member of parliament who had authored the law. I had contacts in the Justice and Foreign Ministries, and also had a working relationship with the federal prosecutor. So I had the whole circle – everybody who had a major stake."[18]

Exercise: Promoting Democracy in the Middle East

Hans Wechsel had a very different challenge when he arrived in Abu Dhabi from Brussels in 2004. He was the first regional director for the Arabian Peninsula of the Middle East Partnership Initiative (MEPI), which the Bush administration had created two years earlier to help build and strengthen civil society, and to support the region's democratic aspirations. His main task was to find local organizations in

Exercise: (cont.)

eight countries – Bahrain, Jordan, Kuwait, Oman, Qatar, Saudi Arabia, Yemen and the United Arab Emirates – and award them grants for projects promoting the U.S. agenda. "The way a society is governed is important to whether extremism develops," Wechsel told Kralev. "So we try to get to the roots of terrorism by addressing not only political rights, but also economic opportunity, education, women's rights, because these are all linked."[19]

Task: What diplomatic skill sets did Wechsel need to accomplish his assignment in Abu Dhabi?

ADDITIONAL RESOURCES

Christopher R. Hill, *Outpost: A Diplomat at Work* (Simon & Schuster, 2014).
Harry W. Kopp and John K. Naland, *Career Diplomacy: Life and Work in the US Foreign Service*, 3rd ed. (Georgetown University Press, 2017).
Dante Paradiso, *The Embassy: A Story of War and Diplomacy* (Beaufort Books, 2016).

4   The Interagency Foreign Policy Process

DANIEL FRIED AND JOHN TEFFT

One of the biggest U.S. political scandals of the 20th century started with a story in a Lebanese magazine. In November 1986, the Ash-Shiraa weekly broke the news that the United States had been secretly selling weapons to Iran in breach of a U.S. arms embargo against the Islamic Republic. The two countries had broken off diplomatic relations after U.S. diplomats in Tehran were taken hostage, following the 1979 Islamic Revolution. It soon became clear that the money from the weapons sales was being funneled to Nicaraguan right-wing rebels known as Contras.[1]

That second operation was illegal, too. In 1984, the U.S. Congress had passed legislation banning direct funding to the Contras. The Reagan administration was in a bind – its policy was to support the overthrow of the left-wing Sandinista government in Managua by financing and arming the rebels. In 1985, officials on the National Security Council (NSC) staff designed a scheme to continue that support, using part of the proceeds from the arms sales to Iran, in violation of the ban. The operation, called "the Enterprise," was spearheaded by Lieutenant Colonel Oliver North, who was on detail to the NSC staff from the U.S. Marine Corps.

After the scandal broke, the administration tried to defend its actions. First, it said that the weapons shipments were part of an effort to free seven American hostages being held in Lebanon by the militant group Hezbollah, which had close ties to the regime in Tehran. Then it argued that the law did not apply to the NSC, because it stated that "no funds available to the Central Intelligence Agency, the Department of Defense or any other agency or entity of the United States involved in intelligence activities may be obligated or expended" in support of the Contras. The White House also claimed that Congress had no right to block funding, because the Constitution gave the authority to conduct foreign policy to the executive branch. Lawmakers countered that the Constitution gave Congress control of the budget, and it had every right to enact the ban. Through all that, Reagan insisted that he had not approved the diversion of funds to the Contras.

The majority of legal and constitutional scholars said that the NSC did fall within the purview of the law, which is known as the Boland Amendment. Many scholars were also astonished that the NSC, created by the National Security Act of 1947 as an advisory body that staffs and assists the president in formulating foreign policy,[2] had "gone operational" by carrying out policies on its own. Several administration officials, including North, were eventually indicted, and some went to prison. The debate about how operational the NSC should be continues to this day.

Why does that matter to diplomats? Because they work in a large and complex bureaucracy, in which structures, duties, responsibilities and authorities should be clearly defined – the alternative is a recipe for chaos at best and disaster at worst. Thomas W. Simons, a former U.S. ambassador to Poland and Pakistan, and one of our mentors in the Foreign Service, used to say that a good officer should be able to work in any bureaucratic situation and be effective. To achieve that, one must have solid knowledge and understanding of policy structures, as well as the parallel, informal policymaking culture that each administration develops. That should be the backdrop against which diplomats inform and influence decision-making and implementation.

This applies to every government, not just that of the United States. If officials whose job is to advise a head of state or government suddenly start carrying out policies on their own, that directly affects the daily work of the people actually responsible for policy implementation, including diplomats.

What is the interagency?

In foreign policy and national security, most governments have a policymaking structure. In democracies, that structure is generally more transparent and inclusive than in autocracies. In dictatorships, there is usually only one person who matters. The U.S. government uses the term "interagency" to describe both a structure and a mechanism through which policies are supposed to be developed, debated and presented to relevant Cabinet members,[3] who head executive departments, and ultimately to the president for a decision. The foreign policy interagency process is managed by the NSC staff, which is part of the Executive Office of the President (EOP). The role assigned to the NSC by the National Security Act is to "advise the president with respect to the integration of domestic, foreign and military policies."

The interagency has its origins in the early post-World War II period, when the United States recognized the leading role it would have to play in the world, somewhat reluctantly accepting that it could not retreat into isolationism, as it had after World War I. The modern national security bureaucracy took shape during the Gerald Ford administration, thanks largely to Brent Scowcroft.[4] He served as national security adviser for less than 15 months, beginning in 1975, but was reappointed to the position by President George H. W. Bush in 1989 and held it during Bush's entire four years in office. The interagency structure and process Scowcroft established still exist as of this writing, although stylistic differences may emerge from one administration to another, as we will see later in the chapter.

In terms of structure, the interagency brings together departments and other agencies with responsibility in foreign affairs to discuss and flesh out policy in committees at several levels of seniority and authority. Those levels start from deputy assistant secretary and gradually go up to assistant secretary, undersecretary and deputy secretary, culminating at the secretary or Cabinet level. The higher-level committees are permanent – they meet regularly to consider either a range of issues or one big issue, and they also hold emergency meetings during crises, as was the case when Russia invaded Ukraine in 2022, and when the Taliban retook power in Afghanistan in 2021. The lower-level committees convene around specific matters in what is much more likely to be an ongoing process than a one-off session.

When it comes to process, it can originate in one of two ways. The first is a formal or informal instruction from the president directing the interagency to explore and draft options for a potential policy. Weeks before Russia's invasion of Ukraine, U.S. intelligence warned that more than 100,000 Russian troops had amassed along the border between the two countries. As President Joe Biden considered a potential response, he tasked the interagency with developing options, using political, economic, military and other tools. Sometimes the president may have decided tentatively to take a certain action, and what he needs from the interagency is a properly formulated strategy to implement that action. After Barack Obama began his second term in the White House in 2013, he wanted to normalize relations with Cuba, which had been broken off in 1961. So he directed a small group on the NSC staff to start exploring creative ways to make it happen. Because the issue was controversial and politically charged, Obama chose to keep it quiet and did not bring most of the interagency into the process until later on.[5]

Figure 4.1 President Barack Obama speaks at an NSC meeting on Ukraine in the White House Situation Room in 2014. Deputy Secretary of State William Burns (third from left) represents Secretary of State John Kerry.
Photo by Universal History Archive/Universal Images Group via Getty Images.

The other way for a policy idea to originate is through a proposal from the Department of State or the Department of Defense – or from one or more of the other foreign affairs agencies. If the proposal involves international finance or economic sanctions, it could come from the Treasury. If it concerns trade, the Department of Commerce would most likely take the lead. If it has to do with a pandemic, it would probably come from the Department of Health and Human Services (HHS). Even though historically HHS was not considered a foreign affairs agency, it became one out of necessity. Long before Covid-19, HIV/AIDS and other global health emergencies, including previous coronaviruses, occupied the attention of policymakers.

The National Security Council

It is important to understand the difference between the NSC and the NSC staff. The NSC is a permanent structure whose composition includes the president, the vice president, and the secretaries of state, defense, the treasury and energy, as prescribed by statute. Additional officials are included at the president's discretion, and they may differ from one administration to another. The NSC staff, which supports the NSC, is made up of career civil servants "detailed" or "seconded" from different federal agencies, including diplomats and military and intelligence officers, as well as professional members recruited from outside the government, such as experts in think tanks, academia and nongovernmental organizations.

The Biden NSC also includes the attorney general, the secretary of homeland security, the U.S. ambassador to the United Nations, the White House chief of staff, the president's national security adviser, the White House science and technology director, and the U.S. Agency for International Development (USAID) administrator. The director of national intelligence and the chairman of the Joint Chiefs of Staff attend NSC meetings in an "advisory capacity" by statute. Specific to the Biden administration is the attendance of the CIA director. In addition, the counsel and deputy counsel to the president, as well as the NSC legal adviser, are invited to every meeting, as is the principal deputy national security adviser, who serves as secretary.[6] The tent is even bigger: "Given the cross-cutting nature of a number of critical national security issues – such as homeland security, global public health, international economics, climate, science and technology, cybersecurity, migration and others" – Biden designated other "regular attendees" of NSC meetings "as appropriate" in a memo soon after taking office in 2021. Modern presidents usually issue a similar memo or directive on the NSC system within days of being sworn in.[7]

The additional attendees are the secretaries of HHS, commerce and labor; the administrator of the Environmental Protection Agency (EPA); the director of the Office of Management and Budget (OMB); the U.S. trade representative (USTR); the national cyber director; the president's economic, domestic and homeland security advisers; the chair of the Council of Economic Advisers; the deputy national security advisers for cybersecurity and international economics; and the special presidential envoy for climate. This list may seem long and tedious, but in the complex pecking order of official Washington, being a member of the NSC is a highly sought-after sign of influence – even more so if one is invited to a restricted meeting on the most sensitive matters known as "rump NSC."

"The NSC shall be the president's principal means for coordinating executive departments and agencies in the development and implementation of national security policy, and in long-term strategic planning," Biden's memo said. "The NSC shall meet regularly and as required. The national security adviser, at the president's direction and in consultation with other members of the NSC, shall be responsible for determining the agenda, ensuring that necessary papers are prepared in advance, and recording and communicating NSC actions and presidential decisions in a timely manner." As the highest level of the interagency structure, the NSC does not meet often. When it does, the president presides, usually in the White House Situation Room. Most interagency meetings take place in committees, as we will see shortly.

The NSC staff

As a member of the NSC and leader of the NSC staff, the national security adviser is a principal. But he or she is also a staffer, whose job is to manage the interagency process and to be a neutral presenter of policy options for the president developed by various agencies. In the Scowcroft model, the incumbent helps the president consider those options, meaning that he or she is usually the last person in the Oval Office after a meeting with all other top officials. Ideally, the national security adviser enjoys the president's full confidence, but it does not always work out that way in practice. Condoleezza Rice had a famously close relationship with President George W. Bush, while James Jones never quite found his place in the Obama White House and left after about 20 months. Reagan went through six advisers in eight years, and Donald Trump had four in four years. Richard Nixon had only one in five and a half years, Henry Kissinger, who served simultaneously as secretary of state for more than two years under both Nixon and Ford. The national security adviser is not supposed to compete with the secretary of state, but in reality there is often tension between the two.

Daniel Fried, a 40-year Foreign Service veteran and one of this chapter's authors, served on the NSC staff during both the Clinton and George W. Bush administrations. One of his successors as senior director for European and Eurasian affairs more than a decade later was Fiona Hill, who gained prominence as a witness in the 2019 Trump impeachment proceedings in Congress. She had joined the NSC staff from the Brookings Institution in Washington.

The National Security Act does not say much about the NSC staff, which is sometimes referred to as the National Security Staff (NSS), and its size and functions are determined by the president and the national security adviser. It has grown enormously in the last half-century, from about 20 members during the John F. Kennedy administration, to about 40 under Nixon and about 100 under Clinton, to more than 200 under

George W. Bush and over 300 under Obama.[8] The pressure to react to fast-breaking events was used as a justification for adding more staff, but it easily became a rationale for quick policy decisions that cut out key voices in the interagency community.[9] In the face of sustained complaints that the NSC risked becoming just another bureaucracy, Obama's last national security adviser, Susan Rice, cut back to about where the numbers were at the beginning of his administration.[10]

The NSC staff's structure is similar to the State Department's: it is divided into regional (e.g. Europe, Asia, etc.) and functional directorates (e.g. counterterrorism, energy, etc.). They are headed by senior directors, who also hold the title of special assistant to the president and are roughly equivalent to the rank of assistant secretary, though they are not confirmed by the Senate. They report to a deputy national security adviser. The deputies, whose number depends on the administration, report to the national security adviser. Under the senior directors, there are directors with various portfolios in the respective geographical region or functional area. Alexander Vindman, who was fired in 2020 for testifying at the Trump impeachment hearings, was a director under Fiona Hill whose responsibility included policy toward Ukraine.[11]

New challenges and crises have added to the complexity of the NSC staff structure. For example, after the 9/11 terrorist attacks, the Bush administration expanded the counterterrorism directorate. The cyber directorate has also grown in recent years, as cyber threats have become a bigger challenge to national security. Counter-disinformation policy illustrates how emerging issues put pressure on the NSC staff and the interagency structure. Dealing with disinformation has both foreign and domestic aspects, and a policy discussion on the subject brings together the cyber, legal, military and intelligence directorates, as well as those responsible for Europe and Asia, because of Russia's and China's roles in producing and spreading disinformation.

What does the NSC staff do? When Daniel Fried worked for Condoleezza Rice, she used to tell her staff that they had three main jobs: to staff the president on foreign affairs, which meant preparing papers and briefings for his meetings, trips and phone calls; to run the interagency policy process by making sure the bureaucracy was dealing with issues and moving them up; and to oversee the implementation of the president's decisions by being a guardian and, when necessary, enforcer. As the NSC staff has grown, more positions have been filled with career civil servants than with outside experts, especially at the director level. On one hand, that ensures a smoother process, because career employees are steeped in the complex Washington bureaucracy. On the other hand, it makes the NSC staff more like other government agencies, without the benefit of new blood and outside perspectives.

NSC policy committees

Much of the work of the interagency takes place in meetings at various levels, and much of it happens outside formal gatherings, as officials from different agencies consult and work things out with their counterparts in other departments. At the top of the process for nearly half a century have been committees of the principals and their deputies. Meetings are held on a regular basis but are also scheduled in advance of major summits and other important international events, and can be called in response to a crisis, such as an attack, a coup d'état or a natural disaster. Below the senior level, the main day-to-day forums for interagency coordination on national security policy are the **Interagency Policy Committees** (IPCs).[12] In some administrations, they are known as policy coordination committees (PCCs). The Biden memo cited earlier said that "they shall provide policy analysis for consideration by the more senior committees of the NSC system and ensure timely responses to decisions made by the president. The IPCs shall be established at the direction of the national security adviser and be chaired by his or her designees."[13]

NSC senior directors typically manage IPCs and chair their meetings, which are usually attended by assistant secretaries from various departments. An IPC on Ukraine policy, for example, would most likely be chaired by the senior director for Europe and include the assistant secretaries for Europe at the Departments of State and Defense, as well as the equivalent-level officials at the CIA and other intelligence agencies, USAID, and given the food and energy implications, the Departments of Agriculture and Energy, among others. Determining which IPC should have responsibility for a certain issue can be complicated. For example, should China trade policy be managed by the IPC headed by the senior director for international economics or for Asian-Pacific affairs? What about Russian disinformation? Should it fall under the purview of the cyber or Russia IPC? Ultimately, the national security adviser decides, but all participants need to work together in the most effective and efficient way, leaving egos aside, to design and carry out the president's policy.

The substantial legwork needed to create and implement a policy has resulted in the emergence of sub-IPCs, even though they are not formally recognized in documents laying out the interagency structure. This is the level at which papers with policy options are drafted and technical expertise is required, forming the basis for higher-level discussions and ultimate decisions. In terms of the hierarchy, the officials participating in sub-IPCs are usually deputy assistant secretaries. Meetings are normally, though not always, chaired by an NSC director, or at times a senior director. Decisions on whether to convene an IPC or sub-IPC to deal with a specific matter or situation are made on a case-by-case basis. These committees are the forums where different agencies lay out their perspectives and policy recommendations. Although the outcomes of their meetings are not dispositive, they can filter out nonviable ideas and provide a sharper focus once the issue is moved up to the more senior committees, especially on technical matters, such as nonproliferation or climate change. They can also serve as a reality check by exposing any disagreements or potential conflicts among agencies.

Once policy options have been drafted, studied and debated, the outcome from the IPC level is moved up to the **Deputies Committee** (DC), the workhorse of the interagency process. A deputy national security adviser chairs its meetings, and its membership includes the deputy heads of the departments that form the NSC. Depending on the topic of a meeting, a deputy secretary might send an under-secretary who specializes in the relevant area, such as arms control or economics. The main purpose of the DC is to set up issues for discussion by the principals once they "have been properly analyzed and prepared for decision." Its job is to "ensure that all papers … fairly and adequately set out the facts, consider a full range of views and options for decision, and fully assess the prospects, risks and implications of each."[14] U.S. ambassadors are often invited to DC meetings via secure video conference from their posts abroad. Their insights about the political and economic situation, as well as their knowledge of historical and cultural sensitivities, in their host-countries can provide significant value to policy debates.

The **Principals Committee** (PC) is the senior interagency forum for consideration of policy issues affecting national security. It is composed of the same principals, such as the heads of Cabinet departments, who are members of the full NSC, with one major difference: instead of the president, the national security adviser chairs PC meetings. He or she must report objectively the participants' views to the president, as well as any differences among them, and ensure that conclusions and decisions are recorded and communicated to the interagency in a timely manner.

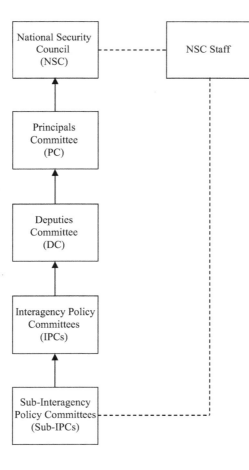

Figure 4.2 The interagency process is coordinated by the NSC staff at every level, and issues and recommendations move from lower-level committees to upper-level ones.

If consensus on an issue has been reached at the DC level, a recommendation can be ratified by the PC through a memo, without the need for a meeting, in a process called a "paper PC." Similar to a rump NSC, there can be a rump PC, and even a rump DC, devoted to particularly sensitive issues, with limited attendance.

Ambassadors are sometimes invited to PC meetings, and once in a while, even to full NSC meetings. During the 2011 Arab Spring protests in Cairo, President Obama asked more than once the ambassador to Egypt, Anne Patterson, to join via video conference. When Russia invaded Georgia in 2008, John Tefft, this chapter's co-author, was ambassador in Tbilisi and joined a full NSC meeting with President Bush on a secure phone line, since the embassy in Georgia did not have a secure video capability. Sometimes other embassy officers have opportunities to participate in meetings at lower levels of the interagency process, such as IPCs and sub-IPCs, especially during fast-developing situations. Some officials in Washington are reluctant to include diplomats from overseas if their views are perceived as not being aligned with those of their home-bureau at headquarters.

For most NSC, PC and DC meetings, the principals or their deputies are accompanied by lower-level officials, known as backbenchers, whom their bosses can consult on certain matters. An assistant secretary who chairs an IPC may be a backbencher at a higher-level meeting, and may even be asked to speak. At an NSC meeting during Bush's second term, Daniel Fried was a backbencher as assistant secretary of state for European and Eurasian affairs. The president turned to him to articulate a particular position regarding Georgia.

When rapidly developing events abroad require a speedy response from Washington, the administration in office may decide to form a working group to coordinate policy formulation and implementation. Such a group may be led by NSC staff or one of the agencies. As a deputy assistant secretary in the State Department's European bureau, Tefft chaired a group on Ukraine at the sub-IPC level during the country's so-called Orange Revolution in 2004, following a disputed presidential election. Fried, who was the NSC senior director for European affairs at the time, deferred to State because it had eyes on the ground, contacts with all the players and made sensible policy recommendations.

Working inside the system

The 2004 Ukraine election campaign was controversial from the start and marred by violence. One of the two main candidates, Prime Minister Viktor Yanukovych, had Russian President Vladimir Putin's backing. The other, former Prime Minister Viktor Yushchenko, ran on an anti-corruption platform and promised to seek Ukrainian membership in the EU and NATO. Two months before the November vote, Yushchenko was poisoned with dioxin and flown for emergency medical treatment to Austria, from where he returned with a disfigured face.[15] Rumors abounded in Ukraine of planned efforts for election fraud. Even though most exit polls gave Yushchenko the lead on election day, Yanukovych was declared the winner. In response, thousands of orange-clad Ukrainians started nationwide protests, and a lawsuit alleging voter fraud was brought before the Supreme Court.

To help U.S. policymakers formulate a response, the U.S. Embassy in Kyiv examined evidence of fraud, including numerous reports of multiple voting and stuffing ballot boxes after the polls had closed. In Washington, Tefft formed a rump interagency team of officials from the Departments of State and Defense, the intelligence community and the NSC staff to analyze the results and prepare recommendations for the principals. The ambassador in Kyiv, John Herbst, could not join the interagency meetings because secure video did not exist, but he sent copious cables and secure emails.

Three days after the election, having determined that the evidence of fraud was credible, Tefft's group drafted a statement declaring that the United States did not accept the result as legitimate. Secretary of State Colin Powell decided to read the statement before the press himself. "If the Ukrainian government does not act immediately and responsibly, there will be consequences for our relationship, for Ukraine's hopes for a Euro-Atlantic integration, and for individuals responsible for perpetrating fraud," Powell said.[16] EU leaders made similar remarks. In early December, the Ukrainian Supreme Court annulled the election results and ordered a revote at the end of the month. This time, Yushchenko defeated Yanukovych with 52 to 44 percent. International monitors declared the election free and fair.

This was a case of the State Department leading the interagency process by keeping on top of fast-moving events and giving the secretary of state influence by empowering him with facts on the ground before they reached other principals. Tefft's group worked within the system, with the full support of Fried, who had no interest in competing with Powell, and with the active participation of the NSC staff. The Pentagon and the intelligence agencies recognized that State was best positioned to take the lead and dutifully fulfilled their roles in the process.

Although there are many examples of a Cabinet department coordinating a particular policy, the NSC staff usually initiates interagency meetings, and drafts and circulates the agenda and relevant papers to the participating agencies in advance. Some materials can be distributed at the meeting by both NSC staff and representatives of various departments, in what is known as "table-dropping," often in an effort to assert policy control or influence. If a department official plans to table-drop, it is wise to check with NSC staff beforehand. Departments can also be asked to prepare policy papers, though it is up to a committee's chair to decide whether to use them. It is standard practice for a meeting to begin with an intelligence briefing, especially during rapidly moving events. The chair may then turn to the State Department representative to give its view on the issue, or the Pentagon participant if the matter is predominantly military, followed by other agencies for their perspectives.

The NSC staff's proximity to the president and the "NSC suite," which includes the national security adviser and the principal deputy, provides a bureaucratic high ground and significant influence over the interagency process. Staff members often use that privilege to advance their own policy preferences and those of their bosses, but they seldom go rogue. Although the staff acts as a transmission belt for the president's views to the interagency, it frequently takes a liberal approach to extrapolating those views. When Fried was a senior director, he would usually seek to advance the interagency process in the direction set by the NSC suite as interpreted by his own directorate.

Senior directors are often in the Oval Office and believe that puts them in a position to speak for the president to the interagency, and to act as a custodian of and advocate for his initiatives. Such power risks distorting judgment. They may be tempted to discount the expertise in the various agencies, which is needed to avoid mistakes. It is a valid concern that too much deference to the agencies can stymie creativity and paralyze decision-making, but too little is fraught with risks as well. Even when the NSC staff believes it is steering the policy process, it must keep in mind that it operates within a context set by the wider interagency and by realities on the ground.

The formal interagency process described above is supplemented by a web of informal contacts, quick discussions, bureaucratic alliances and maneuvering for advantage, handshake deals between agencies and sanity checking. As senior director,

Figure 4.3 Daniel Fried (right), U.S. assistant secretary of state for European and Eurasian affairs, meets with Polish Foreign Minister Radosław Sikorski in Warsaw in 2008.
Photo by Janek Skarzynski/AFP via Getty Images.

Fried checked in regularly with his assistant secretary counterparts at the State and Defense Departments before a meeting to determine their respective positions, and often worked out informal policy understandings. This is a normal, within-the-system coordination that is essential to the functioning of the interagency. Without it, the machinery would work far more slowly and contentiously, if at all. It is necessary no matter what kind of policymaking culture an administration develops.

What is the interagency supposed to do if the NSC staff, with all its institutional advantages in steering the process, is divided on a potential course of action? One such split occurred in 2014, when Russia annexed Ukraine's Crimean Peninsula and invaded the country's eastern Donbas region. With the Obama administration's NSC staff divided on a response, including the wisdom and utility of imposing sanctions, the relevant agencies united and exerted decisive influence. The Departments of State, Treasury and Commerce worked the system from the side, as it were, to craft an offer the NSC staff, the deputies and principals could not refuse.

Interagency dysfunction

The NSC staff divisions in 2014 resulted in a dysfunctional process. Although the administration eventually approved economic sanctions against Russia, it rejected a proposal to send weapons to Ukraine to defend itself, arguing that doing so would be either useless or harmful. This meant that sanctions were left as the principal policy tool to respond to Russia's aggression, rather than being a part of a broader strategy, which history suggests asked more of sanctions than they could achieve. We will discuss further details in the first case study at the end of the chapter.

There were few cases in our careers when the interagency process was as riven with fundamental differences as it was on arms-control policy toward the Soviet Union during the Reagan administration. Not long after taking office in 1981, Reagan signed a series of directives that made it virtually impossible to negotiate serious arms-limitation agreements with Moscow. Opposition to such talks was centered on the office of Secretary of Defense Caspar Weinberger. His assistant secretary for global strategic affairs, Richard Perle, headed a neoconservative group of experts deeply suspicious of the Soviets. Among the agencies advocating in favor of arms control as a useful tool for promoting strategic U.S. interests were the State Department, the Arms Control and Disarmament Agency, and at times the Joint Chiefs of Staff.

Against a backdrop of huge increases in the defense budget, launching Reagan's Strategic Defense Initiative (SDI) – which became known as Star Wars – and his harsh anti-Soviet rhetoric, there were fierce battles over strategic arms, nuclear testing limitations and compliance. The interagency deadlocked. Ironically, as it spent an enormous amount of time bickering over the utility of arms control, Secretary of State George Shultz was making the case for negotiations with Moscow directly to Reagan. Eventually, Shultz persuaded the president that arms-reduction agreements were consistent with his strategic objectives, including SDI.

In 1985, Reagan found a negotiating partner in a new Soviet leader, Mikhail Gorbachev. Meeting in Geneva and Reykjavik over the next two years, they laid the foundation for the Intermediate Range Nuclear Forces (INF) Agreement, which they signed in Washington in 1987. They later developed a framework for the Strategic Arms Reduction Treaty (START) signed by Gorbachev and President George H. W. Bush in Moscow in 1991. As the interagency became disconnected from the larger context of U.S.–Soviet relations and the evolution in the president's views, the NSC staff was unable to resolve the differences and sometimes battled itself. So Shultz decided to work outside the regular interagency process and succeeded. He used to tell his staff that working in a bureaucracy is like sailing across a lake in heavy headwinds – it is critical to keep your eye on the spot you aim to reach, no matter how brutal the wind.

While there has been interagency dysfunction under both Republican and Democratic presidents, an interagency process barely existed under Trump. The NSC staff and Trump's frequently changing national security advisers were not able to function as reliable conveyors of the president's views or as advocates of his policies. A wide gap opened between what the staff and the interagency produced and what Trump seemed to believe. A glaring early example was the 2017 National Security Strategy written during the tenure of Trump's second national security adviser, H. R. McMaster. The document took Washington's foreign alliances seriously, while Trump expressed sympathy for various autocracies' strongmen and contempt for alliances.[17] Many NSC staff members conceded privately that the policy process seemed detached from the president's decisions and was often pointless.

Foreign countries wasted no time in taking advantage of the dysfunction. During a 2020 visit to the White House by Polish President Andrzej Duda, remarks that reflected the partisan views of Poland's ruling Law and Justice party found their way into Trump's public statement without the NSC staff's knowledge.[18] It was not the first time another government had tried to circumvent the established channels and influence the president directly. But in most other administrations, what the Poles pulled off would not have been possible, because White House speechwriters normally work closely with the NSC staff. Moreover, other presidents would not have hosted a foreign leader in the Oval Office just four days before he was up for reelection.

Working around the system

In 1989, Daniel Fried was the country desk officer for Poland at the State Department. Such officers closely follow developments in the country of responsibility and serve as the day-to-day liaison with both the U.S. embassy in the field and the foreign country's embassy in Washington. As we will see in more detail in Chapter 6, they also draft documents for the office director, deputy assistant secretary and assistant secretary in the home-bureau.

The year began with the inauguration of George H. W. Bush as president. There was an overwhelming consensus in the U.S. government that nothing significant would happen in Central and Eastern Europe in the foreseeable future. It viewed the Iron Curtain and the Soviet Union's de facto rule over its satellites, including Poland, Hungary and Czechoslovakia, as permanent facts of life. The Bush administration at first accepted that consensus. It started an exhaustive, months-long interagency review of Soviet policy, and no major decisions would be made until the review was completed. The interagency was divided over how serious Mikhail Gorbachev's reforms were, and whether his signature policies of *glasnost* and *perestroika* were likely to succeed.

Events on the ground, especially in Poland, were outrunning the slow pace of administration thinking. After eight years of martial law, the Polish communist regime faced growing economic stagnation and social unrest. In February, it opened roundtable talks with Solidarity, part trade union and part political opposition movement, on possible economic reforms and some degree of political pluralism.[19] In Washington, however, the interagency was slow to recognize the importance of what was happening. The analytic community viewed the roundtable with skepticism, as a cynical communist effort to co-opt the opposition. The State Department leadership was focused on the review of Soviet policy, although Thomas Simons, the deputy assistant secretary Fried worked for, advocated for U.S. economic assistance to Poland should the talks succeed. The Treasury was hostile to the idea and downplayed the significance of the events in Warsaw. The NSC staff was mostly cool to the negotiations.

While the interagency displayed little interest, Fried read every piece of reporting from the U.S. Embassy in Warsaw, which was well-informed about the thinking of both negotiating sides. He argued that the Polish developments were a once-in-a-generation opportunity with the potential to break the Soviet hold on a third of Europe, a U.S. policy objective since 1945. Few officials shared this assessment – the exceptions were Simons and the new NSC director for Soviet and Eastern European affairs, Condoleezza Rice. A Stanford professor, Rice had studied the Soviet Union and its satellites as an undergraduate and doctoral student at the University of Denver under Josef Korbel, an exiled former Czech diplomat and father of Madeleine Albright, the first female U.S. secretary of state. Rice would become the second.

In March, as part of her contingency planning in case of a breakthrough at the roundtable in Warsaw, Rice asked Fried to draft a speech that Bush might want to give, welcoming an agreement between the communist government and Solidarity, should it happen. With the negotiations moving fast, Rice wanted to be ready. Hers was an unusual request – a mid-level desk officer like Fried was not supposed to draft a presidential speech. But he happily complied, writing a draft that offered "moral, political and economic support" for Poland's reforms and called for a "free and democratic Eastern Europe." Fried hit a roadblock when he tried to send the draft through the normal State-to-NSC channel. The department's Executive Secretariat rejected it, calling him "giddy." He walked to the White House gate and handed the draft to a grateful Rice. In a break with State Department practice, he offered to take instructions directly from her in the future.

Events in Poland moved quickly. On April 5, Solidarity and the regime signed an agreement. There would be free elections for the Senate, the upper house of parliament, and for 35 percent of the seats in the lower house, the Sejm. On April 17, Bush delivered the speech Fried had drafted, pledging support for the new reform process, including economic aid. That provided a thaw to the frozen interagency process, giving Simons room to advance his policy proposals. In the June 4 elections, Solidarity won 99 of the 100 seats in the Senate, and all the seats in the Sejm it was allowed to contest. The enthusiastic rejection of communism sent shockwaves throughout the region.

As Bush planned to visit Poland in July, the NSC staff tasked Fried with developing plans for economic assistance, again outside normal channels. He and a colleague developed a concept paper for an "enterprise fund" for Poland, which became one of the key initiatives announced during Bush's trip. The country quickly became a test case for political transformation behind the Iron Curtain. By September, a Solidarity leader, Tadeusz Mazowiecki, was prime minister. In November, the Berlin Wall fell. By the end of the year, the communist regimes throughout Central and Eastern Europe had collapsed. Two years later, the Soviet Union disintegrated.

This example shows that members of the NSC staff can go around the interagency process by seeking out and empowering allies in the foreign affairs agencies to advance their objectives. Rice reached down in the system to Fried, who took the professional risk of circumventing State Department instructions, and she reached up through the NSC suite to the Oval Office. Fried had been in the Foreign Service for more than a decade when he was assigned to the Poland desk in the State Department's European bureau. He had previously served in the Soviet Union and Serbia, as well as in the department's Office of Soviet Affairs. In 1990, he became political section chief in Warsaw, and three years later joined the NSC staff during the Clinton administration, as mentioned earlier. In 1997, he became ambassador to Poland. When Rice was appointed national security adviser in 2001, she brought him back to the NSC staff as the senior director for Europe, and when she became secretary of state, she named him her assistant secretary for Europe.

Diplomats' role in the interagency

As has become clear by now, career diplomats can participate in the interagency process in multiple ways. Many of them draft briefings papers for interagency meetings at some point in their careers. While serving abroad, they may be invited to meetings at different levels via secure video conference. They may also bid on positions on the NSC staff, just like they do for any other assignment on the Foreign Service bid list. Once they reach the senior ranks, they may represent the State Department on IPCs or sub-IPCs as assistant secretaries or deputy assistant secretaries. In those posts, they may also be backbenchers in DC, PC and even full NSC meetings. Most deputy assistant secretaries and about half of the assistant secretaries tend to be career diplomats, though the latter number may vary significantly from one administration to another. Occasionally, career officers become undersecretaries, which makes them DC members. William Burns was a rare exception as a Foreign Service officer serving as deputy secretary during the Obama administration, and in that capacity he substituted several times for Secretaries of State Hillary Clinton and John Kerry in PC meetings.

Usually, the start of a new administration is rich with opportunities for career officials in all parts of the government. It takes months, if not longer, to fill positions with political appointees, especially those who need to be confirmed by the Senate – at the State Department, they include ambassadors, assistant secretaries, undersecretaries, deputy secretaries and the secretary. During that time, Foreign Service officers are most likely to occupy those posts in an acting capacity. At overseas posts with political ambassadors, who are required to resign as soon as the president who appointed them is out of office, the career deputy chief of mission becomes chargé d'affaires and may be asked to brief the DC or PC.

Once political appointees are in place, career diplomats can lend their expertise to bring them up to speed on issues and events. Outside foreign policy experts, however knowledgeable and experienced, may not be familiar with certain details or nuances of understandings with foreign governments. Some may not know exactly how the interagency process works and may be overwhelmed by the huge bureaucracy. Those coming off the winning presidential campaign may still be in campaign mode and assume that the outgoing administration is as clumsy and clueless as they accused it of being. Some diplomats mistakenly believe that their job is to persuade political appointees that their strategic views are wrong or simplistic. They can be. But a patronizing approach breeds mistrust and betrays a conviction that Foreign Service officers are special guardians of foreign policy truths. They are not. Rather, they can be guardians of expertise, detailed knowledge of realities abroad, and the difference between those realities and what appears in the opinion pages of major newspapers. Understanding that distinction well can make a difference between policy success and failure.

Our experience suggests that good policy can be crafted from more than one set of political assumptions and from a broad range of starting points. The job of Foreign Service officers in the interagency is to help the president, top officials and the network of political appointees that staff key positions to advance their own strategic vision in ways that are productive and sustainable. The first year of a new administration is a learning curve for both career and political appointees. Former campaign advisers come into government from a loose structure during the election season, and their instinct at first is to consult their former colleagues now scattered across agencies, rather than their new co-workers. The process of shifting from campaign to governing mode takes time and is often complicated by new policy issues for which there are no preset campaign positions.

The Trump administration's political appointees had more difficulty making the transition than usual, and in some cases never made it at all. The hostility toward career professionals encapsulated in the pejorative term "Deep State," along with Trump's refusal to consider views different from his own, crippled the interagency policy process. The Biden administration returned to the tested practices of the previous few decades, both formal and informal.

We began this chapter with an example of NSC staff members taking it upon themselves to implement decisions all on their own, or "going operational." Granted, those were highly unusual decisions – selling weapons to Iran and using the money to fund the Nicaraguan Contras – that were deliberately kept secret from both the interagency and the public. But decades later, the NSC staff still faces accusations of being too actively involved in carrying out policies, rather than focusing on its original job of coordinating policy formulation. As we saw earlier, that role has naturally developed to include overseeing implementation, to make sure that policies are carried out as the president intended. Striking the right balance without being too heavy-handed, duplicating other agencies' activities and encroaching on their turf takes a constant effort. The results it produces vary greatly, but there is no doubt that it is an effort worth making.

Case Study 1: Russia Sanctions Over Crimea Annexation

For more than two decades after the Cold War ended and the Soviet Union collapsed in 1991, the U.S. policy toolbox toward Russia did not include sanctions. Every American president came to office with the intention to improve relations with Moscow. That never quite happened, but for about a decade, the relationship was fairly good. At the end of 1999, Vladimir Putin succeeded Boris Yeltsin as president. After George W. Bush took office in Washington, he had big hopes for what he could achieve with Putin. It did not take long for ties to start sliding downhill as Putin's rule grew more authoritarian at home and aggressive abroad, culminating in the 2008 invasion of Georgia.

The Obama administration attempted to "reset" relations in 2009. Its policy produced some important results, such as the New START arms-control treaty, but it was premised on what turned out to be a faulty assumption. The White House believed that Dmitry Medvedev, who had become president months earlier, represented a pro-Western, reformist Russian leadership that would influence Moscow's future direction. In reality, Putin had used Medvedev to engineer a way to stay in power indefinitely. In 2012, after four years as prime minister, Putin reassumed the presidency. That same year, Congress passed a law that mandated Russia-related sanctions for the first time. The Magnitsky Act, as it is known, was named for a Russian lawyer who had died in police custody after uncovering corruption and tax fraud. Obama reluctantly signed the law, which resulted in targeted sanctions against those responsible for Magnitsky's death and a few others viewed as enablers. But he never contemplated a more general confrontation or widespread sanctions.

In early 2014, Putin annexed Crimea and invaded the Donbas region in eastern Ukraine, claiming to be protecting ethnic Russians. In Washington, the interagency

Case Study 1: (cont.)

went into high gear. The NSC staff led the process, but it was divided over how to respond to Putin's aggression. The Russia directorate urged a firm pushback, the European directorate was more cautious, and the economic directorate was split between those who sought a strong response and those who believed that the United States had no compelling interest in Ukraine. These divisions sent mixed signals to the interagency.

The State Department forcefully advocated for economic sanctions. Leading the charge were Victoria Nuland, assistant secretary for Europe, and Daniel Fried, who was then the department's sanctions coordinator. They had the backing of William Burns, the deputy secretary. Nuland also proposed sending weapons to the Ukrainian government to help it defend itself, but the NSC staff rejected that option on the grounds that the Russians already had and would retain the military edge. The department could not develop sanctions on its own and found allies in the Office of Foreign Assets Control at the Treasury. They put together an informal interagency sanctions group, which also included like-minded NSC staff members and the Department of Commerce.

The group quickly drafted options for IPC and DC consideration. The Treasury leadership was willing to support strong measures if they were designed to avoid damaging the global financial system. Commerce was open to restricting exports of certain technologies to Russia, but only if U.S.-friendly governments agreed to replace the United States as suppliers. The NSC suite was inclined to back sanctions in principle but, reflecting internal staff divisions, did not want them to be unilateral – it wanted them imposed in conjunction with the EU. Washington had never coordinated sanctions with another government before, so this was a long shot. Some of those who put that condition assumed that the 27 EU member-states would never reach the required consensus for such penalties on Russia.

Fried received authorization to start working toward an agreement acceptable to the Europeans and, along with Treasury officials, he led delegations to various capitals. Any initial reluctance on the continent did not last long. In July, Moscow's proxy forces in eastern Ukraine shot down a Malaysian airliner, killing all 298 passengers onboard, most of them EU citizens. The EU officials working with the Americans were prepared to discuss general sanctions against key sectors of the Russian economy, including finance, energy and military technology.

With a handshake on a framework for U.S. and EU sanctions that would be announced in parallel, the skeptics in Washington agreed to go ahead and finalize the details. The Europeans were grateful that the United States was willing to coordinate and consult with them, rather than act unilaterally. Throughout the process, the U.S. Embassy in Moscow helped identify the best sanctions targets, including individuals, companies and sectors. The embassy also played a key role in explaining the purpose of the sanctions to the Russian public, and what it would take to get them

Case Study 1: (cont.)

lifted. Although they had some impact, they could not compare with the massive penalties imposed on Russia as a result of its 2022 war against Ukraine.

Figure 4.4 John Tefft presents his credentials as the new U.S. ambassador to Russia to President Vladimir Putin at the Kremlin in 2014.
Photo by Sasha Mordovets/Getty Images.

This experience shows that, in spite of the NSC staff's institutional advantages in steering the interagency process, the foreign affairs agencies, when united, can exert decisive influence – especially when the NSC staff is divided. The divisions over sending weapons, however, could not be overcome, leaving sanctions as the principal policy tool to respond to Russia's aggression, rather than being a part of a broader strategy. The sanctions did cause some harm to the Russian economy, and Putin temporarily abandoned his plan to annex other parts of Ukrainian territory beyond Crimea. But they did not cause him to negotiate an end to the conflict.

When Putin launched his full-scale invasion of Ukraine in 2022, the Biden administration, including the NSC staff, appeared to have learned from the 2014 experience. Although it was slow to recognize the possibility of Ukrainian success on the battlefield, the administration decided early on to provide weapons to Ukraine and kept increasing the arms flow significantly. As of this writing, Ukraine has received U.S. weapons and military equipment worth tens of billions of dollars.[20]

Case Study 2: Russian Invasion of Georgia

The Russian invasion of Georgia in August 2008 came as no surprise to policymakers in Washington. Relations between the two former Soviet republics had deteriorated significantly since the 2003 Rose Revolution, a movement similar to Ukraine's Orange Revolution, which had brought to power a new, young Georgian leadership headed by President Mikheil Saakashvili. Moscow's influence in what it considered part of its sphere of influence had declined immensely.

In February 2008, the United States and 12 EU members recognized the independence of Kosovo from Serbia. A longtime Serbian ally, Russia denounced the move and threatened to offer recognition to Georgia's breakaway regions of Abkhazia and South Ossetia. In April, NATO assured Georgia and Ukraine that they will become members of the alliance eventually. Even though the two countries were not given so-called Membership Action Plans, which usually pave the way for candidates to join, the statement further heightened tensions with Moscow. It had earlier upped the ante by cutting gas supplies, firing missiles and drones inside Georgia, and increasing the number of Russian forces stationed in Abkhazia beyond what had been agreed after the breakup of the Soviet Union in the early 1990s. In May, Russia sent an additional 400 specially trained troops to Abkhazia.

All of this raised the apprehension level in Washington. Daniel Fried, as assistant secretary of state, tasked his deputy for the Caucasus, Matthew Bryza, with heading an interagency group and often attended PC and DC meetings as a backbencher. John Tefft, who was ambassador to Georgia, and his embassy team sent a steady stream of reporting to the State Department and the interagency. In March, President George W. Bush hosted Saakashvili at the White House. Following standard practice, Bush's briefing papers had been coordinated by the NSC staff, with input from the State Department, the Pentagon and the CIA. He assured Saakashvili of U.S. support for eventual NATO membership and offered help in securing European consent for a Membership Action Plan. Under pressure from Moscow, Germany and other NATO allies resisted such a move.

Bush made a point of impressing upon Saakashvili the importance of not falling for Russian provocations in Abkhazia or South Ossetia, which could trigger a war. As much as the United States supported Georgia, Bush made clear that it would not get drawn into a shooting war with Russia. Secretary of State Condoleezza Rice emphasized the same point several times in the following months, including during a visit to Tbilisi in July, which Fried attended.

On August 1, Russian-backed forces in South Ossetia started shelling Georgian villages. On the night of August 7, Saakashvili took the bait and sent his troops into South Ossetia. The next day, Russia launched a full-scale land, air and sea invasion of Georgia. After just a few days of fighting, the Georgian forces retreated, and the Russians marched deep into Georgian territory, with Tbilisi on the path of their advance. From the capital, Tefft briefed a full NSC meeting chaired by Bush on the situation on a secure phone line, not knowing if an evacuation would be necessary. The embassy worked closely with a task force in Washington created by the State Department, with help from military and

Case Study 2: (cont.)

intelligence officials, to assist U.S. citizens in Georgia and protect the embassy. At a press conference, Rice called for an immediate stop to the hostilities.

On August 12, French President Nicolas Sarkozy negotiated a ceasefire agreement. The next day, Bush demanded that the Russians withdraw from Georgia and backed its sovereignty. He also sent Rice back to Tbilisi, as well as to Paris, to help finalize a durable end to the conflict. The U.S. military had already begun humanitarian relief flights, as part of a broad assistance program managed by USAID, which provided food, shelter and medicine to war victims. Even though the fighting had stopped, the White House was concerned that the Kremlin might force Georgia's economic collapse and dispatched a senior interagency delegation to assess the country's needs.

On August 26, Moscow recognized the independence of Abkhazia and South Ossetia. It would take until October for the Russian troops to withdraw from undisputed Georgian territory. On September 3, the Bush administration announced a $1 billion assistance package for Georgia's recovery. That figure had been proposed by Senator Joe Biden, who was running for vice president, which made the issue bipartisan. Key members of Congress visited Georgia, and the emergency appropriation was quickly approved. That marked the beginning of another interagency process designed to coordinate the disbursement of the aid package. U.S. officials were also able to galvanize international fundraising efforts, which resulted in another $3 billion.

The interagency mechanism during the war was led by the principals, who could not afford to wait for the regular machinery. Policy decisions and intelligence assessments were often out of date before they were presented at DC and PC meetings. The key decisions – to support Georgia even after its army had been beaten by the Russians, to back Sarkozy's ceasefire efforts and to offer the aid package – were made by the president and his key principals in real time, based on advice from trusted officials on the NSC staff and at the Departments of State and Defense. The bipartisan support in Congress for the $1 billion was remarkable, especially in such a short time.

Exercise: French Anger Over Australian Submarines

You are serving as director for Western Europe on the staff of the NSC Europe directorate. The United States and Australia have just announced a deal for U.S. nuclear-powered submarines to replace older Australian diesel-electric vessels, as part of a trilateral security partnership with Britain. This means that Australia will break an earlier agreement with France to provide the submarines. The French government is outraged as much over the deal as for being kept in the dark, warning privately and publicly about serious damage to its relationship with Washington.[21]

Exercise: (cont.)

Task: Your boss, the senior director for Europe, has tasked you with drafting an agenda for an IPC meeting to assess the French reaction and recommend to the DC how to handle the situation. As you prepare your memo, consider the following questions:

- Which agencies should be invited to the IPC meeting and at what level?
- Should you or the senior director represent the NSC?
- Which agency should chair the meeting and why?
- What kind of briefing papers should be prepared before the meeting?
- What specific outcomes would you aim for?

ADDITIONAL RESOURCES

John Gans, *White House Warriors: How the National Security Council Transformed the American Way of War* (Liveright, 2019).

Roger Z. George and Harvey Rishikof, eds., *The National Security Enterprise: Navigating the Labyrinth* (Georgetown University Press, 2017).

Karl F. Inderfurth and Loch K. Johnson, *Fateful Decisions: Inside the National Security Council* (Oxford University Press, 2004).

David Rothkopf, *Running the World: The Inside Story of the National Security Council and the Architects of American Power* (PublicAffairs, 2006).

5   How Does an Embassy Work?

CHARLES RAY AND JANICE JACOBS

José Irizarry was a star agent of the Drug Enforcement Administration (DEA), the agency tasked with combating drug trafficking and leading the U.S. government's decades-long war on drugs. For his work in the DEA's Miami Field Division, Irizarry was rewarded with a transfer to the U.S. Embassy in Colombia in 2015. Six years later, he was sentenced to more than 12 years in prison for operating a money-laundering and fraud scheme throughout his assignments in Miami and Colombia. He had diverted about $9 million "from undercover DEA money-laundering investigations to himself and to co-conspirators," according to court documents. In return, he received kickbacks and bribes "worth at least $1 million for himself and his family, which [were] used to purchase jewelry, luxury cars and a home."[1]

The fall from grace of a DEA agent was hardly a surprise to dozens of U.S. ambassadors. As chiefs of mission, they have authority over all representatives of the U.S. government – or official Americans – in their host-country, except for uniformed military personnel serving under a regional commander. If an employee from any agency engages in behavior that harms the mission or U.S. interests, the ambassador can declare "loss of confidence" and send the person home. In the aftermath of the Irizarry scandal and other DEA incidents, two former ambassadors in Central America wrote about witnessing "unprofessional" and "criminal behavior" by DEA staffers. "From the pursuit of unauthorized commercial sex to embezzlement, fraud and even active collaboration with the drug traffickers they are meant to be pursuing, DEA agents are among the most likely candidates to receive loss of confidence," wrote John Feeley and James Nealon, who served in Panama and Honduras, respectively.[2]

They pointed out that the "DEA is hardly an exclusive offender in this realm," and that some agencies are better than others in "adhering to chief-of-mission authority." Officers from the State Department, the U.S. Agency for International Development (USAID), the CIA and the Departments of Agriculture and Commerce – all formally designated as foreign affairs agencies – "generally color between the lines," Feeley and Nealon wrote. Representatives of law-enforcement agencies, such as the DEA and the Departments of Justice (DOJ) and Homeland Security (DHS), sometimes "have their own agendas, which don't necessarily include the president's foreign policy," they added. They did not mean to suggest that such officials are disloyal or try to sabotage the president and, by extension, the chief of mission. "But their actions are no less disruptive for being carried out by loyal and hard-working public servants," Feeley and Nealon wrote. "The root of the problem lies in diametrically opposed bureaucratic cultures and operating environments."

Cases like Irizarry's may not happen every day, but they have become more frequent than anyone outside a small circle realizes. They illustrate a constant struggle to make sure that representatives of multiple government agencies abroad work as one team – perhaps the biggest challenge in a diplomatic mission, whether it is an embassy, consulate or one accredited to a multilateral organization. This chapter focuses on embassies, but much of it applies to other missions as well. They are all outposts representing the home-country through diplomacy, and their structure, culture and challenges are similar.

A diplomatic mission is an organization like no other. Its members live and work away from home, and the line between their professional and personal lives is blurred to an extent most outsiders do not fully understand or appreciate. In the average workplace, a supervisor is not concerned with what employees do at home. That is not the case in a diplomatic mission. Its staff is a community, and excessive drinking, a nasty divorce, threats of violence or a suicide is not just one family's problem. It affects the section in which that person works, and often the entire mission. The chief of mission has not only authority over almost everyone at post, but also responsibility for their security and well-being. So managing such a workplace is a unique and daunting task, made even more difficult by being in a foreign country.

The embassy team

In spite of their fundamental similarities, not all embassies are the same, and a Foreign Service officer's daily duties depend on a variety of factors, such as the host-country, the state of the bilateral relationship and the post's size. Large U.S. embassies, such as those in London, Cairo and Mexico City, have hundreds of official Americans and thousands of local staff, while in small posts like those in Papua New Guinea or Eritrea, the Americans may be only a handful. In 2022, of the 275 U.S. diplomatic missions worldwide, 171 were embassies. The United States had diplomatic relations with 195 countries[3] – as noted in Chapter 1, some embassies are accredited to more than one country. We were Foreign Service officers for three decades, and in our experience, most U.S. embassies are midsize, with an average of 50 to 100 Americans and as many as hundreds of local employees. In the 2010s, we were both ambassadors in Africa. Charles Ray had about 50 official Americans on his team in Zimbabwe, while Janice Jacobs had just over 100 in Senegal.

A typical embassy has political, economic, management, consular and public diplomacy sections, which correspond to the five career tracks for Foreign Service officers. Along with a security section, they are all staffed by State Department employees. Security sections are headed by agents of Diplomatic Security (DS), the department's law-enforcement bureau. They are considered Foreign Service specialists, not officers – this is a way to differentiate between diplomats and other service members. Bureaucratically, the officers are known as generalists. The specialist category also includes office managers, information technology experts, doctors, engineers and accountants, among others. In 2022, there were 7,996 generalists and 5,511 specialists, or a total of 13,507 Foreign Service personnel – 8,843 of them were serving abroad, while the rest worked in the United States.[4]

In addition to the State Department-staffed sections, a typical embassy has at least one that represents other parts of the Foreign Service: USAID, the Foreign Commercial Service (FCS), the Foreign Agricultural Service (FAS) and the Animal and Plant Health Inspection Service (APHIS). Their officers are diplomats as well. The rest of the offices are occupied by officials from other government agencies, some of which we mentioned earlier. The Department of Defense has a significant presence, reflecting the global reach of the U.S. military. As epidemics and pandemics became a bigger threat in recent years, the Centers for Disease Control and Prevention (CDC) increased their personnel abroad. Even agencies traditionally not considered players in foreign affairs, such as the Department of Energy (DOE) and the U.S. Forest Service, have staff overseas. The situation in the host-country, the importance of relevant matters in the bilateral relationship and the available resources determine whether a certain agency is represented in an embassy.

As chiefs and deputy chiefs of mission (DCM), we supervised colleagues from parts of the government that most Americans would never suspect of having a presence overseas. In both Zimbabwe and Cambodia, Ray had an employee of the Library of Congress at each post. Their job was to find and procure books for the library. In Cambodia, there were also two staffers from the U.S. Forest Service, who worked on deforestation issues with the host-government. Jacobs had representatives of the Federal Aviation Administration (FAA) in Senegal, in the only such office in sub-Saharan Africa. In the Dominican Republic, her team included employees of the Treasury Department and the U.S. Marshals Service. The former helped improve the country's financial institutions and combat money-laundering. The latter worked on returning American fugitives to the United States. The FBI and DEA were present as well.

Although the State Department is the custodian of U.S. embassies, its career diplomats are often outnumbered by officials from other agencies. In Chapter 1, Nicholas Kralev called those who are not part of the Foreign Service "transitory diplomats," many of whom spend only one or two tours abroad. In this category, he also included a few domestically based State Department civil servants on occasional "excursion tours" abroad, usually when a position cannot be filled by a Foreign Service member, as well as noncareer appointees in ambassadorial positions.

To sum up, there are three main categories of embassy offices under the authority of the chief of mission and, by extension, the DCM, as shown in Figure 5.1. The first category includes the six core sections staffed by the State Department; the second, the other parts of the Foreign Service; and the third, other government agencies (OGAs). Some embassies have just a few of those agencies, while others have

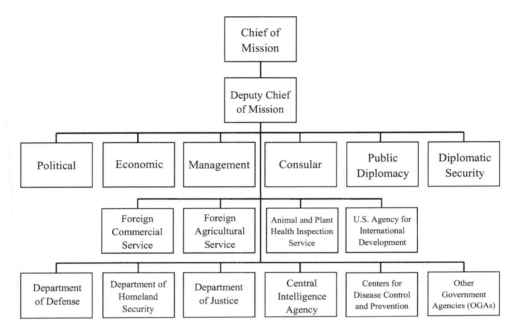

Figure 5.1 Organizational structure of a typical U.S. embassy. Some of the agencies shown here may not be present or there may be others, such as the DOE or the FAA.

dozens. An agency's most senior representative is known as an *attaché*, a French word that means "attached" – the head of the defense office is the defense attaché, and the top DOJ or FBI official is the legal attaché.

The chief of mission, the DCM and the heads of sections and agencies are members of the post's senior management, known as the country team. That team is the overseas version of the interagency structure in Washington. U.S. embassies periodically prepare documents known as Integrated Country Strategies, meant to focus their work on the priorities that matter the most. If all agency representatives work together as intended, the country team functions as a mini-government. It is also a mechanism for the ambassador to exercise oversight, provide guidance and instructions, and to receive information from across the embassy – or to keep a finger on the mission's pulse. At most posts, the team meets once a week, but that is up to the ambassador, as are other details, such as how formal the meetings are and who is invited in addition to the regular participants.

Other countries' embassies follow a similar organization, even if some of the specifics of their operations are different. In general, they tend to be smaller than U.S. embassies, with some exceptions, and their agenda is usually not as ambitious. For example, Russian, Chinese, Cuban and many other embassies are not tasked by their capitals to help improve governance or promote human rights abroad. It is hardly surprising that every country has its own foreign policy priorities, and that most lack the resources of the United States. The U.S. Foreign Service is the largest in the world, with almost 9,000 of its members posted abroad, as noted earlier. The next largest is Britain's Foreign Service, which has an estimated 5,000 personnel overseas (we could not find a precise official figure).[5] Exact numbers were not available for China and Russia, either, but the estimates for both were about 4,500.[6]

The chief of mission

As an ambassador extraordinary and plenipotentiary, the chief of mission is usually considered a personal representative of the sending country's head of state or government. Newly sworn-in U.S. ambassadors receive a letter from the president, which instructs them to exercise authority and oversight over all U.S. government personnel and programs in their receiving countries. The main purpose of that instruction is for the president to have a single point of contact and accountability. Chief-of-mission approval is required before sending any home-country official to the host-country. On paper, ambassadors report to the president through the secretary of state, but in reality, the person with whom they communicate most often – and the one who writes their performance evaluations – is the assistant secretary responsible for their region.

How much power does an ambassador have? When Hillary Clinton was secretary of state in the Obama administration, she wanted to "turn" American ambassadors into chief executive officers (CEOs). "We believe that having a CEO model for the chief of mission will help us manage the myriad of U.S. government assets and activities in every country," she said in 2011.[7] Many ambassadors and other diplomats, however, had doubts that was a realistic prospect. "We don't have the degree of license within our law" to be true CEOs, Francis Ricciardone, who was an ambassador three times – to Turkey, Egypt and the Philippines – told Nicholas Kralev not long after Clinton's remarks. "We have a lot of people looking over our shoulders, who can and do exert statutory authority over what we do. The budget is directed from Washington, and we cannot allocate resources in the way that a CEO can on behalf of the shareholders."[8]

Within those confines, the degree of autonomy chiefs of mission have depends largely on where they are serving. Most countries rarely enjoy attention from the president of the United States. That may seem like a negative, but it usually means that the relationships with those countries are doing just fine and fewer people in Washington may be looking over the shoulders of the ambassadors there. If there is a crisis, however, the White House will likely get involved. "In general, there is an inverse relationship between the amount of autonomy an ambassador has and the degree of controversy around what is happening" in a particular country at a certain time, Jacob Lew told Kralev in 2012, when he was President Obama's chief of staff.[9]

Large countries, especially U.S. adversaries like China and Russia, receive presidential attention almost every day. In the years after the 9/11 terrorist attacks in 2001, both the George W. Bush and the Obama administrations invested heavily in the relationship with Pakistan, because of its importance to the war in neighboring Afghanistan and in the fight against extremism in general. As noted in the previous

Figure 5.2 The U.S Embassy in Berlin, near the Bundestag and next to the Brandenburg Gate. Photo by Sean Gallup/Getty Images.

chapter, routine decisions regarding most countries are typically made in the established interagency process. But during that period, many decisions about Pakistan rose to the presidential level. As a result, U.S. ambassadors there faced constant demands from the White House, which the State Department's inspector general criticized as "intense and at times intrusive" in a 2012 audit. While that "ensures that mission concerns receive both timely and top-level attention, it also consumes extraordinary amounts of time and energy, and adds significantly to the stresses at this already stressed post," the report said.[10]

Cameron Munter was the ambassador during that audit. In Chapter 3, we discussed his involvement in the aftermath of the 2011 raid that killed Osama bin Laden – a chief of mission does not enjoy much autonomy when the stakes are this high. But things were very different at Munter's previous post. He was ambassador to Serbia in 2008, when the United States officially recognized newly independent Kosovo, until then a Serbian province, which had plunged into an ethnic conflict in the late 1990s. In reaction to Washington's move, a mob attacked the U.S. Embassy in Belgrade and set a part of it on fire. Evidence soon surfaced that the prime minister, Vojislav Koštunica, had personally approved the assault. Determined to prevent something like this from happening again, Munter concluded that he needed to "encourage the formation of a less dangerous government."

The key to weakening Koštunica's reelection chances was taking away the support he had from the Socialist Party of Serbia, whose leader was Ivica Dačić.

"We got him to flip and join the pro-Europeans," Munter told Kralev. "We didn't pay him off; we just persuaded him. What he really wanted was international legitimacy." Munter and his team turned for help to José Luis Rodríguez Zapatero, the Spanish prime minister at the time, and George Papandreou, a Greek politician who ran Socialist International, a worldwide organization of leftist parties. They urged Dačić to join a coalition of Serbia's pro-European parties. "He put a knife in Koštunica's back" and the ruling party lost the election, Munter said. Dačić was named deputy prime minister and rose to prime minister four years later. Munter did not ask Washington to approve his plan. "We just did it," he said.[11]

When the policy direction set by headquarters is broad and general, an ambassador's hand is much freer in shaping the home-country's actions in the receiving state. In the 2000s, the Balkans were not high on Washington's agenda, and along with Serbia, Albania was another post where American ambassadors had significant autonomy. The U.S. policy objectives there were a stable, secure and democratic country that developed its economy toward future membership in the EU. Albania was not deemed vital to the U.S. national interest, so when explosive disputes broke out between the government and the opposition in the early part of the decade, Ambassador James Jeffrey saw no reason to bother senior officials in Washington. "Every day during that period, I had to get on the phone with the head of the opposition, the prime minister or the president and say, 'You are about to throw the country into total chaos and violence, and you might drag down the entire Balkans. Could you please take the following six-point action program that we just developed this morning and apply it?' This is what I got to do for almost two years," Jeffrey told Kralev in 2012.[12]

There is an old saying in the Foreign Service that "an ambassador should never receive an instruction he hasn't written." What does this mean? Ideally, policy decisions at headquarters take into account the reporting, analysis and recommendations that come in from embassies and other diplomatic missions. Ambassadors who feel strongly about the direction of policy concerning their host-countries make proposals to their capitals. When those proposals are accepted, they come back to the embassy in the form of instructions, which are naturally familiar to the chief of mission. Instructions are easier and more satisfying to carry out when they reflect one's own views.

Great ambassadors spend most of their time outside the embassy, meeting with officials and people from all walks of life in the host-country, giving speeches, talking to the media and otherwise participating in the public discourse. Traveling outside the capital is essential to both understanding the country and conducting effective diplomacy. But ambassadors should also regularly walk around the embassy and check in with their staff.

The deputy chief of mission

Thousands of American diplomats served in Iraq when it was an active war zone in the 2000s. For many of them, most days were challenging and fraught with security risks. For Cameron Munter, however, one of the most jarring days while serving as deputy chief of mission at the U.S. Embassy in Baghdad in 2010 had nothing to do with the dangers of rocket attacks and suicide bombings. Rather, it concerned a new member of the embassy staff who arrived on a Friday. On Sunday morning, after an apparent night of drinking, he was found "in a stairwell, naked, lying in his own urine," Munter recalled. So he sent the new employee right back home. "He said, 'Give me another chance! Someone must have drugged me when I was having a drink.' I said, 'Maybe, but I'm not going to risk it.' We had no choice in Iraq."[13]

The job of a DCM is arguably the most demanding in any embassy, as noted in Chapter 1. The main reason stems from the DCM's primary responsibility as the top day-to-day manager of mission operations, and it specifically has to do with the fact that managing people working in a diplomatic mission inevitably crosses over into their personal lives. "Where they live can be so defining to people's lives and whether they are happy," Virginia Blaser, a former DCM in Tanzania, Uganda and Mauritius, told Kralev. "And this is particularly true for family members. Are they in a house or an apartment? Do the kids have a room they love? Is there a yard for the dog? These things are very important for people, and everybody's needs are different. If there is anything that will cause more resentment, anger and low morale, it's housing, and especially perceptions that housing is inadequate or unfair."[14] Even though embassies usually have housing boards, whose job is to ensure fairness by considering the interests of single and married, junior and senior employees, DCMs oversee the process.

Other aspects of the personal lives of mission staff and their families, who are known as the embassy community, can be even harder to manage. "I've had everything from drunk driving and road rage to child molestation to weapons incidents to threatened murders and suicides," Blaser said. "I handled them through advocacy committees and other groups. Like the housing boards, they are excellent tools to ensure happiness and fairness in what can be extremely emotional decisions." At U.S. diplomatic missions, the Marine Security Guard is charged with protecting classified material and information. When a marine committed suicide in an African country, "we had to deal with the family and to manage the mental health of the other marines," Blaser said. "We also had to deal with the political ramifications of the local authorities wanting to get involved in the investigation, even though it was on a diplomatic compound." During her tour in a Central American country, "we lost a marine in a drinking incident," she said. "He passed out and choked to death after having too much to drink. It's hard enough when you lose a work colleague, but in the Foreign Service, it's always more than that."

As an embassy's second-in-command, the DCM's authority comes, for the most part, from the chief of mission. A post is best run when the two get along well, but if they disagree, they should do so in private. Generally, the ambassador is the public face of the embassy and the home-country, while the DCM is the internal manager, but that is not set in stone. Some ambassadors may not be comfortable with a highly visible public role – one might wonder why they wanted the position in the first place, but there are examples of such in recent history. Chiefs of mission are entitled to make whatever arrangements with their DCMs they prefer. But a good ambassador gives the DCM space to do their job.

Every country's Foreign Service has a bureaucratic hierarchy, and learning how to manage both up and down is essential to a successful diplomatic career – and especially in a DCM role. You have to make the ambassador happy and ensure the embassy works well, but you may rarely get credit. As chief of mission, Charles Ray had four DCMs. He did not necessarily make their jobs easier, but he did his best not to do anything to make them any harder. He gave each of them clear authority to manage the post, and full credit when things went well.

In the U.S. Foreign Service, DCMs are designated as mentors to entry-level officers. They hold regular informal meetings meant to relax the natural barriers of rank, so the officers can ask any questions to help them navigate both the profession and the bureaucracy. Many DCMs consider this to be their most rewarding responsibility. Counseling sessions should not be limited to new officers. Everyone can do better and can use help. Blaser had such sessions not only with fellow State Department employees, but with colleagues from different agencies, "even if they were doing great," she said. "I felt strongly that I was responsible for every agency for the mission to be successful. I had to look out for them, help them and push them sometimes, when I felt that they were not connecting with each other." The embassy community expects the DCM to be "a fair interlocutor that everybody can trust, and that means you can't have a cabal or best friends" whom you favor over others. "That can be very lonely," Blaser said.[15]

Embassy sections and functions

Official home-country representation, consular services, managing relations with the receiving state, reporting and analysis, and advocacy and negotiation were the main diplomatic duties and responsibilities outlined in Chapter 1. Each embassy section and agency office has concrete functions that, ideally, help to make the mission work and contribute to the national interest. The chapters that follow will examine the tradecraft fundamentals underpinning those functions. But first, we will briefly examine what the different parts of a typical U.S. embassy do.

Political section

The duties most often associated with traditional diplomacy fall on the political section. Its head is usually the third-ranking embassy official, after the chief of mission and the DCM. It has primary responsibility for the day-to-day management of the political relationship with the host-country, as well as for reporting and analysis. Its main interlocutor is the Ministry of Foreign Affairs, but it also works with other parts of the government, including the legislative branch. U.S. embassies in democracies engage with opposition and other parties not in power, as well as civil society groups. Most of the cables sent to headquarters originate in the political section.

The term "political officer" should not be confused with "political ambassador," which is shorthand for a politically appointed chief of mission. Political officers are career Foreign Service members who work in the political section. They maintain and expand a diverse network of contacts, who help them to understand the host-country better and stay abreast of the latest developments. Diplomats gather information overtly, because they are not spies. They use it to report back to their capital and share insights that may help policymakers to formulate decisions. They explain host-country policies to officials at headquarters and home-country policies to the receiving state. They also advocate for positions and actions favored by their government and participate in negotiations.

Economic section

The economic section manages the economic relationship with the host-country, reports on economic and business developments, and helps to negotiate trade agreements and other accords. In some small and midsize U.S. embassies, the political and economic functions are performed by one combined section. Given how interconnected and interdependent economies are nowadays, these issues have become dominant in many bilateral relationships. Advocacy is increasingly prevalent in the duties of economic officers. The most common type of advocacy has to do with protecting and advancing the home-country's economic and business interests, usually by ensuring a level playing field where companies can compete fairly.

Things get more complicated when it comes to protectionism, corruption and other policies and practices that hurt the sending state's economy. In countries with weak or barely functioning economies, a large part of the economic relationship is based on development and foreign aid, not just to help feed people in need but to build institutions and infrastructure, to improve governance and create long-term stability. This approach is characteristic of Western diplomacy but does not apply to all countries. China's economic diplomacy, for example, has been focused mostly on projects in developing states aimed at securing resources for China itself, rather than helping those states.

In most U.S. embassies, the economic section is also responsible for environmental, science, technology and health affairs – with the exception of large posts like those in London and Tokyo, where a separate section takes on these responsibilities. How much emphasis an embassy places on one or more of these areas depends on their importance in the relationship with the host-country. Environmental issues are high on the agenda in Brazil, so the embassy in Brasília has a dedicated section. Science and technology play an increasingly prominent role in diplomacy, and even countries that cannot agree on much else may negotiate agreements in the fields of education and science. U.S. Foreign Service officers who work on these matters are in the economic career track. An embassy can have State

Department officers working on health policy in the economic section, as well as health experts from the CDC in a different office.

Consular section

The only part of an embassy a member of the public may ever see is the consular section. It is tasked with carrying out the post's mission of assisting home-country citizens visiting or living in the receiving state. The services the section provides range from routine (issuing passports, recording births and deaths) to special (helping compatriots who have been hurt or run afoul of local laws) to emergency (evacuations due to natural disasters or armed conflict). The other consular function, as noted earlier, is adjudicating entry visas for travelers who wish to visit the sending country. Visas are typically nonimmigrant or immigrant. The latter are issued to people planning to reside permanently in the home-country. Student and work visas are considered nonimmigrant visas, because they do not grant permanent residency.

Public diplomacy section

While consular officers normally come face-to-face with more members of the public than their colleagues in other parts of the embassy, the activities of the public diplomacy section tend to reach the largest number of host-country citizens. The section's work is designed to inform, engage and influence public opinion, with the goal of supporting specific policy objectives or, more broadly, creating goodwill and boosting the sending state's standing. Public diplomacy officers do that through messaging in traditional and social media, arranging press conferences, briefings with senior officials and other events. They also manage professional, educational and cultural exchanges, as well as other short- and long-term programs meant to expose recognized and emerging local leaders to life in the sending country. The International Visitor Leadership Program (IVLP) and the Fulbright scholarship program are among the best-known U.S. public diplomacy efforts.

Management section

Administration may not sound very exciting, but without a good management section, an embassy cannot run well, if at all. A DCM cannot be a successful manager of the mission if this section is in disarray. Everything from human resources to finance to transportation to building maintenance requires constant attention. How smooth or rough the arrival of new officers at post is depends on their management colleagues, who help them to get settled in their homes, enroll their children in school and adjust to an unfamiliar environment. Taking vacation in the summer, which is moving season in the Foreign Service, is almost impossible in the management section – as its customers, the service's members rely on it to ship their household items, cars, pets and personal effects.

At U.S. embassies, this section gets help in settling down new arrivals from the Community Liaison Office (CLO), which assigns volunteers to meet incoming staffers and their families, stock their refrigerators with groceries and show them the lay of the land. The management section also takes care of local employees, who usually get paid through a separate payroll system. In addition, it is responsible for the embassy's outside contracting of various services.

Security section

Everyone understands the need to provide the most reliable security to both embassies and diplomats – they represent high-level targets that have long appealed to terrorists. Visitors used to walk into U.S. diplomatic missions without any security checks to read or check out library books or attend events. Those days are long gone. In the aftermath of the 1998 bombing of the embassies in Kenya and Tanzania, and especially following the 9/11 terrorist attacks, embassies started resembling fortresses, with ever stricter measures that have angered many host-country officials. Embassy contacts now avoid going there if they can help it and prefer to hold meetings elsewhere. The United States is often accused of adopting a bunker mentality. The new rules have drastically restricted U.S. diplomats' movements in some countries, making the conduct of diplomacy increasingly difficult. These sections, which are known as regional security offices, are headed by DS agents. They supervise the Marine Security Guard Detachment and locally hired guards.

Foreign Commercial Service

The six State Department-staffed sections above are complemented by the other agencies that are part of the U.S. Foreign Service. The first one is the FCS, which is an agency in the Department of Commerce, with about 220 officers and more than 70 offices around the world.[16] While economic officers work mostly on policy matters and try to remove barriers that hurt American businesses in the host-country, their commercial colleagues directly help companies to identify export and investment opportunities abroad and create international sales strategies. Their paid services include market intelligence and analysis, as well as matchmaking with local firms. In embassies without a commercial section, the economic section performs these functions. Commercial diplomacy has developed significantly as a field in recent years and has become many countries' highest diplomatic priority.

Foreign Agricultural Service

The FAS is an agency within the Department of Agriculture (USDA) and has more than 100 offices overseas.[17] Its diplomats gather market intelligence, maintain and expand access to foreign markets, promote U.S. agricultural exports and help developing countries improve their agricultural capacity. The service "provides cost-share funding to U.S. agricultural producers and processors to develop new markets and to mitigate the adverse effects of trade barriers," former officer Susan Phillips wrote in the Washington International Diplomatic Academy's Diplomatic Diary in 2023.[18] The APHIS, another agency within the USDA, is also part of the Foreign Service. With offices in 27 countries, it helps to ensure the health of agricultural imports to the United States and assists foreign governments in building capacity to control, manage and eradicate pests and diseases.[19]

USAID

In recent decades, development has become a de facto part of diplomacy. Foreign aid used to be viewed mainly as an expression of humanitarianism, compassion or charity. Nowadays, donor countries consider it an investment in regional and global stability, and even in their own security. As noted in Chapter 1, in the years after 9/11, both the George W. Bush and Obama administrations argued that poorly governed or failed states often end up giving their territory over to terrorists, traffickers or other criminals. That makes them dangerous places from which transnational threats emerge.

USAID works in more than 100 countries to reduce poverty, strengthen democratic governance, provide disaster relief and help people to emerge from crises.[20] The sectors on which it focuses include health, emergency response, food security, family planning, water supply and environmental protection, among many others. U.S. foreign aid spending has long been less than 1 percent of the federal budget. In 2021, it was about $28 million.[21] USAID sections are called "missions," which can be confusing, since they are still part of the overall U.S. diplomatic mission, or embassy. In many developing countries, the USAID mission is the largest part of the embassy, sometimes almost as big as the rest of the post, and often in a separate location. Its Foreign Service officers manage programs and oversee projects that are contracted to U.S. and local organizations. Those projects may be trying to reduce maternal or child mortality, improve sanitation conditions or water filtration, increase immunization rates or reform rural education.

Defense office

The defense attaché and their team manage the military relationship with the host-country and any military assistance it might receive from the sending state. This section may include representatives of different armed services, such as army, navy and air force. The chain of command can be complicated. In a U.S. embassy, the defense attaché reports to both the chief of mission and the Defense Intelligence Agency (DIA) in Washington. In addition, they may report to a regional military commander, such as the head of U.S. European Command. As the senior defense official at post, the attaché has authority over all military personnel, except the Marine Security Guard Detachment, which, as we saw earlier, is supervised by the regional security officer. An embassy may also have an office of defense cooperation, responsible for sales, delivery and monitoring of military equipment and training in the host-country. Sometimes that office helps during natural disasters, humanitarian operations, and even with goodwill projects like building schools, clinics or bridges.

Intelligence station

The senior intelligence official in an embassy is typically known to the host-government and serves as the main point of contact on intelligence matters. The term "attaché" is not used in this case, and the section has different names, depending on the sending state. Most of us have watched enough spy movies to be familiar with the phrases "CIA station" and "station chief." Unlike diplomats, intelligence officers often collect information covertly – it is raw, unprocessed and does not become intelligence until it has been analyzed and collated. Relations between spies and diplomats are usually complex, challenging and frequently tense. In U.S. embassies, all intelligence activities must be approved by the chief of mission, with rare exceptions. The reason is to ensure that any potentially negative effects would not damage the relationship with the host-country beyond repair. However, intelligence officers are driven chiefly by security interests, rather than diplomatic relations, which can lead to conflict. Competition and friction can also occur between intelligence and defense officials, because the latter collect military intelligence, and both sides sometimes complain about encroachment on their territory.

Law-enforcement agencies

Many embassies have a legal attaché representing the home-country's Ministry of Justice. In the case of the United States, these officials work for the DOJ, and more specifically the FBI. They work with the host-government to obtain information on crimes and criminals that have harmed – or could harm – U.S. citizens or interests. As we saw at the beginning of the chapter, the DEA has offices in some countries. So does the DHS and some of its components, such as Immigration and Customs Enforcement (ICE), which helps the consular section to screen visa applicants, and Customs and Border Protection (CBP), which runs so-called preclearance facilities at several foreign airports. Travelers flying to the United States from those airports undergo immigration and customs procedures before they board a plane, instead of on arrival. Some U.S. embassies form a multiagency law-enforcement group chaired by the DCM to ensure better coordination.

Other agencies

The sections above by no means exhaust the list of government agencies represented at embassies, no matter the sending country. There can be dozens of such agencies in large U.S. diplomatic missions, some of which we mentioned earlier. There are two organizations that are part of the government but, for the most part, tend to stay away from embassies. The first, the Peace Corps, is familiar to most Americans, but the second, the U.S. Agency for Global Media, is not. Peace Corps volunteers in more than 60 countries live and work in local communities to help them tackle their most pressing challenges in health, education, the environment and many other areas. Although they usually go to embassies only on holidays like Independence Day and Thanksgiving, the Peace Corps director is a member of the country team. The Agency for Global Media is the umbrella organization of six government broadcasters, including the Voice of America (VOA), Radio Free Europe (RFE) and the Middle East Broadcasting Network (MBN). To the surprise of many, VOA foreign correspondents with U.S. citizenship, who are professional journalists, are considered members of the Foreign Service.

Constituent posts

Consulates general, consulates, presence posts and other diplomatic offices outside the host-country's capital are an embassy's constituent posts. There may be a constituent post, such as a consulate or embassy office, in a country that does not host an embassy. Before the U.S. Embassy in the Seychelles reopened in 2023 after a 27-year absence, the embassy in Mauritius was also responsible for the Seychelles. An embassy office opened in the Seychelles in 2022, in preparation for the reopening of the new embassy there.

You may have heard of honorary consuls. They are a unique kind of official representatives, who are not considered diplomats, because they are private citizens who may not be nationals of the sending country. Honorary consuls are based in places where the government for which they work does not have a diplomatic mission. They are not paid and usually practice another profession. Germany has honorary consuls in more than 30 American cities, including Orlando, Denver and Honolulu. The only one in California is in San Diego, because there are consulates general in Los Angeles and San Francisco. The assistance they provide is limited to general information and notary services, and some are able to accept passport applications. It is still a good idea to contact an honorary consul even if you need help from an embassy, because they can connect you with the right office and save you time navigating a government bureaucracy.[22] The State Department requires honorary consuls representing foreign countries in the United States to be U.S. citizens or permanent residents. However, they may not "hold an office of profit or trust with the U.S. government."[23]

Local embassy staff

Diplomats rotate in and out of embassies every few years, but local employees often serve for decades. They are a diplomatic mission's institutional memory, and great Foreign Service officers regularly ask for their advice – Francis Ricciardone calls them "the secret to an officer's success." Local staff members "unlock the mysteries and the hidden portals of their societies when treated with respect," he told Nicholas Kralev.[24] Almost every section and agency in U.S. embassies have local staff, who usually outnumber the Americans. For example, in 2023, the CDC had 80 staffers in Tanzania, and only 14 of them were Americans. "Our diplomatic missions simply could not function without our remarkably talented and loyal locally employed colleagues," William Burns told Kralev. "Working with them at posts as diverse as Amman and Moscow has been one of the genuine highlights of my career."[25]

Interagency challenges and solutions

The President's Emergency Plan for AIDS Relief, better known as PEPFAR, is a U.S. program created in 2003 that has invested more than $100 billion in the fight against the Human Immunodeficiency Virus (HIV) and Acquired Immune Deficiency Syndrome (AIDS). According to the State Department, it represents the largest commitment by any government to combat "a single disease in history," having saved 25 million lives, supported antiretroviral therapy for 20 million adults and children, and made it possible for nearly 5.5 million babies of mothers with HIV to be born free of the virus.[26]

Although PEPFAR is housed in the State Department, USAID and CDC usually take the lead in implementation abroad. Most of the $100 billion has been spent in Africa, where in some countries, PEPFAR provides more than 90 percent of the entire U.S. development budget. Every year, there is fierce rivalry between USAID, CDC and sometimes other agencies to get a bigger piece of the resources that have been allocated to a particular country. As a result, chiefs of mission and DCMs have to act as referees between agencies. "USAID may have better connections and more experience in a certain country, but CDC may be more efficient and have a greater impact," Virginia Blaser told Kralev. The ambassador or DCM should not be seen as favoring one agency over another. So it is a serious challenge, and it is made worse by the fact that both agencies provide similar services, sometimes in the same building, but they rarely cooperate, Blaser added.[27]

The importance of running the interagency in diplomatic missions effectively and skillfully cannot be overstated. As noted at the beginning of the chapter, it is an uphill battle, because of the different cultures and agendas of the agencies, the limited experience working in such a unique environment many of their staffers have, and the lack of proper training before they are sent abroad. "It's hard to galvanize and gain the confidence of the interagency, so that you can get them to work together towards one purpose," Blaser said. "I don't think institutionally they are created to do that very well." She recalled a U.S. Secret Service representative briefing her on an operation in a country where she was the DCM. She realized that the embassy's regional security office was working on another case in the same town and thought that they could be connected. The two offices, however, had not talked to each other. "So I had to be essentially a telephone operator," Blaser said.

John Feeley and James Nealon, the former ambassadors in Central America, explored the reasons for the different bureaucratic cultures in 2022. "Most DEA agents have been U.S. street cops. Most DOJ officials sent overseas have served as assistant U.S. attorneys or are career DOJ staff – folks for whom judicial independence, the sanctity of an investigation and the sacrosanct pursuit of a conviction in a U.S. court trump all other considerations," they wrote. "This makes for an extremely bad fit when joining a diplomatic organization, where relationships and policy goals are measured in shades of frustrating gray, and where the ambassador is, by presidential order, the boss." Not only do such officials fail to coordinate and collaborate with other agencies, but they often "freelance," instead of consulting with the chief of mission or the DCM, Feeley and Nealon wrote.[28]

As ambassadors and DCMs, we were confronted with one type of interagency friction or another almost every week. Resolving disputes and finding fair solutions requires patience and perseverance, as well as the ability to communicate a common mission and inspire others to work toward it as one team. The quintessential example of interagency dysfunction in the U.S. government is 9/11, when the failure of the FBI, CIA and other agencies to share information they possessed prevented them from detecting the al-Qaeda plot to hijack commercial aircraft and fly them into buildings. The implementation of some of the post-9/11 policies overseas led to interagency challenges as well.

In 2002, Washington tasked U.S. embassies in countries with Muslim communities to conduct outreach meant to explain that the United States was not at war with their religion, but with terrorism. Charles Ray was the ambassador to Cambodia at the time. He, along with the political and public diplomacy sections, meaning the State Department, wanted to fund an educational program for ethnic Cham, a small Muslim community that was often overlooked by the host-government. Funding, however, had to come from USAID, and its director in Cambodia was not on board with the idea. The agency's policies required it to fund countrywide programs, not specific groups, he explained. A compromise resulted in a program for underserved Cambodians, which did not name any particular groups. It significantly changed the Cham's and others' perceptions of the United States.

A well-run country team is essential to effective interagency cooperation. The weekly team meetings should not be just a briefing for the ambassador by section and agency heads, but a forum for exchange of information, views and ideas, so that everyone knows and understands everything going on that is important to their work. And those meetings should not be where the cooperation stops. If the ambassador hears about a key development or a serious problem for the first time at the meeting, it may already be too late. Team members should keep the front office, as well as each other, in the loop and work together more than once a week. Below the senior leadership, mid-level and even junior officers should also be included in the process, at least as notetakers. That would allow them to see how things work and appreciate the value of the interagency early in their careers, so that one day they can run it more efficiently.

Most U.S. embassies have one or two junior Foreign Service officers assigned as assistants to the front office, which provides the best education on how a diplomatic

Figure 5.3 Charles Ray (left), the U.S. ambassador to Cambodia, with Secretary of State Colin Powell during Powell's 2003 visit to Phnom Penh.
Photo by Hoang Dinh Nam/AFP via Getty Images.

mission works. As key staff aides, they see almost everything that comes to the attention of the ambassador and the DCM and get to attend meetings to which they would have no access otherwise. Since those positions are few, when Blaser was DCM in Uganda, she created a system that allowed junior officers from all parts of the embassy to rotate through the front office for several weeks. "I think every single one of them" took advantage of this opportunity, Blaser said. "They came out much better officers who were easier for us to work with, because they knew even the most parochial issues."[29]

Key relationships at post

Building and maintaining relationships is at the heart of diplomacy, and for an embassy, they are not limited to the host-government. An overseas mission's relations with headquarters are crucial to its ability to perform its functions and carry out policy. Chiefs of mission, DCMs and all other diplomats are often confronted with difficult choices and even ethical dilemmas when the interests and agendas of different institutions and players clash. This is one of the reasons why having a collaborative country team is so important. If an embassy can speak with one voice, problems can be resolved much more effectively.

Managing the relationship with the host-country naturally begins with the government. As noted earlier, the Ministry of Foreign Affairs is typically an embassy's main interlocutor, though a good diplomatic mission works with many other ministries and agencies, as well as directly with the president or prime minister. It also does not limit its engagement to the executive branch. Both institutional and personal relations with legislators and their staff can be critical in achieving policy objectives. Relationships with all major political parties, civil society, the private sector, the media, academia and other parts of society are not only useful but critical. You never know where you may have to turn and who may be in a position to help you in a time of need.

This is especially true when the official relations with the host-government are strained or downright hostile. Suspending all diplomatic activity is rarely a good option in such cases, and the embassy's job becomes even more difficult. For more than two decades, U.S.–Venezuela ties have been in a dire state. When the national government wanted little to do with the U.S. Embassy, contacts and relationships built and cultivated elsewhere in the country helped its diplomats to do their jobs – until 2019, when Caracas broke off diplomatic relations and the embassy had to close.[30]

When it comes to public diplomacy, U.S. embassies in states with unfriendly governments try to reach the public directly, even if the authorities disapprove. Relations between the United States and Zimbabwe were at an all-time low when Charles Ray was ambassador there in the early 2010s. Anti-American hardliners in the government tried to block the embassy's outreach to the Zimbabwean people, especially the youth, which was a priority group in the post's public diplomacy strategy. Those officials intimidated people to keep them from attending embassy meetings and events at outside venues. Aware that many young Zimbabweans accessed the Internet on their phones via providers in South Africa, the embassy communicated with them through text messages and social media chats. It also live-tweeted Ray's speeches and posted videos on YouTube. That neutralized the government's propaganda and bullying efforts.

Career ambassadors are sometimes accused of prioritizing good ties with their host-country over certain policy goals advocated by headquarters, because that makes their job easier. In Washington, most of those accusers tend to be political appointees with a particular agenda or law-enforcement agencies that want to take actions likely to anger the receiving government. Ambassadors who understand how Washington works and know the key players there have the best chance of handling such tricky situations deftly. On one hand, they must speak truth to power and explain to a less-than-receptive audience that a particular domestic constituency's short-term desires could have negative long-term consequences for U.S. national security. On the other hand, they have to realize that policymakers back home have to juggle a wide range of tasks and issues, with an ever-increasing competition for their attention. As diplomats, it falls on them to reconcile cultural, political and bureaucratic differences into a common vision.

Other types of relationships an embassy has are those with other diplomatic missions in the host-country. Sometimes the reason may be simply to exchange information – both for official purposes and to share tips about life as an expat – and other times a collaboration can lead to a common action. In many countries, U.S. and European embassies cooperate on matters of mutual interest, which often gives their efforts more weight and influence.

The Foreign Service way of life

It has become clear by now what a peculiar way of life diplomats lead. They witness history in the making and help to shape it, they dine with presidents and kings and meet fascinating people. But they also contend with hazardous living conditions and security threats in many countries. The downside of moving around every few years is being uprooted and having to start a new life in every place. By spending most of their careers far from home, diplomats give up many of the things their compatriots take for granted, such as the ability to help an aging parent and attend family gatherings.

This is not meant to scare you from choosing to serve your country through diplomacy. Quite the opposite; we hope to encourage more people to consider diplomatic careers. But we want you to know what to expect – both the opportunities and the challenges – and to be prepared for what may come your way. No two Foreign Service officers have the same career path, which depends heavily on where they serve and with whom they work. The more you know about the system and the better you understand its intricacies and quirks, the more control you will have over your career and your family life. Through it all, nothing will be more important than your integrity and reputation.

A diplomatic service is a government bureaucracy, where rank and hierarchy are entrenched and unavoidable. You may not think highly of your bosses, but you have to show them respect and perform the tasks they assign to you. At the same time, in spite of the strict hierarchy, all embassy staff belong to the same unique community, and on a human level, you and your boss may be going through the same personal challenges. Whether you are coping with the effects of pollution or your children are having difficulties adjusting to a new school in yet another country, common circumstances and problems will inevitably lead to relationships with your colleagues outside the office.

You cannot forget, however, that you are still co-workers with various ranks, which makes for a tricky balancing act. So when you arrive at a new post, take special care to forge relationships and friendships that will serve you well both professionally and personally. You may already know someone from a previous tour, and even if you do not, you will most likely have mutual friends with many of your new colleagues. After all, even the world's largest diplomatic service is not that large. Remember to treat everyone kindly, including your subordinates and the staff of the management section responsible for your residence. If you are in a developing country, do not expect conveniences you take for granted in the West, and if something needs fixing in your house, keep in mind that yours is not the only problem that requires attention.

When it comes to rank, the U.S. Foreign Service has both rank in person and in position, which can be confusing. Rank in person means that every officer has a personal grade. With few exceptions, officers come in at the entry level and, when promoted, move up to the mid-level and the senior service. There are three or more grades at each level. For example, once you are a senior officer, you can be a "counselor," "minister counselor," "career minister" or "career ambassador." Separately, every position at an embassy has a grade attached to it. A job may be designated as a minister counselor, and ideally, the officer occupying it is a minister counselor as well. In reality, a match is not always possible, and the person may be less or more senior.

All these grades and ranks are known and used only internally for personnel purposes, and no one outside the U.S. government is aware of them. To make things even more complicated, there is another system that is internationally recognized, so diplomats from different countries know each other's rank without the need of a tutorial in other governments' bureaucracies. For example, almost every embassy – regardless of the sending or receiving state – has one or more first secretaries, who are generally upper-midlevel officers, and some missions have second and third secretaries. Entry-level diplomats are usually third secretaries or vice consuls. And in some countries' embassies, the DCM has the rank of minister, which has nothing to do with a Cabinet minister.

There are few more consequential decisions in a diplomat's career than where they serve. Most countries allow their diplomats at least some say in selecting their next assignment, and in a large organization like the U.S. Foreign Service, there is a complex bidding system. Although service members are required to be available for postings worldwide, they cannot be forced to go to a place against their will, except in extraordinary circumstances. Bidding is a skill that has to be acquired. As a Foreign Service officer, you will have to consider a myriad of professional and personal factors.

First and foremost, you have to decide what your priority is for your next assignment: enhancing your career or making your family happy. Having the best of both worlds is rarely possible. Serving in a developing country may be very satisfying, because you will likely make a big difference. But if your spouse or partner cannot work and has nothing meaningful to do, they will be miserable, which will affect you sooner or later. If you are about to have a baby and need top-notch medical care, or if you have a child with special needs, going to a developed country would make most sense, even though the work there may not be too exciting. If you are single, you need to decide whether you want to remain single or not – that will likely lead to different conclusions about the best assignment. And if you identify as lesbian, gay, bisexual, transgender or queer (LGBTQ), you may want to avoid countries where you might not be welcomed or safe.

Once you have selected your top choices on the bidlist, you will do well to learn as much as possible about each post, its current leadership, your prospective position and your direct supervisor. A job may sound amazing, but if that post is plagued with chaos and dysfunction because of poor management, or if your boss is abusive, you will almost certainly have a bad tour. It is also important to be honest with yourself about whether you are ready for the responsibilities of the position you are seeking.

As ambassador to Russia in 1993, Thomas Pickering offered William Burns the role of DCM. Burns, however, declined. He had just started learning Russian in preparation for an assignment as the political section chief in Moscow, and he had not headed a section before. Without that experience, he did not think that he would make a great DCM. In addition, because Pickering did not speak Russian, Burns believed that the DCM should be fluent. "I wasn't ready," he told Nicholas Kralev. "I wanted to do it right."[31] The following year, he began his previously planned tour as the embassy's political counselor, and in 2005, he returned to Moscow as ambassador.

Most career diplomats choose their profession because of a desire for public service. Their work has little to do with themselves – it is about their country and its interests. At the same time, however, most of us aim to grow professionally, and when it comes to career development for diplomats, governments fail to rise to the task. So you have to be proactive and persistent in securing opportunities for training, bidding on assignments, promotions and other aspects of the diplomatic way of life for which you are at the mercy of the bureaucracy. There is no shame in advocating for yourself, as long as you do it with humility, rather than hubris. If there is a better recipe for success, at least in the U.S. Foreign Service, it has escaped our combined experience of more than six decades.

Case Study: Double Problem in Zimbabwe

In 2010, the governor of Zimbabwe's Masvingo Province imposed restrictions on the operations of foreign nongovernmental organizations (NGOs), which went far beyond previously taken measures by the authoritarian national government of President Robert Mugabe. The United States opposed such actions anywhere in the world and reacted strongly whenever they occurred. The practice was for its ambassador in the country in question to issue a statement condemning the restrictions. Not long before this happened in Zimbabwe, an American tourist had been arrested in the same province and was being threatened with espionage charges. A conviction would have meant a death sentence.

Charles Ray was the U.S. ambassador at the time, and as noted earlier, U.S.–Zimbabwe relations were at an all-time low. He knew that, if he issued a statement against the new NGO restrictions, it was likely to negatively affect

Case Study: (cont.)

the arrested tourist. If he were to forgo voicing a condemnation, there was no guarantee that would benefit the detained American. The State Department's Bureau of Democracy, Human Rights and Labor advocated for a statement, but the department let Ray make the decision. He called a meeting of the country team and asked for recommendations from the political and consular section chiefs, the regional security officer and the USAID mission director. Based on the recommendations and his own assessment, Ray decided against a statement on the NGO matter. If queried by the media, he would respond in a measured tone. He asked the Zimbabwe desk officer at the State Department to block any statement on the specific issue from Washington, at least until the U.S. citizen was released. In the meantime, he approached senior officials of the provincial governor's political party, which ruled the entire country, outlining both problems and requesting their assistance in resolving them.

Within a week, those officials came through. Not only were all charges against the American tourist dropped, but he received an apology and an official escort to the border. The Masvingo governor rescinded his NGO restrictions, under pressure from senior party officials and other governors – assuming his initial announcement had not been just political posturing. The U.S. NGOs that had been caught up in the case thanked Ray for not intervening, because that could have derailed their own efforts to find a solution. Ray and his team leveraged relationships in the host-country's ruling party, in Washington and with American NGOs working in Zimbabwe to resolve two potentially dangerous situations. Bilateral relations did not really improve, but diplomacy is about winning small battles one at a time much more often than scoring an outright victory.

Exercise 1: Vietnam Visa Line

In 1998, the United States opened a consulate general in Ho Chi Minh City, formerly Saigon, for the first time since the Vietnam War. Charles Ray was appointed consul general. The building was on a busy street along which many local Communist Party officials were driven on their way to and from the party headquarters nearby.

The new consulate presented an opportunity for Vietnamese citizens to apply for U.S. visas. There were so many applicants that the consular section could hardly keep up. Before 9/11, there was no appointment system like the one today, and people simply queued up. The line in Ho Chi Minh City became so long that it crowded the street, with applicants waiting outside for hours, often in intolerable

Exercise 1: (cont.)

weather conditions. The state-controlled media complained frequently and loudly, as did the Ministry of Foreign Affairs, which accused the consulate of subjecting the host-country's citizens to unacceptable hardship.

For Ray, the more likely reason for the outrage was that the pictures of so many Vietnamese standing in the long line for a chance to travel to the United States worried and offended the Communist Party. Whatever the motive, he decided that something had to be done and tasked his staff with preparing recommendations. There was not enough room inside the consulate to accommodate all applicants, but there was space on the compound that could be utilized. Ray decided that a waiting area should be built there, so applicants could be inside the fence and not in the street. He wrote an opinion article in a local newspaper explaining the plan and heard no more complaints.

Today, visa interviews are scheduled in advance, and applicants arrive at a specific time, rather than queuing up outside without an appointment.

Task: How would you assess the resolution Ray found? What types of relationships did this case involve? Which sections of the consulate had a stake in it? What were the risks of doing nothing or delaying resolution? What else would you have done?

Exercise 2: Renovating the Ambassador's Residence

You work in the management section of an embassy. The ambassador's spouse wants to renovate the chief of mission's residence, but there are no funds in this year's budget for such a costly project – there may be just enough money to repaint the large house. Your boss, the section chief, has tasked you with working things out with the ambassador's spouse, who does not take "no" for an answer. In deciding how to proceed, consider the following questions:

- Would you try to explore other options to fund a renovation? Would you consult with headquarters? Would you seek to raise funds from the private sector?
- If your attempts to find the necessary resources fail, what will you tell the ambassador's spouse? How would you communicate the message? Would you talk to the ambassador?
- If the ambassador or the spouse wants to divert money inappropriately from another part of the budget, what would you do?
- If the renovation falls through and the ambassador tries to hurt your career, how would you react?

ADDITIONAL RESOURCES

Marshall P. Adair, *Lessons from a Diplomatic Life: Watching Flowers from Horseback* (Rowman & Littlefield, 2012).

Scott Alan Ast, *Managing Security Overseas: Protecting Employees and Assets in Volatile Regions* (CRC Press, 2009).

Shawn Dorman, *Inside a U.S. Embassy: Diplomacy at Work*, 3rd ed. (Foreign Service Books, 2011).

6 Political Tradecraft

EUNICE REDDICK AND GINA ABERCROMBIE-WINSTANLEY

The U.S. ambassador's Cadillac was just steps away, but every time Marie Yovanovitch tried to make a run for it, bullets streaked past the entrance to the ambassador's residence. When she finally made it to the car, she lay on the floor – with four colleagues inside, there was no helmet or bulletproof vest left for Yovanovitch, and sitting up was too dangerous. In the back seat, the ambassador, Thomas Pickering, leaned over her, in part to protect her and in part not to be visible through the windows. When they arrived at the U.S. Embassy, Yovanovitch learned that intense fighting had raged in the streets surrounding the compound the day before. Pickering considered an evacuation, but the local authorities could not guarantee safe passage to the airport for the American staff.

Having served in Somalia, Yovanovitch did not expect to contend with gunfire and shelling in Moscow. Just weeks into her tour as a political officer in 1993, Russian President Boris Yeltsin tried to dissolve parliament, even though the country's constitution did not give him the power to do so. Lawmakers quickly impeached him, and afraid that he might arrest them or take over the legislature if they left, they barricaded themselves in the building, known as the Russian White House. They brought in food, blankets and weapons and settled in for what was likely to turn into a long standoff. Large crowds of supporters gathered outside, and Yeltsin ordered his forces to surround the area and establish a security perimeter to control who went in and out.

The U.S. Embassy ended up inside the security perimeter, but that did not mean it was safe – rather, it was perilously close to the fighting. The army destroyed the White House and hunted down opposition supporters in the streets around both the embassy and Pickering's residence, known as Spaso House. Yeltsin won, but 187 Russian civilians died and 437 were wounded, police said.[1] A sniper shot one of the embassy's marine guards, in an apparent case of mistaken identity, but a fellow marine quickly compressed the wound, saving his life. When hostilities ceased, embassy staff found the compound walls full of bullets. Many other buildings in the area had bloodstains on their facades.

Yovanovitch's job through all this was to report on what was happening and provide analysis in diplomatic cables to Washington. After the standoff was over, she and her colleagues in the political section started "fanning out to discover what the past week's events meant for Russia's future," she recalled in her memoir.[2]

"We had to work hard to find many of our usual contacts. Some were in hiding, while others weren't around, because their offices had been destroyed in the fighting." The experience of that early fall in 1993 was harrowing, and a reminder that diplomats get caught up in dangerous crises more often than the vast majority of the public realizes, including civil unrest, coups d'état, terrorist attacks and even wars. Despite the risk, "I was finally doing exactly what I had joined the Foreign Service to do: reporting on historic change and trying to make sense of it, so that Washington could make the best policy choices," Yovanovitch wrote.

The ability to interpret and navigate an often bewildering world is a core skill of diplomacy. In that endeavor, the role of an embassy's political section is indispensable. Its reporting and analysis help translate – both literally and figuratively – the host-country to headquarters and vice versa. With its finger on the host-society's pulse, and with eyes and ears in government, opposition circles, civil society, the private sector and the media, the political section is also "an early warning radar for troubles and opportunities," in William Burns's words.[3] The information it gathers and provides to officials in the home-capital helps them to formulate policy – and once decisions are made, it helps to carry them out on the ground.

What is political tradecraft?

Political tradecraft is a **set of duties, responsibilities and skills required of diplomats who work in political affairs**. It is the main instrument in the diplomatic tradecraft toolbox, which also includes economic tradecraft, commercial diplomacy, consular affairs and public diplomacy, among other tools. As explained in the previous chapter, political officers are career diplomats, not political appointees. They work both at diplomatic missions abroad and at headquarters, such as their Ministry of Foreign Affairs or the State Department. Although there are some differences in a political officer's daily duties at home compared to those abroad, they all participate in managing international relations and implementing foreign policy. Those who rise to the most senior positions in their ministry or department also take part in the policymaking process.

Political officers need to possess all the skills described in Chapter 3. Managing relations with other countries begins with building and cultivating a diverse network of sources who can provide the most accurate and useful information, for which curiosity, interpersonal skills and language ability are essential. Empathy helps to win the trust and confidence of others, and to understand where they are coming from in their decision-making. Aside from emergencies, political officers rarely send raw information to their capitals or other governments – rather, it has to be processed. This is where mastering the entire set of communication and analytical skills can make a big difference. Whether you are drafting a cable to headquarters, a memo to your boss or a document to a foreign government, your writing must be clear, concise, to the point, grammatically correct and easy to digest. In meetings with foreign interlocutors, active listening is imperative, and adhering to the norms of cross-cultural communication goes a long way.

In policy implementation, judgment and creativity are critical as you try to determine the best ways to carry out decisions made at headquarters in a foreign environment. Whatever those ways are, you will need advocacy and negotiation skills to ensure that your country's policies and actions are correctly understood, and to persuade foreign officials to modify their behavior should that be in your national interest. In all your work as a political officer, you must do your best to align other countries' interests with those of your own government, even if you disagree personally with a particular decision or an entire policy. This is the most difficult part of political tradecraft, and we will discuss it further later on in the chapter.

Traditionally, managing people and programs has been neglected as a skill set required of political officers, who tend to be policy wonks with little zeal for operational matters. That is changing, at least in the U.S. Foreign Service. When Colin Powell became secretary of state in 2001, he was perplexed by what he saw as a paradox: of all career tracks, political officers went on to become chiefs and deputy chiefs of mission more than anyone else. But even though many had to manage local staff, generally, political officers had the least management and leadership experience. So Powell instituted mandatory training to get promoted, which his successors have continued, and opened up more opportunities for officers from other career tracks to compete for leadership positions.

What type of subject matters do political officers work on as they carry out their main duties of reporting and analysis, managing relationships and implementing policy? In the 21st century, bilateral and multilateral issues have become less distinct than they were for much of the previous century, largely because of globalization and technological advances. Security and migration, for example, have long had bilateral aspects to them, but they cannot be effectively addressed today if governments ignore regional and even global conditions and contexts. Other areas of responsibility for political officers include human rights, arms control and nonproliferation, terrorism, trafficking in drugs and persons, as well as other transnational crimes. Even climate change, extreme poverty and infectious diseases have significant political implications.

In managing a country's foreign relations, success is impossible unless the headquarters and its diplomatic missions in the field are on the same page, and ideally, in lockstep. That takes constant coordination and regular communication, at the heart of which are political officers. When the U.S. government needs something from a foreign country, officers at the State Department work with that country's embassy in Washington, and officers posted in the receiving state work with its government through the Ministry of Foreign Affairs. Like all career diplomats, political officers work both at home and abroad during various times in their careers, and they need to master the fundamentals of political tradecraft no matter where they are.

That includes multilateral organizations, whether one represents a particular member-state at its mission to the organization or works as an international civil servant. The United Nations has a political department headed by the undersecretary-general for political affairs, the world body's third-highest position, which is usually occupied by a career diplomat with decades of experience. The officers who work in that department hail from dozens of countries, but in their work, they should be guided by the interests of the organization, not those of their motherlands – this is no easy job, and we will discuss details in the chapter on multilateral diplomacy. In spite of that significant difference, many aspects of political tradecraft apply in this case as well.

The political headquarters

Cameron Munter was seething. His taxi was rapidly nearing the Embassy of Czechoslovakia in Washington, his destination, but he was still struggling to reconcile his personal disagreement with the assignment he had been instructed to carry out. It was September 1989, and Shirley Temple Black, the former child-actor, had just become U.S. ambassador in Prague. Determined to leave a mark, she set out to improve Washington's relations with the communist state by ending an 11-year freeze in ministerial-level contacts. She persistently lobbied Secretary of State James Baker to meet with Czechoslovak Foreign Minister Jaromir Johannes during the annual opening session of the U.N. General Assembly (UNGA) in New York later that month.

Munter was the country desk officer for Czechoslovakia in the State Department's European bureau, responsible for managing the day-to-day relationship with the country, which was still behind the Iron Curtain. "I thought the Baker meeting was a terrible idea," especially without a concession from the Czechoslovaks, Munter told Nicholas Kralev. "But Shirley Temple got Baker to agree, and I was given the job of announcing it to the Czechoslovak Embassy." Only four years into his Foreign Service career, Munter was in no position to argue or refuse to do as told. Still, he wondered if there might be a quid pro quo he could extract from the embassy.

As his taxi sped up a hill on Connecticut Avenue, Munter remembered that the government in Prague had recently prevented a prominent Czechoslovak dissident, Zdenek Urbánek, from visiting the United States on a fellowship he had been awarded. During most of the Cold War, citizens of the so-called Eastern bloc were not allowed to travel abroad without an "exit visa," which was not easy to obtain. Munter quickly devised a plan. "The cab dropped me off at the embassy," he recalled. "I walked in and told my contact, 'I have a deal for you: if you give Urbánek an exit visa, we'll give you a meeting with Baker.' He immediately said, 'Deal.' So Johannes met with Baker, and Urbánek arrived in the United States in October."[4]

On November 9, the Berlin Wall was breached, leading to the collapse of all Soviet-allied authoritarian regimes in Central and Eastern Europe. Three years later, Czechoslovakia broke up into two states, the Czech Republic and Slovakia. Munter never told his bosses about the "deal" he struck, but it did wonders in assuaging his frustration with carrying out an instruction he deemed a mistake. It also gave him a good reason to stay in the Foreign Service.

Politics and policy

The terms "international relations" and "international politics" are not quite the same thing, but they share a significant overlap and heavily influence each other. The political aspect of a bilateral relationship usually receives the most attention by governments and the media, even when economic, commercial or other ties may have a bigger practical importance. This is why many in the public, to the extent they ever think about diplomacy, associate it entirely with what political officers do, unaware of the rest of its toolbox.

The primacy of politics is also the reason the political department is the most powerful in any Ministry of Foreign Affairs, and its head, known as "political director," is typically among the highest-ranking officials. At the State Department in Washington, that is the undersecretary of state for political affairs, usually a professional diplomat from the political career track who oversees all bureaus responsible for the world's geographic regions. Both William Burns and Thomas Pickering have held that position, which sits at the intersection of politics and policy, macromanaging political relations with foreign countries and coordinating policy toward those states.

As chief diplomats, ministers of foreign affairs or secretaries of state naturally lead both bilateral and multilateral political engagement abroad and serve as key policymakers. So what do political directors do? In diplomacy, for something to rise to the ministerial level, a lot of work needs to be done by the bureaucracy first. Position papers, objectives and strategies go through multiple iterations, and political directors and bureau heads oversee that process. It includes consultations with other parts of the interagency with stakes in the issue at hand, which can result in meetings of the policy committees described in Chapter 4. The process may also involve engagement with foreign officials at the working level to gauge what the sides can realistically achieve or to iron out any disagreements before the matter goes up to the minister.

When the George W. Bush administration decided to explore negotiations with Iran alongside five other countries in 2008, Secretary of State Condoleezza Rice put Burns in charge as undersecretary for political affairs. He kept both that position and the Iran portfolio after Hillary Clinton succeeded Rice in the first term of the Obama administration and started direct talks with the Iranians to prevent them from building a nuclear weapons capability. In 2015, not long after Burns retired, another secretary of state, John Kerry, led the negotiations to the finish line, reaching a deal with Tehran.[5]

Career diplomats make a meaningful distinction between politics and policy – they are involved in driving and implementing policy, and they follow and analyze the politics of other countries, but as public servants, they must stay away from domestic politics at home. Still, as noted in earlier chapters, they regularly have to contend with domestic politics, especially when serving at headquarters. For example, those who were involved in the Iran deal saw it as the best way to ensure that Tehran did not develop a nuclear weapon, at least in the short and medium terms. They did not view it through a domestic political lens or as a partisan issue. In 2018, however, Donald Trump withdrew the United States from the deal.[6] Some Foreign Service officers who had worked on the negotiations were forced to retire or were otherwise punished by Trump administration officials. Keeping professional diplomacy and the career Foreign Service apolitical in a decidedly political environment is no easy feat. Political appointees are an asset if they are qualified and put the national interest above that of their party. But injecting partisanship makes diplomacy less effective and hurts the national interest.

Duties of domestic assignments

Cameron Munter was still a junior officer when he served as Czechoslovakia desk officer. Country desk officers at the State Department or in ministries of foreign affairs are usually junior or lower-midlevel diplomats, but they play an outsized role in managing relations with the country or countries in their portfolio on a daily basis. In Washington, one officer staffs the entire Nepal desk, while there are more than a dozen in the Office of India Affairs, responsible for different aspects of the relationship with India, including security, economic, etc. Consequently, not all of them come from the political career track. Most country desks have one or two officers. In many ministries of foreign affairs, several countries or even entire regions may fall under the purview of one diplomat.

Serving as a country desk officer is a rite of passage for career diplomats. It provides unique opportunities to learn how to navigate the bureaucracy, become well-versed in policy issues, experience a high-pressure environment and make useful connections with both home-country and foreign officials. Country desk officers are typically housed in a ministry's regional bureaus or departments. For example, the Nigeria desk is in the Africa bureau. One can also work as a desk officer in what are known as functional bureaus, dedicated not to countries but to issues like human rights, arms control and multilateral organizations. At the State Department, both the regional and functional bureaus are headed by assistant secretaries, and deputy assistant secretaries are responsible for subregions or subtopics.

Another type of position in which one can work as a political officer at headquarters is staff assistant to a senior official. In Washington, these jobs tend to be very career-enhancing. Since the incumbents get a lot of face time with their superiors, if your boss likes you and can rely on you, you will likely have an influential and longtime supporter and promoter, who may even give you important senior positions some day. William Burns was one of two staff aides to the assistant secretary of state for Near East affairs during his second tour in the Foreign Service in the mid-1980s. The other one was David Satterfield, who went on to become ambassador to Turkey and Lebanon.

Duties of Country Desk Officers

- Monitor all major news and other developments in their assigned country and alert their bosses to matters that require higher-level attention. If questions related to that country are raised in meetings or come down the chain from top officials, the desk officer is the person most likely to receive them.
- Draft policy papers, talking points, media guidance and other documents for senior officials. Those include briefings to prepare principals for meetings or trips abroad, as well as memos to superiors that convey and analyze new information or make policy recommendations. On rare occasions when the senior leadership has instructions for a specific post in the field, it tasks the desk officer with writing the first draft.
- Provide oral briefings to the minister or secretary and their deputies. As secretary of state, Colin Powell was known for tasking desk officers with briefing President George W. Bush, which was highly unusual and a morale-booster.
- Serve as the main point of contact and support for their embassy and constituent posts in the host-country, monitoring the cable and email traffic coming from them and keeping them updated on developments at headquarters.
- Coordinate with fellow desk officers in other agencies to make sure that everyone is on the same page and their government speaks with one voice.
- Act as the main liaison with their assigned country's embassy in the home-capital and the go-to staffer when official diplomatic communication has to be delivered, whether electronically, by phone or in person. Such documents include diplomatic notes and notes verbale (see Chapter 8).

Political officers can also work at the State Department's Operations Center, the central node of a global network and a 24-hour communications and crisis-management hub. "The Watch," as it is known, provides a quick but in-depth education on how the department works, as well as invaluable insight into how the secretary of state communicates with leaders from around the world. In addition, political officers serve on the National Security Council staff at the White House, as explained in Chapter 4.

The political section abroad

Taiwan's strategic importance to the United States is no secret. Not only does Washington view the island as critical to its power projection in the Pacific, but as a shining example of a thriving democracy. U.S.–Taiwan relations are complicated, especially since the United States recognized Beijing as the seat of the Chinese government in 1978, as the case study in Chapter 2 explained. When Washington withdrew its formal diplomatic recognition from Taiwan, the U.S. Embassy there was renamed the American Institute in Taiwan, but it has continued to operate as a de facto embassy. The main practical difference is that it is led not by an ambassador but a director.

Although Taiwan has been democratic since 1987, the same party, the Kuomintang (KMT), ruled it for 55 years. In 2000, the opposition Democratic Progressive Party (DPP) won its first presidential election. Its anticipated victory prompted an insatiable appetite for information in Washington in the run-up to the election. U.S. officials wanted to learn as much as possible about the future leader, Chen Shui-bian, and his likely policies, and to figure out how he might change Taiwan's relationship with mainland China. While the United States helps to guarantee Taiwan's security, it does not support its formal independence and favors stable ties with Beijing.

The diplomatic reporting Washington expected from Taiwan naturally fell on the American Institute's political section, formally known as the general affairs section. Eunice Reddick, one of this chapter's authors, was the section chief. She and her staff did not wait for instructions to send a series of in-depth cables. In fact, the section had been writing dispatches about Chen and his views since he was mayor of Taipei, the capital, beginning in 1994. The reporting continued even after he lost his reelection bid four years later, because he was likely to run for president. In addition to Chen's background and political agenda, Reddick's section wrote about media and public reaction to his views and his record as mayor, as well as about political and other figures who could end up in his administration. The section also examined Chen's experience with mainland officials and analyzed the potential impact of his support for Taiwan's independence.

Reporting on elections, new political leaders and governments, cabinet reshuffles and power struggles is among the most frequent cable traffic that diplomats from all countries send to their capitals. The best cables interpret the information they gather to help headquarters understand what a particular development means for the sending state. Along with reporting, the political section is responsible for "gardening" the political relationship with the host-country through its Ministry of Foreign Affairs, as noted earlier. The section's third main duty is to advocate for the home-country's policy priorities and against host-government decisions and actions that hurt its interests. In all this, good political officers seek opportunities to advance their national interests.

The section chief is usually known as the embassy's counselor for political affairs and as its third-ranking official after the chief and deputy chief of mission. The section's composition depends on the size of the post – a U.S. diplomatic mission can have a single political officer responsible for handling all issues in the bilateral relationship; a team of more than a dozen, with each member focusing on just one or two topics; or any number in between. When William Burns was the political counselor in Moscow in the mid-1990s, his section had 27 American officers.[7] That number has dwindled to just a few in recent years, as U.S.–Russia relations

Figure 6.1 Eunice Reddick, the U.S. ambassador to Gabon, takes part in the opening ceremony of a multinational military exchange exercise in 2009.
Photo by Wils Yanick Maniengui/AFP via Getty Images.

deteriorated and each government expelled many of the other's diplomats. The average political section has between three and six officers, plus local staff, and is divided into an internal and external unit. The former reports on internal political affairs, and the latter on the host-country's foreign relations.

Attending conferences, receptions and other events is an important part of political officers' work. All diplomats take part in representing their mission and country, but the more practical benefit of such functions is the opportunity to make new contacts and collect information from old ones in a short period of time. Sometimes officers have to make remarks, which tests their public speaking skills. There are usually journalists at these events who have a job to do, and officers should be aware that anything they say, even off the record, can end up in the press.

The number of taskings the political section – or the embassy as a whole – receives from headquarters can be overwhelming. In such cases, the country desk officer can be very helpful in prioritizing requests or demands from various offices, since that person usually has a better sense of the leadership's agenda, style and preferences. They can also provide heads-up about a forthcoming instruction cable or a visit to the host-country by a senior official, or win support in the home-capital for giving the embassy additional time to complete a task.

Duties and responsibilities in the field

Gina Abercrombie-Winstanley, this chapter's co-author, arrived at the U.S. Embassy in Israel in late 1994 to start an assignment as a political officer reporting on the situation in the Gaza Strip, her fourth tour in the Foreign Service. Palestinian territories occupied by Israel – Gaza, an enclave on the Mediterranean's eastern coast, and the West Bank – were preparing for a phased transition to self-governance, under the first of the Oslo Accords signed by Israel and the Palestine Liberation Organization (PLO) the previous year. The first-ever Palestinian elections, for a legislative council, were scheduled for January 1996.[8]

In addition to leading the embassy's reporting on the vote in Gaza, Abercrombie-Winstanley was tasked with coordinating election monitoring. The United States, as a major player in the Middle East, had a significant stake in the success of the Israeli–Palestinian peace process, and the election commanded the highest level of attention in Washington. Abercrombie-Winstanley started developing two sets of plans, one on setting up the embassy's observer mission and the other on mapping out her section's reporting before, during and after the elections. She had no prior experience with the former, but she had to figure it out. She reached out to international nongovernmental organizations with rich expertise in the field and to embassy contacts on both the Palestinian and Israeli sides. From the Palestinians she learned about likely candidates for office, planned polling stations and anticipated voter turnout. Israeli officials briefed her on plans for security arrangements and managing the risk of potential trouble caused by militant groups.

Abercrombie-Winstanley's next order of business was internal: sharing the information she had collected and consulting with colleagues to draft an embassy-wide plan. She began putting together a list of officers who volunteered to be election observers. The management section helped with logistical support, including vehicles, so the observers could cover as many polling stations as possible. Gaza was designated as a high-threat location, and any visits by U.S. diplomats had to be choreographed in advance and precisely executed, which meant that the security office had to be involved early on. Abercrombie-Winstanley drafted exit-poll questions to ensure that the embassy got a thorough and accurate picture of the vote. She also put together a list of all possible reporting angles to satisfy Washington's interest.

All the planning paid off on election day. Abercrombie-Winstanley and her colleagues fanned out across Gaza, covering sections in different areas and conducting exit interviews with voters that elicited valuable information. They also offered those Palestinians the chance to voice their hopes and concerns to diplomats from a powerful and influential country. As coordinator of the monitoring mission, Abercrombie-Winstanley drove around the strip to make sure the work of all her teams was going smoothly and to assist with anything they needed. Once the polls closed, she returned to the embassy and started drafting the cables that officials in Washington awaited.

Reporting on political developments

The cables that Abercrombie-Winstanley, Eunice Reddick and Marie Yovanovitch wrote from Israel, Taiwan and Russia, respectively, were a small fraction of the traffic that flows from around the world to Washington every day. Reporting is the bread and butter of political tradecraft, even though it is by no means limited to the political section. Because Foreign Service officers from all career tracks write cables, this book has a separate chapter on diplomatic reporting and communication.

Still, the political dispatches are usually more than those on other issues. Reporting officers do not just wait for something to happen so they have an event to cover. They travel around the host-country, because reporting only from the capital does not provide as full a picture as necessary. The best of them dig deep to find out what is really going on below the surface, much like journalists do. The media breaks news much faster than a diplomatic cable can, but a great cable asks and answers the question "So what?" Officials at headquarters will learn about what happened from the press. Why should they also spend time reading a cable? Why should a mayoral election in the host-country matter to them? Perhaps because the winner may become president one day. Why should they care about a draft law that just failed in the local parliament? Maybe because the bill contained provisions that would have hurt the interests of the home-country, and it was voted down by such a razor-thin margin that one day it might be resurrected with cosmetic changes.

William Burns saw his section's job in Moscow as providing "ground truths" and "a granular sense" of realities in the country, "so that policymakers in Washington could weigh them against all the other considerations overflowing their inboxes," he wrote. "We roamed widely across Russia's 11 time zones, trying to convey to Washington as clear an understanding as we could of the unfolding drama of a Russia struggling to absorb simultaneously three immense historical transformations: the collapse of communism and the tumultuous transition to market economics and democracy; the collapse of the Soviet bloc and the security it had provided to historically insecure Russians; and the collapse of the Soviet Union itself, and with it, a Russian empire built gradually over several centuries."[9]

In reporting and writing, smart Foreign Service officers lean on colleagues as a valuable sounding board. Running an analysis or a policy recommendation by fellow officers, including your country desk officer at headquarters, as well as local staff, is likely to answer questions you may have not addressed, but whose answers officials at home are likely to need. That will make your writing clearer and more impactful. In researching a topic or trying to make sense of something about the host-country that puzzles foreigners, local experts are a key resource. Notetaking is a skill not taken seriously enough, but its importance in diplomatic reporting, and diplomacy in general, cannot be overstated. We will discuss details in Chapter 8.

At U.S. diplomatic missions, political officers are also responsible for reporting to Congress in the form of legally mandated annual reports on their host-country's practices in areas such as human rights, religious freedom, trafficking in persons and counterterrorism. Some governments have become so incensed with the criticism in those documents that they have started producing their own reports on the situation in the United States. Many American diplomats complain that the reports Congress requires have proliferated unnecessarily in recent years, costing them valuable time that can be spent more productively.

How far should a political officer go in befriending sources in the host-country? Most sending governments allow and even encourage their diplomats to socialize with local contacts by taking them out to lunch or hosting them in their homes. After all, meaningful relationships cannot be built only in official meetings. Whether they grow into friendships depends on the circumstances. That is usually easier in friendly and allied countries. If the bilateral relationship is plagued with animosity, diplomats have to decide how much they can trust a local government official; in making a decision, consulting with a supervisor often helps. Personal friendships with contacts outside government in such countries are less likely to raise ethical questions.

Several chapters so far have pointed out the importance of building trust in diplomacy, but diplomats do not have the luxury of dealing only with people they trust. Often they cannot be sure whether to believe their interlocutors, so they have to use their judgment and everything they know about them, how their government works and what its interests are. Sometimes diplomats suspect or are certain that they are being lied to, and that is part of the game, too. It is very difficult to design an effective response or strategy without actual facts. If you cannot figure out whether you should trust a contact, share your predicament with colleagues – they bring different experiences to your section and may possess useful instincts you have yet to develop.

While the main purpose of political reporting is to inform policymakers at headquarters, it has the added benefit of helping to build and cultivate relationships. If an officer gets to know an up-and-coming politician early on, and that politician wins a national election, the officer – and by extension, the embassy and the home-country – already has an "in" with the host-country's new leader. Reflecting the experience of many U.S. embassies around the world, the reporting that Reddick's section did in Taiwan lay the foundation for U.S. engagement with Chen and his administration. Things started out well, but it did not take too long for the tide to turn.

Relationship management

After Chen became president, he decided to test how far Washington would go in tolerating his support for Taiwan's independence. Many of his public remarks and actions were seen as provocative to Beijing and irritated the Bush administration, souring a relationship that had begun with hope and high expectations. Although the American Institute in Taipei was able to maintain collegial working-level relations with Chen's administration – by then Reddick had departed Taiwan – official ties at the very top had been poisoned. The White House lost confidence in

Chen and kept him at arm's length. Some U.S. officials even took the unusual step of criticizing him publicly.[10]

Bush's predecessor, Bill Clinton, had a surprisingly close personal relationship with Boris Yeltsin despite their differences in age and political culture. Even when Yeltsin ordered a military invasion of Chechnya, a separatist republic in Russia's North Caucasus region, in 1994, leading to a brutal war that killed thousands of innocent civilians, Clinton was reluctant to let the relationship suffer. "This guy is in a tough spot," Clinton told Burns during a 1995 visit to Moscow, referring to Yeltsin. "We have to give him as much space as we can, because we are not going to find a better Russian partner."[11]

When the home-country's head of state or government is directly involved in managing a foreign relationship, its diplomatic mission in the host-country plays a supporting role. It still has plenty of work to do, because a president or prime minister has many other responsibilities, and much of the daily business between sovereign states can only be done in person. The previous chapter explained why ambassadors to countries like China, India and Russia usually have less autonomy than their colleagues in places that rarely command the head of state's attention. The same logic applies here. If the White House does not follow developments in Botswana, Libya or Malta on a regular basis, that gives the U.S. embassies there a bigger role in managing those relationships. If a crisis erupts, however, higher-level attention is guaranteed.

That was the case when civil war broke out in Libya in 2011 and consistently occupied a top spot on President Obama's agenda. Based on intelligence that Libyan government forces planned to kill scores of civilians, NATO intervened militarily and helped to end the conflict.[12] The following year, the murder of the U.S. ambassador to Libya, Chistopher Stevens, in the city of Benghazi again required Obama to focus on the North African country. So did another civil war there in 2014, which led to the embassy's evacuation. Such emergencies present a serious dilemma before the home-government: do you put relations on hold or try to manage them from afar?

The State Department wanted to maintain at least some engagement with government officials, opposition leaders and civil society members in Libya. But how were the ambassador, Deborah Jones, and her team supposed to do that from Washington? Abercrombie-Winstanley had an idea. As U.S. ambassador to Malta at the time, she thought that her host-country would be the best alternative. Not only was Tripoli, the Libyan capital, a mere 20-minute flight from Malta across the Mediterranean, but Libyans from all walks of life had close ties to the island country. Many frequented a Libyan-Maltese co-owned hotel, the Corinthia, in the capital Valletta.

Abercrombie-Winstanley urged the State Department to send Jones and her core team and offered to host them at her embassy. They would have relatively easy access to Libyan contacts, and their presence would send a strong signal that the United States was not giving up on Libya. There were already precedents of evacuated diplomatic missions being housed in embassies in third countries, as

Figure 6.2 Gina Abercrombie-Winstanley, a former U.S. ambassador to Malta, speaks following Secretary of State Antony Blinken's announcement that she would become the State Department's first chief diversity and inclusion officer in 2021.
Photo by Mandel Ngan/Pool/AFP via Getty Images.

noted in Chapter 1, and the department agreed. But that was not enough. Abercrombie-Winstanley had to secure the consent of Malta's government to accredit Jones and her colleagues. Three decades earlier, Jones had met Abercrombie-Winstanley at Baghdad airport and welcomed her to her first Foreign Service post. Now Abercrombie-Winstanley was eager to return the gesture. Navigating the complexities of two missions in the same building is never easy, but the ambassadors' relationship made the process much smoother than it would have been otherwise. After a year in Malta, the embassy's Tripoli team was relocated to Tunisia.

Whether or not the president is personally engaged in managing a foreign relationship, an embassy's political section has four sets of responsibilities. First, it facilitates communication between the two governments, whose volume can be overwhelming. Previous chapters made clear why diplomats are still essential in the era of email, instant messaging and video calls. Diplomatic notes, non-papers, notes verbale, démarches and other forms of official diplomatic communication between the embassy and the Ministry of Foreign Affairs, examples of which we will examine in Chapter 8, take up significant time.

Second, as part of the "gardening" of the relationship, political officers hold both regular and urgent meetings with local officials and other embassy contacts, and they often accompany their ambassador to higher-level appointments and serve as notetakers. Such encounters provide opportunities to compare notes, clarify positions, resolve misunderstandings and anticipate troubles. Third, the political section frequently sends representatives to conferences and other events, either as speakers or attendees, and its officers give speeches or talks to audiences as diverse as think tank experts, community leaders, and university and high school students.

Fourth, members of the political section serve as "control officers" during visits by senior home-country officials, including but not limited to the head of state or government, cabinet ministers and lawmakers. In that capacity, their job is to plan and execute a program that maximizes the visitor's time and accomplishes their objectives in the most efficient way. A typical schedule features meetings with the host-country's leadership, discussions with civil society groups, public speeches and press conferences. U.S. presidential trips involve a traveling party of hundreds of staffers and security personnel, as well as more than 100 journalists. During such demanding visits, some diplomats serve as "site officers," each responsible for a single event on the president's schedule or as a notetaker in one of his meetings. Working on a high-level visit takes a lot of time, energy, patience and even sleepless nights, but the high-level contacts officers make can bring lasting career benefits.

During the first year of Russia's 2022 invasion of Ukraine, almost no U.S. officials visited Russia, while Poland had more than 200 visitors, including the president, vice president, almost the entire Cabinet and over a quarter of the congressional membership, according to a Foreign Service officer posted to the U.S. Embassy in Warsaw who worked on many of the visits. As an EU and NATO member and one of Ukraine's neighbors, Poland was the main staging ground for arms transfers and humanitarian assistance, as well as the primary gateway for travel to Ukraine. "For us, it has meant hosting visits constantly, which we can provide leverage for our own goals, but it also absorbs all of our time and energy," the officer told Nicholas Kralev.[13]

Not receiving high-level attention on a regular basis means that headquarters does not look over the embassy's shoulder all the time. That gives the post more leeway in setting the agenda with the host-country and responding to events on the ground, as long as it colors within the broad outlines of official policy. The experience of the U.S. Embassy in Albania in the early 2000s, which the previous chapter recounted, is an example of such leeway. U.S. policy called for a stable, democratic and prosperous Albania that would join the EU and NATO one day. Within those contours, the embassy worked directly with Albania's government and opposition to resolve disputes that had the potential to plunge the country into violence. Albania became a NATO member in 2009 and received EU candidate status in 2014.

Advocacy and negotiation

All duties of a political section abroad are organically interconnected. As we saw earlier, reporting helps in managing a bilateral relationship, which in turn is impossible to accomplish successfully without advocacy and negotiation. After the embassy in Albania drafted its proposal to resolve the crisis, it had to advocate for the adoption of the recommendations by the key political players – and because there was significant animosity between the government and the opposition, the Americans also had to mediate and negotiate.

Diplomatic advocacy is a tool of diplomatic tradecraft used to persuade and influence other countries' decisions and actions, in order to align them with the home-country's interests. Great advocacy work shapes the other side's perceptions and calculations so that it does what the diplomat wants it to do, because it comes to see that doing so is in its own best interest, as noted in Chapter 2. Sometimes that necessitates rearranging foreign officials' appraisal of their strategic circumstances, and even the circumstances themselves. One diplomat can hardly achieve such changes in behavior alone – it takes a focused and dedicated team that draws on the assets of all embassy sections and agencies, as well as on support from headquarters.

The first prerequisite for effective advocacy is knowing exactly whom in the host-country to persuade and influence. That means having an accurate and thorough understanding of how the local society works, how strong its institutions are, how the main players in government, civil society, the private sector and the media make decisions, and how other leading opinion-makers affect those decisions. None of this is possible without having a wide network of contacts in all those places whose trust the embassy has already won, which is difficult to pull off without great reporting and skillful relationship management. The second prerequisite is possessing a solid understanding of the subject matter or problem that the advocacy effort seeks to address, as well as the official positions on the issue of both the home-government and the receiving state.

An advocacy endeavor usually starts with an instruction cable from headquarters, though the chief of mission can sometimes take action without specific instructions, as was the case in Albania. If an embassy does receive instructions, it may be wise to modify them based on the conditions on the ground and cultural or other sensitivities – as Chapter 3 noted, instructions may come from political appointees with little experience in diplomatic practice or be drafted by a new desk officer who has never been to your host-country. Initial steps the embassy can take include sending a diplomatic note to the Ministry of Foreign Affairs or an informal meeting with a key local official to gauge how receptive the government might be to the decision or action the embassy is seeking. If the issue is controversial and likely to face resistance, it may be better to design a carefully thought-out strategy before approaching the government. Speedy and half-baked measures can backfire and render the advocacy effort dead on arrival.

A viable strategy may have private and public components. Diplomats often prefer to work things out quietly by engaging with different host-government agencies and legislators, as well as other leading figures who can influence decisions, including advisers to key officials. In such exchanges, listening is more important than talking to fully understand how the matter might resonate with the other side, and what conditions it might attach to potential cooperation. If the embassy's private efforts at persuasion fail, it may take its arguments to the public with a public diplomacy campaign, as we will see in Chapter 9. But even if the government is open to the proposal, it may still be necessary to win public support, especially in a democracy – the party in power may not want to spend political capital without public backing.

An impactful tactic in diplomatic advocacy is forming ad hoc partnerships with like-minded organizations, such as NGOs or other foreign embassies in the host-country that share the same interests and goals. Not every advocacy campaign necessarily involves official negotiations, but negotiating skills can help to win support from potential partners and key stakeholders in the local society. When the Obama administration decided in 2014 to change the nature of the U.S. security relationship with Africa, diplomatic negotiations were essential. The White House envisioned a multilateral framework that would confront challenges such as terror-ism, piracy and trafficking in persons, drugs, weapons and wildlife. Concerned that extremist groups like Boko Haram, al-Shabab and al-Qaeda of the Islamic Maghreb were tearing at the fabric of African societies, Washington wanted the security assistance it provided to yield better results. After consulting with African govern-ments, it determined that the best way to achieve its objectives was by building and strengthening the capacity of institutions in the security sector. That approach differed from the longtime practice of providing mostly training and equipment to a country's security forces.

The plan that emerged was called the Security Governance Initiative (SGI). Based on initial feedback from African leaders and previous partnerships, Washington invited Ghana, Kenya, Mali, Niger, Nigeria and Tunisia to participate, but the formal commitment of their governments had yet to be secured. The State Department instructed the U.S. embassies in the six countries to start working on bilateral agreements. It also created an SGI team for each country to bolster embassy capabilities, with support from the Departments of Defense and Justice and the U.S. Agency for International Development.

Eunice Reddick was the ambassador to Niger at the time. She and her team, which included the deputy chief of mission, the embassy's only political officer and the defense attaché, adjusted some of the particulars in the instructions from Washington to account for Niger's unique security threats, as well as its budgetary and legislative constraints. Then they developed a strategy that began with a comprehensive assess-ment of current conditions on the ground and existing government capacity, with help from local, U.S. and international experts. That made it possible to set realistic priorities and goals. While outreach and advocacy efforts would naturally be focused on the Ministries of Foreign Affairs and Defense, as well as the offices of the president and prime minister, Reddick's team determined that a whole-of-government approach would have the best chance of success. All relevant agencies, including the Ministries of Justice and Finance, had to work together. The importance of transparency prompted the embassy to add public outreach to its strategy.

In 2015, after months of negotiations, Reddick and Niger's deputy foreign minister signed a document called the SGI Joint Country Action Plan, a road map for implementing the initiative. It sought to improve the country's security infrastructure, modernize its communication capabilities and better align human and material resources to address both short- and long-term needs. It also had built-in regular evaluations meant to adjust implementation and produce more effective approaches to U.S. security assistance.

Human rights, democracy promotion and good governance have been staples of American diplomacy for decades, as noted in Chapter 3, and advocacy is the main tool in those efforts. Along with other Western democracies, the United States spends billions of dollars every year to help developing countries hold free and fair elections, fight corruption, reform their justice systems, eradicate extreme poverty, and improve access to education and healthcare. Soft power has been an invaluable advantage in such endeavors, though domestic problems in the United States in recent years have diminished the allure of its political system and limited the goodwill its diplomats encounter in some parts of the world.

A day in a political officer's life

As Marie Yovanovitch began her tour as a political officer in Moscow in 1993, she was thrilled to be working for Ambassador Pickering, a "wickedly smart Foreign Service legend," she wrote in her memoir. "Pickering seemed to work around the clock, and rumor had it that he had so mastered the skill of power-napping that he required only a few hours of sleep a night," she added. "For staying awake during boring meetings, he recommended digging your nails into the palm of your hand or chewing on the inside of your cheek – techniques I found painful but effective."[14] Even in the excitement and, as we saw earlier, risks of serving as a political officer during the early years of post-Soviet Russia, diplomats were not immune to periods of boredom.

For the most part, however, working in a political section keeps officers on their toes and provides many opportunities to make a difference. What does an officer's day look like? The answer must be prefaced by making two things clear. First, no two days are exactly the same. Second, it depends on where you are posted, and on the style and preferences of your section chief. Some posts receive several visitors from headquarters a week, while others may host just a handful for an entire year. That directly affects a political officer's schedule and workload. Your boss may like to hold section meetings daily or weekly, and may require you to write a certain number of cables every month, regardless of what is happening in the host-country. That, too, shapes an officer's day at work.

An average day starts in the office with review of the overnight cable and email traffic from headquarters and other home-country diplomatic missions abroad. Although you may have seen some unclassified emails on your phone before arriving at work, access to all classified communication and materials is restricted to the mission's premises. If you have received requests or instructions that require immediate attention, any plans for the day you may have made previously will likely have to be adjusted. Unless you got caught up on the latest news at home, this is a good time to do so. The local staff in the public diplomacy section often compiles a digest of the most important media stories before the official start of business. You do not want to miss a major development, especially one that might affect your job.

If your section meets every morning, your boss will review the day's tasks, any longer-term projects and potential last-minute assignments, such as delivering an unexpected démarche to the Ministry of Foreign Affairs or drafting an urgent memo for the ambassador. If there is no daily section meeting, you should check in with your boss to see if you might be needed. It is critical to make sure that no task gets lost or neglected. Even though one type of activity – reporting and writing, or internal and external meetings, or a visit by a senior official – may take up most of your day, an average day consists of a variety of duties. Time-management and prioritizing skills are essential to get everything done properly and in a timely manner. If a problem arises, do your best to resolve it, but if you cannot, tell your boss. Do not keep it secret in the hope of a magical or quick solution.

There is a difference between a planned day and an actual day of a political officer – or any diplomat, for that matter. You may have the following scheduled items on your agenda: a section meeting; responding to emails; preparing for an upcoming visit by a senator; lunch with a local official for a cable you need to write; calls to experts on the subject of your cable; drafting the cable. As you are reviewing a speech your future visitor is supposed to give at a university, an announcement about a host-government reshuffle or other breaking news may require you to drop everything and write a cable on the possible impact of what just happened to home-country policies. Then, as you are driving to your lunch, you may be ordered back to the embassy to be a notetaker in a meeting the ambassador is hosting, instead of your section chief, who has to speak at a conference in place of the deputy chief of mission, who has to deal with an internal crisis.

Whatever your day looks like, you must be flexible. Even with all the demands that may need your attention, it is helpful to set aside some time to review meeting notes, jot down ideas for cables or memos, and edit any reports you have in the works. It also pays off to walk around the mission and drop by other sections and agencies, which may have picked up new information from their own sources. Checking in regularly with your most trusted sources and experts will make your job easier in the long run. You must be available to respond to calls and emails from both your post and headquarters outside business hours, and sometimes even to help with urgent taskings. At the same time, if you want to have a personal life, try to limit working at night and on weekends on those assignments that clearly can wait until the next business day, even if that might inconvenience the colleague in your home-capital who asked for your help.

You can scarcely do your job – one might argue that you cannot do it at all – without support from your local staff, whom you also may have to manage. The embassy's agents of continuity and institutional memory, the best of them develop well-placed contacts and can get you the kind of access in the host-country that even ambassadors find challenging to secure. At the same time, you need to have your guard up against potential political bias or agenda among some local employees, which can hurt the embassy. They are not trained diplomats and may find it more difficult than you do to keep their beliefs and opinions private.

What can an officer do to prepare for an assignment in a political section before arriving at their post? Quite a bit. Learning the local language and as much as possible about the receiving country is a must. Do not rely on your government to teach you everything you need to know. Hopefully, it will give you language training, but beyond that, you are responsible for your own preparation. Read all the books you can get your hands on, and watch films and videos and listen to songs from the host-country as your time allows. Try to read the local press, as difficult as that may be in the beginning.

Meet your counterpart and, if you can, the ambassador at the receiving state's embassy in your capital, as well as any media correspondents who may be posted there. Visit your future country desk officer at headquarters and make them your new best friend – they can make your life much easier with early warnings and other tips and insights from headquarters. Paying courtesy calls on colleagues in other relevant parts of your ministry or department, as well as on officials in other agencies of your government, is another worthwhile time investment. Learning about their agenda and any issues they are working on related to your host-country, such as refugee assistance or measures to fight climate change, can be very helpful during your tour. Talk to officers who have previously served at your new post and can give you practical advice about life and work there. Consult with experts at think tanks, NGOs and in academia to gain an even better understanding of the place you will call home for the next few years.

Personal disagreement with official policy

Warren Christopher, a calm and patient man, was very worried. He was facing what increasingly looked like a rebellion. Less than seven months after he had become President Clinton's first secretary of state in 1993, dozens of Foreign Service officers were vocally criticizing the new administration's refusal to intervene in a brutal war in the Balkans. Three officers had already resigned in protest, including the country desk officers for Yugoslavia and Bosnia and Herzegovina – the first one had left the service toward the end of the Republican administration of George H. W. Bush the previous year. In an attempt to stave off a revolt, Christopher met privately with exasperated and frustrated mid-level diplomats, but just 10 days later, the Croatia desk officer quit.

The officer, Stephen Walker, described U.S. policy in his resignation letter to Christopher as "misguided, vacillating and dangerous." The conflict's horrors, following the multiethnic Yugoslav federation's disintegration at the end of the Cold War, dominated the U.S. and foreign media and sparked widespread outrage. Washington's inaction "undermined and threatened not only the fate of the Balkans and the hundreds of thousands of victims there, but also vital U.S. national interests," Walker wrote. "A dangerous precedent is being set. Genocide is taking place again in Europe, yet we, the European Community and the rest of the international community stand by and watch."[15] The United States eventually intervened militarily and brokered the 1995 Dayton Accords that ended the Bosnian War.

In 2003, it was action, rather than inaction, that prompted three Foreign Service officers to resign over the George W. Bush administration's decision to invade Iraq, which it said aimed to rid Saddam Hussein's regime of weapons of mass destruction. Mary Ann Wright, the most senior of the three who was deputy chief of mission in Mongolia at the time, said that leaving the service was a "big step" that changed her life. "Most of my life [now] is dedicated to trying to stop the war," she told Reuters in 2008.[16] A decade earlier, Christopher's spokesman had called resigning from the Foreign Service "an honorable form of protest." But not all administrations react in the same way. Diplomats usually view quitting as their last resort, having exhausted all internal mechanisms, including the State Department's dissent channel. More than 100 used the channel in 2017, when Donald Trump banned Muslims from seven countries from entering the United States on his first full day as president.[17] Trump's spokesman dismissed the officers as "Deep State" and told them to "get with the program or ... go."[18]

The dissent channel has been a unique feature of the U.S. system since 1971, as a result of the Vietnam War, when hundreds of officers resigned in the late 1960s and early 1970s.[19] According to the State Department's "Foreign Affairs Manual" (FAM), the channel was "created to allow its users the opportunity to bring dissenting or alternative views on substantive foreign policy issues, when such views cannot be communicated in a full and timely manner through regular operating channels or procedures." Dissent cables usually go to the department's policy-planning staff and are forwarded to the offices of the secretary of state, the deputy secretary and other senior officials, as appropriate. Their authors cannot be subjected to reprisal, disciplinary action or unauthorized disclosure of their names or the cables' contents. Those who engage in retaliatory actions can be disciplined themselves.[20]

One of the most outspoken Foreign Service officers in the last half-century, who managed not to get himself fired despite repeatedly and sometimes publicly criticizing U.S. policies, was the late Terence Todman. A six-time ambassador, Todman is best remembered for two episodes, in Democratic and Republican administrations. While serving as acting assistant secretary of state for Latin America, Todman questioned the extent of President Carter's human rights agenda. In a 1978 speech, he urged Carter not to punish countries with poor human rights records, including dictatorships, arguing that entire populations should not have to suffer because their rulers misbehaved. In 1986, Todman declined President Reagan's offer to become the first African-American ambassador to South Africa, in protest of U.S. support for the country's racist apartheid regime. During his four-decade career, he also sharply criticized the State Department for almost automatically sending Black diplomats to Africa or the Caribbean on what he called "ghetto" assignments.[21]

There are Democrats and Republicans in the Foreign Service, and there are those who do not identify with any political party. Many have disagreed with official policies or decisions at some point in their careers. As government employees, they are required to carry out the president's policies no matter what. But as citizens of a free and democratic country, they have the right to personal opinions. Some keep their views to themselves, and others dare to speak truth to power. If they are working on matters related to the policy they find problematic, they may try to get reassigned to a mission or office that deals with issues in a different area. We saw earlier how Cameron Munter handled a State Department instruction he thought misguided by extracting a last-minute concession from the Czechoslovak Embassy, which helped to ease his frustration.

In the run-up to the 2003 Iraq invasion, hundreds of Foreign Service officers feared that it would be a mistake, but they defended it in other countries, explaining to both governments and publics why the Bush administration deemed using force necessary. The way they saw it, they were doing their jobs. In this and almost every other case, most officers concluded that their disagreements were not significant enough to justify quitting a profession they loved but could hardly practice anywhere else. After all, if everyone resigned, what would happen to U.S. diplomacy?

Case Study: U.S. Air Base in Kyrgyzstan

In Marie Yovanovitch's three years as U.S. ambassador to Kyrgyzstan, beginning in 2005, one issue took up more of her time than everything else she worked on combined: the Manas Air Base, a military installation that provided logistical support for U.S. operations in Afghanistan. The United States had been renting the base since late 2001, after it attacked Afghanistan's Taliban regime for harboring al-Qaeda and being complicit in the 9/11 terrorist plot. Kurmanbek Bakiyev, the Kyrgyz prime minister who had negotiated the original agreement with the Bush administration, was now the former Soviet republic's president.

In February 2006, shortly after a meeting with Russian President Vladimir Putin, Bakiyev announced that Kyrgyzstan and the United States had reached a deal to increase the annual rent of Manas to exponentially more than the $2 million the Americans were paying. That was news to the U.S. government, including to Yovanovitch. "No such deal had been struck," she wrote. She and her colleagues interpreted the announcement as pressure to negotiate a new deal at a higher price. It was not the first time Bakiyev had demanded more money for the base. He "saw a rich country that he believed had the money to pay big for something he thought was essential for its war effort."[22] Two months later, he issued a public ultimatum: either Washington would pay $200 million or Manas would be closed.

However, the Pentagon was not willing to consider anything approaching that amount. It thought that it was in Kyrgyzstan's interest to help the U.S. military rid

Case Study: (cont.)

the region of terrorists – given that Afghanistan was just a two-hour flight from Bishkek, the Kyrgyz capital – and that the existing rent was fair. "It was an epic culture clash," Yovanovitch wrote. "At the embassy, we started strategizing on how we could help bridge the divide" and established a small team to spearhead the effort. It included the deputy chief of mission, Donald Lu, the political counselor, Liam O'Connell, and Tom Plumb, the defense attaché. It soon became clear that, whatever final number the Pentagon landed on, it was going to appear "humiliatingly far away from Bakiyev's demand," Yovanovitch added. "We needed some creative thinking."

Figure 6.3 Kyrgyz President Kurmanbek Bakiyev, Colonel Joel Reese, commander of the 375th U.S. Air Expeditionary Wing, and the U.S. ambassador to Kyrgyzstan, Marie Yovanovitch, attend a commemoration ceremony for the victims of the 9/11 attacks at the Manas Air Base in 2006.
Photo by Vyacheslav Oseledko/AFP via Getty Images.

Lu and O'Connell had an idea: the United States would redefine the terms of the negotiation and frame its offer "in the context of the totality" of its relationship with Kyrgyzstan – after all, there was much more to it than the monetary compensation for the use of Manas. That included a "large assistance program that added up to about $43.5 million a year," and the United States "pumped a huge amount of money into the local economy through the goods, fuel and services purchased by the

Case Study: (cont.)

embassy and the base." The team calculated that Washington "had infused over $150 million into Kyrgyzstan every year for the past several years," much of which would be lost if it vacated Manas. That number plus a modest increase in rent would be close enough to the $200 million that it might prove a face-saving way for Bakiyev to acquiesce.

Before presenting the proposal to Bakiyev, however, Lu and O'Connell had to win backing from the Pentagon. "There can sometimes be a difference in how diplomats at the embassy and our Defense Department colleagues from Washington view a situation," Yovanovitch noted. The embassy was responsible for "the full breadth of the bilateral relationship," while the defense negotiators "were responsible solely for the military equities – in this case, the base agreement – and they flew in for a couple of days for the negotiations. It fell to the embassy team to help" the two sides "better understand each other's positions, as well as the environment in each country." In this case, the Pentagon's negotiator, Jim MacDougall, understood "the headwinds blowing against the base" and agreed that Lu and O'Connell's plan was the best option under the circumstances.

In May 2006, MacDougall arrived in Kyrgyzstan for an informal round of discussions. The Kyrgyz negotiator was Bakiyev's national security adviser, Miroslav Niyazov. Over a day and a half, MacDougall, Yovanovitch and her three embassy colleagues met with Niyazov and his staff in the presidential office building. The U.S. proposal was not even close to what he had in mind, Niyazov said. But the Americans persevered, explaining that Bakiyev's "maximalist position was a nonstarter," and that their approach "will provide him with a reasonable deal, more rent for the base, and a face-saving way to sell the results to his people." The president did not make it easy – for the Americans or his own negotiator. He "would insist on a point only to rescind it, leaving Niyazov flat-footed and guessing what his boss wanted. But eventually, after a lot of shuttling between his own office and Bakiyev's, Niyazov reported that Bakiyev was interested in continuing the conversation under our proposed framework," Yovanovitch recalled.

A formal second round of negotiations took place in July at the Kyrgyz Ministry of Defense. MacDougall returned and offered $17.4 million for the rent of Manas. To Yovanovitch's relief, Bakiyev accepted the offer, and MacDougall and Niyazov signed a protocol formalizing the agreement.

However, in 2009, exactly a year after Yovanovitch left Kyrgyzstan to become ambassador to Armenia, Bakiyev renewed his demand for $200 million a year for the base. The parliament in Bishkek even voted to close it, but Bakiyev continued to negotiate with the new Obama administration, which eventually agreed to pay the money.[23] After a series of controversies and pressure from Russia, Manas was closed in 2014.[24]

Exercise: South Africa and Russia's War in Ukraine (Part 1)

You are a political officer at the U.S. Embassy in South Africa. In a recent vote in the UNGA condemning Russia's invasion of Ukraine and demanding its pullout, the South African government decided to abstain. Its position was that it did not want to "take sides," although it pointed out that, during the apartheid era of white-majority rule during the Cold War, the Soviet Union supported the African National Congress, which is now the ruling party. Because of that history, some South African officials expressed a sense of "kinship" with Russia.

Washington, however, believes that Russia's invasion was unprovoked and unjustified. It views it as an attack on a sovereign country that must be condemned by the rest of the world, and as a struggle between democracy and autocracy. The State Department has sent an instruction cable to your embassy to persuade the South African government to vote in favor of another UNGA resolution calling for a stop to Russia's killing of civilians and destruction of Ukraine's infrastructure. That vote is scheduled to take place in a week.

Task: The political section chief, your direct boss, has asked you to draft a plan for an advocacy campaign. Consider the following questions:

- How would you define a realistic objective that can be achieved in a week?
- Who would your audience be?
- How would you approach them?
- What arguments would you make?
- Would you involve other embassy sections or outside partners?
- Would you keep your efforts quiet, and if not, at what point would you go public?
- Would you need any support from Washington?

Part 2 of this exercise is at the end of Chapter 9 and involves developing a public diplomacy campaign.

ADDITIONAL RESOURCES

James A. Baker, III, *The Politics of Diplomacy* (Putnam, 1995).
Elizabeth Shackelford, *The Dissent Channel: American Diplomacy in a Dishonest Age* (PublicAffairs, 2020).
Marie Yovanovitch, *Lessons from the Edge: A Memoir* (Mariner Books, 2022).

7 Economic Tradecraft and Commercial Diplomacy

LISA KUBISKE

Mary Ng likes to talk about a "trilateral hamburger." In it, the beef comes from Canadian cows but is processed in the United States. The buns are made from Canadian wheat but are baked in Mexico. The lettuce is American and the tomatoes Mexican. "This is how connected our economies are" on the most basic level, Ng, Canada's minister of international trade, said at a 2021 event to mark the first anniversary of a trade agreement negotiated among the three countries.[1]

Thanks to the unprecedented level of integration in the world economy, much of what we own comes from different parts of the world. A shirt may be designed in Italy, manufactured in Vietnam from Indian fabric and sold in Britain. A German-made car may be assembled in China. On a much larger scale, the Boeing 787 aircraft has parts from at least eight countries, including engines from the United States, center fuselage from Italy, landing gear from France, access doors from Sweden, cabin lights from Germany and lavatory parts from Japan.[2] Such complex and truly global integration does not just happen; to a large extent, it is the result of diplomacy. We take for granted the ability to travel seamlessly to, through and over other countries, but it would not be possible without diplomacy.

When unexpected events in recent years disrupted the integrated economy, diplomacy came to the rescue. Beginning in early 2020, the Covid-19 pandemic threw supply chains in disarray, causing widespread shortages of much-needed materials and products, and significant price increases and high inflation in much of the world two years later. Diplomacy helped to find temporary supply-chain alternatives, and to make some of them permanent. In 2022, Russia's invasion of Ukraine prevented millions of tons of grains from reaching export markets in Africa, the Middle East and elsewhere. Diplomacy helped again to reach an agreement for moving shipments safely through the Black Sea despite the war raging nearby.

International relations have long had economic and commercial aspects. In fact, the first treaties negotiated between many nation-states had to do with trade and navigation.[3] In Chapter 1, Nicholas Kralev identified security and prosperity as the core pillars of the national interest, which can be applied to most countries. To prosper, a country needs a thriving economy, which can come about from what it produces at home, but it can be greatly enhanced by foreign trade and investment. As Kralev also noted, some governments have expanded the concept of national security to include economic security, because they view the lack of economic opportunity as a cause of potential political instability and conflict.

A country's economic might can significantly increase its soft power, as it has done for the United States and Japan, among others. Economic preponderance since World War II has not only made the United States hugely admired and sometimes feared around the world, but it has also brought unprecedented benefits. They include the emergence of English as a de facto global language – the first one in history – and the rise of the U.S. dollar as the principal currency for settling international transactions. For decades, the country's soft power has given it unrivaled diplomatic influence, though it has subsided in recent years as its economy became less dominant.

On the surface, it may appear that a country's economic and commercial diplomats do the same type of work abroad. That is not quite the case. Economic officers inform policymaking at headquarters by monitoring and analyzing economic trends and developments in the receiving state. They also advocate for host-government policies aimed at leveling the playing field for companies from the home-country and against regulations that hurt those businesses. Commercial diplomats directly help industries and individual companies in starting or expanding business and investment in the host-country. Conversely, they facilitate investment by local firms in the home-country.

There is certainly some overlap between economic and commercial work. When I was an economic officer at the U.S. Consulate General in Shanghai in the early 1990s, both I and my commercial colleague Rosemary Gallant researched China's insurance industry, and the laws and regulations governing foreign companies' participation in it. We even interviewed the same local officials, experts and business people. However, we used our findings for different purposes. I sent a series of reports and analyses to Washington to inform deliberations and decision-making regarding China's application to the World Trade Organization (WTO). U.S. negotiators needed to know about any practices in the Chinese insurance industry that were not allowed by WTO rules. Gallant used the information she had gathered to advise U.S. companies already operating in China and those that considered entering the market. We worked together, which doubled our ability to gain as much knowledge and insight as possible, and to secure official meetings that were not easy to arrange.

While much of diplomacy is a long game that takes years to bear fruit, economic and commercial diplomats' work often produces tangible results in a relatively short time. The benefits of a trade agreement that removes tariffs or other barriers can be felt soon after it enters into force. An embassy's assistance in securing a new export market for an industry can lead to more jobs, higher revenues and more taxes in the government's coffers in a year or two. We will focus first on economic tradecraft, and then on commercial diplomacy.

What is economic tradecraft?

Economic tradecraft is **a set of duties, responsibilities and skills required of diplomats working in economic affairs**. It is a key instrument in the diplomatic tradecraft toolbox. As is the case with their colleagues in the political career track, economic officers work both at diplomatic missions abroad and at headquarters, such as their Ministry of Foreign Affairs or the State Department. Their main duties are similar to those in political tradecraft: reporting and analysis; relationship management – in this case, economic relations with the host-country; and implementing policy through advocacy, persuasion and negotiation.

Most of the required skill sets are the same as well. Economic officers need interpersonal skills and language ability to build and cultivate a diverse network of sources who can provide accurate and useful information. They also have to possess good communication and analytical skills to convey information to both headquarters and the host-country. Listening to interlocutors is as important as cross-cultural communication. Managing people and programs is becoming increasingly critical as more governments realize how pivotal economic tradecraft can be in gaining and maintaining diplomatic influence.

The official requirements for becoming an economic officer vary. Some governments make it mandatory to have a university degree in economics, while others, including the United States, do not. The State Department has the same criteria for Foreign Service officers in all career tracks, as noted in Chapter 1. Still, to work as an economic officer, you need to possess or acquire a substantial amount of specialized knowledge in macro- and microeconomics, finance and other fields related to your assignment's portfolio. For example, you should know what a "debt swap" is and how it works. You should also know how to read a balance of payments, and what resources are available to governments facing foreign exchange shortages. It is not difficult to learn all this, or even to understand innocuous terms like "unicorn investments." If your ministry has a training facility, it likely offers economics courses. You have unlimited knowledge at your disposal in books, magazines, on the Internet and other resources. There are also many experts and colleagues you can consult.

What are the issues economic officers deal with? The range can be very wide, depending on the host-country and the mission's size. It includes traditional and universal matters, such as economic growth, monetary and fiscal policy, and investment flows and rules, as well as country-specific issues like inflation, data privacy, corruption and intellectual property rights. Within the economic career track, there are several sub-tracks, including environment, science, technology and health. In large embassies, there may be separate sections focusing on these matters, but in small and midsize posts, they usually fall under the economic section's purview. Later, we will explore the U.S. Foreign Commercial Service and Foreign Agricultural Service, but it is worth remembering that they do not have a presence in every embassy or consulate. Where they are absent, the economic section assumes their responsibilities, as it does with financial matters at posts to which the Treasury Department does not send financial attachés.

Sample Policy Issues in Economic Tradecraft

- Economic growth
- Monetary and fiscal policy
- Trade and investment flows
- Energy policy
- Sovereign debt
- National budget
- Balance of payments
- Labor policy
- Inflation
- Corruption
- Intellectual property rights
- Data privacy and governance
- Antitrust policy
- Commercial sales
- Aviation and transportation
- Expropriation
- Export controls
- Economic sanctions
- Environmental policy
- Health and science
- Economic development and assistance
- International communications
- Regulatory policy
- Digital and cyber policy

Economic officers serving at home and abroad, including those who work in multilateral diplomacy, need to align the interests of other countries and organizations with those of their own government, even if they disagree personally with a particular decision or an entire policy. Given the high level of interdependence in the global economy today, most issues and policies inevitably have multilateral dimensions, even in the context of bilateral relationships. In 2010, for example, a financial crisis in Greece rocked the entire eurozone, which is composed of the countries using the euro as their currency. Multilateral economic diplomacy is the stock-in-trade of organizations like the WTO, the World Bank and the International Monetary Fund (IMF).

The economic headquarters

In 2001, soon after the 9/11 terrorist attacks in New York and Washington, the George W. Bush administration drew up sweeping plans to track down terrorist financing, freeze assets and build an international mechanism for blocking funds from flowing to extremist groups and causes. This undertaking was as overwhelming as it was unprecedented. U.N. resolutions needed to be passed and national laws had to be changed around the world. A sanctions regime had to be designed to punish those who continued to support terrorists. As is typical when economic sanctions are involved, the Treasury Department took the lead, but it could not succeed without the State Department.

Secretary of State Colin Powell instructed the department's economic and multilateral bureaus and other relevant offices to work with the Treasury and the White House to create a comprehensive and realistic strategy, and to start implementing it as soon as the National Security Council (NSC) approved it. The Bureau of International Organizations joined forces with the U.S. Mission to the United Nations in New York to win member-states' backing for a Security Council resolution to criminalize participation in the financing, planning, preparation and perpetration of terrorist acts.[4] The Bureau of Economic and Business Affairs prepared options for helping countries likely to be hurt by the sanctions and reached out to potential international donors. In these efforts, officials in Washington worked with U.S. diplomatic missions in countries on six continents, many of which "designated scores of entities for sanctions, froze more than $100 million in funds and assets, and made it much harder for others to fund terrorists," recalled Tony Wayne, a Foreign Service officer who headed the bureau as its assistant secretary. "Each freeze was implemented globally within 48 hours."[5]

The Bureau of Economic and Business Affairs is the home of the majority of economic officers in the Foreign Service on domestic assignments. It has offices specializing in the various issues listed earlier. One of the offices leads U.S. aviation negotiations, such as those that hammer out "open skies" agreements, which allow for unlimited flights between the United States and other countries. It is a functional bureau, in State Department parlance, though some economic officers serve in regional bureaus, including as country desk officers. On large country desks like the one for China in the Bureau of East Asian and Pacific Affairs, there are usually several economic officers. In both functional and regional bureaus, officers follow all major developments in their respective portfolios, draft policy papers, memos and other documents for their bosses, provide briefings to senior policymakers and act as the eyes and ears of overseas posts in the home-capital.

One of the main benefits of working at headquarters is the ability to participate in the interagency process. Economic officers coordinate with colleagues in other parts of the government, such as the Departments of Commerce, Treasury, Agriculture and Energy, as well as the Office of the U.S. Trade Representative, which leads trade negotiations, and the U.S. Agency for International Development (USAID). At the senior levels, they also take part in meetings of the interagency policy committees discussed in Chapter 4. Another advantage of domestic assignments is their exposure to a wide range of viewpoints not just in the executive branch, but also in Congress, the media and the public, which is difficult to grasp from abroad. A third benefit is the opportunity to help develop new initiatives.

In the mid-1990s, the United States pursued multilateral agreements to fight corruption and bribery around the world, which it viewed as serious impediments to economic development and prosperity. The Bureau of Economic and Business Affairs helped to draft and adopt two major international accords. The Inter-American Convention Against Corruption, passed by the Organization of American States in 1996, was the first of its kind anywhere in the world.[6] A year later, the Organization for Economic Cooperation and Development approved the Convention on Combating Bribery of Foreign Public Officials in International Business Transactions.[7] These early achievements led to the adoption of the 2003 United Nations Convention Against Corruption.[8]

Support for economic reforms and reconstruction in developing countries has been a diplomatic priority for many developed states for decades, including Britain, Canada, Australia, Japan and members of the EU, among others. The lending authority and expertise of the World Bank and the IMF play an indispensable role in these endeavors. One of the first challenges the United States faced after it overthrew the Taliban regime in Afghanistan for its complicity in the 9/11 attacks was how to rebuild the country. In addition to collaborating with USAID to send aid where it was most needed, the Bureau of Economic and Business Affairs took the lead in organizing three international donor conferences, with help from the U.N. Development Programme (UNDP), the World Bank, Japan, the EU and Persian Gulf countries. These events, which raised billions of dollars, were early precursors to similar donor gatherings in the next several years to assist Iraq after the United States toppled Saddam Hussein, and to help rebuilding after natural disasters, such as the 2004 tsunami in Asia and the 2005 earthquake in Pakistan, both of which claimed thousands of casualties.[9]

Like their colleagues in the political career track, economic officers also serve as staff assistants to senior officials and as watch officers in the State Department's Operations Center. They work on the NSC staff at the White House, as well as on detailed assignments in other agencies. From time to time, some of them choose to serve in noneconomic positions – the department expects all diplomats to gain experience in other areas, so they can be better leaders and managers when they rise to the senior ranks. Even if an officer stays only in the economic track, variety is guaranteed, thanks to the mandatory rotations discussed in Chapter 1. Working with or in different countries can lead to very dissimilar experiences, depending on their location, size and level of development, among other factors.

The economic section abroad

The worst pandemic in a century changed everyone's life overnight. The world shut down – countries closed their borders, streets emptied, businesses shattered, schools grew quiet, millions of people lost their jobs and thousands were dying every day. As governments scrambled to evacuate diplomats and their families from some of the worst-hit places, and to figure out how they could continue to perform their duties, economic sections in many U.S. diplomatic missions were as busy as ever. In its path of devastation, fear and despair, Covid-19 ravaged the world economy, starting in early 2020 – and would continue to do so for at least three years. Just like it caused immediate and long-term health damage, so did the disease inflict both instant and delayed pain on the modern way of life.

Across the world, economic officers' first order of business was to take stock of the desolation. How much and how quickly were their host-countries' economies bleeding? What were the unemployment rates? How many companies had gone out of business? How much revenue were governments losing? Was there enough personal protective equipment? Diplomats sent their findings in cables to headquarters, along with analyses of what the crisis meant for the home-country and its economic policies. As it became evident that lockdowns in almost every country were causing major disruptions to supply chains, trade and travel, economic officers began to discuss strategies for identifying alternatives to getting vital supplies where they needed to be, especially face masks, protective equipment and, later on, vaccines.

In Chapter 1, Nicholas Kralev defined national security as the provision, protection and defense of the security of a country and its people. In this case, an easily transmittable respiratory virus killed millions of people and threatened everyone else – it was obviously a matter of national security everywhere. From an economic perspective, supply-chain management is a national security issue at any time, let alone during a pandemic, because overreliance on a single foreign supplier can make a country vulnerable to the whims of businesses and governments it cannot control. As Covid-19 lockdowns continued, millions of people worked from home and their children attended virtual classes, which led to skyrocketing demand for computers and other electronic devices. However, the few manufacturers of semiconductors, or chips, struggled to keep up. Factories with labor-intensive backend operations, such as chip packaging and testing, fared even worse than those with higher levels of automation. Semiconductors are also used in cars. At the start of the pandemic, automakers canceled previous orders, but as low interest rates boosted demand and they ramped up production, chips were not available.[10]

A closer look at supply chains revealed structural problems that were certain to persist after the pandemic was over, unless something was done about them. For example, "just-in-time" or last-minute sourcing practices, though popular among businesses as a way to maintain small inventories and keep storage costs down, ran the risk of immense damage from cyberattacks and other disruptions. In Asia, Latin America and elsewhere, U.S. economic officers sought better solutions. They helped American companies to find more than one reliable supplier and become more resilient, and they encouraged host-governments to adapt and modernize, which would bring higher revenues. Their work also informed the efforts of Washington policymakers to engage with other countries and organizations in international forums dedicated to the issue.

As in the political section, the various duties of economic officers are organically connected, and the Covid-19 experience showed how. Reporting and analyses not only provided much-needed insights to officials at headquarters but also led to advocacy before governments and businesses aimed at averting economic collapse as a result of the pandemic. The response to the crisis quickly became central to U.S. ties with most countries and affected officers' management of those economic relationships. Also like the political section, an economic section's composition depends on the host-country and the size of the post. There may be a single economic officer in a combined political-economic section, or a section may be able to afford to have one officer responsible for following a single sector of the economy. The head of the economic section usually holds the title of counselor for economic affairs, sits on the mission's leadership team and serves as the ambassador's main adviser on economic matters.

Reporting and analysis

The protection of intellectual property rights has featured prominently in Washington's economic agenda with the rest of the world for years, but it has remained an intractable problem that hurts American companies, especially in developing countries. When Julie Chung was economic counselor at the U.S. Embassy in Thailand in the early 2010s, she understood why. Her section's reporting made clear that fundamental cultural differences prevented most Thais from appreciating the American argument against buying pirated products. Consumers had a hard time comprehending what was so wrong about saving money by watching an unauthorized copy of a Hollywood movie. There was another cultural gap at play. For the Thais, it was normal that, if a U.S. company wanted local vendors not to sell pirated items or fake designer clothing, it should pay them compensation for potential losses. For the Americans, however, that amounted to bribery and corruption. At the same time, businesses from other foreign countries had fewer qualms about paying bribes. "We may have high standards," but not everyone has our "value system," Chung told Nicholas Kralev.[11]

Diplomatic missions in other Asian countries reported similar findings. In their cables to Washington, Chung and her colleagues explained why it would take a sustained long-term effort to persuade consumers, businesses and governments to respect and protect intellectual property. Their reporting and analysis naturally led to advocacy. But one needs to be in possession of the facts and understand how they came about before one tries to change them.

Economic reporting helps officials at headquarters to gain insight into the host-country's economy and the forces that affect it, including laws and regulations, key decision-makers, institutional strengths and weaknesses, the extent of corruption, the state of the infrastructure, and the openness of markets, among others. This is done not just to satisfy people's curiosity – as we saw earlier, economic troubles in one country can easily spread to another or even an entire region, and receiving an early warning can give policymakers the time and tools to head off a potential contagion. In addition, the economic situation in the host-country has a direct impact on any home-country businesses investing there, and the sooner they are aware of a looming crisis, the better they can protect their investments.

Economic disruptions and dislocations spill over into many aspects of life beyond national borders, and the reporting of economic sections abroad is widely read by many government agencies at home. A recession, for example, often causes massive migration. High unemployment and economic collapse have forced more than 7 million Venezuelans to move to Colombia, the United States and other countries in the last two decades, in what the U.N. Refugee Agency has called "one of the largest displacement crises in the world."[12] The large numbers of migrants from Central America trying to cross the U.S. southern border leave behind everyone and everything they know to escape desperate economic conditions and lack of opportunity. The U.S. government has made it a top priority to help countries in the region, particularly El Salvador, Guatemala and Honduras, to build up their economies and tackle the problem from its root. Washington policymakers follow closely the reporting coming from the U.S. embassies there.

If the sending state provides financial or other assistance to the host-country, it may impose conditions, such as introducing certain economic reforms. In that case, economic officers report on the state and pace of those measures and assess the need for additional help from the home-capital to speed things along. It has become standard practice for the United States to require transparency, civil liberties, rule of law, the reduction of corruption, and other steps from recipients of U.S. aid. In addition, if the host-country aspires to join the WTO or another organization, it likely needs to implement reforms to qualify, and economic officers monitor its progress. They also alert headquarters about potential problems, as we saw in the example with the Chinese insurance industry at the beginning of the chapter.

Although there are many sources of economic data and analysis today, diplomats must decide which of them are the most accurate, unbiased and reliable. Established and respected institutions such as the World Bank and the IMF put out high-quality products, and experienced media outlets like The Economist, Reuters and the Financial Times are usually trustworthy. There are even more narrowly specialized periodicals that can be very useful. It is always a good idea to talk to proven experts in academia, think tanks, chambers of commerce, banks, reputable consultancies and other private-sector groups. It also helps to run a concept for a cable, analysis or policy recommendation by fellow officers, both at post and at headquarters, as well as by local staff.

The amount of economic data published today can be overwhelming. Analyses by various private firms, governments and nongovernmental organizations have proliferated as well. So what is left for economic diplomats to do? First, precisely because there is so much data out there, senior officials at home hardly have the time to follow all that comes out of any given country. Officers on the ground do have to track almost everything and make judgments about the most consequential facts that should be included in cables. Second, they must explain clearly to non-experts what certain fiscal developments, economic indicators or trends mean for the home-country, and whether there is cause for concern. Third, if they believe the information that has come to light requires action by headquarters, they can recommend options. Put simply, economic reporting officers have to take stock of all that is happening and make sense of it for policymakers. Like their colleagues in the political career track, they have to answer the question "So what?"

For example, Britain's 2016 decision to leave the EU, which became known as "Brexit," was the subject of a torrent of analyses, speculation and predictions in almost every newspaper, magazine and journal in the world, as well as on numerous podcasts, radio and television programs. The value of diplomatic cables from London was not in rehashing details that had already appeared in the media, but in focusing on the likely impact of Britain's departure from the most successful economic bloc in history on the home-country.

Relationship management

Whatever that country was, it would have to negotiate new trade and investment agreements with Britain – EU-wide accords that previously governed such relationships would no longer include the British. Companies from most of the world had offices in Britain. The old EU regulations were no longer valid, so how would the new ones affect those firms? With many European businesses planning to move their headquarters to EU member-states, governments had to rethink London's future as a major global financial center.

Economic relationships need "gardening" as much as political ones. In this respect, an economic section's first duty is facilitating relevant communication between headquarters and the host-government, including phone calls, email traffic, diplomatic notes, non-papers, notes verbale and démarches. Second, economic officers meet regularly with local officials, business people and other embassy contacts, both to discuss pressing matters and to review ongoing developments or projects. Third, officers attend and speak at conferences and other events. Fourth, they serve as "control officers" during high-level visits from the home-country – such trips often open doors to which embassies may not have routine access. The contacts made while carrying out all of these duties help to leverage economic relationships when they are most needed.

The Financial Action Task Force (FATF) is an intergovernmental organization founded in 1989 on the initiative of the Group of Seven (G7) leading industrialized countries to develop policies aimed at combating money-laundering. In the aftermath of the 9/11 attacks in 2001, when Washington was looking for the best mechanism to counter the financing of terrorism, I was chief of the economic-political section at the U.S. Consulate General in Hong Kong. As it happened, Hong Kong held the task force's rotating presidency at the time. I had built a relationship with the official in that position, Clarie Lo, so I requested a meeting with her and suggested that her organization was best placed to take on the challenge, perhaps starting with guidance for governments on how to approach it.

Figure 7.1 Lisa Kubiske, the U.S. ambassador to Honduras, talks to the press in 2013. Photo by Orlando Sierra/AFP via Getty Images.

When the U.S. administration made an official proposal along these lines, Lo was prepared. Before the year was out, the task force's mandate was expanded to include terrorist financing.[13]

Economic sections use their interactions with local officials to both seek and offer advice on developments anywhere in the world that might affect their two economies. At the beginning of the 1997 Asian financial crisis, Indonesia seemed calm, and the authorities assured the U.S. Embassy that the country's economic fundamentals were sound. Ambassador J. Stapleton Roy, however, did not want to be surprised when things came "crashing down." Patricia Haslach, the economic counselor, instructed her section to dig deeper. Her deputy, Judith Fergin, tapped into her large network of contacts and began holding daily phone briefings with officials at the State and Treasury Departments in Washington. Junior officer Brian McFeeters reached out to local bankers he had met a few months earlier, who sounded worried that funds from abroad were drying up. Soon Indonesia's currency was in freefall. Experts in Washington advised the government in Jakarta to negotiate a loan package with the IMF as quickly as possible. Haslach's section suggested that President Suharto had to hear it, and that he would take it more seriously if a senior official from Washington came to deliver it. A few days later, Treasury Secretary Lawrence Summers arrived in Jakarta and Suharto reluctantly agreed to negotiate.[14]

Advocacy and negotiation

The IMF loan, which was finalized in the spring of 1998, was not going to magically solve all of Indonesia's problems. For three decades, Suharto had presided over a corrupt system that was in desperate need of major reform. It was clear to the U.S. Embassy that it had to engage in a serious advocacy campaign in all parts of society. But events far outpaced its planning. By then, the economic crisis and the pent-up discontent with Suharto's rule had unleashed a political storm. Massive protests accompanied by street violence, including a million-person march in front of the presidential palace near the embassy, prompted Washington to evacuate many of its diplomats. Within weeks, Suharto was ousted, clearing the way for policies recommended by the IMF to be carried out. By summer, the worst of the crisis was over.

Economic reforms, a level playing field for foreign businesses and improving the investment climate in the host-country are among the most common objectives of economic advocacy efforts in most of the world. "Some economic decisions made in one country have an outsized impact on jobs and growth here in the United States and around the world," Lael Brainard, a Treasury undersecretary in the Obama administration, said in 2012. "Convincing leaders of other countries to change their domestic economic policies can be challenging and intensely political, yet it is essential when it has an economic impact on our shores."[15] Diplomats often lobby their host-governments to open certain sectors to foreign investors and make the process for bidding on contracts more transparent. The Bureau of Economic and Business Affairs at the State Department publishes investment-climate reports sent by U.S. missions abroad and shares them with the Department of Commerce, which includes the information in its annual Country Commercial Guides.[16] The ultimate goal is increasing U.S. trade and investment, with an eye to prosperity at home.

In recent years, that has been particularly important in Africa, where the United States has competed with China, and American diplomats have been trying to show that the presence of U.S. companies is much more beneficial to African countries than that of Chinese firms. In 2017, the U.S. ambassador to Cameroon, Michael Hoza, and his team devised an advocacy strategy to promote American businesses by contrasting their practices with those of the Chinese. As was the case elsewhere on the continent, China imported its own laborers, "extracted raw materials" without transferring technology to the Cameroonians, stoked corruption and had no interest in corporate social responsibility, Hoza pointed out. The Americans would create local jobs, transfer technology to Cameroon, adhere to the U.S. Foreign Corrupt Practices Act and engage in corporate social responsibility. Not only did U.S. companies win several contracts and other opportunities, but their focus on transparency boosted pro-American sentiment. The Chinese ambassador even thanked Hoza for giving him ideas about how to discipline some of his country's more "wayward" firms.[17]

As the previous chapter noted, diplomatic advocacy can be done quietly by engaging key decision-makers, or it can also include a public campaign. Hoza's embassy did both, and its efforts were bolstered by a reservoir of goodwill the

United States had built in Cameroon for years by helping to eradicate polio, stop outbreaks of bird flu and Ebola, and by training the Cameroonian military to drive away pirates and Boko Haram extremists. Goodwill usually provides a strong jump-start to an advocacy endeavor, but it cannot save a poor strategy and weak execution. Diplomats must remember their bottom line, which is to influence host-country decisions and actions to align them with the home-country's interests.

A winning strategy includes a clear definition of success and an objective way to measure it. Vague goals like increasing awareness of an issue or improving the sending country's image are not nearly as useful as specific outcomes, such as a certain number of contracts going to host-country firms or the local parliament passing anti-corruption and fair-practices legislation. The most persuasive tactic tends to be putting yourself in your foreign interlocutors' shoes and understanding how they think about the matter at hand, why they have not previously done what you want them to do, and what their concerns are. Make sure you have a solid grasp of the subject matter, including any technical details, so you do not come off as a lightweight and miss important nuances in your discussions. Expect the other side's responses and be ready to address them. If your campaign features a public diplomacy component, plan carefully any opinion articles the ambassador might publish in the local press, any media interviews embassy officials or visitors from headquarters might give, and press conferences and other events that are likely to produce a clear benefit.

As it does in political advocacy, partnering with other organizations that share your values and aims in the host-country often multiplies the message. In the 2010s, U.S. embassies in Latin America joined forces with missions from other developed countries in advocating for the elimination of mercury from the region's gold-mining practices. A potent neurotoxin, mercury was used to extract gold, causing severe and lasting pollution in the air, soil and water. Moreover, that problem existed mostly in illegal gold mining, which was controlled by traffickers of drugs and migrants. The lobbying efforts led to agreements between the United States and Peru and Colombia to combat unlawful mining and minimize its negative effects. With American assistance, Peru evicted miners from the epicenter of its illicit gold-mining operations, and the Colombian police seized or destroyed more than $4 million worth of heavy machinery and other mining equipment.[18]

The agreements, of course, had to be negotiated. Earlier chapters noted that high-level negotiations are typically handled by headquarters, but there is still plenty of work to be done by economic officers abroad to grease the skids for a favorable outcome. Since they are the ones on the ground, they are often in possession of facts and insights that officials at home may have no other way of obtaining. They provide advice on the best time to start or pause a negotiation, on reaction in the host-government and the public on the latest negotiating round, and on demands the other side might view as culturally insensitive or even insulting. Economic officers serve as the liaison between their own lead negotiators and those in the receiving state, and sometimes they become part of their country's delegation during formal sessions.

Economic sanctions

U.S. airline executives and shareholders grew more and more frustrated by the day. They were losing business to foreign competitors that flew passengers between the United States and Asia faster and more cheaply, because those carriers had the luxury of using Russian airspace. The American companies had lost access to Russia's skies when Moscow retaliated against the sweeping economic sanctions the West had imposed on Russia after it invaded Ukraine a year earlier. Now, in early 2023, three U.S. airlines – American, Delta and United – estimated that they had lost a collective $2 billion and started lobbying the White House to prevent carriers from China, India and the Middle East from using the polar route that saved them significant time and fuel.

The most draconian sanctions regime in history included banning Russian airlines from U.S. airspace. Many other countries, such as Canada, Japan and the entire EU, issued the same restrictions. The Kremlin closed its skies to airlines from all those countries, and they were forced to alter their flight paths, which necessitated reducing passenger and cargo loads to keep costs down as they flew longer distances. On routes from India to the United States, U.S. carriers often had to stop in third countries, because headwinds and other unfavorable weather depleted their planes' jet fuel supply.[19] Even without a stop, on March 22, 2023, it took American Airlines 15 hours and 15 minutes to fly from New York to New Delhi, while Air India took 13 hours and 31 minutes to fly the same distance.[20] The U.S. carriers saw the disparity as an unfair advantage and wanted Washington to level the playing field by imposing on their foreign competitors the same restrictions on using the polar route that applied to them. No decision has been made as of this writing.

In the last two decades, economic sanctions have become a frequent tool of coercive or hard power, used particularly by the United States. Although they are designed at headquarters, economic diplomats abroad play an important role in informing decisions and helping to monitor implementation. The purpose of sanctions is usually to compel changes in policies and behavior by their targets, but in reality, they can end up inflicting pain without achieving their objectives – and sometimes they have unintended consequences for the country that imposes them, as in the case of the U.S. airlines above. So it is critical for their creators to analyze thoroughly their likely collateral effects and take them into consideration in decision-making, for which economic officers can be very useful. During the wars in the Balkans in the 1990s, Yugoslavia was under U.N. sanctions, including an oil embargo. Cutting off a gas pipeline was proposed at one point as well, but when diplomats realized that it would deprive civilians of heat in the winter, the idea was abandoned.

The targets of sanctions inevitably explore workarounds. They often find alternative suppliers and import substitutions, and even institutionalize smuggling to meet demand. Markets tend to "adjust to the distortions in supply and demand," as Chas Freeman, one of the contributors to this book, has observed.[21] Even though the West banned almost all Russian energy imports in 2022, Moscow found markets in

China, India and elsewhere to sell its oil and gas.[22] For the party imposing the sanctions, monitoring their implementation and being aware of countries and companies that violate them by continuing to do business with the target is as crucial for their effectiveness as it is difficult to accomplish. Economic diplomats in the field try to keep track of all that, and headquarters decides what costs, if any, to impose on the perpetrators. The sanctions' effectiveness ultimately depends on their specific objectives, how widely they are observed internationally, and how successful the targets are at evading them, among other factors.

Thanks to the unprecedented power of its currency, the United States is in a unique position to block trade and investment to countries it accuses of wrong-doing, as it has done to punish Iran and North Korea for pursuing nuclear weapons. Not surprisingly, these states, and some of those that suffer from not being able to trade with the sanctions' targets, have accused Washington of abusing its power as the issuer of the de facto global currency. Some, including Russia and China, have been searching for substitutes to the dollar. During Chinese President Xi Jinping's 2023 visit to Moscow, he and his Russian counterpart, Vladimir Putin, agreed to use the Chinese yuan in trade with the Global South, which includes developing countries that are mainly in the Southern Hemisphere.[23] There have been other attempts to weaken and even replace the dollar as the principal currency for settling international transactions, most prominently with the euro, but none have succeeded as of this writing.

The dollar is not likely to lose its current status in the near term, though the repeated battles in Congress over the U.S. debt ceiling may speed up that process. Were it eventually to do so, experts predict catastrophic consequences for the U.S. economy and financial system. The United States would no longer be able to print money to pay for imports or to run huge deficits, which is made possible by other countries' willingness to buy U.S. debt thanks to the dollar's strength. If that happens, "future generations of American diplomats will have less financial coercive power to work with," Freeman wrote. "This will test their negotiating skills in ways that previous generations have not experienced."[24]

Development and foreign aid

In the early 2010s, Nigeria was the world's sixth most populous country. It had vast oil reserves but struggled to feed its people. Nearly half of the 5 million tons of rice consumed annually were imported. Fertile land was plentiful, but Nigeria lacked a strategy to make agriculture profitable. Most farmers lived on less than $2 a day. "We were producing rice with bad quality, and many people didn't want to buy it," rice farmer Vitalis Tarnongo recalled. A public–private project sponsored by the U.S. government and called "Markets" set out to transform the country's agricultural sector, beginning with rice farms.[25]

The project's team first sought to find out what rice-processing companies wanted to buy, and once those requirements were determined, it trained the farmers how to

Figure 7.2 The World Food Programme and USAID distribute food aid to displaced people fleeing the extremist group Boko Haram's incursions into Niger in 2016.
Photo by Issouf Sanogo/AFP via Getty Images.

produce quality rice. "For the first time, we've been able to grow rice and process it into a product that can compete with imports on both price and quality," Tim Prewitt, the project's director, said in 2012. Next, Prewitt and his co-workers persuaded banks to extend credit to the farmers, which resulted in a significant investor interest in rice production. The farmers' income increased 400 percent in just a few years. The same strategy was applied to the production of corn, sesame, cassava and even to the fish-processing industry. "Markets" trained more than 500,000 Nigerians.

Development and foreign assistance have become a key part of diplomacy, particularly for the largest donors, such as the United States, Germany, Britain, Canada and Japan, which have specialized government agencies that lead these efforts. Development diplomats often serve at missions abroad. The mission of USAID, which sponsored the Nigeria project, is to "save lives, reduce poverty, strengthen democratic governance, and help people emerge from humanitarian crises and progress beyond assistance."[26] Its officers are members of the Foreign Service. "The best ambassadors and deputy chiefs of mission really value what we do, because they see us as a resource in their toolkit for promoting U.S. foreign policy objectives," Andrew Sisson told Nicholas Kralev during his assignment as USAID mission director in Pakistan in 2012. "We believe that stabilization, economic and social development are very much in the U.S. interest."[27]

In 2019, USAID had about 1,700 Foreign Service officers.[28] A major part of their work is supervising and evaluating projects implemented by a significant number of contractors. U.S. aid rarely goes directly to foreign governments. Rather, the money is awarded to nonprofits and businesses from the United States and sometimes from the recipient countries. For example, USAID does not have the capacity to build a clinic or school in an impoverished country, but it can hire a company to do it. The agency has missions in more than 80 countries and programs in more than 100.[29] Where it does not have a presence, the embassy's economic section helps with development activities.

U.S. officials often say that the ultimate goal of foreign aid is to wean recipient countries off that assistance, helping them to prosper and become better U.S. trading partners, as has happened with South Korea and Taiwan, among others. In 2021, USAID spent more than $28 billion worldwide, the largest part of which went to sectors like healthcare, emergency response, civil society, agriculture and education. The agency estimated that 46 million liters of drinking water were disinfected with point-of-use treatment products, 29 million women and children benefited from family planning and maternal, neonatal and child health services, and 12 million babies received postnatal care within two days of birth, among other projects funded by American taxpayer dollars.[30]

A day in an economic officer's life

We have covered a lot of what economic diplomats do, but it by no means exhausts everything they have to deal with at some point in their careers. For example, some exports involve sensitive technology and need special licenses from the home-government, and economic officers verify that exporters comply with their license's conditions. Chapter 5 noted that embassies often send recognized and emerging leaders from the host-country on exchange programs to the home-country. Chapter 9 on public diplomacy will discuss those programs in detail, but it is worth pointing out that economic officers are among those who nominate candidates.

When describing an officer's typical day, the caveats from political tradecraft apply here as well: no two days are exactly the same, it depends on where you are posted, and there is a difference between a planned day and an actual day. You do have to catch up on the overnight news and cable traffic in either case, and to make sure that you complete any work previously assigned to you, but after that, your schedule may diverge from what appears in your calendar. Your planned agenda may include the following items: an internal section meeting; drafting a cable about a démarche the ambassador delivered the previous afternoon, at which you were present; a visit to the offices of a trade union to learn about its political clout; a talk at the monthly lunch meeting of the local chamber of commerce; planning a trip to one of the host-country's provinces the following week to meet with the governor and local business leaders; or working on a long-term report about the host-government's record in fighting corruption.

Here is how your day may take a different turn. As you are writing your cable, the deputy chief of mission stops by unexpectedly with the visiting governor of a state or province from your home-country, who is leading a trade delegation and would like an impromptu briefing on the amount of red tape in the ministry responsible for approving new foreign investment. This causes you to delay finishing your cable until the afternoon, which means that your corruption report will have to wait. Then, while you are speaking at the chamber of commerce, your economic section chief suddenly shows up to whisk you off to a factory owned by a company from your home-country, where workers are staging an improvised protest against low pay. Since you know the factory's management, your boss hopes you can get to the bottom of the dispute and help to defuse it. Now, assuming you will return to the office before the end of the day, your cable may keep you there until well after business hours, unless you can get an extension. It is unusual to make headquarters wait for two days after a démarche has been delivered to read a cable about it.

Hopefully, the protest at the factory or another emergency – they can happen more frequently than you think – will not force you to cancel or delay your out-of-town trip. The importance of such travel cannot be overstated. At the end of the day, the greatest value of having diplomats stationed in a foreign country is their ability to see and hear things with their own eyes and ears, and it is impossible to understand and keep track of the local economy unless one regularly leaves the capital and meets with people from different walks of life in all parts of the country.

The advice in the previous chapter on how to prepare for your assignment even before you arrive in the host-country can also help economic officers, with the addition of acquiring specialized knowledge in the field from respected publications, government policy documents, think tank studies and other materials. Along with consultations with colleagues in your own government and diplomats in your future host-country's embassy in your home-capital, it would be wise to meet economists, bankers, business leaders and other experts. They can help you gain a deeper understanding and wider variety of perspectives than what you can glean from reading, especially if you arrive at your meetings with prepared questions and ask new ones as you listen to the experts. Ideally, you will benefit from their insights and recommendations throughout your tour.

Just like their colleagues in the political section, economic officers sometimes have to carry out policies or instructions with which they disagree. They may believe that certain sanctions their government is considering are doomed to failure, or they may feel that advocating for free trade while their own country is being accused of protectionism is hypocritical. They can certainly try to influence the policy debate, but once decisions are made, they are required to implement them as best they can. U.S. diplomats, of course, can use the State Department's dissent channel to register disagreement or propose policy changes.

What is commercial diplomacy?

During a trip to Nigeria in 2015, Eno Umoh saw drones being used for photography and filming. When he returned home to Baltimore, he began researching other purposes of drone technology and was surprised by its huge potential in agriculture, construction, real estate and many other industries. In agriculture, for example, drones can help map out areas of farmland, spray crops and plant tree seeds with great efficiency. However, few executives in any of these industries realized the promise the technology held. With a business partner, Austin Brown, Umoh founded Global Air Media, a drone education, training and consulting company, and even got it licensed by the Federal Aviation Administration.[31]

After their initial success in the United States, where the drone market was more developed than in most of the world, Umoh and Brown decided to look for opportunities overseas. At an entrepreneur event in Baltimore, they learned about the U.S. Foreign Commercial Service (FCS), which eventually helped them to find foreign markets and connected them with prospective clients in several countries. "We found out about resources we had no idea were available to us," Umoh recalled in 2021.[32] Through its offices in about 70 U.S. diplomatic missions, the FCS provides export-promotion services to American companies of all sizes, including market research, matchmaking and due diligence.[33] Its diplomats helped Global Air Media to find partners in Zambia, Ethiopia and other African countries.

Commercial diplomacy is **the activity of developing and maintaining trade, investment and business relations between and among countries**. It can be bilateral or multilateral, and its mission is the same as that of diplomacy overall: to advance the home-country's national interest of ensuring security, fostering prosperity and promoting its values. More specifically, commercial diplomats help to strengthen the country's economy by identifying business and investment opportunities abroad for its companies and assisting them in entering and navigating foreign markets. They also facilitate host-country firms' investment in the home-country, as noted earlier. The longtime practice of sending trade delegations to foreign countries is perhaps the best-known part of commercial diplomacy. Unlike most of diplomacy, this type of engagement takes place not only at the national level. Governors, mayors and other local officials regularly travel with business executives to find markets abroad and to attract foreign investment to their own states, provinces or cities.

Foreign Commercial Service

As an agency in the U.S. Department of Commerce, the FCS helps to implement trade policies aimed at producing economic growth and increasing employment. It offers services to businesses of all sizes – from startups to major corporations that are household names. Other than free general briefings on the investment climate and particular sectors, those services are paid, and their cost depends on the firm's size. At this writing, an "initial market check" is priced at $350 for small, $900 for midsize and $1,300 for big companies.[34] The fees for an "international partner search" vary from $750 to $2,700.[35]

FCS officers understand what it takes to break into the host-country market, what obstacles need to be overcome, and what local businesses are looking for in a foreign partner. Good commercial diplomats are trained to think like business people. They also have insights into available local financing, tax breaks and other incentives. They advocate directly before the host-government – and publicly – on behalf of American industries or companies and explain the potential benefits of their presence and operations, such as creating jobs and stimulating innovation. The U.S. government does have red lines. Its diplomats do not promote industries and firms that make harmful products, such as tobacco, or have poor corporate governance track records. If two or more American companies are competing for the same contract, U.S. officials do not take sides, though they may advocate for American products and services in general. It can be tricky to determine what exactly an American company is, given all the multinationals with complex ownership structures, and either policymakers in Washington or diplomats in the field must make judgment calls.

The most senior commercial officer at an embassy is a member of the country team and serves as adviser to the ambassador on trade and investment matters. Chiefs of mission are often commercial advocates themselves, especially when American companies are in the running for large and important contracts that could create many jobs at home. Big and well-known corporations like Boeing have the resources to do their own lobbying abroad, but they still need help from diplomats. Embassies view championing Boeing as an act of national pride. They are also aware that a single new plane order can result in hundreds of employment opportunities. In the early 2010s, when the Boeing 787 Dreamliner was still new, the company flew the aircraft to many countries and staged high-profile events in front of it. Almost every time, the U.S. ambassador was a featured speaker, including Kristie Kenney, who served in Thailand at the time. She personally promoted a variety of American brands nearly every day, she told Nicholas Kralev in 2012. "It starts with me wearing a Coca-Cola T-shirt at a basketball game or carrying a Starbucks cup," she said.[36]

If the Department of Commerce, in consultation with the State Department, determines that advocating for a U.S. company is in the national interest, officers from all embassy sections become commercial diplomats – and there is no charge.[37] When the stakes are high, such as winning a large defense or energy contract that would reinvigorate the relationship with the host-country, the post designs an advocacy strategy using political, economic, public diplomacy and other tools. This approach is relatively new in U.S. diplomacy. In the last century, the government was less enthusiastic about helping private companies, unless there was an obvious strategic interest involved. But as the international environment became much more competitive, and businesses from other countries enjoyed increasing support from their own governments, Washington decided to step up its game. It also realized that showcasing and sharing American business practices had political and economic benefits for the United States.

Unlike their State Department colleagues, who take assignments outside their career tracks, the job of FCS officers does not change. Since 1993, Michael Lally has spent each workday helping to build, cultivate and expand U.S. trade and investment relationships on three continents. Lally began his career in the former Soviet republics of Ukraine, Kazakhstan and Azerbaijan, where free markets were a novelty after decades of communist-style planned economies. He later served in Mexico, whose trade with the United States exceeded $1 billion a day. In Turkey, Lally and his colleagues helped facilitate dozens of deals, including a joint venture to manufacture and commercialize carbon fiber and derivatives between the Dow Chemical Company, based in Midland, Michigan, and a Turkish firm, Aksa Akrilik Kimya Sanayii, he told Kralev.[38] Lally's most challenging tour was in Russia, amid tense overall relations. At this writing, he is the minister-counselor for commercial affairs at the U.S. Mission to the EU in Brussels.

Foreign Agricultural Service

Susan Phillips met her husband in lockup – but a lockup of a peculiar kind. In her first job in the U.S. Department of Agriculture (USDA) in the early 1990s, she was a commodities analyst responsible for tracking and analyzing the global trade of wheat and forecasting future production, supply and demand. The data was so sensitive that employees were herded into a secure area, with sealed window shades and all communications blocked. The time she spent in that room was long enough to lead to a romance, and eventually marriage. As a civil servant, Phillips worked in Washington but later became an officer in the U.S. Foreign Agricultural Service and was posted to South Korea and the Netherlands.[39]

With about 100 offices at diplomatic missions abroad, the service gathers market intelligence, maintains and expands access to foreign markets, promotes U.S. agricultural exports and helps developing countries to improve their agricultural capacity, as noted in Chapter 5.[40] Not only does it not charge American producers and processors, but it provides them with cost-share funding to develop new markets and mitigate the adverse effects of trade barriers, mainly through agreements with commodity groups, such as the U.S. Soybean Export Council, the Almond Board of California and the Meat Export Foundation.

The U.S. Animal and Plant Health Inspection Service is also part of both the Foreign Service and USDA. With offices in 27 countries, it helps to ensure the health of agricultural imports to the United States and assists foreign governments in building capacity to control, manage and eradicate pests and diseases.[41]

Because their Foreign Service does not have representatives in every country, U.S. agricultural diplomats are responsible for entire regions. Clay Hamilton, whom Kralev met in Turkey in 2012, also covered Central Asia and had recently come back from Azerbaijan, where he organized training on food safety, plant and dairy health. Having started his career in Bulgaria in 1992, Hamilton also served in Italy and Japan. "American farmers are our main constituency, and we frame everything through how it helps them," he said. Turkey, for example, had relied for years "on excess dairy cattle for meat," and meat prices were among the highest in Europe. Hamilton's office successfully lobbied the Turkish government to open up the market to American cattle bred for meat. In addition to being swayed by the high prices, "they realized that cattle bred for meat tastes better than dairy cattle and started to diversify," Hamilton said.[42]

As the U.S. agricultural attaché in the Netherlands in the 2010s, Susan Phillips covered six countries in Northern Europe with only three local staff members. "We spent a lot of time securing the release of detained shipments at the port of Rotterdam. Because trade policy is usually a slow-moving train, I worked on market-access issues that my predecessor had started, and my successor would finish," she wrote in 2023.[43] In South Korea, Phillips was one of several American officers and had a larger local staff. The size of an embassy's agricultural office depends on how big a market the host-country is for U.S. products. From a developing country after World War II, South Korea has become one of the world's fastest-growing economies.

"They are one of our biggest trading partners," Hamilton said. "We want the rest of the world to develop into better customers."[44]

Case Study: Dominican Banking Crisis

When I became deputy chief of mission at the U.S. Embassy in the Dominican Republic in 2003, a deep crisis consumed most of the post's work for months. The failure of a major Dominican bank had shaken the entire sector and dragged down the economy shortly before my arrival, as Kralev noted in Chapter 1. Even though Washington had invited the Caribbean country to start negotiations for membership in the Central America Free Trade Agreement (CAFTA), it was obvious that it would not qualify while suffering an economic contraction, high inflation and unemployment. We had to help it get back on its feet, so it could become a reliable U.S. partner.

We determined that the fulfillment of three main conditions was essential for an economic recovery. First, the Dominican government had to secure an IMF bailout, which would require painful austerity measures. Second, the authorities had to conduct an impartial and transparent investigation into the banking fraud scandal and punish its perpetrators. Third, elections scheduled in a few months had to be free, fair and clean to restore faith in government and prove that corrupt practices were limited to the banking sector. With these objectives in mind, the embassy's combined political-economic section, the USAID mission and many of the rest of us went into high gear. Our ambassador, Hans Hertell, a noncareer appointee who had been a banker in Puerto Rico, was a valuable asset.

What did we do? Not surprisingly, the government was hesitant to agree to the drastic spending cuts the IMF required, because they would cause hardship among voters, so our economic officers had to advocate and persuade. They explained to officials, legislators and the public how the necessary reforms would help their country to join CAFTA, which in turn would bring significant trade and investment benefits that would bolster the Dominican economy. They also arranged a visit by a senior Treasury official from Washington to reinforce

Case Study: (cont.)

these points. It turned out that the authorities did not know how to do a forensic probe into the banking fraud, so the USAID office hired U.S. experts to train investigators and prosecutors. To make sure the elections were clean and the results legitimate, the embassy provided technical assistance, worked with other foreign embassies and U.N. representatives to bring in international observers, and some of our officers served as monitors.

All aspects of our engagement and advocacy mattered, and the three parts of our strategy affected each other. We cannot claim all the credit, but the government reached an agreement with the IMF and the elections went reasonably well. It took four years, but bank owners and executives were sentenced to prison[45] and the Dominican Republic joined CAFTA in 2007.[46] Thanks to the accord, which also includes Costa Rica, El Salvador, Guatemala, Honduras and Nicaragua, the U.S. trade surplus in goods with the six countries was $7 billion in 2018, and goods exports supported an estimated 134,000 jobs in 2014.[47]

Exercise: Boeing 737 MAX Troubles

The Boeing 737 MAX, the fourth generation of the narrow-body aircraft manufactured by the U.S. company, entered commercial service in 2017. Over the next two years, two planes, one operated by Indonesia's Lion Air and one by Ethiopian Airlines, crashed shortly after takeoff, killing everyone onboard. Although Boeing denied responsibility, it later became clear that a software issue played a role in both accidents, and the FAA grounded the aircraft.[48] The firm's reputation took a big hit. The incident is the subject of "Downfall: The Case Against Boeing," a Netflix documentary film.[49]

It is now three years after the accidents, and Lion Air and Ethiopian Airlines need to renew their fleets. Following changes Boeing has made to the 737 MAX software and the FAA clearance for the aircraft's return to service, both carriers believe it would meet their needs better than its main competitor, the Airbus 320neo. Boeing, recognizing its reputational problem, has offered the airlines significantly discounted prices. However, the Indonesian and Ethiopian governments are pushing for a switch to Airbus. Public opinion in both countries is also opposed to the Boeing aircraft.

Boeing has requested meetings with the U.S. ambassadors to Indonesia and Ethiopia to discuss support from the U.S. government, which is open to advocating on Boeing's behalf.

Task: The class will be divided into two groups, the first of which will represent the economic and commercial sections at the U.S. Embassy in Indonesia, and the

Exercise: (cont.)

second the same sections at the U.S. Embassy in Ethiopia. Each group will prepare recommendations for its ambassador on a strategy to boost the chances of securing Boeing 737 MAX orders. Consider what steps, if any, the embassy should require that Boeing take to receive U.S. government support; which other embassy sections, if any, should take part in your campaign; and whether quiet lobbying or public outreach would lead to a better outcome.

ADDITIONAL RESOURCES

Michael S. Hoza, Kevin McGuire, Brian McFeeters, David R. Gilmour, Preeti Shah, Paul A. Brown, Naomi C. Fellows, Jonathan Addleton, Theodore Lewis, Kimberly Rosen, et al., "From Guitars to Gold: The Fruits of Economic Diplomacy," *Foreign Service Journal*, January–February 2019.

Daniel Immerwahr, *How to Hide an Empire* (Farrar, Straus and Giroux, 2019).

Robert B. Zoellick, *America in the World: A History of U.S. Diplomacy and Foreign Policy* (Twelve, 2020).

8   Diplomatic Reporting and Communication

DOUGLAS SILLIMAN AND EUNICE REDDICK

It was one of a career diplomat's worst nightmares. In November 2010, major U.S. and European media outlets started publishing jaw-dropping details from secret cables sent to Washington by U.S. embassies around the world. The New York Times called the revelations "an unprecedented look at backroom bargaining" and "brutally candid views of foreign leaders and frank assessments of nuclear and terrorist threats."[1] Diplomatic reporting had never received as much public attention.

The documents were part of more than 250,000 State Department cables stolen from a U.S. government computer and released by WikiLeaks. Thousands of Foreign Service officers worried about the prospect of serious damage to diplomatic relationships and physical danger to sources of sensitive information in various countries, whose names were included in many of the cables. The White House condemned "in the strongest terms the unauthorized disclosure of classified documents and sensitive national security information."[2] "There is always an expectation that people talk to us in confidence," Michael Hammer, a Foreign Service officer who was the spokesman for the National Security Council at the time, told Nicholas Kralev. "Diplomacy does need that space behind closed doors to take effect and produce results. People will be more willing to talk to you and do things for you if they are allowed that breathing space."[3]

If there was a silver lining in the leaks, it was that "people suddenly realized three things," said Hammer, who later served as ambassador to Chile and the Democratic Republic of the Congo. "First, that we are pretty good writers and provide sound and interesting analysis. Second, that we are passionate and determined to advance the U.S. national interest. Third, that we do what we say, and there isn't much variance between what we say in private and in public."

Douglas Silliman, one of this chapter's authors, was chargé d'affaires at the U.S. Embassy in Turkey at the time of the WikiLeaks release. He and his colleagues rushed to review thousands of cables sent from the embassy and believed to have been compromised, so they could warn Turkish officials and other sources that what they had told American diplomats could end up on the Internet, and even in the media. Many people outside the U.S. government have found the WikiLeaks cables useful and eye-opening, and university professors use them as a teaching tool. As former career diplomats, however, we have a responsibility to protect classified information, and at this writing, those cables are still considered classified by the State Department. So we will not refer to any of them in this chapter. We will use only documents that have been declassified. Thankfully, there are many.

Although the term "cables" may be an anachronism – they are now sent electronically – digging up information the media has not uncovered, as well as providing insightful analysis of known facts and making influential policy recommendations, are still critical and prized skills for an effective diplomat. Reports, dispatches and memos that are clear, concise, informative and compelling are highly valued by busy policymakers.

Diplomatic reporting

Diplomatic writing and reporting have a long history. As early as the 14th century B.C., the rulers of Egypt's 18th Dynasty corresponded with their representatives to the Amorite Kingdom in Canaan using cuneiform writing on clay tablets.[4] Official diplomatic **dispatches** have been used for centuries. Until the invention of the telegraph in the mid-1800s, dispatches traveled by sea and road, which could take weeks or months. Ebenezer Bassett, the first U.S. ambassador to Haiti and first African-American ambassador, pleaded for assistance from Washington in dispatches in 1870, as Haitians fleeing civil war took refuge on the U.S. diplomatic compound.[5] In the early decades of diplomatic reporting, with long delays in response from headquarters, ambassadors acted without waiting for guidance. In fact, the formal title "ambassador extraordinary and plenipotentiary" was introduced because, given the slow communications, chiefs of mission could make decisions that would bind their home-country on their own authority.

With the creation of the international electric cable system in the 19th century, governments began using **telegrams** for much faster communication. Because they traveled over cable wires, they became known as "cables," a term that has stuck to this day, even though the United States abandoned the wire route in the 1960s.[6] The State Department used telegrams mostly to deal with urgent matters. They were sent in code to protect security. The code work and increasing expenses became a burden, however, and the department introduced **airgrams** in 1942. During the first two decades, they were essentially telegrams, because they used telegraphic style, but were sent in hard copy by air.[7] In 1962, they became longer and written in plain expository language – in other words, they resembled dispatches. The use of airgrams ended in 1991.

The most famous U.S. diplomatic dispatch is the one written in 1946 by George Kennan, at the time chargé d'affaires at the U.S. Embassy in Moscow, which became known as the "Long Telegram."[8] Kennan's 8,000-word message sought to explain the sources of Soviet behavior while recommending a pragmatic policy of containment. Such a long document on any subject is almost unthinkable today. Most Washington policymakers do not have time to read long papers and often repeat to their colleagues and subordinates, "The shorter, the better."

Figure 8.1 George Kennan (left), author of the 1946 "Long Telegram," is sworn in as U.S. ambassador to the Soviet Union in 1952.
Photo by Hulton Archive/Getty Images.

Reporting by telephone

Phone calls are mostly used to report truly urgent breaking news. For example, it is a good idea to call your capital when your embassy is under attack – that is something officials at home need to know immediately. You should also call if there has been a major earthquake, tsunami or another natural disaster, which could affect embassy operations and require immediate steps to secure assistance or other responses. Another reason to call is the need for a back-and-forth conversation with someone responsible for a decision or moving policy in a particular direction. Sometimes a short, direct conversation is better than a written report to clarify points or resolve misunderstandings. In addition to regular phone lines and Internet calls, secure phone lines and videoconferencing capabilities can be used to discuss sensitive topics without fear of leakage. This also makes it possible to have truly private conversations.

While diplomats frequently seek to share urgent information in one-on-one phone calls with an official at headquarters, calls can be expanded to include officials from several offices. The State Department's Operations Center acts as a central connecting service for calls that can start in a diplomatic mission abroad or in Washington. Following an earthquake, for example, an embassy will inform its regional bureau in the department, as well as the bureaus of Consular Affairs and Diplomatic Security, and other offices that may need to send emergency supplies to the affected country or to evacuate U.S. citizens from the disaster area.

Reporting by email

Informal reporting can be done by email outside the official cable system, particularly concerning time-sensitive matters. Email is also useful if you want to provide details or specific explanations to a limited audience, and in circumstances where you want to direct your message to particular individuals. This is a good way to give your capital periodic updates – often called situation reports or "sitreps" – on what is happening on the ground. For example, in the aftermath of a natural disaster, headquarters wants to know on a daily basis the number of casualties, where assistance is coming from, and where there might be more needs. Most governments have both classified and unclassified email systems. Using unclassified email is a good way to reach your audience after business hours or on weekends. The classified system can be accessed only from the office, as noted in Chapter 6.

In 2006, William Burns, then-ambassador to Russia, sent an email message to Secretary of State Condoleezza Rice to urge the Bush administration to sign off on Russia's accession to the World Trade Organization (WTO). It refers to Robert Portman, the U.S. trade representative at the time.[9]

Madam Secretary, I hope you don't mind this informal note, but I wanted to emphasize directly to you my concern that the drift in our WTO negotiations is about to cause severe damage to what is already a troubled relationship with Russia. Please don't misunderstand me. I do not mean any of this as criticism of Ambassador Portman or his team, for whom I have great respect. Nor do I have any illusions about the mood on [Capitol] Hill, or the capacity of the Russians to whine, blame others and deceive themselves.

The problem is that, in my judgment, we have hit the point of diminishing returns in the negotiations. Absent a bold move by the president to close the deal, the Russians are going to slide backwards very quickly, as only they can do, into a swamp of real and imagined grievances. The irony is that Putin himself, for all his many flaws, remains an economic modernizer. He has a genuine interest, not shared by everyone in his inner circle, in integrating into the global economy.[10]

In an attempt to convey Putin's exasperation with the process after 12 years of negotiations, Burns used language that was hardly diplomatic.

He's now at the stage where he's quite capable of shooting himself (and Russia) in the foot by declaring that Russia doesn't need the WTO, and the U.S. can shove it.

After proposing a specific strategy and timeline in a page and a half, Burns ended with this:

I'm convinced that it's time to close the deal, and that the negative consequences of delay far outweigh any possible benefits. I apologize again for bothering you directly, but felt I owed it to you and the president to be straight about my concerns.

A bilateral U.S.–Russia deal to clear the way for Moscow's WTO membership was signed seven months later, though Russia would not join the organization until 2012.

Modern diplomatic cables

Today, we use the term "cable" to describe an official dispatch or message sent instantaneously via a dedicated computer system between headquarters and its diplomatic missions abroad. As with email, most governments have both classified and unclassified cable systems. Almost all U.S. diplomatic cables today are classified. Thanks in no small part to WikiLeaks, officials classify even the most innocuous documents. Cables on an overseas post's management, financial and personnel matters are usually unclassified. Throughout their careers, diplomats – especially reporting officers – must make quick choices about how to provide their government with needed information. This involves the proper and efficient use of language, technology and format to reach the respective target audience.

This chapter will try to give you a sense about how to do that, starting with how to convey information to your capital from abroad – in other words, how to report. We will show you how to structure, write, edit and distribute diplomatic cables. There are four general purposes for messages to be sent as diplomatic cables: reporting on events, reporting on meetings or démarches to a foreign government, influencing a decision or policy, and making explicit policy recommendations. Cables that have real impact are likely to be shared as an email attachment with "heads up" or "read this" in the email's subject line. In the U.S. system, all cables are signed by the chief of mission, even when they were written by someone else. In fact, chiefs of mission do not even have time to read every cable sent out from their mission.

Thanks in part to inaccurate depictions in movies and television shows, diplomatic reporting is often confused with information-gathering by intelligence officers. There are certain similarities – both diplomats and intelligence officers collect information that is shared with policymakers – but the main difference is that the former do so overtly and the latter covertly, as noted in earlier chapters. The CIA has its own cable system separate from that of the State Department, but it also has access to the department's cables, as do other agencies, on a need-to-know basis.

Reporting on events

Diplomatic reports on events are essentially official journalism – you must report on who, what, where, when, how and why. You will have competition from the media, but as a diplomat, you can access resources that many journalists and others cannot, including in governments, other diplomatic missions, international organizations, civil society groups, activists and intelligence. If there is a discrepancy between what appears in the press and in diplomatic reporting, government officials will believe what is in a diplomatic cable, because it is a reporting officer's job to get the facts right and put them in a proper context. As such an officer, you will be seen as the definitive source on what is happening, so do not exaggerate, do not report things from sources that are sketchy, and do not predict the future – even if someone in your capital is pressing you to do all those things. Although you should not predict the future, you should explain the factors that are likely to influence the future.

You do not have to report everything about the beat you are covering and every event that takes place. You should first take into account all available information, and then determine how your reporting would bring added value. As a diplomat, you may be in a faraway corner of the world, where there is no international media presence, and you may be among the first to learn that something of importance has happened. In that case, you need to report on it in detail. Diplomatic reporting on political, social, economic or other events that does not need to be transmitted immediately can be bundled into cables that are sent on a weekly, monthly or more sporadic basis. Some events may require only a paragraph or two in a roundup cable.

We have two examples of cables: one that reported on events in Chile and another on events in Egypt. In the first, events were unfolding as the message was being sent; in the second, they had just happened. On June 29, 1973, the U.S. Embassy in Chile alerted Washington about a military coup attempt against the socialist government of Salvador Allende as it was happening. As mentioned earlier, such breaking news is usually reported by telephone first, but as more details come in, the cable system is utilized to transmit more information. The first sentence here suggests that this may have been a follow-up to an earlier dispatch, or assumes that the reader has heard the news from the media, although only radio would have reported that quickly before the age of cable television and the Internet. The omission of the article "the" throughout the text is unusual in modern cable writing, except in subject lines, as we will see shortly.

It appears that this morning's military rebellion was unplanned and uncoordinated. It was apparently triggered when, at approximately 8:30 a.m., military officers under orders from General [Carlos] Prats arrived at headquarters of Second Armored Regiment to relieve regimental commander, Lt. Col. [Roberto] Souper, of his command. Order apparently connected to alleged plotting, which led to arrests of several army officers and civilians June 26 ...

All businesses have closed and normal civilian activity has shut down. We understand that most international airlines have canceled Santiago landings scheduled for today. Electrical and telephone service, which was disrupted in several large districts of the city, has been partially restored. Up until approximately 2:00 p.m., there were still isolated instances of gunfire.[11]

Prats was the army chief and minister of defense. Souper led the rebellion. The attempt to overthrow the Allende government failed, but it turned out to be the prelude to a successful coup less than three months later, which brought to power General Augusto Pinochet and was backed by the United States, according to declassified documents from that time.[12] Allende committed suicide on the day he was removed from office.[13] Prats fled to Argentina, where Pinochet's agents would assassinate him a year later.[14] Chileans would live under Pinochet's brutal regime for the next 17 years. He was arrested in 1998 for human rights violations but no trial was held before his death in 2006.[15]

The second cable, sent from Cairo on April 11, 1979, consisted of just two sentences.

People's Assembly last night ratified Egypt–Israel peace treaty. According to assembly officials, vote was 328 in favor, 15 against, one abstention and 16 absent.[16]

The treaty, which was a result of the 1978 Camp David Peace Accords, had been signed at the White House two weeks before the ratification.[17]

Reporting on meetings and démarches

Most entry-level diplomats cut their teeth by taking notes in and then reporting on meetings with foreign officials, including démarches. The term comes from the French word *démarche*, one of whose meanings is "step," and in plural it means "proceedings." Even though there are no official rules on how to write cables that report on meetings, we suggest five best practices from our experience.

Summarize conversations and conclusions

Do not attempt to write a verbatim transcript of a conversation. (When Henry Kissinger was secretary of state in the 1970s, he famously demanded verbatim transcripts of his meetings. However, almost no one else does.) You need to interpret the meetings for your capital in a way that is accessible and readable for those who were not in the meeting and may not be familiar with all the details of the substance or the foreign culture in which you work. Report on the atmospherics, body language and other important nonverbal aspects of the meeting, to help you convey your thoughts on the intent of a foreign interlocutor and help the audience at home feel as if they were sitting in the room with you.

Divide the cable by topic

Do not produce a strictly chronological, "he said, she said" recitation. Conversations often touch on different aspects of a topic two or three times at different points in a conversation. Pull together all threads of each topic and place them together, so the conclusions are more coherent. You can even use subheadings, but do not overdo it, as too many can be distracting.

Prioritize topics

The topics during a discussion should be reported in order of importance. The most important should be first, and some topics might not be worthy of putting in a cable at all. This kind of triage may be the most difficult part of reporting on complex conversations. It is essential to filter the information. Your audience may have responsibility for several countries or issues, and it will likely not have more than a few minutes to read a report on an hour-long meeting.

How do you determine which topics to prioritize, which to cover in less detail, and which to leave out? Use your intelligence and judgment, combined with your knowledge of events and priorities in your host-country and your capital, to make educated decisions. If you emphasize something you should not, your boss will let you know. Remember that usually what the other side said in the meeting is more important, because it is likely to make news for your readers at headquarters – they already know what points your side made, because they are familiar with their own policy, and in some cases, they sent the démarche instructions in the first place.

As you attend more and more formal diplomatic meetings, you will find that random topics often pop up as conversation starters or transitions. Topics that do not significantly affect the interests of your country or the host-country can safely be left out. Just because a topic does not make the cut for your cable does not mean that it is not worth reporting in another cable or in some other form. Suppose you are in a meeting on refugee repatriation, and a host-country official brings up child trafficking. Even if you decide to leave the latter out of your immediate reporting, you could include it in a future cable, or even build a cable around it. So save your notes from meetings in a retrievable format.

Use direct and clear language

Try to write the fewest words necessary to get your points across. Make your language clean, clear, declarative and in the active voice. Using passive voice often obscures the actor, and the credit or blame that might flow from an action. Once you have written your first draft, go back through your writing and eliminate redundancies, as well as extraneous adverbs and adjectives.

Be judicious in using quotes

It is tempting to overuse juicy quotes to describe a meeting and build the bulk of your report. Although this can sometimes be entertaining to read, especially if it comes from a contentious conversation, it can lead to misunderstanding. Quotes might not have the same meaning when read at home as they did when delivered in the context of the meeting and the surrounding culture. Reliance on quotes can make a report harder for a reader to understand, since the coherence of quotes often relies on the chronological flow of a conversation, which is not advisable, as mentioned above. Select quotes that encapsulate the essence of a meeting or a response to a particular issue and can be useful and memorable. Block quotes, though appropriate in a book, make diplomatic reports choppy and harder to read.

Not every cable can observe all of the above suggestions, especially if it reports on breaking news and time is of the essence. The cable cited below is one such example.

It was sent from the U.S. Embassy in Iran on January 28, 1979. Two Ministry of Foreign Affairs (MFA) officials in Tehran had reached out to the embassy's political counselor with a remarkable proposal concerning Ayatollah Ruhollah Khomeini, Iran's main opposition leader. He was living in exile in France at the time and was not allowed to return during the reign of Shah Mohammad Reza Pahlavi. The cable also refers to Shapour Bakhtiar, who had become prime minister three weeks earlier.[18] The acronym USG stands for U.S. government. As in the cable from Chile, the articles "a" and "the" are incorrectly omitted here – there were still officers in the Foreign Service at the time who were used to the telegraphic style mentioned earlier in the chapter.

Just before weekend, two high officials of MFA separately told [political] counselor that they earnestly hope USG will support Khomeini, even though they themselves are neither Islamic partisans nor support an Islamic republic as such. ... Over long lunch, [one official] pushed idea that "alternative to Khomeinism is communism." His thesis was that Islamic movement is the only organized group apart from communists and is dedicated to keeping communists from power. In the long run, it is the safest alternative for U.S. and Western world. Army is very slim reed on which to lean, as are others such as Bakhtiar, who does not command any real power. If USG could facilitate takeover by Khomeini forces, it would ingratiate itself with them and improve relations for the future.[19]

The United States, which had helped to reinstall the shah in 1953,[20] did not respond favorably to the MFA officials' overtures. Four days later, and two weeks after the shah went abroad for medical treatment, Khomeini returned to Iran. In late March, Iranians voted in a referendum to abolish the monarchy in favor of an Islamic government. On November 4, the U.S. Embassy was attacked and 52 staff members were held hostage for 444 days.[21] The two countries have not had diplomatic relations since.

Reporting to influence

Diplomats are often asked by their capital – and sometimes take the initiative – to explain the motivations behind foreign government decisions, decipher public reactions or elucidate the political and cultural factors that drive developments overseas. This type of diplomatic writing is designed to analyze more deeply and in greater nuance than just reporting on events and meetings. At the more senior level, it is sometimes used to influence decisions at headquarters without explicitly making a policy recommendation.

Another type of cable often used to influence subtly is called a "scene-setter" in the U.S. Foreign Service. It helps to prepare a senior official from headquarters for meetings with host-government counterparts. Such cables are usually a group effort of the entire embassy or consulate, often with a junior officer compiling different parts contributed by various sections and agencies in the mission. The goal is to shape the upcoming conversations by providing topics that both sides should or are

O 011306Z JUN 07
FM AMEMBASSY MOSCOW
TO SECSTATE WASHDC IMMEDIATE 0806
WHITE HOUSE WASHDC IMMEDIATE
INFO MOSCOW POLITICAL COLLECTIVE IMMEDIATE

~~SECRET~~ MOSCOW 002588

~~EXDIS~~

MILITARY ADDRESSEES TREAT AS SPECAT

FOR THE PRESIDENT AND SECRETARY RICE FROM AMBASSADOR

E.O. 12958: DECL: 05/31/2017
TAGS: PREL, RS
SUBJECT: YOUR MEETING WITH PUTIN AT THE G-8

Classified by: Ambassador William J. Burns.
Reasons: 1.4 (b) and (d).

1. (S) Mr President: Russia's swaggering and pugnacious behavior has reached new lows since Putin's Munich speech in February, and I'm afraid there are greater depths to explore in the months ahead. Your conversations with Putin in Germany next week, and particularly during the Kennebunkport Summit in early July, offer the best opportunities we'll have before Putin leaves office to limit the damage and shore up relations with Russia in the areas that matter most to us, and to Russia's own long-term future. Following are a few informal thoughts on what's driving the Russians, and what to do about it.

Figure 8.2 The beginning of a cable William Burns, the U.S. ambassador to Russia, wrote to President George W. Bush and Secretary of State Condoleezza Rice in 2007.
Source: "The Back Channel: The Archive."

likely to bring up. There is a "points to make" section, recommending the topics the principal should raise with senior host-country officials, along with the approach and even language that might be used. The most important part is the "watch out for" section, which warns of difficult and controversial topics the interlocutor might bring up and provides suggestions on how to respond. Some background information may be included as well. That way, if the principals do not feel conversant on Iran nuclear negotiations or a draft congressional human rights resolution, for example, they can learn the basics.

We have two scene-setter examples sent to Washington shortly before visits of heads of state. In 1994, as the Clinton administration pondered how to support Boris Yeltsin in enacting political and economic reforms less than three years after the collapse of the Soviet Union, it invited Yeltsin to the White House. William Burns was the head of the political section of the embassy in Moscow at the time. In a cable, he wrote the following:

> It is worth emphasizing that Yeltsin needs a strong personal performance at the summit to repair his sagging popular image at home. He drank too much and behaved erratically at the Berlin ceremonies marking Russian troop withdrawal three weeks ago, for which he was roundly criticized in the Russian press. … While the strains of the last year have clearly taken a physical toll on him, and while it is always hard to predict which Boris Yeltsin will emerge at any given moment – the activist leader who thrives on adversity, or the disengaged, increasingly remote head of state – we expect that Yeltsin will rise to the occasion in Washington.[22]

Even though Burns did not say it explicitly, these words were meant to encourage officials in Washington to help make Yeltsin's visit a success. Otherwise, Burns feared that Yeltsin would be weakened at home, which he believed would not be in the U.S. interest. In 2001, as ambassador to Jordan, Burns tried to set the scene for a trip to Washington by King Abdullah, who had succeeded his late father, King Hussein, on the throne two years earlier.

Having survived the Arab summit in Amman without major blow-ups and with a modest boost to his own leadership credentials, King Abdullah arrives in Washington later this week deeply concerned about Jordan's future. The mood amongst Jordanians is increasingly angry and disaffected – a mixture of intense frustration over rising violence across the Jordan river, fury at American policies that are seen to be not just unbalanced but aggressively anti-Arab, and discontent with the meager practical results of economic reform.[23]

Then, having heard directly from the king about his objectives for the trip in a meeting "this past weekend," Burns got straight to the point:

Abdullah wants to come away from Washington with a sense of shared strategic purpose, including a strong mutual commitment to ease Israeli–Palestinian tensions and a sustainable approach to the problem of Iraq. He also wants very much to come away with a clear commitment to obtaining congressional approval of the U.S.–Jordan Free Trade Agreement by early summer, which is widely viewed here as a critical signal of American confidence in Abdullah and in Jordan.

On rare occasions, reporting with the purpose to influence may be done to affect internal policies and procedures. Soon after Douglas Silliman arrived in Kuwait as ambassador in 2014, he learned from his management counselor that the salaries the embassy was paying many local employees put them below both the Kuwaiti and U.S. poverty lines. Nearly all of those employees were from third countries, including India, the Philippines and Egypt. Using the normal administrative process at the State Department, Silliman tried to raise the salaries of the lowest-paid employees, but the department, which looked at worldwide trends and salary comparators from Kuwait's labor market, rejected the request.

Instead of giving up, Silliman took a different tack. He asked the embassy's political and economic sections to begin working on a series of reports and analyses on trafficking in persons, abusive labor practices and the living conditions of underpaid workers in Kuwait, including some at the embassy (with their explicit permission). Over six weeks, those reports, written and transmitted as diplomatic cables to Washington, sensitized decision-makers there to the difficulties in the labor market and the exploitative nature of the comparators the State Department used to set salary levels in Kuwait, treating third-country nationals much worse than Kuwaiti citizens. Not long after the cables reached their audience in Washington, Silliman met with some of the department's top officials. His plea no longer fell on deaf ears, because he had sent solid and compelling facts to back up his arguments. The department significantly increased the employees' salaries and benefits. One undersecretary later told Silliman that the cables had shifted the perception of how local employees were treated and finally drove decision-makers to understand the embassy's point of view.

Direct policy recommendations

Direct policy recommendations – "do this" or "don't do that" – are not made in diplomatic cables as often as one might think. The responsibility for setting policy resides in the capital, not the embassy, and many senior officials at home do not like to be told what to do. They see themselves as better positioned and more in line with the political direction of the president, prime minister or monarch. Most of the time, career diplomats provide several policy options and may note at the end which one they believe would yield the best result. When officers do make direct recommendations, they often come in the form of a first-person message from the chief of mission to a decision-maker at headquarters.

Earlier during his tenure as ambassador to Jordan, Burns teamed up in 2000 with Daniel Kurtzer, who was ambassador to Egypt, to write a series of three cables about the direction of the Israeli–Palestinian peace process. It followed failed negotiations at Camp David and the outbreak of a Palestinian uprising that became known as the Second Intifada. "We felt a responsibility to inject our perspective into the negotiating process from the outside, if we could not provide our views from the inside," Burns recalled in his memoir.[24] This is how the two ambassadors' third cable began:

As seen from Cairo and Amman, U.S. policy in the peace process and our overall posture in the region are still heading in exactly the wrong direction. With our interests under increasing scrutiny and attack, we are acting passively, reactively and defensively. There is no guarantee that a bolder, more activist American approach will stop the hemorrhaging – but it seems clear to us that things could get a lot worse unless we regain the initiative.[25]

Then Burns and Kurtzer outlined specific options for U.S. policy:

One option is to follow [Israeli Prime Minister Ehud] Barak's lead. That may serve what he sees to be his tactical interests at this point, but it's hard to see how it serves ours. A second option is to see if we can extract from the Palestinians a clearer sense of how far they are prepared to go right now, and then use that to craft an approach to Barak. But it's unlikely that [Yasser] Arafat will level with us at this point; and while recent Egyptian and Jordanian efforts with the Palestinians have been helpful, it's not at all clear that they will produce a workable starting point. That leaves it to us to lay out the hard truths – for all parties – that must underpin any enduring political solution.

With only a month left in office for President Clinton, the ambassadors urged the White House to "articulate a 'Clinton vision' for the peace process."

We have a unique but wasting opportunity to take advantage of a remarkable asset: the personal reputation and demonstrated commitment of President Clinton. He has built up substantial personal credit with the parties over the years, and now is the time to use it.

Weeks later, the White House unveiled the Clinton Parameters, a groundbreaking proposal for a two-state solution.[26] It is not clear if Burns and Kurtzer's cables played a role in the initiative's formulation, but it is likely that they at least informed the decision-making. It was too late, however, for the parameters to make any difference, as they were not adopted by the incoming Bush administration.

Figure 8.3 Douglas Silliman (left), the U.S. ambassador to Iraq, holds a press conference in Erbil, Iraq, with Qubad Talabani, deputy prime minister of the Iraqi Kurdish Regional Government (center), and USAID contractor John Lister in 2018.
Photo by Yunus Keles/Anadolu Agency via Getty Images.

When Douglas Silliman arrived in Baghdad as ambassador in 2016, he started working on a series of cables covering the political, security, social and economic aspects of U.S. relations with Iran, as well as Iraq's relations with Iran. These cables included specific recommendations for the outgoing Obama administration and the incoming Trump administration. The embassy sent separate cables on Iran's economic relations with Iraq and what could be done to reduce Iran's economic influence in Iraq, on Iranian social and cultural influence, on Iran's political influence, and on its military and security influence. Silliman worked with the political, economic and public diplomacy sections to draft the messages, which took more than a month to conceptualize, put together, review, rewrite and polish. He gave lower-level officers great leeway in drafting the cables, but coordinated all four cables to make sure that the tone reflected his own, the recommendations were as specific as possible, and that they would be well received in Washington.

Elements of a diplomatic cable

Diplomatic reports in most governments contain several common elements, such as a subject line, a summary or introduction, main body of text, a comment or conclusion, and some form of indicator to route the message to the appropriate audience. A practical note: if you have reviewed the originals of any of the cables discussed so far, you will have noticed that they were written entirely in uppercase letters. That is not the case in the current electronic system, which the State Department has been using for two decades.

Subject line

The subject line, like the headline of a news story, is the most important part of a cable, because it determines whether officials at headquarters will open it in the long queue of cables on their computer screens. How can you get them to open and read it? The same way that journalists get readers to read their stories: pull them in with a short, focused, compelling and meaningful subject line. You have to grab their attention.

As a young diplomat in the 1980s, Silliman served as a staff assistant in the front office of the State Department's Bureau of Near Eastern Affairs. His first duty every day was to get the assistant secretary's morning intake of cables from the communications center. It was an unsorted stack of paper that was often six inches deep. Silliman would sort through hundreds of cables and tell his boss what needed his action, what he should read urgently or carefully, and what he should look at if he had more time. Usually, about two-thirds of the stack ended up in the burn bag – it was impossible for anyone to read that much cable traffic. If the subject line was not snappy or compelling, the cable went in the trash.

Technology has made swift communication easier and more reliable. It has also increased the volume of cable traffic. Instead of a large stack of paper, readers now have to scroll through dozens, if not hundreds, of cables on their computer screens every day, with one line per cable. The subject is only part of that one line, and much of it runs off the screen. To get your cable read, the first few words of your subject must grab the readers' attention. Many young diplomats try to pack everything from their cable into the subject line. But if you put too much in the subject line, you will lose your punch – and often your point. If you take up space with names, titles and adjectives, the message will get lost.

Rules of Thumb: Subject Line

- Be concise.
- Use active verbs; substitute interesting action verbs for dull ones.
- Avoid adjectives and adverbs.
- Place key clues to the cable's substance early in your subject line.
- Pull the most important topic in a multi-subject meeting.
- Employ well-known acronyms and abbreviations, such as U.S., U.N., EU, etc.
- Just like in a newspaper headline, you can leave out the articles "a" and "the."

We have several examples of subject lines. Those of the cables from Tehran and Cairo we discussed earlier reflected the above advice. They were clear, concise and straightforward.

IRANIAN MFA OFFICIALS ASK THAT USG SUPPORT KHOMEINI

PEOPLE'S ASSEMBLY RATIFIES PEACE TREATY

The 1973 cable from Chile cited earlier had the following subject line:

ATTEMPT COUP

It is certainly short and to the point, even if not grammatically correct – it sounds more like an appeal to the reader to attempt a coup. Ideally, it would have said either "coup attempt" or "attempted coup."

The joint cable Burns and Kurtzer sent in 2000 had a subject line that may not be very exciting, but the reader might detect implicit criticism of previous U.S. peace efforts.

PEACE PROCESS: RELAUNCHING AMERICAN DIPLOMACY

Even less attention-grabbing is the subject line of a 1974 cable from the U.S. Embassy in Paris.

ANALYSIS OF FRENCH–INDIAN NUCLEAR COOPERATION[27]

Although there is no active verb – or any verb – it is relatively short and straightforward. Not every piece of the advice above can be heeded every time, so use your best judgment.

Summary

In another parallel to journalism, once your subject line has convinced your target audience to open your cable, you have to further draw them in, so they read the entire report. If you are writing about a long meeting that covered several topics, it can be overwhelming for a busy bureaucrat with hundreds of cables waiting in the queue. That is why the first paragraph is second in importance only to the subject line, and it is best that it provides a concise summary of its most important points. As noted earlier, the U.S. military uses the acronym BLUF – bottom line up front. You do not have to summarize everything the cable covers, just the most important takeaways.

The notes you took during the meeting or event you are writing about are your best friend. Always carry two pens and paper – electronic devices are not allowed in certain spaces – and take extensive notes. If you are having coffee with a contact and it might be rude to write during the conversation, do so as soon as you depart. Then make good use of your notes. Silliman took detailed notes throughout his Foreign Service career, which helped him organize his thoughts before starting to write. He would mark topics using different colored pens and put big stars in places that were decisive points in the meeting – agreement on an idea, refusal to agree or alternate proposals. Then he would prioritize the topics and decide on the most important to include in his summary. He would edit for clarity and brevity, removing extraneous language and unnecessary detail that might detract from the main point.

Here is the summary of the previously discussed cable from Tehran. It mentions the National Front, an opposition party not associated with Khomeini:

Speaking privately, two MFA officials support Khomeini and downgrade Bakhtiar. They represent a sizable number of MFA officials who sympathize with the National Front. Their basic message is that Khomeini's "Islamic republic" would be best buffer against communism and not essentially unfriendly to the U.S.

And here is the summary of the Paris cable on French–Indian nuclear cooperation:

The French have provided substantial assistance to the development of Indian nuclear capability by agreeing to build two heavy-water plants in India and an experimental sodium-cooled fast-breeder reactor, similar to the 40-megawatt Rapsodie reactor. We cannot yet corroborate reports that the French propose selling to India 400 kg of highly enriched uranium, except to note that the French have said they will insist on safeguarding both initial fuel loading of the Indian fast-breeder reactor and its plutonium products. However, it seems to us that 400 kg is rather high for a single fuel loading of a Rapsodie-type reactor. The probable motivation for the French nuclear assistance to India is their hope of establishing a future international market for sales of French nuclear technology.

A summary is not necessary if your cable is only four or five paragraphs long, though the first paragraph is always important. It should convey concisely the most important information, just like a news story's lead, but it does not have to include more than one topic. The cables from Chile and Egypt did not have a summary.

Main body

While a principal will most likely not have time for anything beyond the summary, there are lower-level officials, such as desk officers and intelligence analysts, who will read closely the main body of your cable, because their job requires them to know details. Still, it is a good idea to follow another acronym, KISS, which stands for "keep it short and simple." As you convey the details of a conversation or event, try to get across the main ideas clearly, so that readers who are not subject-matter experts can understand them. Do not get bogged down in details. Again, use the active voice, which does not mask the person or thing responsible for an act. As noted earlier, if your cable is long or covers several topics, it is best to divide it into sections that are clearly labeled with an appropriate short phrase or sentence (subheading). Burns's 2001 scene-setter from Amman before King Abdullah's visit to Washington had three sections: "Regional Crises on Two Fronts," "More Troubles at Home" and "Abdullah's Washington Agenda."

You can also have a little fun with this. When Silliman was a mid-level officer in Islamabad, he wrote a somewhat irreverent cable trying to explain the positions and frustrations of Pakistani political parties. To break up what was otherwise a rather tiresome list of complaints and boasts, and to capture their spirit, Silliman used Rolling Stones song titles as section headers, including "19th Nervous Breakdown," "(I Can't Get No) Satisfaction," "Wild Horses" and "Mother's Little Helper." Sometimes, a little creativity and humor can help make reporting more enjoyable and understandable, but keep in mind that your boss may not get your humor.

Comment

If you think that your cable needs to be put in a certain context, you can add a comment as the concluding paragraph. If you are reporting on a meeting with a newly appointed or elected senior host-country official, you might end with a biographical note. This would help a principal at headquarters who is preparing to meet with that official. You could include standard and simple information, such as the person's age, language ability and personality traits. Here is the comment the embassy in Tehran included in the 1979 cable about the meetings with the MFA officials who urged the United States to support Khomeini.

Both sources are very much establishment types, and neither is an extremist or communist-oriented. They represent sizable numbers of MFA officials who sympathize with the National Front, but have been keeping quiet all these years. They are urging U.S. recognition of a reality in the overwhelming power of the Islamic movement led by Khomeini. While they may be drawing too rosy a picture of the situation which would emerge from a Khomeini takeover, they believe they are being realistic in recognizing its inevitability and believe the result would be reasonably satisfactory from the U.S. and Western point of view.

Finally, make sure to spell-check your cable and read it from beginning to end one final time. Keep in mind that, despite what you learn from this chapter, your boss may have a different style or standards. Learn their pet peeves and what they like and dislike. Silliman had bosses who refused to accept the use of passive voice, turned purple at the sight of a split infinitive and hyperventilated when encountering improper verb-tense progression.

Cable distribution

In reporting back to your capital, you need to keep in mind who would be interested in each of the topics in your cable, and how you can get it onto their computer screens. Nearly all cable distribution systems have markings and tags that are used to deliver messages to audiences that would find them useful in their work. Your job is to determine who those people are and to mark your cables appropriately. Does the president or prime minister need to see this? Perhaps the secretary of state or foreign minister? Be realistic and honest with yourself.

If your cable involves another country or region, you might want to send it to your colleagues posted there. The cable from Paris on French–Indian nuclear cooperation was naturally shared with the U.S. Embassy in India and the U.S. Mission to U.N.

organizations in Vienna, one of which is the International Atomic Energy Agency. You can also include government agencies outside the State Department or MFA, such as the Ministries of Defense, Trade or Energy. In addition to the State Department, the Paris cable was sent to the Department of Defense, the CIA, NASA and other agencies. Cables from the U.S. Mission to the EU in Brussels are often shared with the Departments of Commerce and Agriculture.

Diplomatic writing at headquarters

Every MFA has its own style of writing, but the types of documents used to drive decisions and create historical records are similar. In the State Department, there are three main types: information memorandum; decision memorandum; and instructions to U.S. missions abroad, usually in the form of a cable, to deliver démarches to host-country officials.

An **information memorandum** (or info memo) is a note, as short as one page, describing an event or issue that senior officials need to understand. It is usually compiled using reports from embassies abroad, but may also include information garnered from other departments and agencies. The hardest part of writing such a memo is balancing all the various parts of the bureaucracy that want to get their particular viewpoint into it, while also keeping it short and focused on what the reader needs to know.

A **decision memorandum** (or action memo) makes specific recommendations to a senior official and asks for a decision, usually in one or two pages. The author presents short arguments for and against various courses of action, as well as background needed to support a decision. This format is used for many issues that are not decided in interagency discussions. Many such documents become what are called "split memos," where one part of the bureaucracy supports one policy choice and another part favors a different option. It is vitally important to present all sides of an issue, including the pros and cons of the various options. Some decisions are complex and require a lot of information. They can be controversial or affect different parts of the government – some positively and others negatively. In such cases, decision memos often include longer attachments with more extensive background or longer reasoning for or against the various alternatives.

The term **démarche cable** can be confusing. American diplomats abroad often say that Washington "sent a démarche" – in fact, this is shorthand meaning that Washington sent instructions for a démarche to be delivered to the host-government. "Démarche" is the act of making a request or demand, though it can also be used to describe the request itself.[28] The instructions are usually included in a cable from headquarters. After an embassy delivers a démarche, it sends back to the capital a cable of its own, reporting on the meeting during which the démarche was delivered.

Every year, before the U.N. General Assembly (UNGA) convenes in New York in September, the State Department instructs embassies around the world to deliver démarches on various matters expected to be discussed during the session. For example, the UNGA Third Committee deals with a broad range of social, humanitarian and human rights issues. In 2019, it considered 63 draft resolutions, more than half of which were submitted under the human rights agenda. The committee also deals with the matter of self-determination of the Palestinian people. The State Department routinely directs embassies to deliver démarches asking that countries oppose resolutions it believes unfairly criticize Israel.

Some démarches can get very technical, such as what is informally known as "the sauce démarche" to the EU and its member-states. The EU imposes various tariffs on U.S.-made products based on their ingredients, and the content of one ingredient over another can make a significant difference. The State Department and the Department of Commerce, in consultation with the respective industry, notify the EU of minute details, such as the sugar content or viscosity of ketchup, that might place a product in a lower tariff category. Exporting companies can make or lose billions of dollars because of a change in tariff category.

Official communication between countries

There are more frequently used forms of communication between countries than démarches, and they do not have to be delivered in person. A **diplomatic note** (often called "dip note") is the most formal communication between governments, and "a first-person note is used for the most important correspondence," according to the "Foreign Affairs Manual."[29] At headquarters, a diplomatic note can be signed by the minister or secretary of state, deputy minister or deputy secretary or an undersecretary. Abroad, it is usually signed by the chief of mission and is addressed to the minister of foreign affairs. Here is the first sentence of a diplomatic note the Japanese foreign minister sent the U.S. ambassador in Tokyo in 2008:

Excellency, I have the honor to refer to the Mutual Defense Assistance Agreement between Japan and the United States of America signed at Tokyo on March 8, 1954.[30]

After citing two paragraphs from the accord regarding Japan's share of the costs of maintaining U.S. military bases and personnel in Japan, the minister continued:

Accordingly, I have the honor to propose on behalf of the Government of Japan the following arrangements concerning the amount of the cash contribution referred to above for the Japanese fiscal year 2008: In consideration of the contributions in kind to be made available by the Government of Japan during the Japanese fiscal year from April 1, 2008, to March 31, 2009, the amount of the cash contribution to be made available by the Government of Japan for the said fiscal year shall be one hundred and twenty-five million one hundred and sixty-nine thousand yen.

The minister's final sentence is standard for any diplomatic note:

I avail myself of this opportunity to extend to Your Excellency the assurance of my highest consideration.

A **note verbale** is less formal than a diplomatic note written in the third person. It is not signed but initialed by an officer authorized by the chief of mission, or by an office director at headquarters. The U.N. Secretariat in New York regularly sends notes verbale to the missions of its member-states. Here is one from 2022:

The Protocol and Liaison Service of the Department for General Assembly and Conference Management (DGACM) of the United Nations presents its compliments to the Permanent and Observer Missions accredited to the United Nations and has the honor to inform them of the following: In order to maintain an accurate inventory of flags at the United Nations Headquarters, the Protocol and Liaison Service, with the support of the Security and Safety Service, will be conducting a digital flag verification exercise during the month of January.[31]

The phrases "presents its compliments to" and "has the honor to inform them" are standard for any note verbale, as is the final sentence, which is similar to the ending of a diplomatic note:

The Protocol and Liaison Service of the Department for General Assembly and Conference Management (DGACM) of the United Nations avails itself of this opportunity to renew to the Permanent and Observer Missions accredited to the United Nations the assurances of its highest consideration.

An **aide memoire** (also known as non-paper) is less formal than the two forms above and summarizes an informal diplomatic conversation, serving as an aid to memory. There is no accepted standard for the language or structure of such a document.

Notetaking

William Burns was ambassador to Russia when Condoleezza Rice visited Moscow in October 2006. Putin extended to her a rare invitation to join an "elaborate dinner" celebrating the birthdays of two of his Security Council members. There was no American in the room less senior than Burns, so he acted as the notetaker. Based on his notes, he later wrote a nine-page "memo for the record" – a remarkable account of unusually frank conversations behind closed doors with relatively relaxed Russian officials by an observant and experienced diplomat. The memo was written much like a cable, though it was not sent to Washington through the cable system.[32] Here are some insights from a post-dinner conversation between Rice and Putin:

Putin then turned to Georgia, and turned much testier. He began by stating bluntly that "if [Georgian President Mikheil] Saakashvili uses force in South Ossetia, which we are convinced he is preparing to do, it would be a grave mistake, and the Georgian people would suffer most." Pointing to the dining room where his Security Council was still gathered, Putin said, "I'm going to tell you something that no one in there knows yet. If Georgia causes bloodshed in Ossetia, I will have no alternative to recognizing South Ossetia and Abkhazia, and responding with force."
  Putin insisted that Russian public opinion would compel him to act. He said he respected Georgia's territorial integrity, and did not want conflict. He did not intend to initiate any use

of force, and understood that everyone would lose from armed conflict. But he didn't want there to be any misunderstanding about the seriousness of the situation. The Secretary responded very directly. She said we had repeatedly urged the Georgian leadership to de-escalate, and would continue to do so. But Russia has responsibilities of its own to calm the situation. Any Russian move to recognize South Ossetia or Abkhazia would cause serious problems in U.S.–Russian relations, and undoubtedly for the Europeans too. The key now is to reduce tensions. Putin was unmoved. . . . "I understand that there will be problems in U.S.–Russian relations if we act in South Ossetia, but what good is a strong U.S.–Russian relationship to me if I lose Russia?

Notetaking is a skill whose importance cannot be overstated, no matter what your job is and how senior you are in the hierarchy, as noted in Chapter 6. Reporting officers write cables based on conversations with government officials or other sources all the time, but recording those conversations is almost never an option – it is not an accepted practice, and even if it were, many sources would not agree to being taped. So officers can rely only on their notes and memory. Sometimes you may not be allowed to take notes in a meeting. In such cases, write down everything you remember as soon as the meeting is over, before you forget key details.

In diplomacy, insights like Burns's are invaluable. Your reporting is only as good as the information you put in it. Be inquisitive – the questions you would like your contacts to answer are likely to be the ones a reader at home would ask. Pose the same questions to several contacts and compare responses; they could lead to a different line of questioning or confirm certain conclusions. No matter how good a writer you are, your reporting is of little use in your capital if it is based on incorrect information.

Exercise 1: Prioritizing Reporting Topics

Your boss is the intrepid and peripatetic U.S. Ambassador John Smith. You are accompanying him on a visit to Prague, where he just had lunch with the Czech foreign minister's chief of staff, who is an old friend. They discussed the following topics:

1. good restaurants in Prague;
2. recent violence on the Saudi–Yemeni border;
3. best elementary schools in town for English-speaking students;
4. an Iranian diplomat's revelations about attempts to access U.S. dollar accounts in Europe;
5. personnel changes in the Ministry of Foreign Affairs;
6. EU consideration of a new tariff on imported ketchup;
7. the foreign minister's new wife;
8. Chinese Belt and Road Initiative successes in Eastern Europe;
9. terrorism-related arrests in Prague;
10. a new Rolls Royce dealership that will open soon.

Exercise 1: (cont.)

Task: Divide these topics into three categories for your reporting cable: high importance, low importance, can be left out.
Here is our suggested prioritization:

- High importance: Topics 4, 8 and 9.
- Low importance: Topics 2, 5, 6 and 7.
- Can be left out: 1, 3 and 10.

Exercise 2: Writing a Subject Line

Ambassador Smith had a lunch meeting with U.N. Undersecretary-General (U/SYG) for Political Affairs Jane Doe, whom he knows well, at the Waldorf Astoria Hotel in New York to discuss Iran's nuclear weapons program. The following topics came up:

- the weather, their spouses, children, pets and vacation plans;
- the U/SYG hates her tiny apartment in Manhattan;
- the U.N. Secretary General's discomfort with an ongoing political scandal in his country;
- an internal U.N. debate about U.S. cost-savings proposals;
- an Arab initiative to get one permanent and rotating Security Council seat;
- the Iranian nuclear program, which Doe agrees is potentially military in nature and could not have been developed without assistance from another country, noting that the United States sold Iran its first nuclear reactor decades ago.

Task: Write a subject line for a reporting cable on the meeting.

Bad Example:
Ambassador Smith's Productive Lunch Discussion with U.N. Undersecretary General for Political Affairs Jane Doe

Good Example:
Top U.N. Official Affirms Danger of Iran Nuke Program

Exercise 3: Writing Concise, Active Sentences

Task: Rewrite the sentences below in the active voice and make them concise.

1. It may not have been possible for the prime minister to have his travel schedule altered in order to attend the president's birthday party, but he nonetheless had

Exercise 3: (cont.)

someone purchase a gift that was delivered by a member of the prime minister's staff.

2. The refugees were unable to depart the camp because of the ongoing violence, which had been initiated by local sectarian militias.
3. It was learned from sources inside the Interior Ministry that all criminal penalties have been removed by the prime minister for violent actions against the LGBTQ community.

Here are our suggestions:

1. The prime minister's schedule could not accommodate the president's birthday party, but an aide delivered the PM's gift.
2. Sectarian militia violence prevented the refugees from leaving the camp.
3. Interior Ministry sources say the PM has decriminalized anti-LGBTQ violence.

ADDITIONAL RESOURCES

William J. Burns, *The Back Channel: A Memoir of American Diplomacy and the Case for Its Renewal* (Random House, 2019).

Donna Marie Oglesby, "Diplomatic Language," in Costas M. Constantinou, Pauline Kerr and Paul Sharp, eds., *The Sage Handbook of Diplomacy* (Sage Publications, 2016), 242–54.

Raymond F. Smith, *The Craft of Political Analysis for Diplomats* (Potomac Books, 2011).

9　Public Diplomacy

BRUCE WHARTON AND NICOLE FINNEMANN

Along with the rest of the world, U.S. diplomats watched the attack on Capitol Hill in Washington on January 6, 2021, in disbelief, as a mob tried to overturn the results of a legitimate election. The episode reflected one of the most serious challenges to American public diplomacy in decades. Promoting democracy, good governance and human rights has been a staple of U.S. foreign policy for half a century. Foreign Service officers have helped dozens of countries to hold free and fair elections, fight corruption and establish the rule of law. Now it appeared as if their own country flouted the very ideals they were preaching abroad. Would it be hypocritical to continue to do so?

"I witnessed the positive impact our advocacy for democracy and good governance had on other countries," former Foreign Service officer Robert Downes wrote in the Washington International Diplomatic Academy (WIDA)'s Diplomatic Diary in 2021. "But it gets tough" when Americans behave in a way for which "the U.S. embassy in a foreign country would criticize" it. "The United States sends its diplomats and citizens to observe numerous elections overseas," Downes noted. "Their presence improves voter access, especially for marginalized communities, and levels the playing field for opposition participation. I personally observed more than a dozen elections abroad, most of them free and fair, but some less so. So it was deeply disturbing that a sitting president attempted to overturn the results of a free and fair election at home. Against this backdrop, diplomats find it difficult to encourage other nations to place confidence in the ballot box."[1]

However, Downes did not advocate abandoning the promotion of U.S. values and ideals abroad. "Although the hypocrisy accusations are not without merit, it is important to remember" that the "American ideal is not that we live in a perfect union, but that we recognize its imperfections and must work to improve the country," he said. Most Americans acknowledge "our deficiencies and are working to correct them. This is not hypocrisy, but growth and understanding. U.S. diplomats should point that out overseas."

Thanks in part to the events of January 6, the state of U.S. democracy and governance is a frequent topic in the interactions of U.S. diplomats with officials around the world. Those discussions are not confined to meetings behind closed doors. They take place in the public sphere as well, and it often falls on public diplomacy officers to handle questions about Washington's "right to lecture others," as some call it. Foreign public perceptions about both U.S. politics and global leadership have a direct impact on the effectiveness of American diplomacy and its ability to help ensure the country's security and prosperity.

Every country, regardless of its size or weight in international politics, cares about how it is perceived abroad, precisely because that affects its ability to influence events and further its interests. Almost every embassy has at least one staff member – some have dozens – responsible for external activities, whether they call them public relations, public affairs, public outreach or public diplomacy.

What is public diplomacy?

Put simply – although nothing about it is simple – public diplomacy is diplomacy carried out in public, as opposed to most of diplomacy, which is done in private. It is **a set of activities that inform, engage and influence international public opinion to support policy objectives or create goodwill for the home-country**. It is important to understand what public diplomacy is not. It is not an advertising campaign to get foreigners to like your country – even if they dislike it, they can still support, or at least accept, a particular policy or action. It is not a propaganda effort to mislead or lie to audiences for tactical or other advantage. It is a sustained endeavor that advances your country's policies and reflects a solid understanding of the host-country's language, culture, history and traditions.

The phrase "winning hearts and minds" has been used widely, including during the U.S. wars in Afghanistan and Iraq launched after the 9/11 terrorist attacks. In 2002, in an attempt to improve the U.S. image in the Muslim world, the State Department produced a $15 million series of five short documentaries, which was overseen by Charlotte Beers, an advertising executive appointed as undersecretary of state for public diplomacy.[2] The project failed, mainly because it showed how well Muslims lived in the United States, rather than address the issues that concerned its intended audiences.[3] The hearts and minds of Muslims – or any other audiences – are not likely to be "won" anytime soon, no matter how expensive or glitzy an advertising campaign might be. A public diplomacy strategy does not necessarily need such a win. Sometimes the best you can hope for is that a foreign public comes to understand your country and see it in a light it has not considered before, even if it does not like or agree with its policies. Many people in various countries say that they like Americans, but not the U.S. government's policies. A good public diplomacy officer would use such an attitude to bridge the gap.

The term "public diplomacy" is relatively new – it was used in the West during the Cold War, but gained global acceptance after the 1989 fall of the Berlin Wall. Attempts to influence foreign audiences date back centuries, if not longer. Displays of art, architecture, engineering and administrative prowess helped expand the Roman Empire across Europe, northern Africa and western Asia, and to sustain it for more than 1,000 years.[4] The Great Chinese Fleet of the early 15th century became a symbol of the Ming Dynasty's influence across Southeast Asia, the Indian subcontinent and eastern Africa, bolstering China's reputation as a trading power and great civilization.[5] Two centuries later, Jesuits used their knowledge of astronomy and ability to predict eclipses to impress China's rulers and gain approval to set up missions in the country.[6]

In the 20th century, the U.S. government institutionalized public diplomacy beyond the presence of cultural attachés in embassies with the creation of the United States Information Agency (USIA) in 1953. President Dwight D. Eisenhower defined the agency's mission this way: "To submit evidence to people of other nations by means of communication techniques that the objectives and policies of the U.S. are in harmony with and will advance their legitimate aspirations for freedom, progress and peace." According to an internal document at the time, "USIA carries out this mission primarily by: 1. Interpreting policies of the U.S. government. 2. Showing the correlation between U.S. policies and the legitimate aspirations of other peoples. 3. Unmasking and countering attempts to distort U.S. objectives. 4. Portraying aspects of U.S. life and culture, which facilitate understanding U.S. policies and objectives."[7]

In 1963, the John F. Kennedy administration described USIA's mission as "influencing public attitudes in other nations" and "advising the president, his representatives abroad and the various departments and agencies on the implications of foreign opinion for present and contemplated United States policies, programs and official statements."[8] It also said that "the influencing of attitudes is to be carried out by overt use of various techniques of communication," in contrast to Soviet propaganda efforts, which USIA was meant to counter. The agency was folded into the State Department in 1999. Almost six decades before the January 6 riot, the Kennedy administration was cognizant of what has become known as the "say–do gap" – the discrepancy between what the United States says and does. In 1957, Louis Armstrong, tapped by the State Department as a "jazz ambassador," canceled a visit to the Soviet Union[9] when Black students in Arkansas were prevented from entering a racially segregated high school.[10] He told the media that he would not defend the U.S. Constitution abroad if it was not enforced at home.[11]

How is public diplomacy different from propaganda?

Was Armstrong concerned about being used as a propaganda tool by the U.S. government? If the State Department's goal was to show the Soviet people how successful a Black person could become in the United States as a way to hide the true state of racism in the country, that would have been propaganda. But if the musician was free to discuss segregation and race relations – and any other topic – the department could claim that its only aim was to build cultural ties with the people of the main U.S. political foe at the time. Given that Armstrong traveled to other countries on similar trips before and after 1957, he likely did not see himself as being used for propaganda.[12]

Art, peace, education and justice are universal human aspirations that can serve as entry points for programs uniting people across cultures and political systems.

Initiatives like the one that allowed Armstrong and many other American musicians and artists to engage with foreign audiences have proven successful for decades. Some countries have created educational and cultural institutions to serve as platforms for such engagement, including the British Council, France's Alliance Française and Germany's Goethe-Institut, among others. The impact of public diplomacy lies in the power of example and personal experience. When a country fails to live up to its values, acknowledging those failures, along with evidence that efforts are being made to address them, can become a positive message. When public diplomacy is called upon to help mitigate the negative consequences of bad policy, it can design programs highlighting the measures being taken to correct the problem.

Both public diplomacy and propaganda are means to project power. Usually, it is not hard to see how they are different, although sometimes a propaganda effort can be so masterful and sophisticated that the line gets blurred. Even though there are exceptions, propaganda normally consists of short-term efforts with a specific objective that are not constrained by the truth, while public diplomacy requires a long-term strategy that strives for sustained credibility. Legendary journalist Edward R. Murrow, whom Kennedy appointed as head of USIA, said that "truth is the best propaganda and lies are the worst."[13] As noted in Chapter 2, "soft power" lies in a country's ability to attract and persuade. Public diplomacy works best when it is based on values and aspirations, but that is not always possible – that is why "soft power" and "public diplomacy" are not the same thing.

When the United States waged an intensive diplomatic campaign in early 2022 to prevent Russia, which had amassed more than 100,000 troops along its border with Ukraine, from attacking its neighbor, public diplomacy played a key role. In addition to a series of private meetings and exchanges of letters between leaders, the Biden administration mounted a sustained messaging effort, using speeches, press conferences, media interviews, targeted "leaks" and social media posts. The initial themes focused on standing up for democratic values and the principle that a country should be free to choose its own path. Before long, however, officials started talking about the "massive costs" they would impose on Russia, should it invade Ukraine, and about the military equipment they were sending to Ukraine to help it counter potential Russian aggression. At the same time, Russian officials insisted repeatedly that there would be no invasion and accused the Biden administration of stoking "hysteria," saying that their troops had been sent to the border for long-planned exercises.[14] Once Russia invaded, it was reasonable to conclude that what its officials had done in the run-up to the attack was propaganda.

A long game

Public diplomacy relies on shared experiences in literature, art, science and other areas to overcome fear or suspicion of others, bridge differences, and build respect and friendship. This is vital to securing a good relationship with a foreign country – and it is a long game. In an era when information can reach billions of people in seconds and elicit frantic reactions just as quickly, we have become used to instant gratification. Truly effective public diplomacy does not indulge in chasing speedy results, even if it makes use of modern technology.

This does not mean that pursuing short-term outcomes should be ignored. We still live in the real world and cannot afford to drop the ball on matters and developments that affect our national interest today, just so we can focus on the future. By responding to media inquiries, arranging press conferences, overseeing social media outreach and writing speeches for ambassadors and other senior officials, public diplomacy officers support current policies and initiatives. The effectiveness of those efforts can be measured in accurate media reporting on an embassy's work, positive editorial reaction to an event, or a sustained online conversation about an issue that is important to the embassy. However, such individual efforts must amount to something bigger and more meaningful. They have to be consistent and thought-out elements of a big-picture investment, which must also include long-term components, such as cultural programs, educational and professional exchanges, and teaching English or another language. The results of these efforts may not be seen or felt for years. Measures of success might be reflected in eventual changes to host-country policies, as envisioned or desired by the home-country.

In the early 2000s, the U.S. Embassy in Zimbabwe started an effort to increase the number of female editors in media organizations. Why? One of the embassy's priorities was a more diverse media, which it believed would provide better and more inclusive coverage, and that, in turn, would better serve the public interest. Few countries' diplomats concern themselves with such matters abroad. But when Samuel Kaerezi, a Zimbabwean staff member of the embassy's public affairs section, pointed out that almost no women occupied senior editorial positions, Bruce Wharton, the section chief and one of this chapter's authors, decided to do something about it. Wharton's section provided training to female journalists to help them gain the editing and management skills that would make them more competitive. It also advocated before publishers and top editors to start hiring more women in positions of higher responsibility. It took years, but newsrooms began moving toward a gender balance.

It can take decades to see the impact of the best public diplomacy investment. In the 1950s, about a decade after South Africa adopted the apartheid system, the U.S. Embassy there decided to allow people of color to use its library in Johannesburg, known as the Reading Room. It provided American newspapers, magazines and books, as well as information about U.S. universities and other organizations. The reason at least partially had to do with racial injustice in the United States featuring prominently in anti-American Soviet propaganda. In this particular case, Black South Africans were treated better at an official U.S. facility in their country than Black Americans were treated in the United States. Don Mattera was one of the Reading Room's early Black visitors who became a regular. More than three decades later, as a renowned poet and one of the most influential anti-apartheid voices, he told Wharton how grateful he was that the U.S. library had opened the world to him.

Figure 9.1 Bruce Wharton (right), acting U.S. undersecretary of state for public diplomacy, meets with Italian Culture Minister Dario Franceschini in Florence in 2017.
Photo by Carlo Bressan/Anadolu Agency via Getty Images.

In the 1970s, still in South Africa, the U.S. Embassy selected a junior member of parliament from the ruling National Party to participate in a professional exchange program in the United States – an opportunity to learn about the country's government, politics, economy and culture, and to engage with Americans from various backgrounds. Nominations for such programs are made by U.S. diplomats who detect leadership potential in some of their contacts and believe they are worth the investment because of what they might accomplish in the future. The United States opposed the white-majority party's apartheid policy, but the embassy hoped the young politician might make a difference someday. His name was F. W. de Klerk. In 1989, he became South Africa's president, and two years later he presided over the repeal of the apartheid laws.[15] In 1995, as Nelson Mandela's vice president, he told his U.S. counterpart, Al Gore, at a reception hosted by the U.S. Embassy in Pretoria which Wharton attended, that the exchange program had helped him understand what the U.S. civil rights movement could do for American society – and eventually, to draw lessons applicable to his own country.

As the currency of diplomacy, credibility is indispensable when it comes to public diplomacy. A press officer who misleads or lies to the media instantly loses effectiveness. An exchange program that prevents participants' exposure to inconvenient or embarrassing realities and curtails interaction with government critics is not persuasive. An outreach strategy that is tone-deaf to local culture and history is unlikely to succeed. With a multitude of communications platforms today, a message or a voice stands little chance unless it is perceived as authentic. While the mission of influencing international public opinion is relatively constant, the environment in which public diplomacy officers operate changes all the time, and they must adapt to its demands. Media landscapes, technology and even bilateral relationships shift over time. What worked in Brazil three years ago may not be effective in China next year. Adaptation starts with study and listening.

Key public diplomacy skills

The public diplomacy career track attracts journalists, artists, and marketing and public relations professionals, among others. Although experience in those fields helps, an officer must develop a much more diverse set of skills. Language proficiency is even more important in public diplomacy than in other Foreign Service specialties, because its job is to engage with parts of the host-society that do not belong to the elite and speak only their native tongue. Engaging with complete strangers and quickly finding common ground by listening closely to their interests and concerns is a key skill for a public diplomacy officer.

The interpersonal skills described in Chapter 3 help diplomats to build effective relationships with peers, subordinates and supervisors, as well as host-country interlocutors. The ability to understand and articulate the policies of the home-government takes on an extra dimension in public diplomacy, because its impact is multiplied exponentially in the public space and discourse. An embassy spokesperson is asked about a wide range of issues on a regular basis, unlike colleagues in other sections, who tend to specialize. As well-versed and informed as a spokesperson may be, no one knows everything about everything – that is why one should know where to find guidance and the details necessary to answer a media question.

Standing in front of a group of people or a thicket of microphones and clearly delivering information or communicating ideas is an essential skill in its own right. Having to implement a policy you personally disagree with is challenging enough, but defending that policy publicly in front of television cameras and large audiences represents a whole other level, and few people can do it well. Building and cultivating relationships in the media, academia, cultural institutions and civil society, as well as organizing press conferences, educational and cultural programs, receptions and other events, are all key instruments in the public diplomacy toolbox. The ability to manage budgets, people and programs is essential, as is the skillful use of technology. Simply maintaining a social media presence, putting out information, and holding occasional virtual events is not enough in the 21st century. Being tech-savvy means actively engaging with an audience several times a day and using the latest digital tools, from messaging apps to social media networks to streaming platforms.

The paramount importance of listening and constant learning bears a strong emphasis in public diplomacy. Edward R. Murrow used to emphasize the critical role of "the last three feet" in international communication and understanding – the personal contact in which one person talks to another.[16] You cannot truly influence someone without knowing them well, whether you are dealing with government officials or private citizens. Failure to understand and appreciate the nuances of other cultures and traditions may inadvertently damage otherwise reasonable initiatives. As the press attaché at the U.S. Embassy in Bolivia in the late 1980s and early 1990s, Bruce Wharton worked on a public diplomacy campaign aimed at explaining the dangers of the drug trade to Bolivians, particularly farmers who produced coca used to make cocaine, and many of whom could not read. One of the elements of the campaign almost caused a diplomatic incident, as we will see in the case study at the end of the chapter.

Understanding another culture does not imply agreement with its values. Diplomats, especially those dealing with the public, need to be able to express disagreement without giving offense. The more closely they listen and the more fully they understand a country's history and culture, the greater their ability to have a thoughtful and productive conversation about difficult matters. A European diplomat may disapprove of American gun culture or the death penalty, and a U.S. diplomat may be opposed to the treatment of women in Saudi Arabia, but knowing the context and conditions that produced and continue to sustain those societal traits would help their work. To facilitate a better understanding of the host-country for their staff, embassies can create advisory groups of local experts that meet regularly to discuss key issues, with the added benefit of building important relationships.

Public opinion polls can be a useful reflection of a society's short-term concerns, which can help an embassy to evaluate a program's effectiveness or popularity. If conducted by a reputable firm with a proven method and track record, polling can provide valuable insight. On the other hand, poorly developed or administered questions can skew the results, as can unrelated external events. It is worth keeping in mind that some societies are suspicious of polling and, if commissioned by another country, it may be seen as a form of espionage. Good public diplomacy officers also practice "maven-watching" – identifying and following experts and influential figures through their work, public activities, media appearances and social media posts. It is helpful to pay attention to what local comedians say, what musicians sing about, and what appears in gossip columns. To be truly tuned in to the latest trends and concerns among the locals, diplomats must talk to taxi drivers, shopkeepers and other ordinary people, who may have a better sense of a country's direction than a government minister.

The information and knowledge gained through listening and study should be codified in some way to serve as a guide for public diplomacy programs and set a benchmark against which results can be measured. One approach could be an analysis of important institutions and organizations in the host-country in an unclassified document to which local staff can contribute – and which will not cause embarrassment if leaked. Such analysis should be done once or twice a year and include the following elements: media landscape; academic environment; leading nongovernmental organizations (NGOs) and other civil society groups; prominent religious and cultural organizations; influential thinkers, opinion-makers and pop-culture figures; and social media.

The public diplomacy headquarters

In 2009, three years after Judith McHale stepped down as president and CEO of Discovery Communications, she was appointed to lead the State Department's public diplomacy efforts globally.[17] In several positions during her two decades at Discovery, she helped to grow it from a small company with a single U.S. cable channel to a media giant, with more than 100 channels in 35 languages and over 1 billion subscribers in 170 countries. It had succeeded in part by providing programs in those countries' languages that were also influenced by cultural nuances – not simply feeding them subtitled American content.

In her new position as undersecretary of state for public diplomacy and public affairs, McHale realized that U.S. public diplomacy lacked a strategic focus and had to be better aligned with foreign policy objectives. So she set out to secure a seat for public diplomacy at the policy table. "Public diplomacy needs to be at the front of policy formulation, so decisions can be informed from the beginning as far as foreign attitudes towards a particular subject," she told Nicholas Kralev at the time. "This is not to say that our foreign policy is driven by foreign popular opinion at all. But with an understanding of it, we can better formulate policies and have a greater chance of success. If you are doing something, you want to understand how it's going to impact the people who will be directly affected by it. If you are going to have a negative reaction, wouldn't you want to know that up front?"[18]

During the Cold War, USIA was deliberately separated from the policy process. A 1948 law, known as the Smith-Mundt Act, banned domestic dissemination of information intended for foreign audiences.[19] The Voice of America (VOA) and other U.S. government-funded broadcasters were not available to Americans. The advent of the Internet, followed by social media and mobile technology, made that separation impossible to sustain. In 2012, Congress amended the law to allow U.S. audiences access to materials and information prepared for foreign publics.[20] That freed the State Department to explain to Americans what their tax dollars help to achieve overseas and to encourage them to get involved in what has become known as "citizen diplomacy" with people in other countries.

Having an effective public diplomacy operation at headquarters to provide policy guidance and support is essential for the success of missions abroad. The State Department has two bureaus in Washington that report to the undersecretary for public diplomacy: Global Public Affairs, which focuses on messaging, communication and policy articulation, and Educational and Cultural Affairs, which manages exchanges and other programs. Global Public Affairs runs a 24-hour global media operation. It publishes every word the secretary of state and other top officials utter in public, holds press briefings with officials and facilitates interviews with them, comments on breaking news and foreign countries' statements and actions, manages a wide internet platform and maintains several active social media feeds.

"We have to be aware that the media is so much a part of foreign policy," Michael Hammer, the former ambassador to Chile and the Democratic Republic of the Congo, who served as assistant secretary of state for public affairs in the early 2010s, told Kralev. "There are numerous reports that are erroneous, and it's important to correct as many of them as possible, so people have accurate information about our policies and actions."[21] The bureau operates regional media hubs in London, Brussels, Dubai, Tokyo, and Johannesburg, as well as one in Miami for Latin America. Its activities are separate from the U.S. government's international broadcasts, such as VOA, Radio Free Europe, Radio Free Asia, Radio Sawa and the Arab-language TV network Al Hurra. Centralized mass dissemination of information from the capital is useful, but audience size alone is rarely a good measure of a message's effectiveness. With the possible exception of major events, messaging is most effective when tailored to a specific country or region. Good diplomats translate their headquarters' policy ideas and strategic goals across linguistic, political, cultural and historic divides.

The same principle applies to educational and cultural diplomacy. The capital may develop a program open to participants from anywhere in the world, but embassies should be allowed to customize it to the particular needs, interests and culture of the host-country and the embassy's priorities, while staying true to the overall objectives and strategy.

The public diplomacy section abroad

Many countries' embassies have only one public diplomacy officer, and perhaps a couple of local staffers. Some do not have even a single full-time officer but assign those duties to a member of another section. Big countries, such as the United States and Germany, tend to have bigger public diplomacy – or public affairs – sections. The average section in a U.S. embassy usually includes three official Americans, as well as a dozen or more local employees. Just like in other parts of the mission, the head of the section is a member of the post's leadership team and an adviser to the ambassador.

In addition to overseeing all section activities, budget and personnel, the counselor for public diplomacy is responsible for making sure that those activities are aligned with the mission's priorities, the policies of the administration in office at home and the national interest. A wide network of trusted contacts in the media, academia, government and across civil society is essential to the counselor's ability to develop and expand partnerships. Public diplomacy is much more effective when local partners have a stake in a program or project and can claim some ownership of it. That amplifies the message and makes them work harder to achieve better results, compared to being just players in someone else's show – or worse, passive observers. A local buy-in is also an indication of genuine interest in a topic or initiative in the host-country, and people participate not only because the U.S. embassy invited them.

In certain cases and with approval from headquarters, the public diplomacy chief may offer counsel or support to host-country officials. For example, if the embassy has set as a priority strengthening the capabilities of law-enforcement agencies, that might include media training for police officers, or finding a way to help the host-government develop more direct communication channels between elected officials and their electorate.

One of the other two officers in a typical U.S. public diplomacy section usually manages the embassy's messaging through traditional and social media. Doing that job effectively depends on establishing and cultivating good professional relationships with reporters, editors, publishers, bloggers and opinion-makers. Even though such relationships are mostly transactional – a journalist needs information and the diplomat is in a position to provide it – the longer-term they are, the bigger the benefits for both sides. Knowing what type of message resonates with what audience, and how to craft it, is key to effective communication. The work in this field tends to be reactive, with a focus on the embassy's immediate or short-term needs. An officer must be able to explain and defend policies and programs, in what can be described as "declarative diplomacy."

Cultural and programmatic work, on the other hand, is the realm of "experiential diplomacy," and the responsibility of the third officer in an average section. A longer-term effort than messaging and media work, it brings people together to share ideas and experiences, to learn from and about each other. An officer managing cultural and educational programs spends a lot of time preparing, awarding and monitoring grants to both host-country and home-country organizations, which implement those programs. A grant can be given to a local business incubator to conduct training for entrepreneurs or to a coalition of journalists seeking to improve their investigative skills. Administering exchange programs and recruiting potential participants is another significant part of cultural work, as we will see later in the chapter.

Large U.S. embassies, such as those in London, Tokyo and Beijing, have more than three American officers in the public diplomacy section. On the messaging and communications side, there may be an officer responsible only for print media or only for broadcast networks. On the cultural side, one officer may be in charge of grants, and another of exchange programs. The local staff is indispensable, even more so than in other embassy sections, since the goal of public diplomacy is to engage and connect with the people in the host-country and influence public opinion. Local members of the section are extraordinary resources and reliable advisers to Foreign Service officers, who cannot possibly acquire all the knowledge

Figure 9.2 Nicole Finnemann, director of strategic communications for the State Department's Bureau of Western Hemisphere Affairs and the chapter's co-author, speaks at a conference in Washington, D.C., in 2023.
Photo by Arizona State University.

their local colleagues have or develop even a tiny part of their network. Those assets make a huge difference, from putting together a seating chart for an important dinner to concluding a vital negotiation. Local staff are also the face of the embassy to their communities, and that is where public diplomacy begins.

Speaking to the media

Part of understanding the dynamics of the relationships a diplomat builds in the media is being aware of their usefulness and limitations. While building trust with journalists is important, cultivating such relationships does not mean that one should speak to the press all the time or without a clear objective. Unless you are the ambassador or the official embassy spokesperson, it is usually best not to comment on the record. If you are responsible for messaging and communications in the public diplomacy section, you are likely to be the spokesperson, though your section chief can assume that role as well. Your headquarters may want you to explain a policy decision to the press, or a reporter may ask for comment on a certain development. In both cases, you can use press guidance prepared by the embassy or headquarters. If you do not have the information you need to respond to an inquiry, you can arrange for the reporter to talk to an expert on the topic in another embassy section. If you are trying to publicize a policy initiative, you can write press releases, draft speeches for the ambassador and other embassy officials, and set up interviews and press conferences.

All these efforts should be part of a communication strategy created by your team, with input from the post's leadership, other sections and headquarters – and it should support the Integrated Country Strategy. You can base it on a calendar of major events, such as summits, meetings and anniversaries, and forthcoming policy decisions expected from your capital. It should include medium and long narrative arcs and leave ample flexibility to be able to respond to events and adapt to unforeseen circumstances. In addition to the main strategy, you may be asked to develop and manage separate ad hoc campaigns focused on specific issues.

Imagine that you are serving at the U.S. Embassy in Brazil. The leftist president's government is considering joining China's efforts to replace the U.S. dollar as the world's reserve currency, and Washington has instructed you to design a campaign to explain to the Brazilian public why that is a bad idea that would not serve Brazil's own interests. Whatever your long-term communications strategy might have required you to be doing at this time, you now have a new task. The tools in your box include social media, speeches by the ambassador, media interviews, a press conference and opinion articles by the ambassador in leading Brazilian newspapers.

Where would you begin? That would depend on your assessment of conditions on the ground and public opinion. You might commission a poll to find out how many Brazilians are aware of the issue and how they feel about it. This is a complex matter that requires at least some knowledge of finance and economics, so the questions must be worded carefully and the respondents selected prudently. Once you have answers, you can develop a plan to explain the issue in relatable terms to nonexperts and figure out the best channels to engage the public, using some or all of the tools listed above.

Levels of Attribution in the U.S. Media

On the record
You can be quoted and identified by name and title.
On background
You can be quoted only as a government official, without a name.
On deep background
The information you provide can be used but cannot be attributed to you.
Off the record
What you say cannot be used at all.

We suggest five rules of thumb when talking to the media:

1. **Set the ground rules**.
   Before starting a conversation or discussion, tell the reporters whether you are speaking on the record, on background, on deep background or off the record.

This is your responsibility. If you forget, the reporter can use everything on the record.

2. **Have an agenda in mind**.

   Whether you are giving or facilitating an interview, or holding a press conference or another event, think about your desired outcome, including what headlines you want to see in the media.

3. **Think twice about using humor**.

   Laughter may be universal, but something you find funny may be very serious or even offensive in another country or culture. Unless you speak the local language like a native and have confidence in your grasp of cultural and societal norms, avoid humor.

4. **Beware of potential distractions**.

   You may not be able to control everything at a media event, such as noise from outside, a poor sound system or lighting, and non-camera-friendly backgrounds or backdrops. Risking such distractions may be worth it, if holding an event outside the embassy – for example, in a school or hospital – would make it more authentic and engaging and help you to better convey your message.

5. **Include local partners in your events**.

   Having host-country representatives co-host or actively participate in your events would show that they have a stake in the issue you are highlighting.

Digital communication and social media

When Laura Dogu arrived in Nicaragua as the new U.S. ambassador in 2015, the typical lag between arrival and presentation of credentials in any country, which is required to do official business, was prolonged by the tense relationship between the United States and the government of President Daniel Ortega. During that waiting period, meant to signal Ortega's displeasure with American criticism of his autocratic rule, Dogu could not do much, but she could use social media. With help from the embassy's public diplomacy team, she introduced herself virtually to the Nicaraguan people – she was not allowed to hold in-person events – and asked for recommendations about places to visit, traditional food to try and things to do in their country. Then she went to some of those places, accompanied by the person or people who recommended them, and documented her visits on social media. By the time Ortega accepted her credentials, she had built up goodwill with the Nicaraguan public, which helped when she had to deliver messages the government did not want to hear.

As of this writing, social media networks have been around for about two decades. Even in the poorest countries with low internet penetration rates and slow speeds, the younger generation has integrated electronic devices into everyday life and is considered "digitally native."[22] More and more people get their news from social media mobile apps. So it should be no surprise that, in many countries, almost everyone – including government officials and journalists – is much more likely to respond quickly to a WhatsApp message than to an email. Getting social media right has become key to effective public diplomacy. It provides a digital path to bridge Murrow's "last three feet." It helps diplomats to expand their network of contacts exponentially and get a much better sense about various developments, trends, views, opinions and concerns in the host-society than the traditional media can cover.

A new skill that most diplomats have yet to master is empowering opinion and thought leaders in the digital space who share the embassy's values and interests to become influencers with a significant following. In 2019, the U.S. Embassy in London sent a group of "young social media influencers" to the United States "to learn more about the values that shape American society" and share their findings with their followers. The program's objective was to help the participants find out how life in Washington, Indianapolis and Albuquerque matched up with their depictions in three television series set in those cities: "The West Wing," "Parks and Recreation" and "Breaking Bad." The trip ended with a visit to Universal Studios in Los Angeles.[23]

Instead of spending money on travel expenses, the Chinese Consulate General in New York had another idea in 2021. According to press reports based on Foreign Agent Registration Act records, the consulate paid a New Jersey firm $300,000 to recruit social media influencers to counter a Western diplomatic boycott of the 2022 Winter Olympics in Beijing.[24] The United States, Britain, Australia and other countries had decided not to send official delegations to the games' opening ceremony to protest abuses against minority Uyghurs in Xinjiang Province[25] and democratic crackdowns in Hong Kong.[26] You can judge whether such an effort counts as public diplomacy or propaganda.

Just like an influencer, a diplomat responsible for messaging and communications must build rapport and credibility with audiences, so when the time comes for an official announcement, the message resonates as authentic and well-intentioned. Retaining and growing followers requires constant engagement and a team effort. Someone from the section should be accessible, respond to questions quickly and otherwise make sure the audience feels heard. It is a good idea to allocate time for such engagement every day, for which resources and effective team management are critical. A public diplomacy officer must be tech-savvy, develop an affinity for data and use the latest analytical tools to keep abreast of audience demographics and other characteristics. It is important to understand the significant amount of data one can wrangle and to be careful and precise in its analysis. For example, a social media post might get thousands of "likes" and comments, but where are those people? Are some of them robots? If most are outside the embassy's host-country, you have not reached your target audience. When exactly did you post your message? Perhaps that time is not the best for optimal reach.

Countering misinformation and disinformation

In an age of "fake news," "alternative facts" and "post-truth," technology enables the rapid proliferation of misinformation, disinformation, hate speech and propaganda. Countering such attempts is one of the biggest challenges to public diplomacy in any country. To deal with it, several governments have established task forces in recent years, such as the Global Engagement Center in Washington and the Government Communication Service in London. There is an important distinction between misinformation and disinformation. Misinformation is usually unintentional, and sometimes even well-meaning. Disinformation, on the other hand, is deliberate and often targeted. Governments use it as a tool of both domestic and foreign policies. The most popular messaging platform in the world at this writing, WhatsApp, is used to spread both misinformation and disinformation. They are easily propagated because the technology feels comfortable and trusted, even though its parent company, Meta, the owner of Facebook, has tried to make product changes and educate users about their digital hygiene.

How can public diplomacy counter false information? Educational efforts, including lectures, discussions and seminars, could be a good start, particularly with young audiences – although many adults find themselves at no less of a loss when it comes to what sources of information to trust than their children. Digital and media literacy is essential today no matter one's career choice, and few schools teach it. An embassy cannot properly fill that void, but it can bring attention to it. A diplomatic mission can also provide training to media organizations to improve their fact-checking and investigative capabilities, and it can partner with local civil society groups to carry out long-term campaigns with specific examples of the consequences of misleading or untrue information.

In the immediate and short term, diplomats have to utilize the same tools and platforms on which the false information appears in the first place in order to counter it. Correcting the record, exposing the agenda of those engaging in disinformation and providing context should be an embassy's daily activity, although using your judgment applies here as much as it does in other aspects of diplomacy. If an unknown blogger with few followers posted a false claim on social media, you may not want to bring attention to it. That is why it is important to have staff members dedicated to social media engagement – they would know when it is in the embassy's interest to respond. An official government account should be a credible and trusted voice, so your staff should use credible and trusted sources of information.

U.S. law requires that American public diplomacy, including messaging, be overt. Embassies are allowed to provide financial and other support to local media organizations and advocacy groups they consider independent to promote free expression, and that funding is transparent as well, meaning that any awarded grant is a matter of public record.

Cultural diplomacy

Bringing people together is not just a slogan – that is literally what cultural affairs officers do through a wide variety of programs, including lectures and discussions, concerts and art exhibits, language instruction, teacher training, sports and educational and professional exchanges. Fulbright is a name known around the world, thanks to a program that every year brings thousands of students, researchers and faculty to the United States – and sends thousands of Americans to other countries. It bears the name of the late Senator J. William Fulbright, the longest-serving chair of the Senate Foreign Relations Committee in history, from 1959 until 1974. More than 400,000 people have received a Fulbright scholarship since the first grants were awarded in 1946.[27]

The U.S. government believes that exchange programs have created a deep well of goodwill for the United States, despite anti-American sentiment in certain regions and disapproval of official U.S. policies in many countries. More than 500 participants in the State Department's flagship professional exchange, the International Visitor Leadership Program (IVLP),[28] have gone on to become heads of state or government. Among them are former British Prime Ministers Margaret Thatcher, Tony Blair and Gordon Brown, as well as South Africa's F. W. de Klerk, as noted earlier. "Every time there is a Cabinet reshuffle in a country, the embassy tallies up how many of the new ministers have been on an American program," former public diplomacy officer Walter Douglas told Nicholas Kralev.[29] The IVLP, which began in 1940, brings nearly 5,000 people to the United States every year. Among the best-known cultural exchanges are the Iowa Writers Workshop and Jazz Ambassadors.

Not every visitor, however, draws positive conclusions about the United States. One of those who did not was the Egyptian Sayyid Qutb. After studying in Colorado for much of 1949, Qutb denounced the United States as a soulless place where no Muslim should live. He later became a well-known writer whose work provided the theoretical basis of radical Islamic groups, including al-Qaeda.[30]

The success of exchanges is due in part to providing unfiltered experiences to foreign visitors, as well as a country's willingness to acknowledge and reflect on its problems, shortcomings, challenges and mistakes. The United States makes sure that what visitors hear during their trips is neither scripted nor censored. The State Department schedules all meetings, briefings and other activities, but the host-organizations and interlocutors are not chosen for their support of government policies or their political beliefs – in fact, the department does not even ask what a speaker or host-family might say to foreign guests. Many countries have academic exchange programs, but professional exchanges like the IVLP are few. They can be bilateral or multilateral. For example, the German government regularly brings groups of Americans from a particular field to Germany to share ideas, expertise and experience. A U.S. embassy can also design a custom program for a single visitor, with help from the State Department. The biggest programs are multilateral – they can be global or regional, such as the department's Young African Leaders Initiative (YALI).

YALI participants fall in the 25–35 age group, while IVLP candidates tend to be mid-career professionals from the social sciences, politics, media, arts and other areas, who are vetted and selected in a public application process, though embassy officials can make nominations as well.[31] Embassies seek diverse groups representative of the host-society, with an equal number of men and women, and people with disabilities.

Embassies and headquarters work to put together engaging and enriching programs, and they usually encourage visitors to propose their own ideas – they know best what would be most useful to them. It is essential that cultural officers prepare visitors for their programs in advance, both logistically and substantively.

What happens after a program is over is no less important. An embassy's public diplomacy section should harness the knowledge, experience and goodwill to produce a multiplier effect. Upon their return, participants become alumni, and as figures of emerging and growing influence, they can engage with peers and other fellow citizens to share their takeaways and recruit candidates for future exchanges. Since the inaugural YALI program in 2014, applications have increased significantly, which is a good measure of success. Things do not always go according to plan. In the early 2000s, the State Department found out that about two-thirds of Ethiopian exchange participants ended up staying in the United States after their programs ended. The terms of the grants they had received stipulated that they had to return home – otherwise, the U.S. government's investment was in vain. It was very difficult to track those Ethiopians down once they disappeared, usually aided by the large Ethiopian diaspora in the United States. So the State Department suspended one of the youth exchanges with the East African country, and as of this writing, it has not resumed.

In addition to exchange programs and other traditional cultural activities, a unique tool in the American public diplomacy toolbox has been recruiting celebrities to visit other countries and share their experiences with local audiences.

Figure 9.3 President Obama addresses YALI participants in Washington, D.C., in 2016.
Photo by Chip Somodevilla/Getty Images.

In 2006, Olympic skater Michelle Kwan became the State Department's first "public diplomacy envoy" and traveled to Russia, China and other countries to tell her story to young people. She was followed by former baseball star Cal Ripken Jr. and actress Fran Drescher.

"If you use icons of American culture judiciously and selectively, you can have a big impact," Charles Rivkin, a former U.S. ambassador to France, told Kralev. When actor Samuel L. Jackson was in Paris, "I asked him to come with me to the *banlieues*," the French term for suburbs that has become synonymous with low-income housing areas, Rivkin said. "He got out of the car, and these kids in one of the most disadvantaged suburbs of Paris yelled, 'Le Big Mac, Le Big Mac!'" – a reference to one of the actor's famous lines in the 1994 film "Pulp Fiction." Another celebrity Rivkin took to a *banlieue* was singer William James Adams Jr., better known as Will.i.am. He talked to the youngsters about his upbringing in the housing projects of East Los Angeles by a single mother. Other distinguished guests of Rivkin's in Paris included filmmaker Woody Allen and actress Jodie Foster. "Celebrities are two-dimensional figures when they are on screen or in your headphones," Rivkin said. "But when they appear in person and say, 'I'm proud to be an American,' and 'America is a good place,' that has a huge impact."[32]

Planning, measurement and evaluation

When an embassy writes its Integrated Country Strategy, along with identifying its priorities in the relationship with the host-country, it establishes objectives and benchmarks for measuring progress. Public diplomacy should be an integral part of most objectives, and sometimes it merits its own section in the strategy. A general rule of thumb is that the more difficult the relationship is, the more important public diplomacy programs are. With a place at the creation of the country strategy – and at the policy table in general – public diplomacy can help to inform decisions as they are made, rather than being an afterthought. That does not mean that a particular course of action deemed to be in the national interest should not be taken, just because it may not be popular in the host-country. But the expertise and experience of public diplomacy officers can help the embassy leadership anticipate and prepare for local reactions to whatever it decides to do.

Being included in the strategy also helps the public diplomacy section to better align its programs and other activities with policy goals and mission priorities – it gives the staff a sense of purpose and ensures that taxpayer funds are spent in the service of policies that protect and promote the national interest. Moreover, it provides public diplomacy officers with the opportunity to evaluate their work against the objectives and benchmarks set out in the strategy, and to make course corrections if they are not achieving the desired results.

As difficult as measuring the effectiveness of public diplomacy may be, developing both qualitative and quantitative metrics is a must. We mentioned earlier the superficial analysis of speeches, press conferences and other events, such as donation ceremonies, based on media coverage. Benchmarks for assessing the results of a long-term campaign should be determined as well, with the understanding that various things can derail the plan. For example, a campaign to promote a public health project may be overshadowed by an unrelated outbreak of disease. Beginning in early 2020, the Covid-19 pandemic made holding in-person public events and exchange programs impossible and had a significant negative impact on public diplomacy overall for about three years.

Every year, U.S. embassies around the world award thousands of grants to host-country and American organizations for projects in almost all possible fields one can imagine – journalism, economic development, law-enforcement, agriculture, education, food security, water irrigation, public health, and fighting crime and corruption, to name just a few. Starting in 2004, giving out grants was Hans Wechsel's job as the first regional director for the Arabian Peninsula of the Middle East Partnership Initiative, which the State Department had created two years earlier to help build and strengthen civil society and to support the region's democratic aspirations. Based at the embassy in Abu Dhabi, as noted in the exercise at the end of Chapter 3, Wechsel was tasked with identifying potential grant recipients in eight countries: Bahrain, Jordan, Kuwait, Oman, Qatar, Saudi Arabia, Yemen and the United Arab Emirates.

One of the organizations Wechsel and his small team came across was a group in Yemen called Women Journalists Without Chains. Co-founded by 26-year-old Yemeni Tawakkol Karman to promote human rights and press freedom, it had great ambitions but no funds and was unable to make a difference – until Wechsel's office nominated the group for a $50,000 grant for a pilot project to seek freedoms, rights and protections for journalists in nondemocratic Yemen. "I don't want to overstate the case, but she was this woman who had never done a program before, with this small, nonconsequential organization, so we did launch her as an activist with capacity," Wechsel told Kralev.[33] That capacity increased so much that Karman emerged as the public face of Yemen's uprising when the country joined the Arab Spring pro-democracy movement in 2011, with massive protests against the rule of then-President Ali Abdullah Saleh, who had been in power longer than Karman had been alive. She was even called "the mother of the revolution." That same year, Karman became the first Arab woman to receive the Nobel Peace Prize, which she shared with two Liberian women, then-President Ellen Johnson Sirleaf and peace activist Leymah Gbowee.[34]

Not every public diplomacy grant leads to a Nobel Prize, and the impact of some is more difficult to measure. The one area of public diplomacy where metrics for quantitative measurement abound is social and digital media – strong analytical skills can help you wrangle the data to inform your communications strategy, while laziness with the numbers can get you into trouble. But you have to decide in advance what a successful campaign means. Is the number of eyeballs enough or is the number of people who take a specific action as a result of a social media post what really matters? For example, if the U.S. Embassy in Indonesia promotes an upcoming free English language course for underprivileged students, how should success be measured? By the number of "likes" and comments, or by the number of applications to the program?

Jok Abraham Thon was 26 in 2016, when he founded the Promised Land School near a cattle camp outside Juba, the capital of South Sudan, to educate children affected by conflict, who otherwise would not have had the opportunity to study. Two years later, the U.S. Embassy selected Thon for a YALI fellowship. Since then, he has improved the school significantly through a support network established and strengthened through his YALI experience. "There is no better example of the return on our investment than Thon, who played an instrumental role in helping the embassy's public affairs section to reestablish reciprocal cultural exchanges," Tom Hushek, a former U.S. ambassador to South Sudan wrote in WIDA's Diplomatic Diary in 2021. "During more than three decades as an American diplomat, much of it serving in conflict or post-conflict zones, I learned the same lesson over and over: cultural and educational interactions, in a low-cost and bottom-up approach, have a positive impact on millions of people and make U.S. diplomacy stronger."[35]

Teaching English has been among the most successful U.S. public diplomacy efforts for decades. It is a classic win-win scenario of helping others while helping yourself. English proficiency significantly increases a person's chances of getting a good job in just about any country, which results in a higher living standard. But what is in it for the United States? Understanding English exposes people in other countries to American sources of information and values. "If people are dependent on the local media and a relatively limited and controlled set of resources, they are more likely to be swayed in one direction," Craig Dicker, a former language officer in the Foreign Service, told Kralev. There are about two dozen such officers in the service. "We care, because ignorance is our number one enemy."[36]

Case Study: Anti-Drug Campaign in Bolivia

The U.S. government's "war on drugs" started in 1971 and expanded greatly in the 1980s, resulting in much more severe criminal punishment for nonviolent offenses. Congress passed the Anti-Drug Abuse Act of 1986, which established mandatory minimum prison sentences, and increased media coverage focused the public's attention on the issue. In 1984, First Lady Nancy Reagan began what would become her signature "Just Say No" campaign, a privately funded effort to educate schoolchildren about the dangers of drug use.[37] The United States made the "war on drugs" the primary facet of its relations with Bolivia, Colombia and Peru, the main suppliers of coca and cocaine for the American market.

This was the main focus of all sections and offices at the U.S. Embassy in Bolivia when Bruce Wharton was its press attaché in the late 1980s and early 1990s. The political section worked with the Bolivian leadership to win

Case Study: (cont.)

cooperation on U.S. counternarcotics programs, and the State Department's Bureau of International Narcotics and Law Enforcement Affairs provided funding for the Bolivian counternarcotics police and court systems. The Drug Enforcement Administration, which already had a significant staff presence at the embassy, brought in a large number of special agents on temporary duty. The U.S. military supported the efforts with training for the police and a dozen helicopters. The U.S. Agency for International Development (USAID) worked with the Ministry of Agriculture, local communities and businesses to provide alternative crops and markets for the small farmers in Bolivia's subtropical regions who grew coca.

The public diplomacy section was responsible for helping to reduce drug production through outreach that would inform the Bolivian public's understanding of the dangers of the drug trade. A substantial part of that effort was the promotion of USAID's program to encourage coca farmers to stop producing coca and switch to coffee, bananas and macadamia nuts. The already tall order was further complicated by the illiteracy of many farmers. How could they be persuaded to abandon their longtime livelihood in favor of the uncertainty of growing cheaper crops they were not necessarily familiar with?

After discussions with the public diplomacy staff and other colleagues, Wharton and Robert Callahan, the section chief, decided to start by producing a poster that would visually make the point that farmers should not be supporting the drug trade. With help from an illustrator and a graphic artist in a U.S. military support team, they developed a poster that showed a farmer standing at a crossroads – one road led to trafficking, addiction and ruin, and the other to prosperity, peace and joy. The initial sketch was a simple colorless pencil drawing, which Wharton and Callahan showed to Bolivian Embassy employees and staff at a local NGO working in the counternarcotics area. All agreed that the message was clear, and the sketch was sent to the graphic artist to add color and design the poster.

When the galley arrived from the printer, it looked ready to go to the Americans' eyes. A last check with a Bolivian employee, however, exposed a serious flaw. The dominant color used to depict the path leading to ruin was burnt orange, which was also the main color in the Bolivian ruling party's logo and banners. An illiterate or semiliterate audience used to casting ballots based on graphics and party colors would most certainly see a connection between the party and the road to drug trafficking and addiction. The poster, of course, was sent back to the graphic artist. The embassy relied heavily on the host-government's cooperation to carry out its programs, and antagonizing it was the last thing the public diplomacy section wanted. But had no one noticed the red flag, the embassy would likely have been accused of either embarrassing the ruling party or incompetence.

Case Study: (cont.)

The dangerously close call showed the risk of developing public diplomacy programs without sufficient knowledge and understanding of host-country culture, traditions and values. Even a simple color on a poster can result in a diplomatic crisis and jeopardize a law-enforcement effort as consequential as fighting drug trafficking. The poster incident was not the only ill-fated outreach attempt. At about the same time, Washington sent to several embassies in the region anti-drug public service announcements produced in the United States to run on local television. The test audiences were puzzled. "Why are those nice-looking American kids in prison?" some audience members asked. In fact, the video was set in a high school hallway, but Latin American students had never seen lockers in schools and could not relate. The anti-drug message was lost before it started.

Even with different colors, the poster did not make much of a difference to the levels of coca production. Although the embassy generated a good amount of positive media coverage of USAID and other programs, and those efforts helped Bolivia to diversify its agriculture and deal with its own narcotics problems, huge supplies of drugs continued to flow to the United States. It is important to understand that public diplomacy can rarely compensate for bad policy. The "war on drugs" is widely viewed as a failure, largely because the U.S. government has not been able to curb the demand for narcotics at home and reduce the highly seductive profitability of their production and trafficking.

Exercise: South Africa and Russia's War in Ukraine (Part 2)

In the first part of this exercise at the end of Chapter 6, the U.S. Embassy in South Africa was tasked with trying to persuade the South African government to vote in favor of a U.N. General Assembly resolution calling for a stop to Russia's killing of civilians and destruction of key infrastructure in Ukraine. In a previous vote to condemn Russia's invasion of its neighbor and demand its pullout, South Africa had decided to abstain. Its position was that it did not want to "take sides," although it pointed out that, during the apartheid era of white-majority rule during the Cold War, the Soviet Union supported the African National Congress, which is now the ruling party. Because of that history, some South African officials expressed a sense of "kinship" with Russia.

Washington believes that Russia's attack on a sovereign country is a threat to the United Nations and must be condemned. After the State Department's instruction cable to your embassy to secure South African support for a new U.N. resolution, the post's leadership and the political section developed a political strategy. With

Exercise: (cont.)

only a week left until the next vote, they decided that there was not enough time for a public diplomacy component to the plan. Their efforts to persuade the host-government to back the resolution quietly were not successful, and South Africa abstained again. Now the ambassador wants the public diplomacy section, where you work, to design a campaign to explain to the South African public why it is important that no country can attack another without impunity – and why their government's U.N. abstention sends the wrong message.

Task: Draft a public diplomacy strategy considering the following questions:

- Will you devise a national campaign aimed at the public at large, several local campaigns, or one focused on a community of influential people? South Africa is a big country, with several major cities.
- Who exactly is your audience and how can you most effectively reach it?
- What is your desired and realistic outcome and what benchmarks will you set to measure progress?
- What balance of print, broadcast and online media would work best for your audience?
- What role will in-person and virtual events or experiences play in this campaign?
- What role will your ambassador play? What about officials from your capital?
- How will you coordinate this campaign with the other diplomats in your embassy?
- What other embassies, organizations or people will you recruit as partners to enhance the reach and influence of the campaign?
- How will you respond to South Africans who may accuse you of meddling in their internal affairs?

ADDITIONAL RESOURCES

Nicholas J. Cull, *Public Diplomacy: Foundations for Global Engagement in the Digital Age* (Polity Press, 2019).

Justin Hart, *Empire of Ideas: The Origins of Public Diplomacy and the Transformation of U.S. Foreign Policy* (Oxford University Press, 2020).

Alan Hunt, *Public Diplomacy: What It Is and How To Do It* (United Nations Institute for Training and Research, 2016).

Ilan Manor, *The Digitalization of Public Diplomacy* (Palgrave Macmillan, 2019).

Nancy Snow and Nicholas J. Cull, eds., *Routledge Handbook of Public Diplomacy*, 2nd ed. (Routledge, 2020).

10 Consular Affairs and Crisis Management

JANICE JACOBS AND JAMES ZUMWALT

Some of the most urgent and memorable phone calls in a diplomat's career rarely come during regular business hours. For Matthew Keene, a former U.S. Foreign Service officer in the consular career track, the wee hours of the morning were much more common, no matter where he was posted. "We found the body of a young American male at the airport hotel. It appears to be suicide," one caller reported. "I'm 14 years old," pleaded another. "My parents brought me here on vacation to visit family. But it turns out they want to marry me off to a 50-year-old man I don't even know. Please help!" Yet another was no less desperate: "My husband has hidden my passport and my daughter's passport. He is abusive, he won't let me out of the house, he won't let me call my family back home, and I'm worried he might kill me."

Consular work is perhaps the best example of diplomacy with a human touch, because consular officers touch people's lives around the world every day, often in moments of great need, trauma or desperation. They serve on the front lines of diplomacy, guarding against threats far away from the home-country's physical borders. They protect those borders through the entry visas they decide to grant or deny, and assist home-country citizens in harm's way. They provide what are known as cradle-to-grave services, including everything from issuing reports of birth abroad to visiting detained or imprisoned compatriots to issuing death certificates. Consular matters affect every bilateral relationship, and their impact is felt globally.

"Far from the glamor often associated with diplomacy, the life of a consular officer ... is a daily rollercoaster – from the routine to the sensitive to the catastrophic," Keene wrote in the Washington International Diplomatic Academy's Diplomatic Diary in 2021. "Diplomacy is a complicated business. It requires years of building trust and cultivating relationships in the host-country, creating a respectful expectation of reciprocity and incremental progress toward mutually beneficial goals – all of this hopefully culminating in formal arrangements and lasting agreements."[1]

Consular relations between states are governed by the Vienna Convention on Consular Affairs of 1963, as noted in Chapter 1.[2] In some countries, such as Japan, consular professionals do not carry out any other duties during their careers. There is a limit to how far they can advance in the hierarchy, and they usually do not rise to chief or even deputy chief of mission positions. In other diplomatic services, the consular career track is treated the same as all other specialties, including political and economic. Moreover, the U.S. Foreign Service requires all new officers, regardless of their chosen track, to spend at least one year doing consular work, though in practice, that takes a full first or second two-year tour. Those who have selected nonconsular specialties may never perform consular work for the rest of their careers.

That mandatory requirement may seem odd. It was meant to address significant staff shortages in consular sections, particularly after the 9/11 terrorist attacks, when new requirements increased the burden of the visa process on both line officers and managers. Because the 19 hijackers, who killed nearly 3,000 people, had entered the United States on legally obtained visas, the entire process was overhauled to make it more rigorous and as bulletproof as possible. As a result, all visa applicants, with very few exceptions, had to be interviewed in person for the first time ever. There were not enough consular officers to do all those interviews, and requiring new-comers to step in appeared to be the best solution.

Not surprisingly, many officers were – and still are – not happy about that requirement, because it was not why they became diplomats. Even former secre-taries of state have criticized that policy, though none of them changed it while in office. "I've always thought that having officers stamp visas for two years really does turn off a lot of very smart people" from the Foreign Service, Condoleezza Rice told Nicholas Kralev.[3] The reality, however, is that consular work is a highly effective education for new diplomats, which will serve them well throughout their careers. Almost every diplomatic skill comes into play – from using a foreign language to collecting and analyzing information to communicating and negoti-ating with a wide range of people to quick decision-making. In addition to global and regional knowledge, you must have a good understanding of the economic, social and political conditions in the host-country. Consular work will test you as an individual, including your ability to empathize while fairly applying laws and procedures.

What do consular officers do?

It has become clear by now that consular work is much more than stamping visas in passports. Its two-fold mission is to assist home-country citizens abroad and to adjudicate visa applications. Citizen services can be as routine as issuing tempor-ary passports or as stressful as evacuations because of armed conflict or natural disasters. Visa services are offered both to travelers wishing to visit the home-country for short periods and those intending to immigrate. To be effective and efficient, consular officers must first understand the full extent of both the author-ities and responsibilities that come with the job. Their decisions and actions directly affect people's lives. It is critical that they possess a solid knowledge of their host-country – the government and all parts of society – and maintain and constantly expand their network of contacts, with whom they ideally communi-cate in the local language.

Good networking with the local community is key to dealing with citizen services. Knowing how the host-government is organized and the right people to contact in an emergency is part of crisis preparedness. Visits to government offices, hotels, hospitals and even local morgues to meet those who will help in an emergency is a smart move. Developing an effective warden system, whereby private home-country citizens abroad can help disseminate information or check on others, is another essential responsibility of the consular section. One can do all the planning in the world and be prepared for various contingencies, but unless the officers executing the plan have excellent communication skills, things can easily go wrong.

Visa work can be overwhelming. In countries with huge demand for U.S. visas, such as Mexico and China, consular sections interview as many as 3,000 a day, meaning that individual officers see more than 100 applicants every day.[4] That, in turn, means that an officer has just a couple of minutes to review all the information contained in the documents submitted by the applicant, and to receive any additional information from the candidate verbally, before making a decision. In that sliver of time, the officer has to figure out if the applicant's story makes sense, and to detect any suspicious nervousness, dishonest answers and outright lies. An officer who knows what the average salary of a school teacher is in the host-country will quickly recognize that a document claiming the applicant makes double that amount is fake. If a request must be denied, your public diplomacy skills will be tested as you deliver the news in a way that allows the applicant's dignity to remain intact. Officers must not take applicants' reactions to being denied a visa personally, even if the person on the other side of the window spits in their face – or on the window between the officer and the applicant – as has happened in U.S. embassies.

Consular work will also test your leadership abilities, because officers manage people and resources very early on – as David Lindwall noted in Chapter 3, he managed local employees with much more experience when he was posted to Colombia at age 26. While challenging, consular work can also be fun and rewarding. Unlike in most other areas of diplomacy, you see tangible results quickly and know that you are making a difference.

The consular headquarters

A government's consular operations are usually led by a division of its Foreign Ministry or, in the U.S. case, the State Department's Bureau of Consular Affairs. The bureau, which is responsible for issuing passports to U.S. citizens both at home and abroad, has the distinction of being almost fully funded by the fees collected from the services it provides. It formulates policy related to those services, as well as to immigration, and oversees policy implementation. Apart from issuing passports, its main functions include protecting U.S. citizens abroad and adjudicating visas. Responsibility for these functions is vested in the assistant secretary of state for consular affairs.[5] Janice Jacobs, one of this chapter's authors, held that position from 2008 to 2014.

Figure 10.1 Janice Jacobs, assistant secretary of state for consular affairs, testifies before the U.S. Senate in 2009.
Photo courtesy of C-SPAN.

The consular headquarters in a ministry or department often works with various interagency partners. The Bureau of Consular Affairs' most important relationship is with the Department of Homeland Security (DHS), including its divisions, such as Customs and Border Protection (CBP), U.S. Citizenship and Immigration Services (CIS) and Immigration and Customs Enforcement (ICE). The Department of Defense (DOD) may be called on to provide military flights during an evacuation of Americans. Visa work can involve the FBI or the National Counterterrorism Center. The Centers for Disease Control and Prevention (CDC) provide advice during a pandemic that is included in the State Department's travel advisories. The Federal Aviation Administration may assist after an airplane crash overseas. The Department of Health and Human Services (HHS) is sometimes called on to help a destitute U.S. citizen returning home. Understanding the interagency process is an important part of consular work.

Another major part of the Bureau of Consular Affairs' daily work is to support the consular sections of U.S. embassies and other diplomatic missions around the world, which are key players in the bureau's operations. It is important to understand that a "consular section" is not the same as a "consulate," which can be confusing. As explained in Chapter 1, a consulate is an embassy's constituent post located in a city other than a country's capital. For example, there are U.S. consulates in nine Mexican cities, and they are all part of the U.S. Mission in

Mexico, which is led by the embassy in Mexico City. A consular section can be located in an embassy or consulate, and it provides consular services to the public. Just like an embassy, a consulate can have various other sections, such as political, economic, public diplomacy, etc. As it happens, the U.S. and British consulates in Hong Kong are bigger than many embassies.

The consular section abroad

Most embassies have a consular section – in the U.S. case, a rare exception is the embassy in Pretoria, South Africa, which is a mere 35 miles from the consulate general in Johannesburg, which handles consular services. The size of a consular section can vary wildly – an embassy in a small country may have only one consular officer and a couple of local assistants, while posts in India and the Philippines have dozens of U.S. officers and as many local employees. In a big embassy, the consular section is divided into two units – citizen services and visa services – with dedicated officers assigned to each. A unit may even have subunits, such as nonimmigrant and immigrant visas. Regardless of a post's size, it provides the same types of services (routine, special, emergency, etc., as shown in Figure 10.2). If a section is very small and does not have formally defined units, every officer may perform all types of duties.

The head of the consular section is part of the mission's leadership team. Consular officers see all cross-sections of the local society and often have valuable information and insights on trends and developments, which may have escaped the attention of other sections. Consular sections also play an important public diplomacy role. Most visitors to an embassy or consulate come for a consular service, and many have never met an American. Treating each visitor with dignity and respect, even if a request cannot be granted, is imperative to maintaining a positive home-country image. U.S. law mandates that only consular officers have the authority to issue or deny visas. Not even an ambassador can order that a visa be issued.[6] Each post is required to have a written visa referral system, which allows officials from other parts of the mission to recommend visa issuance to the consular section when it is deemed in the national interest to do so. All referred applicants are

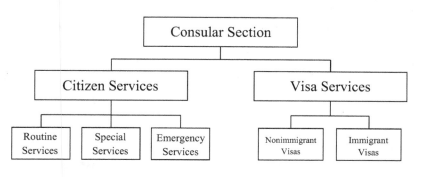

Figure 10.2 Types of services provided by a typical consular section.

subject to the standard checks and requirements, and consular officers are held personally responsible for visa decisions.

Beginning in early 2020, the Covid-19 pandemic disrupted all consular services. Consular sections overseas handled only emergency U.S. citizen and visa cases, with all routine services suspended for months, and in some cases, for more than a year. That led to a huge backlog of applications and meager revenues, which presented an existential challenge for the Bureau of Consular Affairs. When embassies reopened to the public, it became clear that operations would not be fully restored for some time, as pandemic restrictions continued to linger and the backlog kept increasing. To ease the burden, the State Department allowed consular sections discretion to waive visa interview requirements for certain applicants.

Routine citizen services

Assisting the home-country's citizens abroad is – or should be – priority number one, not just for consular officers, but for every embassy and consulate. All U.S. ambassadors are instructed to ensure the safety and welfare of American citizens in their host-country. Routine operations shut down during a crisis to enable everyone in the consular section to provide emergency services. The best known of the routine services is passport issuance. According to U.S. law, only emergency American passports valid for one year can be issued by an overseas post. Regular applications are forwarded to the United States, where the passport is produced at a passport agency. In 2022, there were 26 such agencies around the country, run by the Bureau of Consular Affairs, and about 146 million passports and passport cards were in circulation.[7] A passport card is a credit card-size document that can be used to enter the country by land at border crossings with Canada and Mexico, as well as at sea ports of entry; it cannot be used for international air travel. There is a national security aspect to passports that requires checks of databases and other records to ensure there is no fraud or abuse.

Other routine services include documenting the birth of citizen children, disseminating voter information, helping the destitute secure funds, checking on the welfare of citizens in hospitals and prisons, assisting with the adoption of foreign-born children and issuing reports of death. Although consular officers regularly visit detained Americans, they cannot serve as attorneys, even if they have law degrees. They can provide a list of local lawyers and information on what to expect from authorities. They also perform regular welfare checks to ensure that health and nutrition needs are being met, and that prisoners are not being mistreated. Guidance on how to perform the various services is based on U.S. law and procedures outlined in the "Foreign Affairs Manual" and consular training resources. Local embassy staff often provide an important historical perspective to U.S. officers, who rotate in and out of consular sections every two to three years.

The Bureau of Consular Affairs' Office of Children's Issues handles child adoptions from other countries by American parents,[8] which have decreased drastically in the last two decades – from 22,985 in fiscal year 2004 to 1,622 in 2020.[9] Some of the reasons have to do with certain countries, such as Russia, banning adoptions by U.S. citizens,[10] as well as with rampant corruption in the developing world, which led to tightening of U.S. rules and regulations.[11] The bureau and consular officers overseas work with families, foreign governments and adoption service providers to ensure a transparent process. The office also partners with DHS, as well as with local and airport authorities, to prevent international parental child abductions.[12] Passport regulations make such kidnappings difficult, because they require both parents to accompany a child under 16 filing a new passport application. If both parents cannot be present, proof of sole legal authority over the child is needed. Still, abductions happen more often than most of us realize.

International adoptions and parental child abductions

Sean Goldman was born in the United States in 2000 to an American father, David Goldman, and a Brazilian mother, Bruna Bianchi Carneiro Ribeiro. When Sean was 4 years old, his mother took him to Brazil for what was supposed to be a short vacation, but soon after their arrival, she decided to remain there with Sean indefinitely, without his father's consent. David took swift legal action to recover his son, obtaining a court order in New Jersey giving him temporary custody and filing an action under the Hague Convention on the Civil Aspects of International Child Abduction.[13]

Parties to the convention, such as the United States and Brazil, have agreed that a child removed from one member-state to another in violation of a left-behind parent's custodial rights shall be returned promptly. The convention does not address who should have custody of the child, but in which jurisdiction the custody case should be heard. In this case, it was clear that custody and any visitation rights should be decided in New Jersey, Sean's place of habitual residence. Bruna eventually divorced David and married a Brazilian attorney. When she later died during childbirth, Sean's new stepfather obtained a Brazilian custody order and refused to return him to his father.

Each Hague Convention country has a designated central authority to handle cases. In the United States, that is the Office of Children's Issues. In Brazil, it is the Special Secretariat for Human Rights. The former filed a petition with the latter, and U.S. consular officers in Brazil – at the embassy in Brasilia and the consulate in Rio de Janeiro, where Sean lived – actively followed the case, attended court hearings and frequently reminded the local authorities about the requirements of the Hague Convention. In Washington, Janice Jacobs, as the assistant secretary of state for consular affairs, as well as Secretary of State Hillary Clinton and President Obama, got involved, privately raising the case with the Brazilian government, including the president.

For five years, however, the Brazilian courts sided with Sean's stepfather, who specialized in family law, and the government refused to take action to return the boy to his father, who was prevented from seeing Sean. Finally, following persistent pressure from U.S. consular officers, Brazil's highest court ruled in David's favor, and he brought Sean back to the United States on Christmas Eve in 2009. They were accompanied by Chris Smith, a member of Congress from New Jersey who had brought additional attention to the case. Smith later sponsored a 2014 law, the Sean and David Goldman International Child Abduction Prevention and Return Act, which mandated sanctions against Hague Convention countries that violate the agreement.[14]

Not all Hague Convention cases are this high-profile or drawn-out. Many children are returned promptly to their country of habitual residence. Sean's story demonstrates how important it is that consular officers have solid knowledge of convention procedures and the host-country's judicial system. These cases also require patience, empathy, good persuasive skills and effective working relationships with host-government officials. There was one particular Brazilian official who proved crucial to a successful resolution. This official was well- and positively known to U.S. consular officers, and a sense of mutual trust and shared interests facilitated progress. Having a contact well-versed in and supportive of Hague Convention requirements, who was able to work quietly behind the scenes to obtain a favorable outcome, made all the difference. When it comes to helping U.S. citizens abroad, building and cultivating such ties are essential.

Special citizen services

"Most of the cases consular officers deal with rarely make news," Matthew Keene wrote. "Our embassies and consulates field thousands of distress calls every day, often from people in a heightened emotional state. Among the calls I received was one from a mother of a Fulbright scholar in my consular district who had just been raped. Another came from an irate congressional staffer in Washington, who didn't seem to grasp that I lacked much of the legal authority and firepower necessary to extricate a constituent of her boss's from a village in Yemen. Because of the war there, the U.S. Embassy was closed in 2015, and the State Department has strongly discouraged travel to the country for years."

The following is a sample of other memorable calls Keene received over the years.

"I'm in Ramallah. I'm hiding under my kitchen table, and there is an Israeli tank outside! What should I do?"

"Sir, there is a woman who just arrived at the embassy in a taxi. Her abaya is covered with blood. She has what looks like a knife wound to her neck."

"I'm in jail. My local business partner stole all my money and had me arrested. He is threatening to keep me in jail until I sign over my business to him."

"The American we are holding is on hunger strike. He is in failing health, and we are going to have to force-feed him, unless you can help."

"I'm at the airport. I flew here with my brother to visit my uncle, but now the police are forcing me to go away with someone else. I don't know them! I don't know what's going on! You have to get down here right away!"

"I'm calling from the police station. I got caught up in a protest last night and was
badly beaten by police. I need help."

"My mother is out of her insulin and can't get it and her other medication locally.
She will die without it. How can I get her out of Somalia?"

"I've been assaulted and robbed, and I've lost everything. The police want me to go
to the hospital and have an examination. I just want to forget this ever happened
and go home. Tell them I can go home."

It is the consular officer's job to find the most effective lawful way to help a citizen
in need – or to explain why the U.S. government cannot assist, though most officers
do their best to calm the citizen down and offer general advice. Often those in
trouble just need someone to listen to them. "For the consular officers and local
staff who handle these cases, the work is arduous, demanding, often frustrating,
frequently thankless and exhausting," Keene wrote. "Positive outcomes require
extensive and advance contact work with police and immigration officials, nongovernmental organizations and civil society, developing relationships with local
hotels and homeless shelters, and engagement with anyone who can offer mental
health and emergency aid to victims of domestic abuse and sexual assault. In many
countries, such professionals are nonexistent. Assisting Americans in need is the
most challenging but also the most rewarding part of consular work."[15]

Emergency citizen services

When Covid-19 was declared a pandemic in 2020 and countries around the
world started closing their borders, tens of thousands of Americans abroad
flocked back to the United States. Some U.S. diplomats deemed "nonessential"
and their families did as well. But not consular officers. As "essential personnel,"
they stayed behind – they always do, even when others at an embassy or consulate
are allowed to leave for safety reasons. Whether it is an earthquake, hurricane,
political unrest or a health emergency, consular officers are trained to assist in
getting home-country citizens out of harm's way. Essential staff include members
who are necessary for the post to continue to function, such as the front office, the
heads of the main sections and those needed to complete urgent tasks like an
evacuation.

The Bureau of Consular Affairs has a warning system for travelers about potential risks abroad. It issues advisories for every country, ranging from Level 1
(exercise normal precautions) to Level 4 (do not travel). Its website, travel.state.
gov, also includes information on how to prepare for an emergency, and how the
nearest U.S. embassy or consulate can help during a crisis. Travelers who want to be
informed about the situation in the countries they are visiting, or to be contacted in
case of a family emergency at home, can enroll in the Smart Traveler Enrollment
Program (STEP). The bureau coordinates with other government agencies, such as
the CDC, to provide the best up-to-date information.

Despite warnings, however, disasters happen, and every U.S. diplomatic mission has an emergency action plan that lays out roles and responsibilities during a crisis. Naturally, the host-government is in charge in its own country, and all embassy actions must be closely coordinated with local authorities. While consular sections take the lead, every official at post can be called on to help. In the aftermath of the massive 2010 earthquake in Haiti, the U.S. ambassador, Kenneth Merten, helped to get flight clearances for aircraft delivering relief, among other things.

U.S. embassies have a division of responsibilities in a crisis. The political section works with the host-government's executive and legislative branches, while the management section looks after the welfare of official Americans and their families, including assistance with authorized or ordered departures. The security section ensures the official community's safety and provides every official residence with an emergency radio. The public diplomacy section manages the messaging through traditional and social media. The U.S. Agency for International Development (USAID) mission provides emergency funding, disaster relief, and technical and humanitarian assistance. In order to respond to a crisis swiftly and effectively, advance preparation is crucial. A post should have established and maintained regular contacts with appropriate local authorities, and the consular section must produce written standard operating procedures for how to react in various scenarios, such as earthquakes and flooding. In countries with multiple posts, those procedures should include close coordination and sharing of responsibilities. The case study at the end of the chapter provides further details on how a diplomatic mission responds in a crisis.

Headquarters plays an essential role as well. In Washington, the State Department's Operations Center receives and disseminates information from overseas posts. In addition, a dedicated task force is often formed, with members from various bureaus, as well as other government agencies. Efforts to save lives and minimize casualties are much more likely to succeed as a result of a whole-of-government response. The DOD operates military evacuation flights. USAID provides emergency funding and technical assistance. A second task force may be set up in the Bureau of Consular Affairs to handle inquiries from family and friends of U.S. citizens in the crisis area and pass them on to consular officers overseas for investigation and follow-up. The bureau also has "flyaway teams" ready to leave at a moment's notice to assist in affected areas.

Social media has become vital in sharing information during a crisis and warnings about potential threats. If the U.S. government informs embassy employees about a dangerous situation in the host-country, it is required to give the same warning to unofficial Americans there. This is known as the "no double standard" rule. When individual U.S. citizens are caught up in a situation abroad, such as being hospitalized or detained, the 1974 Privacy Act does not allow for information about their status to be released publicly unless they sign a waiver. There are exceptions in certain emergency cases, when a citizen is unable to complete a written form.

Crises that required a massive response in the last two decades include the following:

In 2021, the State Department and the U.S. military airlifted more than 120,000 people, including about 6,000 Americans, from Afghanistan in six weeks, as the U.S.-backed government fell to the Taliban.[16]

In 2020, the State Department repatriated more than 100,000 U.S. citizens and permanent residents from 137 countries to the United States on over 1,140 flights during the first six months of the Covid-19 pandemic.[17]

In 2011, Americans in Japan were affected by a triple disaster – an earthquake, tsunami and nuclear power plant meltdown. See more details in the case study at the end of the chapter.

In 2010, more than 21,000 U.S. citizens, permanent residents and family members were evacuated following the magnitude 7.2 earthquake in Haiti. The local government was paralyzed and needed significant U.S. help, including search-and-rescue teams, emergency food relief and long-term reconstruction assistance. American consular officers posted around the world volunteered to travel to Haiti, where many slept on couches or on the floor of the U.S. Embassy.[18]

In 2006, almost 15,000 Americans were evacuated from Lebanon by sea and air during an armed conflict with Israel.[19]

In 2004, a tsunami in the Indian Ocean killed at least 225,000 people from dozens of countries, including tourists in Thailand and the Maldives. U.S. consular officers on holiday in Thailand, who were not personally harmed, sent their families home and joined efforts to locate U.S. citizens, some of whom had died and others had lost loved ones.[20]

Visa services

The visa process is the first line of defense in border security, but it has an economic aspect as well. International travel can contribute significantly to a country's economy. According to the World Travel and Tourism Council, international visitor spending amounted to $1.7 trillion globally in 2019.[21] In 2020, because of Covid-19, that figure plummeted by 69 percent. It is the job of consular officers to balance two seemingly competing priorities: encouraging travel and helping to increase the number of visitors while keeping away those who pose a threat.

Fraud prevention is another important aspect of visa work, particularly in poor countries with high unemployment, where many citizens seek opportunities in the United States and other Western countries. Fraud can take many forms, from presenting fake documents to a consular officer to lying in the officer's face. That makes it critical for officers to have all the necessary resources to detect and counter such attempts. The State Department's Bureau of Diplomatic Security assigns some of its special agents to consular sections to assist with anti-fraud efforts. Another serious problem is what amounts to selling U.S. visas by consular officers. That is not a frequent occurrence, but several officers have been convicted in recent years for engaging in such activity. Diplomatic Security usually leads those investigations, with help from the FBI, the DOJ and other agencies.

In 2019, the State Department issued 8.7 million nonimmigrant and 462,422 immigrant visas.[22] Once applicants submit online applications and pay a fee, they schedule appointments at the respective consular section, which collects digital photographs and electronic fingerprints, and also conducts interviews. Then automated checks are performed in various databases. If any red flags are raised, cases can be referred to the State Department for additional checks. By law, consular officers are held liable if they approve someone who is in the lookout system without clearance from Washington. Once a visa is issued, all records, including the biometric data, are shared with CBP inspectors at U.S. ports of entry, who also photograph and fingerprint travelers and match the data with that collected abroad.

Nonimmigrant visas

Most international travelers apply for nonimmigrant visas for temporary stays, and the most common category is the visitor visa, which is used for tourism and business purposes. Every country determines its own visas' periods of validity, the number of entries allowed, and how long a traveler can remain in the country on each visit – all these variables may be different for visitors from different countries, depending on bilateral agreements or reciprocal measures. For example, a Chinese visa may allow a German citizen to stay in China longer than a U.S. citizen. There are many nonimmigrant visa categories. Current U.S. law provides for over 20 types that cover, among others, students and exchange visitors, journalists, athletes and temporary workers.[23] As part of the transformation of the U.S. visa process after the 9/11 attacks, in addition to the new interview and biometric requirements, Congress mandated a more robust lookout system, which resulted in expanded databases among various agencies. Even though the State Department issues visas, visa policies are determined by DHS, which deploys visa security units housed in consular sections at certain overseas posts.

In spite of all the vetting and data-sharing procedures, however, the system does not work perfectly 100 percent of the time. In 2009, Umar Farouk Abdulmutallab, a 23-year-old Nigerian, boarded a flight from Amsterdam to Detroit and attempted to explode a homemade bomb hidden in his underwear shortly before landing.[24] He had a valid U.S. visa in his passport, issued a year earlier by the embassy in London, where he was a student. At the time, there was no information in the system linking Abdulmutallab to terrorist groups. A month before his trip, his father reported him missing to the U.S. Embassy in Nigeria and expressed concern that he might have fallen under the influence of extremists in Yemen.

The State Department shared these details with the National Counterterrorism Center, which determined that "the information was insufficient to make a judgment" about revoking the visa, Patrick Kennedy, the undersecretary of state for management at the time, told Nicholas Kralev.[25] "The U.S. government had the information – scattered throughout the system – to potentially uncover this plot and disrupt the attack," President Obama said days after the incident. "Rather than a failure to collect or share intelligence, this was a failure to connect and understand the intelligence that we already had."[26]

There is a misperception about what a visa allows its holder, with the phrase "overstaying a visa" often used incorrectly to describe people who are in the United States illegally. A visa allows a traveler to show up at a U.S. border and "knock on the door." Upon arrival, it is a CBP inspector at the port of entry or land-border crossing who decides whether the visitor will be admitted. Even though a visa can be valid for up to 10 years – meaning that the holder can travel at any time during that period and "knock on the door" – once admitted, a visitor is given a limited period before they must depart, usually six months. Those found inadmissible have their visa canceled and are returned home. So travelers who stay longer than permitted and fall into illegal status have "overstayed" not their visa, but the period specified by the inspector on the arrival stamp in their passport.

Over the years, visa applicants around the world have told consular officers numerous stories about the reasons for their intended travel to the United States, hoping to boost their chances for approval. Misperceptions about when officers are more likely to grant visas than deny them have resulted in various internet forums and chat rooms claiming to offer advice to candidates, which is usually inaccurate and often borders on the comical. In 2001, a rumor spread in Colombia that applicants wearing suits at interviews were getting approved, and people were renting suits not far from the embassy, Eric Watnik, an officer who served there at the time, told Kralev.[27]

The most common reason for a nonimmigrant visa to be refused is section 214(b) of the Immigration and Nationality Act, which presumes that all applicants are intending immigrants, until they present sufficient evidence that shows strong ties to a home outside the United States.[28] The burden of proof is on the applicants, and consular officers must deny visa requests if they are not persuaded that the candidates will return to their home-country. A consular officer must be familiar with local conditions and trends to determine if an applicant's travel story makes sense. According to section 212(a) of the law, visa applicants may be found permanently ineligible if they willfully misrepresent material facts (waivers may be available in rare cases). If a visa is denied, the officer is required to give the reason in writing, in addition to explaining the decision to the applicant. Since this affects people's lives, these are not always easy decisions.

At this writing, citizens of 40 countries – most of them in Europe and a few in Asia – are permitted to travel to the United States for business or tourism without a visitor visa for stays of up to 90 days, although they must receive Electronic System for Travel Authorization (ESTA) by applying on a CBP website.[29] The condition of this so-called Visa Waiver Program is that travelers hold valid electronic passports with an embedded chip containing biometric data. A country's participation in the program depends on various factors, including the security of its passports and the refusal rate of visa applications. Even if visitors come from visa-waiver countries, they still need visas to study or work in the United States, or if they intend to stay longer than 90 days.

Student and work visas, contrary to some perceptions, are nonimmigrant visas. They come with strict conditions. Students must study at the university that sponsored the visa and are not allowed to work, except for short-term practical training. Workers must be employed by the company that sponsored them and cannot work elsewhere. During the 2020–21 academic year, there were nearly 1 million international students at U.S. colleges and universities, and they contributed $28.4 billion to the U.S. economy, a decline of nearly 27 percent from the prior year, largely due to the Covid-19 pandemic.[30]

Immigrant visas

Consular officers issue immigrant visas to foreign nationals who intend to live and work permanently in the officers' home-country. In the case of the United States, it is usually a relative or employer who can sponsor a candidate by filing a petition with CIS.[31] Certain applicants, such as workers with extraordinary ability and investors, can petition on their own behalf. Approved family- and employment-based petitions are forwarded to the Bureau of Consular Affairs' National Visa Center for further processing. Immigrant visas are also issued to orphans adopted abroad by U.S. citizens, as well as to those selected through what has become popularly known as a green-card lottery, whose official name is the Diversity Visa Program.[32]

How long an applicant waits before receiving an immigrant visa depends on the specific visa category and their citizenship. Immediate relatives of the sponsoring U.S. citizen, such as a spouse, child or parent, are not subject to annual limits. However, other relatives and employer-sponsored candidates are. If the limit to the number of visas for a certain country has been reached, applicants from that country have to wait until the following year – or longer, if the same situation has occurred repeatedly, and there is a large backlog. In late 2020, there was a 22-year wait before a Mexican sibling of a U.S. citizen could immigrate to the United States.

The National Visa Center preprocesses cases by ensuring that documents are in order and all other requirements are met, before scheduling interview appointments at embassies and consulates. Consular officers abroad guard against fraud and the likelihood that the applicant will become a "public charge," meaning they would be primarily dependent on the government for subsistence. Once a visa is approved and the intending immigrant arrives in the United States, a CBP officer checks the consular electronic visa records, biometrics and accompanying paperwork before granting admission.

In 2009, Congress established a Special Immigrant Visa (SIV) program to resettle Afghans at risk because of their work for the U.S. government. By 2020, more than 18,000 such visas were issued, but just as many cases were still in the pipeline, due to delays caused by staffing shortages and lack of proper documentation to verify applicants' identities.[33] Many of those applicants, as well as others who were eligible but had not applied, were airlifted to the United States when the U.S. military withdrew from Afghanistan in 2021. Thousands of others were relocated to third countries to await possible admission to the United States.

Public perceptions and expectations

Goverdhan Mehta, a highly respected professor of organic chemistry in India, prepared for a two-week lecture tour in the United States in 2006 at the invitation of the American Chemical Society. He went to the U.S. Consulate in Chennai for a nonimmigrant visa interview. At 75 and with a good track record of multiple visits to the United States, Mehta had no reason to be nervous. So he was stunned when his visa was not approved on the spot. The consular officer said that his application needed additional processing, because he worked with "sensitive technologies," the embassy in New Delhi told Kralev at the time.[34]

Mehta, however, went to the media and said that he had been refused a visa, because the consular officer had determined that he posed a risk of chemical warfare and bioterrorism. Even though, as we pointed out earlier, only consular officers have the authority to adjudicate visas, the case had taken on a public diplomacy dimension and went up to the ambassador, David Mulford. There is no evidence that Mulford interfered with the process, which involved various security checks in Washington. When they were completed a couple of days later, Mulford personally called Mehta to apologize and offer him a visa.[35] But Mehta had already canceled his trip and declined the offer. "In spite of my track record, I was surprised to be denied a visa this time, though all the relevant papers were in order. I was embarrassed at the way they conducted the interview. I felt humiliated. I decided there was no point in arguing," he said at a press conference, in spite of the embassy's insistence that a visa was never denied, just delayed. "The issue relates to the free interaction of scientists and their participation in various international activities without being subject to any restriction or humiliation. It is not only an issue concerning scientists in India but all over the world."

Mehta is one of thousands of visa applicants who require special security clearances every year, because their field of study or work is deemed highly sensitive by the U.S. government. The journal Physics Today wrote in 2003 about Irving Lerch, director of international affairs at the American Physical Society, who had become "a clearinghouse for those fighting the visa wars and has personally intervened in about 200 visa cases." Lerch told the publication about a Chinese student in the United States who went back to China when his parents were killed in an accident and was refused a visa to return to school. He also cited the case of a Russian woman who had worked as an associate scientist at the U.S. Department of Energy's (DOE) Ames Laboratory in Iowa for 11 years. "She went to Germany with her 2-year-old child and was not allowed to return. Her husband hired an attorney who used loopholes in the law to reunite the family," the journal wrote.[36]

The list of sensitive fields and technologies was expanded after 9/11 to include "everything from nuclear engineering and chemistry to biotechnology and urban planning," Physics Today wrote, and most such cases are referred to Washington for review. It was not unusual for that process to last several months in the years following the 9/11 terrorist attacks, though it was gradually shortened to weeks or even days as the backlog decreased and more resources became available to the government.

When it comes to consular services, the perceptions and expectations of the public – both in the host-country and at home – can be difficult to manage. Most people in any country think that a visa entitles them to entry, not realizing that it only allows them to get on a plane and "knock on the door." Some believe they can stay until their visa expires, even if that takes years, ignoring the six-month limit stamped in their passport. Many Americans who get evacuated on government planes by the State Department are surprised to learn that they will be charged for those flights, because the department does not have a budget for such assistance.

To avoid confusion, misunderstanding and hardship, governments must do a better job of educating their citizens. But the public also has a responsibility to find all necessary applicable information before undertaking a trip or making an important decision. In this century, a shortage of information sources is rarely a problem.

Case Study: Crisis Management During Japan's 2011 Triple Disaster

Northeastern Japan was bitterly cold on the afternoon of Friday, March 11, 2011, as thousands of people in coastal fishing and farming villages went about their daily lives. At 2:46 p.m., the region was rocked by the second-largest earthquake ever recorded, measuring 9.0 on the Richter scale, with an underwater epicenter about 60 km (37 miles) from the coast. In less than an hour, a destructive tsunami as high as 40 meters (131 feet) struck, inundating towns and villages. More than 20,000 people were killed and about 500,000 were left homeless. Millions of residents lost access to electricity, running water and telecommunications. Severe damage to roads, bridges and airports blocked early relief efforts.

The U.S. Embassy in Tokyo immediately set up a round-the-clock operation to assist Americans in distress, and to help Japan cope with the disaster. U.S. citizens in Japan often rely for information and assistance on the Japanese government, but since it was overwhelmed, the embassy had to take the lead. The earthquake caused skyscrapers to sway and prompted the evacuation of the embassy chancery building and housing compound, which went smoothly, because the mission was prepared, having completed a fire drill just three days earlier. Within an hour of the quake, all employees were accounted for, and everyone was safe.

James Zumwalt, the deputy chief of mission and this chapter's co-author, was charged with overseeing the response to the disaster. The first step in managing such an operation is to prioritize wisely, and Zumwalt's immediate goal was to protect the health and welfare of the staff at the embassy and five consulates, so they could help family members and unofficial Americans. Most embassy children were at school when

Case Study: (cont.)

Figure 10.3 James Zumwalt (right), deputy chief of mission at the U.S. Embassy in Japan, hands historical documents about the 1923 Great Kanto Earthquake recorded by an American missionary to Kazuo Ueyama, chief of the Yokohama Archives of History, in 2011.
Photo by Kyodo News Stills via Getty Images.

the earthquake struck. Tokyo's mobile phone network was overwhelmed, and making calls was impossible. Thanks to proper planning, the embassy had installed two-way radios on all of its school buses not long before, and the security office successfully contacted every bus – all children were safe. The news provided a much-needed morale boost.

After cracks were discovered in the nine-story chancery's exterior walls, and as large aftershocks continued to rock Japan, the staff moved to the site of an emergency command center, which every U.S. mission has – in this case, that was the gymnasium on the embassy's housing compound, located in a one-story building with no visible damage. The management section speedily converted it into office space and brought in all necessary equipment, as well as food and water from the compound's warehouse. It also set up a satellite phone line to communicate with Washington.

The next day, a major nuclear power station in Fukushima, about 150 km (93 miles) north of Tokyo, was having trouble maintaining its cooling system. Another day later, the Japanese government decided to mobilize its Self-Defense Forces to evacuate citizens living within 10 km (6 miles) of the plant. Fears of nuclear radiation were

Case Study: (cont.)

exacerbated when three of the plant's units exploded in the following days. These new developments forced the embassy to adjust its response efforts and make decisions with incomplete information about radiation levels.

As the nuclear crisis worsened, many employees experienced stress from not knowing the amount of radiation in the atmosphere or its effect on their health. To allay those fears, the mission's leadership consulted some of the world's leading experts on the subject and shared their assessment and recommendations with the staff. The embassy also hired an engineering company to determine when the chancery building was structurally sound. Once it was, operations resumed there three days after the earthquake, and the embassy stepped up its operation of helping U.S. citizens. The consular services it provided included identifying Americans in need of assistance, facilitating travel for those who wished to depart Japan, and disseminating timely and accurate health and safety information to all Americans in Japan.

Helping Americans in Need

After the earthquake, Americans in the Tokyo area and in western Japan were generally out of immediate danger. There were very few reports of injuries or deaths, and though there were shortages of food and consumables, as well as a few power blackouts, the capital remained habitable. It was closer to the disaster zone in eastern Japan where a small population of U.S. citizens needed assistance. The embassy was prepared. Its emergency action plan had been updated in 2010 to reflect lessons learned from that year's annual disaster exercises, which had included the Tokyo city government's disaster preparedness office, the police and fire departments, and local hospitals. The contacts developed during these exercises proved critical in coordinating the response to the real disaster with Japanese officials. The emergency action plan had not, however, prescribed how to react to a complex triple disaster, and consular officers had to adapt and remain flexible to the changing conditions.

Japan is generally a safe country, with good healthcare and communications systems, so in a typical year, the consular section might assist a few dozen U.S. citizens who run out of money, need medical help or get into legal trouble. The situation was very different in 2011. Just hours after the earthquake, the consular staff began fielding calls and emails from Americans worried about family members living or traveling in Japan – these are known as welfare and whereabouts cases. Within a few days, as many as 9,000 calls came in, including from people who thought that a friend or relative was traveling somewhere outside the United States, but were not sure where. Could they, perchance, be in Japan?

The volume became impossible for the consular staff to handle, let alone go and find missing Americans. The Bureau of Consular Affairs established a task force in Washington and set up a global hotline and an email address for worried relatives, which were answered by consular officers around the world. The consular section in Tokyo had to follow up on any credible information, and it set up a 24/7 shift system to

Case Study: (cont.)

contact Americans or determine the whereabouts of those who did not answer. The most worrisome cases involved Americans living in the three coastal regions directly affected by the disaster, and the embassy dispatched consular teams to each of them. Every team had two minivans and a truck, with three drivers and a mechanic, two consular officers, two Japanese consular employees, and enough supplies for a week, including communications equipment, tents, blankets, first-aid kits, extra gasoline, spare auto parts, food, water, camp stoves and lanterns.

One of the teams went to Sendai, a city of 1 million people that was devastated by the tsunami. The road trip, which normally took four hours, now lasted over 12 hours, due to debris blocking highways, damaged bridges and flooded secondary roads. From their base, which was a hotel with no electricity or running water, the team members would head out every day at dawn to look for missing Americans. They had come with a list of names compiled by the task force from information received from relatives and friends. If there was no known address for a particular person, they would seek information from the police or social welfare organizations. They also went to morgues and Buddhist temples, where residents were posting notices. At one point, they encountered an Australian consular team looking for missing Australians, so they exchanged lists and divided the search areas. As a result, the Americans found Australians and vice versa.

A few days later, the embassy in Tokyo sent buses to bring about 100 Americans from Sendai, so they could return to the United States. The consular section issued emergency passports to those who had lost theirs and arranged for money transfers from relatives for those who had lost their savings. None of the three rescue teams was able to locate two missing Americans, whose bodies were later discovered by police. The consular section issued reports of death abroad and arranged for repatriation of the remains. It took the embassy five weeks to resolve the thousands of cases. It also dispatched consular teams to Tokyo's two main airports, Haneda and Narita, to assist U.S. citizens trying to leave Japan on commercial flights. In the end, few Americans needed help, because the airports were well organized, but the U.S. help desks there sent an important message to the expatriate community, as well as to citizens of other countries, about the embassy's concern and offers of assistance.

Surging Routine Consular Services

The alarming news reports about elevated radiation levels as a result of the nuclear disaster prompted many Americans who were not otherwise in danger to leave Japan. Many of them realized that their passports had expired, or they had not yet obtained reports of birth abroad for their children. That tripled the demand for consular services, and the section had to provide them, even as some of its employees were busy looking for missing U.S. citizens. The post's management decided to extend the section's hours until 8 p.m. and to keep it open on weekends. At a time when other foreign embassies were shutting down and their diplomats were fleeing Tokyo, the U.S.

Case Study: (cont.)

Embassy's actions ended up enhancing its public image by earning praise in the Japanese media.

The increased demand for services and the round-the-clock disaster-response effort made it clear that embassy staffing had to surge as well, even though the consular section discontinued immigrant visa interviews and stopped issuing all but emergency nonimmigrant visas. Both U.S. officers and local employees in those units were cross-trained to perform citizen services, but they were not nearly great enough in number. Their colleagues in consulates outside the capital who were brought in were not sufficient, either. So the embassy asked for volunteers at other posts in Asia to come to Tokyo to help. Although many arrived soon, still more were needed, and the Bureau of Consular Affairs in Washington asked for volunteers among consular officers serving around the world to go to Tokyo on two-week temporary duty. Eventually, the embassy staff grew from about 250 official Americans on March 11 to about 400.

Figure 10.4 Members of a search-and-rescue team from Fairfax County, Virginia, search for survivors in the city of Kamaishi after the March 11, 2011, earthquake and tsunami in Japan. Photo by Nicholas Kamm/AFP via Getty Images.

The work of the mission's Japanese employees, especially in locating and contacting every American who had been reported missing, was indispensable. One such key staff member had an outstanding network of contacts in the affected regions and worked overtime to track down as many people as possible. She told Zumwalt that her parents lived in a village inundated by the tsunami, and she had yet to hear from them and was

Case Study: (cont.)

very worried. Zumwalt gave her permission to take a few days off to manage her personal situation, but she replied, "I don't know if my parents are alive or dead, but there is nothing I can do for them now. My place is here, where I can help others." She later learned that her cousin had rescued her parents.

Keeping Americans Informed

Thousands of Americans in Japan wanted to know whether they should change their routines or leave the country because of radiation from the crippled nuclear plant. They were not sure how much they could trust the various media reports. They needed accurate and credible information about the rapidly changing situation, and the embassy was responsible for providing it. But the leadership quickly realized that its staff lacked the necessary expertise and requested that experts from the Nuclear Regulatory Commission and the DOE be sent from Washington. In addition, a leading expert on how radiation affects the human body arrived from the National Institutes of Health (NIH), and a health-risk communications specialist came from the CDC. They explained the situation and risk levels in layman's terms to both embassy staff and private U.S. citizens during town-hall meetings.

Because of the "no double standard" policy, the embassy shared all the information conveyed to its employees with the wider American community, both on its website and through social media. The Japanese media also came to rely on those updates and advisories. The State Department issued two travel warnings about Japan, one for Americans living close to the nuclear crisis, and one for those outside Japan to defer nonessential travel to the country.

Lessons Learned

Be Prepared

Advance planning, training, developing and updating extensive contact lists of local authorities, and maintaining emergency supplies enabled the embassy to respond to the crisis quickly.

Communicate, Communicate, Communicate

Management must communicate with employees, particularly about workplace safety and managing stress, as well as with the wider American community. The communication must be timely, relevant, clear, consistent and credible. The embassy used a range of tools: State Department travel advisories, town-hall meetings, press releases, its website and social media.

Case Study: (cont.)

Rely on the Local Staff

The expertise, connections and selfless work of the embassy's local staff were indispensable for the success of the response to the disaster.

Promote Employees' Morale and Wellbeing

Leaders must manage the mental health of their staff as they respond to a crisis, which affects them directly or indirectly. It is important to be sensitive to any stress they may be experiencing, and to provide access to mental healthcare for those who need it.

Sustain a Long-Term Response to the Crisis

Leaders must manage their staff's workflow to sustain a crisis response over the long term. Those responders are human beings who need time for regular meals, enough sleep, some exercise, as well as for their families, if they are to continue working effectively. Moving quickly to a shift system and augmenting staff levels to meet increased workload requirements is essential.

Make Timely Decisions, Then Adjust

During a crisis, leaders have to make decisions with imperfect information. As more information becomes available, it may be necessary to change course, so flexibility is key. It makes little sense to criticize past actions during the crisis. There will be time for a lessons-learned exercise after the response. For now, focus on the present and future, not the past.

Bring in Expertise, Then Listen

The CDC, NIH and other experts who traveled to Tokyo were critical to evaluating information and forging effective responses to the triple disaster.

Ensure a Whole-of-Government Response

No consular section can manage a large-scale crisis alone. It is important to consult, communicate and coordinate, and to organize all relevant agencies' contributions in a coherent whole-of-government response.

Exercise: Dominican Minister's Visa

The minister of finance of the Dominican Republic is an important contact of the U.S. Embassy, because it manages important economic and financial assistance programs aimed at helping the country. The minister and his family are applying for U.S. visas to go to Disney World. The minister has traveled to the United States many times to attend World Bank and IMF meetings. As a young adult, he obtained a tourist U.S. visa, when in fact his real intention was to work at his brother's technology firm. He misrepresented material facts on his application (intention to work and having a sibling in the United States), making him permanently ineligible for a visa in the future. This is not an uncommon situation in the Dominican Republic, where a struggling economy creates pressure to seek employment abroad. The U.S. Embassy has an ongoing public campaign to warn of the importance of being truthful when applying for a visa, and of the consequences of not doing so. There is a high visa refusal rate because of fraud.

According to U.S. immigration law, the earlier misrepresentation by the minister does not apply when he travels on official business, but the finding of ineligibility does apply to personal travel. The only way to grant him a visa for his family trip to Disney World is to secure a waiver from CBP.

Task: You are a consular officer. Would you recommend issuing a waiver to CBP, where a final decision will be made? You must make a persuasive case about why a waiver should be granted. Consider the following questions:

- If you decide to recommend a waiver, what arguments would you make in support of CBP granting it?
- If a waiver is approved, would this affect the embassy's public outreach program of discouraging visa applicants from making fraudulent claims?
- How does the U.S.–Dominican diplomatic relationship factor into your decision?

ADDITIONAL RESOURCES

Ana Mar Fernández Pasarín, "Consulates and Consular Diplomacy," in Costas M. Constantinou, Pauline Kerr and Paul Sharp, eds., *The Sage Handbook of Diplomacy* (Sage Publications, 2016), 161–70.

Donna Hamilton, "The Transformation of Consular Affairs: The United States Experience," in Jan Melissen and Ana Mar Fernández, eds., *Consular Affairs and Diplomacy* (Brill, 2011), 143–72.

Halvard Leira and Iver B. Neumann, "Consular Diplomacy," in Pauline Kerr and Geoffrey Wiseman, eds., *Diplomacy in a Globalizing World: Theories and Practice*, 2nd ed. (Oxford University Press, 2017), 170–84.

Maaike Okano-Heijmans, "Consular Affairs," in Andrew F. Cooper, Jorge Heine and Ramesh Thakur, eds., *The Oxford Handbook of Modern Diplomacy* (Oxford University Press, 2013), 473–92.

11 Diplomatic Protocol, Privileges and Immunities

EUNICE REDDICK

German leaders seem to have really bad luck with the greetings that welcome them to foreign countries. In 1995, during President Roman Herzog's arrival ceremony in Brazil, a military orchestra played what was supposed to be the German national anthem – except that it was the anthem of East Germany, a country that no longer existed. In 2018, Chancellor Angela Merkel's Senegalese hosts got the anthem right, but they followed it with a song titled "Beautiful Maiden, Do You Have Time for Me Today?" On a 1997 visit to Britain, one of Merkel's predecessors, Helmut Kohl, was greeted by Queen Elizabeth II's husband, Prince Philip, with "Hello, Herr Reichskanzler!" A key detail had escaped His Royal Highness's otherwise fluent German. *Reichskanzler* was a title used during the country's imperial past, when it was a *reich*, most recently by Adolf Hitler. As a federal republic (*bundesrepublik* in German), it has had a *bundeskanzler* since 1949.[1]

All these gaffes were breaches of diplomatic protocol. As the officials responsible for observing certain rules and norms know well, their work is usually remembered only when something goes wrong. Unlike her husband, Queen Elizabeth was very disciplined, but she was often on the receiving end of protocol mishaps. Although the monarch was not supposed to be touched unless she offered her hand, in 2009, First Lady Michelle Obama put her hand on Her Majesty's back during a trip to London. On his own visit in 2018, President Trump made the queen wait 12 minutes in the sun and then walked ahead of her during the reviewing of the guard at Buckingham Palace. Back in 1991, when the queen traveled to Washington, she made remarks with President George H. W. Bush, who towered over her. Since the White House had neglected to put a footstool behind the lectern to give the much shorter Elizabeth a boost, several microphones hid the lower half of her face.

That embarrassment taught U.S. protocol officials a valuable lesson. When the president of the Philippines, Gloria Macapagal Arroyo, made a state visit to Washington in 2003, her host was Bush's son, George W. Bush. At each event where she was scheduled to speak, there was a footstool behind the lectern. A state visit is the highest honor a national leader can receive from a foreign counterpart, and it is reserved only for heads of state – not for heads of government. The British prime minister cannot be invited on a state visit, because the monarch is the head of state. In the United States, such a visit includes a full-honors arrival ceremony on the south lawn of the White House with a 21-gun salute, a state luncheon at the State Department and a state dinner in the White House's State Dining Room. The visitor usually stays at Blair House, the U.S. president's official guest house, located across the street from the White House.

A state visit is not only an elaborate and glamorous affair, but a major diplomatic event that can strengthen or reinvigorate a bilateral relationship. It takes long and detailed planning, both in terms of protocol and specific diplomatic deliverables. As director of the State Department office overseeing the daily management of relations with the Philippines before and during Arroyo's visit, I helped to coordinate some of the meetings and other events. This was only the second state visit since the 9/11 terrorist attacks, and Arroyo's own government was fighting a militant group, Abu Sayyaf, which had kidnapped Filipinos and Americans. So Bush decided that counterterrorism would be the main topic of discussion, and particularly how the United States could help to strengthen the Philippine security forces' capacity to combat violent extremism.

A state dinner usually invokes images of fancy place settings and multiple knives, forks and spoons, each with a particular purpose. The elaborate menu inevitably makes it into the media, as does the guest list. At the dinner in Arroyo's honor, the menu was created by Cris Comerford, an assistant White House chef born in the Philippines, who said she sought to "marry" American and Filipino cuisines. Maryland and the Philippines are both known for crabs, which were featured in the first course, she added. For the main course, she prepared lamb, achiote polenta, fava beans and cipollini onion. Mango sorbets, filled with coconut mousse, were draped with brightly colored leis made of sugar and chocolate, said pastry chef Roland Mesnier. "Bouquets of pink and white peonies graced each table and flanked a portrait of Abraham Lincoln," the Associated Press reported.[2] The 130 guests included officials from both countries, Americans of Philippine descent and celebrities like television news anchor Tom Brokaw. In his toast, Bush highlighted the contributions of "more than 2 million Americans [with] family ties to the Philippines" who "strengthen America's culture, our economy and government."[3]

Protocol is typically associated with etiquette, though the two terms are not the same. "Etiquette" is a code of polite behavior that prescribes how to do certain things, such as how to sit in a particular setting, how to arrange silverware and how to greet a guest. In the 18th century, *étiquette* was a list of ceremonial observances in the French royal court[4] and was later used by the upper classes more broadly. The French became known as the connoisseurs of etiquette copied by elites across Europe and beyond. French was the language of international diplomacy for centuries until it gave way to English. In 2001, the United Nations asked all its member-states to name the language in which correspondence to their missions should be addressed. More than 120 countries chose English, compared with about 40 listing French.[5]

Etiquette is an integral part of protocol. The word "protocol" comes from the ancient Greek *prōtokollon*, meaning "first page" or "flyleaf" – from *prōtos* ("first") and *kolla* ("glue"). In 19th-century France, the word *protocole* was used to describe a collection of set forms of etiquette to be observed by the government.[6] This definition is very close to the main meaning we ascribe to the term today, as a system or set of rules governing professional and social interactions, which are not limited to any one walk of life. Organizations as different as universities and prisons can have their own protocols. A procedure for carrying out a scientific experiment or a course of medical treatment can also be called a protocol.

What is diplomatic protocol?

As this book has made clear, diplomacy is a highly complex, multifaceted and often unpredictable profession. By definition, it seeks to overcome differences between and among countries, and those distinctions run the risk of turning into discord, or even conflict, without a playing field that has mutually accepted rules and norms. This is the role of diplomatic protocol, **a system of standards, rules and regulations governing the conduct of international relations**. It brings order and predictability to the work of diplomats by providing a road map or framework, so they can focus on the substance of negotiations and high-stakes decisions. It has been called "the oil in the gears of diplomacy" and credited with creating a "safe space that allows diplomacy to succeed."[7]

While tradition has always had a special place in diplomacy, protocol's role is hardly limited to old-fashioned pomp and circumstance. It has practical aspects meant to make diplomatic work more effective. For example, adhering to protocol is widely seen as a sign of respect, and violating it can be taken as a slight. Why does it matter if you serve pork at a dinner to which you have invited Muslim guests? Because the message it sends is that you do not respect their religion, which prohibits the consumption of pork, and consequently, that you disrespect them. Claiming ignorance is no excuse – not bothering to prepare properly is offensive in itself. Why is it a big deal if you wear jeans at an official function? Because it is likely to be interpreted as a sign of disregard for the host and the importance of the occasion. And why is showing respect so critical? Because without it, you almost certainly will not make diplomatic progress. At least some measure of respect is necessary even when interacting with an adversary – your interlocutor represents a country, and there is no need to insult its people just because you disagree with the government.

Is arriving late for a meeting or keeping a guest waiting a breach of protocol, a diplomatic power play or just a snub? It depends on whom you ask. During a summit of the Group of 20 (G20) largest economies in Mexico in 2012, President Obama hosted a bilateral meeting with Vladimir Putin, for which Putin was nearly half an hour late. As the State Department's chief of protocol, Capricia Penavic Marshall, stood at the hotel gate, she wondered if this was a "power play meant to throw the U.S. delegation off kilter."[8] Officials in Marshall's position are usually political appointees, but as career diplomats know well, Putin is notorious for

Figure 11.1 Queen Elizabeth II speaks at the White House during a visit with President George H. W. Bush in 1991. There was no footstool behind the lectern.
Photo by Arnie Sachs/CNP/Getty Images.

deliberately being late, regardless of whether he is the host or guest. Chapter 8 mentioned a 2006 meeting in Moscow between Putin and Condoleezza Rice, where William Burns was the notetaker. Putin kept Rice waiting for almost three hours. When he was finally ready, he changed the venue from the Kremlin to his compound on the city's outskirts, about a 45-minute drive away. According to Burns, who was ambassador to Russia, Rice was not surprised by the delay and shrugged it off as a "trick play."[9]

Protocol also has practical benefits for diplomats' daily work in their own mission, not only at public events or high-level negotiations. It provides guidelines on how to address ranking officials, when to speak in a meeting and how to write memos or emails to your boss. Some of those rules may seem archaic or too formal, but you cannot forget that diplomacy is a hierarchical system and seniority matters. Americans are known for being casual, which in diplomacy is sometimes viewed as rudeness, indifference or lack of respect. Your intention to skip small talk at the beginning of a meeting and get down to business may save time, but it can also be taken as disinterest in your host's wellbeing or in important developments in the host-country on which the host may want to opine. Unless you know the person you are about to meet very well, you should consult with your local embassy staff about the expectations to which you are supposed to live up. As David Lindwall noted in Chapter 3, when he served in Latin America, he started every meeting with small talk and waited for his host to switch to substance. In Sweden, however, his interlocutors much preferred cutting right to the chase.

Diplomatic protocol has both written and unwritten rules. Much of it is codified in the Vienna Convention on Diplomatic Relations of 1961[10] and the 1963 Vienna Convention on Consular Relations,[11] which were agreed by all members of the United Nations, as explained in Chapter 1. The former provides a framework for establishing and maintaining diplomatic missions, for the rights and responsibilities of sending and receiving states, and for the treatment of diplomats and their possessions, among other necessities in the conduct of diplomacy. For example, it says that "if diplomatic relations are broken off between two states, or if a mission is permanently or temporarily" closed, "the receiving state must, even in case of armed conflict, respect and protect the premises of the mission, together with its property and archives." The sending country "may entrust the custody of the premises of the mission," as well as "the protection of its interests" to a third state acceptable to the receiving state.

The Vienna Convention on Consular Relations defines terms like "consular district," "consular agency" and "vice consul." Both conventions also codify the privileges and immunities to which diplomatic and consular officers are entitled, as we will see later. Individual governments can have their own protocol documents. In the United States, the Foreign Service Institute publishes a guide titled "Protocol for the Modern Diplomat," on which the next two sections are based in part.[12] In spite of the word "modern" in the title, many of the rules in this handbook are outdated, and chiefs of mission today ask their subordinates to observe much more pragmatic procedures and use their judgment, depending on what a situation requires.

Rules within a diplomatic mission

Every country has its own regulations and customs when it comes to the internal practices of its missions abroad. For example, even before arriving at a new post, U.S. diplomats need to inform the management section of their travel plans, so it can make arrangements for housing, shipping their belongings, enrolling their children in school and other logistical matters. U.S. posts usually assign a sponsor to meet new arrivals at the airport, help them through customs, take them to their residences and meet any other immediate needs.

When you arrive at a new post, your sponsor will introduce you to the embassy or consulate community, but it is your responsibility to meet with an administrative officer, who will give you an orientation packet, explain everything you need to know to start working and help you schedule a security briefing. In addition to potential safety risks and ongoing threats, diplomats are often subject to surveillance and even harassment by host-country intelligence and security services, and knowing how to deal with them is essential. The administrative officer will also give you a tour of the compound or building and will introduce you to key members of the country team, if they are in their offices at the time. If they are not, you will need to make official introductory calls on them later. You should also call on the chief of mission.

The hierarchy in a diplomatic mission can be very confusing. As Chapter 5 noted, there are separate ranks in person and position in the U.S. Foreign Service, and an officer with a personal rank of "counselor" can occupy a "minister counselor" position – or the other way around. These ranks or grades are part of the service's internal personnel system. There is a separate and parallel diplomatic hierarchy that is internationally recognized and includes titles such as first, second and third secretary, as also pointed out earlier. In Chapter 1, Nicholas Kralev explained that a deputy chief of mission can serve as a *chargé d'affaires ad interim* in the absence of an ambassador, and that sometimes headquarters can appoint another senior diplomat to that role. In the case of two countries that do not have ambassador-level relations, the chief of mission's title is *chargé d'affaires ad hoc*.

You should address the ambassador either as "Mr./Madam Ambassador" or "Ambassador Jones" and refer to them in conversations with others as "the ambassador." It is proper to rise when the ambassador or their spouse enters a room and to remain standing until they sit down or invite you to take a seat; in reality, many ambassadors today do not require that courtesy. When introducing a guest or someone else to the ambassador, you should state the ambassador's name first, unless the other person is a head of state. For example, "Ambassador Jones, may I present Mr. Juan Lopez?" On less formal occasions, it is acceptable to say just "Ambassador Jones, Mr. Juan Lopez." The ambassador and their spouse precede all others when entering or leaving a room. The official place for the ambassador in a car is the backseat, curbside. If you are accompanying the ambassador in a car, enter first and move to the far side or go around and enter on the far side, though if the ambassador's spouse comes along, there will not be space for you – the front passenger seat is usually occupied by a security officer. When going through doorways, the ambassador and the spouse go in first and come out first.

If your embassy is hosting an event, arrive 15 minutes before the scheduled time, unless you have a role in the preparations and need to be there earlier. If there is a receiving line, the host usually stands first, followed by their spouse, though the spouse may defer to the guest of honor and stand after them. You may be assigned to introduce guests to the ambassador or to greet them as they come off the receiving line. Before introducing a guest, the ambassador would appreciate a quick background on the person as they approach the line. You may also be responsible for tending to guests relevant to your embassy portfolio. As the event draws to a close, inform the ambassador when you are leaving, though it is best not to be the employee whose departure would leave the ambassador alone.

International norms and etiquette

As a diplomat, you will attend many receptions, dinners, conferences and other official functions, along with representatives of other countries. You will receive such invitations as part of your official responsibilities. This does not mean that you cannot have a good time and look forward to attending. It does mean that you should use these opportunities to engage with diplomats from other embassies, host-country officials and citizens, and build relationships to advance your embassy's goals. Adherence to protocol will ensure uniform treatment and dispel any notion of bias toward a particular country.

When making introductions, for example, honor is recognized by the name spoken first, and that courtesy is given to those who are older, higher in rank, titled or female. If ambassadors from several countries must be recognized, their order of precedence is determined by the order in which they presented their credentials to the host-country's head of state. The ambassador who has served in the receiving state the longest is the dean of the diplomatic corps. The term "diplomatic corps" refers to all foreign diplomats posted in the host-country – that state's own diplomats make up its diplomatic service, usually known as the Foreign Service. If the home-country has more than one ambassador in the same foreign capital – one accredited to the receiving state and one or more to international organizations, as is the case in Brussels – their order of precedence is decided by the customs of the sending government.

You can prepare in advance for effective engagement at an official function by securing access to the guest list and determining whom you should meet. Once at the venue, find your seat before high-ranking guests and other VIPs arrive to avoid scrambling at the last minute or as the event begins. If you are taking notes, you may need to move your seat to where you can better see and hear the proceedings, if possible. In case notetaking is not possible, try to remember as much as you can and write it down as soon as is practical.

Depending on the culture of the host-country and any high-ranking officials in attendance, greetings may include a handshake, a nod of the head, a bow, kisses or other gestures. There may also be gender differences. In some countries, men show affection when greeting each other, while they do not touch women's hands in professional circles, and a woman should know this before holding out her hand to avoid embarrassment or disrespect. It is never a good idea to socialize only with your own colleagues during a reception. The goal is to meet and obtain information from others. That said, if your ambassador is present, keep alert to make sure you notice should they need assistance.

Attending events as a guest

There are cultural differences here as well. In most cases, an invitation is addressed to all the family members invited, and if a spouse is not specifically named, he or she is most likely not invited. It is inappropriate to bring a date to a work event. However, in some countries, one invitation addressed to the family is meant to include everyone in the house, even guests and visitors. Keep in mind the different concepts of time in various countries, which Chapter 3 mentioned. In Northern

Europe, an invitation for 7 p.m. means that you should arrive exactly at 7 p.m., but in Latin America, showing up before 8:30 p.m. may be considered rude.

Dress-code concepts vary, too. In diplomatic circles, "casual" almost never includes jeans or shorts, and "informal dress" means "business attire" – a suit and tie for men, and a business suit or conservative dress for women. Black tie is generally not worn in the daytime, and white tie requires the additional formality of "tails," with a white tie for men and a floor-length ball gown for women. Your invitation should be your main guide. Women should be mindful of conservative rules, such as skirt length, low necklines and covering their arms. The acceptability of conversation topics at an official function also depends on culture. In some countries, asking someone about their age or income is appropriate, while discussing children is not. The local embassy employees are your best consultants.

Table Etiquette[13]

Napkin

The dinner napkin should be placed on your lap by unfolding it halfway, with the fold facing your body. Luncheon-size napkins are smaller and are unfolded completely. When the meal is over, the napkin should be casually folded from the center and placed on the left side of the plate. If the plate has been removed, put the napkin in front of you. Leave it on the chair when you step away from the table during a meal, not on a saucer.

American Style of Eating

Hold the knife in the right hand and the fork in the left to cut food, then put the knife down and transfer the fork to the right to lift food to the mouth. Cut no more than two pieces of food at a time.

Continental Style of Eating

Keep the knife in the right hand and the fork in the left throughout the meal. Cut one piece of food at a time.

Service

Waiters serve from the left and remove from the right. Drinks are poured from the right and removed from the right.

It is polite to accept the food and drink a host offers you, and if unsure or apprehensive, try a small portion. Remember that tasting different countries' food is as much a cultural experience as a means of feeding yourself. If you cannot eat something for health or religious reasons, it is acceptable to refuse with a short explanation. In the United States, alcohol is generally not consumed at a business lunch, but it is in most of Europe. Even if you do not wish to drink, you can still take a little to have in your glass for toasts. If you do drink, do so responsibly, so as not to embarrass yourself or your country.

Hosting events

Many diplomats other than the ambassador and deputy chief of mission have entertaining responsibilities. You may be tasked with planning and executing an embassy event or hosting a dinner in your home. The type of entertainment you choose depends on what you would like to achieve. Its purpose can be to introduce a visiting home-country official or expert, to discuss an important matter, or to welcome a newly arrived diplomat from your mission or another country. Other than at the ambassador's residence or another private home, an event can be held at a restaurant, club or another venue. Before scheduling it, always consult the embassy calendar, which is typically kept by the protocol officer or the ambassador's assistant, to make sure that your proposed date is appropriate. Weekday evenings are the most common times for official functions.

If your section does not have sufficient representational funds, another agency at post may be able to help, especially if you secure the attendance of host-government officials or others to whom that agency's staff does not have regular access. When local officials are invited, the event becomes an official function, and international protocol is in order. Consult with the embassy's protocol officer and your co-hosts on seating arrangements and review plans for food and drinks, decorations and floral displays. It is best to use unscented flowers, in case some of the guests have allergies.

Informal entertaining, such as family-style meals, buffet lunches, barbecues, picnics and tea parties, is not only appropriate but the easiest to organize, and is also preferred by many guests. Although there is not much protocol involved, high-ranking officials should be recognized and shown respect. The key is to move the guests around, so they can talk to different people. Tables of six or eight are more conducive to conversation than tables of four. Tableware may be part of the buffet service or set on the tables. If you choose not to have dining tables, at least clear out any coffee tables and end tables, so the guests can put down their dishes.

As a general rule, couples sit across the table from each other, not side by side, and an even number of men and women alternate seats at a table. If an unequal number of men and women are in attendance, alternate the sexes. A seating chart in the entrance hall – and a table chart, if there are several tables – helps guests to find their seats as they arrive. Place cards are used when there are more than eight guests. One waiter for every six to eight guests is usually sufficient. Guests may be served either in sequence around the table, or women may be served before men. Hosts of diplomatic dinners often offer two toasts – one to all guests, after the first course has been served to everyone, and another to the guest of honor, at the beginning or the end of dessert. When giving a toast, rise in place, speak to the entire room and be brief. At the end of the event, the host should be available near the exit to say goodbye to the guests.

Official summits and negotiations

The day before Obama's 2012 meeting with Putin in Mexico, Capricia Penavic Marshall, the U.S. chief of protocol, walked into the venue of the U.S.-hosted session. The low ceiling of the room, which the hotel where Obama was staying had provided, "was just about right," Marshall thought. "People in rooms with lower ceilings tend to think more concretely than those under higher ceilings, which seem to prime people to think more abstractly," she wrote in her memoir. "I was also relieved that the overall space was small and spare," she added. "There was just enough space to fit the countries' flags at one end, the main table in the middle, and a curtained entrance at the other end to allow for the discreet movements of the stewards of the presidential food service."[14]

The U.S. Secret Service required that the room had hard walls on at least three sides – one wall could have windows, but the president's back and that of his guest could never be against it. The windows had been blacked out for security reasons and the room was too dark, so Marshall and her staff found standing lamps to "avoid an oppressive feel." Next, they needed to find a table "large enough to fit the 12 key delegates – six Russians and six Americans – but small enough to create closeness." They located one that fit the bill and placed it in the center of the room. As "nondistracting table decor," Marshall wanted unscented white and green flower arrangements, whose stems were clipped "to lower the height, so they wouldn't block sight lines, and ran them down the center of the table for a streamlined effect. The flowers also softened the vibe" – she observed that "greenery has a well-known relaxing effect." Finally, she requested water and "nibbles of local breads, cookies, spreads and nuts."

One of the primary goals of protocol is to make visitors feel welcomed, and Marshall "wanted the room to have a bit of a Zen quality, especially since the meeting was anticipated to be long and intense." Her Russian counterpart, however, had a different view, as she discovered when the Russians hosted the next Obama–Putin meeting in Northern Ireland the following year. The venue was "a huge open tent" that "swallowed up the leaders and delegates," and the "bleak" lighting made it feel stark. The chairs for the two presidents "had been placed side by side, with only a tiny side table between them," making a face-to-face conversation very difficult. Moreover, "because the room was large and sparse, there was only empty space in front of them to look at." No food or water was to be served. "This was a hard configuration for such a long meeting," Marshall recalled.[15]

The impact that a setting for an official meeting or negotiation can have on the substance of the engagement with another country is proof that diplomatic protocol matters more than we realize. Perhaps the most famous example of that in history is the 10-week argument in late 1968 and early 1969 over the shape of the table at peace negotiations in Paris to end the Vietnam War. The table, of course, had an outsize significance in diplomatic and political terms. As the parties prepared for the talks, they all agreed that the governments of the United States, North Vietnam and South Vietnam should participate, even though North Vietnam did not formally recognize the government of South Vietnam. A dispute erupted, however, when North Vietnam demanded that the Viet Cong, a guerrilla movement fighting South Vietnamese and American forces in the south, take part with a separate delegation, which would lead to a four-party negotiation. The United States and South Vietnam countered that, as a pawn of North Vietnam, the Viet Cong should participate as part of the North Vietnamese delegation, and insisted on a trilateral format.[16]

The question was not yet settled when the negotiators arrived in Paris, but a decision had to be made about the shape of the table for the first meeting – at that point, what was a matter of protocol turned into a rather substantive negotiation of its own. Not surprisingly, North Vietnam proposed a rectangular table to make it clear that there were four parties to the talks, and an alternative with four tables arranged in a circle or a diamond-shaped pattern. After South Vietnam rejected that proposal, the American delegation suggested a long, two-sided table, or alternatively, two rectangular tables, which North Vietnam dismissed and countered with the idea of a round table. The United States was inclined to accept, because it blurred the notion of four distinct delegations. When the North Vietnamese pointed out that a round table would emphasize the equal footing of the four parties, the Americans came up with modifications to dispel the impression that the Viet Cong was equal to the government of South Vietnam. They included a round table divided in the middle by a long strip, a round table cut in half, two semicircular tables and a flattened ellipse.

Figure 11.2 Negotiators from the United States, South Vietnam and North Vietnam gather around the newly installed round table for initial talks to end the Vietnam War in Paris in 1969. Photo by Rolls Press/Popperfoto via Getty Images.

The impasse, which became known as "the battle of the tables," was finally resolved after a Soviet diplomat proposed a round table with no flags, names or other markings, papering over the number and identity of the delegations. The negotiations formally started in early 1969 and ended with the 1973 Agreement on Ending the War and Restoring Peace in Vietnam, signed by all four parties. However, fighting soon resumed, and two years later, the South fell to North Vietnamese and Viet Cong forces. Henry Kissinger, the U.S. secretary of state at the time, later observed that "in every revolutionary conflict, the acceptance of the guerrillas as a negotiating partner has proved to be the single most important obstacle to negotiations, for it obliges the government to recognize the legal status of the enemy determined to overthrow it."[17]

Matters such as the shape and configuration of the tables during negotiations may seem trivial, but they are not just internal logistical arrangements. It is a longtime tradition to invite the media for a photo opportunity at least at the beginning, and the negotiating parties have to be conscious of how the world sees their positions and competence. Each country's delegation uses procedural details to advance its objectives and prevent the other side from accomplishing its own goals. This is why questions about the rules of the game must be answered in the preliminary stage of a negotiation, including the place and schedule, the composition of the delegations, the issues that must be discussed or excluded, and the role a third party might play in the talks.

In 1983, following Israel's invasion of Lebanon, the two countries agreed to start peace talks, with meetings to be held alternately in Israel and Lebanon. The latter would host the first round, and it demanded that the United States participate as well, to which U.S. and Israeli officials raised no objections. When their delegations arrived at the venue, they were surprised to find three tables in a U-shaped pattern, with the American table in the center. The Lebanese expected the United States to chair the meeting and lead the discussions. The Israelis protested, pointing out that the diplomatic protocol in such cases called for the head of the hosting delegation to be the chair. The Americans stressed that, though they would play an active role in the discussions and propose compromises, this should be a bilateral Israeli–Lebanese negotiation. As the scheduled start time came and went, and with the press waiting impatiently outside the conference room, the parties finally agreed to move the tables into a triangular formation.[18]

Procedural matters are usually addressed in letters of invitation and negotiated in advance of substantive talks, but last-minute bargaining over previously neglected details happens often. Another issue in 1983 was Lebanon's insistence that the negotiations produce simply an "agreement," not a "peace treaty." The latter would mean establishing full diplomatic relations with embassies, and the government in Beirut was ready to open only "liaison offices." Israel and Lebanon signed an agreement in 1983, but the Lebanese parliament failed to ratify it because of pressure from Syria, so it never entered into force. Israel began instead a unilateral, phased withdrawal of its forces, which ended in 2000. The two countries still have no peace treaty as of this writing. Another Middle East peace conference, which convened in Geneva in 1973, prompted an even longer dispute over procedural matters and furniture, as we will see in the case study at the end of the chapter.

Diplomatic privileges and immunities

The last thing Devyani Khobragade expected when she dropped off her daughter at school one day in 2013 was to get arrested. As India's deputy consul general in New York, she enjoyed diplomatic privileges and immunities. So she was shocked when she was handcuffed, strip searched, detained and ordered by a judge to post a $250,000 bail if she wanted to go home. The district attorney for the Southern District of New York charged Khobragade with falsifying a U.S. visa application for her Indian maid, on which she said that she paid the worker three times more than she actually did. About a month later, in early 2014, a grand jury indicted Khobragade, as noted in Chapter 1. The incident outraged the Indian government and caused a full-blown diplomatic crisis, throughout which Khobragade claimed that she was protected by immunity and could not be prosecuted.[19]

Many of us have heard the term "diplomatic immunity," but few, including diplomats, understand what exactly it means and when it can be applied. In Khobragade's case, both she and the New York authorities failed to grasp some of the nuances. The Vienna Convention on Diplomatic Relations says that a "diplomatic agent" accredited to a foreign country "shall not be liable to any form of arrest or detention" and "shall enjoy immunity from the criminal jurisdiction of the receiving state."[20] Khobragade, however, was not considered a diplomatic agent, because she did not work at an embassy or multilateral mission. Rather, as a consulate employee, she was subject to the Vienna Convention on Consular Relations. According to that document, "consular officers shall not be liable to arrest or detention pending trial, except in the case of a grave crime and pursuant to a decision by the competent judicial authority." In addition, "consular officers and consular employees shall not be amenable to the jurisdiction of the judicial or administrative authorities of the receiving state in respect of acts performed in the exercise of consular functions."[21]

In other words, there is a difference between immunity for diplomatic agents and consulate employees, and the latter enjoy only partial protection. Khobragade was entitled to immunity only when she carried out her official duties, and the district attorney argued that she committed a crime in her private life. Had she worked at the Indian Embassy in Washington or the Indian Mission to the United Nations in New York, all her activities in both her official and private capacities would have been covered by the Convention on Diplomatic Relations. The Convention on Consular Relations, on the other hand, allows for consular officers to stand trial, even if it exempts them from arrest or detention. So the New York authorities had the right to indict Khobragade and put her on trial, though they should not have arrested and detained her – what she was accused of was obviously not a "grave crime."

When it became apparent that the district attorney had legal grounds to pursue the case and was backed by the judge assigned to it, the State Department stepped in to diffuse the crisis, which had strained U.S.–Indian relations. It agreed to accredit Khobragade to the Indian Mission to the United Nations, which automatically conferred full diplomatic immunity on her. To avoid the appearance of interfering in the judicial process, the department then asked the Indian government to waive immunity. When it refused, as expected, the department demanded that Khobragade leave the United States, which she did. The district attorney wrote in a letter to the judge that "the charges will remain pending until such time as she can be brought to court to face the charges, either through a waiver of immunity or the defendant's return to the United States in a nonimmune status."[22] No one expected that would ever happen. It was a face-saving way for both sides to resolve the impasse and move on – Khobragade did not face trial and was welcomed home as a victor, while the Southern District did not give in as the case was not dismissed.

The importance of learning the intricacies of diplomatic immunity before starting an overseas assignment cannot be overstated. The type and scope of immunity depend on the status of the mission to which diplomats are posted and how exactly they are accredited by the host-government. For example, the family members of a diplomat working at an embassy are covered by the same immunity as the diplomat, but that is not the case for the family of an officer at a consulate. The meaning of "consular officer" can be confusing in the context of the Vienna Convention on Consular Relations. Generally, the document uses the term to refer to officials assigned to a consulate, not officers providing consular services in an embassy. In other words, consular officers posted to an embassy are still considered "diplomatic agents" and have full immunity in both their official and personal capacities. To make the distinction clearer, it is more practical to use the term "consulate officers" as opposed to "consular officers" in this particular context.

The first formal attempt to codify diplomatic privileges and immunities dates back to the 1815 Congress of Vienna – the Austrian capital has hosted many international meetings of diplomatic significance for centuries, as evidenced by the titles of a plethora of agreements and other official documents. One of the norms adopted at the congress established the rules of diplomatic precedence that are still used today, ranking envoys of equal title based on the date and time when they presented their credentials to the host-government.[23] Although the 1961 and 1963 conventions provided an indispensable framework for the conduct of international relations, states sometimes strike bilateral agreements to grant certain privileges and immunities to the other country's diplomats that go beyond what the conventions require. So it is possible that Khobragade could have enjoyed immunity for acts performed in her private capacity had she been serving in another country with which India had such an agreement.

Diplomatic immunity does not give diplomats permission to do whatever they want. They should abide by host-country laws and regulations, and if they commit a crime, the local government will most likely expel them – unless the sending state agrees to waive immunity, which happens, but rarely. If the crime is very serious, such as murder, a diplomat may be tried in the home-country.

The privileges and immunities codified in the two Vienna conventions do not apply to diplomats serving in their own country, contractors from the sending state working at embassies and consulates, or employees of diplomatic missions who are host-country citizens. Diplomats with dual citizenship who represent one of the two countries to the other are not protected, either. Many governments do not allow their diplomats to hold a second citizenship at all, even if they never serve in the country of their other nationality. Some, such as the United States, do not impose a blanket ban on dual citizenship, but they almost never assign their diplomats to states where they are citizens. Certain citizenships may also raise red flags during the security clearance process.[24] Of course, there are countries that do not allow dual nationality for anyone, let alone diplomats.

Other than immunity from prosecution, what are the main privileges afforded by the Vienna conventions? Among the better-known ones is the exemption from host-country taxation, which applies to both diplomatic agents and consulate officers. They usually carry a special card showing their status and present it when they pay in stores and restaurants. There are a few exceptions, such as for taxes on "immovable property" owned by a diplomat in the receiving country. Another major privilege in both conventions is the "inviolability" of official correspondence. A diplomatic bag "shall not be opened or detained" – diplomatic couriers "shall be protected by the receiving state in the performance" of their functions and "shall not be liable to any form of arrest or detention." A diplomatic bag "may be entrusted to the captain of a commercial aircraft scheduled to land at an authorized port of entry," but the captain "shall not be considered to be a diplomatic courier." The same rules apply to consular bags.

The receiving state is also required to "permit and protect free communication" among diplomats, and between them and their headquarters, for all official purposes, including "messages in code or cipher." However, wireless transmitters may be installed and used only with the host-government's consent. Diplomats' papers and correspondence are "inviolable" as well, including in their homes. In fact, according to the Convention on Diplomatic Relations, their private residences "shall enjoy the same inviolability and protection as the premises of the mission."[25] The Convention on Consular Relations, however, does not bestow that right on consulate officers.

One of the most consequential norms set out in the consular convention concerns the ability of consular officers to assist their compatriots in the host-country. The document requires that, when local authorities arrest or detain a foreign citizen, they inform the respective consular post and forward any communication from the suspect. "Consular officers shall have the right to visit a national of the sending state who is in prison, custody or detention, to converse and correspond with him and to arrange for his legal representation," the convention says. "If the relevant information is available to the competent authorities of the receiving state, such authorities shall have the duty, in the case of the death of a national of the sending state, to inform without delay the consular post in whose district the death occurred."[26]

There are many other elements of diplomatic protocol you will discover in your work in diplomacy and international affairs, and you can look up those not familiar to you in the two conventions, other documents and books. It is impossible and impractical to know and remember all of them all the time. This chapter has tried to lay a foundation. "Protocol can sound both stuffy and mysterious at the same time, and most of us believe we have had little experience in our nongovernment lives to prepare us," the U.S. Foreign Service Institute's "Protocol for the Modern Diplomat" says. "In fact, the rules and processes of diplomatic protocol are based in pragmatic thinking, common sense and good manners – areas where we all have had some experience. Protocol makes the job of representing our nation easier by facilitating our work as a mission team, making our relationships and interactions within the diplomatic and host-country communities more predictable, and by providing a basic social framework and hierarchy to follow."[27]

Case Study: "Battle of the Tables," Middle East Edition

Former Syrian President Hafez al-Assad was not known as an amicable, polite or patient man, or for possessing many other diplomatic attributes, but he was notorious for his brinkmanship. In 1973, after initially appearing to accept an invitation to a peace conference, following an attack on Israel by Syria and Egypt, he pulled out just three days before the ceremonial opening session in Geneva. It had been agreed that the talks would be held under the auspices of U.N. Secretary-General Kurt Waldheim, with Henry Kissinger and his Soviet counterpart, Foreign Minister Andrei Gromyko, serving as co-chairs. Kissinger and Gromyko invited the parties that fought in what became known as the Yom Kippur War – Israel, Egypt and Syria – as well as Jordan, which stayed out of the conflict but was deemed a "concerned party," having lost the West Bank when Israel launched the 1967 Six-Day War.

In spite of Syria's absence, the other parties decided to proceed with the conference at the level of foreign ministers, and to keep an empty table for the Syrians as a visible reminder that they could still join the talks later. The arrangement of the tables, however, had not been determined before the ministers met on the morning of the opening session, becoming a source of intense negotiations. Gromyko initially proposed placing Waldheim at a table in the middle, with the Soviet Union, Egypt and the empty Syrian table on Waldheim's right, and the United States, Israel and Jordan on his left, Kissinger recalled in his memoirs. Concerned that separating Jordan from the other Arab states would offend Amman, Kissinger rejected Gromyko's plan. Waldheim then suggested arranging the tables in alphabetic order, consistent with protocol at U.N. meetings, but that would put Egypt next to Israel, which the Egyptian delegation would not accept. So it demanded that the empty Syrian table be inserted between the Egyptian and Israeli tables, meaning that Jordan would be next to Israel. Not surprisingly, Jordan objected.[28]

There was still no resolution at the time the conference was scheduled to begin. Finally, an Israeli official made a proposal that was acceptable to everyone: placing Israel between the Soviet Union and Jordan, and the empty Syrian table between

Case Study: (cont.)

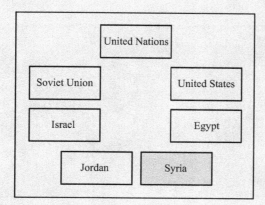

Figure 11.3 The table arrangement at the 1973 Middle East peace talks in Geneva.

Jordan and Egypt. The arrangement would be the following: the United Nations, the Soviet Union, Israel, Jordan, the empty Syrian table, Egypt and the United States, as shown in Figure 11.3. The opening session could start at last. The conference, however, ended the day it began, with no agreement other than the table setting. Still, many experts view it as the first step toward the peace treaties Israel would sign with Egypt in 1979 and Jordan in 1994.[29]

In 1991, emboldened by its speedy victory over Iraq in the Gulf War, the United States embarked on the most ambitious quest for peace in the Middle East to date. The process, which would officially start with a conference in Madrid, would involve bilateral and multilateral negotiations between Israel and several Arab states. This time, Syria agreed to participate, but there was another problem that resulted in a new battle of the tables. Washington wanted to invite the Palestinians, and Israel would agree only if they did not have an independent delegation, because they did not represent a country, and were included instead in the Jordanian team. The Palestinians found that limitation insulting. Even after U.S. assurances that they would be "free to announce the component of the joint delegation and to make a statement during the opening of the conference,"[30] they were concerned about the visual expression of their participation. How would the world know that they were even there from a photo or television news footage? Would they have their own table? Would their flag be displayed?

U.S. Secretary of State James Baker and his team had learned a lesson from the 1973 Geneva conference and were determined to preempt another battle of the tables. Having considered every small detail, they selected a T-shaped table. The two co-chairs, the United States and the Soviet Union, would be seated at the head of the table, with the other delegations occupying both sides of the lower part of the "T" – that way, there would be no argument over whether the Palestinians would sit at the Jordanian table or have one of their own. To avoid a quibble over whether the Palestinian flag would be allowed, no national flags would be displayed, other than those of the two conference co-sponsors.[31]

This case study clearly shows the need for diplomats and other officials to plan carefully and well in advance of any official meetings and negotiations, if they want to

Case Study: (cont.)

Figure 11.4 Negotiators gather around a T-shaped table at the Middle East peace conference in Madrid in 1991.
Photo by Dirck Halstead/Getty Images.

avoid delays because of bickering over furniture or other seemingly logistical matters. In addition to understanding key elements of diplomatic protocol, the hosts and chairs of such events must be familiar with the history, policies and grievances of all negotiating parties, so they can anticipate potential problems and try to resolve them before they erupt.

Exercise: Reception at the Ambassador's Residence

This book has just been published, and the State Department's Speaker Program, which sends U.S. experts to speak to audiences around the world, has invited Nicholas Kralev to travel to several countries and deliver U.S. embassy-sponsored programs on best practices in diplomatic training and the future of diplomacy. One of Kralev's stops will be Bulgaria, where the public diplomacy section is planning to arrange for him to speak at the Ministry of Foreign Affairs, a think tank and two universities. In addition, the ambassador, who knows Kralev, would like to host a

Exercise: (cont.)

reception at his residence for foreign diplomats, host-government officials, the NGO and academic communities, and the media.

You are serving as a public diplomacy officer, and your boss has given you responsibility for organizing the reception. Using all available resources, prepare a plan that answers the following questions:

- What objectives would the reception serve and how would it complement the rest of Kralev's program?
- How big should the reception be, whom would you invite, and what would the dress code be?
- How would you arrange the reception room and what would you serve?
- Who should be in the receiving line, who should speak and for how long, and should there be a toast?
- Would this book be promoted at the reception, and would you need permission from anyone?

ADDITIONAL RESOURCES

Moyra Bremner, *Modern Etiquette* (Chartwell Books, 1994).
Chas W. Freeman, *The Diplomat's Dictionary* (National Defense University Press, 1994).
Mary Mel French, *United States Protocol* (Rowman & Littlefield, 2010).
The Vienna Convention on Diplomatic Relations, 1961.
The Vienna Convention on Consular Relations, 1963.

12 Multilateral Diplomacy

JEFFREY DELAURENTIS AND TRESSA RAE FINERTY

Rena Lee's broad smile could not hide the tears of exhaustion in her eyes. The 36-hour marathon session of nonstop negotiations among 193 countries in a windowless New York conference room, which Lee chaired, was almost over. "The ship has reached the shore," said Lee, a Singaporean diplomat and president of the United Nations Intergovernmental Conference on Marine Biodiversity of Areas Beyond National Jurisdiction (BBNJ). After 19 years of negotiations, Lee's late-night announcement in March 2023 that the delegates had reached an agreement on a historic treaty to protect oceans that lie outside national borders drew thunderous applause and long-awaited relief in the auditorium.[1]

Discussions on a "high seas treaty" began soon after the U.N. Convention on the Law of the Sea entered into force in 1994, but no formal action was taken until 2004, when the United Nations established a group to study marine conservation in the nearly two-thirds of the world's oceans considered international waters. As those areas do not fall under any state's jurisdiction, they are not legally protected. In 2015, a U.N. committee recommended the adoption of a legally binding document on the conservation and sustainable use of marine biological diversity in the high seas, and two years later, the U.N. General Assembly (UNGA) decided to convene the intergovernmental conference that ultimately sealed the deal in 2023.[2] U.N. Secretary-General António Guterres hailed the breakthrough as "a victory for multilateralism and for global efforts to counter the destructive trends facing ocean health, now and for generations to come,"[3] and Greenpeace proclaimed it "the biggest conservation victory ever."[4]

The agreement in New York, however, by no means marked the end of the process. The Convention on the Law of the Sea took 12 years to be ratified by the necessary number of signatories – and some, including the United States, have yet to do so. Although the BBNJ conference reached an accord on the substance of the new treaty, the next step was creating an informal working group to "undertake technical edits to ensure uniformity of terminology throughout the draft text and harmonize its versions in the six official languages of the United Nations" – English, French, Spanish, Arabic, Chinese and Russian – Lee told the delegates. The treaty was signed in June 2023 and will enter into force 120 days after ratification by at least 60 signatories.[5]

However long it takes for the document to become part of international law, there was no doubt that the 2023 negotiations were an example of multilateral diplomacy at its best. Key players understood the urgency of protecting marine life in the high seas, which for years had been under threat from unregulated exploitation, including overfishing, pollution from ships and other human activity causing climate change. Those players built coalitions of like-minded countries and organizations and put the issue on the agenda of major high-level international forums. For example, the EU made the adoption of a BBNJ treaty a key priority, and European Commission President Ursula von der Leyen formed a 51-party "high-ambition coalition" committed to negotiating a pact at a 2022 conference of ocean industries.[6] That same year, G20 leaders expressed support for a "legally binding instrument."[7] The decision of the United States to join von der Leyen's coalition in early 2023 provided a significant boost to the momentum built in the run-up to the New York meeting. But it owes its ultimate success to dogged determination, unwavering tenacity, painstaking diplomacy and active civil society engagement.

All these elements do not come together very often in negotiations, especially among so many countries, which is hardly surprising. This book has made clear how complex, unpredictable and sometimes frustrating diplomacy can be, and when you have many participants, each with their own interests and values, those difficulties are heightened exponentially. The world's simultaneous globalization and fragmentation require that this game be played in spite of the hurdles. Just like climate change and marine conservation, most of today's challenges do not recognize national borders and cannot be resolved by any one country alone. To have any influence in the 21st-century international system of multiple centers of power, a country must engage in skillful multilateral diplomacy.

Most diplomats spend their careers serving in bilateral missions, such as embassies and consulates accredited to a single nation-state. The two of us, on the other hand, have worked for years in multilateral missions or on multilateral issues. Negotiations, on which Chapter 15 will focus in more detail, are certainly an essential part of multilateral diplomacy, but there are many other facets that affect the conduct of international relations and the results that countries seek to achieve.

What is multilateral diplomacy?

In 1568, the Dutch took up arms to win their independence from Spain. Except for a 12-year truce, the war that broke out raged on for 80 years, during the last three decades of which various other European countries also fought wars for religious, territorial, commercial and dynastic reasons. In 1648, all warring parties negotiated the end of hostilities in what became known as the Peace of Westphalia, and one of its two treaties resulted in the establishment of the Netherlands. Some scholars of international relations credit the settlement with providing the foundation of the modern nation-state system and the concept of territorial sovereignty.[8] It was also an early attempt at multilateral diplomacy, as envoys from several countries met to negotiate, including France, Sweden and the Holy Roman Empire, even if there was never a session with all of them in the same room.[9]

Multilateral diplomacy has evolved significantly since then, thanks to the many technological inventions of the industrial and information revolutions, as well as to scientific advancements and human development in general. For instance, diplomats no longer have to sail for weeks to cross an ocean or wait for days for a letter to reach another country. Negotiators today can work on a draft agreement, joint statement or another document in person or remotely from different locations around the world. But at its core, multilateral diplomacy is still defined as **the management of relations among three or more nation-states**, both within and outside international organizations, as Nicholas Kralev noted in Chapter 1. One substantive novelty is the growing influence of nongovernmental institutions, such as prominent advocacy groups and rich foundations.

The main value of multilateral diplomacy is its ability to reduce the complexity of international relations in everyday life, including traveling, sending mail and solving crimes across borders. It produces agreements that are much more practical and less costly than a web of bilateral arrangements between individual countries, and it sets common standards that enable collaboration among scientists, engineers and businesses around the world. The average citizen in any country hardly ever thinks about what it takes for a letter or package to reach its recipient thousands of miles away, and few have heard of the Universal Postal Union (UPU). But before it was founded in 1874, if a country wanted its people to send and receive international mail, it had to negotiate an accord with every other country.[10] Phone calls, email and texting across borders would not be possible without the International Telecommunications Union (ITU), which was established in 1865 to facilitate and standardize telegraph exchanges. It estimates that 95 percent of today's wireless, broadband and multimedia technologies are powered by ITU standards.[11]

In addition to formal international organizations, multilateral diplomacy is practiced in informal or ad hoc groups and coalitions. When the West sought to place checks on Iran's nuclear program and prevent it from developing an atomic weapon in the early and mid-2000s, European officials urged the United States to talk to the Iranians. However, given the historical animosity between Washington and Tehran and the absence of official diplomatic relations, a multilateral format was necessary for any engagement. In 2006, the United States, China and Russia joined Britain, Germany and France, which had been negotiating with Iran, for what became an informal group known as both the "E3+3" – the European three plus the other three – and the "P5+1," the five permanent members of the U.N. Security Council (UNSC) plus Germany. Nearly decade-long negotiations in this format led to the 2015 deal that suspended Iran's nuclear weapons program.[12]

Sometimes informal coalitions evolve into formal groupings. A major international effort to bolster the Israeli–Palestinian peace process resulted in four key players – the United States, the United Nations, the EU and Russia – coming together to help mediate between the two parties in 2002. The Middle East Quartet, as it was called, was institutionalized as a permanent organization five years later, headed by former British Prime Minister Tony Blair. With hopes for a peace agreement dashed, Blair quit in 2015, and the quartet shifted its focus to assisting the Palestinians' economic development. It still exists and has an office in Jerusalem as of this writing.[13]

There are few things in multilateral diplomacy more important than who writes the rules, who sets the agenda, and who holds the pen during negotiations. The multilateral system created in the aftermath of World War II, which today we in the West call the "rules-based international order," was shaped mainly by the United States, because no other country had the capacity and both the military and economic power to play that role at the time. Even though the American statesmen of the era tried to build some fairness into the system to give a chance to other countries to achieve the level of security and prosperity they wanted, it is hardly surprising that the rules they set favor the United States and its allies. Washington continued to exercise outsize influence for decades, because it took a long time for other states to recover from the war and start to exert meaningful sway and leadership. U.S. primacy was reinforced after the end of the Cold War and the Soviet Union's collapse. Even as Western Europe, Japan and other countries grew into economic powerhouses, they benefited considerably from the U.S.-led order and had no interest in changing the system.

Although Beijing and Moscow were initially eager to join multilateral structures, such as the World Trade Organization (WTO), after the end of the Cold War, it became clear by the following decade they had concluded that the existing world order did not benefit them to the extent they thought they deserved. Soon,

Figure 12.1 Ukrainian President Volodymyr Zelenskyy addresses the UNSC via video link in 2022.
Photo by Spencer Platt/Getty Images.

separately and jointly, they sought to reshape it,[14] forming multilateral groupings to compete with U.S.-led institutions and holding rival summits. Having realized that the ability to set the agenda in multilateral forums carries substantial influence, Beijing mounted a concerted effort to win leadership positions for its diplomats and experts in a myriad of agencies in the U.N. system – something that Moscow had already mastered. As of this writing, Chinese nationals hold the top positions in four of the 15 specialized U.N. agencies.[15]

The U.S. government now makes it a priority to ensure that no Chinese or Russian candidates run unopposed for key positions, and to nominate representatives of the United States or like-minded countries. U.N. agency heads have a direct impact on their agencies' agendas and policies. They decide which issues deserve more attention than others, and they can fast-track or slow-pedal an agenda item. That matters in a world where power is as diffused as it is today.

For most of our Foreign Service careers, work in multilateral missions was not considered as important as that in bilateral posts, but that is changing. In addition to the skill sets discussed in Chapter 3, multilateral diplomacy requires a much higher level of multitasking and the ability to consider the interests of multiple states – unlike in a bilateral mission, where the focus is on a single country. The multilateral playing field is much more crowded, with a wide range of national objectives, values and grievances, which makes negotiations and other dealings more challenging and time-consuming. You must keep track of your government's relationships with other concerned parties, as well as their views and the interactions among them, and build a network of contacts much larger than the one needed at a bilateral post.

Working at international organizations

The League of Nations was the short-lived predecessor of the United Nations, founded in the aftermath of World War I in 1920. The following year, the League established the High Commissioner for Refugees (HCR), an agency tasked with helping more than 1 million Russian refugees who had fled political persecution in their country after the 1917 Bolshevik Revolution. However, the first high commissioner, Fridtjof Nansen, a famed Norwegian thinker and explorer, saw no reason to confine his new organization, given the millions of other refugees in urgent need of assistance. Emboldened by his personal stature, he unofficially expanded the mandate imposed by the league's member-states to include nationals of Greece, Turkey and other countries. The agency also created a refugee travel document, the "Nansen passport," and drafted a treaty widening the definition of a refugee.

Some members of the League of Nations were aghast. The mandate they had granted the HCR was limited to coordinating assistance, but the agency was providing direct operational support. They had specifically left out refugees fleeing religious, ethnic and other types of persecution, yet that restriction was disregarded. As great as the need to help non-Russians was, and as unique as Nansen's qualifications were, those members thought that he lacked the formal authority to make such drastic changes.[16] The lesson they learned was that, when you appoint a larger-than-life figure, such as the man who led the first team to cross Greenland and was about to receive the Nobel Peace Prize, you should not be surprised when he acts as his own boss. Today, international organizations' member-states are not keen on entrepreneurial candidates to lead them and prefer those who are not likely to "freelance" and operate outside their formal responsibilities and the organizations' official mandates. It is a safe bet that someone like Nansen would not be chosen to head up the HCR's successor, the U.N. High Commissioner for Refugees (UNHCR), which is known today as the U.N. Refugee Agency.

Global intergovernmental organizations

Modern multilateral diplomats work at both global and regional intergovernmental organizations (IGOs) composed primarily of sovereign states and can be divided into two categories. The first one includes national diplomats who represent their country at its missions to multilateral organizations, most of whom are career Foreign Service officers. Diplomats who are employed directly by the organization – usually its secretariat – are international civil servants who are supposed to represent the interests of the institution, not those of any particular nation-state, as noted in Chapter 1. In practice, it is not easy to separate oneself from one's national identity, which can deliberately or inadvertently affect institutional policies and operations. This is why it matters which countries hold leadership positions.

There are hundreds of IGOs working in areas that reflect almost all facets of life. In addition to mail, communications and refugees, such areas include labor and women's rights, trade, culture and education, among others. Since 1923, the International Criminal Police Organization, better known as Interpol, has served as a central repository of information from its 195 members, which share it to catch criminals across borders.[17] The WTO is one of the youngest multilateral organizations, founded in 1995 to help negotiate global agreements, create norms and standards that facilitate smooth, predictable and free trade flows, and to settle trade disputes. The successor to the General Agreement on Tariffs and Trade (GATT), which was established by 23 countries in 1947, the WTO has 164 members at this writing.[18]

Groups like the Organization of Islamic Cooperation (OIC) are based on religion. With 57 member-states in Europe, Asia, Africa, Latin America and the Middle East, the OIC is the largest intergovernmental grouping outside the United Nations system, founded in 1969 as "the collective voice of the Muslim world."[19] Other entities are based on specific economic interests, such as the Organization of the Petroleum Exporting Countries (OPEC). It is sometimes described as a cartel, because its mission is to "coordinate and unify" the policies of its 13 members to maximize their profits.[20]

The G7 started as an informal gathering of the finance ministers of the United States, Japan, Britain, Canada, Germany, France and Italy in 1973, but it grew into an annual summit of heads of state and government and began addressing political and other global challenges. It still has no secretariat or office, and its members rotate as president every year, during which the incumbent presides over the group's priorities and hosts the leaders' summit and ministerial meetings. Although the G7 has no formal authority and its decisions are not legally binding, it wields significant influence. The EU attends all its gatherings but is not an official member. The bloc does have full membership in the G20, which was created in 1999 as a forum for finance ministers and central bank governors, and was upgraded to the level of leaders in 2008. Apart from the EU, members are nation-states and include China, Russia, India, South Africa, Australia and South Korea, among others.

When a country holds the rotating presidency of either the G7 or the G20, it usually designates a senior diplomat to manage the process, coordinating the alignment of policy priorities and overseeing preparations for the leaders' summit. Other diplomats are involved in drafting documents, participating in consultations and planning the summit, either on a full-time or part-time basis. As leaders and ministers get ready for meetings, diplomats from all member-states have responsibilities in supporting their principals and delegations. If a country wants to exert influence, its representatives must arrive at these forums prepared, with clear objectives and a strategy that is as specific as it is flexible. There is ample opportunity to make participants' voices heard in formal deliberations, informal conversations and drafting joint statements.

Regional IGOs

Years before the British diplomat Hastings Ismay was appointed secretary-general of NATO, he said that the political and military alliance was founded in 1949 "to keep the Soviet Union out, the Americans in and the Germans down."[21] In other words, it was conceived with a specific purpose, whose more proper formulation was to guarantee Europe's security during the Cold War, four years after the end of World War II.[22] The best-known part of the treaty, signed in Washington by 12 countries, is its Article 5, which says that an attack on one of the alliance's members is considered an attack on all. Its main effect was to commit the United States to protecting the European members of NATO, since no one expected that the Americans would need the Europeans' help. Ironically, the only time Article 5 has been invoked came a day after the 9/11 terrorist attacks in 2001. It has remained open to new members since its creation and has 31 of them at this writing.

Like NATO, the European Coal and Steel Community, the EU's predecessor, was founded in 1952 for a specific reason: to integrate the coal and steel industries of its six member-states.[23] Today, the EU is a 27-member supranational organization, meaning that its laws and regulations supersede those of its individual member-states, and its reach extends to areas of political, economic, social and cultural life. The initial purpose of regional blocs on other continents, such as the African Union (AU) and the Organization of American States (OAS), was broader than that of either NATO or the EU and focused on political cooperation, but not on integration. The AU is the successor to the Organization of African Unity, which was established in 1963, and has 55 members today.[24] The OAS was formed in 1948, and its current membership includes all 35 countries in the Western Hemisphere.[25]

Although there is no pan-Asian bloc like the AU and the OAS, there are subregional entities, such as the Association of Southeast Asian Nations (ASEAN) and the Asia-Pacific Economic Cooperation (APEC). The former started out with five members in 1967 and expanded to 10. Its initial focus on trade and development has widened to include political matters.[26] The latter has preserved its original 1989 mandate to ensure that goods, services, investment and people move easily across borders.[27] The China-led Shanghai Cooperation Organization was founded in 2001 to address development and security issues and currently has eight members.[28] Subregional groups exist in other parts of the world as well. The Community of Latin American and Caribbean States (CELAC) was established in 2011 to mitigate U.S. influence in the region.[29] The Economic Community of West African States (ECOWAS) is a political and economic grouping of 15 countries created in 1975.[30]

Inner workings and practices

All IGOs have founding documents, such as a treaty, charter or compact, which outline their mission, principles, membership requirements, rights and duties of member-states, official organs, budget, regulations and procedures. Those with a secretariat generally do not like its head or other officers to take actions unless authorized by the members. This can create tension when the secretariat is a large bureaucracy. On one hand, international civil servants must operate within the mandate granted by the membership and receive approval for major activities. On the other hand, their job is to run the organization on a day-to-day basis, with at least some autonomy, and it is impractical at best and crippling at worst to seek consent from the member-states too often. So striking a balance is essential.

Procedural rules, oversight authorities and funding mechanisms are typically the most challenging and critical aspects of intergovernmental organizations' work for both the body itself and its membership. Diplomats with deep knowledge of these three areas and intricate understanding of how they influence each other have a big advantage in molding policy goals and securing support for their priorities. The most consequential procedural rule has to do with how an organization makes policy decisions. Some like the EU and NATO use consensus as their most common method – for a proposal to be adopted, every single member has to agree. They rarely hold formal votes before agreement has been reached, which is done in negotiations at the working level. In most groups with a large membership, the majority decides. This is the case in the UNGA and the UNSC, though in the latter, each of the five permanent members has veto power, as noted in Chapter 1. Meeting procedures include rules on how agenda items are put forward and agreed upon, as well as on quorums, transparency, making motions, debating and voting. Rules on membership govern the process for suspending members and admitting new ones.

Dedicated boards or committees usually exercise oversight authority over multilateral entities to ensure transparency, efficiency and compliance with rules and regulations. Internal audit committees, or in some cases external auditors, oversee financial controls and reporting. Some institutions have inspector-general offices that investigate allegations of fraud, waste or abuse.

The main source of funding for most intergovernmental organizations is a membership-dues mechanism, though some receive voluntary contributions – or both. Dues are assessed using formulas based on the relative size of a country's economy or other methods. In the United Nations, assessed contributions by member-states pay for peacekeeping, the management and operational expenses of the U.N. secretariat and other purposes. Specialized U.N. agencies like the International Organization for Migration (IOM) and the International Civil Aviation Organization (ICAO) are autonomous and are financed by both dues and donations. On the other hand, U.N. groups designated as programs and funds, such as the World Food Programme and the U.N. Development Programme, are funded entirely by voluntary contributions. Private foundations and other donors also support intergovernmental organizations.

Nongovernmental organizations

Some non-state donors can take on the weight of sovereign states in international agenda-setting, such as the Bill and Melinda Gates Foundation. Regularly ranked as the largest or second-largest private charity in the world, with an endowment of more than $50 billion,[31] it is also perhaps the most influential in the fields of international development and global health. In recent years, the Gates Foundation has been among the top three funders of the World Health Organization (WHO).[32] But its impact reaches far beyond funding, thanks to its extensive work in scientific research, project implementation and policy recommendations. It has been lauded for its data-driven approach to fighting poverty, disease and inequity, but also criticized for making decisions with public policy implications without sufficient and transparent public discussion. Some experts have expressed concern that it exerts too much influence over the WHO in particular.[33]

The Gates Foundation is just one – albeit the most prominent – example of the ever-increasing role that international nongovernmental organizations (INGOs) play in multilateral diplomacy. Although their officials and experts are not considered diplomats, they often work with diplomats, and sometimes can help or hurt the latter's efforts. Independent of government involvement, INGOs usually act as either advocates or service providers. The first category includes well-known groups like Greenpeace and the World Wildlife Fund, whose focus is on environmental protection, as well as Amnesty International, which promotes human rights. In the second category, Médecins Sans Frontières, also known as Doctors Without Borders, provides humanitarian medical care, and Lutheran World Relief works on disaster relief and recovery. INGOs are funded either by a few large benefactors, as is the case with the Gates Foundation, or by tens of thousands of small donations, like World Central Kitchen, which provides meals in the wake of natural and humanitarian disasters.

In addition to nonprofit organizations, multinational corporations sometimes get involved in aspects of multilateral diplomacy. Many of them have offices in capitals around the world, some of which resemble diplomatic missions. They may not have the same formal structure, but they do have a similar goal, in that they seek to influence a country's or an organization's policies and actions, and to advance their own interests. While companies benefit from lobbying, their presence, perspectives and expertise provide value to governments on challenges that cannot be addressed effectively without the private sector, such as climate change, pandemic management, and information and new technologies.

Diplomacy at the United Nations

It was the most dramatic meeting of the UNSC since the United States presented evidence of Soviet missiles secretly stationed in Cuba in 1962, which led to what became known as the Cuban Missile Crisis, the closest Washington and Moscow came to nuclear confrontation during the Cold War. This time, the U.S. secretary of state, Colin Powell, had been dispatched to show the world proof that Iraqi President Saddam Hussein had active weapons of mass destruction programs that posed grave danger. It was a crisp New York morning in February 2003, and the air crackled with tension as Powell, a widely admired hero of the 1991 war that liberated Kuwait from Iraqi occupation, began his hour-long presentation, complete with slides and audio recordings. He said that Iraq had "sophisticated" mobile labs for "anthrax and botulinum toxin" that could "produce enough dry biological agent in a single month to kill thousands" of people. He talked about systems Iraq was "developing to deliver weapons of mass destruction, in particular ballistic missiles and unmanned aerial vehicles."[34]

Because of Hussein's previous use of chemical and biological weapons, as well as his documented pursuit of nuclear arms, many officials and experts in the West believed that at least some of those programs were still active and dangerous. Iraq had defied 17 UNSC resolutions demanding that it dismantle the programs or prove that they had already been scrapped. Powell's list had been compiled by U.S. intelligence, and its purpose that day was to make the case that, unless Iraq was disarmed by force, the world would pay dearly. "Leaving Saddam Hussein in possession of weapons of mass destruction for a few more months or years is not an option," the secretary said. "Not in a post-September 11 world." The United States, Britain and Spain sponsored another UNSC draft resolution that would have authorized the use of force in Iraq, but when it became clear that it would fail, they withdrew it and maintained that the council's 1990 authorization of force was still in effect.[35]

After the U.S.-led invasion resulted in Hussein's removal from power in April 2003, both U.N. and U.S. inspectors had plenty of time to look for Iraq's suspected illicit weapons – but they did not find any. Western officials and intelligence analysts had not considered the possibility that Hussein might have ended his onetime programs but decided to keep that secret. Now they realized that the deposed leader most likely feared that acknowledging the dismantling of those programs would have made Iraq seem weak and invited an attack by its neighbor Iran, against which it fought a war in the 1980s. In the years that followed, Powell regretted making his 2003 presentation, saying it was a "blot" on his record and its assertions were "a great intelligence failure."[36]

From Powell's point of view, he did everything he could to resolve the Iraq problem through multilateral diplomacy by seeking U.N. approval for military intervention, just like the administration of Bush's father, George H. W. Bush, had done before the 1991 war.[37] Critics, however, saw a big difference between the two cases. While they considered the first conflict justified because of Iraq's invasion of Kuwait, they viewed the second as a war of choice, not necessity. Russia was particularly vexed that the UNSC could do nothing to prevent the use of force in 2003, because the United States had veto power as a permanent council member. When Russia invaded Ukraine in 2022, it used its own veto to block the council from condemning its actions and demanding withdrawal, as we will see in the case study at the end of the chapter. We do not mean to equate the two examples, but to point out the limitations of the body charged with maintaining global peace and stability.

As the largest global organization, the United Nations sees the largest share of multilateral diplomacy in the world. In addition to its headquarters in New York and its European headquarters in Geneva, it has large offices in Montreal, Nairobi, Rome and Vienna. United Nations diplomats work in a kinetic environment, especially in New York, where in recent years the UNSC has met nearly every day. Most governments send some of their best diplomats to the United Nations, which provides a rare opportunity for both multilateral and bilateral engagement at the same time. This is especially valuable to smaller countries that do not have embassies in every capital, and their envoys can interact with the world and have an impact well beyond their country's size. Good multilateral diplomats build a global network of colleagues they will likely meet again throughout their careers, some of whom are bound to become foreign ministers, prime ministers or presidents some day.

Apart from their missions to the United Nations, many governments place great importance on having their nationals hold key positions inside the U.N. system. The largest dues to the organization fall on the United States, but when it comes to filling positions, Americans have long been underrepresented. In 2021, they made up less than 7 percent of the total staff of the U.N. secretariat of more than 35,000 worldwide.[38] Some countries, such as the United Arab Emirates and the Marshall Islands, were not represented at all. There are serious politics around the most senior appointments in the secretariat and some informal arrangements among key member-states. For example, the undersecretary-general for political affairs, the third-ranking U.N. position, historically has been given to an American, while the undersecretary-general for peacekeeping has been French. A Russian national has often held the post of director-general of the U.N. office in Geneva.

The UNSC and the UNGA are the principal organs of the United Nations. All 193 U.N. member-states have one vote each in the assembly, whose resolutions are not legally binding. Votes on important matters, such as the admission, suspension and expulsion of members, require a two-thirds majority, while other questions are decided by a simple majority. In the council, the five permanent members are the United States, Britain, France, China and Russia, and the 10 rotating members are elected for two-year terms. Votes require a majority of nine to pass, but the permanent members hold veto power.[39] Many of the council's resolutions are legally binding. For example, a country can be sanctioned for a certain reason, and if it violates the sanctions, the council can hold it accountable. The body elects the U.N. secretary-general for a renewable five-year term and observes an unwritten rule that the chosen candidate may not be a national of the five permanent member-states.

The calendar in Figure 12.2, officially known as a "program of work" (POW), shows what a month for the UNSC looks like. It includes formal meetings, briefings and mandate renewals on a variety of topics. In a typical month, a working-level diplomat might be responsible for preparing their delegation's participation in two

Provisional Program of Work of the Security Council – March 2023 *(as of 28 March 2023)*

Monday	Tuesday	Wednesday	Thursday	Friday	Saturday	Sunday
27	28 February	1 March *PR Breakfast* **10:30 A.M.** Coordinators' meeting Consultations (**11:30 A.M.**) - Programme of work	2 TCC meeting (**P.M.**) - UNMISS	3 *1718 Cttee. PoE final report due*	4	5
6 Briefing (**A.M.**) - UNMISS Consultations (**A.M**) - UNMISS Briefing (**P.M.**) - Middle East Consultations (**P.M.**) - Middle East (Syria) [cw]	7 Open debate (**A.M.**) - Women and peace and security: Towards the 25th anniversary of resolution 1325 (2000)	8 Briefing (**A.M.**) - UNAMA Consultations (**A.M.**) - UNAMA Adoption (**P.M.**) -Sudan sanctions	9 *1701 report due*	10	11	12
13 Private meeting (**P.M.**) - Myanmar	14 Briefing (**A.M.**) - Threats to international peace and security	15 Adoption (**A.M**) - UNMISS Briefing (**A.M.**) - Middle East - 2140 Committee Consultations (**A.M.**) - Middle East (Yemen) - 2140 Committee *UNMISS mandate ends*	16 Adoption (**A.M**) - UNAMA Consultations (**A.M.**) - 1701 report Adoption (**P.M**) - Libya Briefing (**P.M.**) - Maintenance of international peace and security: Security sector reform	17 *S-G luncheon* Consultations (**P.M.**) - Ukraine Briefing (**P.M.**) - Ukraine *UNAMA mandate ends* *UNDOF report due*	18	19
20 Consultations (**A.M.**) - Programme of work Briefing (**A.M.**) - Non-proliferation/DPRK Briefing (**A.M.**) - 1591 Committee Briefing (**A.M.**) - UNITAMS Consultations (**A.M.**) - UNITAMS *MONUSCO report due*	21 *UN floating holiday*	22 Briefing (**A.M.**) - Middle East [2334] Consultations (**A.M**) - Middle East	23 Briefing (**A.M.**) - Middle East Consultations (**A.M.**) -Middle East (Syria) [pol/hum] Adoption (**P.M**) - Non-proliferation/DPRK Briefing (**P.M.**) - 1540 Committee	24	25	26
27 Private meeting (**A.M.**) - Somalia Adoption (**P.M**) - Threats to international peace and security *Colombia report due* *OPCW report due*	28 Debate (**A.M.**) - Threats to international peace and security caused by terrorist acts: Countering terrorism and preventing violent extremism conducive to terrorism by strengthening cooperation between the United Nations and regional organizations and mechanisms	29 Briefing (**A.M.**) - Security Council mission Briefing (**A.M.**) - MONUSCO Consultations (**A.M**) - MONUSCO Consultations (**P.M.**) - UNDOF *MINUSMA report due* *PSC Framework report due*	30 Open debate (**A.M.**) - Peace and security in Africa: The impact of development policies in the implementation of the Silencing the Guns agenda	31 March Briefing (**A.M.**) - Threats to international peace and security *Wrap-up session (P.M.)*	1 April	2

Figure 12.2 Source: U.N. Security Council[40]

or three events. It takes days to get ready for each of them, first coordinating with their own government, and then with other countries. For a diplomat working in their country's mission to the United Nations in New York whose portfolio included Afghanistan, March was a busy month in 2023. They had to prepare for the March 8 briefing on the U.N. Assistance Mission in Afghanistan (UNAMA), which faced insurmountable challenges under the Taliban regime.

The diplomat would have had to draft their ambassador's remarks at the council meeting, which are known as an "intervention," or at least to send the ambassador a memo providing an update on UNAMA. They would have sought input from officials in the sending country's capital and its embassy in Afghanistan, unless it was closed when the Taliban returned to power in 2021, as was the case with many foreign missions. The resolution scheduled for a vote on March 16 to renew the UNAMA mandate would have required weeks of negotiations and another memo to the ambassador, outlining the contours of the negotiations and anticipated challenges, as well as any expectations for the ambassador's personal involvement.

The growing need for multilateral diplomacy has long been accompanied by criticism of the United Nations as ineffective, and of the UNSC as dysfunctional. The council's failure to deal with Russia's invasion of Ukraine was just one recent example of that dysfunction. In the 1990s, it was unable to prevent or stop genocide in Rwanda and ethnic cleansing in Bosnia and Herzegovina. Many politicians and experts around the world believe that the United Nations and other institutions created after World War II are outdated and incapable of responding to today's challenges – and almost impossible to reform.

We have no intention to wade into the debate in this chapter, but it is worth pointing out that the United Nations is not some distant self-reliant entity with its own mind. It is a membership organization that is as good or bad as its member-states, and it is up to them to improve or revitalize it – if only they could agree how. They would do well to remember that, in spite of the ineffectiveness and dysfunc-tion, millions of people around the world have food and shelter today thanks to the United Nations, and that its peacekeeping operations are the only thing standing between stability and chaos in many parts of the world.

Multilateral diplomatic duties and skills

Chaos, panic and desperation ruled Afghanistan as the Taliban returned to power on August 15, 2021, nearly 20 years after it had been ousted by a U.S.-led military campaign. Hundreds of thousands of people were evacuated, and as thousands more descended on the airport in the capital Kabul even without flight reservations, suicide attacks not far from the terminal killed hundreds of civilians and dozens of military personnel on August 26.[41]

At the United Nations in New York, several member-states proposed UNSC action to bring more public attention to the events in Afghanistan and protect the Afghan people. Some countries suggested that the council issue a press statement, while others pushed for a resolution condemning the terrorist attacks. The next day, Washington instructed the U.S. Mission in New York to draft and circulate a broad council resolution that spelled out what the international community expected of the Taliban. It had to include three main elements: denouncing the bombings and demanding the Taliban ensure that Afghanistan's territory is not used to threaten or attack another country; holding the Taliban to its stated commitment to allow safe passage to those who wanted to leave the country; and calling for increased efforts to provide humanitarian access and protect human rights. Although such a document would usually take a week or two to adopt, and it was Friday, the White House wanted the resolution passed by Monday.

For the staff of the U.S. mission, that meant intense negotiations through the weekend. Jeffrey DeLaurentis, one of this chapter's authors who at the time served as the U.S. alternate representative at the United Nations for special political affairs, came up with a plan. First, he and his colleagues, working with officials at the State Department and the National Security Council (NSC) staff, drafted the initial text, which became the "zero draft" the Americans distributed to the other 14 members of the UNSC on Friday evening, August 27. As they often do, U.S. diplomats also consulted with colleagues from Britain and France, their closest P5 allies. On Saturday morning, working-level P5 diplomats, known as "experts," held a teleconference to review the American draft, during which it became apparent that Russia and China did not see an urgent need for such a document. The UNAMA mandate was coming up for renewal in a few weeks, and they preferred to wait until then to consider a resolution on Afghanistan.

All 15 council members met at the working level that afternoon for a broader discussion. Several changes were made to the draft to reflect comments and suggestions by various participants in the meeting, and the text was "put under silence" in the evening to allow members to consult with their capitals – the typical "silent" period of 24 to 48 hours was shortened because of the imminent deadline. Russia and China "broke the silence" on Sunday morning. The Russians indicated that they would most likely abstain, while the Chinese opposed the resolution but did not reveal how they would vote. In an unusual move, the Americans immediately escalated the negotiations to the level of permanent representatives with a meeting of the P5. The U.S. ambassador, Linda Thomas-Greenfield, a 35-year veteran of the Foreign Service, pointed out that the rapidly deteriorating situation in Afghanistan required council action without delay. The goal of the meeting was to determine how the text could achieve its original objectives without triggering a veto from China or Russia. Hours of back-and-forth language proposals followed, during which each delegation was in constant consultations with its capital.

With most council members expressing support for the resolution, even if Russia and China were still unmoved by the arguments in favor of it, on Sunday night, the Americans put the draft "in blue," meaning that no more changes were allowed. That forced a vote on Monday, August 30. The outcome depended entirely on China – it was not clear whether it would use its veto until the Chinese ambassador, Zhang Jun, joined his Russian colleague, Vasily Nebenzya, in abstaining. U.N. Security Council Resolution 2593 was adopted with 13 votes.[42]

Figure 12.3 Jeffrey DeLaurentis, U.S. alternate representative for special political affairs, speaks during a UNSC meeting in 2022.
Photo by Spencer Platt/Getty Images.

There are many similarities between work in a bilateral and multilateral diplomatic mission. Both promote and advance the sending country's national interests and carry out the policies of the administration in office at home. Both are led by a chief and deputy chief of mission and have most of the same sections, although the management section is usually smaller at a multilateral post, and it has no consular section, as noted in Chapter 10. A mission to NATO has a big political section but no economic section, while a mission to the EU has both, but the latter is typically larger than the former. In general, there are fewer home-government resident agencies at the average multilateral post compared with the average embassy. There is significant overlap between the duties of bilateral and multilateral diplomats. Both build and cultivate contact networks; report on and analyze important developments; write memos, talking points and speeches for their superiors; and manage visits by senior officials from headquarters.

An embassy receives its marching orders mainly from the bureau or department at the Ministry of Foreign Affairs in the home-capital responsible for the respective geographic region. A multilateral mission falls under the purview of the part of the ministry charged with managing multilateral affairs. At the State Department in Washington, that is the Bureau of International Organization Affairs, which develops and coordinates policy concerning the United Nations and many of the other intergovernmental organizations of which the United States is a member.[43]

Other U.S. government agencies are engaged with such groups with increasing regularity and widening scope. For example, the Department of Health and Human Services works with the WHO, the Office of the U.S. Trade Representative works with the WTO, and the Department of Homeland Security with Interpol. The NSC staff also has a directorate dedicated to multilateral affairs.

In the field, diplomats representing their country to an international organization have some unique duties that, while partly dependent on the particular entity, have much in common. Both of us have served at the U.S. missions to the United Nations in New York and Geneva. In the former, American diplomats protect and advance a wide range of U.S. political, economic, social, legal, military, public diplomacy and management interests.[44] In the latter, they represent the United States at dozens of U.N. programs and specialized agencies working in areas as diverse as refugees, global health, trade, arms control, human rights and the environment.[45] There are also U.S. missions to the United Nations in Montreal, Nairobi, Rome and Vienna.

For the purposes of this section, we will focus on work at the U.S. Mission in New York, which resembles playing three-dimensional chess. You may be arguing with the Russians over Ukraine, trying to understand China's motivation behind a certain move, and grappling with the climate-change predicaments of small island-countries. Your schedule is structured around meetings of the UNSC and the UNGA, and depending on the matters at hand, as well as your expertise and seniority, your work can be reactive or proactive. Your interaction with Washington is likely to be more frequent and substantive compared to that in a bilateral mission, because senior officials there usually attach high importance to U.S. activities and influence at the United Nations. That leads to their personal involvement in issuing instructions or editing draft documents and speeches.

As an officer in the field, you are on the receiving end of the instructions, which may require you to convene a meeting, hold a press conference or lobby another country to support a U.S. candidate in a leadership election at a specialized U.N. agency. If you detect opportunities to further your government's policy priorities, you can be the one recommending a particular course of action to officials in Washington. Security Council members rotate in the president's chair every month, and in advance of your country's turn, you might suggest preparing a presidential statement on the use of artificial intelligence in peacekeeping or another topic. Such statements, which are made on behalf of the entire council, are not legally binding and do not have the force of council resolutions.[46] Still, this would attract attention to a critical matter and signal U.S. leadership in addressing it. If your proposal is approved, you are likely to be tasked with writing the statement's first draft, to which other officials in both New York and Washington will contribute. Once it is cleared by the interagency, it becomes the official U.S. "zero draft." You might also be the one to start initial negotiations with other council members, who will have to vote on the document.

Perhaps the main difference between serving in a bilateral and a multilateral mission is that the latter requires much more negotiating. Although few of the highest-profile UNSC resolutions, such as those before the two wars with Iraq, may be negotiated between capitals – sometimes by foreign ministers and even heads of state or government – usually negotiations originate in New York and are managed by diplomats there. You might start seeking support for your draft statement with like-minded countries, and even find a co-sponsor of the document. Then you can try cajoling other council members. If they have conditions for their backing that you are not authorized to accept, you would have to run them by officials in Washington, who may have to consult the U.S. embassy in the country in question. It helps to identify a "sweet spot" in the text that is phrased in such a way as to satisfy the largest number of member-states and make them feel like they scored a win. Then you have to ensure that the countries unwilling to support the draft at least will not oppose it – an abstention is much better than a vote against it.

You have to be prepared for surprises, as officials in capitals can change their minds and shift positions. Some may demand adjustments that can throw off the carefully negotiated balance. This game requires dexterity and flexibility. It can be frustrating and even infuriating at times, but it is necessary if decisions are to be made and action is to be taken. You can minimize the frustration by making it a point to understand the interests and motivations of the different countries before you even begin negotiating – in other words, to practice empathy. Sometimes arguing and bargaining with officials in your own government may be more challenging than with your foreign interlocutors, so it is wise to be familiar with the personalities and styles of key figures in Washington, and to know how to navigate your bureaucracy.

Writing outside of UNSC resolutions and presidential statements also consumes a significant amount of time, including the various types of cables, memos, diplomatic notes and other documents discussed in Chapter 8. Preparing an intervention for the ambassador at a council meeting has complex choreography. These remarks are supposed to last just five minutes, so all points must be made clearly and effectively, and in a way that is appealing to other members. Once in a while, the ambassador may signal a change in policy and make news. But more often, drafting officers struggle to come up with slightly different wording to convey unchanged positions painfully familiar to everyone in the UNSC chamber.

The preparation choreography starts with a brainstorming session the drafting officer has with a colleague at the State Department's Bureau of International Organization Affairs in Washington to outline the key points the ambassador should make, as well as the process for writing, editing, clearing and finalizing the speech. After an edited draft comes back from Washington, it may need another round of revisions, because parts of it may not be in the ambassador's voice. Some additions or amendments may require a consultation with a lawyer. This back-and-forth between New York and Washington can go on for days. Once the staff and the bureaucracy have finalized the text, it undergoes a review by the deputy ambassador and lands in the ambassador's "night book," a huge binder the boss takes home to prepare for the next day. In the morning, if the staff notices any last-minute edits or questions, that sets off yet another round of calls and emails to Washington.

A day in a multilateral diplomat's life

Tressa Finerty, this chapter's co-author, joined the U.S. Foreign Service in 2002 and served at the mission in New York from 2009 to 2012, first as deputy counselor and then as acting minister-counselor for political affairs. Her time at the United Nations was the most exhausting, but also the most rewarding, of her career so far. A typical day during her tour started at home, with a review of the morning news and responding to urgent overnight emails. She was out the door of her East Village apartment by 7:30 a.m. and biked up to the U.S. mission across the street from the iconic U.N. building on First Avenue, with a quick stop for a bagel and coffee. She needed to put away her mobile phone in a lock box before entering her office, which was designated as a classified area.

Once at her desk, Finerty replied to emails from U.S. embassies around the world providing readouts from meetings of American ambassadors in various countries related to the United Nations. For example, messages might shed light on the host-governments' upcoming U.N. votes, give advance warning of new initiatives certain member-states might raise in the UNSC, or ask about negotiations of a council resolution. At 8:30 a.m., Finerty attended her ambassador's morning coordination meeting, which included four other senior diplomats with ambassadorial rank serving in the mission – DeLaurentis was one of them. The NSC senior director for multilateral affairs and the assistant secretary of state for international organizations joined via teleconference from Washington. Representing the political section, Finerty highlighted any potential surprises in the UNSC sessions that day, as well as key negotiations or press statements, though she was there mostly to answer questions and receive taskings.

The political section's 15-minute morning "huddle" was next. Finerty would pass down any assignments or queries from the earlier meeting to section staff, and the team would review the day's meetings, negotiations and challenges. The U.S. mission's size dwarfed all other UNSC members' delegations, and three issues for which three American diplomats had responsibility might fall under the purview of a single diplomat from another country. This meant that the Americans had to coordinate their outreach to foreign colleagues among themselves, so that, if one of them had a meeting with a Guatemalan diplomat to discuss sanctions against Syria, another one might join briefly to ask for Guatemala's position on Rohingya refugees in Bangladesh, because the Guatemalan would cover both matters in their mission.

The remainder of Finerty's day was punctuated by just such meetings, as well as calls with Washington and writing cables, memos, policy papers and remarks for the ambassador. She and her co-workers made a significant effort to be accessible to representatives of most of the other 192 U.N. member-states, explaining and reiterating U.S. positions, trying to understand other countries' interests and objectives, and seeking common ground and opportunities to collaborate. Most of Finerty's meetings were with a single foreign interlocutor at a time, although she participated in plenty of multilateral negotiations and discussions. The Delegates Lounge in the U.N. building was a favorite place to meet for many diplomats.

Figure 12.4 Tressa Finerty, the State Department's deputy executive secretary, with Secretary of State Antony Blinken in 2023.
Photo by Andrew Harnik/Pool/AFP via Getty Images.

Every political officer at the U.S. Mission to the United Nations in New York has at least one ongoing or upcoming visit by an official from Washington to manage at any given time. The visitor can be the president, the vice president, the secretary of state or another Cabinet officer, an assistant secretary or a technical expert. The close proximity of the two cities makes such trips much easier than foreign travel. Finerty was often the "control officer" for then-Secretary of State Hillary Clinton, including during the annual opening session of the UNGA. Those 10 days, when heads of state and government from around the world descend on the United Nations, are packed with back-to-back high-level bilateral and multilateral meetings, press events and galas. Managing it all can be head-spinning.

Case Study: U.N. Response to Russia's Invasion of Ukraine

It took the UNGA just six days to adopt a resolution condemning Russia's invasion of Ukraine, which began on February 24, 2022 – 141 countries voted yes, only 5 opposed the document, 35 abstained and 12 skipped the session.[47] Over the next year, the assembly passed five more resolutions, which demanded Russia's immediate withdrawal, suspended it from the U.N. Human Rights Council, reaffirmed Ukraine's sovereignty and territorial integrity, and created a register of damages inflicted by the Russian aggression.

Case Study: (cont.)

The sixth resolution's specific purpose was to call on "member-states and international organizations to redouble support for diplomatic efforts to achieve a comprehensive, just and lasting peace in Ukraine." It also urged all members "to cooperate in the spirit of solidarity to address the global impacts of the war on food security, energy, finance, the environment, and nuclear security and safety."[48] Like all important multilateral initiatives, the process began with a small group of like-minded countries, which then recruited a cross-regional working group – in this case led by the EU – to draft a carefully crafted text that avoided asking member-states to pick sides, and to coordinate lobbying and negotiating efforts around the world. The draft was introduced or "tabled" on February 16, 2023, by 56 co-sponsors. Throughout the negotiations, Ukraine showed flexibility and made many accommodations in response to requests from other countries.

Two days before the scheduled February 23 vote, Belarus, Russia's staunchest ally, proposed a package of amendments to the document. It wanted to delete a reference to "the full-scale invasion of Ukraine" and replace "aggression by the Russian Federation against Ukraine, including the continuous attacks against critical infrastructure across Ukraine" with "hostilities in Ukraine." Belarus also suggested dropping the UNGA's "demand that the Russian Federation immediately, completely and unconditionally withdraw all of its military forces from the territory of Ukraine within its internationally recognized borders."[49] In addition, it wanted to insert a sentence calling on "member-states to refrain from sending weapons to the zone of conflict" to help Ukraine.[50] Belarus's action produced an additional flurry of lobbying, but the proposals received backing from only 15 countries and were rejected. In the end, the draft negotiated by the co-sponsors was approved with 141 votes for and 7 against. Nearly half of the 32 abstentions came from African countries, showing a lingering disquiet that the West focused too much on the war in Ukraine at the expense of climate change, food security, economic development and other urgent challenges.

International organizations outside the U.N. system issued their own condemnations of Russia's invasion soon after it started, including NATO, the EU, AU and OAS. But the body tasked by the U.N. Charter with the "primary responsibility" in maintaining global peace and stability, the UNSC, failed to take action, as noted earlier.[51] Although it met more than 60 times during the first year of the war, every draft resolution was blocked by Russia.[52] In the view of the U.N. leadership and many in the West, the irony that the perpetrator of the biggest armed conflict in Europe since World War II holds veto power in the council made a mockery of the U.N. Charter. But could anything be done to overcome the council's paralysis? Article 27 of the charter says that "a party to a dispute shall abstain from voting." Yet neither

Case Study: (cont.)

has Russia abstained, nor have any of the other members insisted that it does so.

Some legal experts and diplomats have pondered the possibility of removing Russia from the UNSC's permanent membership, pointing to another part of Article 27.[53] It says that decisions "on procedural matters shall be made by an affirmative vote of nine members," but does not require "the concurring votes of the permanent members," meaning that vetoes are not allowed. Is expelling a member a "procedural matter"? An affirmative answer would have precedent-setting implications, which is why the other permanent members – the United States, Britain, France and China – have to consider their calculations very carefully. If all it takes to deprive them of their seats is a nine-vote majority, with no country able to block such a motion, whose turn will it be next?

In 1950, as the UNSC voted to condemn North Korea's invasion of South Korea and authorize a U.N. intervention to repel the North's aggression,[54] the communist North, a client state of the Soviet Union, expected Moscow to veto such action. The Soviets, however, were absent from the council. They were in the middle of an eight-month boycott to protest the United Nations' unwillingness to transfer China's U.N. seat from the Republic of China, whose government had lost the civil war and retreated to the island of Taiwan, to the People's Republic of China, founded by the Communist Party, which had won the war. Since then, the Soviet Union and Russia, which inherited the Soviet U.N. seat at the end of 1991, have not missed a single vote in the UNSC.

Exercise: U.N. Security Council Action on Sudan

You are serving as a political officer at your country's mission to the United Nations in New York, and your portfolio includes African affairs. Your ambassador is this month's president of the UNSC. Over the past week, forces loyal to two rival Sudanese generals – one from the country's military and the other leading a rebel group – have been fighting violently for control of the government. Hundreds of civilians have been killed, and thousands have fled their homes. The generals are former allies who orchestrated a military coup two years earlier but are now feuding over if and how to integrate the rebel group into the official army.[55]

Your ambassador has asked you to write a memo proposing how the UNSC should respond to the crisis. Consider the following questions:

Exercise: (cont.)

- Is a council meeting with a debate on the matter sufficient for the time being, or would you also suggest a presidential statement or resolution?
- Would you invite to the meeting any representatives of countries that are currently not members of the council, and why? Would there be outside speakers, such as experts on Sudan or conflict resolution?
- If you recommend a presidential statement or resolution, what would its exact purpose be?
- Which other council member(s) would you seek as your potential co-sponsor(s), and why?
- What potential opposition to the document can you anticipate?
- How would you go about building support from other countries once you have a "zero draft"?

ADDITIONAL RESOURCES

Madeleine K. Albright, *Madam Secretary* (Miramax Books, 2003).

Margaret P. Karns, Karen A. Mingst and Kendall W. Stiles, *International Organizations: The Politics and Processes of Global Governance*, 3rd ed. (Lynne Rienner, 2015).

James P. Muldoon Jr., JoAnn Fagot Aviel, Richard Reitano and Earl Sullivan, eds., *Multilateral Diplomacy and the United Nations Today*, 2nd ed. (Routledge, 2005).

13   Health and Science Diplomacy

JIMMY KOLKER

It was one of the finest examples of Sino-U.S. cooperation. When an outbreak of avian influenza caused by the H7N9 virus in China sparked fears of a possible pandemic in 2013,[1] the U.S. Centers for Disease Control and Prevention (CDC) sent 40 experts to Beijing, nearly doubling its staff there, to work at the Chinese CDC. By studying the virus and its effects, which resulted in severe respiratory illness, the American and Chinese scientists and public health officials helped to devise a response to the epidemic. Their joint efforts contained the spread of infections in a relatively short time and prevented a pandemic. In the four years after the outbreak started, fewer than 1,000 human cases of avian flu were reported to the World Health Organization (WHO), mostly in people who had visited live poultry markets in China. There were 35 fatalities.[2]

Even after the U.S. CDC staffers who had been dispatched to Beijing returned home, the agency continued to maintain a substantial presence on the Chinese CDC campus. At the time, I served as assistant secretary for global affairs at the Department of Health and Human Services (HHS) in Washington. The CDC is an agency under the HHS umbrella. When I left my position in early 2017, we had 47 CDC employees in Beijing. We also had three bilateral health cooperation agreements with China, which authorized and facilitated sharing technical information. Over the next two years, however, all diplomatic agreements were allowed to expire, and the CDC staff was cut to 14 and moved to the U.S. Embassy, about an hour away from the Chinese CDC. So it was hardly a surprise that, after a novel coronavirus was first detected at the end of 2019, also in China, the events that ensued were very different from those in 2013.

Although the Chinese promptly shared the genetic sequence of the SARS2 virus that causes Covid-19, enabling the global scientific community to get to work immediately on diagnostic tests, treatments and vaccines, they failed to provide timely information about its transmission, severity and symptoms. They also withheld samples of the original pathogen, which remains the case at this writing, feeding suspicion of the initial theory that the virus had originated in a wet seafood market in the city of Wuhan.[3] Just when they were most needed, the U.S. health attaché and representatives of the National Institutes of Health and the Food and Drug Administration (FDA) were evacuated to the United States, along with other embassy staff.

There is no way to know for sure whether a repeat of the 2013 collaboration would have stopped Covid-19 from becoming a devastating pandemic, which has infected more than 770 million people and killed nearly 7 million globally, as of this writing.[4] We cannot be certain that having more American experts in Beijing working at the Chinese CDC and renewing the bilateral agreements would have made China share more vital information or mitigated the wreckage the disease left behind. But the chances of that would have been higher had those measures still been in place. Why were they not? The diplomatic agreements expired not because the Trump administration, which took office in early 2017, found fault with them or because China had violated them. The reason was that health cooperation with Beijing was simply not a diplomatic priority. In fact, in 2018, the White House disbanded the National Security Council's directorate responsible for global health, even though some experts remained on staff.[5]

Few scientists, health professionals or diplomats have any doubt that international cooperation in the fields of science, technology and health makes a big difference for the better. The pursuit of objective knowledge is a universal human endeavor that knows no borders and is not confined by the concept of nationality. Science and health diplomacy have a long history. For example, the first International Sanitary Conference was held in Paris in 1851 to standardize international quarantine regulations against the spread of cholera, plague and yellow fever – until then, individual countries had conflicting and costly maritime quarantine requirements.[6] Each national delegation to the conference included a diplomat and a technical expert, an early realization that this dichotomy is inherent in science and health diplomacy.

Technical expertise and diplomatic skill inform and complement each other to advance and apply scientific knowledge, and to prevent and combat diseases. Even though viruses do not recognize national borders, healthcare has always been a national – and in many cases, subnational – responsibility, which strengthens the case for international cooperation and multilateral diplomacy. This is a two-way street: diplomacy promotes and facilitates scientific and technological progress, while collaborating on science and technology fosters closer ties and better understanding between countries and people. Even political and strategic enemies like the United States and the Soviet Union during the Cold War had diplomatic agreements and cooperated in several scientific areas.

What is science diplomacy?

Andrew D. White, the U.S. ambassador to Germany, was obsessed with pork. In the final days of 1897, as the United States prepared for war with Spain, nothing was more important for White than getting the German government to lift a ban on American pork imports. He was convinced that the scientific rationale the Germans used to justify the restrictions was faulty, but he and his embassy's diplomats lacked sufficient knowledge to sway their hosts. So White, who had co-founded Cornell

University three decades earlier, requested that the State Department ask the Department of Agriculture (USDA) to send to Berlin "one or more thoroughly trained experts fit to deal with the whole subject, and especially accustomed to the use of the microscope."[7] USDA soon selected Charles W. Stiles, a 31-year-old zoologist whose research focused on intestinal parasites in cattle and poultry, and the State Department arranged for his accreditation with the German authorities.[8] He arrived at the embassy in early April 1898, two weeks before the Spanish–American War broke out.

Stiles enthusiastically embraced the assignment White had given him. When a shipment of American swine livers docked in Hamburg, the Germans declared that it carried trichinosis, a disease caused by a parasite called Trichinella, and refused to allow it in the country. Stiles immediately set off for the port city. He examined both the American goods and German pork. The former had no signs of trichinosis, but the latter did. In his report to Washington, he wrote that half of the 6,300 German cases recorded in the previous two decades appeared "to have been due to faults of the German inspection."[9] Although Stiles suspected that the affair was a smoke-screen for protectionism, he decided that hostility and confrontation would not accomplish what White wanted. He chose instead to build rapport and trust with his interlocutors, and to rely on empathy and persuasion. Having seen progress in their relations, he gradually began urging the Germans to ease the restrictions – and they did. White was so impressed that he refused to send Stiles back to Washington and kept him in Berlin for a year and a half. No one replaced him after he left.

Stiles had been brought to the embassy entirely for his scientific expertise, but when he realized that it was not enough to influence the Germans' decision-making, he resorted to using diplomatic tools. Combining science and diplomacy was a novelty at the time, and Stiles is considered the first U.S. science diplomat. By the time one of his successors, Earl A. Evans, was posted to the U.S. Embassy in London almost half a century later, the State Department had introduced the title of science attaché. But the Americans occupying those positions were not usually career Foreign Service officers. Most either came from academia, as was the case with Evans, who chaired the department of biochemistry at the University of Chicago,[10] or worked as technical experts in other government agencies like Stiles.

World War II unleashed unprecedented scientific advances, leading Washington to recognize that basic research resulted in new technologies and industries. After nuclear fission was discovered in Germany, and the United States later used it to build the first atomic weapon, the U.S. government grew ever more cognizant of the role of science in foreign affairs.[11] It significantly increased federal funding of research and development and took a serious interest in the international exchange of scientific information, partly as a way to avoid duplication. In an influential report, Vannevar Bush, an engineer and inventor who headed the Office of Scientific Research and Development during the war, suggested that, "as an experiment," science attachés serve in selected embassies.[12]

When Evans was sent to London in 1947, he was assigned the following duties: to aid and facilitate the exchange of scientific personnel between the United States and

Britain; develop and maintain "close personal contact" with British government agencies and other research institutions; obtain answers to questions asked by government and other scientific agencies in the United States; and stimulate the exchange of scientific and technical reports, especially those not generally available by usual channels.[13]

This is essentially what science diplomats do to this day. Science diplomacy is **the activity of deploying international cooperation in the service of science, and using science to achieve foreign policy goals**. The explosion of scientific and technological breakthroughs, along with globalization, has markedly expanded the agenda of science diplomats in recent decades. Yet many political leaders view science diplomacy as a "soft" or "technical" subject and do not consider it a priority. The vast majority of governments barely have any full-time science diplomats.

The United States has more than any other country, but "science counselors" can be found in fewer than a third of its embassies. The State Department has increasingly sought to link its science diplomacy to policy objectives and align it directly with the national interest. It prioritizes "projects that will have significant positive impact on [U.S.] national security and economic prosperity," and it is open about pursuing "international cooperation with partners to preserve American dominance in key sectors of interest." Its recent efforts in the field include "managing dry lands in Africa, developing regional drinking water systems in Latin America, researching climate-change mitigation efforts in Europe and the Caribbean, and preparing for disaster response in East Asia."[14]

Science and public policy

Science diplomats quickly discover that science rarely speaks for itself. Its findings have to be interpreted and analyzed, sometimes leading to different conclusions. When it comes to using the results of scientific research to make public policy, things can get complicated, since political, social and cultural factors and considerations come into play as well. The science behind climate change is a case in point. The overwhelming majority of the scientific community agrees that human activity has caused temperatures to rise, and that those changes threaten life on Earth as we know it, unless certain measures are taken to minimize the damage. Politicians in various countries, however, criticize such views as exaggerated and alarmist, citing analyses by scientists and other experts who disagree with the majority. Even among countries whose leaders champion green policies, reaching formal accords with accountability has long been excruciatingly difficult.

Another prominent example of political decisions based on conflicting interpretations of scientific findings concerns genetically modified organisms (GMOs), whose genetic material is artificially altered to give it a new property, such as resisting disease, insects or drought, or to increase crop productivity. The scientists who design GMO crops, including maize, soybeans and cotton, claim that the technology is safe for humans, better for the environment and is the only way to feed the planet's rapidly growing population. At the same time, opponents argue that GMOs cause health problems for both humans and animals and destroy the environment. While the United States generally agrees with the former and uses GMOs extensively, the EU shares the concerns of the latter and imposes significant restrictions. It has an almost total ban on GMO cultivation, and in 2021, it authorized the use of only 10 GMO crops as food and animal feed.[15]

France is one of the countries where GMOs have been most controversial, and the issue figured prominently in U.S.–French relations when Anthony Rock served as the science counselor at the U.S. Embassy in Paris at the turn of this century. Rock started out as a physical scientist at the National Oceanic and Atmospheric Administration (NOAA) before spending more than two decades in the Foreign Service. After one in a series of droughts in Africa, the United States proposed GMO cultivation as a means of overcoming serious food shortages. American experts expected that a country using GMOs would not only be self-sufficient within two years following the drought, but would produce enough food to become an exporter, Rock told students at the Washington International Diplomatic Academy in 2020. The U.S. proposal met "tremendous resistance from Europe, ostensibly on scientific grounds," because once African countries "were ready to export, they would be exporting to Europe," Rock added.[16]

African governments often looked to the United States and the EU for guidance on food safety, so the conflicting advice they received in this case was not helpful. Confident that scientific data and experience would strengthen the U.S. case, Washington decided to help the Africans build their own capacity and determine whether GMO cultivation was worthwhile. U.S. diplomats arranged training for science advisers at various ministries, started expert exchanges and urged the African Development Bank to support more science-based programs. They also encouraged the Organization of African Unity and its successor, the African Union, to establish science-based committees to provide guidance to national governments.

The continent's capacity has since improved, but hesitation about GMOs persists, and compared to the Americas and Asia, Africa has been slow to utilize them. South Africa was first in 1996, with only a handful of countries following suit. Concerns about adverse effects from GMOs continue, even though no confirmed harm has been reported in the three decades since the technology was first commercialized.[17] Decisions about GMOs, climate change and other controversial matters tend to be made by politicians, not scientists, with strong commercial and economic influences, and science diplomats have to navigate these waters. Like Charles Stiles in Germany, they need to understand fully the technical side of the issues, but the key diplomatic skills described in this book are likely to prove more decisive.

What is health diplomacy?

My experience with health diplomacy faced the other side of this coin: how to understand scientific evidence, and especially uncertainty, and to make program decisions of huge consequence. Historically, international health has been the domain of biomedical researchers and development specialists. Health diplomacy is **the activity of deploying international cooperation in the service of public health, and using global health efforts to achieve foreign policy goals**.

I had no intention of being a health diplomat. I possessed no medical expertise, and during much of my career in the Foreign Service, health diplomacy was not a well-defined concept. Like most diplomats, I was a generalist interested in a variety of subjects. However, in 2003, while I was serving as ambassador to Uganda, the U.S. government launched the President's Emergency Plan for AIDS Relief (PEPFAR), its largest-ever health diplomacy program, with Uganda as its show-piece.[18] Although the embassy had on staff some of the leading experts in the field from the CDC and the U.S. Agency for International Development (USAID), we needed partners from the political, economic, academic and logistical sectors in both Uganda and the United States to develop and sustain the initiative. Scaling-up of HIV treatment nationwide required a multi-sector effort. The program changed many lives, and mine was one of them. After three years in Uganda, I spent the rest of my career working on global health.

The first cases of AIDS in the United States were detected in 1981. When I arrived in Uganda in 2002, about 5 percent of adult Ugandans were estimated to be suffering from AIDS, and many more adults and children were living with the Human Immunodeficiency Virus (HIV) that causes AIDS.[19] In all of Africa, about

Figure 13.1 Jimmy Kolker, principal deputy assistant secretary of health and human services, speaks before the Pan-American Health Organization (PAHO) in 2013.
Photo by PAHO.

25 million people had the disease, and it was the leading cause of death on the continent.[20] In its first 15 years, an infection was considered a death sentence – the virus suppressed patients' immune systems to such an extent that they could die from virtually any microbial or medical infection. But in the mid-1990s, U.S. scientists developed a three-drug cocktail of antiretroviral therapy (ART) that was able to reduce the immune deficiency, lowering the risk of opportunistic infections.[21]

By 2003, only a few thousand Africans had access to the drugs. The therapy was prohibitively expensive. In the United States, it was administered only by specialists, and patients needed to be under strict and regular medical supervision, with viral-load tests performed in specialized laboratories required at least once every quarter. The combined cost of the therapy and the tests was about $10,000 a year, clearly out of reach for most patients in Africa. Normally, a strong cocktail like ART would not be used commercially until a multiyear study of its long-term effects has produced encouraging results, but the standard practice was not followed in this case, because the drugs were saving lives and patients accepted the risks. Not surprisingly, many of them suffered severe side effects.

Through PEPFAR, Washington wanted the drugs to reach as quickly as possible all 50,000 Ugandans whose lab results showed that their HIV had progressed to AIDS. The challenge was more formidable than it may sound, and things could have easily gone wrong. Africans were not in the habit of taking multiple pills at precise times, a requirement thought to be important for efficacy at the time. In Uganda, most AIDS patients lived in the remote countryside, far from medical centers in big cities, but even those centers lacked medical specialists or sophisti-cated labs that were an integral part of the antiretroviral treatment in the United States. Some Ugandans were so sick that they had stopped eating and were not cultivating food for subsistence. They were dying of malaria and diarrhea, diseases that were rare and almost never fatal in the United States.[22]

We knew about side effects among Americans, but Ugandans had a different way of life and could develop other reactions to the cocktail, which would be very difficult to monitor, especially in areas where doctors or other experts were not available. In many places, the monitoring would be done by paraprofessionals, who were high school graduates with bicycles. They would visit patients and complete a simple checklist of potential side effects, which turned out to be effective.

In addition to scientific uncertainty, there were political risks. Setting up a system to deliver lifesaving drugs fairly and with transparent recordkeeping would be a tall order amid pervasive corruption. We would need the government's cooperation, and would work with and allocate resources through reliable partner organizations, at least initially. The political stakes were high. If there was widespread treatment failure, unexpected side effects or an inability to reach needy patients, the main consequence would be personal tragedies, but the reputation of the United States would be severely damaged as well. We decided that it was a moral imperative to assume the risk and provide the drugs as fast as we could to as many people as possible, trying to anticipate problems and making necessary adjustments as we monitored the situation. Our strategy paid off, and the scaling-up met its targets for coverage. Adverse individual reactions to treatment were below expectations, with nearly immediate feedback from patients and treatment centers that the impact was evident and lifesaving.

Unlike American patients, Ugandans benefited from not having taken earlier experimental drugs, and the ART cocktail worked better than expected, with fewer side effects. Most patients showed dramatic improvement within weeks.[23] In less than two years, almost every family in Uganda seemed to know someone who would have died but was still alive and returning to a normal life because of PEPFAR. At this writing, the program, which is still active, has saved 25 million lives, supported ART for 20 million adults and children, and made it possible for nearly 5.5 million babies of mothers with HIV to be born free of the virus, as noted in Chapter 5.[24]

Why is PEPFAR a health diplomacy, and not just a foreign aid, program? There is no doubt that, without the scientific advancements that produced the ART treatment, PEPFAR would not have been possible, but neither could it be carried out without diplomacy. The collaborative work of U.S. diplomats and medical experts with Ugandan authorities at all levels – including the country's top leadership, as well as its medical community – saved hundreds of thousands of lives. It also created a reservoir of goodwill for the United States and bolstered its diplomatic influence.

What did we do? We started with a review of the small HIV/AIDS programs we already had in Uganda and determined which could be scaled up quickly, where we had gaps and which did not fit the criteria for PEPFAR funding, such as coupling AIDS education with the introduction of new crops for export. We presented our plan to the host-government and made adjustments, though our mandate from Washington for rapid results did not allow time for a comprehensive review by government and other stakeholders, which would become the norm in subsequent years. As the U.S. ambassador, it was my responsibility to lead the ambitious endeavor in Uganda. We had about a dozen priority issues, including a rebellion by the Lord's Resistance Army – a militant group that controlled 20 percent of the country – challenges to democratic practices, and Ugandan involvement in a war in the Democratic Republic of the Congo. But health matters ended up consuming more of my time than any other.

Duties of health and science diplomats

In 2019, about 95 percent of deaths from terrorism occurred in the Middle East, Africa and South Asia, with 0.25 percent in the United States.[25] Yet almost half of Americans worried that someone in their family would become a victim of a terrorist act,[26] and the U.S. government's counterterrorism spending exceeded $100 billion that year.[27] The issue has figured prominently in Washington's diplomatic priorities around the world for decades, particularly since the 9/11 attacks in 2001. According to expert estimates, the chance that an asteroid will hit the Earth by 2095 is about 5 percent.[28] There rarely are opinion polls measuring public concern about being killed by such an object, but the risk has not compelled any of us to adjust our habits or budgets. Both terrorism and impact with an asteroid are low-probability, high-consequence events, but we are clearly conditioned to antici-pate each of them in a very different way.

Pandemic disease, which is defined as a widespread occurrence of infectious disease over more than one country at a particular time, is the same type of event. Before Covid-19, we thought of it much like we viewed asteroids: not something we allowed to affect our daily lives, nor a threat that required preemptive and proactive government funding. The statistics about pandemics, however, have long been eerily similar to terrorism. More than 13 million people globally died from infectious diseases, other than Covid-19, in 2019,[29] though rare viruses affected a few thou-sand, and like terrorism, mostly in Africa, the Middle East and South Asia. But spending on tracking, prevention and preparedness was a fraction of the money the United States spent on counterterrorism. Stockpiles of materials and response drills were nonexistent or woefully inadequate to deal with a pandemic when one actually hit.

Scientific and health matters rarely capture the attention of ambassadors or ministries of foreign affairs, and few people seek diplomatic careers to specialize in science and health. No diplomatic service has career tracks dedicated to them – at best, there are sub-tracks, such as those within the economic track in the U.S. Foreign Service, as noted in Chapter 7. In Washington, the State Department's Bureau of Oceans and International Environmental and Scientific Affairs has long been the home of officers specializing in these areas. In 2023, the department established the Bureau of Global Health Security and Diplomacy,[30] to elevate and promote health at State and in bilateral and multilateral relations.

Science and health diplomats are not required to hold science or medical degrees, but they have to acquire certain technical knowledge, just like diplomats need proficiency in foreign languages for many assignments. Scientists and public health professionals serving abroad usually work for other government agencies, such as HHS, NOAA and NASA. Because they are not members of the Foreign Service and many do only a couple of overseas tours during their careers, Nicholas Kralev called them "transitory diplomats" in Chapter 1. When I was at HHS, we had health attachés at six embassies, including in India, Brazil and South Africa. That number has since risen to nine.

Putting scientific priorities on policymakers' agendas

Because these issues rarely cross the radar screens of government leaders, the main set of duties of science and health diplomats is putting their priorities on policy-makers' agendas, both at home and abroad. A health attaché, for example, main-tains regular contact with biomedical experts and other scientists on the front lines of diagnosing and fighting disease. The results of their work serve as an early warning system. If they determine that an outbreak has an epidemic or pandemic potential, or that it might create other public health problems that could cause economic or political damage, the attaché recommends to senior officials at head-quarters certain diplomatic engagement with the host-country. Once approved, the attaché might work with the Ministry of Health and other specialized agencies in the host-government to alert decision-makers to the issue and offer help. If the problem warrants, the ambassador might get involved and, when necessary, engage the Ministry of Foreign Affairs and even the head of government.

As a bridge between the scientific community and decision-makers in govern-ment, a science or health diplomat must understand the work of both and, ideally, how they think. The skills of maintaining relationships with policymakers at home and host-country interlocutors are similar to those described in the previous chap-ters. As for scientists, they certainly think differently from diplomats. Scientists see a pattern or anomaly in nature and try to gather data and evidence to explain it. They publish their findings in peer-reviewed scientific journals, such as Science, The New England Journal of Medicine and The Lancet. But those findings also have to be packaged and communicated to nonscientists, because the data rarely speaks for itself, as noted earlier. This is where science diplomats come in. They need to understand the evidence and incorporate it into persuasive arguments that can influence policymakers to elevate the potential threat as a priority and take action.

A typical scientific article makes it clear that there is a degree of uncertainty in the results it describes, and further research, which usually takes years, is needed for more definitive conclusions. Diplomats, on the other hand, go to work every day alert to breaking news and what needs to be done about it that same day. They also try to minimize uncertainty. These different cultures have to come together to create the political will to ensure that health is not crowded out by the many other competing priorities – this is the only way to stop the spread of a virus or eradicate a disease.

Bringing first-world standards to developing countries

A lot has changed since PEPFAR started. Before 2003, health diplomacy was limited mostly to aid programs that provided primary care and other services to developing countries for the purpose of fighting infectious diseases, as well as to research and exchange initiatives, such as the Fulbright Fellowship mentioned in Chapter 9. The U.S. government still awards research grants predominantly to American scholars, who work with local partners on subjects chosen by U.S. officials. Foreign aid programs tend to be on a relatively small scale, including proof of concept and pilot projects, but they leave scaling-up and sustaining them to others – and often to no one. At the start of the century, countries with a high disease burden often lacked the capacity to sustain and grow successful models and implement projects started by others.

In the last 20 years, however, most developing countries have significantly expanded their ranks of qualified experts and moved to consolidate national respon-sibility for their health systems, reducing dependence on foreigners for basic ser-vices. Students from low- and middle-income countries make up a large part of enrollees in Western graduate public health programs, and the quality of universities in those countries has improved markedly.[31] In addition, while foreign donors focused on infectious diseases in the past and they remain a major problem, more people today die of chronic and noncommunicable illnesses, such as heart disease, strokes and diabetes – not counting Covid-19 deaths.[32]

These new realities have changed the nature of assistance developing countries seek from advanced ones. As assistant secretary at HHS, more and more of the requests I received from officials and scientists were not for providing services, but for sharing expertise and experience to address a specific challenge. They would ask how we solved a particular problem in the United States, and who the best experts were. They wanted to partner with those experts and bring their own healthcare systems up to first-world standards. Helping to create and manage such partnerships, which often have political, economic and security components, is another major set of duties for science and health diplomats.

Balancing resources, ethics and expectations

The WHO was overwhelmed as it tried to help Liberia, Guinea and Sierra Leone deal with an Ebola outbreak in 2014. The virus was spread by contact with bodily fluids and had a fatality rate between 25 percent and 90 percent in past outbreaks, depending on the circumstances and the response.[33] Being deferential to the affected countries' governments, which tried to avoid acknowledging the severity of the disease for weeks, the WHO delayed declaring a health emergency.[34] In Washington, the first questions the White House asked us at HHS were, "What are the U.S. interests?" and "Is this our problem?" Although two American aid workers had been infected with Ebola in Liberia and we evacuated them to the United States,[35] there had been no domestic transmissions and the immediate risk for Americans was almost nonexistent. So was the crisis in West Africa our problem to solve? CDC personnel flew to West Africa to assist with response efforts, including surveillance, contact tracing, data management, laboratory testing and health education.[36] But what about treatment of infected patients?

Based on reports from the field, our experts projected that the spread of Ebola was outstripping any ability to treat it, and that it posed a serious threat to all of Africa, with substantial risk to Europe and North America, due to travel patterns. It became apparent that, sooner or later, the virus would cross the Atlantic unless we did something. But what would be the most effective approach? The charity Doctors Without Borders was treating about half of the Ebola patients in the three African countries, and its physicians and nurses needed to double the number of treatment centers. They knew that additional health workers, especially from overseas, would be much more likely to step up if there was a modern facility where they could receive skilled care in case they got infected. Since such a center did not exist, it had to be built. In spite of its longtime reluctance to cooperate with armed forces, the charity became an unlikely advocate for using the U.S. military's logistical capacity to deliver materials for treatment facilities, including an Ebola-care field hospital.

President Obama authorized the military to help build rural treatment outfits and a more sophisticated center in Liberia. Britain and France would convert existing hospitals in Sierra Leone and Guinea, respectively. The facility in Liberia would be staffed by the U.S. Public Health Service (PHS), a uniformed corps of about 6,000 with military rank, under HHS authority. Its members had full-time jobs, and we could deploy only a limited number at a time – we decided on 75 for six-week rotations. But before they could go to Liberia, there were 16 conditions we had to fulfill. Some of them were medical, such as specialized training for Ebola, but most had to be addressed by diplomats and policymakers.

We had to arrange authorization for the PHS workers to practice medicine and prescribe medication in Liberia. We had to determine whether the new center would provide the same standard of care as the few U.S. hospitals that offered Ebola treatment, as well as who would have access to the facility if they were infected with the virus. It was supposed to be only for health workers who themselves needed advanced care. But who counted as a health worker? Did a cleaner at a rural clinic count? What about a financial officer for a health organization with an office in the capital, Monrovia? We decided that a cleaner should be eligible, but not the financial officer. There were other urgent questions that had to be answered: Who would provide security at the new hospital? Where would the PHS staff be housed? How would they be transported? How would they get fresh water? The U.S. Embassy took the lead on making those arrangements, and my office in Washington provided guidance on other potential scenarios that could arise.

Even before the facility opened, it gave confidence to health workers from several countries that they would have access to excellent care if they contracted Ebola, and hundreds of them went to Liberia to treat those who had fallen ill. In the end, thousands of patients received treatment thanks for the unified U.S.–Liberian response to the crisis. While we consulted with scientists and medical experts every step of the way, the majority of the decisions we faced were policy and diplomatic ones. We made them with help from the U.S. ambassador to Liberia, Deborah Malac, and her embassy colleagues, as we balanced resources, ethics and expectations. By the time the Liberian government declared an end to the epidemic in 2016, 4,810 Liberians had died, a number that was much lower than expected at the start of the outbreak. In the United States, in addition to the 2 health workers mentioned above, 11 people were treated for Ebola, most of whom had been infected in West Africa. Two of them died.[37]

Health and national security

Even after the Ebola epidemic, few political leaders thought of public health as a national security issue. The U.S homeland had not been affected materially, and the definition of national security as the provision, protection and defense of the security of a country and its people, long interpreted in more traditional hard-power terms, did not seem to apply. That changed dramatically with Covid-19, when many governments acknowledged that an easily transmittable virus that killed millions of people and threatened everyone else was, indeed, a national security concern. It also became clear that the initial response to the pandemic had to include diplomacy.

The fact that healthcare systems have always been a national responsibility is another reason both politicians and the public do not usually associate health with foreign and security policy. But as the coronavirus ravaged economies and rendered global supply chains inadequate, it was again up to diplomats to figure out how to deal with the challenges discussed in Chapter 7. Diplomacy was also needed in the production and distributions of vaccines. The State Department's decision to create a new bureau dedicated to global health is a clear recognition that permanent and systematic international collaboration is vital in responding to epidemic and pandemic disease.

Global health governance

The existence of the WHO and the sporadic examples of international cooperation in the public health area in recent years do not mean that there is a formal system of global health governance. Although the WHO has convening power, Covid-19 made clear that, in the event of a serious outbreak, there is no one in charge globally. One of the first specialized U.N. agencies founded in 1948, the WHO has an outdated operational and governing model. Its role and mandate are widely misunderstood, and it is chronically underfunded. It was not set up to provide healthcare or manage health programs. It is a normative organization that offers guidance and technical support through regional and country offices. Most important, it is not an independent body but derives its authority from its 194 member-states.

As a result, there is no clear hierarchy of public health rights or responsibilities that supersede national determinations, which are discussed and aligned in principle at meetings of health ministers at the WHO headquarters in Geneva. Its consensus-based decision-making processes often fall victim to conflicting interests and regional rivalries, and the organization's leadership is deferential to member-state views and priorities. That often makes it slow to react to fast-moving developments, as was the case with declaring Ebola an emergency – a pattern that was repeated at the beginning of the Covid-19 pandemic. The WHO leadership's aversion to upsetting its members led to accusations that it trusted the information China provided too much and failed to challenge Beijing's initial underreporting of coronavirus infections. There was something else at play in this particular case. For the first time in WHO history, several candidates for director-general competed in 2017, with each country having one vote. China strongly supported Tedros Ghebreyesus, a former Ethiopian foreign and health minister. After he won and planned to run for reelection, he likely wanted to remain sensitive to Chinese concerns. In 2022, he was unopposed for a second term and received both U.S. and Chinese backing.[38]

The WHO has probably been more deferential to the United States than to any other country, refraining from criticism even when Washington, which is

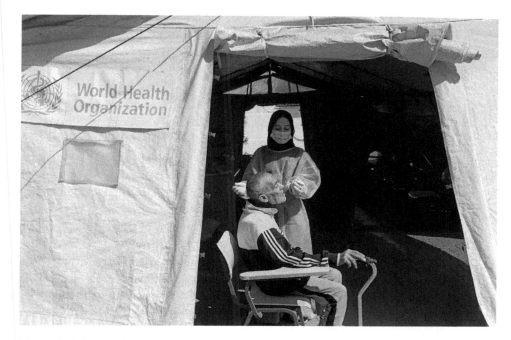

Figure 13.2 A Palestinian man gets tested for Covid-19 in a WHO tent in Gaza City in 2021. Photo by Mohammed Abed/AFP via Getty Images.

responsible for the largest share of membership dues, has made decisions that ignored science. Member contributions totaling about $1 billion a year cover only 20 percent of the organization's budget, though there is a plan to increase that to 50 percent by 2028.[39] The rest comes from voluntary donations, which are mostly earmarked for specific programs like polio eradication and regional immunizations. In 2023, the entire WHO budget of about $3 billion[40] was barely a third of the funds Congress enacted for the U.S. CDC.[41]

One of the WHO's biggest weaknesses is a lack of flexibility to adjust to the reality that many key actors in global health today are not governments, but philanthropic foundations, religious and patient advocacy groups, other NGOs, private companies, and academic leaders and institutions. The Bill and Melinda Gates Foundation is often among the top three funders of the WHO, as noted in Chapter 12, yet the agency has not found a way to include such organizations in its governance structures.

The danger of preparing for the last crisis

Governments learned key lessons from the Ebola epidemic in West Africa, and many used them to prepare for future crises. But there was a problem: they assumed that the next emergency would be similar to the last one. That failure of imagination caught every country by surprise when Covid-19 hit and led to disaster. When it turned out that the hospital preparedness for Ebola in the United States, which cost millions of dollars, was not necessary, since only 11 cases materialized, the authorities concluded that financing such readiness need not be a priority. But as soon as Covid-19 patients started filling hospital wards, it was clear that had been the wrong conclusion.

The U.S. domestic structures mobilized to fight Covid-19 were ill-adapted to deal with such a widespread disease. The National Biodefense Strategy[42] and the National Health Security Strategy[43] called for a task force chaired by the secretary of health and human services. HHS, however, had no mandate to convene agencies on matters of economic and security importance, and the Department of Defense and USAID were not on the task force. Moreover, HHS does not have the authority to instruct U.S. embassies. So after just a week in 2020, the White House replaced the task force envisioned in the strategy documents by one led by the vice president. But some important diplomatic tools were never deployed.

Work with the G7, which has long been a key organizing forum on biomedical issues, was given low priority. The Trump administration's accusation of pro-Chinese bias in the WHO resulted in a missed opportunity to leverage the U.S. expertise in public health surveillance with the WHO's high standing in low- and middle-income countries. Washington paid little attention to preparedness in Africa and Latin America and no attention at all to migrant and humanitarian emergencies, where it has been the lead donor. Engagement with international partners on the development of vaccines and other countermeasures was not a priority, either.

National rivalries and global equities

There has hardly been a public health rivalry among countries as fierce as the race to develop a Covid-19 vaccine. The public health community maintains that vaccines for such a widespread disease should be a "global public good." But given the weakness of global health governance, international collaboration and equity were often secondary considerations in vaccine procurement and distribution.

In the competition to create a vaccine, hundreds of attempts were made by companies in several countries, with dozens of them reaching human trials to test their safety and efficacy. Even though Russian and Chinese vaccines showed positive results, the two that proved most effective were those developed by Pfizer in the United States with BioNTech in Germany, and by Moderna in the United States. While many vaccines contain a weakened or inactivated germ to trigger an immune response, for the first time those two companies used mRNA, a genetic material that teaches the body how to make a protein. Even a piece of a protein can trigger an immune response, which produces antibodies and helps to protect us from getting sick.[44] The U.S government subsidized the Pfizer and Moderna vaccines through a commitment to buy huge quantities if they proved effective,[45] but the firms were free to negotiate prices with prospective buyers.

To ensure equitable access to Covid-19 vaccines, in 2020, the WHO and two other organizations established an initiative called COVAX.[46] All countries had equal access to its supply. Because of the mRNA vaccines' high prices, manufacturing bottlenecks and heat sensitivity, COVAX's largest commitment was to AstraZeneca (AZ), an Anglo-Swedish company whose vaccine was less expensive and was manufactured in India. The bet on that product, however, turned out to be problematic. Its efficacy raised concerns, and although they were alleviated, India battled a deluge of Covid-19 cases in early 2021, and the government ordered the manufacturer to stop deliveries to COVAX for several months.[47] At the same time, a handful of small, wealthy countries, including the United Arab Emirates, Israel and Qatar, essentially outbid the rest of the world for some of the earliest available mRNA vaccines.[48]

In 2021, the WHO established an intergovernmental negotiating body to strengthen pandemic prevention, preparedness and response. Equity and need-based access to vaccines and pharmaceuticals are key elements of the negotiations, with a draft agreement expected in 2024.[49] The Pandemic Influenza Preparedness Framework, which the WHO adopted in 2011 after a multiyear negotiation, mandates that vaccine producers pay a certain amount of money to the organization to be shared with developing countries that provide viral sequences and samples to be used in vaccine manufacturing.[50] Some of those countries had previously called for compensation. For example, during a 2007 bird flu outbreak, Indonesia claimed "viral sovereignty" over a treatment developed from a virus that came from the Southeast Asian nation. It argued that companies using the sequence or samples of that virus should provide free vaccines or other countermeasures to Indonesia.

Intellectual property rights are a major barrier to widespread access to vaccines and medications. When U.S. developers and manufacturers secure FDA approval, they hold patents for many years and can usually charge whatever the market can bear. As a major customer that subsidizes vaccine development, the U.S. government is in a strong position to influence prices and distribution, but that is not a role it has often played in the past. Another global challenge highlighted by Covid-19 is that vaccines do not prevent disease – vaccinations do. Once vaccines were widely available in 2022, distribution was delayed by supply bottlenecks and a shortage of cold-chain storage facilities and health workers. Moreover, misinformation and disinformation about their safety hampered their acceptance.

Still, the Covid-19 vaccination campaign was one of the largest in history. By the spring of 2023, more than 13 billion doses had been administered, and nearly 70 percent of the world's population had received at least one dose. In developing countries, however, that number was less than 30 percent,[51] in spite of hundreds of millions of donated doses by rich countries and private organizations. The United States sent more than 687 million doses.[52] This points to the urgent need to recognize that strengthening national health systems should be a top priority of governments and the scientific community.

It is hard to imagine a future in which global health will seem as remote a concern for diplomats as a killer asteroid. The real question is how often it will make it onto the agenda of policymakers and generate political will to act – and when that happens, how long it will last. Will health security be a political, diplomatic and budget priority in the absence of a widespread outbreak? After all, the next pandemic is as unpredictable as it is inevitable.

Case Study: Zika Virus in Brazil

Zika fever is a mosquito-borne viral disease caused by Zika virus, whose symptoms – which include mild fever, headaches, rash, conjunctivitis, and muscle and joint pain – occur about two to seven days after the mosquito bite. During a large epidemic in Brazil in 2015, scientists found a link between Zika and a condition called microcephaly, which caused babies to be born with smaller-than-normal heads. Zika infections could also lead to preterm birth and miscarriages. An estimated 5 to 15 percent of infants born to women infected with Zika during pregnancy had evidence of Zika-related complications.[53]

On February 1, 2016, the WHO declared a public health emergency. That same day, the Brazilian president, Dilma Rousseff, called President Obama and asked him to send the best U.S. experts to Brazil. Although the Brazilians knew how to handle the problem, she said, the Americans would ensure that the Brazilians were on the right track. As the assistant secretary for international affairs at HHS, I was eager to collaborate with Brazil, which had not agreed to our requests to share samples and cooperate on vaccine development. Our CDC scientists studying the birth defects needed to go to Brazil, but their visas had not been approved. It appeared that the Brazilian government did not want to be seen as dependent on the United States in its response to the crisis.

Two weeks later, I led a delegation to the capital Brasilia that included the top 12 U.S. government experts. The Brazilian health minister, Marcelo Castro, and I co-chaired the meeting. The Brazilian experts spoke at length but were reluctant to make any requests in front of their minister. That left it to us to propose areas of cooperation and map out the way forward. We needed access to the Zika-affected regions, and we had to decide who would own the information that would come out of the studies we would conduct. We suggested points of contact on both sides in each area who would regularly keep in touch. Most important, the minister and I signed an agreement formally launching a research partnership to develop better testing methods and a vaccine against the virus, and to eradicate the mosquito that spread it.[54]

Less than three months later, the Brazilian Senate suspended Rousseff's powers and removed her from office in August. Our agreement survived the government transition. As an official diplomatic document, it gave the Brazilian agencies involved in the process political cover to collaborate with their U.S. colleagues, without being accused of overreliance on the United States in their research and response to the epidemic. In other words, the

Case Study: (cont.)

agreement was an expression of political will to collaborate and provided the technical experts with a platform on which they could make scientific advances and battle the virus.

The partnership with Brazil allowed the U.S. government to fight Zika cases in the United States. There were just 231 in U.S. states, but more than 37,000 in U.S. overseas territories in 2016 and 2017.[55] The CDC awarded more than $100 million to about a dozen NGOs and other organizations for a wide range of activities, including surveillance and epidemiology, vector control, communication and outreach to pregnant women and vulnerable populations, and planning with key stakeholders.[56]

Exercise: Liberian Plans for Future Ebola Outbreaks

You are serving at the Embassy of Liberia in Washington, which has a small staff, and one of your responsibilities is covering the science and health portfolios. Your government is working on a plan to respond to future Ebola outbreaks more effectively than it did in the past, and as part of the planning, it wants to strengthen existing partnerships with research and public health institutions, as well as the private sector, in countries with advanced expertise in fighting infectious diseases, and Ebola in particular. You have been tasked with helping to improve collaborations with U.S. government agencies, NGOs and companies, and to explore new associations with key players. Your ambassador has scheduled a meeting on the matter in a month, where you are expected to present your initial proposal.

Based on what you learned from this chapter and additional research, draft a proposal addressing Liberia's need for assistance in the following areas:

- gathering and reporting accurate data during an outbreak;
- information-sharing with the WHO and other countries, including genetic virus sequence, symptoms and transmission;
- securing a reliable supply chain for personal protective equipment;
- enabling U.S. and other foreign health workers to provide treatment in Liberia;
- ensuring priority access for Liberia to U.S.-produced vaccines and medicines.

As you prepare, consider the following questions:

- Which agency in the U.S. government should be your main point of contact and what other parts of the government should be involved?
- What type of initial engagement would you suggest between the U.S. and Liberian governments, what forms should that engagement take in the long term, and how frequent should it be?

Exercise: (cont.)

- Would you seek an increase of CDC personnel at the U.S. Embassy in Liberia, and if so, how would you justify it?
- Which academic, research and advocacy organizations would you seek to engage, and what would their contributions be?
- Which private companies would you approach, and what would you need from them?

ADDITIONAL RESOURCES

Sara E. Davies, Adam Kamradt-Scott and Simon Rushton, *Disease Diplomacy* (Johns Hopkins University Press, 2015).

Ilona Kickbusch, Graham Lister, Michaela Told and Nick Drager, eds., *Global Health Diplomacy: Concepts, Issues, Actors, Instruments, Fora and Cases* (Springer, 2013).

Colin McInnes and Kelley Lee, *Global Health and International Relations* (Polity, 2012).

14 Cyber Diplomacy

HELI TIIRMAA-KLAAR

The Bronze Soldier is the informal name of a Soviet-era World War II memorial in Estonia's capital, Tallinn. In 2007, nearly 60 years after the statue was erected, the government of independent Estonia made plans to relocate it from the city center to the nearby Tallinn Military Cemetery. On the night of April 26, following false information in Russian-language media about the monument's imminent demolition, Russian-speaking youth started rioting in front of it. As the situation escalated, shops were looted and cars set on fire – scenes that were out of character for the quiet Baltic city.

It soon became clear that the riot was not as spontaneous as it first appeared, but the prelude to a carefully orchestrated anti-Estonian campaign. Its first phase also included a siege of the Estonian Embassy in Moscow, a suspension of shipments from Russian to Estonian ports and a demand by a visiting delegation from the Duma, the lower house of the Russian parliament, that Estonia's democratically elected government resign. Meanwhile, the campaign also unfolded in cyberspace, initially in support of the rioters. Hackers defaced the websites of Estonian government agencies and other organizations and posted messages in Russian celebrating the riots. They also disseminated instructions and relatively simple hacking tools on Russian sites for others to take down Estonian sites and attack servers with millions of requests. As one of the world's most wired countries, Estonia relied heavily on online services and other Internet-based solutions, and such disruptions affected much of its population.

After a week, the campaign entered its second phase, with more sophisticated cyberattacks, including what is known as "distributed denial of service" that targeted the servers of government agencies and media outlets. In the third phase, large botnets, which had been rented from international cybercrime groups before the Bronze Soldier riots, crippled financial institutions, government ministries, media organizations and other key providers across Estonia. To prevent further damage to the country's information and communications technology (ICT) infrastructure at the height of the attacks, the government limited internet connectivity, so that no one could access Estonian websites from abroad. That created the impression that the entire country was under digital siege. In reality, online services were restored relatively quickly and continued to function inside Estonia. After 16 days, the last botnets used in the final stage of the campaign stopped their attacks at 11 p.m. on

May 13, or midnight Moscow time. With their rental period apparently over, Estonia's cyberspace returned to normal and has run smoothly ever since.[1] The World War II memorial was moved to the military cemetery when the riots started.

The events of 2007 marked the first politically motivated, large-scale, coordinated cyberattack against an entire country. Its objectives included disinformation, political coercion and inciting violence. Fortunately for Estonia, it was as prepared as any state was at the time. It had held its first online elections the previous year and conducted exercises simulating cyberattacks against both public and private organizations. It is noteworthy that the Russian campaign had been calibrated as a "below-the-threshold operation" – it was significantly disruptive and harmful, but it fell short of armed conflict. Had it crossed that threshold, it would have provoked a NATO response – as a member of the alliance, Estonia would have benefited from the collective security clause of Article 5 of the Washington Treaty, as explained in Chapter 12.

One of the major lessons of the Estonian experience was that governments around the world must have highly qualified cyber experts guarding their most critical networks, anticipating crises and fighting back when they occur. Not long after the 2007 attacks, the Estonian government asked me to lead the development of the country's first Cyber Security Strategy, and I later coordinated its implementation while managing the National Cyber Security Council. In 2011, I started working on cyber defense policy at NATO, and beginning in 2012, I headed cyber policy coordination at the EU's External Action Service, the bloc's diplomatic service. I returned to Estonia in 2018 as ambassador-at-large for cyber diplomacy at the Ministry of Foreign Affairs. In these positions, I watched subsequent cyberattacks on two other former Soviet republics, one during Russia's 2008 invasion of Georgia, which was very similar to the anti-Estonian campaign, and the other – more sophisticated – during Russia's annexation of Crimea and invasion of eastern Ukraine in 2014.

Western publics became more aware of politically motivated Russian cyber operations during and after the 2016 U.S. election campaign. Similar operations targeted many European countries' elections both before and after 2016. As Moscow prepared for its 2022 invasion of Ukraine, it attacked the country's critical civilian infrastructure and continued to do so after the war broke out, but the damage it inflicted was limited, because the Ukrainian government had strengthened its cyber defenses following the 2014 events. Russian information warfare as a political tool is not a new phenomenon but an updated construct that continues to evolve, develop and adapt. For other countries' responses to be effective, they must be innovative and ahead of Russia's game.[2]

Although Russia is by no means the only country trying to weaponize cyberspace, its long history of attacks is a vivid example of the need for rules governing international behavior in this relatively new domain.[3] The U.S. National Institute of Standards and Technology defines cyberspace as consisting of an "interdependent network of information systems infrastructures, including the Internet, telecommunications networks, computer systems and embedded processors and controllers." It results from "the interaction of people, software and services ... by means of technology devices and networks connected to it, which does not exist in any physical form."[4] Not all elements of cyberspace are connected to the Internet – those that are not connected include industrial control systems of critical infrastructure that provide essential services, such as electricity, water and transport, as well as closed military, intelligence and other systems.

What is cyber diplomacy?

Actions in cyberspace by governments, businesses, nongovernmental organizations (NGOs) and other players have become part of international relations and international security. Those actions reflect countries' national interests and affect their bilateral and multilateral diplomatic relationships. This has led to the rise of cyber diplomacy, **the activity of deploying international cooperation in cyberspace and using actions in cyberspace to achieve foreign policy goals**. The main focus of cyber diplomacy in its still early stage is trying to forge a way to regulate state behavior and prevent and regulate conflict in cyberspace. Some governments have extended their cyber diplomacy portfolios to include the foreign policy implications of new technologies. Both traditional tools from the diplomacy toolbox and new technologies are needed to build and maintain international cooperation in cyberspace.

Figure 14.1 Heli Tiirmaa-Klaar (third from left), head of cyber policy coordination at the European External Action Service, speaks at a cybersecurity conference in Washington, D.C., in 2014.
Photo by Brendan Smialowski/AFP via Getty Images.

In addition to the skill sets outlined in Chapter 3, diplomats in this field must possess expertise in digital technologies and understand cyber risks.

It is important to understand what cyber diplomacy is not. It is not the activity of using digital tools to accomplish traditional foreign policy objectives – that is the definition of digital diplomacy. For example, when the Covid-19 pandemic shut the world down, diplomats could rely only on digital communications and virtual interactions to do their work, but that did not mean that they engaged in cyber diplomacy, unless their focus was on cyberspace stability and Internet governance. Although all of international diplomacy includes certain interactions between nation-states and the private sector, civil society and other non-state actors, such interactions between and among a variety of stakeholders are much more prevalent in cyber diplomacy. The absence of borders in cyberspace requires a multi-stakeholder governance approach where diplomats pursue a challenging agenda, which includes promoting peace and stability, protecting human rights and conducting economic and other relations in the nonphysical realm. For that, governments need help from businesses, academia, NGOs and other organizations.

A multi-stakeholder model already exists in the governance of the Internet. As the single interconnected worldwide system of commercial, government, educational and other computer networks that share a set of protocols, it is governed by no single body, but by a myriad of technical, civil society and governmental entities.[5] Internet protocols are specified by the Internet Architecture Board (IAB), and the name and address spaces are managed by the Internet Corporation for Assigned Names and Numbers (ICANN).[6] The origin of the Internet dates back to a 1960s computer network known as ARPANET, which was built by the U.S. government and academia. In 1985, the National Science Foundation started to develop a university network backbone called NSFNET. By the mid-1990s, the Internet had evolved into a large-scale network, which commercial service providers took public. In 1989, British computer scientist Tim Berners-Lee invented what is known as the World Wide Web, a collection of webpages found on the network of computers that constitutes the Internet. All major technologies Berners-Lee created, such as HTML, URL and HTTP, are still in use today.[7]

It may be useful to think of the Internet as a global highway where most cyber activities take place, whether benevolent or malicious. It was developed into a complex ecosystem by the public and private sectors, academia and civil society, while harnessing the shared technical expertise of the global engineering community. To keep it reliable, it is important to maintain integrity, openness and interoperability as its key attributes that facilitate social and economic progress. Unlike air, space, land and sea, cyberspace is a man-made domain and access to it is not automatic – it is dependent on thousands of ICT components produced by different companies, often in different countries. The cumulative complexity of such systems and the relative novelty of cyberspace lead to vulnerabilities that can be exploited for nefarious and malicious purposes.

With 5.3 billion Internet users worldwide in 2023,[8] humankind depends on this technology more than ever. But with enough resources and determination, most IT systems can be accessed by an outside party. Large organizations and those of particular value or prominence are especially vulnerable, because attacks against them usually attract the most attention. Personal devices and systems tend to be less appealing targets to states and criminal groups, although individual users with high visibility and responsibility, such as public officials and celebrities, can become victims of hacking and other malignant activities.

Threat levels and malicious actors in cyberspace

Diplomats help their governments to counter threats and take advantage of opportunities, as noted in previous chapters. In cyber diplomacy, at least in its current phase, the bigger emphasis is on threats, because of their overwhelming number and potential to wreak enormous havoc. It may be helpful to both policymakers and diplomats to think of different levels of threats, based on their impact, and to consider different approaches in trying to mitigate them.

In June 2017, novel malware called NotPetya infected computers around the world. It started in Ukraine – it was designed to infiltrate ICT systems via a popular piece of Ukrainian accounting software – where the authorities blamed Russia, as the cyberattack was an apparent part of the ongoing conflict between the two countries. But the devastation spread far beyond Ukraine, causing more than $10 billion in damages globally. One of its largest victims in the private sector was Mondelez International, a Chicago-based multinational food company, whose products include Oreos and Triscuits, among other well-known snacks. NotPetya disrupted Mondelez's email systems, file access and logistics for weeks.[9] The company's insurance provider quickly denied its claim, saying that its policy did not cover damages caused by war, resulting in a $100 million lawsuit against the insurer, Zurich, which settled it in 2022. The case set off a shake-up of the cyber-insurance industry with far-reaching and lasting consequences.[10] NotPetya also managed to seriously disrupt the global shipping industry by knocking out the systems of one of its largest companies, Maersk of Denmark, for a week.[11]

Ransomware, malware and other cyberattacks on a **global level** like those perpetrated by NotPetya and WannaCry, which paralyzed Britain's National Health Service in 2017, can inflict large-scale economic loss and cause crippling disruptions.[12] For example, Covid-19 unleashed an avalanche of cybercrime that touched many parts of the world. "Cybercriminals are taking advantage of the widespread global communications on the coronavirus to mask their activities," Interpol warned in 2020. "Malware, spyware and Trojans have been found embedded in interactive coronavirus maps and websites. Spam emails are also tricking users into clicking on links that download malware to their computers or mobile devices."[13]

On a **national level**, governments are mostly concerned with cyber threats emanating from other states or state-sponsored actors with various purposes, such as supporting conventional warfare, playing a part in hybrid conflicts, espionage, interfering in elections or other internal affairs. On an **industry level**, cyberattacks can affect entire industries or sectors of the economy, as was the case with NotPetya's and WannaCry's impact on the insurance, healthcare, transport and other sectors. Economic espionage in cyberspace is another serious threat that can cause significant economic losses and distort markets.[14] On an **individual level**, most end-users have been targets of cyber incidents, and millions have become victims. Home computers with weak cybersecurity protection are susceptible to hijacking and inclusion in "botnet armies" used for illegal activities like the 2007 attacks on Estonia.

Actors Posing Threats in Cyberspace

Nation-States

They employ technologically sophisticated methods; have established special governmental cyber structures; may have developed destructive or offensive cyber capabilities, but will exploit those capabilities as responsible international actors within the boundaries of international law.

State-Sponsored Non-State Actors

Alongside the military and intelligence structures in nation-states, a number of quasi-state entities use highly skilled non-state actors for politically motivated cyber operations, either for deniability purposes or due to the lack of skilled in-house personnel.

Organized Crime

Well-resourced global criminal organizations, motivated by economic gain, provide illegal cyber activities as a service, using loopholes in national legal frameworks.

Other Criminal Groups

Due to lax cybersecurity in many organizations, cybercrime remains a lucrative business for many criminal groups operating on a local or regional level. They are not well organized, and their targets tend to be in countries that are linguistically similar to those of the aggressors.

Hacktivist Groups

These groups of hackers engage in cyber protests or similar activities, usually for a cause, rather than economic gain. They can use sophisticated methods but have no hierarchical command chain and can act unpredictably.

Individual Hacktivists

Activists who are not frequent hackers can be rallied by fellow activists or political groups to fight for a cause or political goal. They use less sophisticated methods.

When consumers are affected by cyber incidents, they seek help from private companies – usually, Internet providers or IT firms. But when the victim is a government agency or an entire country, most firms lack the capacity to respond to such crises. So it is crucial for governments to understand the level of cyber sophistication of state and state-sponsored actors, as well as that of organized crime and motivated groups of criminal hackers, which are known as high-end actors. Cyber diplomats can be useful in creating and improving that expertise, tracking those actors' behavior and monitoring what other states may be doing in response. They can also identify and engage outside experts with superior skills in the field. Many countries have invested in building cyber structures in their armed forces, such as U.S. Cyber Command, one of 11 combatant commands under the Department of Defense. Its mission is to "direct, synchronize and coordinate cyberspace planning and operations . . . in collaboration with domestic and international partners."[15] While some governments have been fairly transparent about such actions, others have chosen to be opaque.

Duties of cyber diplomats

Addressing threats in cyberspace is largely viewed as the purview of law-enforcement and defense authorities, and the field of cyber diplomacy is less developed and known than cyber military commands or high-tech police operations. More than 20 states have nascent cyber diplomacy units in their ministries of foreign affairs. The United States led the way in 2012, during the Obama administration, by establishing a small office at the State Department headed by a special coordinator on cyber issues, a senior position reporting to the secretary of state. By 2022, the office had grown into the Bureau of Cyberspace and Digital Policy, with an ambassador-at-large at the helm.[16] In the mid-2010s, Britain, France and Germany created cyber diplomacy offices, followed by others.

Even as more and more governments realize the high importance of having at least one full-time diplomat dedicated to cyber issues, many lack the expertise and resources to establish such positions. Such expertise must include in-depth understanding of international security, cyber threats, new technologies, Internet governance, capacity-building and Internet freedom. Knowledge of defense and intelligence structures and operations helps as well. Direct access to the Foreign Ministry leadership is essential to make sure that cyber matters are taken seriously, given the priority they deserve and addressed in a timely manner. The ability to communicate quickly with diplomatic missions abroad is critical as well. International cooperation and activities related to state behavior in cyberspace must become part of the mainstream foreign policy agenda – both at headquarters and overseas – if a country wants to exert meaningful diplomatic influence on a global scale. Senior officials across the ministry should be educated about how cyber matters affect their respective portfolios.

The duties of cyber diplomats are still being defined and refined, but at this stage they are focused on international security, state behavior, prevention, and establishing and enforcing rules of the road in cyberspace.

Conflict prevention in cyberspace

Joseph Nye, the Harvard political scientist who coined the term "soft power," has described governance of the cyber domain as a "regime complex of managing cyber activities."[17] In that complex, the role of cyber diplomats is to use the diplomacy toolbox to prevent and diffuse inter-state conflicts in the domain. Cybersecurity has become a key part of international security and global stability, and diplomatic skill and strategy remain indispensable in conflict prevention, no matter how advanced a country's technological capabilities may be. In their work, diplomats utilize existing bilateral and multilateral relationships to raise issues, monitor behavior and seek solutions to existing and potential problems. They also build new ties specifically to address cyber matters and participate in various permanent and ad hoc international forums, such as working groups, cooperation frameworks and events hosted by governments, private business, academia and NGOs. This means that cyber diplomats are frequent globe-trotters.

Because of the inherent dual-use nature of ICT systems, meaning that they can be used for both peaceful and offensive purposes, building an arms-control regime in cyberspace is next to impossible. Such an approach works only when one can verify that the signatories to a treaty adhere to their legal obligations, as in the case of nuclear, biological and chemical weapons. That is not an option when it is difficult even to define what a cyber weapon is, so the only realistic approach is to rely on regulating state behavior. In other words, just like with climate accords, one has to trust that governments will fulfill their commitments and behave responsibly by observing the rules of the road in cyberspace, which represent a normative framework for cyber stability.

Agreeing rules of the road

Those rules and commitments were codified in four reports by the U.N. Group of Governmental Experts (GGE), under the U.N. Disarmament Committee. Three reports on "Developments in the Field of Information and Telecommunications in the Context of International Security" were published in 2010, 2013 and 2015, and "Advancing Responsible State Behaviour in Cyberspace in the Context of International Security" in 2021.[18] In these documents, which were endorsed by the U.N. General Assembly (UNGA), all 193 member-states of the United Nations committed to follow the principles of existing international law, norms of responsible state behavior and confidence-building measures (CBMs) in cyberspace. Members also pledged to bolster efforts to build and strengthen cyber capabilities – some still lack the capacity to detect and mitigate cyber threats.

The 2015 GGE report outlined 11 "nonbinding norms, rules or principles of responsible behavior of states aimed at promoting an open, secure, stable, accessible and peaceful ICT environment." They included respect for "the promotion, protection and enjoyment of human rights on the Internet," as well as "the right to privacy in the digital age to guarantee full respect for human rights, including the right to freedom of expression." The document also described principles for protecting critical infrastructure and supply-chain integrity. "States should not knowingly allow their territory to be used for internationally wrongful acts using ICTs," it said. "States should consider how best to cooperate to exchange information, assist each other, prosecute terrorist and criminal use of ICTs and implement other cooperative measures to address such threats."[19] The 2021 report clarified that international humanitarian law applies in cyberspace.[20]

In 2018, the UNGA established a three-year Open-Ended Working Group on ICT issues in the context of international security, in which all of its member-states were eligible to participate. As a more inclusive body than the GGE, it became a useful forum for raising awareness of the importance of responsible state behavior and CBMs in cyberspace, and for sharing information and best practices among countries.[21] Its success led to the creation of another, similar group in 2021.[22]

Enforcing the rules of the road

Given that a traditional arms-control treaty would not work in regulating state behavior in cyberspace, how are the above measures enforced? Although most states follow these norms, some flout them flagrantly, as we saw earlier, attacking both critical public infrastructure and private companies – even if they never admit to doing so. A much-publicized cyberattack on Sony Pictures, the Hollywood studio, in 2014 was attributed to North Korea, in apparent revenge for a feature film mocking the communist country's leader, Kim Jong-un.[23] The following year, the United States accused China of being behind a massive data breach targeting the Office of Personnel Management in Washington.[24] What response do such activities, which stay below the threshold of armed conflict but seriously affect national security and economic interests, warrant? In short, finding proportionate and effective responses remains a major challenge.

The United States, the EU and other like-minded countries have been searching for the right tools for years, both separately and together. In 2017, the EU said that its "diplomatic response to malicious cyber activities" would be "proportionate to the scope, scale, duration, intensity, complexity, sophistication and impact" of the attacks.[25] In its 2023 National Cybersecurity Strategy, the White House vowed to "make malicious cyber actors incapable of threatening the national security or public safety of the United States."[26] In the past decade, both the United States and the EU have sanctioned Russian, Chinese and North Korean entities and individuals, but the number of cyberattacks has not decreased. It falls to diplomats and law-enforcement officials to actively monitor and anticipate trends and activities in cyberspace, and to design and execute responses on a case-by-case basis.

Promoting Internet freedom

Not all governments around the world appreciate – or even tolerate – the free flow of information, and cyber diplomats can play a key role in promoting the right to freedom of expression online. They can do so in their private interactions with foreign officials or in public speeches and other engagements. Although they should avoid self-indulgent confrontation with the host-government, as in all of diplomacy, they must find the right balance between respecting the receiving state's laws and traditions and advocating for free speech.

Freedom House, a U.S. watchdog NGO that publishes annual reports on the state of Internet freedom, warned of an "authoritarian overhaul of the Internet" in 2022. "Global Internet freedom declined for the 12th consecutive year. The sharpest downgrades were documented in Russia, Myanmar, Sudan and Libya," it said. "Governments are breaking apart the global Internet to create more controllable online spaces. A record number of national governments blocked websites with nonviolent political, social or religious content, undermining the rights to free expression and access to information. A majority of these blocks targeted sources located outside the country. New national laws posed an additional threat to the free flow of information by centralizing technical infrastructure and applying flawed regulations to social media platforms and user data."

Freedom House named China as having "the world's worst environment for Internet freedom" for the eighth year in a row. "The government continued to tighten its control over the country's booming technology sector, including through new rules that require platforms to use their algorithmic systems to promote Chinese Communist Party ideology," the 2022 report said. At the same time, "a record 26 countries experienced Internet freedom improvements," it noted. "Civil society organizations in many countries have driven collaborative efforts to improve legislation, develop media resilience and ensure accountability among technology companies. Successful collective actions against Internet shutdowns offered a model for further progress on other problems like commercial spyware."[27]

Strengthening cooperation mechanisms

When the massive 2007 attacks against Estonia took place, there were no formal international cooperation mechanisms on cyber issues. The following year, NATO became the first organization to create a cyber policy, and it updated its Strategic Concept in 2009 to include a focus on cyberspace. The alliance was also the first to establish a cyber defense covering all IT services in its entire command structure at its Brussels headquarters and in other countries. Its decision in 2016 to declare cyberspace a domain of NATO operations was an important milestone, which accelerated the introduction of cyber elements into defense planning and military operations. It also facilitated the creation of dedicated cyber forces in member-states' national military structures.

In 2008, the Estonian government hosted the first regional cybersecurity discussion at the Organization for Security and Cooperation in Europe (OSCE), bringing

ATTACK TARGETS   LIVE ATTACKS

Figure 14.2 Exercises on cyberwarfare and cybersecurity took place during NATO's Coalition Warrior Interoperability Exercise in 2017 in Poland.
Photo by Jaap Arriens/NurPhoto via Getty Images.

together diplomats, military officers, heads of national cyber agencies and academic experts – a prelude to the OSCE Intergovernmental Working Group, which was formed in 2009 to lower tensions and foster collaboration in cyberspace. Its CBMs include early warning and information-sharing mechanisms.[28] They served as a template for regional organizations in other parts of the world, such as the Association of Southeast Asian Nations (ASEAN) and the Organization of American States (OAS). In 2001, the Council of Europe, which was founded in 1949 to uphold human rights, democracy and the rule of law on the continent, adopted the Budapest Convention on Cybercrime. It provides comprehensive guidelines for investigating and prosecuting crimes, as well as a 24-hour law-enforcement network to facilitate information-sharing and operational collaboration among its members.

As a supranational organization, the EU began developing cyber policies later than NATO and the OSCE, but it now has the most extensive cooperation mechanism in cybersecurity at the regional level. Despite the late start, the bloc has built up an impressive volume of cyber regulations since the adoption of its first cybersecurity strategy in 2013. The majority of its policies and legislative initiatives aim to increase overall cyber resilience and strengthen the union's cyber ecosystem by enhancing cooperation, improving technological capabilities and creating a higher level of cyber preparedness. That has led the 27 members to streamline investigations and harmonize penalties in fighting cybercrime. The EU established two entities to address cyber threats: the European Cybercrime Center, which is colocated with Europol, the bloc's law-enforcement arm, and the European Union Agency for Cybersecurity, which is dedicated to technical issues. As an economic powerhouse, the EU has set high cyber standards for key economic sectors and public administrations across its territory.[29]

The OAS has punched above its weight in cyber diplomacy for more than a decade, holding workshops and exercises and promoting peer learning. Its programs have significantly benefited many Latin American countries, and its work has won much praise globally.[30] In Southeast Asia, ASEAN introduced voluntary cyber norms and opened a Cybersecurity Center in Singapore in 2018.[31] The African Union Convention on Cyber Security and Personal Data Protection provides a framework for cooperation and capacity development.[32]

Cyber capacity-building and coordination

Governments around the world are still building their cyber capabilities across bureaucracies large and small, with multiple agencies involved in cyber policymaking and operations in every country. Cyber diplomats can not only help educate their less experienced colleagues, but ensure that they understand and fully appreciate the need for international cooperation in addressing the challenges of cyberspace. In particular, cyber diplomats should engage with the development and foreign assistance community to make sure that funders and investors dedicate resources to cyber programs and causes. The Global Forum of Cyber Expertise is a key knowledge collector and community builder, striving to become a global clearinghouse on capacity-building.[33] Many development organizations provide cyber assistance, and the World Bank has set up a special cybersecurity multi-donor trust fund.[34]

It is critical that cyber diplomats regularly coordinate various international issues with domestic agencies and follow their relationships with similar entities in other countries. An effective national cyber ecosystem works as one team to protect and advance the country's interests, with a mix of domestic and international policy tools and operational programs. A whole-of-government approach is essential, as is having an agency in charge of coordinating cyber resilience and overseeing critical information infrastructure protection, such as the U.S. Cybersecurity and Infrastructure Security Agency (CISA), which is part of the Department of Homeland Security (DHS). It is "at the center of the exchange of cyber defense information and defensive operational collaboration among the federal government and state, local, tribal and territorial governments, the private sector and international partners."[35]

In many countries, Computer Emergency Response Teams (CERTs) serve as "cyber fire brigades," preventing, mitigating and helping to recover from cyber incidents 24 hours a day. In law enforcement, most organizations today have cybercrime units, as well as prosecutors and judges dedicated to cyber matters, using the Budapest Convention as a framework for international cooperation. The role of the intelligence community in uncovering sophisticated cyber threats cannot be overstated. Together with military cyber structures, they are the state's eyes and ears in cyberspace. All these stakeholders operate under the authority of different ministries or departments, but more and more governments tend to bring experts from various agencies together under one umbrella to improve coordination and streamline responses to cyber threats.

In 2023, the State Department offered a reward of up to $10 million for information leading to the arrest and conviction of Russian national Mikhail Pavlovich Matveev for transnational organized crime. "We are taking these actions against Matveev for his role in ransomware incidents targeting U.S. law-enforcement, businesses and critical infrastructure around the world," the department said.[36] Such rewards, which have been offered for decades for the capture of criminals in the physical world, are now used to catch cybercriminals. They are usually accompanied by legal indictments by the Department of Justice that require a trove of information to make a persuasive case in a court of law. It takes multiple agencies of the U.S. government to gather that information, and to process and analyze it. In this complex and time-consuming undertaking, cyber diplomacy plays an increasingly important role.

Case Study: Iranian Cyberattacks Against Albania

Camp Ashraf, a small town of Iranian exiles in Iraq with its own university, was the headquarters of the People's Mujahedin of Iran, which is also known as Mojahedin-e Khalq or MEK. An Iranian resistance group, it was designated by the State Department as a foreign terrorist organization for the assassination of U.S. military personnel and civilians in the 1970s. Following the 2003 U.S. occupation of Iraq, the U.S. military disarmed the camp, which had about 3,400 residents. The Iraqi government was under pressure from Iran to close Ashraf for years, but the MEK refused to leave. The Iraqi army attacked the camp more than once, killing several Iranians. In 2012, U.S. diplomats tried to find a new home for the refugees and close Ashraf. David Lindwall, one of the co-authors of Chapter 3, led the effort. The following year, Albania agreed to provide refuge to the MEK, which built another camp there in 2019.

In July 2022, Iranian state cyber actors identifying as "HomeLand Justice" launched a destructive cyberattack against Albanian government websites and online services. An FBI investigation found that the Iranians had acquired initial access to the victim's network about 14 months earlier, thanks to a "ransomware-style file encryptor and disk-wiping malware." The intruders maintained continuous network access for about a year, periodically accessing and exfiltrating email content. Between May and June, the Iranians "conducted lateral movements, network reconnaissance and credential-harvesting from Albanian government networks," CISA said.[37]

In July, they launched ransomware on the networks, leaving an anti-MEK message on desktops. When the Albanians identified and began to respond to

Case Study: (cont.)

the ransomware activity, the cyber actors deployed a version of ZeroCleare destructive malware. On July 18, HomeLand Justice claimed credit for the attack and posted videos of it online five days later. From late July to mid-August, social media accounts associated with HomeLand Justice repeatedly advertised Albanian government information for release. In September, the Iranians launched another wave of cyberattacks against the Albanian government, likely in retaliation for public attribution of the July attacks and the severing of diplomatic ties between Albania and Iran.

The United States, which not only had asked Albania to take in the refugees but had strongly encouraged the government there to digitize many of its services, decided to help the small country to respond to the Iranian attacks. Nathaniel Fick, ambassador-at-large and head of the State Department's Bureau of Cyberspace and Digital Policy, and Linda Thomas-Greenfield, the U.S. permanent representative to the United Nations, flew to the capital Tirana and met with Albania's national cyber coordinator, Igli Tafa. The Americans wanted to "remind the Iranian attackers that Albania is a member of NATO, and this is a problematic path that we don't want to go too far down," Fick said in 2023. They also offered $25 million in immediate cyber assistance to Albania.[38]

"We marshaled a bunch of private sector partners to come in and work with the Albanian government," Fick added. "We got [the affected websites and services] back online, put basic security measures in place and then started the process of long-term capacity building."

In June 2023, the Albanian authorities raided the MEK camp and seized 150 computers suspected of being used for "prohibited political activities," the Associated Press reported. "Albanian Interior Minister Bledi Cuci and the head of the national police, Muhamet Rrumbullaku, said both police officers and Iranian dissidents were injured during the raid." The agreement the Albanian government and the MEK had signed in 2013 prohibited political activity, but MEK members "have proudly told local journalists how they have hacked or penetrated communication systems of the Tehran government and Iranian institutions," the AP said.[39]

Exercise: U.N. Response to Manula Cyberattack

Manula, a small island-state, has been hit by a malicious cyberattack. Many critical services, including the electricity supply, have been disrupted and the entire country has been blacked out, which is affecting other parts of the critical civilian infrastructure, such as water and waste management, banking, telecommunications and healthcare. Some services continue on generators, but not for long. There is no

Exercise: (cont.)

way to tell when power will be restored. The government has suspended all air, rail and sea travel.

Three days later, there is still no power, and riots have broken out. Undersea telecommunications cables appear to have lost functionality, and backup satellite-based commercial telecommunications links are not working properly, either. Manula is in dire condition, and the economic damage is incalculable. No one has claimed responsibility for the attack and there are no ransom demands, but the government blames the neighboring country of Draconia.

Task: You are serving as Manula's ambassador to the United Nations in New York, and your government has asked you what the world body can do to help your country. Draft a memo to the foreign minister outlining options and recommending a course of action.

ADDITIONAL RESOURCES

Richard A. Clarke and Robert K. Knake, *The Fifth Domain* (Penguin Press, 2019).

Thomas Rid, *Active Measures: The Secret History of Disinformation and Political Warfare* (Farrar, Straus and Giroux, 2020).

David E. Sanger, *The Perfect Weapon: War, Sabotage and Fear in the Cyber Age* (Crown, 2018).

15 Diplomatic Negotiation

THOMAS R. PICKERING AND NICHOLAS KRALEV

War was all but certain. After Iraq ignored 11 U.N. Security Council (UNSC) resolutions demanding its pullout from Kuwait, which it had invaded nearly four months earlier, the council voted to authorize "all necessary means" – a diplomatic euphemism for the use of force – to expel the Iraqis. As a career diplomat and the U.S. permanent representative to the United Nations at the time, Thomas R. Pickering, one of this chapter's authors, did not take the threat of military action lightly, but all other options had been exhausted. The three years of his ambassadorship, beginning in the spring of 1989, saw the biggest upheaval of the international system in decades as the Cold War came to an end. But the hectic pace of U.N. diplomacy reached a new level after Iraq attacked Kuwait at the beginning of August 1990. Those four months of marathon negotiations of resolutions were perhaps the most intense of Pickering's tenure.

Sitting behind the United States' placard at the horseshoe-shaped table in the UNSC chamber in New York is the honor of a lifetime for a diplomat, and it never gets old. But as the council's rotating president for the month of November, Pickering was happy to turn his seat over to Secretary of State James Baker when the 15-member body met to vote on the 12th and most consequential Iraq resolution on November 29. At the start of the crisis, President George H. W. Bush had made clear that the invasion "will not stand" – with American power at its height, every country understood what that meant.[1] Although Bush was prepared to use force, his preference was diplomacy, and even if war could not be avoided, diplomacy would still be needed to build an anti-Iraq coalition and set the post-conflict peace terms. Baker crisscrossed the world to meet with the foreign ministers of the 14 other UNSC member-states and win their support.[2] In New York, Pickering and his staff worked to make sure that all delegations would vote in favor of the resolution, which invoked Chapter VII of the U.N. Charter, authorizing the council to declare war in a legally binding document.

Resolution 678 offered Iraq one last chance to withdraw from Kuwait unconditionally by January 15, 1991, or face the consequences.[3] It was adopted with 12 votes in favor, two against – by Cuba and Yemen – and an abstention by China. Baker made a point of bringing the Soviet Union onboard, and his close relationship with Foreign Minister Eduard Shevardnadze helped to win Moscow's vote. Baker's effort to secure Yemen's support was not successful, even though he warned that it "would pay a price" and risk $70 million a year in U.S. aid.[4] After his meeting with the Yemeni president, Baker flew to Colombia, which wanted the resolution to include a face-saving gesture to Iraqi President Saddam Hussein, such as the pullout of the U.S. military from the region, if the Iraqi forces were to leave Kuwait. Baker rejected the Colombian proposal, saying that it would reward Iraq's "brutal aggression," but in the end, Colombia voted with the United States.

Even as the 39 countries in the coalition Baker and Bush had assembled prepared for war, the White House remained open to negotiations with Iraq.[5]

U.N. Security Council Resolution 678[6]

Adopted on November 29, 1990

The Security Council,

Recalling and reaffirming its resolutions 660 (1990) of 2 August 1990, 661 (1990) of 6 August 1990, 662 (1990) of 9 August 1990, 664 (1990) of 18 August 1990, 665 (1990) of 25 August 1990, 666 (1990) of 13 September 1990, 667 (1990) of 16 September 1990, 669 (1990) of 24 September 1990, 670 (1990) of 25 September 1990, 674 (1990) of 29 October 1990 and 677 (1990) of 28 November 1990,

Noting that, despite all efforts by the United Nations, Iraq refuses to comply with its obligation to implement resolution 660 (1990) and the above-mentioned subsequent relevant resolutions, in flagrant contempt of the Security Council,

Mindful of its duties and responsibilities under the Charter of the United Nations for the maintenance and preservation of international peace and security,

Determined to secure full compliance with its decisions,

Acting under Chapter VII of the Charter,

1. *Demands* that Iraq comply fully with resolution 660 (1990) and all subsequent relevant resolutions, and decides, while maintaining all its decisions, to allow Iraq one final opportunity, as a pause of goodwill, to do so;
2. *Authorizes* Member States cooperating with the Government of Kuwait, unless Iraq on or before 15 January 1991 fully implements, as set forth in paragraph 1 above, the above-mentioned resolutions, to use all necessary means to uphold and implement resolution 660 (1990) and all subsequent relevant resolutions and to restore international peace and security in the area;
3. *Requests* all States to provide appropriate support for the actions undertaken in pursuance of paragraph 2 above;
4. *Requests* the States concerned to keep the Security Council regularly informed on the progress of actions undertaken pursuant to paragraphs 2 and 3 above;
5. *Decides* to remain seized of the matter.

Adopted at the 2963rd meeting by 12 votes to 2 (Cuba and Yemen), with 1 abstention (China).

Just six days before the January 15 deadline, Hussein dispatched his foreign minister, Tariq Aziz, to meet with Baker in Geneva, but the meeting failed to produce a diplomatic breakthrough, and the war started on January 16. After Kuwait was liberated on February 28, negotiations on yet another UNSC resolution began, and they turned out to be much more complex than those a few months earlier.

Negotiating with other countries, as both a duty and a skill set, accompanies diplomats throughout their careers, as Nicholas Kralev noted in Chapter 1. Just like diplomacy as a whole, diplomatic negotiation – the dealmaking subset of diplomacy – is **a form of application of national power by measures short of war**. However, if the purpose of a negotiation is to reach agreement with the other side, the purpose of diplomacy is to achieve an end state required by a government's overall strategy that advances its interests. Success depends in large part on diplomats' ability to reshape the other side's perceptions and calculations, so that it does in whole or in part what one wants it to do, because it comes to see that doing so is in its own best interest, as Chas Freeman pointed out in Chapter 2.

What makes a negotiation diplomatic?

We participate in various forms of negotiation throughout our lives. Companies negotiate business deals, trade unions and executives negotiate labor contracts, car buyers negotiate with dealers, children negotiate curfew times or vacation destinations with their parents. The goal is to persuade the other side to accommodate one's demands. Many of the fundamentals of these types of negotiation apply to diplomacy as well. Parties participate in them because they believe they have something to gain by bargaining and something to lose in the absence of a negotiated solution. Such absence deprives them of the influence and insights that only face-to-face talks afford. Willingness to negotiate "does not necessarily foreshadow concessions," as Freeman has observed.[7]

What makes diplomatic negotiation different is that it takes place between or among nation-states through their representatives, and the stakes are usually higher than those in a domestic context. In addition, while other types of negotiation tend to be mostly transactional, negotiating in diplomacy cannot be isolated from the overall relationship with the other party. A truly successful diplomatic negotiation is one that not only resolves an immediate problem, but ensures that the state of relations with the other side will serve one's interests in the long run. That does not mean that ties must necessarily be close or friendly, as long as they are civil and respectful, and the countries can work together in the future. Another feature of negotiation that is essential in diplomacy is its ability to build a basis for empathy. On one hand, it helps to convey one's own motivations and interests directly, which can reduce misunderstanding, and on the other hand, it provides insight into the other side's motivations and perceptions.

Diplomatic negotiation should not be viewed as a favor to an adversary, but as an opportunity to gain and exercise leverage, conduct reconnaissance and build or improve personal relationships. It offers the benefit of using and observing body language, as well as a form of communication that facilitates the kind of engagement written messages do not. The failure of a diplomatic negotiation preserves the status quo – or it can result in a protracted impasse, sanctions or other forms of escalating tensions, and even armed conflict. For economic sanctions and other penalties to be effective, the prospect of their removal must be linked to a conducive deal achievable through serious negotiation.

There is a place for negotiation even in wars with a clear winner on the battlefield – more precisely, the terms of the peace that follows a war are determined in a diplomatic negotiation, unless they are subject to diktat by the winning side. The larger the number of countries fighting in the war, the more complicated the negotiation. After the 1991 Gulf War, instead of a peace treaty, it fell to the U.N. Security Council to set the terms of Iraq's capitulation in what was called "the mother of all resolutions." It created a demilitarized zone of 10 km inside Iraq and 5 km inside Kuwait, with a small U.N. "observer unit" to "deter violations of the boundary."[8] The resolution also found Iraq liable "for any direct loss, damage – including environmental damage and the depletion of natural resources – or injury to foreign governments, nationals and corporations as a result of its unlawful invasion and occupation of Kuwait," ordering the establishment of a fund to collect compensation. In addition, for the first time at the end of a war, the council set up an arms-control mechanism through weapons inspections conducted by a special commission.

Although negotiations at the United Nations are multilateral, the average diplomatic career is characterized mainly by bilateral negotiations, as bilateral relations are the largest slice of the diplomatic business. Negotiating with friendly governments is not always easier, even if friends have a higher propensity to avoid bitterness and belligerence for the sake of their long-term relations. As many experienced diplomats like to say, timing in negotiation is as important as location is in real estate. If you have previously built a relationship of trust and good rapport with a foreign interlocutor, you will have a better idea when the time is ripe for a negotiation. You have to make sure that your own government is ready as well, which is usually more challenging than it might seem. Being ready does not only mean being willing – it means that the highest levels of government and the preponderant parts of the bureaucracy with a stake in the negotiation have agreed on what it should achieve.

Dealmaking with an adversary is naturally much more difficult, especially when the adversary is an enemy on the battlefield. At this writing, the war in Ukraine is well into its second year, but peace negotiations are nowhere on the horizon despite calls for such talks from various quarters. For negotiations to begin, both Russia

Figure 15.1 Former Undersecretary of State Thomas R. Pickering and former Secretary of State Madeleine K. Albright testify before the 9/11 Commission in Washington, D.C., in 2004. Photo by Alex Quesada/*Los Angeles Times* via Getty Images.

and Ukraine have to believe that they have more to gain by bargaining than what they think they can accomplish on the battlefield. As of mid-2023, that is not the case. For now at least, each side's objectives far exceed what the other appears ready to concede: for Russia, control of all of Ukraine, and for Ukraine, return of all its territory. The absence of full agreement on the substance, however, should not preclude prior preparations for eventual talks by third parties, such as the United States, the EU or China. Like battle plans, peace plans may not survive first contact with the enemy, but the groundwork laid in advance will inform decision-making and improve the odds of a favorable outcome.[9]

Major categories of diplomatic negotiations

No matter the type of negotiation, in a diplomatic context, you will almost never get everything you want. At least some level of compromise is inevitable in diplomacy, however masterful a negotiator one may be. All skill sets outlined in Chapter 3 and discussed throughout the book are essential for success in diplomatic negotiation, including empathy, language ability, intellectual curiosity, communication, judgment, advocacy and interpersonal skills. As a career diplomat, the biggest challenge you will most likely face on a regular basis is the necessity to get ready for a negotiation in a hurry, especially if your knowledge of the subject is limited or barely existent. You will rarely have much time to prepare, which Pickering experienced very early on in his career, when he was assigned to the U.S. delegation to arms-control talks in Geneva in the 1960s and quickly had to learn a lot about the testing of nuclear weapons, how to detect it, and how inspections worked. One of his duties was to write a speech for the head of the delegation almost every day.

Routine and informal negotiations

In a Foreign Service career, negotiations take place at almost every turn. You do not have to be sitting at a table with official delegations, reading scripted talking points or making formal announcements. A routine activity like delivering a démarche frequently becomes a negotiation – as soon as your interlocutor responds to the request or demand you have been instructed to make, the bargaining begins. You may have to negotiate at a cocktail party to secure consular access to a jailed fellow citizen, or make a deal as you await the arrival of a key home-country lawmaker at the airport to ensure that the guest will not be harassed by the host-government's intelligence services. Such informal meetings can sometimes lead to the greatest progress. Officers in every section of an embassy or consulate have negotiating responsibilities.

Political work is most often associated with negotiations, because the majority of them tend to be political. But economic officers are consistently called on to negotiate as well – both on policy issues, such as supply chains or intellectual property rights, and to help home-country businesses benefit from investment opportunities in the host-country, as noted in Chapter 7. The management section is perhaps the last place an outsider to diplomacy would consider to be steeped in negotiations. In reality, the effective and secure operations of a diplomatic mission require constant negotiations with local authorities, whether it has to do with a building's safety, a diplomatic compound's renovation or the shipment of incoming officers' personal effects. Chapter 9 showed the need for public diplomacy officers to negotiate with non-governmental organizations (NGOs), academic institutions and media organizations, and Chapter 10 depicted the numerous reasons consular officers have to negotiate with various parts of the host-government to assist fellow citizens.

A task you are given that is not meant to be a negotiation may turn into one, and you have to be ready for it. Sometimes certain information you dig up may lead in that direction. When, during his tour in Brussels in the early 2000s, Hans Wechsel started researching the Belgian law that allowed any citizen to sue foreign officials for crimes against humanity anywhere in the world, he had no plans to negotiate with the Belgian government, as recounted in Chapter 3. But when it became clear that U.S. concerns about the risk the law posed to American officials had to be addressed, Washington instructed the embassy to work toward a repeal. Since Wechsel had become an expert on the matter, he found himself participating in negotiations with the prime minister, the federal prosecutor and members of parliament, including the author of the law he was trying to overturn. The negotiations achieved the desired outcome.

If you are serving at headquarters, rather than abroad, you may have to negotiate with foreign embassies in your capital on issues ranging from preparing a state visit to granting diplomatic privileges to same-sex spouses. Although Cameron Munter was not sent to the Embassy of Czechoslovakia in Washington in 1989 to negotiate, but simply to inform his interlocutor that James Baker had agreed to bring their foreign minister in from the cold, Munter decided to bargain, as noted in Chapter 6. As a result, in exchange for the meeting with Baker after 11 years without high-level contacts between the two governments, Munter won permission for a Czechoslovak dissident to visit the United States before the end of the Cold War.

These examples represent official negotiations in the sense that they were conducted by government officials, but they were informal because there was no strict format or predetermined structure – rather, they were carried out quietly as developments necessitated negotiated solutions. Even the talks in Brussels that eventually required a meeting with the prime minister took place mostly in a series of sessions with one Belgian official at a time. In contrast, the next five subsections will focus mostly on high-profile negotiations with a formal structure and official delegations, which tend to attract media attention.

Political and security negotiations

By the 1970s, Black-majority rule in Southern Africa had been a cause and aspiration for millions of people for decades, but it had never been translated into an operational policy. South Africa was ruled by the apartheid regime, and Namibia was its possession. In 1976, Ian Smith, the white prime minister of Rhodesia (today's Zimbabwe), which was still a British colony, proclaimed that he did not "believe in black-majority rule ever. ... Not even in a thousand years."[10] About a decade earlier, Smith had declared "independence," but no other country had recognized it. Barely six months after his bombastic pronouncement, in one of the most stunning reversals in modern political history, Smith accepted the principle of majority rule, to take effect within two years.[11]

The shock that reverberated around the world was the result of complex negotiations in the region led by Henry Kissinger in 1976, his last year as U.S. secretary of state. He persuaded South Africa's apartheid regime to apply decisive pressure on Smith to abandon his policy, even though the white-minority government in Pretoria had little doubt that Smith's acquiescence would accelerate the end of its own rule.[12] Kissinger had three main reasons to undertake his mission: to prevent Washington's Cold War rival, the Soviet Union, and its ally Cuba from dominating the region; to advance democracy by promoting Black-majority rule; and to avert a race war, as a 2018 analysis of his negotiating record pointed out.[13] The talk of a race war was far from hyperbolic. In 1976, the Associated Press reported that "most worrying to whites is the prospect that Soviet arms and Cuban troops in Angola might be used in Rhodesia to back militant Black movements in a conflict that could spill over borders to engulf the entire region."[14]

Instead of the more common approach of direct talks with Smith at the negotiating table, Kissinger chose an indirect strategy away from the table. Understanding that acceptance of majority rule would deprive the white minority of its power and wealth, while rejection would give it at least a chance of retaining its privileges, Kissinger decided to change Smith's circumstances, so agreement would become more attractive and refusal more costly. To orchestrate such incentives and penalties, the secretary conducted a web of negotiations with the leaders of a dozen countries across Africa and in Europe. He did not meet with Smith until he had devised a plan and secured the other countries' support for it – and felt confident that the Rhodesian leader would have no choice but to accept it. Kissinger's strategy, which we will discuss later, paid off. Smith called his agreement to Black-majority rule "my own suicide note."[15]

Such high-profile and dramatic political negotiations conducted on multiple fronts are usually led by a ministerial-level official or a special envoy, as was the case with Richard Holbrooke, whom President Clinton tasked with finding a negotiated solution to the war in Bosnia and Herzegovina in 1995.[16] Their teams are staffed mostly by career diplomats. Pickering worked with Kissinger on his disengagement negotiations between Egypt and Israel after the 1973 Yom Kippur War, which was mentioned in Chapter 11. Foreign Service officers typically play a bigger role in bilateral negotiations that take place mainly in their host-country's capital, such as the talks on the Manas Air Base in Kyrgyzstan, as noted in Chapter 6. In that and many other cases, political and security matters are inextricably linked.

As ambassador to Jordan in the mid-1970s, Pickering was involved in negotiations to conclude a sale of Hawk missile batteries to the Jordanians for their air defense, which Kissinger had promised them. Not surprisingly, Israel, whose peace treaty with Jordan would not be completed until two decades later, opposed the sale and tried to restrict the batteries' capabilities. After the United States signed a contract with Jordan, Pickering was told that an undersecretary of state in Washington had prepared a letter to the U.S. Senate at the behest of the Israelis, saying that the limits Israel sought on the equipment would be imposed. This was a major problem for the Jordanian government. To head it off, Pickering suggested that Amman make clear in the Jordanian press – the letter had leaked in the U.S. media – that it had signed a contract and intended to fulfill its terms fully, and it would not feel bound to do anything that was not in the agreement. It was not the most profound proposal, and not something that ambassadors regularly recommend to their host-governments, but Pickering heard nothing further from Washington.

Economic, financial and trade negotiations

Economic and financial negotiations can be divided into four main categories. The first involves strengthening cooperation or integration between or among states for their mutual benefit, and it often leads to detailed accords in various sectors. The "open skies" agreements, which allow for an unlimited number of commercial flights between the United States and other countries, are examples of such negotiations. Candidates for membership in the EU must undergo lengthy and exhaustive negotiations to meet the bloc's numerous standards and requirements.

The second category aims to resolve disputes over policy issues, such as currency manipulation, data privacy and barriers to foreign investment. It also includes dealing with historical injustices in the form of reparations or restitution. In the 1990s, Stuart Eizenstat, who held senior positions at the U.S. Departments of State, Treasury and Commerce, led highly complex and emotionally charged negotiations with Germany, Switzerland, Austria and France to return billions of dollars to both Jewish and non-Jewish victims of the Nazi regime. Eizenstat's mission exposed deep wounds in the four countries five decades after World War II, but it also helped them to face their roles in enabling or assisting the Nazi crimes, including slave labor, confiscated property and looted art. He succeeded in the face of stiff resistance, and without causing long-term damage to relations with some of the best U.S. allies.[17]

The third category of economic and financial negotiations covers designing and enforcing sanctions, where collaboration among countries is essential. When the United States started its campaign to track down terrorist financing, freeze assets and build an international mechanism for blocking funds from flowing to extremist groups and causes after the 9/11 attacks in 2001, it had to put together a sweeping sanctions regime. That meant a series of tough negotiations to deter both governments and companies from aiding activities that could benefit terrorists, which required U.N. resolutions to be passed and national laws to be changed around the world, as noted in Chapter 7. The fourth category involves assistance by developed countries to states with poorly functioning economies, as was the case in that same chapter in which the United States helped the Dominican Republic to resolve its banking crisis in the early 2000s. This category also includes negotiations with the IMF and the World Bank over loans, economic reforms and other measures. The lender usually has the upper hand in these talks, and the diplomatic skills and experience of the negotiators from the countries in need of help can make a big impact.

There is a difference between trade deals and trade agreements. The former are struck routinely between private companies, or between a government and a company, and include almost every industry. For example, the aircraft maker Boeing, where Pickering was senior vice president for international relations in the early 2000s, regularly signs deals with both airlines and governments. Trade agreements are broad accords that govern trade relations between and among countries. Such negotiations are usually led not by the Ministry of Foreign Affairs, but by a specialized government entity.[18]

Trade agreements can be bilateral or multilateral, and their purpose is to minimize or eliminate trade barriers while protecting a country's interests, such as intellectual property rights. As of this writing, the United States has bilateral free trade accords with 20 countries. The central tension in such negotiations is typically between free trade and protectionism, which is the main reason the World Trade Organization, the primary multilateral trade forum, has not been as successful as its founding member-states hoped. Its so-called Doha Development Round failed after nearly 15 years of negotiations, chiefly because of disagreements between developed countries and those in the Global South over opening up agricultural and industrial markets.[19]

Climate negotiations

On a typically cold December day in 2009 in Copenhagen, President Obama grew utterly frustrated. Yet another multilateral round of climate talks aimed at reducing greenhouse gas emissions appeared all but dead over measures like transparency and monitoring. The main disagreements were again between developed nations and the Global South. Obama wanted to meet with Chinese Premier Wen Jiabao and Indian Prime Minister Manmohan Singh, but he was told they had left the convention center that hosted the negotiations, formally known as Conference of the Parties (COP). Obama also tried to meet with Brazilian President Luiz Inácio Lula da Silva and South African President Jacob Zuma, but they were reluctant without the Chinese and the Indians. Obama was told that the Indian delegation was on its way to the airport.[20]

Suddenly, however, U.S. officials began hearing that all four leaders were meeting together in secret, in an apparent attempt to isolate the United States. Obama and his secretary of state, Hillary Clinton, decided to crash the session. "So off we went, charging up a flight of stairs and encountering surprised Chinese officials, who tried to divert us by sending us in the opposite direction," Clinton wrote after leaving office. "We were undeterred."[21] The "real negotiations," as she called them, led to explicit emission pledges by all major economies, including, for the first time, China, even though the accord charted no clear path toward a treaty with binding commitments. In climate negotiations, victories like the one at COP15 in Copenhagen have been small but critical nonetheless.

Climate negotiations are based on the 1992 United Nations Framework Convention on Climate Change.[22] At COP21 in Paris in 2015, the parties reached the first-ever universal, legally binding global climate agreement. Its goal was to hold "the increase in the global average temperature to well below 2°C above pre-industrial levels" and pursue efforts "to limit the temperature increase to 1.5°C above pre-industrial levels."[23] Since then, however, scientists have stressed the need to limit global warming to 1.5°C by the end of the century.[24]

Many governments have designated climate envoys or negotiators, who are usually backed up by a bureau or department in their Ministry of Foreign Affairs. For example, in Washington, the State Department's Bureau of Oceans and International Environmental and Scientific Affairs, which Pickering headed in the late 1970s and early 1980s as assistant secretary of state, has handled climate negotiations for decades. In 2021, the Biden administration created a special presidential envoy position to lead the process and appointed John Kerry, Obama's second secretary of state, as its first occupant.

Arms-control negotiations

Talks to limit the proliferation of weapons of mass destruction are often viewed as quintessential diplomatic negotiations, featuring formal, structured and sometimes tedious proceedings that can drag on for years, usually in Geneva. The city, a symbol of Swiss neutrality, has hosted the U.N. Conference on Disarmament since the dark days of the Cold War. That forum and its predecessors have produced such major multilateral agreements as the Nuclear Non-Proliferation Treaty (NPT), the Biological Weapons Convention (BWC), the Chemical Weapons Convention (CWC) and the Comprehensive Nuclear Test-Ban Treaty (CTBT).[25]

Attempts at arms control date back to the days following the U.S. use of atomic bombs against Japan at the end of World War II in 1945. Having won the race for nuclear weapons, Washington had little doubt that other countries would acquire them and resolved to control their spread through the United Nations. By the time the NPT was signed in 1968, the Soviet Union, Britain, France and China had built atomic bombs. The NPT negotiations included efforts by non-nuclear states to strictly govern the behavior of the five nuclear-armed countries, which were permanent members of the UNSC. In the end, all signatories agreed to work toward "the cessation of the manufacture of nuclear weapons, the liquidation of all their existing stockpiles, and the elimination from national arsenals of nuclear weapons and the means of their delivery." The P5 committed not to transfer nuclear weapons technology to other countries or assist them in obtaining a weapon. All other states pledged not to receive such technology or assistance.[26] Safeguards were later established to ensure that peaceful nuclear programs undertaken to address legitimate energy needs would not be weaponized.

It is no secret that countries other than the P5 have since developed or acquired nuclear weapons, and others have tried to do so. Even though the global arms-control regime is not perfect, multilateral organizations like the International Atomic Energy Agency have made a significant difference for the better. During the Cold War, bilateral agreements between the United States and the Soviet Union to reduce their nuclear arsenals and limit the number of missiles that could carry warheads helped to ease tensions, especially in the 1980s, as noted in Chapter 4. Those agreements took years of painstaking negotiations. Compliance and verification are key elements of arms control, and an inspection regime is essential for a treaty's success. The 1991 Strategic Arms Reduction Treaty (START) and its 2010 successor, known as New START, reduced and eliminated U.S. and Russian strategic nuclear delivery vehicles and launchers, and took warheads out of deployment. The monitoring and verification provisions included on-site inspections; technical means of verification, such as national satellites and radar; and exchanges of data and telemetry information.[27] In 2023, Russia "suspended" its participation in New START.[28]

Arms-control matters are usually handled by headquarters, rather than by diplomatic missions abroad. In Washington, that responsibility falls to the State Department's Bureau of Arms Control, Verification and Compliance and the Bureau of International Security and Nonproliferation. However, as ambassador to Russia in the 1990s, Pickering was involved in a long negotiation to prevent Moscow from supplying India, which had conducted a nuclear test in 1974, ostensibly for peaceful purposes, with a third-stage maneuvering engine for a satellite vehicle. That would have given the Indians the capacity to build MIRV warheads, a step that would have improved and weaponized their nuclear program. MIRV stands for multiple independently targetable reentry vehicles, which allow a country to deploy multiple warheads on top of individual missiles.[29] The Russians eventually agreed not to transfer the technology in exchange for U.S. consent to the launch of a dozen Russian satellites in cooperation with a U.S. satellite program. Nevertheless, India successfully completed the nuclear weaponization process in 1998,[30] and Pakistan followed suit just 17 days later.[31]

War termination negotiations

In the Russian–Ukrainian war, neither side has a realistic expectation of military victory or unconditional surrender at this writing, and both sides have made clear that they believe it is too soon for diplomacy. But at some point, the time will come for negotiations, and it is essential to be prepared for them. A war can end with capitulation, and with the United Nations or other third parties dictating the peace terms, as was the case with Iraq in 1991. Absent a clear winner on the battlefield, war termination occurs in three phases: prior preparations, pre-negotiations and the negotiations themselves. In each phase, decisions lead to forks in the road, opening some possibilities and closing off others. Political circumstances, leverage and changing military realities all influence preparations.[32]

No process is a template for others, but in general, the first phase involves resolving internal differences of opinion within one's own government, opening communications with other parties, and reviewing their positions and attitudes to determine priorities and strategy. Prior preparations do not require the parties to agree on issues of substance. It is not even necessary that all relevant agencies of a government agree among themselves. Early resolution, or even just understanding, of differences among key players in a bureaucracy, such as the National Security Council (NSC) staff, the State Department, the Department of Defense (DOD) and the intelligence community, is vital for diplomatic readiness. For a third party, informal and confidential contacts with the warring sides and other interested parties can gauge their attitudes toward diplomacy.

The second phase of peacemaking involves laying the groundwork for official negotiations, including by deciding where and when they will take place and who will participate in them. The task of pre-negotiations is to persuade the warring sides that diplomacy can support and even advance their interests by emphasizing that a positive military outcome will be time consuming, expensive and uncertain, and that talks may be a surer path to getting what they want. The goal should be to focus both sides on the punishing realities of further combat and the opportunities of negotiation, and to develop a common understanding of the situation. One practical way to do this is to hold so-called **proximity talks**, which bring both sides to the same city but not the same room, and allow intermediaries to shuttle between them, exchanging information on positions, preparing ideas and working to foster direct contacts. To start, one or more third parties deemed acceptable by both sides could meet individually with their two leaders or their trusted designees, eventually identifying areas of overlap that could form the basis of agreements.

The third phase of war termination involves the direct talks that most people associate with diplomacy. The warring sides' willingness to move from pre-negotiations to direct negotiations depends partly on events on the battlefield and perceptions of who is winning and who is losing, as well as on pressures created by everything from sanctions to shifts in public opinion to morale. Territorial questions are usually the most difficult, and as a result, likely to be resolved last. They are influenced by military realities and other sources of leverage. The safest and fairest way to settle territorial disputes is to ask the people of the contested region what they want. Referendums are not always perfect, but carefully handled by the United Nations, they can be the best approach to facilitating self-determination.

Although the contours of any deal are determined in large part by leverage, reciprocity, negotiating skill and quid pro quos, there are some basic principles that could help facilitate a fair and lasting agreement. Once negotiations commence, they should continue regularly with only short, mutually agreed recesses, until a final agreement is reached. Both sides should be allowed to invite a limited number of states and international organizations to assist in negotiation, verification, monitoring, observation and peacekeeping. The principle that "nothing is agreed until everything is agreed" should apply, unless the parties agree to implement some measures early – for example, a ceasefire to enable humanitarian access. All agreements should be made at the negotiating table, put in writing, signed by the parties, guaranteed by a UNSC resolution and registered under the U.N. Charter.

Preparing for a diplomatic negotiation

Kissinger's 1976 negotiating process on allowing Black-majority rule in Southern Africa is a textbook example of how meticulous preparation and a carefully designed strategy can make all the difference between success and failure. The process began with an extensive analysis of the interests of all stakeholders in Africa, Europe and the United States. "We needed to distill a strategy from the partially overlapping, partially incompatible objectives of the various parties," Kissinger wrote.[33] Those parties included four "frontline states" – countries bordering or close to Rhodesia: Mozambique, Tanzania, Zambia and Botswana – as well as South Africa, Ian Smith's staunchest ally, other African states, Britain and France. The strategy that emerged had seven parts.

First, Kissinger would offer the frontline states the benefit of "a shortcut to majority rule" in Rhodesia "by throwing the weight of American diplomacy behind their goals. They would be spared the destruction attendant on a prolonged struggle and the risk to their domestic stability of establishing large guerrilla units on their soil." In return, those governments would have to "keep foreign forces out of the conflict, assume responsibility for the negotiating positions of the Rhodesian liberation movements and guarantee" white-minority rights once whites were out of power.[34] This was a reference to the role of the four countries, on whose territory guerrillas were organizing, as "the conduit for arms from outside the continent and for foreign advisers or Cuban troops."

Second, Kissinger would work with moderate African leaders in Kenya, Zaire (today's Democratic Republic of the Congo), Senegal, Côte d'Ivoire and other members of the Organization of African Unity, the predecessor to the African Union, "to help shape a consensus" in support of his plan and to "protect the frontline presidents from radical African and international pressures."

Third, securing South Africa's backing would require perhaps the most skillful diplomacy. On one hand, the regime in Pretoria "feared that armed struggle in Rhodesia might turn into the prelude to an assault on South Africa itself," so it had an interest in a peaceful solution. On the other hand, it also had leverage, because "all the frontline states recognized that South African assistance was indispensable to a Rhodesian solution," Kissinger recalled – "without it, the transition would be bloody, the outcome uncertain, and the radicalization of the whole region inevitable." So he would finesse his proposal this way: he would tell the leaders in Pretoria that they "would be given a responsible role in helping shape an Africa of peace, stability and racial justice." South Africa "would be treated as a valuable interlocutor and given a breathing space in dealing with its own problems, provided it helped move Southern Africa toward a new political dispensation." At the same time, Kissinger would make it "very clear that our support of majority rule did not stop at the borders of South Africa."

Fourth, Kissinger would deal with Ian Smith "only after the other parties' commitments had been agreed" and would "ease the transition" to Black-majority rule by treating Smith with respect. Previous efforts to win acceptance for such rule "had failed because they could not generate the balance of rewards and penalties to reconcile the conflicting motivations comprising the cauldron of Southern Africa," Kissinger wrote. For him, the Rhodesian leader was "a problem to be dealt with, rather than an enemy to be overcome."[35]

Fifth, Kissinger would secure support from Britain and propose that it orchestrate a conference that "would be the culmination of the breakthrough" he hoped to achieve, where all relevant parties would negotiate the specific terms of the transition to majority rule in Rhodesia. The tricky part was that those negotiations would also result in the creation of a newly independent successor-state called Zimbabwe – in other words, the British Empire would lose another colony.

Sixth, Kissinger would engage France, the "European country with perhaps the strongest continuing involvement in Africa." French President Valéry Giscard d'Estaing argued that "the task of relating Africa to the West" was too great for the United States alone, Kissinger wrote. Giscard "was prepared to put forward a joint Western program for the economic development" of the region, which would be "designed to rally the moderate states," the program's principal beneficiaries.[36]

Seventh, Kissinger would "make a major effort to build domestic support" for his plan in the United States during an election year in which the sitting president, Gerald Ford, tried to fend off a mounting challenge in the Republican primaries from Ronald Reagan. Although the advances of the American civil rights movement had helped to make Black-majority rule in Southern Africa a liberal cause, many conservatives opposed U.S. efforts to weaken the white-minority regimes in the region. Fortunately for Kissinger, he had in his corner the person who mattered the most, the president. "I cannot judge whether the political impact will be good or bad, but we must do this because it is the right thing to do," Ford wrote of Kissinger's campaign.[37] The secretary was determined to consult extensively with Congress throughout the process and to meet with prominent African-American leaders.

Kissinger's plan was far from a case of "making it up as you go along" – it was a "carefully conceptualized strategy ... implicitly designed to overcome the barriers he had identified in his assessment," as James Sebenius, Nicholas Burns and Robert Mnookin pointed out in their 2018 book *Kissinger the Negotiator*.[38] Rather than limit his focus on the people who would be signing an agreement or their direct agents, Kissinger employed a "wide-angle lens" to include all parties that had the potential to influence a favorable outcome, the authors noted. That allowed him to both "zoom out" to the big picture and "zoom in" on individual players. While Kissinger was the principal driver of his complex negotiation scheme, he had a skilled team of eight diplomats.[39] We will see how the strategy was executed later on.

Know what you want and what you need

Kissinger understood the importance of having a unified U.S. position from which he could negotiate in Africa, which is why he constantly kept Ford abreast of what he was doing – and wanted to do. It may seem obvious that the main requirement in preparation for a diplomatic negotiation is knowing what you want, but it is not heeded properly by governments around the world more often than they care to admit. What exactly does it mean to know what you want in this context? It means that your government has resolved all differences among the relevant agencies and key players on the matter in question and has determined what outcome from the negotiation it will seek. Chapter 4 showed how dysfunctional the interagency process on arms-control negotiations with the Soviet Union was in the Reagan administration in the early 1980s.

Agreeing on a unified position is critical not only to deciding what you want in a negotiation, but what you need – the threshold below which a deal would not be worth it. "It rarely seems to happen that those who go into a negotiation do that," Dennis Ross, a veteran of Middle East negotiations over several Democratic and Republican administrations, told students at the Washington International

Diplomatic Academy (WIDA) in 2022. "Before the negotiations with the Iranians in the Obama administration, we never really had a thorough discussion on what it was we had to be able to have coming out of these discussions," Ross said in reference to talks on Tehran's nuclear program during his time working on Iranian affairs on the NSC staff from 2009 to 2011. As a result, the objective kept shifting.

"We went from focusing on having no uranium enrichment as the outcome to accepting some level of enrichment," he recalled. To prevent Iran from weaponizing its program, the size of its nuclear infrastructure had to shrink, which was the initial U.S. goal. But then the Americans decided that they could live with the existing infrastructure, as long as it could be monitored, so the Iranians could not cheat. "That was an evolution, because we did not enter the negotiations with a very clear sense of what we really had to have," Ross said. "It is true that your idea of what you have to have can change," and "your negotiating partner may change your view of what you can live with."[40] But you have to know what you want (your best realistic outcome, also known as "aspiration") and what you need (your least acceptable outcome or "reserve") going into a negotiation. The latter is also known as a "red line" or "walk-away point."

It is crucial that negotiators possess a deep, thorough and sophisticated understanding of their country's interests. For example, U.S. diplomats about to participate in talks with Japan on the future of the American military bases in the country must understand why the United States has such a large presence there, why it is important to Washington that the arrangement with the Japanese government continue, and how it benefits the American people. On a deeper level, they must also understand the role of the bases in the overall U.S. security strategy and projection of power in the Pacific, as well as existing and potential threats in the region that affect the bases and the troops stationed there. Finally, they have to be aware of the impact the U.S. installations have on the local population and the Japanese public in general, and how it affects their attitudes toward the United States.

Diplomats must also understand how the domestic politics of their own country have shaped its interests, as they pertain to the upcoming negotiations, and how that might influence the negotiating strategy. In May 1976, four days after Kissinger officially outlined his negotiation plans in Southern Africa, Reagan defeated Ford in the Texas Republican primary election, gaining a significant boost. Kissinger's diplomacy was an inflammatory issue during the campaign, and Reagan sided with those conservatives who opposed it. CBS Radio reported that Reagan "accused the secretary of preparing a bloodbath in Rhodesia."[41] Kissinger recalled that "some political experts subsequently claimed that it was our support for majority rule, interpreted as abandonment of the white populations of Southern Africa, that transformed Ford's probable setback into a debacle."[42]

Realizing that his initiative could cost Ford the Republican nomination and end his presidency, Kissinger came up with a "strategy for the benefit of restive conservatives," framed in the context of Cold War great-power rivalry in Africa. "We are trading our diplomatic support" for Black-majority rule for keeping the Soviets and

Cubans out of the region, he wrote at the time, adding that his approach "gives us a platform to prevent future Angolas,"[43] a reference to the Cuban troops there. He stepped up his consultations with Congress and meetings with civil society leaders. In spite of the political risk, Ford continued to back his secretary of state, stressing publicly that Kissinger was carrying out the president's policy. As Ford saw it, Kissinger was trying to "head off a race war."[44]

Know your opponents and build trust in advance

If you treat a diplomatic negotiation as a transaction with someone you barely know, you are not likely to get what you want or need. On the other hand, the more you know about the other side and the better rapport and level of trust you have with them, the more likely you are to succeed. You should try to learn everything you can about your interlocutors – and the decision-makers, if they are not part of the negotiating team. That includes where they come from, what defines and shapes them, what their fears and hopes are, who influences them inside and outside their government, how they see their national interests, how they assess threats and opportunities, and what they want and need from the negotiation.

It is usually a good idea to meet, or otherwise communicate, with your interlocutors in advance; it is even better if you know each other already. There is little more important in building a rapport and trust than being a good listener. Active listening has three principal objectives: to assess what the other side says, to understand what it means, and to derive – with some luck – what they might settle for. Getting your counterpart to talk may not be easy; like you, they do not want to reveal too much, because that may put them at a disadvantage.

Speaking their language, literally and figuratively, as well as understanding their cultural background, will give you a leg up. People tend to use certain phrases and idiomatic expressions in their native tongue to convey feelings, and the ability to pick up hints can be very beneficial. If your command of that language is at a level that allows you to use such phrases effectively yourself, and especially if you get their sense of humor, you may be able to put them at ease and have relaxed conversations. In all this, you should not be pushy or intrusive, because that will arouse suspicion. Instead, just show curiosity by making clear you want to understand where your interlocutor is coming from.

Set realistic expectations

Early in the Clinton administration, King Hussein of Jordan wanted the United States to forgive Jordan's $700 million debt and provide F-16 fighter jets to the Jordanian military. But before any negotiations could start, Dennis Ross made clear to the government in Amman that neither of its requests could be considered unless the king was willing to meet publicly with Israeli Prime Minister Yitzhak Rabin – and ideally, negotiate a peace treaty with Israel. At first, King Hussein was not prepared to make such a commitment and sent Clinton a 10-page memo outlining how Washington could help Jordan, short of giving it everything it wanted, so he did not have to meet with Rabin. The proposals included restructuring the debt to ease its burden without completely writing it off, and other measures.[45]

When the king and the president met on June 22, 1994, Hussein was "blown away" that Clinton discussed each point in the memo in minute technical detail – he did not expect the president of the United States to take the time "to learn about all those things," Ross said. "This was Clinton's way of proving that he was investing himself in these matters." At the end of the meeting, Clinton said he had no objections to the proposals in the memo, but what he preferred was to go back to Hussein's initial requests. "What I really want is to be able to give you F-16s and full debt forgiveness," Ross recalled the president saying. "But you need to meet with Rabin." Anything less would not have the support of the U.S. Congress, whose approval was essential. Convinced that Clinton genuinely cared about Jordan's needs, Hussein promised to think seriously about meeting with the Israeli leader.[46]

"Within a week, he got back to us and said he was ready to do it," Ross added. "Clinton did not just say how much he appreciated Jordan or how important the bilateral relationship was. He demonstrated it by marrying those assurances with a level of detail, which had a profound effect." On July 9, Hussein told the Jordanian parliament that it was time to end the state of war with Israel, and negotiating teams from the two countries met first on their border and later in Jordan. After Hussein and Rabin met at the White House on July 25, the U.S. Congress approved debt relief, followed by further debt reductions when Israel and Jordan signed a peace treaty later in the year. The debt was fully forgiven by 1997. A deal for a squadron of F-16s was reached in 1995.[47]

By being honest and direct with the Jordanian government, the United States set realistic expectations from the very beginning about what was possible to achieve. This does not mean that one has to give away all cards in a negotiation, but that one should not make promises that cannot be kept, which will not help in building trust.

Conducting diplomatic negotiations

Initially, Kissinger's negotiations in Southern Africa unfolded according to plan. Beginning in April 1976, after reaching an understanding with Britain about its role in the process, he visited Kenya, Tanzania, Zambia, Zaire, Liberia and Senegal, and received provisional support for his strategy. Next, he negotiated with South Africa, the key to pressuring Ian Smith to accept Black-majority rule in Rhodesia. Kissinger understood how vital Pretoria's economic and military backing was for Smith. With Mozambique having closed its border to Rhodesia weeks earlier amid worsening relations, transport links to South Africa provided the only access to the outside world. "Incongruously, pariah South Africa, the citadel of apartheid, was emerging as the key to progress toward majority rule," Kissinger recalled.[48]

No U.S. secretary of state had met – let alone negotiated – with a South African leader in more than three decades, and Kissinger knew that a meeting with Prime

Figure 15.2 U.S. Secretary of State Henry Kissinger (right) meets with South African Prime Minister John Vorster in Pretoria in 1976.
Photo by Central Press/Getty Images.

Minister John Vorster would be seen as a significant diplomatic gesture. A visit to South Africa would be an even bigger favor, but Kissinger did not think it was warranted yet. He invited Vorster to meet in Germany, leaving open the possibility of a trip to South Africa later, pending its cooperation. Kissinger constructed his argument to Vorster around three main points. First, agreeing to assist the United States, Britain and the frontline states would ease South Africa's international isolation, which included sanctions and a stain on its reputation. Second, the situation in South Africa was unsustainable, with an economy in steep decline, an increased risk of domestic instability and rising costs of fighting guerrillas in Namibia and underwriting Smith's regime in Rhodesia. Third, majority rule was inevitable, and it was in South Africa's interest to help achieve a peaceful transition, in which it might have some influence – the alternative was the white minority being overrun by Black guerrillas and a "radical tide" that would soon reach South Africa's borders.[49]

Kissinger did not lecture or threaten Vorster but expressed "compassion" for his "agonizing dilemmas" – the prime minister had to face reality. "The opportunity I was offering Vorster was to achieve a certain breathing space, in which his country might solve its problems peacefully, not a means for escaping them," Kissinger wrote. He offered Vorster two carrots. First, the United States would press for certain rights for Rhodesia's white minority under a Black-dominated government. Second, by separating the issue of majority rule in Rhodesia from the prospect of such rule in South Africa, Kissinger was "buying time" for the South Africans, so they could control their own eventual transition. Vorster agreed in principle to support Kissinger's mission. Another negotiator might have been tempted to announce publicly this potentially major shift in South African policy. Not Kissinger. He decided to keep it secret and use it as leverage in further talks with the frontline states to firm up their support for his plan.[50]

That support soon started to erode, with leaders in several countries having second thoughts and others trying to delay the process, hoping that anticipated guerrilla pressure on Rhodesia would weaken the bargaining position of the white minority. The British wavered, too, growing increasingly conflicted about the active role they were supposed to play in the negotiations. They were evasive on major details in the American proposal, including the Black–white balance in a future Rhodesian government, the extent of property and political protections and any compensation for whites.[51] In Washington, more and more Republicans pressured Kissinger to abandon his negotiations. But instead of quitting, he changed his strategy, reversing the sequence of his plan's elements. The initial order – working out a common position with the frontline states, taking it to Vorster, and then imposing it on Smith – was no longer realistic. Now, Kissinger would put together a detailed proposal with the British, "obtain Vorster's support, clear the principles of it with the frontline presidents, convince Smith with Vorster's help, and then bring it back to the frontline presidents for their final approval."[52]

A key detail Kissinger grasped, thanks in part to a steady flow of information he was receiving from various countries throughout his campaign, would make all the difference: he concluded that, if the proposal were seen as coming from South Africa or Rhodesia, the frontline leaders would not accept it. "It was a complicated scenario, depending crucially on our stage-managing it in such a way as to have the final breakthrough emerge as Smith's acceptance of terms proposed by Britain and the United States, to which the frontline states were invited to respond, and not as African concessions to Smith," Kissinger noted.[53]

The negotiation process was back on track. By the end of August, four months after it had begun, a joint U.S.–British working group produced the detailed proposal Kissinger had in mind. During another meeting with Vorster in early September, this time in Pretoria, Vorster firmly committed to pressuring Smith, which the secretary again withheld from the frontline presidents – he used the prospect of Vorster's consent to push them to provide their full support. They were deeply skeptical that Kissinger would be able to persuade Vorster to turn on Smith, but in the end, they said that, if he did, they would back the plan. Of course, they did not know that Vorster had already agreed. He soon delivered an ultimatum to Smith to accept the U.S.–British proposal or lose all South African economic and military support for his regime. Now that Smith's every escape route was closed off, Kissinger was ready to meet with the Rhodesian prime minister.

Show respect and empathy

Kissinger's offer to Smith was straightforward. The United States and Britain would support provisions to protect white-minority property and political rights, and to discuss the prospect of compensation for those forced off their lands. In exchange, Smith would have to participate in all-party negotiations and publicly agree that Black-majority rule would prevail within two years.[54] Kissinger "stressed that his heart was heavy for us," Smith wrote. "If we rejected this offer, there would be understanding and sympathy, never recrimination from him. ... He spoke with obvious sincerity, and there was great emotion in his voice."[55] For his part, Kissinger noted that he "did not relish having to tell my interlocutors that their way of life was coming to an end."[56] Smith decried "South African eagerness to throw us to the wolves in their desperate panic to try to buy time and gain credit for solving the Rhodesian problem. ... We were confronted by the one country in the world that controlled our lifeline, and which had now issued an ultimatum, leaving us no alternative."[57]

Being on the opposite side of an issue or negotiation does not have to result in acrimony or malice. Empathy and respect are much more likely to produce a satisfactory outcome. If you have to negotiate with someone who has a record of lying or not carrying out obligations undertaken in the past, it is very difficult to be empathetic, but showing at least some sign of respect might help your own objectives. Under most circumstances, you can benefit greatly by showing the other side that you understand their interests and motivations, just like Clinton did in his 1994 meeting with King Hussein. Clinton was known for his unique ability to relate to people by sending an "I feel your pain" message. Another part of being empathetic is demonstrating that you appreciate your interlocutor's need to explain any concessions or flexibility you are requesting from them to their own capital – just like you, they have to be able to sell whatever deal you come up with together to their leadership and other domestic constituencies.

As one of the most intense parts of diplomacy, negotiations often hinge on personal relationships. In the 1980s, a breakthrough in U.S.–Soviet arms-control talks did not occur until the second half of the decade, after President Reagan and Soviet leader Mikhail Gorbachev had built as solid a relationship as was possible between the world's largest adversaries at the time. In 1982, during negotiations in Geneva over intermediate-range missiles, U.S. negotiator Paul Nitze, a big believer in developing a personal rapport, took a "walk in the woods" with his Soviet counterpart, Yuliy Kvitinsky, so they could get to know each other better. In such moments away from the negotiating table, they drafted possible concessions on each side for Reagan and then-Soviet leader Leonid Brezhnev to discuss later in the year. Reagan and Brezhnev did not have much of a relationship and the proposals fizzled, but the experience helped to prepare the conditions for Reagan's negotiations with Gorbachev later.[58]

Reagan's successor, George H. W. Bush, already knew Gorbachev fairly well when he became president in 1989, from his time as Reagan's vice president.

Although the United States was at the height of its power after the Berlin Wall fell, while the Soviet leader was struggling to hold his country together, Bush showed Gorbachev a lot of empathy by including him in all major negotiations on Europe's future, such as the reunification of Germany. Bush was willing to change NATO's doctrine and no longer consider the Soviet Union – and later Russia – an enemy, which paved the way for the establishment of the NATO–Russia Permanent Joint Council in 1997. Moscow was even invited to open a diplomatic mission at NATO headquarters in Brussels. Russia closed the mission in 2021.

You do not have to like your opposite number, but you should show respect for their leadership position in their country and the authority that comes with it. That should not be viewed as a favor to the other side, but as creating a path to achieving your goals. You should not lie knowingly, bluff or make promises you cannot deliver, even if that would produce short-term gain, because if the other party can no longer trust you, it will be very difficult to reach agreement. Your word is your bond.

Expect the unexpected

As we saw in Pickering's negotiation on Hawk missile batteries for Jordan in the 1970s, surprises can threaten even a signed agreement. Unlike the military, diplomacy lacks estimative precision, and negotiators should be prepared for unexpected events, moves and revelations before, during and after the talks. When Kissinger encountered a roadblock that presented a risk to his negotiations in Southern Africa – the erosion of support for his plan by Britain and the frontline states – he reversed his strategy, which likely saved the process. A surprise may come not just from an unpredictable or capricious interlocutor, but from a stable and reliable one. It may be a planned or spontaneous move. It may come from one of the negotiating parties or from an outside development unrelated to the talks that affects them nonetheless.

In 1998, Clinton led negotiations at Wye River, Maryland, between Palestinian leader Yasser Arafat and Israeli Prime Minister Benjamin Netanyahu on transferring control of 13 percent of the West Bank from Israel to the Palestinians. After a week of tense talks, the parties seemed to have reached an agreement. Suddenly, Netanyahu refused to close the deal unless Clinton released Jonathan Pollard, an U.S. naval intelligence officer who had been serving a life sentence since 1985 for selling numerous U.S. state secrets to Israel. As Clinton considered Netanyahu's demand, Dennis Ross advised him against tying it to the West Bank agreement. "If you want to release Pollard, do it separately," Ross recalled saying to the president during his WIDA lecture. "He has already served more than 12 years, so there are reasons to do this. But don't tie it to this agreement." Because of Clinton's talent for empathy and Netanyahu's propensity to hear what he wanted to hear, a rushed response risked being "a perfect prescription for misunderstanding," Ross said. "In the end, the deal was held up for about four hours."[59]

In a one-on-one meeting with Clinton, Netanyahu agreed to drop his Pollard demand, though he brought up another issue. He wanted to change "the mix of Palestinian prisoners" Israel would release in three tranches as part of the deal. "The idea was that there would be 750 total prisoners released in the last tranche," and they would be security prisoners, rather than petty criminals. Arafat agreed, but "I had some unease about it – I knew there had to be something more," Ross added. "Sure enough, Netanyahu said that he would release only petty criminals. I went along with it, because we had been up for 48 hours, we were close to Friday sundown, and if we didn't close the deal by the Shabbat, it could unravel." Leaving the language on prisoners ambiguous would become one of the reasons the agreement would not be fully implemented, Ross noted.

He also warned the WIDA students about the value and limitations of deadlines. Generally, "deadlines don't produce agreements," he said. In other words, "you won't get an agreement just because of a deadline." Few negotiators are prepared to take the blame for giving up for the sake of observing a time limit, and many continue talking to see if they can get more from the other side. On the other hand, depending on the type of negotiation, "you may not be able to reach agreement without a deadline," Ross said. "When continuing the negotiation will not result in a better outcome, playing for time may put the whole thing at risk, and it is helpful to impose a deadline." For example, when Richard Holbrooke and Warren Christopher, Clinton's first secretary of state, were negotiating the Dayton Accords in 1995, "they reached a point where" they had the outlines of an agreement that all sides – the leaders of Serbia, Croatia, and Bosnia and Herzegovina – "could live with, but there was hesitancy to close the deal." Concerned that, if the negotiations went on, what they had achieved might unravel, the Americans "created a deadline," Ross said. It was risky, but it worked. The deal ended a war.

Write down everything you agree on

Five days after his talks with Kissinger in 1976, Ian Smith announced in a televised address his acceptance of Black-majority rule within two years, as well as his agreement to participate in negotiations in Geneva. Although there was a written initial U.S.–British proposal, neither the frontline states nor any other party had produced an official document to codify their commitments to Kissinger, or the understandings among them, beyond oral statements. That was supposed to happen at the Geneva conference, for which Kissinger had high hopes. But they were soon dashed.

In the November U.S. election, Jimmy Carter defeated Ford, making Kissinger a lame-duck secretary of state, which diminished Britain's commitment to the Geneva process. Carter's tough stance against apartheid meant that he would not be nearly as accommodating of South Africa as Kissinger and Ford had been, which lessened John Vorster's incentives to maintain pressure on Rhodesia. The Geneva conference failed to produce a regional agreement on a transition to majority rule. That would not happen for another three years. When Margaret Thatcher became British prime minister, she convened successful negotiations in London that largely followed Kissinger's blueprint and ended in December 1979 with a new constitution for an independent Zimbabwe.[60] Although Kissinger's goals were achieved eventually, his inability to translate the results of his negotiations into a formal written multilateral agreement at the end of 1976 stopped the process in its tracks.

Even before signing an official agreement, it is essential in diplomatic negotiation that everything the sides agree on, as small as it may seem, is written down, so they know where they stand and can move on to other issues, rather than rehash what has already been discussed. Every session should end with a summary of what was accomplished in that time, with or without agreement. When Gorbachev visited Washington in May 1990, the United States and the Soviet Union were at odds on whether the process to reunite Germany should lead to the country's membership in NATO. At the time, West Germany was a NATO member, while East Germany belonged to the Warsaw Pact, a Soviet-led military alliance.

Although Moscow's influence had decreased significantly since the fall of the Berlin Wall, President Bush tried to find common ground with Gorbachev wherever possible. During a meeting in the Oval Office, Bush attempted a different approach to the NATO question from the way it had been addressed before, invoking the 1975 Helsinki Final Act, which was signed by all members of the Conference for Security and Cooperation in Europe (CSCE), including the Soviet Union. Under the CSCE principles, all countries had the right to choose their alliances, so Germany should be able to decide whether it should join NATO, the Warsaw Pact or neither, Bush said. Gorbachev nodded in an apparent agreement, according to an account of the exchange by Philip Zelikow and Condoleezza Rice, Bush administration officials who worked on Germany's reunification. As the conversation moved to another matter, Robert Blackwill, senior director for European affairs on the NSC staff, thought that Gorbachev's consent should not be glossed over. He passed a note to Bush suggesting that he get the Soviet leader to say he agreed that Germany should be able to choose its alliance.

"I'm gratified that you and I seem to agree that nations can choose their own alliances," Bush reopened the issue. Gorbachev replied, "So we will put it this way: the United States and the Soviet Union are in favor of Germany deciding herself in which alliance she would like to participate." Bush proposed a different phrasing: "The United States is unequivocally advocating Germany's membership in NATO. However, should Germany prefer to make a different choice, we will respect it." Gorbachev agreed with this formulation. Now everyone understood what Blackwill had meant – Gorbachev had consented to a united Germany in NATO. "Many of his aides could not conceal their distress," Zelikow and Rice wrote in 1995. "There was a palpable feeling – conveyed through expression and body language – among Gorbachev's advisers of almost physically distancing themselves from their leader's words."[61] It was quite a moment, and a turning point. Thanks to Blackwill, it was part of the official record of the meeting.

Another related matter from that time has been the subject of much controversy ever since, particularly since Russia's 2022 invasion of Ukraine. Vladimir Putin has

Figure 15.3 Soviet leader Mikhail Gorbachev discusses Germany's reunification with President George H. W. Bush in the Oval Office in 1990.
Photo by Ron Sachs/CNP/Getty Images.

repeatedly claimed that James Baker had promised his Soviet counterpart, Eduard Shevardnadze, that NATO would not expand to the east. Putin first made this claim at a conference in Munich in 2007 and resurrected it when he annexed Crimea in 2014, in an attempt to portray his aggression as a response to a supposed NATO threat.[62] There is no evidence, however, that such a promise was ever made. Baker and other Bush administration officials have denied it was, and Gorbachev said in a 2014 interview with Russian media that the issue did not even come up at the time.

"The topic of NATO expansion was not discussed at all," said Gorbachev, who died in 2022. "Not a single Eastern European country raised the issue, not even after the Warsaw Pact ceased to exist in 1991. Western leaders didn't bring it up, either. Another issue we brought up was discussed: making sure that NATO's military structures would not advance, and that additional armed forces from the alliance would not be deployed on the territory of then-[East Germany] after German reunification. Baker's statement was made in that context."[63] He referred to a pledge not to station non-German NATO forces in the east, which was honored.

Maintain a lessons-learned mechanism

Governments around the world conduct multiple negotiations at any given time, yet a formal mechanism to take stock of past experiences and learn from successes and failures is a rarity. The State Department does not have such a process as of this writing. The benefits are obvious: best practices offer policymakers and diplomats options that have and have not worked before, inform or remind them of precedents and save them the time of reinventing the wheel – all of which they can reimagine and adapt for their own specific purposes. In fact, a lessons-learned process should be used even during negotiations, especially when a certain approach is not working, to look for alternate permutations and combinations that could turn things around. Today, if a U.S. diplomat leads a negotiation with a particular country or on a given issue that echoes a negotiation from 30 years ago, the only way to learn potentially helpful details of the past effort is to find someone who worked on that team. But as more time passes, fewer and fewer people with such memories will still be around.

It is also useful to analyze both the intended and unintended consequences of past negotiations, which of course could only be guessed at the time. For example, Kissinger's negotiations on Black-majority rule bought the apartheid regime in South Africa some time, as he expected – the white minority ruled there until Nelson Mandela was elected president in 1994. On the other hand, Ian Smith's acquiescence to the historic change brought to power in Zimbabwe the repressive, violent and corrupt regime of Robert Mugabe, which would not have been Kissinger's preferred option. And as noted above, the negotiations on Germany's reunification among the two German states, the United States, Britain, France and the Soviet Union in 1990 had consequences that still reverberate and raise thorny questions more than three decades later.

A lessons-learned mechanism on negotiation should be a key part of any diplomatic doctrine, if and when one is created. Consistent with this volume's purpose, we tried to focus on practical knowledge – from Pickering's own experience of more than half a century, as well as from other illustrative examples – that will help you prepare to negotiate as career diplomats or in other capacities inside and outside government. There are certainly many other resources on this subject, including incisive and useful books, some of which are listed at the end of the chapter. Negotiating skills will serve you well in whatever path you choose.

Case Study: Negotiating "Plan Colombia"

In the 1990s, Bogotá, the capital of Colombia, was one of the most dangerous cities in the world. A violent, decades-long conflict between the government and a Marxist-Leninist guerrilla group, the Revolutionary Armed Forces of Colombia (FARC), had killed tens of thousands of civilians around the country and devastated its economy. The FARC's operations were funded by kidnapping and ransom, illegal mining, extortion, taxation of various forms of economic activity, and the production and distribution of illegal drugs. By the decade's end, Colombia supplied nearly 90 percent of the world's

Case Study: (cont.)

cocaine, most of which ended up in the United States.[64] To say that the situation was unsustainable would be an understatement. Its impact had caused significant regional instability and hurt U.S. political, security and economic interests.

After Pickering became undersecretary of state for political affairs in 1997, the NSC asked him to lead an effort to help Colombia find a way out of its intractable problems. He declined, mainly because he did not consider the Colombian president at the time sufficiently honest or effective, which would have made him a bad partner. But when Andrés Pastrana was elected president in 1998 and President Clinton's national security adviser, Sandy Berger, asked Pickering, he accepted. They agreed that he would lead an interagency committee of all relevant parts of the U.S. government, with authority delegated to him by Berger and the full backing of Secretary of State Madeleine Albright. The committee's objective was to devise a plan and negotiate a joint strategy with the Colombians to end the conflict with the FARC, reassert the government's authority and strengthen democratic institutions, revive the economy and reduce drug production – and to do it in a way that did not result in the United States taking over the entire effort.

During the preparations for the committee's first visit to Bogotá, its members realized that the Colombians were doing a lot of what was necessary, but not in a fully coordinated manner, which left significant holes in the process. Part of the U.S. task was to fill those gaps and help financially. It also quickly became clear that various U.S. government agencies were working separately on Colombia-related matters and competed for funding, but what was needed was a unified effort with new funding from Congress. In the committee's first meeting, the participants were relieved that there was finally a coordinated, whole-of-government approach to the problem. The United States would be prepared to provide monetary assistance, as well as both military and civilian assets to Colombia, including equipment to build up their capacity to fight the FARC insurgency. But it would require a series of major reforms in the Colombian justice system, a reduction in corruption, human rights protections, a retraining of the military and law enforcement to meet higher standards, and substantial cuts to drug production.

The Americans shared their ideas with the Colombians in their first meeting in Bogotá, which Pickering led as the senior U.S. representative. Pastrana and most of his Cabinet were on the other side of the table. Pickering was principally supported by the State Department's Bureau of Western Hemisphere Affairs and the Bureau of International Narcotics and Law Enforcement Affairs, with the active participation of other agencies, including the DOD and the Joint Chiefs of Staff. The White House's drug czar, Barry McCaffrey, took part as well. Based on the discussions, the Colombians moved quickly to

Case Study: (cont.)

develop what became known as "Plan Colombia" – the Americans suggested the name and were committed to helping the Colombians, but it had to be their plan. Once the plan was completed, the two sides began a series of monthly bilateral meetings to flesh out the strategy and discuss implementation.

This was an unusual kind of negotiation, because it did not quite fit into the major categories outlined earlier. The United States did not have a disagreement with Colombia – in fact, they were on the same side of the issue at hand. Still, in a complex international engagement involving almost the entire governments of both countries, all details have to be negotiated. Although there were many overlapping interests, the United States and Colombia were two sovereign states, each with its own political, economic and financial considerations. Complete agreement on every element of such a large endeavor is not realistic, and any misunderstanding had to be cleared up to avoid unfulfilled expectations, and any wrinkles had to be ironed out before they became a problem. For example, for the U.S. reform requirements to be effective, both governments had to be on the same page regarding Colombia's current capacity and potential in a particular area, such as economic development, military readiness and human rights.

The Colombians estimated that "Plan Colombia" would cost about $7.5 billion. Pastrana's government pledged $4 billion and called on the international community to help with the rest. The initial U.S. contribution was $330 million, and an additional $1.3 billion would be provided later.[65] The U.S. assistance included five major components. The first was support for human rights and judicial reform, with specific initiatives to protect NGOs working on human rights; establishing human rights units in the Colombian National Police and the attorney general's office; and training judges, prosecutors and law-enforcement personnel in anti-corruption, anti-money laundering and anti-kidnapping measures. The second component was expansion of anti-drug operations into southern Colombia, with funding for 59 helicopters for the Colombian military, as well as humanitarian assistance for people displaced by the conflict with the FARC and developmental aid. The third element was alternative economic development, to help small farmers who grew coca and opium poppies make the transition to legal economic activity, and to protect fragile lands and watersheds from environmental threats.

Fourth, the U.S. package provided funds for enhanced U.S. and Colombian narcotics interdiction efforts. That included support for the Colombian navy's intelligence infrastructure and upgrading the radar systems in four U.S. Customs Service early-warning interdiction aircraft used to detect and monitor suspected targets from cocaine source zones destined for the United States. Fifth, assistance for the Colombian police included funding for helicopters,

Case Study: (cont.)

agricultural spray aircraft, communications equipment, ammunition, spare parts, training and logistics.

All this required extensive negotiations and ongoing monitoring of implementation. "Plan Colombia" was agreed on and approved by the U.S. Congress in 2000. It outlived the Clinton and Pastrana administrations and Pickering's involvement, lasting about a decade. It achieved almost all of its initial goals: it helped to end the conflict with the FARC, restore the government's authority, rebuild democratic institutions and revitalize the economy. However, its success in reducing drug production, beginning in 2007, was only temporary, and those levels recovered by 2015.[66]

Exercise: Preparing for U.S.–China Negotiations

Relations between the United States and China are at their lowest point in decades, and a diplomatic way forward seems difficult to find. The bilateral relationship affects not only the two countries, but the rest of the world. A conflict between the two would have devastating consequences for global security and prosperity and must be avoided through diplomacy.

The class will be divided into two groups – one representing the Chinese Ministry of Foreign Affairs and the other the U.S. State Department. Each group will draft initial ideas about prior preparations for an eventual series of U.S.–China negotiations on the future of their relationship. Similar talks used to take place as part of the U.S.–China Strategic and Economic Dialogue, which was last convened in 2016.[67] In the current hostile context, there is an increasing need for the two governments to articulate their respective interests on the world stage and visions for the future of the international system. That will show how conflicting those interests and visions are, which can be used as the basis for exploring ways to identify the underlying factors that drive them and hone in on resolving specific problems and disagreements. The current deficit of trust will have to be overcome, and each side will have to learn how to practice empathy for the other. Your job is to suggest how to begin creating the conditions for that to happen.

Draft a proposal outlining your ideas, with the following questions in mind:

- Which agencies of your government should be involved at this initial stage of the process? Would you keep it in the Ministry of Foreign Affairs or the State Department, or expand the circle?
- When would you open informal contacts with the other side and who would initiate them? How informal would they be? Would you use Track II diplomacy?

Exercise: (cont.)

- How much substance would you discuss at this point? What topics would you plan to address and how?
- What third parties would you like to have as partners and why? Would you seek countries that have good relations with both sides?
- What would be the objective of this phase and how would you measure progress? What would you do to avoid failure?

ADDITIONAL RESOURCES

Richard Holbrooke, *To End a War* (Random House, 1998).

Henry Kissinger, *Years of Renewal* (Simon & Schuster, 1999).

Dennis Ross, *The Missing Peace* (Farrar, Straus and Giroux, 2004).

James K. Sebenius, R. Nicholas Burns and Robert H. Mnookin, *Kissinger the Negotiator: Lessons from Dealmaking at the Highest Level* (Harper, 2018).

Brigid Starkey, Mark A. Boyer and Jonathan Wilkenfeld, *International Negotiation in a Complex World*, updated 4th ed. (Rowman & Littlefield, 2016).

Afterword
Diplomacy Is the World's Best Hope
NICHOLAS KRALEV

We often give students at WIDA an assignment to write an essay titled "Diplomacy Is the World's Best Hope." Now it is my turn. The good news for me is that, if you have come this far in the book, you do not need to be persuaded in the value of diplomacy. Many political leaders around the world profess to appreciate diplomacy, too, but few bother to build or strengthen their countries' diplomatic capacities, perhaps hoping that problems will somehow work themselves out. I will never stop repeating that the world needs highly skilled and effective diplomats, and the sooner those in power realize that — and do something about it — the better we all will be. I know of no better recipe to make the world less of a mess.

It took more than two years to complete this book, but the process was invigorating and I am happy with the result. I am profoundly grateful to all contributors for their time, insights and enthusiasm for our mission. Their skill, integrity and decades of public service are inspiring and deserve the highest respect. You have seen their names and I will not list them all again, but I have to single out Ambassador Thomas Pickering, whose name has become synonymous with the best the U.S. Foreign Service has produced in its century-long history. It was an honor to co-author the last chapter with him. I am also thankful to the hundreds of other Foreign Service officers I have met over the years, and to the four U.S. secretaries of state I covered as a journalist, all of whom taught me something about diplomacy. We lost two of those former secretaries, Madeleine Albright and Colin Powell, while I was working on the book, and I thought of them often. The memories I have from my travels with them, as well as from our conversations after they left office, are never far from my mind.

As textbooks go, this one is rather unusual: I tried to make it as interesting as it had to be insightful, informative and instructional. If it succeeded, the credit goes to all contributors. If it did not, the failure is mine. I thank Cambridge University Press for understanding and accepting my vision, and for giving me complete freedom to determine the book's approach, structure and content. I am also grateful to Charlie Keohan, my research assistant, who is better prepared for the Foreign Service than most candidates, having been a student at WIDA and then an intern. I hope the book will help other applicants to learn almost as much as he knows about what to expect in a diplomatic career and what diplomatic tradecraft entails. That would make their lives much easier and the quality of their work much higher.

Not intentionally, the book's publication coincides with the 100th anniversary of the U.S. Foreign Service. The decision of American statesmen in the executive and legislative branches in 1924 to create a professional cadre of apolitical public servants who put the country's interests first and protect them abroad has served the United States well. However, the service is in desperate need of major reform — it should not be undertaken simply for the sake of reform, but with the objective of making the organization more flexible, resilient and focused on results. That would require rare vision, creativity and imagination. The needed outcome will not be achieved in one or even two presidential terms, so it will take a president and a secretary of state who are less concerned with their legacy and more with the country's long-term international leadership to begin a lengthy and meaningful overhaul.

The book focused on diplomatic tradecraft as practiced by humans, but the frantic development of artificial intelligence (AI) in recent years makes me wonder how much of that tradecraft can be performed by AI. The State Department has created a data and analytics hub to deliver insights that can be used in policy-making, and it has integrated AI into the Foreign Service selection process, as I mentioned in Chapter 1. Some countries use AI in migration forecasting and management,[1] and others in determining where they should invest government resources abroad.[2] Various levels of automation reduce the amount of time spent performing repetitive tasks, and writing software that predicts words, phrases and sentences is widely deployed in drafting speeches, reports and other documents; some can write entire documents. There is, of course, much more to come. But should diplomats be worried about being replaced by machines?

In a 2022 study, the U.S. companies Google and Deloitte proposed an AI strategy for the State Department with four major elements: automating rules-based work; detecting patterns of data that humans might miss; predicting outcomes, events and metrics; and simulating complex systems to identify possible courses of action. "In most situations, AI augments rather than replaces human decision-making," the study said. "Rather than simply funneling crystal-ball predictions for action, AI reshapes how experts evaluate a problem at hand, stimulating and speeding the delivery of new insights. Combining a machine's ability to make predictions based on millions of inputs with a human's intuition, insight and creativity is among the most virtuous and productive applications of AI."[3]

However, it is one thing to use machines in bureaucratic and analytical processes at headquarters, and quite another in persuading and influencing other governments abroad. I can see how AI could help Foreign Service reporting officers in their research by analyzing troves of texts, images and videos too large for a human to read or watch, which would allow them to uncover hidden patterns, make elusive conclusions and anticipate future trends.[4] But some of the most valuable information diplomats collect by talking to other humans, as noted in Chapter 6. AI can also be employed in consular work. For example, screening of visa applications can be done by a machine, and interviews by chatbots or avatars, but U.S. law would have to be changed for that to happen, because it currently requires that consular officers interview almost all visa applicants, as pointed out in Chapter 10. Several companies have claimed that AI can help to prepare diplomats for negotiations, and even to advise them on how to respond to moves by the other side during negotiations by simulating various scenarios.[5]

Whether governments use AI in negotiations, reporting, analysis, policy recommendations or other aspects of diplomatic tradecraft, machines will need to be fed massive amounts of data and instructions before they can be reliable replacements of human diplomats. Perhaps the contents of this book can provide some fodder. Still, some diplomatic duties and responsibilities, such as those affecting the lives of real people, are too important to be left entirely to AI, and even if parts of those duties are performed by machines, they should be supervised by people.

A more realistic hope than providing input for AI is that the book will inspire many young people from around the world to choose diplomacy as their profession and will give them a realistic idea about what they would be getting themselves into should they make that choice. I also hope that the book will help ministries of foreign affairs in many countries to improve the training they provide to their diplomats. Whether you are an aspiring or working diplomat and want to expand your knowledge and hone your diplomacy skills after reading the book, you might want to consider applying for one or more of the courses we offer at WIDA.

We look forward to meeting you.

Glossary

Aide memoire (also known as non-paper) The least formal type of diplomatic communication that summarizes a diplomatic conversation, serving as an aid to memory.

Ambassador The head of an embassy and personal representative of the sending country's head of state in the receiving country; a senior diplomat holding a position at headquarters that carries the rank of ambassador without being a chief of mission.

Bilateral diplomacy The management of international relations between two nation-states.

Clientitis The acquired tendency to think and act from the point of view of a diplomat's host-country.

Consulate A diplomatic mission located outside a capital city; a constituent post of an embassy that provides limited consular services.

Consulate general A diplomatic mission located outside a capital city; a constituent post of an embassy that provides full consular services.

Cyber diplomacy The activity of deploying international cooperation in cyberspace and using actions in cyberspace to achieve foreign policy goals.

Decision memorandum A document that makes recommendations to a senior official and asks for a decision, usually in one or two pages. Also known as an action memo.

Deputies Committee A U.S. interagency forum convening the deputy heads of the Cabinet departments whose heads are members of the National Security Council.

Diplomacy The profession or activity of managing international relations with measures short of war; a tool for implementing a country's foreign policy by engaging and influencing nation-states, multilateral organizations and other actors on the world stage.

Diplomatic cable An official dispatch or message between headquarters and its diplomatic missions abroad sent via a dedicated computer system.

Diplomatic démarche A request or demand from one government to another, usually delivered orally and in person by an ambassador or another diplomat to the host-country's Ministry of Foreign Affairs.

Diplomatic mission A country's official outpost in another country, including embassies, consulates general, consulates, representative offices, presence posts or permanent missions to international organizations.

Diplomatic negotiation The dealmaking subset of diplomacy; a form of application of national power by measures short of war.

Diplomatic note The most formal type of communication between governments, usually written in the first person.

Diplomatic protocol A system of standards, rules and regulations governing the conduct of international relations.

Diplomatic tradecraft A set of skills, duties and responsibilities required in the daily work of modern diplomacy.

Economic tradecraft A set of duties, responsibilities and skills required of diplomats working in economic affairs.

Embassy A diplomatic mission located in a foreign capital, usually headed by an ambassador.

Expeditionary diplomacy Diplomatic service in conflict zones and other high-risk locations.

Foreign Service A country's diplomatic service.

Foreign Service cone A career track, such as political, economic, consular, management and public diplomacy.

Hard power The ability to coerce, which grows out of a country's military or economic might.

Health diplomacy The activity of deploying international cooperation in the service of public health and using global health efforts to achieve foreign policy goals.

Information memorandum A note, as short as one page, describing an event or issue that senior officials need to understand. Also known as an info memo.

Interagency Policy Committee A U.S. interagency forum convening assistant secretaries or their deputies from the Cabinet departments whose heads are members of the National Security Council.

Multilateral diplomacy The management of international relations among three or more nation-states, within or outside multilateral organizations.

Multilateral diplomatic mission A mission accredited to an international organization similar to an embassy, without a consular section.

National security The provision, protection and defense of the security of a country and its people.

National Security Council The highest U.S. interagency forum that includes the president, vice president and the heads of several Cabinet departments.

Note verbale A less formal note than a diplomatic note written in the third person.

Off the record What you say cannot be used at all.

On background You can be quoted only as a government official, without a name.

On deep background The information you provide can be used but cannot be attributed to you.

On the record You can be quoted and identified by name and title.

Political tradecraft A set of duties, responsibilities and skills required of diplomats who work in political affairs.

Principals Committee A U.S. interagency forum that convenes the heads of the Cabinet departments that are members of the National Security Council.

Proximity talks Indirect talks between two parties through an intermediary or mediator.

Public diplomacy A set of activities that inform, engage and influence international public opinion to support policy objectives or create goodwill for the home-country.

Science diplomacy The activity of deploying international cooperation in the service of science and using science to achieve foreign policy goals.

Soft power The ability to attract and persuade, not to threaten and intimidate; arises from the attractiveness of a country's culture, political ideals and policies.

Statecraft The skillful management of state affairs.

Strategy A plan of action designed to achieve a desired objective through the lowest possible investment of effort, resources and time, and the fewest adverse consequences for oneself.

Acronyms

AFSA American Foreign Service Association

AIDS Acquired Immune Deficiency Syndrome

AIT American Institute in Taiwan

APHIS Animal and Plant Health Inspection Service

ART Antiretroviral Therapy

APEC Asia-Pacific Economic Cooperation

ASEAN Association of Southeast Asian Nations

AU African Union

BBNJ U.N. Intergovernmental Conference on Marine Biodiversity of Areas Beyond National Jurisdiction

BLUF Bottom Line Up Front

CAFTA Central America Free Trade Agreement

CBM Confidence-Building Measure

CBP Customs and Border Protection

CDC Centers for Disease Control and Prevention

CELAC Community of Latin American and Caribbean States

CIA Central Intelligence Agency

CIS Citizenship and Immigration Services

CLO Community Liaison Office

DC Deputies Committee

DCM Deputy Chief of Mission

DEA Drug Enforcement Administration

DGACM Department for General Assembly and Conference Management of the United Nations

DHS Department of Homeland Security

DIA Defense Intelligence Agency

DOD Department of Defense

DOE Department of Energy

DOJ Department of Justice

DS Diplomatic Security

ECOWAS Economic Community of West African States

EOP Executive Office of the President

EPA Environmental Protection Agency

ESTA Electronic System for Travel Authorization

EU European Union

FAA Federal Aviation Administration

FAM State Department's Foreign Affairs Manual

FAO Food and Agriculture Organization

FAS Foreign Agricultural Service

FATF Financial Action Task Force

FBI Federal Bureau of Investigation

FCS Foreign Commercial Service

FDA Food and Drug Administration

FSOA Foreign Service Oral Assessment

FSOT Foreign Service Officer Test

G20 Group of 20

G7 Group of Seven

GATT General Agreement on Tariffs and Trade

GMO Genetically Modified Organism

HHS Department of Health and Human Services

HIV Human Immunodeficiency Virus

IAEA International Atomic Energy Agency

ICAO International Civil Aviation Organization

ICC International Criminal Court

ICE Immigration and Customs Enforcement

ICT Information and Communications Technology

IGO Intergovernmental Organization

IMF International Monetary Fund

INGO International Nongovernmental Organization

IOM International Organization for Migration

IPC Interagency Policy Committee

ITU International Telecommunications Union

IVLP International Visitor Leadership Program

KISS Keep It Short and Simple

MFA Ministry of Foreign Affairs

NASA National Aeronautics and Space Administration

NATO North Atlantic Treaty Organization

NGO Nongovernmental Organization

NIH National Institutes of Health

NOAA National Oceanic and Atmospheric Administration

NSC National Security Council

NSS National Security Staff

OAS Organization of American States

OECD Organization for Economic Cooperation and Development

OIC Organization of Islamic Cooperation

OMB Office of Management and Budget

OSCE Organization for Security and Cooperation in Europe

P5 The five permanent members of the U.N. Security Council

PC Principals Committee

PEPFAR President's Emergency Plan for AIDS Relief

PHS U.S. Public Health Service

PLO Palestine Liberation Organization
PRT Provincial Reconstruction Teams
QEP Qualification Evaluations Panel
RFE Radio Free Europe
SDI Strategic Defense Initiative
SGI Security Governance Initiative
SIV Special Immigrant Visa
STEP Smart Traveler Enrollment Program
U/SYG United Nations Undersecretary-General
UNAMA United Nations Assistance Mission in Afghanistan
UNDP United Nations Development Programme
UNESCO United Nations Educational, Scientific and Cultural Organization
UNGA United Nations General Assembly
UNHCR United Nations High Commissioner for Refugees
UNSC United Nations Security Council
UPU Universal Postal Union
USAID United States Agency for International Development
USDA United States Department of Agriculture
USG United States Government
USIA United States Information Agency
USTR United States Trade Representative
VOA Voice of America
WHO World Health Organization
WIDA Washington International Diplomatic Academy
WTO World Trade Organization
YALI Young African Leaders Initiative

Notes

Foreword

1 Nicholas Kralev, *America's Other Army: The U.S. Foreign Service and 21st-Century Diplomacy*, 2nd ed. (Amazon, 2015), xxi.
2 Nicholas Kralev, "Diplomats Are Made, Not Born," *New York Times*, February 1, 2018, www.nytimes.com/2018/02/01/opinion/diplomats-training-foreign-policy.html.

Chapter 1

1 "Amnesty International Report 1996 – Sierra Leone." www.refworld.org/docid/3ae6aa0528.html.
2 Kevin Sullivan, "Bank Scandal Ruins Dominican Economy," *Washington Post*, September 5, 2004. https://archive.seattletimes.com/archive/?date=20040905&slug=dominican05.
3 Henry Kissinger, *Diplomacy* (Simon & Schuster, 1994), 836.
4 Valerie Hansen, "Old World Order: The Real Origins of International Relations," *Foreign Affairs*, September 6, 2022. www.foreignaffairs.com/reviews/old-world-order-origin-international-relations.
5 Peter H. Sand, "Mesopotamia 2550 B.C.: The Earliest Boundary Water Treaty," *Global Journal of Archaeology & Anthropology*, June 27, 2018. https://juniperpublishers.com/gjaa/pdf/GJAA.MS.ID.555669.pdf.
6 Jovan Kurbalija, "Ancient Greek Diplomacy: Politics, New Tools, and Negotiation," *Diplo*, 2021. www.diplomacy.edu/histories/ancient-greek-diplomacy-politics-new-tools-and-negotiation.
7 Chas W. Freeman and Sally Marks, "Diplomacy," *Britannica*. www.britannica.com/topic/diplomacy.
8 Thomas R. Pickering, "After Two Decades of War, It's Time to Shift Our Focus on Diplomacy," *Responsible Statecraft*, October 13, 2020. https://responsiblestatecraft.org/2020/10/13/after-two-decades-of-war-its-time-to-shift-our-focus-on-diplomacy.
9 "National Security Strategy," Obama Administration, The White House, February 2015. https://obamawhitehouse.archives.gov/sites/default/files/docs/2015_national_security_strategy_2.pdf.
10 Nicholas Kralev, *America's Other Army: The U.S. Foreign Service and 21st-Century Diplomacy*, 2nd ed. (Amazon, 2015), 8.
11 Budget of the United States Government, 2023. www.whitehouse.gov/wp-content/uploads/2022/03/budget_fy2023.pdf.
12 "GTM Fact Sheet," Bureau of Global Talent Management, U.S. Department of State, June 30, 2022. www.state.gov/wp-content/uploads/2022/08/GTM_Factsheet0622.pdf.

13 Zoe Manzanetti, "2021 Active-Duty Military Personnel, Civilians by State," *Governing*, February 1, 2022. www.governing.com/now/2021-military-active-duty-personnel-civilians-by-state.

14 Nicholas Kralev, "Congressional Staff Attitudes Toward the Foreign Service and the Department of State," American Foreign Service Association, June 1, 2013. https://afsa.org/sites/default/files/Portals/0/2013_Congressional_Attitudes.pdf.

15 "In a Politically Polarized Era, Sharp Divides in Both Partisan Coalitions, 6. Views of Foreign Policy," Pew Research Center, December 17, 2019. www.pewresearch.org/politics/2019/12/17/6-views-of-foreign-policy.

16 Michael S. Pollard, Charles P. Ries and Sohaela Amiri, "The Foreign Service and American Public Opinion," Rand Corporation, 2022. www.rand.org/pubs/research_reports/RRA1845-1.html.

17 "Diplomacy," *Merriam Webster Dictionary*. www.merriam-webster.com/dictionary/diplomacy.

18 "Diplomacy," *Cambridge Dictionary*. https://dictionary.cambridge.org/us/dictionary/english/diplomacy.

19 Nicholas Burns, "The Diplomat as Gardener," *Foreign Affairs*, February 19, 2021.

20 Otto von Bismarck, *The Man & the Statesman*, vol. 2 (Cosimo Classics, 2013).

21 Chas W. Freeman, "Diplomacy: A Rusting Tool of American Statecraft," Speech at Brown University, February 7, 2018. https://chasfreeman.net/diplomacy-a-rusting-tool-of-american-statecraft.

22 "The Foreign Ministry's State Secretary Welcomes to Riga the Former Temporary Head of Mission at the Ukrainian Embassy in Moscow," Ministry of Foreign Affairs, Republic of Latvia, March 4, 2022. www.mfa.gov.lv/en/article/foreign-ministrys-state-secretary-welcomes-riga-former-temporary-head-mission-ukrainian-embassy-moscow.

23 Tom Balmforth, "Zelenskiy Decree Rules Out Ukraine Talks With Putin as 'Impossible,'" *Reuters*, October 4, 2022. www.reuters.com/world/europe/zelenskiy-decree-rules-out-ukraine-talks-with-putin-impossible-2022-10-04.

24 Vienna Convention on Diplomatic Relations, April 18, 1961. https://legal.un.org/ilc/texts/instruments/english/conventions/9_1_1961.pdf.

25 "Adding a Family Member to Orders," Global Community Liaison Office, U.S. Department of State, 2023. www.state.gov/global-community-liaison-office/foreign-service-life/adding-a-family-member-to-your-orders.

26 Dustin Jones, "Why a Submarine Deal Has France at Odds With the U.S., U.K. and Australia," *NPR*, September 19, 2021. www.npr.org/2021/09/19/1038746061/submarine-deal-us-uk-australia-france.

27 "The Cabinet," Biden-Harris Administration, The White House, 2023. https://whitehouse.gov/administration/cabinet.

28 Ryan Scoville, "Unqualified Ambassadors," Marquette University Law School Legal Studies Paper No. 19-02, February 19, 2019. https://papers.ssrn.com/sol3/papers.cfm?abstract_id=3333988.

29 *United States of America* v. *Devyani Khobragade*, United States District Court, Southern District of New York, March 25, 2015. www.justice.gov/sites/default/files/usao-sdny/legacy/2015/03/25/Khobragade%2C%20Devyani%20Indictment.pdf.

30 Krishnadev Calamur, "Indian Diplomat at Center of Row with U.S. Indicted, Leaves Country," *NPR*, January 9, 2014. www.npr.org/sections/thetwo-way/2014/01/09/261106904/indian-diplomat-at-center-of-row-with-u-s-leaves-the-country.

31 Vienna Convention on Diplomatic Relations.

32 Bureau of Global Talent Management Fact Sheet.

33 "Main Bodies," United Nations. www.un.org/en/about-us/main-bodies.

34 William J. Burns, *The Back Channel: A Memoir of American Diplomacy and the Case for Its Renewal* (Random House, 2019), 10.

35 Vienna Convention on Diplomatic Relations.

36 Vienna Convention on Consular Relations, April 24, 1963. https://legal.un.org/ilc/texts/instruments/english/conventions/9_2_1963.pdf.

37 Kralev, *America's Other Army*, 163.

38 Ibid., 159.

39 Ibid., 160–61.

40 Ibid., 166.

41 Condoleezza Rice, "Farewell Remarks to Employees," U.S. Department of State, January 16, 2009. https://2001-2009.state.gov/secretary/rm/2009/01/115155.htm.

42 "Young Professionals Programme," United Nations. https://careers.un.org/young-professionals-programme?language=en.

43 "Careers," United Nations. https://careers.un.org.

44 Robert Hutchings and Jeremi Suri, "Developing Diplomats: Comparing Form and Culture Across Diplomatic Services," University of Texas at Austin, May 1, 2017. https://repositories.lib.utexas.edu/bitstream/handle/2152/62371/prp_194-developing_diplomats-2017.pdf.

45 "Foreign Service Officer Selection Process," U.S. Department of State. https://careers.state.gov/career-paths/worldwide-foreign-service/officer/fso-test-information-and-selection-process.

46 Charlie Keohan and Nicholas Kralev, "Want To Be a Diplomat? You Must Make it Past an A.I. 'Gateway,'" Diplomatic Diary, Washington International Diplomatic Academy, August 7, 2022. https://diplomaticacademy.us/2022/08/07/foreign-service-exam.

47 Kralev, *America's Other Army*, 185.

48 Cameron Munter, Email to Nicholas Kralev, May 27, 2023.

Chapter 2

1 Treaty of Paris, 1783. www.archives.gov/milestone-documents/treaty-of-paris.

2 Chester A. Crocker, *High Noon in Southern Africa* (W. W. Norton, 1993).

3 "Statecraft," *Oxford Learner's Dictionaries*. www.oxfordlearnersdictionaries.com/us/definition/english/statecraft?q=statecraft.

4 Nicholas Kralev, *America's Other Army: The U.S. Foreign Service and 21st-Century Diplomacy*, 2nd ed. (Amazon, 2015), 40.

5 "Décret No. 2022-561," Légifrance, April 16, 2022. www.legifrance.gouv.fr/jorf/id/JORFTEXT000045592729.

6 Maïa De La Baume, "Anger Over France's Diplomatic Corps Overhaul as War Rages in Ukraine," *Politico*, April 22, 2022. www.politico.eu/article/france-diplomat-ukraine-war-emmanuel-macron.

7 John Irish, "Macron Seeks to Calm Diplomats Amid Overhaul of Foreign Service," *Reuters*, March 16, 2023. www.reuters.com/world/macron-seeks-calm-diplomats-amid-overhaul-foreign-service-2023-03-16.

8 Juan Cole, "Glaspie Memo Vindicates Her, Shows Saddam's Thinking," *Informed Comment*, January 3, 2011. www.juancole.com/2011/01/glaspie-memo-vindicates-her-shows-saddams-thinking.html.

9 Conor Friedersdorf, "Churchill on Appeasement," *The Atlantic*, August 31, 2010. www .theatlantic.com/daily-dish/archive/2010/08/churchill-on-appeasement/182952.

10 Chas W. Freeman, *The Diplomat's Dictionary*, revised ed. (United States Institute of Peace Press, 1997), 221.

11 Louisiana Purchase Treaty, 1803. www.archives.gov/milestone-documents/louisiana-pur chase-treaty.

12 "Check for the Purchase of Alaska (1868)," National Archives. www.archives.gov/mile stone-documents/check-for-the-purchase-of-alaska.

13 Joseph S. Nye Jr., "Soft Power," *Foreign Policy*, Autumn 1990. www.jstor.org/stable/1148580.

14 "Confucius," ScienceDirect. www.sciencedirect.com/topics/psychology/confucius.

15 Scott Shane and Andrew W. Lehren, "Leaked Cables Offer Raw Look at U.S. Diplomacy," *New York Times*, November 28, 2010. www.nytimes.com/2010/11/29/ world/29cables.html.

16 *União Nacional para a Independência Total de Angola* in Portuguese.

17 Joint Communiqué of the People's Republic of China and the United States of America, Shanghai, February 28, 1972.

18 Susan V. Lawrence, "President Reagan's Six Assurances to Taiwan," Congressional Research Service, October 8, 2020. https://sgp.fas.org/crs/row/IF11665.pdf.

19 22 U.S. Code § 3302, "Implementation of United States Policy With Regard to Taiwan," Cornell Law School Legal Information Institute. www.law.cornell.edu/uscode/text/22/3302.

20 Brian Spegele, Chun Han Wong and Joyu Wang, "As Pelosi Leaves Taiwan, China's Military Looms Larger," *Wall Street Journal*, August 3, 2022. www.wsj.com/articles/as-pelosi-leaves-taiwan-chinas-military-looms-larger-11659531357.

Chapter 3

1 Rome Statute of the International Criminal Court, July 17, 1998. https://legal.un.org/icc/ statute/99_corr/cstatute.htm.

2 "Article 98 Agreements," U.S. Department of State. https://www.state.gov/subjects/ article-98.

3 Nicholas Kralev, *America's Other Army: The U.S. Foreign Service and 21st-Century Diplomacy*, 2nd ed. (Amazon, 2015), 179–80.

4 Ibid., 28.

5 Ibid., 23–24.

6 "Culture," *Merriam-Webster Dictionary*. www.merriam-webster.com/dictionary/culture.

7 "Culture," *Cambridge Dictionary*. https://dictionary.cambridge.org/us/dictionary/english/ culture.

8 Edward T. Hall, *Beyond Culture* (Anchor Books, 1977).

9 Thomas R. Pickering, Lecture at the Washington International Diplomatic Academy, July 16, 2018.

10 Kralev, *America's Other Army*, 3.

11 "Osama bin Laden Killed," Special Series, *NPR*, 2011. www.npr.org/series/135908383/ osama-bin-laden-dead.

12 Mark Mazzetti, "How a Single Spy Helped Turn Pakistan Against the United States," *New York Times Magazine*, April 9, 2013. www.nytimes.com/2013/04/14/magazine/ray mond-davis-pakistan.html.

13 Kralev, *America's Other Army*, 187–88.
14 Ibid., 189.
15 Ibid., 29.
16 Ibid., 82–83.
17 "Belgium: Universal Jurisdiction Law Repealed," Human Rights Watch, August 1, 2003. www.hrw.org/news/2003/08/02/belgium-universal-jurisdiction-law-repealed.
18 Kralev, *America's Other Army*, 83.
19 Ibid., 148.

Chapter 4

1 Bruce Hicks, "Presidential Foreign Policy Prerogative After the Iran-Contra Affair," *Presidential Studies Quarterly*, 1996.
2 National Security Act, 1947. https://dni.gov/index.php/ic-legal-reference-book/national-security-act-of-1947.
3 "The Cabinet," Biden-Harris Administration, The White House, 2023. https://whitehouse.gov/administration/cabinet.
4 John Gans, *White House Warriors* (Liveright, 2019).
5 Daniel Trotta and Steve Holland, "U.S., Cuba Restore Ties After 50 Years," *Reuters*, December 17, 2014. www.reuters.com/article/us-cuba-usa-gross-idUSKBN0JV1H520141217.
6 "Memorandum on Renewing the National Security System," Biden-Harris Administration, The White House, February 4, 2021. https://whitehouse.gov/briefing-room/statements-releases/2021/02/04/memorandum-renewing-the-national-security-council-system.
7 "Organization of the National Security Council System," Obama Administration, The White House, February 13, 2009. https://irp.fas.org/offdocs/ppd/ppd-1.pdf.
8 Jerry Hendrix, "Reducing NSC Staff Places Trump on Right Side of History," *The Hill*, October 11, 2019. https://thehill.com/opinion/national-security/465320-reducing-nsc-staff-places-trump-on-right-side-of.
9 Kathleen J. McInnis, "'Right-Sizing' the National Security Council Staff?" Congressional Research Service, June 30, 2016. https://fas.org/sgp/crs/natsec/IN10521.pdf.
10 Susan Rice, "Reflecting on the National Security Council's Greatest Asset: Its People," Obama Administration, The White House, January 17, 2017. https://obamawhitehouse.archives.gov/blog/2017/01/17/reflecting-nscs-greatest-asset-its-people-0.
11 Alexander Vindman, "Opening Statement Before the House of Representatives," *NPR*, October 28, 2019. www.npr.org/2019/10/28/774256868/read-ukraine-expert-lt-col-alexander-vindmans-opening-statement.
12 Organization of the National Security Council System.
13 Memorandum on Reviewing the National Security Council System.
14 Ibid.
15 "Viktor Yushchenko: Ukraine's Ex-President on Being Poisoned," *BBC News*, April 2, 2018. https://www.bbc.com/news/av/world-europe-43611547.
16 Colin Powell, "Briefing by Secretary of State Colin L. Powell," U.S. Department of State, November 24, 2004. https://2001-2009.state.gov/secretary/former/powell/remarks/38738.htm.
17 "National Security Strategy," Historical Office, Office of the Secretary of Defense. https://history.defense.gov/Historical-Sources/National-Security-Strategy.

18 Donald Trump and Andrzej Duda, "Remarks by President Donald Trump and Polish President Andrzej Duda," Trump Administration, The White House, June 24, 2020. https://trumpwhitehouse.archives.gov/briefings-statements/remarks-president-trump-president-duda-republic-poland-joint-press-conference-3.

19 Brian Porter, "The 1989 Polish Round Table Revisited: Making History," *The Journal of the International Institute*, 1999. https://quod.lib.umich.edu/j/jii/4750978.0006.301?view=text;rgn=main.

20 "Biden Unveils New $375 Million Military Aid Package for Ukraine," *Reuters*, May 21, 2023. www.reuters.com/world/biden-unveils-new-us-military-package-up-375-mln-ukraine-2023-05-21.

21 Dustin Jones, "Why a Submarine Deal Has France at Odds With the U.S., U.K. and Australia," *NPR*, September 19, 2021. www.npr.org/2021/09/19/1038746061/submarine-deal-us-uk-australia-france.

Chapter 5

1 "Former DEA Special Agent Sentenced to Prison for Money Laundering and Fraud Scheme," Office of Public Affairs, U.S. Department of Justice, December 9, 2021. www.justice.gov/opa/pr/former-dea-special-agent-sentenced-prison-money-laundering-and-fraud-scheme.

2 John Feeley and James Nealon, "Diplomats Frustrated by DEA's Dark Side," *Univision News*, November 22, 2022. www.univision.com/univision-news/opinion/oped-foreign-policy-and-the-role-of-dea.

3 "GTM Fact Sheet, Bureau of Global Talent Management, U.S. Department of State, June 30, 2022. www.state.gov/wp-content/uploads/2022/08/GTM_Factsheet0622.pdf.

4 Ibid.

5 "Annual Report and Accounts 2021–22," Foreign, Commonwealth and Development Office, March 31, 2022. https://assets.publishing.service.gov.uk/government/uploads/system/uploads/attachment_data/file/1095304/FCDO_Annual_Report_2021_2022_Accessible_290722.pdf.

6 Robert Hutchings and Jeremi Suri, "Developing Diplomats: Comparing Form and Culture Across Diplomatic Services," Lyndon B. Johnson School of Public Affairs Policy Research Project Report 194, University of Texas, May 2017. https://repositories.lib.utexas.edu/bitstream/handle/2152/62371/prp_194-developing_diplomats-2017.pdf.

7 Hillary Rodham Clinton, "Opening Remarks at the President's Export Council," U.S. Department of State, March 11, 2011. https://2009-2017.state.gov/secretary/20092013clinton/rm/2011/03/158181.htm.

8 Nicholas Kralev, *America's Other Army: The U.S. Foreign Service and 21st-Century Diplomacy*, 2nd ed. (Amazon, 2015), 77.

9 Ibid., 75.

10 "Audit Report of Embassy Islamabad," State Department Inspector General, June 2012. https://english.alarabiya.net/articles/2012%2F06%2F22%2F222083.

11 Kralev, *America's Other Army*, 76.

12 Ibid., 76.

13 Sal Cerrell, "Deputy Chief of Mission: The Toughest Job in an Embassy," Diplomatic Diary, Washington International Diplomatic Academy, July 24, 2022. https://diplomaticacademy.us/2022/07/24/deputy-chief-of-mission.

14 Virginia Blaser, Interview with Nicholas Kralev, November 5, 2021.

15 Ibid.
16 "Services for U.S. Exporters," U.S. Foreign Commercial Service. www.trade.gov/let-our-experts-help-0.
17 "About Us," U.S. Foreign Agricultural Service. www.fas.usda.gov/about-fas.
18 Susan Phillips, "How Agricultural Diplomats Help to Feed Americans, and the World," Diplomatic Diary, Washington International Diplomatic Academy, January 8, 2023. https://diplomaticacademy.us/2023/01/08/agricultural-diplomats.
19 "Foreign Service," Animal and Plant Health Inspection Service. www.aphis.usda.gov/aphis/ourfocus/internationalservices/foreign-service/foreign-service.
20 "How to Work with USAID," U.S. Agency for International Development. www.usaid.gov/partner-with-us/how-to-work-with-usaid.
21 "Why Our Work Matters," U.S. Agency for International Development. https://results.usaid.gov/results.
22 "Honorary Consuls in the U.S.," Embassy of Germany. www.germany.info/us-en/service/12-Honorarkonsuln.
23 "Honorary Consular Officers," U.S. Department of State. www.state.gov/honorary-consular-officers-posts.
24 Kralev, *America's Other Army*, 46.
25 Ibid.
26 "Results and Impact – PEPFAR," U.S. Department of State, September 30, 2022. www.state.gov/results-and-impact-pepfar.
27 Blaser.
28 Feeley and Nealon.
29 Blaser.
30 "Venezuela to Close U.S. Embassy, Consulates," *Reuters*, January 24, 2019. www.reuters.com/article/us-venezuela-politics-maduro/venezuela-to-close-u-s-embassy-consulates-maduro-idUSKCN1PI2V6.
31 Kralev, *America's Other Army*, 186.

Chapter 6

1 "New Compensation Plan for Victims of Russia's 1993 Crisis," *The Moscow Times*, October 4, 2016. www.themoscowtimes.com/2016/10/04/new-compensation-plans-for-victims-of-russias-1993-crisis-a55592.
2 Marie Yovanovitch, *Lessons from the Edge: A Memoir* (Mariner Books, 2022), 89–93.
3 William J. Burns, *The Back Channel: A Memoir of American Diplomacy and the Case for Its Renewal* (Random House, 2019), 10.
4 Nicholas Kralev, *America's Other Army: The U.S. Foreign Service and 21st-Century Diplomacy*, 2nd ed. (Amazon, 2015), 33.
5 Burns, *The Back Channel*, 337–87.
6 Kali Robinson, "What Is the Iran Nuclear Deal?" Council on Foreign Relations, July 20, 2022. www.cfr.org/backgrounder/what-iran-nuclear-deal.
7 Burns, *The Back Channel*, 88.
8 "Gaza Strip," *Britannica*. www.britannica.com/place/Gaza-Strip.
9 Burns, *The Back Channel*, 88.
10 Michael D. Swaine, "Taiwan's Management of Relations with the United States," Carnegie Endowment of International Peace, 2005. https://carnegieendowment.org/

2005/05/05/taiwan-s-management-of-relations-with-united-states-during-first-chen-shui-bian-administration-pub-18670.

11 Burns, *The Back Channel*, 104.

12 "Libya Revolt of 2011," *Britannica*. www.britannica.com/event/Libya-Revolt-of-2011.

13 Email to Nicholas Kralev, April 6, 2023.

14 Yovanovitch, 82.

15 Norman Kempster, "4th State Dept. Officer Quits Over Bosnia," *Los Angeles Times*, August 24, 1993. www.latimes.com/archives/la-xpm-1993-08-24-mn-27481-story.html.

16 Adam Tanner, "Anti-Iraq War U.S. Diplomats Poorer but Proud," *Reuters*, March 18, 2008. www.reuters.com/article/us-usa-iraq-diplomats/anti-iraq-war-u-s-diplomats-poorer-but-proud-idUSN1822857420080318.

17 Felicia Schwartz, "State Department Dissent, Believed Largest Ever, Formally Lodged," *Wall Street Journal*, February 1, 2017. www.wsj.com/articles/state-department-dissent-believed-largest-ever-formally-lodged-1485908373.

18 Mark Landler, "State Dept. Officials Should Quit if They Disagree With Trump, White House Warns," *New York Times*, January 31, 2017. www.nytimes.com/2017/01/31/us/politics/sean-spicer-state-dept-travel-ban.html.

19 David T. Jones, "Advise and Dissent: The Diplomat as Protester," *Foreign Service Journal*, April 2000. www.afsa.org/sites/default/files/vietnamArchivedContentFromFSJ007.pdf.

20 *Foreign Affairs Manual*, U.S. Department of State. https://fam.state.gov/fam/02fam/02fam0070.html.

21 Douglas Martin, "Terence Todman, an Envoy to 6 Nations, Is Dead at 88," *New York Times*, August 20, 2014. www.nytimes.com/2014/08/21/world/terence-todman-an-envoy-to-6-nations-is-dead-at-88.html.

22 Yovanovitch, 144–51.

23 "U.S. Talks on Kyrgyzstan's Manas Continuing," *Radio Free Europe/Radio Liberty*, January 17, 2013. www.refworld.org/docid/51223577c.html.

24 Abdujalil Abdurasulov, "Kyrgyzstan Happy to Drop Hot Political Potato," *BBC News*, June 19, 2014. www.bbc.com/news/world-asia-27903358.

Chapter 7

1 "USMCA at One," Wilson Center, Washington, D.C., July 14, 2021 (video). www.wilsoncenter.org/video/usmca-one.

2 Parija Kavilanz, "Dreamliner: Where in the World Its Parts Come From," *CNN*, January 18, 2013. https://money.cnn.com/2013/01/18/news/companies/boeing-dreamliner-parts.

3 Robert B. Zoellick, *America in the World: A History of U.S. Diplomacy and Foreign Policy* (Twelve, 2020), 1.

4 U.N. Security Council Resolution 1373, adopted on September 28, 2001. https://documents-dds-ny.un.org/doc/UNDOC/GEN/N01/557/43/PDF/N0155743.pdf.

5 Tony Wayne, "What Is Economic Diplomacy and How Does It Work?" *Foreign Service Journal*, January–February 2019.

6 Inter-American Convention Against Corruption, March 29, 1996. www.oas.org/en/sla/dil/inter_american_treaties_B-58_against_Corruption.asp.

7 Convention on Combating Bribery of Foreign Public Officials in International Business Transactions, December 17, 1997. www.oecd.org/corruption/oecdantibriberyconvention.htm.

8 United Nations Convention Against Corruption, October 31, 2003. www.unodc.org/unodc/en/corruption/uncac.html.

9 Wayne.

10 "Supply Chain Issues and Autos: When Will the Chip Shortage End?" J. P. Morgan Research, August 11, 2022. www.jpmorgan.com/insights/research/supply-chain-chip-shortage.

11 Nicholas Kralev, *America's Other Army: The U.S. Foreign Service and 21st-Century Diplomacy*, 2nd ed. (Amazon, 2015), 88.

12 "Venezuela Situation," U.N. Refugee Agency, August 2023. www.unhcr.org/venezuela-emergency.html.

13 "What We Do," Financial Action Task Force. www.fatf-gafi.org/en/the-fatf/what-we-do.html.

14 Brian McFeeters, "The Asian Financial Crisis: The Ground View From Jakarta," *Foreign Service Journal*, January–February 2019. https://afsa.org/guitars-gold-fruits-economic-diplomacy.

15 Lael Brainard, Speech Before the Women's Foreign Policy Group, Washington, D.C., June 25, 2012. www.wfpg.org/assets/documents/2012-06-25-Brainard-Transcript.pdf.

16 "Country Commercial Guides," Department of Commerce. www.trade.gov/ccg-landing-page.

17 Michael Hoza, "Ebony for Taylor Guitars," *Foreign Service Journal*, January–February 2019.

18 Richard Glenn, Testimony Before Senate Foreign Relations Subcommittee, December 5, 2019. https://2017-2021.state.gov/illicit-mining-threats-to-u-s-national-security-and-international-human-rights/index.html.

19 Kate Kelly and Mark Walker, "Banned From Russian Airspace, U.S. Airlines Look to Restrict Competitors," *New York Times*, March 17, 2023. www.nytimes.com/2023/03/17/us/politics/russia-us-airlines-ukraine.html.

20 American Airlines 292 and Air India 102, Flightaware.com, March 22, 2023.

21 Chas W. Freeman, "Diplomacy as Tactics," Speech at Brown University, April 5, 2018. https://chasfreeman.net/diplomacy-as-tactics.

22 Christiaan Triebert, Blacki Migliozzi, Alexander Cardia, Muyi Xiao and David Botti, "Fake Signals and American Insurance: How a Dark Fleet Moves Russian Oil," *New York Times*, May 30, 2023. www.nytimes.com/interactive/2023/05/30/world/asia/russia-oil-ships-sanctions.html.

23 Thomas Graham, "Putin-Xi Summit Reinforces Anti-U.S. Partnership," Council on Foreign Relations, March 24, 2023. www.cfr.org/in-brief/putin-xi-summit-reinforces-anti-us-partnership.

24 Freeman, "Diplomacy as Tactics."

25 "Markets," Archived Content, USAID, July 3, 2012 (video). https://2017-2020.usaid.gov/news-information/videos/node/5616.

26 "Mission, Vision and Values," USAID. www.usaid.gov/about-us/mission-vision-values.

27 Kralev, *America's Other Army*, 147.

28 Julie Nutter, "Where We Stand," *Foreign Service Journal*, January–February 2020. https://afsa.org/foreign-service-numbers.

29 "How to Work with USAID," USAID. www.usaid.gov/partner-with-us/how-to-work-with-usaid.

30 "Dollars to Results," USAID. https://results.usaid.gov/results.

31 Global Air Media Website. https://globalairmedia.com.

32 "Global Air Media Finds Success in Africa," U.S. Department of Commerce, February 9, 2021 (podcast). www.trade.gov/success-story/global-air-media-finds-success-africa.

33 "U.S. Commercial Service – Virtual Services," U.S. Department of Commerce. www .trade.gov/virtual-services.

34 "Initial Market Check," U.S. Department of Commerce. www.trade.gov/initial-market-check.

35 "International Partner Search," U.S. Department of Commerce. www.trade.gov/international-partner-search.

36 Kralev, *America's Other Army*, 86.

37 "Policy Requirements for U.S. Advocacy," Department of Commerce. www.trade.gov/us-government-advocacy-policy.

38 Kralev, *America's Other Army*, 89–90.

39 Susan Phillips, "How Agricultural Diplomats Help to Feed Americans, and the World," Diplomatic Diary, Washington International Diplomatic Academy, January 8, 2023. https://diplomaticacademy.us/2023/01/08/agricultural-diplomats.

40 "About Us," U.S. Foreign Agricultural Service. www.fas.usda.gov/about-fas.

41 "Foreign Service," Animal and Plant Health Inspection Service. www.aphis.usda.gov/aphis/ourfocus/internationalservices/foreign-service/foreign-service.

42 Kralev, *America's Other Army*, 92–93.

43 Phillips.

44 Kralev, *America's Other Army*, 92.

45 "Bank Bosses Jailed for Crippling Dominican Economy," *Irish Examiner*, October 22, 2007. www.irishexaminer.com/business/arid-30333098.html.

46 "U.S.–CAFTA–DR Free Trade Agreement," International Trade Administration. www .trade.gov/us-cafta-dr-free-trade-agreement.

47 "CAFTA–DR," Office of the U.S. Trade Representative. https://ustr.gov/trade-agreements/free-trade-agreements/cafta-dr-dominican-republic-central-america-fta.

48 Thomas Kaplan, Ian Austen and Selam Gebrekidan, "Boeing Planes Are Grounded in U.S. After Days of Pressure," *New York Times*, March 13, 2019. www.nytimes.com/2019/03/13/business/canada-737-max.html.

49 Rory Kennedy, dir., "Downfall: The Case Against Boeing" (Netflix, 2022).

Chapter 8

1 Scott Shane and Andrew W. Lehren, "Leaked Cables Offer Raw Look at U.S. Diplomacy," *New York Times*, November 28, 2010. www.nytimes.com/2010/11/29/world/29cables.html.

2 Robert Gibbs, "Statement by the Press Secretary," Obama Administration, The White House, November 28, 2010. https://obamawhitehouse.archives.gov/the-press-office/2010/11/28/statement-press-secretary.

3 Nicholas Kralev, *America's Other Army: The U.S. Foreign Service and 21st-Century Diplomacy*, 2nd ed. (Amazon, 2015), 68.

4 "Amarna Letters," *Britannica*. www.britannica.com/topic/Amarna-Letters.

5 Nancy Gordon Heinl, "America's First Black Diplomat," *Foreign Service Journal*, August 1973. www.afsa.org/sites/default/files/fsj-1973-08-august_0.pdf.

6 David Langbart, "Foreign Service Friday! The Telegram," National Archives, March 18, 2011. https://text-message.blogs.archives.gov/2011/03/18/foreign-service-friday-the-telegram.

7 David Langbart, "Foreign Service Friday! The Airgram," National Archives, March 25, 2011. https://text-message.blogs.archives.gov/2011/03/25/foreign-service-friday-the-airgram.

8 George Kennan, "Long Telegram," George Washington University Archives, February 22, 1946. https://nsarchive2.gwu.edu/coldwar/documents/episode-1/kennan.htm.

9 A collection of documents Burns wrote or co-wrote as a Foreign Service officer was declassified in 2017 for use in his memoir, *The Back Channel*. https://carnegieendowment.org/publications/interactive/back-channel.

10 William J. Burns, "Note for the Secretary From Bill Burns," U.S. Department of State, April 11, 2008. https://carnegieendowment.org/pdf/back-channel/2006EmailtoRice.pdf.

11 "Santiago 2850," U.S. Department of State, 1973. https://nsarchive2.gwu.edu/NSAEBB/NSAEBB188/AAD-1.pdf.

12 "Intelligence Report on Planned Coup," National Security Archive, September 8, 1973. https://nsarchive.gwu.edu/document/22020-document-04.

13 "Salvador Allende," *Britannica*. www.britannica.com/biography/Salvador-Allende.

14 "Prats González, Carlos (1915–1974)," *Encyclopedia.com*. www.encyclopedia.com/humanities/encyclopedias-almanacs-transcripts-and-maps/prats-gonzalez-carlos-1915-1974.

15 "Augusto Pinochet," *Britannica*. www.britannica.com/biography/Augusto-Pinochet.

16 "Cairo 07271," U.S. Department of State, 1979. http://diplomaticacademy.us/wp-content/uploads/2022/01/Cairo1979.pdf.

17 "Central Foreign Policy File (CEPF), 1973–1979," National Archives. www.archives.gov/research/foreign-policy/state-dept/rg-59-central-files/1973-1979.

18 "Shahpur Bakhtiar," *Britannica*. www.britannica.com/biography/Shahpur-Bakhtiar.

19 "Tehran 01375," U.S. Department of State, 1979. http://diplomaticacademy.us/wp-content/uploads/2022/01/Tehran1979.pdf.

20 Malcome Byrne, "CIA Confirms Role in 1953 Iran Coup," National Security Archive, August 19, 2013. https://nsarchive2.gwu.edu/NSAEBB/NSAEBB435.

21 "The Iranian Hostage Crisis," Office of the Historian, Foreign Service Institute, U.S. Department of State. https://history.state.gov/departmenthistory/short-history/iraniancrises.

22 "Moscow 27483," U.S. Department of State, 1994. https://carnegieendowment.org/pdf/back-channel/1994Moscow27483.pdf.

23 "Amman 01658," U.S. Department of State, 2001. https://carnegieendowment.org/pdf/back-channel/2001Amman1658.pdf.

24 William J. Burns, *The Back Channel: A Memoir of American Diplomacy and the Case for Its Renewal* (Random House, 2019), 143.

25 "Amman 06760," U.S. Department of State, 2000. https://carnegieendowment.org/pdf/back-channel/2000Amman6760.pdf.

26 "The Clinton Parameters," Bicom. www.bicom.org.uk/timeline/the-clinton-parameters.

27 "Paris 13729," U.S. Department of State, 2001. http://diplomaticacademy.us/wp-content/uploads/2022/01/Paris1974.pdf.

28 "Diplomatic Communications," Harvard University. https://projects.iq.harvard.edu/files/hks-communications-program/files/pp_sri_kulkarni_and_yotam_goren_4_10_17.pdf.

29 "5 FAH-1 H-600, Diplomatic Notes," U.S. Department of State, February 2, 2023. https://fam.state.gov/fam/05fah01/05fah010610.html.

30 Hirofumi Nakasone, "Letter to Ambassador John Thomas Schieffer," Ministry of Foreign Affairs of Japan, November 18, 2008. https://2009-2017.state.gov/documents/organization/121124.pdf.

31 "Flag Verification," Protocol and Liaison Service, United Nations, January 6, 2022. www.un.org/dgacm/sites/www.un.org.dgacm/files/Documents_Protocol/nv_for_flag_verification_2022.pdf.

32 William J. Burns, "A Birthday Dinner with Putin's 'Politburo': Secretary Rice's October 21 Discussions With Putin and Senior Advisors," U.S. Department of State, October 22, 2006. https://carnegieendowment.org/pdf/back-channel/2006MemoforRecord.pdf.

Chapter 9

1 Robert Downes, "U.S. Diplomats Preach Ideals Their Country Flouts. Is That Hypocrisy?" *Diplomatic Diary*, Washington International Diplomatic Academy, August 1, 2021. https://diplomaticacademy.us/2021/08/01/diplomats-ideals-hypocrisy.

2 Merrie Spaeth, "Words Matter: Ads Don't Work," *United Press International*, March 19, 2003. www.upi.com/Odd_News/2003/03/19/Words-Matter-Ads-dont-work/51951048105704.

3 Sheldon Rampton, "Shared Values Revisited," Center for Media and Democracy, October 17, 2007. www.prwatch.org/node/6465.

4 Bryan Ward-Perkins, *The Fall of Rome and the End of Civilization* (Oxford University Press, 2005).

5 Robert Finlay, "The Voyages of Zheng He: Ideology, State Power and Maritime Trade in Ming China," *Journal of the Historical Society*, 2008. https://doi.org/10.1111/j.1540-5923.2008.00250.x.

6 Lü Lingfeng, "Eclipses and the Victory of European Astronomy in China," *East Asian Science, Technology and Medicine*, 2007. www.jstor.org/stable/43151255.

7 Dwight Eisenhower, "USIA," Eisenhower Presidential Library, March 13, 1954. www.eisenhowerlibrary.gov/sites/default/files/file/people_to_people_BinderR.pdf.

8 John F. Kennedy, "Organization of Foreign Policy; Information Policy; United Nations; Scientific Matters (Document 144)," Memorandum to the Director of the U.S. Information Agency, U.S. Department of State, Office of the Historian, *Foreign Relations of the United States, 1961–1963*, Vol. XXV.

9 Billy Perrigo, "How the U.S. Used Jazz as a Cold War Secret Weapon," *Time Magazine*, December 27, 2017. https://time.com/5056351/cold-war-jazz-ambassadors.

10 Lina Mai, "'I Had a Right To Be at Central': Remembering Little Rock's Integration Battle," *Time Magazine*, September 22, 2017. https://time.com/4948704/little-rock-nine-anniversary.

11 Ricky Riccardi, "'I'm Still Louis Armstrong-Colored': Louis Armstrong and the Civil Rights Era," Louis Armstrong House Museum Virtual Exhibits, May 11, 2020. https://virtualexhibits.louisarmstronghouse.org/2020/05/11/im-still-louis-armstrong-colored-louis-armstrong-and-the-civil-rights-era.

12 "Louis Armstrong: Satchmo Blows Up the World," Meridian International Center, 2008. www.meridian.org/jazzambassadors/louis_armstrong/louis_armstrong.php.

13 J. Michael Waller, ed., *The Public Diplomacy Reader* (Institute of World Politics Press, 2007), 158.

14 Jack Guy, Anna Chernova and Nathan Hodge, "Kremlin Accuses U.S. of Stoking 'Hysteria' Over Ukraine, as U.N. Security Council meets," *CNN*, January 31, 2022. www.cnn.com/2022/01/31/europe/ukraine-russia-latest-news-monday-intl/index.html.

15 F. W. de Klerk, "Repeal of Population Registration Act," C-SPAN, June 17, 1991 (video). www.c-span.org/video/?19041-1/repeal-population-registration-act.

16 Nancy Snow, *Information War: American Propaganda, Free Speech and Opinion Since 9/11* (Seven Stories Press, 2003).

17 "Biography: Judith McHale," U.S. Department of State, May 26, 2009. https://web.archive.org/web/20090530030044/http://www.state.gov/r/pa/ei/biog/124007.htm.

18 Nicholas Kralev, *America's Other Army: The U.S. Foreign Service and 21st-Century Diplomacy*, 2nd ed. (Amazon, 2015), 96.

19 U.S. Information and Educational Exchange Act, January 27, 1948. www.usagm.gov/who-we-are/oversight/legislation/smith-mundt.

20 Smith-Mundt Modernization Act, May 10, 2012. www.congress.gov/bill/112th-congress/house-bill/5736.

21 Kralev, *America's Other Army*, 99.
22 "Median Country Speeds," Speedtest Global Index, April 2023. www.speedtest.net/global-index.
23 "Exploring American Values," U.S. Embassy & Consulates in the United Kingdom, April 3, 2019. https://uk.usembassy.gov/exploring-american-values-applications-now-open-for-2019-program.
24 Anna Massoglia, "Chinese Government Deploying Online Influencers Amid Beijing Olympics Boycotts," Open Secrets, December 13, 2021. www.opensecrets.org/news/2021/12/chinese-government-deploying-online-influencers-amid-beijing-olympics-boycotts.
25 Jen Kirby, "Concentration Camps and Forced Labor," *Vox*, September 25, 2020. www.vox.com/2020/7/28/21333345/uighurs-china-internment-camps-forced-labor-xinjiang.
26 Jen Kirby, "China's National Security Legislation Is Destroying Hong Kong's Rule of Law," *Vox*, July 1, 2021. www.vox.com/22554120/hong-kong-national-security-law-tong-ying-kit-trial.
27 "About Fulbright," U.S. Department of State. https://eca.state.gov/fulbright/about-fulbright.
28 "International Visitor Leadership Program," U.S. Department of State. https://eca.state.gov/ivlp/about-ivlp.
29 Kralev, *America's Other Army*, 102.
30 Robert Siegel, "Sayyid Qutb's America," *NPR*, May 6, 2003. www.npr.org/templates/story/story.php?storyId=1253796.
31 "Young African Leaders Initiative," U.S. Department of State. https://yali.state.gov/about.
32 Kralev, *America's Other Army*, 104.
33 Ibid., 148.
34 "Tawakkol Karman" The Nobel Prize, 2011. www.nobelprize.org/prizes/peace/2011/karman/facts.
35 Tom Hushek, "He Founded a School in South Sudan at 26, and U.S. Bet on Him," Diplomatic Diary, Washington International Diplomatic Academy, June 20, 2021. https://diplomaticacademy.us/2021/06/20/south-sudan-exchange-programs.
36 Kralev, *America's Other Army*, 102.
37 "War on Drugs," *Britannica*. www.britannica.com/topic/war-on-drugs.

Chapter 10

1 Matthew Keene, "For Americans in Trouble Abroad, a Consular Officer May Be the Only Hope," Diplomatic Diary, Washington International Diplomatic Academy, March 21, 2021. https://diplomaticacademy.us/2021/03/21/consular-american-citizen-services.
2 Vienna Convention on Consular Relations, April 24, 1963. https://legal.un.org/ilc/texts/instruments/english/conventions/9_2_1963.pdf.
3 Nicholas Kralev, *America's Other Army: The U.S. Foreign Service and 21st-Century Diplomacy*, 2nd ed. (Amazon, 2015), 130.
4 "Visa Statistics," U.S. Department of State. https://travel.state.gov/content/travel/en/legal/visa-law0/visa-statistics.html.
5 "U.S. Visa Law & Policy," U.S. Department of State. https://travel.state.gov/content/travel/en/legal/visa-law0.html.

6 Immigration and Nationality Act, 1952. www.uscis.gov/laws-and-policy/legislation/immi gration-and-nationality-act.

7 "Passport Agencies," U.S. Department of State. https://travel.state.gov/content/travel/en/ passports/get-fast/passport-agencies.html.

8 "Intercountry Adoption," U.S. Department of State. https://travel.state.gov/content/ travel/en/Intercountry-Adoption.html

9 "Adoption Statistics," U.S. Department of State. https://travel.state.gov/content/travel/ en/Intercountry-Adoption/adopt_ref/adoption-statistics-esri.html?wcmmode=disabled.

10 "Russia Intercountry Adoption Information," U.S. Department of State. https://travel .state.gov/content/travel/en/Intercountry-Adoption/Intercountry-Adoption-Country-Info rmation/RussianFederation.html.

11 E. J. Graff, "The Lie We Love," *Foreign Policy*, October 6, 2009. https://foreignpolicy .com/2009/10/06/the-lie-we-love.

12 "International Parental Child Abduction," U.S. Department of State. https://travel.state .gov/content/travel/en/International-Parental-Child-Abduction.html.

13 "Goldman Case," Bring Sean Home Foundation. http://bringseanhome.org/goldman-case.

14 Sean and David Goldman International Child Abduction Prevention and Return Act, August 8, 2014. www.congress.gov/bill/113th-congress/house-bill/3212/text.

15 Keene.

16 Ben Fox, "What Happened to the Afghanistan Evacuation?" *Associated Press*, November 26, 2021. www.usnews.com/news/politics/articles/2021-11-26/explainer-what-happened-to-the-afghanistan-evacuation.

17 "State Carried Out Historic Repatriation Effort but Should Strengthen Its Preparedness for Future Crises," U.S. Government Accountability Office, November 2, 2021. www .gao.gov/products/gao-22-104354.

18 "United States Government Haiti Earthquake Disaster Response," Obama Administration, The White House, March 10, 2010. https://obamawhitehouse.archives .gov/the-press-office/united-states-government-haiti-earthquake-disaster-response.

19 "State Department: The July 2006 Evacuation of American Citizens from Lebanon," U.S. Government Accountability Office, June 7, 2007. www.gao.gov/products/gao-07-893r.

20 "Indian Ocean Tsunami of 2004," *Britannica*. www.britannica.com/event/Indian-Ocean-tsunami-of-2004.

21 "Economic Impact Reports," World Travel & Tourism Council. https://wttc.org/ Research/Economic-Impact.

22 "Summary of Visas Issued by Issuing Office, Fiscal Year 2019," U.S. Department of State. https://travel.state.gov/content/dam/visas/Statistics/AnnualReports/FY2019Annu alReport/FY19AnnualReport-%20TableIV.pdf.

23 "Directory of Visa Categories," U.S. Department of State. https://travel.state.gov/con tent/travel/en/us-visas/visa-information-resources/all-visa-categories.html.

24 "'Underwear Bomber' Umar Farouk Abdulmutallab Pleads Guilty," U.S. Immigration and Customs Enforcement, October 11, 2011. www.ice.gov/news/releases/underwear-bomber-umar-farouk-abdulmutallab-pleads-guilty.

25 Kralev, *America's Other Army*, 123.

26 Barack Obama, "Remarks on the Terror Plot Review," *New York Times*, January 7, 2010. www.nytimes.com/2010/01/08/us/politics/08obama.text.html.

27 Kralev, *America's Other Army*, 127.

28 "Visa Denials," U.S. Department of State. https://travel.state.gov/content/travel/en/us-visas/visa-information-resources/visa-denials.html.

29 "ESTA Application," U.S. Customs and Border Protection. https://esta.cbp.dhs.gov/esta.

30 Erica Stewart and Matt Ruffner, "Impact of Covid-19 Pandemic Significant," NAFSA, November 15, 2021. www.nafsa.org/about/about-nafsa/new-nafsa-data-show-largest-ever-drop-international-student-economic.

31 "Processes for Cubans, Haitians, Nicaraguans and Venezuelans," U.S. Citizenship and Immigration Services. www.uscis.gov/CHNV.

32 "Diversity Visa Program," U.S. Department of State. https://travel.state.gov/content/travel/en/us-visas/immigrate/diversity-visa-program-entry/diversity-visa-submit-entry1.html.

33 "Review of the Afghan Special Immigrant Visa Program," Report AUD-MERO-20-35, Office of Inspector General, U.S. Department of State, June 2020. www.oversight.gov/sites/default/files/oig-reports/AUD-MERO-20-35.pdf.

34 Kralev, *America's Other Army*, 124.

35 "U.S. Issues Visa and Apology to Scientist," *NBC News*, February 24, 2006. www.nbcnews.com/id/wbna11546142.

36 Jim Dawson, "Post-September 11th Visa Woes Still Plague International Students and Scientists," *Physics Today*, 2003. https://physicstoday.scitation.org/doi/full/10.1063/1.1595044.

Chapter 11

1 "Diplomatic Oops! Embarrassing State-Visit Blunders," Deutsche Welle, February 9, 2018. www.dw.com/en/diplomatic-oops-embarrassing-state-visit-blunders/g-45328087.

2 Scott Lindlaw, "White House Hosts State Dinner for Arroyo," *Associated Press*, May 18, 2003. www.ctinsider.com/news/article/White-House-Hosts-State-Dinner-for-Arroyo-7100508.php.

3 George W. Bush and Gloria Macapagal Arroyo, "Remarks by President Bush and President Arroyo in an Exchange of Toasts," George W. Bush Administration, The White House, May 19, 2003. https://georgewbush-whitehouse.archives.gov/news/releases/2003/05/20030519-17.html.

4 "Etiquette," *Oxford Languages*. https://languages.oup.com/google-dictionary-en.

5 Barbara Crossette, "Diplomatically, French Is a Faded Rose in an English Garden," *New York Times*, March 25, 2001. www.nytimes.com/2001/03/25/world/diplomatically-french-is-a-faded-rose-in-an-english-garden.html.

6 "Protocol," *Oxford Languages*. https://languages.oup.com/google-dictionary-en.

7 Capricia Penavic Marshall, "Diplomacy After Hours," National Museum of American Diplomacy, September 23, 2020. https://diplomacy.state.gov/events-listing/diplomacy-after-hours-the-power-of-protocol-with-capricia-marshall-and-cam-henderson.

8 Capricia Penavic Marshall, *Protocol* (Ecco, 2020), 5.

9 William J. Burns, *The Back Channel: A Memoir of American Diplomacy and the Case for Its Renewal* (Random House, 2019), 200.

10 Vienna Convention on Diplomatic Relations, April 18, 1961. https://legal.un.org/ilc/texts/instruments/english/conventions/9_1_1961.pdf.

11 Vienna Convention on Consular Relations, April 24, 1963. https://legal.un.org/ilc/texts/instruments/english/conventions/9_2_1963.pdf.

12 "Protocol for the Modern Diplomat," Foreign Service Institute, U.S. Department of State, January 2011. https://2009-2017.state.gov/documents/organization/176174.pdf.

13 Ibid.

14 Marshall, *Protocol*, 3.
15 Ibid., 8.
16 Philip C. Habib, "1960s – More Talk Than Peace," Association for Diplomatic Studies and Training. https://adst.org/oral-history/fascinating-figures/philip-habib-cursed-is-the-peacemaker.
17 Henry Kissinger, *Ending the Vietnam War* (Simon & Schuster, 2003), 52.
18 Joel Singer, "Where You Sit Is Where You Stand," *International Negotiation*, January 2021. www.joelsinger.org/wp-content/uploads/Where-You-Sit.pdf.
19 *United States of America* v. *Devyani Khobragade*, United States District Court, Southern District of New York, March 25, 2015. www.justice.gov/sites/default/files/usao-sdny/legacy/2015/03/25/Khobragade%2C%20Devyani%20Indictment.pdf.
20 Vienna Convention on Diplomatic Relations.
21 Vienna Convention on Consular Relations.
22 Krishnadev Calamur, "Indian Diplomat at Center of Row with U.S. Indicted, Leaves Country," *NPR*, January 9, 2014. www.npr.org/sections/thetwo-way/2014/01/09/261106904/indian-diplomat-at-center-of-row-with-u-s-leaves-the-country.
23 "Congress of Vienna," *Britannica*. www.britannica.com/event/Congress-of-Vienna.
24 "Dual Citizenship – Security Clearance Applications," U.S. Department of State. https://careers.state.gov/wp-content/uploads/2016/02/Dual-Citizenship.pdf.
25 Vienna Convention on Diplomatic Relations.
26 Vienna Convention on Consular Relations.
27 "Protocol for the Modern Diplomat, " 1.
28 Henry Kissinger, *Years of Upheaval* (Simon & Schuster, 2011), 795–96.
29 Singer.
30 William B. Quandt, *Peace Process* (University of California Press, 1993), Appendix M.
31 Singer.

Chapter 12

1 "'The Ship Has Reached the Shore,' President Announces, as Intergovernmental Conference Concludes Historic New Maritime Biodiversity Treaty," United Nations, March 3, 2023. https://press.un.org/en/2023/sea2175.doc.htm.
2 Intergovernmental Conference on Marine Biodiversity of Areas Beyond National Jurisdiction, United Nations. www.un.org/bbnj.
3 Stéphane Dujarric, "Statement Attributable to the Spokesperson for the Secretary-General – On Int'l Legally Binding Instrument Under the UN Convention on the Law of the Sea," United Nations, March 9, 2023. www.un.org/sg/en/content/sg/statement/2023-03-04/statement-attributable-the-spokesperson-for-the-secretary-general-intl-legally-binding-instrument-under-the-un-convention-the-law-of-the-sea.
4 Gaby Flores, "How People Power Helped Protect the Oceans," Greenpeace International, March 9, 2023. www.greenpeace.org/international/story/58596/how-people-power-helped-protect-oceans.
5 "U.N. Adopts World's First Treaty to Protect High Seas Biodiversity," *Reuters*, June 20, 2023. www.reuters.com/world/un-adopts-worlds-first-treaty-protect-high-seas-biodiversity-2023-06-19.
6 "Treaty of the High Seas: The United States of America Join the High Ambition Coalition on Biodiversity Beyond National Jurisdiction," Directorate-General for Maritime Affairs

and Fisheries, European Commission, January 24, 2023. https://oceans-and-fisheries.ec .europa.eu/news/treaty-high-seas-united-states-america-join-high-ambition-coalition-biodiv ersity-beyond-national-2023-01-24_en.

7   "Leaders' Declaration," Group of 20, Bali, Indonesia, November 16, 2022. www.g20.org/ content/dam/gtwenty/gtwenty_new/about_g20/previous-summit-documents/2022-bali/G20 %20Bali%20Leaders%27%20Declaration,%2015-16%20November%202022.pdf.

8   "Peace of Westphalia," *Britannica*. www.britannica.com/event/Peace-of-Westphalia.

9   Jonathan I. Israel, *Conflicts of Empires* (Hambledon Press, 1997), 330.

10 "History," Universal Postal Union. www.upu.int/en/Universal-Postal-Union/About-UPU/History.

11 "About ITU," International Telecommunications Union. www.itu.int/en/about/Pages/ default.aspx.

12 William J. Burns, *The Back Channel: A Memoir of American Diplomacy and the Case for Its Renewal* (Random House, 2019), 337–87.

13 "About Us," The Office of the Quartet. www.quartetoffice.org/page.php?id= 4e3e7y320487Y4e3e7.

14 "Competing Visions of International Order in the South China Sea," International Crisis Group, November 29, 2021. www.crisisgroup.org/asia/north-east-asia/china/315-compet ing-visions-international-order-south-china-sea.

15 Courtney J. Fung and Shing-Hon Lam, "China Already Leads 4 of the 15 U.N. Specialized Agencies," *Washington Post*, March 3, 2020. www.washingtonpost.com/polit ics/2020/03/03/china-already-leads-4-15-un-specialized-agencies-is-aiming-5th.

16 Arthur C. Helton, "The Emergence of the International Refugee Regime," *International Migration Review*, September 1997.

17 "Interpol 100," Interpol. www.interpol.int/en/Who-we-are/INTERPOL-100.

18 "Overview," World Trade Organization. www.wto.org/english/thewto_e/whatis_e/wto_ dg_stat_e.htm.

19 "History," Organization of Islamic Cooperation. www.oic-oci.org/page/?p_id=52&p_ ref=26&lan=en.

20 "Our Mission," Organization of Petroleum Exporting Countries. www.opec.org/opec_ web/en/about_us/23.htm.

21 "NATO Leaders: Lord Ismay," North Atlantic Treaty Organization. www.nato.int/cps/ en/natohq/declassified_137930.htm.

22 "Why Was NATO Founded?" North Atlantic Treaty Organization. www.nato.int/weare nato/why-was-nato-founded.html.

23 "European Coal and Steel Community," *Britannica*. www.britannica.com/topic/ European-Coal-and-Steel-Community.

24 "Member States," African Union. https://au.int/en/member_states/countryprofiles2.

25 "Member States," Organization of American States. www.oas.org/en/member_states/ default.asp.

26 "About ASEAN," Association of Southeast Asian Nations. https://asean.org/about-asean.

27 "About APEC," Asia-Pacific Economic Cooperation. www.apec.org/about-us/about-apec.

28 "Shanghai Cooperation Organization," U.N. Political and Peacebuilding Affairs. https:// dppa.un.org/en/shanghai-cooperation-organization.

29 Community of Latin American and Caribbean States. https://celacinternational.org.

30 "About ECOWAS," Economic Community of West African States. https://ecowas.int/ about-ecowas.

31 "Consolidated Financial Statements," Bill and Melinda Gates Foundation, December 31, 2021. https://docs.gatesfoundation.org/documents/f_331060e-1a_billmelindagatesfounda tion_fs.pdf.

32 "United States of America: Partner in Global Health," World Health Organization, May 19, 2022. www.who.int/about/funding/contributors/usa.

33 Mark Suzman, "Annual Letter," Bill and Melinda Gates Foundation, January 16, 2023. www.gatesfoundation.org/ideas/articles/2023-gates-foundation-annual-letter.

34 Colin Powell, "U.S. Secretary of State Colin Powell Addresses the U.N. Security Council," George W. Bush Administration, The White House, February 5, 2003. https://georgew bush-whitehouse.archives.gov/news/releases/2003/02/20030205-1.html.

35 "U.S., Britain and Spain Abandon Resolution," *Associated Press*, March 17, 2003. https://archive.globalpolicy.org/component/content/article/167-attack/35373.html.

36 Jason M. Breslow, "Colin Powell: U.N. Speech 'Was a Great Intelligence Failure,'" *PBS Frontline*, May 17, 2016. www.pbs.org/wgbh/frontline/article/colin-powell-u-n-speech-was-a-great-intelligence-failure.

37 U.N. Security Council Resolution 678, adopted on November 29, 1990. https://docu ments-dds-ny.un.org/doc/RESOLUTION/GEN/NR0/575/28/PDF/NR057528.pdf.

38 "Composition of the Secretariat (2021)," United Nations, December 7, 2022. https:// documents-dds-ny.un.org/doc/UNDOC/GEN/N22/677/81/PDF/N2267781.pdf.

39 "Main Bodies," United Nations. www.un.org/en/about-us/main-bodies.

40 Provisional Program of Work of the Security Council, March 2023. www.un.org/secur itycouncil/sites/www.un.org.securitycouncil/files/programme_of_work.pdf.

41 "Instability in Afghanistan," Council on Foreign Relations, August 15, 2023. www.cfr .org/global-conflict-tracker/conflict/war-afghanistan.

42 U.N. Security Council Resolution 2593, adopted on August 30, 2021. https://documents-dds-ny.un.org/doc/UNDOC/GEN/N21/238/85/PDF/N2123885.pdf.

43 "Our Mission," Bureau of International Organization Affairs, U.S. Department of State. www.state.gov/bureaus-offices/under-secretary-for-political-affairs/bureau-of-inter national-organization-affairs.

44 "About the Mission," U.S. Mission to the United Nations. https://usun.usmission.gov/ mission.

45 U.S. Mission to International Organizations in Geneva. https://geneva.usmission.gov/ usmissiongeneva.

46 "Presidential Statements," U.N. Security Council. www.un.org/securitycouncil/content/ presidential-statements.

47 U.N. General Assembly Resolution A/RES/ES-11/1, tabled on March 1, 2022, adopted on March 2, 2022. https://documents-dds-ny.un.org/doc/UNDOC/GEN/N22/293/36/ PDF/N2229336.pdf.

48 U.N. General Assembly Resolution A/RES/ES-11/6, tabled on February 16, 2023, adopted on February 23, 2023. https://documents-dds-ny.un.org/doc/UNDOC/LTD/ N23/048/58/PDF/N2304858.pdf.

49 Proposed Amendment to U.N. General Assembly Resolution A/ES-11/L.8, tabled on February 21, 2023. https://documents-dds-ny.un.org/doc/UNDOC/LTD/N23/054/37/ PDF/N2305437.pdf.

50 Proposed Amendment to U.N. General Assembly Resolution A/ES-11/L.9, tabled on February 21, 2023. https://documents-dds-ny.un.org/doc/UNDOC/LTD/N23/054/44/ PDF/N2305444.pdf.

51 United Nations Charter. www.un.org/en/about-us/un-charter/full-text.

52 "Russia Blocks Security Council Action on Ukraine," United Nations, February 25, 2022. https://news.un.org/en/story/2022/02/1112802.

53 Robert Downes, "Can Russia Be Removed From the U.N. Security Council?" Diplomatic Diary, Washington International Diplomatic Academy, April 24, 2022. https://diplomaticacademy.us/2022/04/24/russia-un-security-council.

54 U.N. Security Council Resolution 82, adopted on June 25, 1950. https://digitallibrary.un.org/record/112025?ln=en.

55 "Death Toll From Sudan War Rises to More Than 600," Voice of America, May 10, 2023. www.voanews.com/a/death-toll-from-sudan-war-rises-to-more-than-600/7086508.html.

Chapter 13

1 "Asian Lineage Avian Influenza A(H7N9) Virus," Centers for Disease Control and Prevention. https://web.archive.org/web/20230225185149/www.cdc.gov/flu/avianflu/h7n9-virus.htm.

2 "Human Infection With Avian Influenza A(H7N9) Virus – China," World Health Organization, January 17, 2017. https://web.archive.org/web/20170118143706/http://www.who.int/csr/don/17-january-2017-ah7n9-china/en.

3 Sheryl Gay Stolberg, Benjamin Mueller and Carl Zimmer, "The Origins of the Covid Pandemic," *New York Times*, March 17, 2023. www.nytimes.com/article/covid-origin-lab-leak-china.html.

4 "WHO Coronavirus (Covid-19) Dashboard," World Health Organization. https://covid19.who.int.

5 "NSC Directorate for Global Health Security and Biodefense Dissolved," Sabin Center for Climate Change Law, Columbia Law School. https://climate.law.columbia.edu/content/nsc-directorate-global-health-security-and-biodefense-dissolved.

6 "International Sanitary Conferences," Curiosity Collections, Harvard Library. https://curiosity.lib.harvard.edu/contagion/feature/international-sanitary-conferences.

7 Cable from Andrew D. White to Secretary of State John Sherman, December 27, 1897, cited in James H. Cassedy, "Applied Microscopy and American Pork Diplomacy," *Isis, A Journal of the History of Science Society*, Spring 1971. https://doi.org/10.1086/350704.

8 "Charles W. Stiles: Biography," National Agricultural Library, U.S. Department of Agriculture. www.nal.usda.gov/exhibits/speccoll/exhibits/show/parasitic-diseases-with-econom/item/8206.

9 James H. Cassedy, "Applied Microscopy and American Pork Diplomacy," *Isis, A Journal of the History of Science Society*, Spring 1971. https://doi.org/10.1086/350704.

10 "Earl Evans, 1910–1999," University of Chicago Medicine, October 5, 1999. www.uchicagomedicine.org/forefront/news/earl-evans-1910-1999.

11 John Lisle, "The Origins, Work and Legacy of the World War I Science Attachés," University of Texas Paper, 2017. https://sites.nationalacademies.org/cs/groups/pgasite/documents/webpage/pga_190086.pdf.

12 Vannevar Bush, "Science: The Endless Frontier," U.S. Government Publishing Office, 1960.

13 "Report of Subcommittee on Dissemination of Information," Committee to Assist U.S. Mission on Science and Technology, National Academy of Sciences, October 3, 1947.

14 "Embassy Science Fellows Program," U.S. Department of State. www.state.gov/programs-office-of-science-and-technology-cooperation/embassy-science-fellows-program.

15 "The Commission Authorizes Ten Genetically Modified Crops for Use as Food and Animal Feed," European Commission Press Release, August 17, 2021. https://ec.europa.eu/commission/presscorner/detail/en/MEX_21_4262.

16 Anthony Rock, "Science Diplomacy," Lecture at the Washington International Diplomatic Academy, July 24, 2020.

17 Lanre Anthony Gbadegesin, Emmanuel Ayodeji Ayeni, Carlos Kwesi Tettey, Victoria Anthony Uyanga, Oluwaseun Olayemi Aluko, John Kojo Ahiakpa, Charles Obinwanne Okoye, Jane Ifunanya Mbadianya, Modinat Adejoke Adekoya, Raheem Olatunji Aminu, et al., "GMOs in Africa: Status, Adoption and Public Acceptance," *Food Control*, November 2022. https://doi.org/10.1016/j.foodcont.2022.109193.

18 Jimmy Kolker, "A Diplomat's Perspective on Use of Science and Evidence in Implementing PEPFAR," *Science & Diplomacy*, April 2018. www.sciencediplomacy.org/sites/default/files/kolker_march_2018.pdf.

19 Thomas Goliber, "The Status of the HIV/AIDS Epidemic in Sub-Saharan Africa," Population Reference Bureau, July 2, 2002. www.prb.org/resources/the-status-of-the-hiv-aids-epidemic-in-sub-saharan-africa.

20 "The Global HIV and AIDS Epidemic," Centers for Disease Control and Prevention, June 8, 2001. www.cdc.gov/mmwr/preview/mmwrhtml/mm5021a3.htm.

21 "Antiretroviral Drug Discovery and Development," National Institute of Allergy and Infectious Diseases. www.niaid.nih.gov/diseases-conditions/antiretroviral-drug-development.

22 Grant Dorsey et al., "Prevention of Malaria and HIV Disease in Tororo," University of California San Francisco and Makerere University, March 6, 2012.

23 Elliot Marseille, James G. Kahn, Christian Pitter, Rebecca Bunnell, William Epalatai, Emmanuel Jawe, Willy Were and Jonathan Mermin, "The Cost-Effectiveness of Home-Based Provision of Antiretroviral Therapy in Rural Uganda," *Applied Economics and Health Policy*, 2009. www.ncbi.nlm.nih.gov/pmc/articles/PMC2912402.

24 "Results and Impact – PEPFAR," U.S. Department of State, September 30, 2022. www.state.gov/results-and-impact-pepfar.

25 "Global Terrorism Overview: Terrorism in 2019," National Consortium for the Study of Terrorism and Responses to Terrorism, July 2020. www.start.umd.edu/pubs/START_GTD_GlobalTerrorismOverview2019_July2020.pdf.

26 "Concern About Being Victim of Terrorism," Gallup. https://news.gallup.com/poll/4909/terrorism-united-states.aspx.

27 Bipartisan Budget Act, August 2, 2019. www.congress.gov/bill/116th-congress/house-bill/3877.

28 Scott A. Johnson, "There's a New Asteroid Deflection System in the Works and It Could Be Up by 2025," *Science Alert*, May 2, 2022. www.sciencealert.com/china-is-building-an-asteroid-deflection-defense-system-to-launch-in-2025.

29 Authia Gray and Fablina Sharara, "Global and Regional Sepsis and Infectious Syndrome Mortality in 2019," *The Lancet*, March 2022. https://doi.org/10.1016/S2214-109X(22)00131-0.

30 "Bureau of Global Health Security and Diplomacy, U.S. Department of State. https://www.state.gov/bureau-of-global-health-security-and-diplomacy-about-us/"

31 Prisca Zwanikken, Lucy Alexander and Albert Scherpbier, "Impact of MPH Programs: Contributing to Health System Strengthening in Low- and Middle-Income Countries," Human Resources for Health, August 22, 2016. https://human-resources-health.biomedcentral.com/articles/10.1186/s12960-016-0150-7.

32 Thomas Bollyky, Tara Templin, Matthew Cohen, and Joseph L. Dieleman, "Lower Income Countries That Face the Most Rapid Shift in Non-Communicable Disease Burden Are Also the Least Prepared," *Health Affairs*, November 2017. https://doi.org/10.1377/hlthaff.2017.0708.

33 "Ebola Virus Disease," World Health Organization. www.who.int/news-room/fact-sheets/detail/ebola-virus-disease.

34 Maria Cheng, "Emails: U.N. Health Agency Resisted Declaring Ebola Emergency," *Associated Press*, March 20, 2015. https://apnews.com/article/2489c78bff86463589b41f3faaea5ab2.

35 Alan Blinder and Denise Grady, "American Doctor With Ebola Arrives in U.S. for Treatment," *New York Times*, August 2, 2015. www.nytimes.com/2014/08/03/us/kent-brantley-nancy-writebol-ebola-treatment-atlanta.html.

36 "2014–2016 Ebola Outbreak in West Africa," Centers for Disease Control and Prevention. www.cdc.gov/vhf/ebola/history/2014-2016-outbreak/index.html.

37 Ibid.

38 Jennifer Rigby, Emma Farge, Mrinalika Roy and Paul Carrel, "Tedros Reelected as Head of World Health Organization," *Reuters*, May 25, 2022. www.reuters.com/business/healthcare-pharmaceuticals/tedros-re-elected-who-director-general-german-minister-2022-05-24.

39 "How WHO Is Funded," World Health Organization. www.who.int/about/funding.

40 "WHO's Budget Segments," World Health Organization. www.who.int/about/accountability/budget.

41 "Centers for Disease Control and Prevention Funding Overview," Congressional Research Service, March 28, 2023. https://crsreports.congress.gov/product/pdf/R/R47207.

42 "National Biodefense Strategy," Trump Administration, The White House, 2018. https://trumpwhitehouse.archives.gov/wp-content/uploads/2018/09/National-Biodefense-Strategy.pdf.

43 "National Health Security Strategy," Department of Health and Human Services, 2019. https://aspr.hhs.gov/ResponseOperations/legal/NHSS/Documents/2019-2022-nhss-ip-v508.pdf.

44 "Understanding How COVID-19 Vaccines Work," Centers for Disease Control and Prevention, February 3, 2023. www.cdc.gov/coronavirus/2019-ncov/vaccines/different-vaccines/how-they-work.html.

45 "Explaining Operation Warp Speed," Department of Health and Human Services, December 31, 2020. www.nihb.org/covid-19/wp-content/uploads/2020/08/Fact-sheet-operation-warp-speed.pdf.

46 "COVAX: Working for Global Equitable Access to COVID-19 Vaccines," World Health Organization. www.who.int/initiatives/act-accelerator/covax.

47 "COVAX Updates Participants on Delivery Delays," World Health Organization, March 25, 2021. www.who.int/news/item/25-03-2021-covax-updates-participants-on-delivery-delays-for-vaccines-from-serum-institute-of-india-(sii)-and-astrazeneca.

48 "Coronavirus (Covid-19) Vaccinations," Our World in Data. https://ourworldindata.org/covid-vaccinations.

49 "Intergovernmental Negotiating Body," World Health Organization. https://inb.who.int.

50 "Pandemic Influenza Preparedness Framework," World Health Organization. www.who.int/initiatives/pandemic-influenza-preparedness-framework.

51 "Coronavirus (Covid-19) Vaccinations."

52 "Covid-19 Vaccine Donations," U.S. Department of State. www.state.gov/covid-19-recovery/vaccine-deliveries.

53 "Zika Virus," World Health Organization, December 8, 2022. www.who.int/news-room/fact-sheets/detail/zika-virus.

54 Anthony Boadle, "U.S., Brazil Researchers Join Forces to Battle Zika Virus," *Reuters*, February 18, 2016. www.reuters.com/article/us-health-zika-brazil/u-s-brazil-researchers-join-forces-to-battle-zika-virus-idUSKCN0VR2P8.

55 "Zika Cases in the United States," Centers for Disease Control and Prevention. www.cdc.gov/zika/reporting/index.html.

56 "CDC Awards $6.8 Million to Partners to Support Zika Response," Centers for Disease Control and Prevention, August 24, 2016. www.cdc.gov/media/releases/2016/p0824-cdc-zika-award.html.

Chapter 14

1 Jason Healey, *A Fierce Domain: Conflict in Cyberspace, 1986 to 2012* (Cyber Conflict Studies Association, 2013).

2 Keir Giles and Anthony Seabroyer, "The Russian Information Warfare Construct," Defense Research and Development Canada, March 2019. https://cradpdf.drdc-rddc.gc.ca/PDFS/unc341/p811007_A1b.pdf.

3 Roland Heickerö, "Emerging Cyber Threats and Russian Views on Information," Swedish Defence Research Establishment (FOI), March 2010. https://foi.se/rest-api/report/FOI-R–2970–SE.

4 "Cyberspace," Computer Security Resource Center, National Institute of Standards and Technology. https://csrc.nist.gov/glossary/term/cyberspace.

5 "Internet," Computer Security Resource Center, National Institute of Standards and Technology. https://csrc.nist.gov/glossary/term/Internet.

6 "Internet Governance," ICANN. www.icann.org/resources/pages/internet-governance-2013-06-14-en.

7 "History of the Web," World Wide Web Foundation. https://webfoundation.org/about/vision/history-of-the-web.

8 Ani Petrosyan, "Number of Internet Users Worldwide from 2005 to 2022," Statista, February 23, 2023. www.statista.com/statistics/273018/number-of-internet-users-worldwide.

9 Josephine Wolff, "How the NotPetya Attack Is Reshaping Cyber Insurance," the Brookings Institution, December 1, 2021. www.brookings.edu/articles/how-the-notpetya-attack-is-reshaping-cyber-insurance.

10 Suzanne Smalley, "Insurance Giant Settles NotPetya Lawsuit, Signaling Cyber Insurance Shakeup," *Cyberscoop*, November 4, 2022. https://cyberscoop.com/insurance-giant-settles-notpetya-lawsuit.

11 Lee Matthews, "NotPetya Ransomware Attack Cost Shipping Giant Maersk Over $200 Million," *Forbes*, August 16, 2017. www.forbes.com/sites/leemathews/2017/08/16/notpetya-ransomware-attack-cost-shipping-giant-maersk-over-200-million.

12 Alex Hern, "WannaCry, Petya, NotPetya: How Ransomware Hit the Big Time in 2017," *The Guardian*, December 30, 2017. www.theguardian.com/technology/2017/dec/30/wannacry-petya-notpetya-ransomware.

13 "Covid-19 Cyberthreats," Interpol, 2020. www.interpol.int/en/Crimes/Cybercrime/COVID-19-cyberthreats.

14 "Foreign Economic Espionage in Cyberspace," National Counterintelligence and Security Center, 2018. https://fas.org/irp/ops/ci/feec-2018.pdf.

15 "Our Mission and Vision," U.S. Cyber Command. www.cybercom.mil/About/Mission-and-Vision.

16 "Our Mission," Bureau of Cyberspace and Digital Policy, U.S. Department of State. www.state.gov/bureaus-offices/deputy-secretary-of-state/bureau-of-cyberspace-and-digital-policy.

17 Joseph S. Nye Jr., "The Regime Complex for Managing Global Cyber Activities," Global Commission on Internet Governance, May 20, 2014. www.cigionline.org/publications/regime-complex-managing-global-cyber-activities.

18 "Developments in the Field of Information and Telecommunications in the Context of International Security," U.N. Office for Disarmament Affairs. www.un.org/disarmament/ict-security.

19 "Group of Governmental Experts on Developments in the Field of Information and Telecommunications in the Context of International Security," United Nations, July 22, 2015. https://documents-dds-ny.un.org/doc/UNDOC/GEN/N15/228/35/PDF/N1522835.pdf.

20 Heli Tiirmaa-Klaar, "The Evolution of the U.N. Group of Governmental Experts on Cyber Issues," The Hague Center for Strategic Studies, December 9, 2021. https://hcss.nl/report/the-evolution-of-the-un-group-of-governmental-experts-on-cyber-issues-from-a-marginal-group-to-a-major-international-security-norm-setting-body.

21 "Open-Ended Working Group," U.N. Office for Disarmament Affairs. https://disarmament.unoda.org/open-ended-working-group.

22 "Open-Ended Working Group on Information and Communications Technologies," 2021–23 Session Schedule, U.N. Office for Disarmament Affairs. https://meetings.unoda.org/open-ended-working-group-on-information-and-communication-technologies-2021.

23 "North Korean Regime-Backed Programmer Charged With Conspiracy to Conduct Multiple Cyber Attacks and Intrusions," Office of Public Affairs, U.S. Department of Justice, September 6, 2018. www.justice.gov/opa/pr/north-korean-regime-backed-programmer-charged-conspiracy-conduct-multiple-cyber-attacks-and.

24 Ellen Nakashima, "Chinese Breach Data of 4 million Federal Workers," *Washington Post*, June 4, 2015. www.washingtonpost.com/world/national-security/chinese-hackers-breach-federal-governments-personnel-office/2015/06/04/889c0e52-0af7-11e5-95fd-d580f1c5d44e_story.html.

25 "Draft Council Conclusions on a Framework for a Joint EU Diplomatic Response to Malicious Cyber Activities," Council of the European Union, June 7, 2017. https://data.consilium.europa.eu/doc/document/ST-9916-2017-INIT/en/pdf.

26 "Biden-Harris Administration Announces National Cybersecurity Strategy," Biden-Harris Administration, The White House, March 2, 2023. www.whitehouse.gov/briefing-room/statements-releases/2023/03/02/fact-sheet-biden-harris-administration-announces-national-cybersecurity-strategy.

27 Adrian Shahbaz, Allie Funk and Kian Vesteinsson, "Countering an Authoritarian Overhaul of the Internet," Freedom House, 2022. https://freedomhouse.org/report/freedom-net/2022/countering-authoritarian-overhaul-internet.

28 "Cyber/ICT Security," OSCE Secretariat. www.osce.org/secretariat/cyber-ict-security.

29 "Directive on Measures for a High Common Level of Cybersecurity Across the Union," European Commission. https://ec.europa.eu/digital-single-market/en/directive-security-network-and-information-systems-nis-directive.

30 "Inter-American Cooperation Portal on Cybercrime," Organization of American States. www.oas.org/en/sla/dlc/cyber-en/homePortal.asp.

31 "The ASEAN–Singapore Cybersecurity Centre of Excellence," Cyber Security Agency of Singapore. www.csa.gov.sg/News-Events/Press-Releases/2021/asean-singapore-cybersecurity-centre-of-excellence.

32 African Union Convention on Cyber Security and Personal Data Protection, June 27, 2014. https://au.int/en/treaties/african-union-convention-cyber-security-and-personal-data-protection.

33 Global Forum of Cyber Expertise Website. https://thegfce.org.

34 "Cybersecurity Multi-Donor Trust Fund," The World Bank. www.worldbank.org/en/programs/cybersecurity-trust-fund.

35 Cybersecurity and Infrastructure Security Agency. www.cisa.gov.

36 "The Department of State Announces Reward Offer Against Russian Ransomware Actor," U.S. Department of State, May 16, 2023. www.state.gov/the-department-of-state-announces-reward-offer-against-russian-ransomware-actor.

37 "Iranian State Actors Conduct Cyber Operations Against the Government of Albania," U.S. Cybersecurity and Infrastructure Security Agency, September 23, 2022. www.cisa.gov/news-events/cybersecurity-advisories/aa22-264a.

38 Kimberly Underwood, "Cyber Diplomacy Is in High Demand," *The Cyber Edge*, April 12, 2023. www.afcea.org/signal-media/cyber-edge/cyber-diplomacy-high-demand.

39 Llazar Semini, "Police Raid Iranian Opposition Camp in Albania, Seize Computers," *Associated Press*, June 20, 2023. https://apnews.com/article/albania-mek-iranian-opposition-police-raid-851dcb5fc32cd6bc60206e342eea7b16.

Chapter 15

1 "The Gulf War," Miller Center, University of Virginia. https://millercenter.org/statecraft movie/gulf-war.

2 "Oral History: James Baker," *PBS Frontline*, www.pbs.org/wgbh/pages/frontline/gulf/oral/baker/1.html.

3 U.N. Security Council Resolution 678, adopted on November 29, 1990. https://documents-dds-ny.un.org/doc/RESOLUTION/GEN/NR0/575/28/PDF/NR057528.pdf.

4 James A. Baker III, *The Politics of Diplomacy* (Putnam, 1995), 317–18.

5 "Gulf War Fast Facts," *CNN*, July 24, 2022. www.cnn.com/2013/09/15/world/meast/gulf-war-fast-facts/index.html.

6 U.N. Security Council Resolution 678, adopted on November 29, 1990. https://documents-dds-ny.un.org/doc/RESOLUTION/GEN/NR0/575/28/PDF/NR057528.pdf.

7 Chas W. Freeman, "Diplomacy as Tactics," Speech at Brown University, April 5, 2018. https://chasfreeman.net/diplomacy-as-tactics.

8 U.N. Security Council Resolution 687, adopted on April 9, 1991. https://peacemaker.un.org/sites/peacemaker.un.org/files/IQ%20KW_910403_SCR687%281991%29_0.pdf.

9 Thomas R. Pickering, "How to Prepare for Peace Talks in Ukraine," *Foreign Affairs*, March 14, 2023. www.foreignaffairs.com/united-states/how-prepare-peace-talks-ukraine.

10 Elizabeth Knowles, *The Oxford Dictionary of Modern Quotations* (Oxford University Press, 2008), 296.

11 Henry Kissinger, *Years of Renewal* (Simon & Schuster, 1999), 1011.

12 James K. Sebenius, R. Nicholas Burns and Robert H. Mnookin, *Kissinger the Negotiator* (Harper, 2018), 4.

13 Ibid., 10.

14 "Whites in Africa Fear Race War," *Associated Press*, February 27, 1976, cited in Ibid., 9.

15 Bernard Gwertzman, "Rhodesian Response to Kissinger Ringed on an Ambiguity," *New York Times*, November 16, 1976. www.nytimes.com/1976/11/16/archives/rhodesian-response-to-kissinger-hinged-on-an-ambiguity.html.

16 Richard Holbrooke, *To End a War* (Random House, 1998).

17 Stuart E. Eizenstat, *Imperfect Justice* (Public Affairs, 2003).

18 "Trade Agreements," Office of the United States Trade Representative. https://ustr.gov/trade-agreements.

19 "Global Trade After the Failure of the Doha Round," *New York Times*, January 1, 2016. www.nytimes.com/2016/01/01/opinion/global-trade-after-the-failure-of-the-doha-round.html.

20 Lisa Lerer, "Obama's Dramatic Climate Meet," *Politico*, December 18, 2009. www.politico.com/story/2009/12/obamas-dramatic-climate-meet-030801.

21 Hillary Rodham Clinton, *Hard Choices* (Simon & Schuster, 2014).

22 United Nations Framework Convention on Climate Change, June 1992. https://unfccc.int.

23 Paris Agreement, United Nations Framework Convention on Climate Change, December 12, 2015. https://unfccc.int/process-and-meetings/the-paris-agreement.

24 "It's 'Now or Never' to Limit Global Warming to 1.5 Degrees," United Nations, April 4, 2022. https://news.un.org/en/story/2022/04/1115452.

25 Conference on Disarmament, United Nations. https://disarmament.unoda.org/conference-on-disarmament.

26 Treaty on the Non-Proliferation of Nuclear Weapons, March 5, 1970. www.iaea.org/sites/default/files/publications/documents/infcircs/1970/infcirc140.pdf.

27 Rose Gottemoeller, "U.S.–Russian Nuclear Arms Control Negotiations," *Foreign Service Journal*, May 2020. https://afsa.org/us-russian-nuclear-arms-control-negotiations-short-history.

28 Shannon Bugos, "Russia Suspends New START," *Arms Control Today*, March 2023. www.armscontrol.org/act/2023-03/news/russia-suspends-new-start.

29 Gottemoeller.

30 John F. Burns, "India Sets 3 Nuclear Blasts, Defying a Worldwide Ban," *New York Times*, May 12, 1998. www.nytimes.com/1998/05/12/world/india-sets-3-nuclear-blasts-defying-a-worldwide-ban-tests-bring-a-sharp-outcry.html.

31 John Ward Anderson and Kamran Khan, "Pakistan Sets Off Nuclear Blasts," *Washington Post*, May 29, 1998. www.washingtonpost.com/archive/politics/1998/05/29/pakistan-sets-off-nuclear-blasts/be94cba3-7ffc-4ecc-9f67-ac6ddfe2a94c.

32 Pickering, "How to Prepare for Peace Talks in Ukraine."

33 Kissinger, *Years of Renewal*, 916.

34 Ibid., 918.

35 Ibid.

36 Ibid., 955.

37 Gerald R. Ford, *A Time to Heal* (Harper & Row, 1979), 380.

38 Sebenius, Burns and Mnookin, 20.

39 Ibid., 23.

40 Dennis Ross, Lecture at the Washington International Diplomatic Academy, April 12, 2022.

41 Marvin Kalb, "First Line Report," CBS Radio, May 4, 1976, cited in Sebenius, Burns and Mnookin, 32.

42 Kissinger, *Years of Renewal*, 940.

43 Ibid., 941.

44 Ford, 380.

45 Ross, Lecture at WIDA.

46 Ibid.

47 Bruce Riedel, "25 Years On, Remembering the Path to Peace for Jordan," the Brookings Institution, October 23, 2019. www.brookings.edu/blog/order-from-chaos/2019/10/23/25-years-on-remembering-the-path-to-peace-for-jordan-and-israel.

48 Kissinger, *Years of Renewal*, 961.

49 Ibid., 958.

50 Ibid., 968–69.

51 Sebenius, Burns and Mnookin, 42.

52 Kissinger, 980.

53 Ibid.

54 Sebenius, Burns and Mnookin, 47.

55 Ian Smith, *The Great Betrayal* (Blake Publishing, 1997), 202–3.

56 Kissinger, *Years of Renewal*, 998.

57 Smith, 207, 209.

58 "Paul Nitze and a Walk in the Woods," Association for Diplomatic Studies and Training, March 30, 2016. https://adst.org/2016/03/paul-nitze-and-a-walk-in-the-woods-a-failed-attempt-at-arms-control.

59 Ross, Lecture at WIDA.

60 Sebenius, Burns and Mnookin, 56–57.

61 Philip Zelikow and Condoleezza Rice, *Germany Unified and Europe Transformed* (Harvard University Press, 1995), 277–78.

62 Steven Pifer, "Did NATO Promise Not to Enlarge?" The Brookings Institution, November 6, 2014. www.brookings.edu/blog/up-front/2014/11/06/did-nato-promise-not-to-enlarge-gorbachev-says-no.

63 Maxim Kórshunov, "Mikhail Gorbachev: I Am Against All Walls," *Russia Behind the Headlines*, October 16, 2014. www.rbth.com/international/2014/10/16/mikhail_gorba chev_i_am_against_all_walls_40673.html.

64 Claire Klobucista and Danielle Renwick, "Colombia's Civil Conflict," Council on Foreign Relations, January 11, 2017. www.cfr.org/backgrounder/colombias-civil-conflict.

65 "Plan Colombia: Fact Sheet," U.S. Department of State, March 14, 2001. https://2001-2009.state.gov/p/wha/rls/fs/2001/1042.htm.

66 Klobucista and Renwick.

67 "U.S.–China Strategic and Economic Dialogue," U.S. Department of State. https://2009-2017.state.gov/e/eb/tpp/bta/sed/index.htm.

Afterword

1 "The Use of Digitalisation and Artificial Intelligence in Migration Management," European Commission, February 2022. www.oecd.org/migration/mig/EMN-OECD-INFORM-FEB-2022-The-use-of-Digitalisation-and-AI-in-Migration-Management.pdf.

2 Jason Lemon, "China Is Using Artificial Intelligence to Help Make Diplomatic Decisions," *Newsweek*, July 30, 2018. www.newsweek.com/china-using-artificial-intelli gence-help-make-diplomatic-decisions-1048734.

3 "Using Artificial Intelligence (AI) to Modernize American Statecraft," Google Cloud and Deloitte, November 2022. www2.deloitte.com/content/dam/Deloitte/us/Documents/public-sector/us-using-artificial-intelligence-to-modernize-american-statecraft.pdf.

4 Janosch Delcker, "Where AI Can Replace Diplomats – And Where It Shouldn't," *Internationale Politik Quarterly*, June 29, 2023. https://ip-quarterly.com/en/where-ai-can-replace-diplomats-and-where-it-shouldnt?mc_cid=68f312b3d7&mc_eid=da1659bfd9.

5 Ibid.

Index

Abdullah, king of Jordan, and
    Clinton 184
Abercrombie-Winstanley, Gina 137,
    138
    in Israel 134
Abkhazia 97
advocacy
    diplomatic mission duty 23
    as diplomatic skill 73–75
    economic officers 160–62
    for human rights 73
    identification of contacts 140, 161
    and instructions 140
    and partnerships with other
        agencies 141–42, 162
    and personal views 75
    and persuasion 73, 140
    political officers 139–42
    public commercial 169
    and specific goals 162
    see also influence; negotiations
Afghanistan 24, 57, 146
    economic rebuilding 155
    fall to Taliban (2021) 231, 276–77
    Special Immigrant Visa program
        234
    U.N. and 276–77
    weapons-abatement programs 72
Africa
    and black-majority rule in
        southern Africa 326, 332,
        338
    economic policy in 161
    Security Governance Initiative 141
    use of GMOs in 290
    see also Namibia; South Africa;
        southern Africa; Uganda;
        Zimbabwe
African Development Bank 290
African Union (AU) (formerly
    Organization of African Unity)
    20, 270, 290, 333
African Union Convention on Cyber
    Security and Personal Data
    Protection 316

agency employees
    ambassadorial loss of confidence
        in 100
    relations with diplomats 100
Agency for Global Media (U.S.) 114
aide memoire, between countries 193
AIDS
    antiretroviral therapy (ART) 292
    relief programs 115–17
    in Uganda 291
    see also President's Emergency
        Plan for AIDS Relief
        (PEPFAR)
airgrams, for dispatches (cables) 175
Alaska, purchased from Russia
    (1867) 38
Albania
    ambassadorial autonomy 106, 139
    Iranian cyberattacks on (case
        study) 317–18
Albright, Madeleine 64, **324**, 346, 350
Allen, Woody 215
Allende, Salvador 179–80
Alliance Française 200
ally, alliance 41
ambassadors 17
    autonomy of 104–6, 139
    balancing national policy and
        relations with host country 118
    as chief of mission 104–6
    contact with the U.S. president 104
    local participation 106
    at NSC Principals Committees 86,
        87
    order of precedence 251
    and policy instructions 106
    power of 104
    proposed CEO model 104
    protocol 250
    relations with DCMs 107
    see also political appointees
Amnesty International 272
analytical skills 59–60
    avoidance of bias 60
    and diplomatic reporting 59

Angola, and Cuba 46
Anti-Drug Abuse Act (1986) 217
APEC (Asia-Pacific Economic
    Cooperation) 271
APHIS (Animal and Plant Health
    Inspection Service) 102, 170, 364
Arafat, Yasser, Palestinian
    Authority 185, 341
arms-control
    negotiations 325, 330–31
    START treaties 90, 94
Armstrong, Louis 199
Arroyo, Gloria Macapagal, state
    visit 245, 246
artificial intelligence (AI) 351–52
    for analysis 351
    possible use in negotiations 352
    strategy for State Department 351
ASEAN (Association of Southeast
    Asian Nations) 20, 271
    and cyber diplomacy 316
Ash-Shiraa, Lebanese weekly
    magazine 78
Asian financial crisis (1997) 160
Assad, Hafez al- 260
AstraZeneca, Covid-19 vaccine 301
attachés 103
    defense 112
    legal 113
Australia
    and France 13, 78–99 (exercise)
    numbers of diplomatic missions 15
avian influenza (H7N9), outbreak in
    China (2013) 286–87
aviation 154
    and effect of sanctions on Russia
        163
    "open skies" agreements 328
    see also Boeing
Aziz, Tariq 322

Baghdad, U.S. embassy 25
Baker, James 128, 261, 326
    and NATO 344
    and U.N. resolution on Iraq 320

Bakhtiar, Shapour 182
Bakiyev, Kurmanbek 146, **147**
Balkan wars 144
    sanctions 163
Banco International, Dominican
    Republic 6
Barak, Ehud 185
Bashir, Salman 66
Bassett, Ebenezer, Haiti 175
Beers, Charlotte 198
Beijing, 2022 Winter Olympics 211
Belarus, and U.N. response to
    Russian invasion of Ukraine
    283
Belgium, repeal of law on crimes
    against humanity (*case study*)
    75–76
Benghazi, Libya, attack on U.S.
    consulate **15**
Berger, Sandy 346
Berlin, U.S. Embassy **105**
Berlin Wall, fall of (1989) 128
Berners-Lee, Tim 308
Biden, Joe
    and NSC 81
    and presidential envoy on climate
        negotiations 329
    as senator 98
    and Ukraine 80, 200
bilateral diplomacy 14
    negotiations 323
Bill and Melinda Gates Foundation
    272, 299
Biological Weapons Convention 330
BioNTech, Covid-19 vaccine 300
Bismarck, Otto von 11
Black, Shirley Temple 128
Blackwill, Robert 343
Blair, Tony 213, 266
Blaser, Virginia 107, 115
Blinken, Antony, Secretary of State
    138, **282**
body language 55, 62
Boeing 150, 169
    and 737 MAX problems (*exercise*)
        172–73
Bolivia, anti-drug campaign (*case
    study*) 204, 217–19
borders
    expansion of 38
    trade and investment across 38
Bosnia and Herzegovina war in 327
Brainard, Lael 161

Brazil
    environment 109
    numbers of diplomatic missions *15*
    parental child abduction case 227
    public diplomacy strategy 209
    Zika virus outbreak (*case study*)
        302–3
Brexit 159
Brezhnev, Leonid 340
bribery, and fake merchandise 157
British Council 200
Brown, Austin 168
Brown, Gordon 213
Bryza, Matthew, and Georgia 97
Budapest Convention on
    Cybercrime 315, 316
Bureau of Arms Control 331
Bureau of Consular Affairs 223
Bureau of Cyberspace and Digital
    Policy 311
Bureau of East Asian and Pacific
    Affairs 154
Bureau of Economic and Business
    Affairs 154
    and accords on corruption 155
    investment-climate reports 161
Bureau of International Narcotics
    and Law Enforcement Affairs
    218, 346
Bureau of International
    Organizations Affairs 154, 278,
    280
Bureau of International Security and
    Nonproliferation 331
Bureau of Oceans and International
    Environmental and Scientific
    Affairs 329
Bureau of Western Hemisphere
    Affairs 346
bureaucracy, navigating 69, 79, 108
Burns, William J. 21, **27**, 29, 121, 130
    cable from Jordan 184
    cable from Russia **183**, 183
    cables on Israeli–Palestinian peace
        process 185, 188
    and Iran 129
    and note-taking 193
    and NSC 26, 80, 93, 95
    reporting 135
Bush, George H. W.
    and Gorbachev 340, 343, **344**
    and Iraq War (1991) 274
    and Poland 91, 92

    and Queen Elizabeth II 245, **248**
    and START treaty (1991) 90
    and U.N. resolution on Iraq 320
Bush, George W. 37
    and Belgian law 76
    and Georgia 97
    and ICC 51
    invasion of Iraq 145
    and Iran 129
    and Putin 94
    and visit of President Gloria
        Arroyo 245, 246
Bush, Vannevar 288

cables (dispatches) 23, 59, 186–91
    checking 190
    classified and unclassified 178
    in code 175
    comment (conclusion) 190
    distribution (recipients) 190–91
    electronic 187
    by email 177–78
    from headquarters 191–92
    main body 189–90
    modern 178
    prioritizing topics 180–81, 194–95
        (*exercise*)
    reports of meetings and
        conversations 180–82, 193
    "scene-setters" 182
    subject line **187** (box), 187–88, 195
        (*exercise*)
    summary 188–89
    by telegram 175
    telegraphic language 175, 179
    use of humor 189
    and use of telephone 175–77
    Wikileaks disclosures 45, 174
    writing style 181, 189, 195–96
        (*exercise*)
Callahan, Robert 218
Cambodia **117**
Cameroon 161
Camp Ashraf 317
Camp David Peace Accords (1978)
    180
Canada, numbers of diplomatic
    missions *15*
capability and readiness 43–45
Capitol Hill, January 2021 attack on
    197–98
career paths 27–29
    choice of tracks 28

Carter, Jimmy 73
  and human rights agenda 145
  and Kissinger's negotiations in
    Africa 342
Castro, Marcelo 302
CELAC (Community of Latin
  American and Caribbean
  States) 271
celebrities, as public diplomacy
  envoys 214–15
Centers for Disease Control and
  Prevention (U.S.) (CDC) 102,
  115, 224
  and avian influenza (China 2013)
    286
Central America Free Trade
  Agreement (CAFTA) 171
Chechnya, Russian invasion 137
Chemical Weapons Convention 330
Chen Shui-Bian 132, 136
Chiang Kai-shek 48
Chile, cable reporting coup attempt
  against Allende 179–80, 188
China
  and Africa 161
  application to WTO 151
  avian influenza outbreak (2013)
    286–87
  cyberattacks 313
  decision-making 34
  and economic diplomacy 109
  insurance industry 151
  and Internet freedom 314
  Ming dynasty 198
  Nixon and 36
  numbers of diplomatic missions 15
  and postwar multilateral system
    267
  relations with United States 54
  size of Foreign Service 104
  and Taiwan 49, 131
  and Track II diplomacy 29
  and U.N. Security Council
    resolution on Afghanistan
    (2021) 277
  U.S. negotiations with (exercise)
    348–49
  use of social media influencers
    211
  and WHO 298, 300
Christopher, Warren 144, 342
Chung, Julie 157
Churchill, Winston 11, 36

CIA (Central Intelligence Agency),
  cable system 178
Citizenship and Immigration
  Services (CIS) 224
client–state relationships 42
"clientitis" 14, 54
climate change
  negotiations 329–30
  science of 289
Clinton, Bill
  and Balkan War 144
  and Israeli–Palestinian peace
    process 185, 341
  and King Hussein of Jordan
    336–37, 340
  and Yeltsin 137
Clinton, Hillary 9, 282
  and CEO model for ambassadors
    104
  at COP15 329
coalitions and alliances, diplomacy
  to preclude hostile 38
coercion, and persuasion 39
Cold War 35
  and deterrence 43
  end (1989) 41
  examples of statecraft 36
  and spheres of influence 35,
    41
Colombia 52
  anti-drug operations 345, 347
  DEA fraud in 100
  end of conflict with FARC
    345
  negotiations on "Plan Colombia"
    (case study) 345–48
Comerford, Cris 246
commercial diplomacy 167–71
  defined 168
commercial diplomats 151, 169
communication 22, 190
  between countries 192–93
  essential during war 37
  see also cables
communication skills 60–66
  cross-cultural 64–66
  and language ability 65
  listening 62, 204
  public speaking 63
  (box), 62–64
  writing 61–62
Comprehensive Nuclear Test Ban
  Treaty 330

Computer Emergency Response
  Teams (CERTs) 316
Conference for Security and
  Cooperation in Europe (CSCE)
  343
conflict zones, expeditionary
  diplomacy 24
Congress of Vienna (1815) 258
consular affairs 221–36
  crisis information for citizens
    241
  crisis management (Japan 2011)
    (case study) 236–41, 241–42
  (box)
  diplomatic mission duty 22
  emergency citizen services
    229–31
  headquarters 223–25
  interagency partners 224
  routine citizen services 226–27,
    239–41
  special citizen services 228–29
  travel warnings 229
  see also visas
consular officers
  assistance to home-country
    citizens 222, 226, 238–39
  and child adoptions 226
  and detained citizens 226
  and diplomatic immunity
    258
  documenting birth of citizen
    children 226
  importance of local contacts 222,
    325
  leadership abilities 223
  and parental child abductions
    227–28
  responsibilities 222–23
consular sections, in embassies 110,
  224, 225–26
  head of section 225
  and public diplomacy 225
  services 224
consulates 18, 224
consulates general 18
Contras, Nicaraguan rebels 78
Convention on Combating Bribery
  of Foreign Officials in
  International Business
  Transactions (1997) 155
Copenhagen, COP15 climate
  negotiations 329

corruption 109
  and economic development 155
Council of Europe, and Budapest
    Convention on Cybercrime 315,
    316
counterterrorism
  National Counterterrorism Center
    224, 232
  NSC directorate 83
countries, and nations 64
country desk officers **131** (box),
    130–31
  and section chiefs abroad 133
country teams 103, 116
Covid-19 pandemic 231, **299**
  and consular services 226, 229
  and cybercrime 309
  development of vaccines 300–1
  economic consequences 155–57
  effect on public diplomacy 216
  and equitable access to vaccines 300
  and global supply chains 150, 156
  lack of information from China
    286
  and lack of preparedness 299
  lockdowns 156
  and national security 297
  vaccination campaign 301
creative solutions 69
Crimean Peninsula
  Russian annexation 6, 89
  Russian cyberattack 306
  Russian sanctions over annexation
    (*case study*) 94–96
Crocker, Chester A. 31, 35, **47**
  and "linkage diplomacy" (*case
    study*) 46–48, 69
Cuba
  and Angola 46, 326
  U.S. relations with 80
Cuban Missile Crisis (1962) 273
Cuci, Bledi 318
cultural differences 33, 218
  gender differences 251
  greetings 251
  and respectfulness 65, 203, 204
  when a guest at events 251
cultural diplomacy 212–15
  use of celebrity envoys 214–15
  see also exchange programs
culture 64
  knowledge of host country 57
  and public diplomacy 199

Customs and Border Protection
    (CBP) 113, 224
cyber diplomacy 305–17
  capacity-building and
    coordination 316–17
  cooperation mechanisms 314–16
  description 307–9
  international cooperation 307,
    311, 312, 316
  multi-stakeholder governance 308
cyber diplomats
  and conflict prevention 312
  coordination with domestic
    agencies 316
  duties of 311–12
  enforcement of rules 313
  need for expertise 311
  promotion of Internet freedom
    313–14
  and rules and norms of behavior
    312–13
cyber policy
  armed forces structures 311
  NATO 314
  NSC directorate 83
cybercrime
  actors 310
  attack on Estonia 305–6, 314
  by China 313
  Computer Emergency Response
    Teams (CERTs) 316
  global 309
  individual level 310
  industry level 309
  Iranian attack on Albania (*case
    study*) 317–18
  national 309
  need for expert response to
    311
  by North Korea 313
  Russian attacks on Ukraine
    306
  U.N. response (*exercise*) 318–19
cyberspace
  complexity of 308
  conflict prevention 312
  defined 306
  enforcement of rules 313
  humanitarian law in 313
  impossibility of arms-control
    regime 312
  rules and norms of behavior
    312–13

threat levels 309–10
  see also Internet
Czechoslovakia 128–29

Dačić, Ivaca 105
Davis, Raymond 66
Dayton Accords (1995) 145, 342
de Klerk, F. W. 202, 213
DEA (Drug Enforcement
    Administration) 113, 218
  agents 100
decision memorandum (action
    memo), from State Department
    191
decision-making
  by consensus 271
  cultural differences 33
  intergovernmental organizations
    271
Defense Intelligence Agency (DIA)
    112
DeLaurentis, Jeffrey 277, **278**
Deloitte 351
démarches
  cable from State Department 191
  delivery of 67, 325
democracy
  effect of attack on Capitol Hill on
    U.S. reputation 197–98
  promotion of 76 (*exercise*), 142
  see also elections
Department of Agriculture (U.S.)
    170, 288
Department of Commerce (U.S.)
    169
  Country Commercial Guides 161
Department of Defense (DOD) 102,
    224
  emergency evacuation flights 230
  and U.S. Cyber Command 311
Department of Energy (U.S.) 102
Department of Health and Human
    Services (HHS) 224
  and CDC 286
  and Covid-19 300
Department of Homeland Security
    (DHS) 113, 224
  and cybersecurity 316
Department of Justice (U.S.) 113
Deputies Committees, in NSC 84
deputy chief of mission (DCM) 18,
    106–8
  authority from ambassador 107

management responsibilities 107
  as mentors 108
desk officers 16
deterrence 43
developing countries
  economic reforms 155, 328
  health and science diplomacy in
    295–96
  national responsibility for
    healthcare 295
development
  and democracy 142
  as diplomatic policy 112
development aid 109, 112, 164–66, 295
  and economic reforms 158
  Nigeria 164–65
  see also USAID
Dicker, Craig 217
digital diplomacy 308
diplomacy
  as alternative to war 38
  capability and readiness 43–45
  defined 7, 10–12
  limits of 12
  origin of term 7
  as risk management 40–43
  as strategy 35–37
  as tactics 37–39
  value of 350
  see also diplomatic missions;
    diplomats; reporting
"Diplomacy Is the World's Best
  Hope", WIDA essay
  assignment 350
diplomacy system
  bilateral 14
  see also multilateral diplomacy
"diplomatic bag" 259
diplomatic doctrine
  need for 45–46
  and review of experience 46, 345
diplomatic immunity 257–58
  for consulate employees 257
  for diplomats 257
  family members 258
  limits on 258–59
  see also diplomatic privileges
diplomatic missions 11–19, 101
  categories of officers 102
  chief of mission (ambassador)
    104–6
  Community Liaison Office 111
  constituent posts 114

country teams 103, 116
deputy chief of mission 18, 106–8
duties and responsibilities 21–24
Emergency Action Plans 230, 238
hierarchy within 250
involvement of head of state 137
management negotiations 325
numbers 15, 101
protocol within 249–50
relations with headquarters 117
relations with host country 118
relations with other missions 119
size of 101
specialists 102, 152, 167, 294
staff and families 107, 110
see also ambassadors; consulates;
  consulates general; diplomats;
  embassies; permanent missions;
  presence posts; representative
  offices
diplomatic notes 192
diplomatic privileges 258
  exemption from host-country
    taxation 259
  free communication among
    diplomats 259
  inviolability of official
    correspondence 259
  see also diplomatic immunity
diplomatic protocol 245–57
  breaches of 245
  description of 247–49
  and etiquette 246–47
  and guidelines for meetings and
    negotiations 248
  international norms 250–51
  making introductions 250, 251
  official summits and negotiations
    254–57
  reception at ambassador's
    residence (exercise) 262–63
  and respect 247
  role of 247
  and rules of precedence 258
  state visits 245–46
  table arrangements for
    negotiations 254–56, **255**,
    260–62, **261–62**
  timing of arrival 247
  Vienna Convention rules 249
  within diplomatic missions 249–50
  see also diplomatic immunity;
    etiquette

Diplomatic Security 101, 111
diplomats 12–14
  assignments and bidding process
    120–21
  career paths 27–29
  consular work 58, 222
  and domestic politics 129
  frequent moves 119
  in government agencies 15
  lack of training 52
  permanent (career) 13
  political opinions 146
  ranks and hierarchy 119–20, 250
  recall of 13
  relations with political appointees
    93
  role in NSC 92–94
  skill sets 25–27
  transitory 13, 102, 294
  at U.N. 274
  way of life 119
Discovery Communications 205
disinformation, countering 211–12
dispatches
  diplomatic 175
  see also cables; communication
"dissent channel", for criticism of
  policy 60, 145, 167
Diversity Visa Program 234
Dogu, Laura 210
dollar, and power of economic
  sanctions 164
Dominican Republic 6
  banking crisis (case study) 171–72,
    328
  IMF loan 171
  visa waiver (exercise) 243
Douglas, Walter 213
Downes, Robert, on Capitol Hill
  attack (2021) 197
Drescher, Fran 215
drone technology 167
drugs
  Bolivia campaign 204, 217–19
    (case study)
  Colombian campaign 345, 347
  U.S. "war on" 217, 219
  see also DEA
Duda, Andrzej 90

Eagleburger, Lawrence 68
Ebola outbreak (2014) 296–97,
  299

economic measures
  and monitoring of reforms 158
  power of 38
economic officers 151
  advocacy and negotiation 160–62
  daily routine 166–67
  duties and responsibilities abroad
    155–62
  and interagency process 154
  liaison role in negotiations 162
  and local officials 160
  local travel 167
  personal disagreement with policy
    167
  preparation for assignments 167
  relationship management 159–60
  reporting and analysis 157–59
  skills required 152
  specialist knowledge 152, 167
economic sanctions 39, 162–64
  as hard power 39, 163
  negotiations on 328
  and power of dollar 164
  on Russia (2022) 12, 39, 89, 163
  workarounds 163
economic tradecraft 109–10, 150–67
  and commercial diplomacy 151
  description 152–53
  development and foreign aid 164–66
  and headquarters 153–55
  policy issues **152** (box), 152–53
economy
  data analysis 158
  disruptions and crises 158
  global integration 150
  supply chains 150, 156
ECOWAS (Economic Community
  of West African States) 271
education
  to counter disinformation 212
  and public diplomacy 199
Educational and Cultural Affairs
  bureau 206
Egypt
  Arab Spring 86
  cable on Egypt–Israel peace treaty
    (1979) 180, 188
  and Israel 36
Egypt, ancient 175
Eisenhower, Dwight D. 199
elections
  monitoring 134
  reporting on 132

Electronic System for Travel
  Authorization (ESTA) 233
Elizabeth II, and breaches of
  protocol 245, **248**
email, reporting by 177–78
embassies 17–18, 100–21
  chief of mission (ambassador)
    104–6
  and commercial advocacy 169
  deputy chief of mission 18, 106–8
  interagency challenges 115–17
  inviolability of 19
  local staff 19, 111, 114
  Marine Security Guard 107, 111
  organizational structure 101–4,
    103
  renovations for ambassador's
    residence (*exercise*) 123
  weekly team meetings and
    interagency cooperation 116
  see also ambassadors
embassy sections 18, 101, 108–15
  consular 110, 224, 225–26
  crisis responsibilities 230
  defense office 112
  economic 109–10, 150–67
  Foreign Commercial Service
    111
  intelligence station 113
  law-enforcement agencies 113
  management 110–11
  other agencies 111, 112, 113–14
  political 108–9, 125–46
  public diplomacy 110, 206–8
  security 111
  and USAID 112
Emergency Action Plans 230, 238
empathy 53–55
  and diplomatic negotiations 322,
    340
English
  as *lingua franca* 55, 151
  public diplomacy teaching
    schemes 217
ententes, limited partnerships 42
environment
  Brazil 109
  see also climate change
Estonia
  Bronze Soldier in Tallinn 305
  Cyber Security Strategy 306
  Russian cyberattack on 305–6,
    314

Ethiopia, and exchange programs 214
etiquette 246–47
  dress code 252
  greetings 251
  as guest at events 251
  seating 253
  table 252 (box)
European Coal and Steel
  Community 270
European Cybercrime Center 316
European Union Agency for
  Cybersecurity 316
European Union (EU) 20, 270
  and cyber security 313, 315
  External Action Service, cyber
    policy 306
  and G7 270
  and G20 270
  and GMOs 290
  negotiations with candidates for
    membership 328
  permanent missions to 17
  and Russia 6
  and tariffs on American products
    192
  and U.S. sanctions on Russia
    95
Evans, Earl A. 288
examinations, to join Foreign
  Service 28
exchange programs 110, 166, 213
  academic 213
  professional 213
  South Africa 202
Executive Office of the President
  (EOP) (U.S.) 79
expeditionary diplomacy 24–25
expertise
  and cyber security 311
  economic 152, 167
  and exercise of judgment 68
  and intellectual curiosity 59
  scientific 287, 294
exports, licenses for 166

Facebook 212
families
  and choice of assignment 120
  and diplomatic immunity 258
  in diplomatic missions 107,
    110
FAO (U.N. Food and Agriculture
  Organization) 20

FARC (Revolutionary Armed
    Forces of Colombia) 345
FBI (Federal Bureau of
    Investigation) 102, 113
  representatives 13
  and visas 224
Federal Aviation Administration
    (FAA) 102, 224
Feeley, John 100, 116
Ference, Matthew 24, 25
Fergin, Judith 160
Fick, Nathaniel 318
Financial Action Task Force 159
Finerty, Tressa, at U.N. 281, **282**
Finneman, Nicole **208**
Ford, Gerald, Kissinger and 334, 335
Foreign Agricultural Service (FAS)
    102, 111, 170–71
  regional responsibility 170
  role of 170
foreign aid
  aim of 166
  see also development aid
Foreign Commercial Service (U.S.)
    102, 111, 168–70
  services to business 168
Foreign Corrupt Practices Act (U.S.)
    161
foreign languages *see* languages
foreign ministries
  as career path 27, 28
  civil servants 15
  desk officers 16
  foreign policy 14
  regional organization 15
  see also U.S. Foreign Service
foreign policy
  and diplomacy 11
  and national security 8–10
  purpose of 40
  responsibility for 14
  see also interagency foreign policy
    process
Foreign Service Officer Test (U.S.) 28
Foreign Service Oral Assessment
    (U.S.) 28
Foster, Jodie 215
France
  and Australia 13, 78–99 (*exercise*)
  Foreign Service 33
  French–Indian nuclear
    cooperation, cable from Paris
    on 188, 189

and GMOs 290
and Kissinger's negotiations in
    southern Africa 333
and Louisiana Purchase 38
Franceschini, Dario **202**
Franco-Prussian War 11
Freedom House, watchdog NGO
    314
Freeman, Chas W. 11, **34**, 67, **68**,
    163, 322
  in China 57
French language 246
Fried, Daniel 6, 23
  and Georgia 97
  and NSC 82, 83, 86, 88, **88**
  and Poland 90–92
  and sanctions on Russia 95
Fukushima nuclear power station
    237
Fulbright scholarship program 110,
    213

G7 (Group of Seven) 269
  and biomedical issues 300
G20 (Group of Twenty) 270
Gallant, Rosemary 151
GATT (General Agreement on
    Tariffs and Trade) 269
genetically modified organisms
    (GMOs), science of 289–90
Geneva, arms-control talks 325, 330
Georgia
  Russian cyberattack 306
  Russian invasion (2008) 86, 94–98
    (*case study*)
Germany 11, 287
  exchange programs 213
  honorary consuls in U.S. 114
  membership of NATO after
    reunification 343
  numbers of diplomatic missions *15*
Ghani, Ashraf 57
Ghebreyesus, Tedros 298
Giscard d'Estaing, Valéry 333
Glaspie, April 33
Global Air Media 168
Global Engagement Center,
    Washington 212
Global Forum of Cyber Expertise
    316
Global Public Affairs bureau 206
globalization
  and economic integration 150

and "just-in-time" sourcing 156
and multilateral dimensions of
    economic issues 153
and multilateral diplomacy 265
and supply chains 150, 156
Goethe-Institut 200
Goins, Traci 59
gold-mining, and elimination of
    mercury 162
Goldman, David, and son Sean 227
Google 351
Gorbachev, Mikhail 90, 91
  NATO and German reunification
    343, **344**
  and Reagan 340
Gore, Al 202
government agencies
  and foreign policy 14
  lack of training for staffers abroad
    115
Government Communication
    Service (U.K.) 212
Greece, 2010 financial crisis 153
Greece, ancient 7
Greenpeace 272
Gromyko, Andrei 260
Group of Seven (G7) 159
groupthink 54
Guatemala 51, 72
Gulf War (1991) 11, 320, 323
Guterres, António 264

hacktivists, groups and individuals
    310
Hague Convention on Civil Aspects
    of International Child
    Abduction 227
Haiti 175
  earthquake (2010) 70, 230, 231
Hall, Edward T. 65
Hamilton, Clay 170
Hammer, Michael 206
  on Wikileaks 174
hard power
  economic sanctions as 39, 163
  see also war
Haslach, Patricia 160
heads of state 14
health and science diplomacy
    286–302
  and developing countries 295–96
  health diplomacy 290–93
  and international cooperation 287

health and science diplomacy
(cont.)
   and national security 297–98
   not seen as priority 289, 294
   science diplomacy 287–89
   see also science and technology
health and science diplomats
   duties of 293–94
   interpretation of scientific research
   295
   managing resources and
      expectations 296–97
   need for technical knowledge 294
   specialists 294
healthcare
   global governance 298–99, 300
   as national responsibility 287, 295
   see also pandemic disease
Helsinki Final Act (1975) 343
Herbst, John, Ukraine 87
Hertell, Hans 171
Herzog, Roman 245
Hezbollah, in Lebanon 78
High Commissioner for Refugees
   (HCR) 268
Hill, Fiona, on NSC staff 82
Holbrooke, Richard, and Bosnia and
   Herzegovina (1995) 327, 342
HomeLandJustice cyberattack on
   Albania 317
Hong Kong
   consulates 225
   and terrorist financing 159
honorary consuls 13, 114
Hoza, Michael 161
Hu Jintao **34**
human rights, U.S. advocacy 142
human rights abuses 73
   China 211
humor, use of
   in cables 189
   in talking to media 210
Hushek, Tom 217
Hussein, King 336–37
   meeting with Yitzhak Rabin 337

IAEA (International Atomic Energy
   Agency) 20
ICC (International Criminal Court) 51
IMF (International Monetary Fund)
   41, 155
   and conditional loans 158, 171
   negotiations 328

immigrant visas 234–35
   and Diversity Visa Program 234
   Special Immigrant Visa program
   234
   sponsorship 234
   see also visas
Immigration and Customs
   Enforcement (ICE) 113, 224
Immigration and Nationality Act
   233
India
   and Covid-19 301
   French–Indian nuclear
      cooperation, cable from Paris
      on 188, 189
   nuclear weapons 331
   numbers of diplomatic missions *15*
Indonesia 160
   2007 bird flu outbreak 301
   IMF loan 161
influence
   of diplomatic missions 23
   reporting and analysis 182–84
influencers, social media 211
informal diplomacy (Track II
   diplomacy) 29–30
information
   and diplomatic reporting 178
   overt gathering 109
   see also intelligence
information memorandum, from
   State Department 191
information security 45
insurance, against cyberattacks
   309
Integrated Country Strategies 103,
   209, 215
integrity 54, 65
intellectual curiosity 57–59
   and expertise 59
   of host-country's culture 57
   regional travel 58
intellectual property rights 157
   vaccines and medications 301
intelligence 33
   diplomats' reports 45
intelligence operatives
   declaration of 13
   relations with diplomats 113
intelligence station, within embassy
   113
Inter-American Convention Against
   Corruption (1996) 155

interagency challenges, within
   diplomatic missions 115–17
   difference in bureaucratic culture
   115
   and weekly team meetings 116
interagency foreign policy process
   78–94
   dysfunction 89–90, 116
   and intergovernmental
      organizations 279
   and policy-making 79–81
   role of diplomats 92–94
   structure 79, *80*
   working around dysfunction
   90–92
   see also National Security Council
   (U.S.)
Interagency Policy Committees
   (IPCs) 84
   lower-level committees 80
   permanent committees 80
   sub-committees 84
intergovernmental organizations
   269–70
   decision-making 271
   funding 272
   leadership positions in 268, 269
   and national diplomats 269
   oversight authority 272
   regional 270–71
   rotating presidencies 270
   structure and practices 271–72
Intermediate Range Nuclear Forces
   agreement (1987) 90
International Atomic Energy
   Agency (IAEA) 330
International Child Abduction
   Prevention and Return Act
   (2014) 228
International Civil Aviation
   Organization 272
international law, and norms of
   behavior 41
International Organization for
   Migration 272
international organizations 20,
   268–73
   regional 20
   see also intergovernmental
   organizations; NATO; United
   Nations
international relations 7
   adversarial 44, 118

need for constant engagement 43
relationship categories 41
and trade treaties 150
see also intergovernmental
    organizations; international
    organizations; multilateral
    diplomacy
International Sanitary Conference
    (1851) 287
International Telecommunications
    Union (1865) 266
International Visitor Leadership
    Program 110, 213
Internet
    and access to information for
        foreign audiences 205
    and cyberspace 307
    global dependency on 308
    Internet Architecture Board (IAB)
        308
    multi-stakeholder governance
        308
    origin 308
    promoting freedom 313–14
    see also cyberspace
Internet Corporation for Assigned
    Names and Numbers 308
interpersonal skills 70–71
    in crises 70
    for public diplomacy 203
Interpol (International Criminal
    Police Organization) 269
Iran
    cable from (1979) 182, 188, 189,
        190
    cyberattacks against Albania
        (*case study*) 317–18
    economic sanctions 39
    and multilateral diplomatic
        groupings 266
    nuclear program negotiations 335
    U.S. relations with 129
    U.S. sale of arms to 78
Iraq 24, 106
    Gulf War (1991) 323
    invasion of Kuwait 11, 320
    and U.N. approval of U.S.
        intervention 273–74, 320–22,
        321 (box)
    U.S. invasion (2003) 37, 145, 146
    weapons-abatement program 72
Irizarry, José 100
Ismay, Hastings, NATO 270

Israel
    and Egypt 36
    and Jordan 327
    peace talks with Lebanon (1983)
        256–57
    see also Palestine
Israeli–Palestinian peace process
    cables on 185, 188
    Clinton and 185
    and Middle East Quartet 266

Jackson, Samuel L. 215
Jacobs, Janice, consular affairs 5, 69,
    223, **224**
Japan
    consular officers 221
    decision-making 33
    diplomatic note on U.S. military
        bases 192, 335
    earthquake, tsunami and nuclear
        plant meltdown (2011) 231,
        236–41, **240** (*case study*)
Jefferson, Thomas, and Louisiana
    Purchase (1803) 38
Jeffrey, James 106
Johannes, Jaromir 128
Jones, Deborah 137
Jones, James 82
Jordan
    and peace treaty with Israel 327
    visit of King Abdullah to
        Washington 184
journalists, female 201, 216
judgment 67
    and expertise 68
    and knowledge of policy 69
    and noncompliance with orders 68
    testing 69
judiciaries, role in foreign relations
    17

Kamaishi, Japan **240**
Karman, Tawakkol, Nobel Peace
    Prize 216
Kayani, General Ashfaq Parvez
    66
Keene, Matthew 221, 228–29
Kennan, George, and 1946 "Long
    Telegram" 175, **176**
Kennedy, John F., and USIA 199
Kenney, Kristie 72, 169
Kerry, John 329
    and Iran 129

Khobragade, Devyani, and
    diplomatic immunity 17, 257
Khomeini, Ayatollah Ruhollah 182
Kissinger, Henry 6, 180, 256, 260
    as national security adviser 82
    and Jordan 327
    conduct of southern Africa
        negotiations 337–39, 341
    and Ian Smith 327
    negotiations in southern Africa
        (1976) 326–27
    preparations for southern Africa
        negotiations 332–34
    and U.S. support for southern
        African negotiations 334
    and Vorster **338**
Kohl, Helmut 245
Kolker, Jimmy, and Pan-American
    Health Organization **291**
Korean War 48
Kosovo, independence from Serbia
    97, 105
Koštunica, Vojislav 105
Kralev, Nicholas **10**
Kubiske, Lisa 6, **160**
Kurtzer, Daniel, cables on Israeli–
    Palestinian peace process 185,
    188
Kuwait 11
    cable on payment of local embassy
        staff 184
    Iraqi invasion (1990) 11, 320
Kvitinsky, Yuliy 340
Kwan, Michelle 215
Kyrgyzstan, U.S. air base (*case
    study*) 146–48, 327

Laden, Osama bin, death of 66, 105
Lagos, Nigeria 5
Lally, Michael 169
language(s)
    and cross-cultural communication
        65, 336
    lack of fluency 56
    machine translation 55
    for public diplomacy 203
    as requirement 28
    as skill set 55–57
    ways to improve 56
Latin America 65
    elimination of mercury in gold-
        mining 162
    U.S. diplomatic advocacy 73

law-enforcement agencies, within
    embassies 113
League of Nations 268
    and High Commissioner for
        Refugees 268
Lebanon
    American hostages in 78
    conflict with Israel (2006) 231
Lee, Rena, U.N. Intergovernmental
    Conference (BNNJ) 264
Lerch, Irving, and visas 235
Lew, Jacob 104
Liberia
    Ebola treatment facility 297
    plans for future Ebola outbreaks
        (*exercise*) 303–4
Library of Congress, employees in
    diplomatic missions 102
Libya
    civil war 137–38
    and Internet freedom 314
Lindwall, David 248
    in Afghanistan 57, **58**, 59, 71, 72
    in Colombia 52, 62, 71, 223
    in Guatemala 51, 72
    in Haiti 70
    in Iraq 317
    in Nicaragua 60
    in Paraguay 56
    in Spain 62
    in Sweden 65
"linkage diplomacy"
    and empathy 54
    southern Africa (*case study*) 46–48
Lister, John, USAID **185**
Livingston, Robert 38
Lo, Clarie 159
local staff 19, 111, 114, 240
    and management skills 71
    pay rates 184
    political officers and 143
    public diplomacy section 207
Louisiana Purchase (1803) 38
Lu, Donald, Kyrgyzstan 147
Lula da Silva, Luiz Inácio 329
Lutheran World Relief 272

McCaffrey, Barry 346
MacDougall, Jim 148
McFeeters, Brian 160
McHale, Judith 205
McMaster, H. R. 90
Macron, Emmanuel 33

Magnitsky Act (2012) 94
Malac, Deborah 297
Maldives, 2004 tsunami 231
Malta, and U.S. Libyan embassy 137
malware
    NotPetya 309
    ZeroCleare 318
managing people 71–72, 127
    audit mechanism 71
    local staff 71
Mao Zedong 48
Marine Security Guard 107, 111
Marshall, Capricia Penavic 247, 254
Mattera, Don 201
Matveev, Mikhail Pavlovich,
    ransomware attacks 317
Mazowiecki, Tadeusz 92
Médecins Sans Frontières (Doctors
    Without Borders) 272
    and Ebola outbreak 296
media 114
    broadcasts to foreign countries
        205
    and diplomatic reporting 135, 178
    levels of attribution **209** (box)
    photo opportunities 256
    and press guidance 208
    relationships with 207
    speaking to **209** (box), 208–10,
        209–10
    training in fact-checking 212
    trusted contacts in 206
    see also social media
mediation 75
Medvedev, Dmitry 94
meetings
    reporting on 180–82
    summarizing conversations
        180
Mehta, Goverdhan, and visa 235
MEK (Mojahedin-e Khalq), Iranian
    resistance group 317
mentors, choice of 69
Merkel, Angela 245
Merten, Kenneth 230
Mesopotamia 7
Meta, and Facebook 212
Mexico, consulates 224
Middle East
    clash of interests and values 8
    Geneva peace conference (1973)
        256
    (*case study*), 260–61, **261**

Madrid peace conference (1991)
    (*case study*) 261–62, **262**
    promoting democracy (*exercise*)
        76
    see also Iran; Iraq; Israeli–
        Palestinian peace process;
        Jordan; Lebanon
Middle East Partnership Initiative
    (MEPI) 76, 216
migration, economic causes 158
military doctrine 46
Miller, James 24
misinformation 212
mission operations, diplomatic
    mission duty 23
Moderna, Covid-19 vaccine 300
Mondelez International, malware
    attack 309
money-laundering, mechanism to
    counter 159
Monroe, James 38
moralism, Confucian 40
Mulford, David 235
multilateral diplomacy 19–21,
    264–82
    coalition building 264
    description 265–68
    evolution of 266
    and globalization 265
    influence of nongovernmental
        institutions 266
    influence of United States 267
    informal groupings 266
    international organizations
        268–73
    multitasking 268
    rules 267
    structure of missions 277
    value of 266
    see also intergovernmental
        organizations; international
        organizations; United Nations
multilateral diplomats
    daily routine 280–82
    duties and skills 276–80
    at U.N. in New York 279–80
multilateral missions 18, 277
multinational corporations 273
Munter, Cameron 24, 29
    and Czechoslovakia 128–29, 326
    in Iraq 107
    in Pakistan 66, 105
Murrow, Edward R. 200, 204

Muslim world, U.S. image in 198
Myanmar, and Internet freedom 314

Namibia, independence 31, 46
Nansen, Fridtjof 268
NASA (National Aeronautics and
    Space Administration),
    representatives 13
nation-states, as cybercrime
    perpetrators 310, 313
National Biodefense Strategy 300
National Counterterrorism Center
    224, 232
National Health Security Strategy 300
National Health Service (U.K.),
    cyberattack (2017) 309
National Institute of Standards and
    Technology (U.S.), and
    cyberspace 306
national interest 7–8
    definition 8
    effect of domestic politics on 335
    understanding of 335
    and values 8
national security
    and economic security 151
    and foreign policy 8–10
    health and 297–98
    threats to 9
    see also cyberspace
National Security Act (1947) 78
National Security Strategy, (2017)
    90
National Visa Center 234
nations, and countries 64
NATO (North Atlantic Treaty
    Organization) 20, 270
    Article 5 270
    cyber policy 314, **315**
    expansion of 343–44
    and Georgia 97
    and Russian cyberattack on
        Estonia 306
    Strategic Concept 314
    and Ukraine 97
NATO–Russia Permanent Joint
    Council (1997) 341
natural disasters
    Haiti earthquake 70, 230, 231
    Indian Ocean tsunami 231
    Japan earthquake and tsunami
        231, 236–41, **240** (*case study*)
    reporting 176

Nazi regime, negotiations on return
    of property to victims 328
Nealon, James 100, 116
    political officers' role 139–42
Nebenzya, Vasily 277
negotiations, diplomatic 322–24
    active listening 336
    with adversaries 44, 323
    analysis of past negotiations 345
    on arms-control 330–31
    bilateral 323
    with China (*exercise*) 348–49
    choice of venue 254
    clear objectives 334–36
    on climate 329–30
    compromise 324
    and deadlines 342
    direct dialogue 44
    economic, financial and trade
        327–29
    and empathy 322, 340
    with foreign embassies 326
    with friendly governments 323
    Israeli–Lebanese peace talks
        (1983) 256–57
    mechanism to learn from
        precedents 344–45
    multilateral 279–80, 323
    multilateral coalition building 264
    need for written records 342–44
    nondiplomatic 322
    personal connection with
        opponents 336, 340–41
    and persuasion 75
    photo opportunities 256
    "Plan Colombia" (*case study*)
        345–48
    political and security 326–27
    and possible use of AI 352
    preparation for 324
    purpose of 322
    realistic expectations 336–37
    and respect 339–41
    role of economic officers 162, 325
    routine and informal 325–26
    skill set 73–75, 324
    stalling for time 44
    training 75
    U.N. approval of U.S.
        intervention in Iraq (1990)
        273–74, 320–22, **321** (box)
    and unexpected events 341–42
    in war 323

on war-termination 331–32
    see also Kissinger, Henry
Netanyahu, Benjamin 341
Netherlands 171
    independence from Spain 265
news media 59
Ng, Mary 150
Nicaragua
    and social media 210
    and U.S. sale of arms to Iran 78
Niger 141, **165**
Nigeria, development aid 164–65
Nitze, Paul 340
Nixon, Richard, and China 36
Niyazov, Miroslav 148
nongovernmental institutions,
    influence of 266
nongovernmental organizations
    272–73
nonstate (state-sponsored) actors,
    cybercrime by 310
North Korea
    cyberattack on Sony Pictures 313
    U.S. impasse with 36, 43–44
North, Lieutenant Colonel Oliver 78
note verbale, between countries 193
note-taking 135, 143, 180, 193–94
    and incidental topics 181
    at official functions 251
    value of 188
    and written record of negotiations
        342–44
NSC (National Security Council,
    U.S.)
    backbenchers 86
    and Nicaraguan Contras 78
    operations by 78
    policy committees 80, 83–86
    policy-making role, [advice to
        president] 79
    role of diplomats 92–94
    and Russian invasion of Ukraine
        80
    structure 81–82
    under Biden 81
NSC (National Security Council,
    U.S.) staff 82–83
    counterterrorism directorate 83
    cyber directorate 83
    divided opinions 89
    influence over policy 78, 87, 94
    and interagency meetings 87
    numbers 82

NSC (National Security Council,
U.S.) staff (cont.)
  regional and functional
    directorates 83
  and working around dysfunction
    90–92
Nuclear Non-Proliferation Treaty 330
nuclear weapons 330
  agreements on 90, 330
  see also Strategic Arms Reduction
    Treaty (START)
Nuland, Victoria **74**, 74
  and sanctions on Russia 95
Nye, Joseph 39, 312

OAS (Organization of American
    States) 20, 155, 270
  and cyber diplomacy 316
Obama, Barack 66, **80**, **214**
  and Africa 141
  at COP15 329
  and Cuba 80
  and Egyptian Arab Spring 86
  and Libya 137
  and Putin 247, 254
  and Russia 94
Obama, Michelle 245
objectivity 60
O'Connell, Liam, Kyrgyzstan 147
OECD (Organization for Economic
    and Social Development) 20,
    155
Office of Children's Issues (Bureau
    of Consular Affairs) 226, 227
OPEC (Organization of the
    Petroleum Exporting Countries)
    269
Organization of African Unity see
    African Union
Organization of Islamic Cooperation
    269
organized crime, and cybercrime 310
Ortega, Daniel 210
OSCE (Organization for Security
    and Cooperation in Europe) **74**
  and regional cyber security 314
Oslo Accords (1993) 134

Pahlavi, Shah Mohammad Reza, of
    Iran 182
Pakistan 66
  nuclear weapons 331
  U.S. relations with 104

Palestine
  elections (1996) 134
  and peace process 185, 188
pandemic disease
  early warning to policymakers 294
  preparation for 299
  as risk 294
  see also Covid-19
Papandreou, George 106
Paraguay 56
Paris
  COP21 negotiations 329
  negotiations to end Vietnam War
    (1968–69) 254–56
Paris, Treaty of (1783) 31
passport cards 226
passports
  consular section and 110, 226
  emergency 239
Pastrana, Andrés 346
Patterson, Anne 86
Peace Corps 114
Pelosi, Nancy 50
permanent missions 17, 18
persuasion
  advocacy and 73, 140
  and coercion 39
  and negotiation 75
Pew Research Center, 2019 survey
    [xx] 10
Pfizer, Covid-19 vaccine 300
Philip, HRH Prince 245
Phillips, Susan 112, 170, 171
Pickering, Thomas 26, 65, 121, **324**,
    350
  ambassador to Moscow 125
  and arms-control talks 325
  in Colombia 346–47
  and Iraq 320
  and Israeli–Egyptian negotiations
    327
  and Jordan 327
Pinochet, General Augusto 179
PLO (Palestine Liberation
    Organization) 134
Plumb, Tom, Kyrgyzstan 147
Poland
  and NSC under Trump 90
  talks with Solidarity 90–92
  and war in Ukraine 139
policy, study of 69
policy coordination committees see
    Interagency Policy Committees

policymaking
  government structure 79
  informal cultures 79
  origination 80
  role of political officers 129
political appointees (U.S.
    ambassadors) 16, 33
  and NSC 93–94
  and partisanship 130
  Trump administration 93
political officers 109
  advocacy and negotiation 139–42
  areas of responsibility 127
  daily routine 142–44
  in diplomatic missions 131–33
  domestic assignments (country
    desk officers) 130–31
  duties and responsibilities in the
    field 133–42
  personal disagreement with policy
    144–46
  as political counselor 132
  politics and policy 129–30
  preparation for assignments 144
  relationship management 136–39
  reporting by 125, 134–36
  skills required 126–27
  staff assistants 130
  and trusted sources 136
  and visits of officials 139
political parties, host-country 118,
    136
political tradecraft 108–9, 125–46
  description 126–28
  and headquarters 128–29
politicians, relations with diplomats
    32
politics, lack of empathy in 54
Pollard, Jonathan 341
Portman, Robert 177
Powell, General Colin 26, **68**, **117**,
    127, 350
  and economic strategy against
    terrorism 154
  and Ukraine election 87
  at U.N. (2003) 273–74
power 39–40
  public diplomacy and 200
  see also hard power; soft power
presence posts 18
President's Emergency Plan for
    AIDS Relief (PEPFAR) 115
  in Uganda 291–93

Prewitt, Tim, Nigeria 165
Principals Committee, in NSC 85
Privacy Act (1974) 230
program management 72–73, 203
    mechanism to monitor success and
        integrity 72
propaganda
    and power 200
    and public diplomacy 199–200
    Soviet Union 199
protectionism 109
protectorates 42
protocol see diplomatic protocol
public diplomacy 110, 197–217
    analysis of information 204
    and Bolivian anti-drug campaign
        218
    commercial advocacy 169
    and consular sections 225
    and cultural diplomacy 212–15
    defined 198–99
    in diplomatic missions 206–8
    and exchange programs 213
    grants 207, 216
    and headquarters 205–6
    and Integrated Country Strategy
        209, 215
    key skills 203–5
    as long-term strategy 200–3, 207
    need for adaptability 203
    need for credibility 202, 211
    origin of term 198
    as overt 212
    planning, measurement and
        evaluation 215–17
    and propaganda 199–200
    short-term needs 201, 207
    use of celebrity envoys 214–15
    "winning hearts and minds" 198
    see also USIA
public diplomacy officers
    and countering disinformation
        211–12
    cultural and educational programs
        207
    in diplomatic missions 206
    and exchange programs 207
    grants 207
    need to be tech-savvy 211
    need to build rapport 211
    network of trusted media contacts
        206

public speaking 63
    (box), 62–64, 203
    reading speeches 63–64
    self-confidence 63
public-opinion polls 204
Putin, Vladimir 12, 94, 96
    annexation of Crimea (2014) 94
    and Condoleezza Rice 193, 248
    deliberate lateness 247
    and expansion of NATO 343–44
    on Georgia 193
    and Obama 247, 254
    and Xi Jinping 164

Qualitative Evaluations Panel (U.S.)
    28
Qutb, Sayyid 213

Rabbani, Salahuddin 58
Rabin, Yitzhak 336
    meeting with King Hussein 337
ransomware, cyberattacks 309, 317
Ray, Charles 5, 117
    in Zimbabwe 121
Reagan, Nancy 217
Reagan, Ronald
    and Brezhnev 340
    and Gorbachev 90, 340
    and Kissinger 334, 335
    and national security advisers 82
    and Nicaragua 78
    and Soviet Union 89
    Strategic Defense Initiative 89
    and Taiwan 49
recall, of diplomats 13
Reddick, Eunice 133
    in Niger 141
    in Taiwan 132
Reese, Col. Joel 147
relationship management
    diplomatic mission duty 22,
        117–19
    economic officers 159–60
    political officers 136–39
reporting and analysis 174–94
    collaboration in 135
    to Congress 135–36
    diplomatic mission duty 22
    direct policy recommendations
        184–86
    by economic officers 157–59
    by email 177–78
    on events 178–80

history of 175
    to influence 182–84
    on meetings and démarches 180–82
    by political officers 125, 134–36
    by telephone 175–77
    see also cables (dispatches); note-
        taking
reporting officer, need for accuracy
    178
representation, diplomatic mission
    duty 21
representative offices 18
Republican Party (U.S.), relations
    with Foreign Service 32
resignation, in protest at policy 144,
    145
respect
    for cultural difference 65, 203, 204
    and diplomatic protocol 247
    and negotiations 339–41
Rhodesia
    Ian Smith and 326
    Kissinger's negotiations on
        337–39
    protections and compensation for
        whites 339, 340
Ricciardone, Francis 55, 104
    on local embassy employees 114
Rice, Condoleezza 9, 343
    and Georgia 97
    and Iran 129
    meeting with Putin 193, 248
    as national security adviser 82, 83,
        91, 92
    on visas 222
Rice, Susan, as national security
    adviser 83
rice production project, Nigeria
    164–65
Ripken, Cal, Jr. 215
risk, perception of 293
risk management, diplomacy as 40–43
Rivkin, Charles 215
Rock, Anthony 290
Rodríguez Zapatero, José Luis 106
Roman Empire 198
Rome Statute (ICC) 51
    Article 98 exemption 51
Ross, Dennis 334
    and Clinton 341
    and Jordan 336
Rousseff, Dilma 302
Roy, J. Stapleton, Indonesia 160

Rrumbullaku, Muhamet 318
Russia
    annexation of Crimean Peninsula
        6, 89, 94–96 (*case study*)
    cyberattack on Estonia 305–6
    cyberattacks 306
    economic sanctions (2022) 12, 39,
        89, 163
    and Internet freedom 314
    invasion of Georgia (2008) (*case
        study*) 94–98
    invasion of Ukraine (2022) 12, 80,
        96, 200
    and New START 330
    numbers of diplomatic missions *15*
    possibility of expulsion from U.N.
        Security Council 283
    and postwar multilateral system
        267
    reporting from 135
    retaliatory sanctions on airspace 163
    and sale of Alaska (1867) 38
    size of Foreign Service 104
    suspension from Human Rights
        Council 282
    and U.N. 274
    and U.N. General Assembly
        resolution 282
    and U.N. Security Council
        resolution on Afghanistan
        (2021) 277
    and U.N. Security Council
        response to invasion of Ukraine
        (*case study*) 282–84
    Yeltsin and 125
    see also Soviet Union

Saakashvili, Mikheil 97, 193
Sadat, Anwar, and Israel 36
Saddam Hussein 11, 33, 273
    fall of 37
    and U.N. Resolution (1990) 321
Saleh, Ali Abdullah 216
Sarkozy, Nicolas, peace negotiations
    in Georgia 98
Satterfield, David 130
Saudi Arabia 67
Schwarzkopf, General Norman **68**
"science counselors" 289
science diplomacy
    defined 287–89
    see also expertise; health and
        science diplomacy

science and technology 109
    and climate change 289
    GMOs 289–90
    and public policy 289–90,
        294–95
scientific attachés 288
scientific knowledge, and health 287
Scowcroft, Brent, and national
    security structure and process
    79
Sebenius, James, Nicholas Burns and
    Robert Mnookin, *Kissinger the
    Negotiator* 334
Secure Traveler Enrollment Program
    229
security 8, 111
    see also counterterrorism;
        Diplomatic Security; national
        security
Security Governance Initiative,
    Africa 141
Sendai, Japan 239
September 11, 2001 terrorist attacks
    9
    and interagency dysfunction 116
    and terrorist funding 153, 328
    and visa process 222, 232
Serbia, and independence of Kosovo
    97, 105
Seward, William, acquisition of
    Alaska 38
Seychelles 114
Shanghai Cooperation Organization
    271
Shevardnadze, Eduard 320, 344
Shultz, George 11, 31
    and Soviet Union 89
Sierra Leone 5
Sikorski, Radoslaw **88**
Silliman, Douglas 25
    and cable on Iran–Iraq relations
        185, 186
    cable from Kuwait 184
    and Wikileaks 174
Simons, Thomas W. 79, 91
Singh, Manmohan 329
Sisson, Andrew, USAID 165
skill sets 25–27, 51–77
    advocacy and negotiation 73–75
    analytical skills 59–60
    communication 60–66
    cyber diplomacy 308
    diplomatic negotiations 324

empathy 53–55
    importance of 52
    intellectual curiosity 57–59
    interpersonal skills 70–71, 203
    languages 55–57
    managing people 71–72, 127
    public diplomacy 203–5
    public speaking **63**
        (box), 62–64
    versatility 25
Smith, Chris 228
Smith, Ian, Rhodesia (Zimbabwe)
    326, 339, 342
    and Kissinger 327, 333, 340
Smith–Mundt Act (1948) 205
social events
    at embassies 250
    to exchange information 58
    as guest 251
    hosting 253
    to improve language facility 56
    informal entertaining 253
    preparation for official functions
        251
    reception at ambassador's
        residence (*exercise*) 262–63
    seating 253
    see also etiquette
social media
    and influencers 211
    and information in crises 230
    measurement of campaign impacts
        216
    as news source 210
    public diplomacy and 210–11
    staff engagement with 212
soft power 39, 142
    economic 151
    and public diplomacy 200
Solidarity, Poland 91
South Africa
    and Angola 47
    apartheid 326
    and GMOs 290
    and Kissinger's negotiations 333,
        337–39, **338**
    and Namibian independence 31,
        46
    public diplomacy programs 201–2
    and war in Ukraine (*exercises*)
        149, 197–220
South Korea 171
South Ossetia 97

South Sudan 217
southern Africa, "linkage
    diplomacy" (*case study*) 46–48
southern Africa, Kissinger's
    negotiations 326–27
    conduct of 337–39
    preparation strategy 332–34
Soviet Union
    China and 49
    collapse (1991) 41
    and interventions in Africa 31, 46,
        326
    and Poland 91
    propaganda 199
    U.S. arms-control policy 89
    see also Russia
specialists, Foreign Service 102, 152,
    167, 294
spheres of influence 35, 41
spies *see* intelligence operatives
State Department *see* U.S. Foreign
    Service (State Department)
state visits (of heads of state) 245–46
statecraft
    in Cold War 36
    diplomacy as instrument of 31,
        32–35
Stevens, J. Christopher **15**
    murdered in Libya 137
Stiles, Charles W. 288
Strategic Arms Reduction Treaty
    (START) (1991) 90, 330
    new treaty (2009) 94, 330
strategy
    defined 35
    diplomacy as 35–37
Sudan
    and Internet freedom 314
    U.N. Security Council action on
        (*exercise*) 284–85
Suharto 160
Summers, Lawrence 160
superpowers 41
Sweden 65

tactics, diplomacy as 37–39
Tafa, Igli 318
Taiwan
    2000 presidential elections 132
    relations with China 49
    U.S. arms sales to (*case study*)
        48–50
    U.S. relations with 131–32, 136

Talabani, Qubad, Iraqi Kurdish
    regional government **185**
Tanzania 115
tape recordings 194
Tefft, John
    and 2004 Ukraine election 87
    ambassador to Georgia 86, 97
    ambassador to Russia **96**
    and NSC 86
telegrams (cables) 175
telephone, reporting by 175–77
Thailand
    2004 tsunami 231
    and intellectual property 157
Thatcher, Margaret 213
    and Zimbabwe 342
Thomas-Greenfield, Linda 318
    U.S. ambassador to U.N. 277
Thon, Jok Abraham 217
Tiirmaa-Klaar, Heli, E.U. head of
    cyber policy **307**
Todman, Terence 145
topics, prioritizing 180–81
    (*exercise*) 194–95
tourism, economic contribution 231
Track II diplomacy 29–30
trade agreements 151
    negotiation of 109, 328
trade deals 328
trade and investment 38, 111
training 352
    lack of formal 52, 115
    language 56
    in negotiation 75
    for political officers 127
transactionalism 42
Treasury Department 102
treaties, earliest 7
Trump, Donald 245
    and Foreign Service resignations 145
    interagency dysfunction 90
    and Iran 130
    and national security advisers 82
    and political appointees 93
trust, building 29, 65, 136
Turkey
    FAS and 170
    numbers of diplomatic missions *15*

Uganda, PEPFAR Aids program
    291–93
Ukraine
    2004 election 86–87

Malaysian airliner shot down over
    95
NotPetya malware 309
Russian cyberattacks 306
U.S. campaign to prevent Russian
    invasion 200
Ukraine, war in
    effect on grain exports 150
    and peace negotiations 323, 331
    Poland and 139
    Russian invasion 12, 80, 96, 274
    South Africa and (*exercises*) 149,
        197–220
    U.N. response to Russian invasion
        (*case study*) 282–84
    weapons for 89, 96
Umoh, Eno, and drone technology
    167
U.N. Assistance Mission in
    Afghanistan (UNAMA) 276
U.N. Conference on Disarmament
    330
U.N. Convention Against
    Corruption (2003) 155
U.N. Convention on the Law of the
    Sea (1994) 264
U.N. Disarmament Committee 312
U.N. Framework Convention on
    Climate Change 329
U.N. Group of Governmental
    Experts (GGE) 312
U.N. Intergovernmental Conference
    on Marine Biodiversity of Areas
    Beyond National Jurisdiction
    (BBNJ) 264–65
UNDP (United Nations
    Development Program) 155, 272
UNESCO (U.N. Education,
    Scientific and Cultural
    Organization) 20
UNHCR (U.N. High Commissioner
    for Refugees) 269
UNITA (National Union for Total
    Independence of Angola) 47
United Kingdom
    and Brexit 159
    Government Communication
        Service 212
    and Kissinger's negotiations in
        southern Africa 333, 339
    numbers of diplomatic missions *15*
    size of Foreign Service 103
    and social media influencers 211

United Nations 20, 273–76
  and 2003 presentation on Iraq
    (weapons of mass destruction)
    273–74
  agency leadership positions 268
  career paths, Young Professionals
    Program 28
  criticism of 276
  in Geneva 279
  and Namibian independence 46,
    48
  permanent missions to 17
  permanent observers 20
  political officers and 128
  politics of senior appointments
    274
  resolutions on terrorist funding
    154
  response to cyberattack on
    "Manula" (exercise) 318–19
  Secretary General 275
  U.S. mission in New York
    279–80, 281
  see also United Nations, General
    Assembly; United Nations
    Security Council
United Nations, General Assembly
  275
  condemnation of Russian invasion
    of Ukraine 282
  and cyberspace rules 312
  decision-making 271
  démarches from embassies 191
  Open-Ended Working Group on
    ICT 313
  vote on war in Ukraine (exercises)
    149, 197–220
United Nations Security Council
  266, 275
  action on Sudan (exercise) 284–85
  and approval of U.S. intervention
    in Iraq (1990) 273–74, 320–22,
    321 (box)
  as dysfunctional 276
  negotiations 279–80
  and North Korean invasion of
    South Korea (1950) 284
  and nuclear-armed states 330
  possibility of expulsion of Russia
    283
  president's chair, monthly rotation
    279
  "program of work" 275, 275

proposals 279, 280
Resolution 678 320, 321 (box)
response to Russian invasion of
  Ukraine (case study) 282–84
and Taliban takeover in
  Afghanistan (2021) 276–77
and veto power 271
United States
  and 2004 Ukraine election 86–87
  and 2014 Ebola outbreak 296–97
  2016 election campaign 306
  and alliances 41
  arms sales to Taiwan (case study)
    48–50
  and assistance with reforms in
    Colombia (case study) 346–48
  bilateral trade agreements 328
  and Brazilian Zika virus outbreak
    (case study) 302–3
  and campaign to prevent Russian
    invasion of Ukraine 200
  and Central American free trade
    agreement 6
  and Cold War 43
  debt ceiling 164
  defense budget 9
  and development of vaccines 300
  and EU 6
  and ICC Article 98 agreements
    51–52
  independence 31
  influence on postwar multilateral
    diplomacy 267
  and Iranian cyberattack on
    Albania 318
  and lack of preparedness for
    Covid-19 300
  modern view of 40
  National Cybersecurity Strategy
    313
  National Security Council 14
  National Security Strategy 8
  need for diplomatic excellence 45
  numbers of diplomatic missions 15
  and Pax Americana 41
  and power of dollar 164
  relations with China 49, 54, 104,
    286
  relations with Pakistan 104
  relations with Russia 104
  reputation for virtue 40
  sanctions on Russia 12, 39, 89
  and scientific research 288–89

  and Security Council resolution on
    Afghanistan (2021) 277
  and Soviet Union 89
  "war on drugs" 217, 219
  and weapons for Ukraine 89
  see also Departments; interagency
    foreign policy process; National
    Security Council; U.S. Foreign
    Service (State Department)
Universal Postal Union (1874) 266
Urbánek, Zdenek 128
U.S. Congress
  responsibilities 16
  see also U.S. Senate
U.S. Cybersecurity and
  Infrastructure Security Agency
  (CISA) 316
U.S. Foreign Service Institute,
  "Protocol for the Modern
  Diplomat" 249, 260
U.S. Foreign Service (State
  Department) 15, 351
  AI strategy 351
  career paths 28
  dispatches from 191–92
  "dissent channel" 60
  and economic tradecraft 153–55
  Foreign Affairs Manual 145, 226
  lack of training 52
  language instruction 56
  need for major reform 351
  negotiations with China (exercise)
    348–49
  Operations Center 131, 155, 176,
    230
  political appointees 16, 33
  and political tradecraft 128–29
  and public diplomacy 205–6
  senate-approved posts 10
  size of 9, 103
  staff at U.N. 274, 279–80
  undersecretary of state for
    political affairs 129
  see also Bureaus
U.S. Forest Service 102
U.S. Marshals Service 102
U.S. Senate, and diplomatic
  appointments 10, 16
USAID (U.S. Agency for
  International Development) 9,
  102, 112, 115
  and Bolivian anti-drug campaign
    218

emergency funding 230
Foreign Service officers 166
in Niger **165**
Nigeria 165
USIA (United States Information
Agency) 199
Cold War 205

values, and national interest 8
Venezuela
migration from 158
relations with U.S. 118
Vienna Convention on Consular
Relations (1963) 7, 221, 249
and diplomatic immunity 257, 259
Vienna Convention on Diplomatic
Relations (1961) 7, 12, **21** (box),
249
and diplomatic immunity 257
on diplomatic missions 17, 21
Vietnam
Paris negotiations (1968-69)
254–56
visas (*exercise*) 122–23
Vindman, Alexander 83
visas 22, 110, 222, 231–35
AI screening 351
Electronic System for Travel
Authorization (ESTA) (visa-
waiver) 233
errors 232
fraud prevention 231
high demand for 223
immigrant 234–35
misperceptions about 233
nonimmigrant (visitor) 232–34
numbers issued 232
personal interviews of applicants
222, 351
public perceptions and
expectations 235–36
refusals 233
and "sensitive technologies" 235
and special security clearance
235
student 234
time limits 233, 236
and tourism 231
waivers (*exercise*) 243
work 234
Voice of America 205
von der Leyen, Ursula 265
Vorster, John 337–39, **338**, 342

Waldheim, Kurt 260
Walker, Stephen 144
Wall, Marc 59
WannaCry malware attack 309
war
and commitment to peace 37
diplomacy as alternative to 38
diplomacy to end 31, 323
and lines of communication 12
provoked by diplomacy 11
war, termination negotiations
331–32
direct negotiations 332
final agreement 332
pre-negotiations 331
prior preparations 331
proximity talks 332
territorial negotiations 332
Watnik, Eric 233
Wayne, Tony 154
Wechsel, Hans 216
and Belgian law (*case study*)
75–76, 325
Weinberger, Caspar 89
Wen Jiabao 329
Wechsel, Hans, and Middle East
Partnership Initiative (MEPI)
(*exercise*) 76
Westphalia, Peace of (1648) 265
Wharton, Bruce **202**
in Bolivia 204, 217, 218
WhatsApp 210
disinformation on 212
White, Andrew D. (1890s) 287
WHO (World Health Organization)
20, 272
and 2014 Ebola outbreak 296
and avian influenza (China 2013)
286
COVAX initiative for equitable
access to vaccines 300
and Covid-19 pandemic 298
deference to U.S. 298
director-general election 298
Pandemic Influenza Preparedness
Framework (2021) 301
relations with China 298, 300
shortcomings 298, 299
and Zika virus outbreak 302
Wikileaks, 2010 disclosures 45, 174
Wilhelm I, Emperor 11
Will.i.am (William James Adams)
215

Winthrop, John 40
World Bank 41, 155
negotiations 328
World Central Kitchen 273
World Food Program 272
Niger **165**
World Travel and Tourism Council
231
World War II
entente between Allies 42
postwar order 40, 41
World Wide Web 308
World Wildlife Fund 272
Wright, Mary Ann 145
writing 61–62
brevity 61, 181, 195–96 (*exercise*)
style 61, 189
and use of quotes 181
WTO (World Trade Organization)
269
China and 151
Doha Development Round 329
Wuhan, China, origin of Covid-19
286

Xi Jinping 34
and Putin 164

Yanukovych, Viktor 86
Yeltsin, Boris 125, 137
visit to Washington 183
Yemen, Women Journalists Without
Chains 216
Yom Kippur War, peace conference
260, 327
Young Africans Leadership
Initiative (YALI) 213–14, **214**,
217
Yovanovitch, Marie 125–26
and Kyrgyzstan air base (*case
study*) 146–48, **147**
Yugoslavia, disintegration 144
Yushchenko, Viktor 86

Zelenskyy, Volodymyr 12
and U.N. Security Council **267**
Zelikow, Philip 343
ZeroCleare malware 318
Zhang Jun 277
Zika virus outbreak, Brazil 302–3
Zimbabwe
female journalists 201
restrictions on NGOs 121

402   Index

Zimbabwe (cont.)
  U.S. relations with 118, 121–22
    (*case study*)
  see also Rhodesia
Zuma, Jacob 329
Zumwalt, James, Japan 236, **237**

case studies
  anti-drug campaign in Bolivia
    217–19
  arms sales to Taiwan 48–50
  cyberattacks on Albania
    317–18
  Dominican Republic banking
    crisis 171–72
  Geneva peace conference on
    Middle East 260–61, **261**

Japan earthquake and tsunami
  236–41
Madrid peace conference on
  Middle East 261–62, **262**
"Plan Colombia" negotiations
  345–48
repeal of Belgian law 75–76
Russian invasion of Georgia
  94–98
sanctions on Russia 94–96
Southern Africa "linkage
  diplomacy" 46–48
U.N. Security Council response to
  invasion of Ukraine 282–84
U.S. air base in Kyrgyzstan 146–48
Zika virus outbreak Brazil 302–3
Zimbabwe 121–22

exercises
  Boeing 737 Max 172–73
  cables (dispatches) 194–96
  cybercrime 318–19
  diplomatic protocol 262–63
  Dominican Republic visa waiver
    243
  Ebola in Liberia 303–4
  embassy renovations 123
  France and Australia 98–99
  negotiations with China
    348–49
  promotion of democracy 76
  U.N. action on Sudan 284–85
  U.N. votes on war in Ukraine 149,
    219–20
  Vietnam visa line 122

Printed in the USA
CPSIA information can be obtained
at www.ICGtesting.com
CBHW080854270324
PP15016700001B/1